P9-DCR-341

RELIGIOUS LIBERTY
IN THE
SUPREME COURT

TERRY EASTLAND is the editor of *Forbes MediaCritic* and a fellow at the Ethics and Public Policy Center. He is the author of *Energy in the Executive: The Case for the Strong Presidency* (The Free Press, 1992) and *Ethics, Politics, and the Independent Counsel: Executive Power, Executive Vice 1789-1989.*

RELIGIOUS LIBERTY
IN THE
SUPREME COURT

*The Cases That Define the
Debate Over Church and State*

Edited by
TERRY EASTLAND

ETHICS AND PUBLIC POLICY CENTER
WASHINGTON, D.C.

WILLIAM B. EERDMANS PUBLISHING COMPANY
GRAND RAPIDS, MICHIGAN / CAMBRIDGE, U.K.

Copyright © 1993 by the Ethics and Public Policy Center
1015 Fifteenth St. N.W., Washington, D.C. 20005

First published 1993 by the Ethics and Public Policy Center
This edition published jointly 1995 by the Ethics and Public Policy Center and
Wm. B. Eerdmans Publishing Co.
255 Jefferson Ave. S.E., Grand Rapids, Michigan 49503 /
P.O. Box 163, Cambridge CB3 9PU U.K.

All rights reserved

Printed in the United States of America

00 99 98 97 96 95   7 6 5 4 3 2 1

Library of Congress Cataloging-in-Publication Data

Religious liberty in the Supreme Court : the cases that define the
debate over church and state / edited by Terry Eastland.
p.   cm.
Originally published: Washington, D.C. : Ethics and Public Policy Center, 1993.
Includes bibliographical references and index.
ISBN 0-8028-0838-7 (pbk. : alk. paper)
1. Freedom of religion—United States—Cases. 2. Church and
state—United States—Cases. I. Eastland, Terry.
[KF4783.A7R45 1995]
342.73′0852—dc20

[347.302852]   95-19180
                                                              CIP

Contents

PART TWO *Reflections*

Preface

"C ongress shall make no law respecting an establishment of religion or prohibiting the free exercise thereof." The language of the religion clause of the First Amendment seems simple enough, but Americans time and again have contended in court over the proper interpretation and application of these sixteen words. A substantial number of the cases have reached the highest court of the land, and anyone interested in the political debate over church and state needs to become acquainted with the litigation.

This volume brings together twenty-five leading religion-clause cases, in chronological order. For each there is a brief introduction that summarizes the facts and suggests how the case relates to others and to evolving judicial doctrine. The majority opinion and some other opinions are then presented, in full or in substantial excerpts. The concurring and dissenting opinions that are included were selected because they add something important to the debate over the proper interpretation and application of the Constitution.

A Supreme Court decision, Abraham Lincoln once said, is not a "thus saith the Lord." Citizens may agree or disagree with what the justices decide; if they disagree, they may try to change the ruling, either by asking the Court to reconsider its decision or by seeking a new law—even, if necessary, amendment of the Constitution through the process spelled out in Article V. On matters of church and state, an argument broader than the one between justices in a given case has not infrequently ensued, on occasion leading to new law. To give the reader a sense of the debate beyond the Court, we have included, with fifteen of the cases, one or more contemporaneous editorial responses, drawn from both the secular and the religious press. Among the publications included in this sampling are the *Washington Post*, the *New York Times*, the *Wall Street Journal*, the *Dallas Morning News*, *The New Republic*, *The Christian Century*, and *America*.

Part Two takes a longer look at these matters. Mary Ann Glendon of the Harvard Law School, Michael Sandel of Harvard University, and Michael McConnell of the University of Chicago Law School focus on certain trends in the Court's religion-clause jurisprudence and their implications for the health of our public life.

Special thanks are in order for several staff members of the Ethics and Public Policy Center. In editing this volume, Carol Griffith has done her usual superb job. And in executing the many tasks that go into the making of a book, including researching, manuscript typing, proofreading, and indexing, Todd Shy, Marianne Geers, Derek Mogck, and William Brailsford, as well as former staff member Dan Maclellan and former interns Sarah Birmingham, Hunter Boyd, Lawrence Florio, Robert Palladino, Ethan Reedy, and James Warner, have all done excellent work.

This book is a basic reader on the church-state debate. We hope it will be useful to lawyers and government officials, to journalists, to students of law, religion, politics, and American history, and also to non-specialists for whom religious liberty is an area of abiding concern.

Acknowledgments

We are grateful to the publishers for permitting us to reprint all or part of the following editorials and op-ed pieces in our sampling of editorial responses to fifteen of the Supreme Court cases:

America: "The Constitution and American Education," 6-22-68; "The Walz Case," by Charles M. Whelan, 5-16-70. Reprinted by permission of America Press, Inc., 106 West 56th Street, New York NY 10019; © 1968/70; all rights reserved.

The Christian Century: "The Flag Salute Case," 6-19-40; "Court Upholds Freedom of Conscience," 6-23-43; "The Champaign Case," 4-7-48; "Public Schools Can Teach Religion!," 4-28-48; "The Court Concurs," 5-15-52; "The Court Decides Wisely," 7-3-63; "The Court Concludes a Term," 7-17-68; "New Ruling on School Prayer," by Donald L. Drakeman, 6-19-85. Reprinted by permission; © 1940/43/48/52/63/68/85 by the Christian Century Foundation.

Christianity and Crisis: "Regents' Prayer Decision," 7-23-62; "The Court's Church-State Confusion," 8-9-71. Reprinted by permission; © 1962/71 by Christianity and Crisis, 537 W. 121st Street, New York, NY 10027.

Commonweal: "A Matter of Tradition," 5-16-52. Reprinted by permission; © Commonweal.

Dallas Morning News: "School Prayer," 6-26-92. Reprinted by permission.

The New Republic: "Engel v. Vitale," 7-9-62; "Parochial School Aid," 7-10-71. Reprinted by permission; © The New Republic, Inc.

New York Times: "Court on the Flag Salute," 6-19-43; "Time Off for Religion," 4-30-52; "Prayer Is Personal," 6-27-62; "Freedom of Religion," 6-19-63; "Of Bible Groups and Scuba Clubs," 6-6-90. Reprinted by permission; © 1943/52/62/63/90 by The New York Times Company.

Wall Street Journal: "In the Name of Freedom," 6-27-62; "The Establishment of Confusion," 6-14-68; "School Rule," 7-1-83; "Trivial Pursuits," 3-7-84; "Reading Between the Lines," by Peter J. Ferrara, 6-11-85. Reprinted by permission; © 1962/68/83/84/85 Dow Jones & Company, Inc.; all rights reserved.

Washington Post: "Religious Freedom," 6-16-43; "Church and State," 2-13-47; "Moment of Silence," 6-28-62; "The Supreme Court and the Churches," 5-11-70; "Safeguarding Religious Freedom," 6-30-71; "The Court, Education, and Religion," 6-30-83; "Religious Meetings in Schools," 6-6-90; "Religion and Absurdity in the Schools," by Edwin M. Yoder, Jr., 6-9-90; "Graduation Prayers," 6-25-92. Reprinted by permission; © 1943/47/62/70/71/83/90/92 The Washington Post.

Washington Post Writers Group: Column by George F. Will, 6-9-85. Reprinted by permission; © 1985 by the Washington Post Writers Group.

ix

Summary of the Cases

Elementary and Secondary Education

2. *Minersville* v. *Gobitis* (1940). Government may require a child to participate in a flag-salute ceremony despite his religious objections.

3. *West Virginia* v. *Barnette* (1943). Government may not require a child to salute the flag in violation of his religious scruples.

4. *Everson* v. *Board of Education* (1947). Government may reimburse parents for fares paid to transport their children to public or Catholic schools.

5. *McCollum* v. *Board of Education* (1948). Religious instruction given in public schools under a "released time" arrangement violates the First Amendment.

6. *Zorach* v. *Clauson* (1952). Religious instruction given away from public school premises under a "released time" arrangement does not violate the First Amendment.

8. *Engel* v. *Vitale* (1962). Government may not sponsor prayers in public schools.

9. *Abington* v. *Schempp* (1963). Government may not sponsor Bible reading and recitation of the Lord's Prayer in public schools.

11. *Board of Education* v. *Allen* (1968). A state may require local schools to lend textbooks free of charge to secondary school students, including those in religious schools.

13. *Lemon* v. *Kurtzman* (1971). Government may not support instructors who teach secular subjects in church-related elementary and secondary schools.

14. *Wisconsin* v. *Yoder* (1972). Government may not require Amish parents to send their children to school beyond the eighth grade if they object to doing so on religious grounds.

15. *Stone* v. *Graham* (1980). A state law requiring posting of the Ten Commandments in public schoolrooms violates the First Amendment.

18. *Mueller* v. *Allen* (1983). A state law providing tax deduction for public and private school expenses does not violate the First Amendment.

21. *Wallace* v. *Jaffree* (1985). A state law authorizing a moment of silence in public schools for "meditation or voluntary prayer" for the sole express purpose of returning voluntary prayer to the schools violates the First Amendment.

22. *Grand Rapids* v. *Ball* and *Aguilar* v. *Felton* (1985). *Grand Rapids*: Shared Time and Community Education programs that at public

expense provide classes to non-public school students in classrooms located in non-public schools violate the ban on establishment. *Aguilar*: Local government use of federal funds to pay salaries of public employees who teach in parochial schools violates the ban on establishment.

24. *Board of Education* v. *Mergens* (1990). Under the Equal Access Act of 1984 a public school that maintains a "limited open forum" may not discriminate against a student club on the basis of its religious content.

25. *Lee* v. *Weisman* (1992). The practice of including clergy who offer prayers as part of an official public school graduation ceremony violates the ban on establishment.

HIGHER EDUCATION

17. *Widmar* v. *Vincent* (1981). A state university may not refuse a student religious group access to university facilities generally open to other student groups.

OTHER

1. *Cantwell* v. *Connecticut* (1940). A state's conviction of Jehovah's Witnesses who were peaceably spreading their faith on a public street violates the First Amendment.

7. *Torcaso* v. *Watkins* (1961). A state requirement that an appointee to office must declare his belief in God violates the First Amendment.

10. *Sherbert* v. *Verner* (1963). Government may not refuse unemployment compensation to a person unwilling to work on Saturday, the Sabbath of her faith.

12. *Walz* v. *Tax Commission* (1970). Tax exemptions to religious organizations for property used solely for religious purposes do not violate the First Amendment.

16. *Thomas* v. *Review Board* (1981). Denial of unemployment compensation to a Jehovah's Witness who quit his job because of his religious beliefs violates the free-exercise provision.

19. *Marsh* v. *Chambers* (1983). A state legislature's practice of opening each legislative day with a prayer by a chaplain paid by the state does not violate the ban on establishment.

20. *Lynch* v. *Donnelly* (1984). A municipality's inclusion of a Nativity scene in an annual Christmas display does not violate the First Amendment.

23. *Employment Division* v. *Smith* (1990). Government may deny unemployment benefits to persons discharged from their jobs for illegal drug use even if the use of the drug is religiously based.

Introduction

Terry Eastland

T he twenty-five cases included in this book were decided between 1940 and 1992. This choice of only *modern* cases should not be taken to imply chronological snobbery. Although the First Amendment, along with the rest of the Bill of Rights, was added to the Constitution in 1791, the Supreme Court decided very few religion-clause cases before 1940, and only one—*Reynolds* v. *United States*, 98 U.S. 145 (1879)—of major doctrinal importance. One reason is that, before the New Deal, the federal government played a relatively small role in American life, and there were few possibilities for litigation claiming that the government somehow had established religion or prohibited its free exercise.

More importantly, as long as the First Amendment was understood to apply to only the federal government, religion-clause cases could not arise in connection with state governments. The broadening of the application of the religion clause came in the first and fourth cases in this volume, *Cantwell* v. *Connecticut* (1940) and *Everson* v. *Board of Education* (1947). *Cantwell* is a free-exercise case, *Everson* an establishment case; together they made possible religion-clause litigation involving actions of the states. The Supreme Court had paved the way for this extension by holding that, in effect, the Fourteenth Amendment, added to the Constitution in 1868, had changed the legal landscape. That amendment provides, in part, "No State shall . . . deprive any person of life, liberty, or property, without due process of law." In a series of cases commencing in 1897, the Supreme Court established the principle that the due-process clause "incorporates" or absorbs certain provisions of the Bill of Rights, which the states, like the federal government, must therefore respect.

In *Cantwell*, a case arising from Connecticut, the Court continued this process by declaring that because "[t]he fundamental concept of liberty embodied in [the Fourteenth] Amendment embraces the liberties guaranteed" by the religion clause, "the legislatures of the states

1

[are] as incompetent as Congress to enact" the kinds of laws that the religion clause forbids. *Cantwell* concerned the free exercise of religion; any doubt about whether the Court believed that the ban on establishment also applied to the states was erased in *Everson*, a New Jersey case involving an establishment-of-religion claim. Most of the other religion-clause cases that the Court has decided in the past half century have concerned the states.

In a recent case included in this volume, *Wallace* v. *Jaffree* (1985), the district judge held that states do have the authority to establish religion. That decision was overruled on appeal, and it is most unlikely that the Supreme Court will ever change course on whether the no-establishment and free-exercise provisions of the First Amendment (or, for that matter, other already applied provisions of the Bill of Rights) bind the states. This much of the debate over church and state may be deemed a closed matter within the Court.[1]

What is not a closed matter is the substantive meaning and application of the religion clause. Obviously there is agreement, as there always has been, that neither the federal government nor the states may establish religion by granting to any particular church or religious organization a political or governmental privilege, such as those extended to the Anglican Church in England. The United States, in a sharp break with the practice in the West since Constantine, has never had an established church. Those first states in the Union that began with some elements of an established church had gradually done away with them by 1833. They did this through their normal political processes, not through First Amendment litigation (for the Bill of Rights was then understood to limit only the federal government). This quite voluntary movement is strong evidence that the people themselves believed in one of the fundamental reasons for the adoption of the First Amendment: that a state-supported church violates religious liberty.

Justice Hugo Black, writing for the Court in *Everson*, may be said to have declared the enduring sense of the American people when he said that the First Amendment means "at least" that "[n]either a state nor the Federal Government can set up a church" and "at least" that no government "can force or influence a person to go or to remain away from church against his will, or force him to profess a belief or disbelief

---

1. Those interested in learning more about the incorporation doctrine might consult such standard reference works as *The Constitution of the United States of America: Analysis and Interpretation* (Washington: U.S. Government Printing Office, 1973), especially pp. 900–907, or "Incorporation Doctrine" in Kermit Hall, ed., *The Oxford Companion to the Supreme Court of the United States* (New York: Oxford University Press, 1992).

in any religion," or punish him "for entertaining or professing religious beliefs or disbeliefs, for church attendance or non-attendance."

The First Amendment's religion clause means "at least" that much. But beyond this point lies controversy, as the cases since *Cantwell* and *Everson* show. Indeed, in *Everson* itself, all nine justices agreed with the broad interpretation of the First Amendment set forth in the Court's opinion, written by Justice Black, but four disagreed with its conclusion that New Jersey could underwrite the bus transportation of school-age children attending public *and* parochial schools. For the dissenters, that funding arrangement violated the Constitution.

Everson's importance lay less in its result than in its doctrine. For Justice Black also said that government, whether federal or state, must be absolutely neutral, not just among Protestant churches (the predominant religious force in the founding period on through the early twentieth century) or even among all religious groups, but also between religious believers and non-believers. "Neither a state nor the Federal Government," Black wrote, ". . . can pass laws which aid . . . all religions." The First Amendment, he added, "was intended to erect 'a wall of separation between church and State.' "

Everson's doctrines of neutrality and separation, which the majority claimed were rooted in the nation's founding history, shaped a test gradually devised by the Court to assess the constitutionality of governmental action. First, the Court said that the action had to be both secular in purpose and secular in primary impact. Later, the Court added a third requirement — the action could not excessively entangle government with religion. In *Lemon* v. *Kurtzman* (1971), a case involving public aid to teachers of secular subjects in parochial and other non public schools, the Court declared that these three conditions had to be met for a challenged governmental action to be constitutional. The three-part "*Lemon* test" has not always been applied in establishment cases. Most notably, in *Marsh* v. *Chambers* (1983), the Court effectively placed the *Lemon* test on hold as it used another approach in upholding Nebraska's legislative chaplaincy.

This refusal to use the *Lemon* test suggests dissatisfaction about it within the Court, and in fact at least six justices have criticized it. No one has done so more sharply than Chief Justice William Rehnquist in his dissent in the *Jaffree* case. Rehnquist said that the test has not provided "adequate standards" for decision, with the result that the Court has tended "to fracture into unworkable plurality opinions, depending upon how each of the three factors applies to a certain state action." Many observers of the Court expected it to jettison the *Lemon* test, and in 1992 in *Lee* v. *Weisman*, the graduation school-prayer case, the moment appeared to have come. But the Court did not abandon the *Lemon* test. Debate about the test and the doctrines of neutrality and separation it seeks to further is certain to persist both within and outside the Court.

One reason it will persist is that the Court's approach to establishment questions has forced the elimination from the nation's public life of religious elements that prior to *Everson* had not been thought by most Americans to violate the First Amendment. The Court has allowed some leeway in non-public-school settings: for example, the Court has said that under certain—in effect, secularizing—circumstances the display of a city-owned Nativity scene is constitutionally permissible. But in regard to public elementary and secondary schools, the Court has ruled out virtually all institutional involvements with religion.

One year after *Everson*, in *Illinois ex rel. McCollum* v. *Board of Education* (1948), the Court for the first time found that a state practice established religion. It struck down an Illinois school board's "released time" program under which teachers from all religious groups choosing to participate were allowed to offer religious instruction in the school for one hour a week. Many states had long had similar programs, just as many also had long allowed classroom teachers to say a prayer and read aloud a Bible passage at the start of the school day. In *Engel* v. *Vitale* (1962), the landmark school-prayer case, the Court found that state-sponsored school prayer violated the First Amendment; the next year, in *Abington School District* v. *Schempp*, state-sponsored Bible reading and other devotional exercises in the schools were struck down. In its most recent ruling on public schools and religion, the *Weisman* case, the Court told public school authorities in Providence, Rhode Island, that they may not invite area clergy to give prayers at middle and high school graduation ceremonies. In the three decades between *Engel* and *Weisman*, other public school involvements in religion, such as display of the Ten Commandments, had been declared unconstitutional. Such involvements, in the Court's view, endorse religion and thus violate *Everson*'s rule that government may not prefer religion over non-religion.

The modern divorce of religion from the public schools still does not sit well with a majority of Americans, if polling data over the past thirty years are reliable, and at various times since *Engel*, efforts have been made to write new law that would allow room for prayers or other religious practices in the public schools. Some states enacted statutes allowing for a "moment of silence" during which students may meditate or even pray; but the only successful effort at the federal level came in 1984, with passage of the Equal Access Act. Sustained by the Supreme Court against a First Amendment challenge in *Board of Education* v. *Mergens* (1990), the law requires public high schools receiving federal funds to allow student-led religious groups to meet (and practice their faith) on the same basis and under the same conditions as any other student-led group. For the Court, what matters in an equal-access arrangement is that the individual student chooses to participate in a fellowship of religious believers who are also students. Thus the public school itself is not endorsing religion. This is about as much religion as the Court seems willing to allow into the public schools.

Unquestionably, the Supreme Court's decisions on public schools and religion have led increasing numbers of parents to send their children to church-related schools. These schools are the focus of another type of church-state controversy: May government support such schools or assist those who attend them, and if so, how? The Supreme Court has said that state aid in any form directly given to private religious elementary and secondary schools does not pass constitutional muster, even if the purpose of the aid is secular and its use is carefully monitored. Taking into account such schools' religious mission, the Court has labeled them "pervasively sectarian" and therefore decided that the primary effect of aiding them is the advancement of religion, in violation of the ban on establishment. When states have designed grants in such a way that the money can be spent only for specific educational purposes unrelated to the schools' religious mission, the Court has said that the monitoring necessary to keep track of how the money is spent unacceptably entangles the state with religion. (If one part of the *Lemon* test does not stop the aid, another part will.) By contrast, state aid directly to the students attending such schools and their parents has won approval from the Court, as in *Mueller* v. *Allen* (1983). In that case the Court sustained a Minnesota law allowing taxpayers to deduct from their state taxable income up to $700 per child for tuition, textbook, and school transportation expenses, regardless of whether they attended public or private schools. Most of the Minnesotans taking the deduction were parents of children attending church-related schools.

The Court has distinguished between religious higher education and religious elementary and secondary education. While it views the latter as "pervasively sectarian," it sees the former as not only inculcating religious beliefs but also teaching critical thinking skills, and it regards college-age students as less "impressionable" than younger students. For these reasons, the Court has been willing to uphold state aid directly given to religious colleges. If past decisions concerning tangible aid by government to religious education are a reliable basis for predicting future cases in this area, what stands the best chance of winning Supreme Court approval is aid given to a religious college or provided directly to students enrolled at religious elementary or secondary schools, or to their parents.

One religion-clause case prior to 1940 that bears noting here is *Reynolds* v. *United States* (1879), a free-exercise case. Acting under a federal anti-bigamy statute, the government sought to end Mormon polygamy in what was then the territory of Utah. George Reynolds, secretary to Brigham Young, had been convicted of bigamy, and the Supreme Court declined to reverse, rejecting Reynolds's argument for a First Amendment exemption from the law. The Court distinguished between belief and action: government may not punish citizens on account of their religious beliefs but may regulate religiously motivated actions, provided it has a rational basis for doing so.

The rational-basis test, which in most cases government can easily satisfy, virtually closed the door to constitutionally compelled exemptions that might be carved out by federal courts—until 1963, that is, when in *Sherbert* v. *Verner* the Court changed its mind. Adell Sherbert, a Seventh-day Adventist, was fired by her South Carolina employer because she refused to work on Saturday, her faith's Sabbath. Unable to find work that gave her Saturday off, she filed for unemployment compensation, but the state rejected her claim on grounds that she was disqualified because she had refused to accept suitable work. The Supreme Court agreed with her that South Carolina had abridged her right to the free exercise of religion. *Sherbert* thus stands for the proposition that government may not enact or enforce a law that burdens religiously motivated conduct unless it is protecting a *compelling* interest by the least intrusive means possible. This doctrine has been called "the conduct exemption."

Sherbert was strengthened by *Wisconsin* v. *Yoder* (1972), in which the Court ruled that Wisconsin could not require Amish parents to send their children to school beyond the eighth grade. But in 1990 it was effectively overruled by *Employment Division* v. *Smith*. Alfred Smith and Galen Black ingested the hallucinogenic drug peyote during a Native American Church ceremony in which that drug was sacramentally used. Smith and Black, who worked with a private drug-rehabilitation organization, were then fired from their jobs for using an illegal drug. When they filed for unemployment compensation, Oregon judged them ineligible for benefits because they had been fired for work-related "misconduct"—ingestion of peyote, possession of which is a felony in that state. Smith and Black challenged the state's decision on free-exercise grounds, ultimately losing in the Supreme Court. "[A]n individual's religious beliefs," wrote Justice Antonin Scalia for the Court, "[do not] excuse him from compliance with an otherwise valid law prohibiting conduct that the State is free to regulate."

Thus the Court returned to the pre-*Sherbert* approach of *Reynolds*. That approach does not prevent legislators from granting exemptions based on religiously motivated conduct, and in 1991 Oregon in fact passed a conduct-exemption law under which persons such as Smith and Black would be eligible for unemployment benefits. Still, no free-exercise decision has provoked as much controversy as *Smith*. An unusual coalition of conservatives and liberals has formed in support of federal legislation, endorsed by President Bill Clinton, that would put the conduct exemption back into the Court's free-exercise jurisprudence. As this volume went to press, the Court unanimously reaffirmed *Smith*'s free-exercise jurisprudence in *Church of the Lukumi* v. *Hialeah* (1993). The city of Hialeah, Florida, had prohibited ritual animal sacrifice with an ordinance aimed at the Santeria religion, the only one in Hialeah that engaged in this practice. Because the ordinance was not one of general applicability, the Court found it unconstitutional.

Argument over what it means to establish a religion frequently refers to the nation's founding history. Justice Black's *Everson* opinion located the First Amendment principles of neutrality and separation in the historical events that led to the making of the no-establishment and free-exercise provisions. All his colleagues thought he was right; it was left to later justices to disagree with Justice Black. Justice William Rehnquist's dissent in the *Jaffree* case (thirty-eight years after *Everson*) is a detailed rejoinder to Black's history and thus to the approach to establishment cases that the Court has more or less followed ever since. Rehnquist argues that the original understanding of the First Amendment does not forbid government to prefer religion over non-religion; government may aid religion, so long as it does not prefer one religion over another. Rehnquist's view of the First Amendment, which reflects the work of recent scholars, has been challenged by other scholars and, in a concurrence in the *Weisman* case, by Justice David Souter. One purpose of this volume is to alert the reader, through annotations, to the ongoing debate among the justices over the original meaning of the establishment prohibition.

Given the justices' frequent references to the nation's founding history in deciding establishment claims, one would expect them to be equally interested in what that history has to say about the free exercise of religion. In fact, the justices have rarely demonstrated any such curiosity. *Cantwell* v. *Connecticut*, the first case in this volume and the first free-exercise case in the modern period, does not inquire into history. Neither do the key cases of *Sherbert* v. *Verner* and *Employment Division* v. *Smith*. Readers interested in historical inquiries into the meaning of the free-exercise provision will have to look elsewhere. A good place to begin is Michael McConnell's "The Origins and Historical Understanding of Free Exercise of Religion" (*Harvard Law Review* 103 [1990]: 1409). A vigorous reply to McConnell is Gerard V. Bradley's "Beguiled: Free Exercise Exemptions and the Siren Song of Liberalism" (*Hofstra Law Review* 20 [1991]: 245).

Religion-clause cases typically have come to the Court asserting either that government has (or has not) established religion or that government has (or has not) burdened its free exercise. Justices especially in recent years have recognized that decision-making based on the one provision cannot always be done apart from consideration of the other, and that it makes sense to bear in mind all of what the First Amendment says about religion. For this reason the introductions and notes to the cases refer to the religion *clause*, rather than the religion clauses, although the two provisions are spoken of separately in the opinions.

What in great part led to the religion clause, as a historical matter, was the embryonic nation's commitment to religious liberty and to securing its constitutional protection. Hence the title of this book, *Religious Liberty in the Supreme Court*.

Not every religion-clause case could be included in this volume. The intention has been to present the cases of most doctrinal significance as well as some that enable the reader to see the larger church-state picture being drawn by the Court. Among cases omitted are those involving challenges either to the so-called blue laws, under which all but the most essential businesses were required to close on Sunday, or to laws concerning the teaching of evolution and creation science in public schools. The Sunday closing laws are addressed in *McGowan* v. *Maryland*, 366 U.S. 420 (1961), and *Braunfeld* v. *Brown*, 366 U.S. 599 (1961). A state law banning the teaching of evolution was ruled an establishment of religion in *Epperson* v. *Arkansas*, 393 U.S. 97 (1968), and a state law forbidding the teaching of evolution unless accompanied by instruction in creation science was likewise deemed an establishment of religion in *Edwards* v. *Aguillard*, 482 U.S. 578 (1987).

Among the cases included in this book is *Torcaso* v. *Watkins* (1961), in which the Court unanimously struck down a state constitutional requirement that a candidate for a public job had to avow belief in the existence of God before being appointed. This case is a reminder that the Constitution actually speaks about religion elsewhere than in the First Amendment; there is also the religious-test prohibition in Article VI of the original Constitution: ". . . no religious Test shall ever be required as a Qualification to any Office or public Trust under the United States." *Torcaso* makes it clear that not only the federal government but also the states may not impose a religious test for the holding of a public office.

Another case in this volume, *West Virginia State Board of Education* v. *Barnette* (1943), is not strictly speaking a religion-clause case. Decided on broader First Amendment grounds, it is included here because it overruled *Minersville* v. *Gobitis* (1940), in which the Court upheld a state law under which a student who on grounds of religious belief refused to participate in the daily ceremony of saluting the American flag had been expelled. The Court, sharply criticized for its *Gobitis* decision, does sometimes change its mind.

Barnette is additionally important because Justice Robert Jackson's opinion for the majority contains one of the most famous articulations of the idea of judicial review as the protection of individual rights against majorities: "The very purpose of a Bill of Rights was to withdraw certain subjects from the vicissitudes of political controversy, to place them beyond the reach of majorities and officials and to establish them as legal principles to be applied by the courts. One's right to life, liberty, and property, to free speech, a free press, freedom of worship and assembly, and other fundamental rights may not be submitted to vote; they depend on the outcome of no elections." Part of the controversy over Justice Scalia's majority opinion in the *Smith* case stems from his implicit disagreement with Jackson's understanding of judicial review.

The religion-clause cases are important for many reasons and may be approached from many angles. They raise profound questions about the direction of our public life. As originally understood, the First Amendment did not command the separation of religion from public life, and throughout the nineteenth century and much of the twentieth, a non-sectarian Protestantism provided the foundation of American society. Americans did not wish to contain the public influence of religion; indeed, they saw religion as necessary to the maintenance of a good society. While there was no institutional establishment of religion of the kind clearly forbidden by the First Amendment, elements of religion were present in governmental contexts, especially at the state and local level, and particularly in the public schools. There was what has been called a *de facto* Protestant establishment. Many of the cases in the modern period constitute a challenge to this *de facto* establishment. This challenge reflects certain developments: the advent of a more religiously diverse society, the rise of secularism, especially among educational and political elites, the expansion of interest-group litigation, and a more activist federal judiciary.

There is no going back to the days of the *de facto* Protestant establishment. But does this mean that, as certain modern decisions of the Court imply, religion today should be seen as a purely private phenomenon, of little consequence to our public life? How we answer this question, in future religion-clause cases but also outside them, in the informal understandings we reach and the laws we enact, will have enormous implications for the kind of nation we become.

A Note on the Text

THE OPINIONS The opening section of the opinion for the Court, which typically gives the facts of the case and describes its adjudication in lower courts, has usually been omitted; the editor's introduction to the case summarizes this information. The opinion for the Court and all other opinions have been edited with the intention of preserving the fundamentals of the justices' reasoning in a somewhat abbreviated form. Omissions within the reprinted text are denoted with ellipses, but omissions before or after the reprinted section are not indicated. An ellipsis at the beginning or end of a paragraph or within a paragraph indicates that one or more words or sentences have been omitted. An ellipsis centered in a space between paragraphs indicates that one or more paragraphs have been omitted. Occasionally a summary of omitted material has been supplied, in brackets.

Most brackets and ellipses have been added by the editor. In the relatively few places at which brackets and ellipses are present in an opinion (in quoted material), they have not been distinguished from those added by the editor.

Most footnotes and a few references to other cases and to books and articles have been omitted from the opinions, without ellipses. Most references to other cases are included, however, but often in a shortened form. The footnotes to the opinions that appear in this volume are by the editor, except for a few clearly attributed to the justices.

CASE NAMES AND CITATIONS For each of the twenty-five cases presented in this book, the full citation to the *United States Reports*, the official edition of the Supreme Court's decisions, is given below the case name on the title page. For Case 1, for instance, *Cantwell* v. *Connecticut*, the full citation is 310 U.S. 296 (1940). When one of these twenty-five cases is first mentioned by a justice in an opinion in another case, it is designated here in an abbreviated form, without the volume and page number. A first mention of Case 1 would be *Cantwell* v. *Connecticut* (1940). Subsequent references in the same opinion would mention simply *Cantwell*. A designation such as Case 9 identifies a case and chapter in this book.

For cases other than the twenty-five presented in this book, the full citation to the *United States Reports* is given on first reference, such as *Reynolds* v. *United States*, 98 U.S. 145 (1879). Subsequent references use the most abbreviated form: e.g., *Reynolds*. When a case not included in this book is mentioned in an opinion, a footnote has been added to explain the holding unless it is adequately described in the text of the opinion.

EDITORIAL RESPONSES In the press responses that follow fifteen of the cases, omissions within the reprinted material, but not omissions (if any) before or after the reprinted section, are shown by ellipses.

PART ONE

The Cases

1

Cantwell v. Connecticut

310 U.S. 296 (1940)

During the 1930s and 1940s several First Amendment cases involving Jehovah's Witnesses reached the Supreme Court. In *Cantwell* v. *Connecticut*, the Court reversed the state's conviction of three Jehovah's Witnesses, on grounds of religious liberty. Never before had the Court invalidated the action of a state for this reason. For such a decision even to be possible, the religion clause had to be understood as applying to the states, and *Cantwell's* chief importance lies in the fact that it stands for this proposition. "The Fourteenth Amendment," the Court maintained, "has rendered the legislatures of the states as incompetent as Congress to enact such laws," i.e., laws "respecting an establishment of religion or prohibiting the free exercise thereof."

Cantwell opened the door to federal litigation over religion-clause claims against the states, and most of the religion-clause cases decided by the Supreme Court since 1940 have involved such claims. By contrast, all of the few religion-clause cases the Court decided during its first 150 years involved claims against the federal government.

The facts in *Cantwell* were as follows. On the day of their arrest Newton Cantwell and his two sons, members of Jehovah's Witnesses, were spreading their faith by going from house to house in a New Haven, Connecticut, neighborhood heavily populated by Catholics. The Cantwells sought permission to play, on a portable phonograph, records describing the contents of books they carried with them. When someone granted permission, they played a record and then asked the person to buy

15

the book it described. If they were turned down, they asked for a contribution to defray costs of their publications.

Having stopped two men in the street, one of the sons, Jesse Cantwell, asked and got permission to play a record describing a book entitled *Enemies*, which included an attack on Catholicism. Both men were Catholics, and they testified that they felt like hitting Cantwell or throwing him off the street. Cantwell left without argument.

Newton Cantwell and his sons were charged and then convicted in Connecticut courts under (1) a state law forbidding the unlicensed soliciting of funds on the representation that they were for religious or charitable purposes, and (2) the common law for inciting a breach of the peace. They appealed their convictions to the U.S. Supreme Court on First Amendment grounds, and the Court unanimously sided with them. *Cantwell* stands out as one of the few religion-clause cases since 1940 in which the Court has been of one mind, expressed in one opinion.

While the Court did hold that both provisions of the religion clause apply to the states, the Cantwells based their appeal on the free-exercise provision, and the case is usually understood in those terms. The Court's reasoning and the cases it cited in footnotes suggest that the Court also saw the case in terms of the First Amendment guarantee of freedom of speech.

Participating in *Cantwell v. Connecticut,* decided May 30, 1940, were Chief Justice Charles E. Hughes and Associate Justices Hugo L. Black, William O. Douglas, Felix Frankfurter, James C. McReynolds, Frank Murphy, Stanley F. Reed, Owen J. Roberts, and Harlan F. Stone.

Opinions

Justice Owen J. Roberts delivered the opinion of the Court:

FIRST. We hold that the [Connecticut] statute, as construed and applied to the appellants, deprives [the Cantwells] of their liberty without due process of law in contravention of the Fourteenth Amendment. The fundamental concept of liberty embodied in that Amendment embraces the liberties guaranteed by the First Amendment. The First Amendment declares that Congress shall make no law respecting an establishment of religion or prohibiting the free exercise thereof. The Fourteenth Amendment has rendered the legislatures of the states as incompetent as Congress to enact such laws.[1] The constitutional inhibition of legislation on the subject of religion has a double aspect. On the one hand, it forestalls compulsion by law of the acceptance of any creed or the practice of any form of worship. Freedom of conscience and freedom to adhere to such religious organization or form of worship as the individual may choose cannot be restricted by law. On the other hand, it safeguards the free exercise of the chosen form of religion.[2] Thus the amendment embraces two concepts, freedom to believe and freedom to act. The first is absolute but, in the nature of things, the second cannot be. Conduct remains subject to regulation for the protection of society.[3] The freedom to act must have appropri-

---

1. In *Permoli* v. *First Municipality*, 44 U.S. (3 How.) 589 (1845), the Supreme Court rejected the claim that the free-exercise provision of the First Amendment applies to the states. In *Meyer* v. *Nebraska*, 262 U.S. 390 (1923), the Court said that "the right of the individual to worship God according to the dictates of his own conscience" is among the liberties protected against state infringement by the due-process clause of the Fourteenth Amendment. But this observation was not essential to the holding in the case. In *Hamilton* v. *Regents of the University of California*, 293 U.S. 245 (1934), Justice Pierce Butler opined that the First Amendment protects religious liberty in the states. It is in *Cantwell* that the Court for the first time says that the states are bound by the requirements of the religion clause.

2. Note here that the Court did not consult constitutional history in an effort to determine the meaning of the free-exercise provision. In subsequent free-exercise cases, the Court has never undertaken the kind of historical inquiries into constitutional meaning that have, by contrast, characterized its work with respect to the no-establishment provision, beginning with *Everson* v. *Board of Education* (1947), Case 4.

3. Footnote four occurs at this point in the opinion; the note cites *Reynolds* v. *United States*, 98 U.S. 145 (1879), and *Davis* v. *Beason*, 133 U.S. 333 (1890), two of the so-called Mormon cases in which the Court for the first time encountered free-exercise claims. In

ate definition to preserve the enforcement of that protection. In every case the power to regulate must be so exercised as not, in attaining a permissible end, unduly to infringe the protected freedom. No one would contest the proposition that a state may not, by statute, wholly deny the right to preach or to disseminate religious views. Plainly such a previous and absolute restraint would violate the terms of the guaranty. It is equally clear that a state may by general and non-discriminatory legislation regulate the times, the places, and the manner of soliciting upon its streets, and of holding meetings thereon; and may in other respects safeguard the peace, good order and comfort of the community, without unconstitutionally invading the liberties protected by the Fourteenth Amendment. The appellants are right in their insistence that the Act in question is not such a regulation. If a certificate is procured, solicitation is permitted without restraint but, in the absence of a certificate, solicitation is altogether prohibited.

The appellants urge that to require them to obtain a certificate as a condition of soliciting support for their views amounts to a prior restraint on the exercise of their religion within the meaning of the Constitution. The State insists that the Act, as construed by the Supreme Court of Connecticut, imposes no previous restraint upon the dissemination of religious views or teaching but merely safeguards against the perpetration of frauds under the cloak of religion. Conceding that this is so, the question remains whether the method adopted by Connecticut to that end transgresses the liberty safeguarded by the Constitution.

The general regulation, in the public interest, of solicitation, which does not involve any religious test and does not unreasonably obstruct or delay the collection of funds, is not open to any constitutional objection, even though the collection be for a religious purpose. Such regulation would not constitute a prohibited previous restraint on the free exercise of religion or interpose an inadmissible obstacle to its exercise.

---

these cases the Court drew a distinction between belief and action: so long as it has a rational basis for doing so, the federal government may regulate action regardless of its motivation, including religious belief, but it may not regulate the belief itself. According to the teachings of *Reynolds* and *Davis,* Mormons were free to believe in polygamy, but they could not practice or even advocate it in violation of certain federal laws governing the federal territories. The Court in these cases thus refused to interpret the free-exercise provision as mandating a conduct exemption based on religious faith from otherwise valid law. If *Cantwell* is read as suggesting that the provision may in fact require such exemption, *Minersville School District* v. *Gobitis* (1940), decided later in the same term, plainly does no such thing; see Case 2.

It will be noted, however, that the Act requires an application to the secretary of the public welfare council of the State; that he is empowered to determine whether the cause is a religious one, and that the issue of a certificate depends upon his affirmative action. If he finds that the cause is not that of religion, to solicit for it becomes a crime. He is not to issue a certificate as a matter of course. His decision to issue or refuse it involves appraisal of facts, the exercise of judgment, and the formation of an opinion. He is authorized to withhold his approval if he determines that the cause is not a religious one. Such a censorship of religion as the means of determining its right to survive is a denial of liberty protected by the First Amendment and included in the liberty which is within the protection of the Fourteenth.[4]

The State asserts that if the licensing officer acts arbitrarily, capriciously, or corruptly, his action is subject to judicial correcting. Counsel refer to the rule prevailing in Connecticut that the decision of a commission or an administrative official will be reviewed upon a claim that "it works material damage to individual or corporate rights, or invades or threatens such rights, or is so unreasonable as to justify judicial intervention, or is not consonant with justice, or that a legal duty has not been performed." It is suggested that the statute is to be read as requiring the officer to issue a certificate unless the cause in question is clearly not a religious one; and that if he violates his duty his action will be corrected by a court.

To this suggestion there are several sufficient answers. The line between a discretionary and a ministerial act is not always easy to mark and the statute has not been construed by the State court to impose a mere ministerial duty on the secretary of the welfare council. Upon his decision as to the nature of the cause, the right to solicit depends. Moreover, the availability of a judicial remedy for abuses in the system of licensing still leaves that system one of previous restraint which, in the field of free speech and press, we have held inadmissible. A statute authorizing previous restraint upon the exercise of the guaranteed freedom by judicial decision after trial is as obnoxious to the Constitution as one providing for like restraint by administrative action.

Nothing we have said is intended even remotely to imply that, under the cloak of religion, persons may, with impunity, commit frauds upon

---

4. Apparently of concern to the Court was what David P. Currie, professor of law at the University of Chicago, has called "the undue risk of discriminatory administration," which, as he points out, "is at the heart of the constitutional prohibition" (*The Constitution in the Supreme Court: The Second Century 1888–1986* [Chicago: University of Chicago Press, 1990], 266).

the public. Certainly penal laws are available to punish such conduct. Even the exercise of religion may be at some slight inconvenience in order that the state may protect its citizens from injury. Without doubt a state may protect its citizens from fraudulent solicitation by requiring a stranger in the community, before permitting him publicly to solicit funds for any purpose, to establish his identity and his authority to act for the cause which he purports to represent. The state is likewise free to regulate the time and manner of solicitation generally, in the interest of public safety, peace, comfort or convenience. But to condition the solicitation of aid for the perpetuation of religious views or systems upon a license, the grant of which rests in the exercise of a determination by state authority as to what is a religious cause, is to lay a forbidden burden upon the exercise of liberty protected by the Constitution.

SECOND. We hold that, in the circumstances disclosed, the conviction of Jesse Cantwell on the fifth count [disturbing the peace] must be set aside. Decision as to the lawfulness of the conviction demands the weighing of two conflicting interests. The fundamental law declares the interest of the United States that the free exercise of religion be not prohibited and that freedom to communicate information and opinion be not abridged. The state of Connecticut has an obvious interest in the preservation and protection of peace and good order within her borders. We must determine whether the alleged protection of the State's interest, means to which end would, in the absence of limitation by the federal Constitution, lie wholly within the State's discretion, has been pressed, in this instance, to a point where it has come into fatal collision with the overriding interest protected by the federal compact.

Conviction on the fifth count was not pursuant to a statute evincing a legislative judgment that street discussion of religious affairs, because of its tendency to provoke disorder, should be regulated, or a judgment that the playing of a phonograph on the streets should in the interest of comfort or privacy be limited or prevented. Violation of an Act exhibiting such a legislative judgment and narrowly drawn to prevent the supposed evil, would pose a question differing from that we must here answer. Such a declaration of the State's policy would weigh heavily in any challenge of the law as infringing constitutional limitations. Here, however, the judgment is based on a common law concept of the most general and undefined nature. The court below has held that the petitioner's conduct constituted the commission of an offense under the State law, and we accept its decision as binding upon us to that extent.

The offense known as breach of the peace embraces a great variety of conduct destroying or menacing public order and tranquillity. It includes not only violent acts but acts and words likely to produce violence in others. No one would have the hardihood to suggest that the principle of freedom of speech sanctions incitement to riot or that religious liberty connotes the privilege to exhort others to physical attack upon those belonging to another sect. When clear and present danger of riot, disorder, interference with traffic upon the public streets, or other immediate threat to public safety, peace, or order, appears, the power of the state to prevent or punish is obvious. Equally obvious is it that a state may not unduly suppress free communication of views, religious or other, under the guise of conserving desirable conditions. Here we have a situation analogous to a conviction under a statute sweeping in a great variety of conduct under a general and indefinite characterization, and leaving to the executive and judicial branches too wide a discretion in its application.

Having these considerations in mind, we note that Jesse Cantwell, on April 26, 1938, was upon a public street, where he had a right to be, and where he had a right peacefully to impart his views to others. There is no showing that his deportment was noisy, truculent, overbearing or offensive. He requested of two pedestrians permission to play to them a phonograph record. The permission was granted. It is not claimed that he intended to insult or affront the hearers by playing the record. It is plain that he wished only to interest them in his propaganda. The sound of the phonograph is not shown to have disturbed residents of the street, to have drawn a crowd, or to have impeded traffic. Thus far he had invaded no right or interest of the public or of the men accosted.

The record played by Cantwell embodies a general attack on all organized religious systems as instruments of Satan and injurious to man; it then singles out the Roman Catholic Church for strictures couched in terms which naturally would offend not only persons of that persuasion, but all others who respect the honestly held religious faith of their fellows. The hearers were in fact highly offended. One of them said he felt like hitting Cantwell and the other that he was tempted to throw Cantwell off the street. The one who testified he felt like hitting Cantwell said, in answer to the question "Did you do anything else or have any other reaction?" "No, sir, because he said he would take the victrola and he went." The other witness testified that he told Cantwell he had better get off the street before something happened to him and that was the end of the matter as Cantwell picked up his books and walked up the street.

Cantwell's conduct, in the view of the court below, considered apart from the effect of his communication upon his hearers, did not amount to a breach of the peace. One may, however, be guilty of the offense if he commit acts or make statements likely to provoke violence and disturbance of good order, even though no such eventuality be intended. Decisions to this effect are many, but examination discloses that, in practically all, the provocative language which was held to amount to a breach of the peace consisted of profane, indecent, or abusive remarks directed to the person of the hearer. Resort to epithets or personal abuse is not in any proper sense communication of information or opinion safeguarded by the Constitution, and its punishment as a criminal act would raise no question under that instrument.

We find in the instant case no assault or threatening of bodily harm, no truculent bearing, no intentional discourtesy, no personal abuse. On the contrary, we find only an effort to persuade a willing listener to buy a book or to contribute money in the interest of what Cantwell, however misguided others may think him, conceived to be true religion.

In the realm of religious faith, and in that of political belief, sharp differences arise. In both fields the tenets of one man may seem the rankest error to his neighbor. To persuade others to his own point of view, the pleader, as we know, at times, resorts to exaggeration, to vilification of men who have been, or are, prominent in church or state, and even to false statement. But the people of this nation have ordained in the light of history, that, in spite of the probability of excesses and abuses, these liberties are, in the long view, essential to enlightened opinion and right conduct on the part of the citizens of a democracy.

The essential characteristic of these liberties is, that under their shield many types of life, character, opinion and belief can develop unmolested and unobstructed. Nowhere is this shield more necessary than in our own country for a people composed of many races and of many creeds. There are limits to the exercise of these liberties. The danger in these times from the coercive activities of those who in the delusion of racial or religious conceit would incite violence and breaches of the peace in order to deprive others of their equal right to the exercise of their liberties, is emphasized by events familiar to all. These and other transgressions of those limits the states appropriately may punish.

Although the contents of the record not unnaturally aroused animosity, we think that, in the absence of a statute narrowly drawn to define and punish specific conduct as constituting a clear and present danger to a substantial interest of the State, the petitioner's communication, considered in the light of the constitutional guaranties, raised no such clear and present menace to public peace and order as to render him liable to conviction of the common law offense in question.

The judgment affirming the convictions on the third and fifth counts is reversed and the cause is remanded for further proceedings not inconsistent with this opinion.

2

Minersville School District
v. Gobitis

310 U.S. 586 (1940)

The Supreme Court concluded in this 1940 case that a public school may require students to salute and pledge allegiance to the U.S. flag; a member of Jehovah's Witnesses had objected on free-exercise grounds. The holding in *Minersville School District* v. *Gobitis* had a short life, as it was overruled in 1943 by *West Virginia State Board of Education* v. *Barnette*, Case 3. (See Justice Antonin Scalia's treatment of *Gobitis* in his opinion for the Court half a century later in *Employment Division* v. *Smith* [1990], Case 23.)

Justice Felix Frankfurter, who wrote for the Court in *Gobitis* and filed a lengthy dissent in *Barnette*, saw these cases as presenting free-exercise claims for special exemption from otherwise valid law. Frankfurter did not believe it was the business of the federal judiciary to issue such an exemption; for that, Frankfurter believed, a complaining party must go to the relevant legislative body.

The only other opinion in the case was a dissent by Justice Harlan Stone, who argued that it was indeed the job of the judiciary to demand a reasonable accommodation between the interests of government and the interests of liberty. As will be seen in Justice Robert Jackson's opinion for the Court in *Barnette*, the flag-salute cases may also be understood in a different way: in terms not of a free-exercise claim but of government authority to compel any American to profess certain words or ideas. Both Frankfurter's opinion for the Court and Stone's dissent are presented here, followed by an editorial comment from *The Christian Century*.

Like Case 1, *Cantwell* v. *Connecticut* (1940), and many other civil-liberties cases in the 1930s and 1940s, *Gobitis* involved complaints against a state by Jehovah's Witnesses. Lillian Gobitis, 12, and her brother William, 10, were expelled from the public schools of Minersville, Pennsylvania, because they refused, on grounds of their faith, to salute and pledge allegiance to the U.S. flag as part of a daily exercise mandated by the local school board. Walter Gobitis, their father, sued and won relief in federal district court; the Minersville school board was enjoined from continuing to demand participation in the flag-salute ceremony. This order was affirmed by a federal appeals court—and then reversed by the Supreme Court.

Participating in *Minersville School District* v. *Gobitis*, decided June 3, 1940, were Chief Justice Charles E. Hughes and Associate Justices Hugo L. Black, William O. Douglas, Felix Frankfurter, James C. McReynolds, Frank Murphy, Stanley F. Reed, Owen J. Roberts, and Harlan F. Stone.

Opinions

Justice Felix Frankfurter delivered the opinion of the Court:

A grave responsibility confronts this Court whenever in course of litigation it must reconcile the conflicting claims of liberty and authority. But when the liberty invoked is liberty of conscience, and the authority is authority to safeguard the nation's fellowship, judicial conscience is put to its severest test. Of such a nature is the present controversy.

. . .

We must decide whether the requirement of participation in [the flag-salute] ceremony, exacted from a child who refuses upon sincere religious grounds, infringes without due process of law the liberty guaranteed by the Fourteenth Amendment.

Centuries of strife over the erection of particular dogmas as exclusive or all-comprehending faiths led to the inclusion of a guarantee for religious freedom in the Bill of Rights. The First Amendment, and the Fourteenth through its absorption of the First, sought to guard against repetition of those bitter religious struggles by prohibiting the establishment of a state religion and by securing to every sect the free exercise of its faith.[1] So pervasive is the acceptance of this precious right that its scope is brought into question, as here, only when the conscience of individuals collides with the felt necessities of society.

Certainly the affirmative pursuit of one's convictions about the ultimate mystery of the universe and man's relation to it is placed beyond the reach of law. Government may not interfere with organized or individual expression of belief or disbelief. Propagation of belief—or even of disbelief in the supernatural—is protected, whether in church or chapel, mosque or synagogue, tabernacle or meeting-house. Likewise the Constitution assures generous immunity to the individual from imposition of penalties for offending, in the course of his own religious activities, the religious views of others, be they a minority or those who are dominant in government. *Cantwell* v. *Connecticut* (1940).

---

1. In *Cantwell* v. *Connecticut* (1940), the Court explicitly stated for the first time that the states are bound by the religion clause of the First Amendment. See Case 1.

But the manifold character of man's relations may bring his conception of religious duty into conflict with the secular interest of his fellow-men. Does the constitutional guarantee compel exemption from doing what society thinks necessary for the promotion of some great common end, or from a penalty for conduct which appears dangerous to the general good? To state the problem is to recall the truth that no single principle can answer all of life's complexities. The right to freedom of religious belief, however dissident and however obnoxious to the cherished beliefs of others—even of a majority—is itself the denial of an absolute. But to affirm that the freedom to follow conscience has itself no limits in the life of a society would deny that very plurality of principles which, as a matter of history, underlies protection of religious toleration. Our present task then, as so often the case with courts, is to reconcile two rights in order to prevent either from destroying the other. But, because in safeguarding conscience we are dealing with interests so subtle and so dear, every possible leeway should be given to the claims of religious faith.

. . . The religious liberty which the Constitution protects has never excluded legislation of general scope not directed against doctrinal loyalties of particular sects. Judicial nullification of legislation cannot be justified by attributing to the framers of the Bill of Rights views for which there is no historic warrant. Conscientious scruples have not, in the course of the long struggle for religious toleration, relieved the individual from obedience to a general law not aimed at the promotion or restriction of religious beliefs. The mere possession of religious convictions which contradict the relevant concerns of a political society does not relieve the citizen from the discharge of political responsibilities. The necessity for this adjustment has again and again been recognized. In a number of situations the exertion of political authority has been sustained, while basic considerations of religious freedom have been left inviolate.[2] In . . . these cases the general laws in question, upheld in their application to those who refused obedience from religious conviction, were manifestations of specific powers of government deemed by the legislature essential to secure and maintain that orderly, tranquil, and free society without which religious toleration

---

2. The opinion here cites, among other cases, *Reynolds* v. *United States*, 98 U.S. 145 (1879), which held that the free-exercise provision does not entitle a polygamist to an exemption from an anti-polygamy criminal law in the federal territories, and *Davis* v. *Beason*, 133 U.S. 333 (1890), which held that a law of the Territory of Idaho does not violate the free-exercise provision because it denies the right to vote to any bigamist or polygamist and to anyone who teaches or promotes such practices.

itself is unattainable. Nor does the freedom of speech assured by Due Process move in a more absolute circle of immunity than that enjoyed by religious freedom. Even if it were assumed that freedom of speech goes beyond the historic concept of full opportunity to utter and to disseminate views, however heretical or offensive to dominant opinion, and includes freedom from conveying what may be deemed an implied but rejected affirmation, the question remains whether school children, like the Gobitis children, must be excused from conduct required of all the other children in the promotion of national cohesion. We are dealing with an interest inferior to none in the hierarchy of legal values. National unity is the basis of national security. To deny the legislature the right to select appropriate means for its attainment presents a totally different order of problem from that of the propriety of subordinating the possible ugliness of littered streets to the free expression of opinion through distribution of handbills.

Situations like the present are phases of the profoundest problem confronting a democracy—the problem which Lincoln cast in memorable dilemma: "Must a government of necessity be too *strong* for the liberties of its people, or too *weak* to maintain its own existence?"[3] No mere textual reading or logical talisman can solve the dilemma. And when the issue demands judicial determination, it is not the personal notion of judges of what wise adjustment requires which must prevail.

Unlike the instances we have cited, the case before us is not concerned with an exertion of legislative power for the promotion of some specific need or interest of secular society—the protection of the family, the promotion of health, the common defense, the raising of public revenues to defray the cost of government. But all these specific activities of government presuppose the existence of an organized political society. The ultimate foundation of a free society is the binding tie of cohesive sentiment. Such a sentiment is fostered by all those agencies of the mind and spirit which may serve to gather up the traditions of a people, transmit them from generation to generation, and thereby create that continuity of a treasured common life which constitutes a civilization. "We live by symbols." The flag is the symbol of our national unity, transcending all internal differences, however large, within the framework of the Constitution. . . .

The case before us must be viewed as though the legislature of Pennsylvania had itself formally directed the flag-salute for the chil-

---

3. Compare Justice Robert Jackson's response in his opinion for the Court in *West Virginia Board of Education v. Barnette* (1943), Case 3.

dren of Minersville; had made no exemption for children whose parents were possessed of conscientious scruples like those of the Gobitis family; and had indicated its belief in the desirable ends to be secured by having its public school children share a common experience at those periods of development when their minds are supposedly receptive to its assimilation, by an exercise appropriate in time and place and setting, and one designed to evoke in them appreciation of the nation's hopes and dreams, its sufferings and sacrifices. The precise issue, then, for us to decide is whether the legislatures of the various states and the authorities in a thousand counties and school districts of this country are barred from determining the appropriateness of various means to evoke that unifying sentiment without which there can ultimately be no liberties, civil or religious. To stigmatize legislative judgment in providing for this universal gesture of respect for the symbol of our national life in the setting of the common school as a lawless inroad on that freedom of conscience which the Constitution protects, would amount to no less than the pronouncement of pedagogical and psychological dogma in a field where courts possess no marked and certainly no controlling competence. The influences which help toward a common feeling for the common country are manifold. Some may seem harsh and others no doubt are foolish. Surely, however, the end is legitimate. And the effective means for its attainment are still so uncertain and so unauthenticated by science as to preclude us from putting the widely prevalent belief in flag-saluting beyond the pale of legislative power. It mocks reason and denies our whole history to find in the allowance of a requirement to salute our flag on fitting occasions the seeds of sanction for obeisance to a leader.

The wisdom of training children in patriotic impulses by those compulsions which necessarily pervade so much of the educational process is not for our independent judgment. Even were we convinced of the folly of such a measure, such belief would be no proof of its unconstitutionality.[4] For ourselves, we might be tempted to say that the deepest patriotism is best engendered by giving unfettered scope to the most crotchety beliefs. Perhaps it is best, even from the standpoint of those interests which ordinances like the one under review seek to promote, to give to the least popular sect leave from conformities like those here in issue. The courtroom is not the arena for debating issues of educa-

---

4. This familiar distinction between the folly or wisdom of a law and its constitutionality is found in other religion-clause opinions. See, for example, Justice Antonin Scalia's opinion for the Court in *Employment Division* v. *Smith* (1990), Case 23.

tional policy. It is not our province to choose among competing considerations in the subtle process of securing effective loyalty to the traditional ideals of democracy, while respecting at the same time individual idiosyncrasies among a people so diversified in racial origins and religious allegiances. So to hold would in effect make us the school board for the country. That authority has not been given to this Court, nor should we assume it.

We are dealing here with the formative period in the development of citizenship. Great diversity of psychological and ethical opinion exists among us concerning the best way to train children for their place in society. Because of these differences and because of reluctance to permit a single, iron-cast system of education to be imposed upon a nation compounded of so many strains, we have held that, even though public education is one of our most cherished democratic institutions, the Bill of Rights bars a state from compelling all children to attend the public schools. *Pierce* v. *Society of Sisters*, 268 U.S. 510 (1925). But it is a very different thing for this Court to exercise censorship over the conviction of legislatures that a particular program or exercise will best promote in the minds of children who attend the common schools an attachment to the institutions of their country.

What the school authorities are really asserting is the right to awaken in the child's mind considerations as to the significance of the flag contrary to those implanted by the parent. In such an attempt the state is normally at a disadvantage in competing with the parent's authority, so long—and this is the vital aspect of religious toleration—as parents are unmolested in their right to counteract by their own persuasiveness the wisdom and rightness of those loyalties which the state's educational system is seeking to promote. Except where the transgression of constitutional liberty is too plain for argument, personal freedom is best maintained—so long as the remedial channels of the democratic process remain open and unobstructed—when it is ingrained in a people's habits and not enforced against popular policy by the coercion of adjudicated law. That the flag-salute is an allowable portion of a school program for those who do not invoke conscientious scruples is surely not debatable. But for us to insist that, though the ceremony may be required, exceptional immunity must be given to dissidents, is to maintain that there is no basis for a legislative judgment that such an exemption might introduce elements of difficulty into the school discipline, might cast doubts in the minds of the other children which would themselves weaken the effect of the exercise.

The preciousness of the family relation, the authority and independence which give dignity to parenthood, indeed the enjoyment of all freedom, presuppose the kind of ordered society which is summarized by our flag. A society which is dedicated to the preservation of these ultimate values of civilization may in self-protection utilize the educational process for inculcating those almost unconscious feelings which bind men together in a comprehending loyalty, whatever may be their lesser differences and difficulties. That is to say, the process may be utilized so long as men's right to believe as they please, to win others to their way of belief, and their right to assemble in their chosen places of worship for the devotional ceremonies of their faith, are all fully respected.

Judicial review, itself a limitation on popular government, is a fundamental part of our constitutional scheme. But to the legislature no less than to courts is committed the guardianship of deeply-cherished liberties. Where all the effective means of inducing political changes are left free from interference, education in the abandonment of foolish legislation is itself a training in liberty. To fight out the wise use of legislative authority in the forum of public opinion and before legislative assemblies rather than to transfer such a contest to the judicial arena, serves to vindicate the self-confidence of a free people.

Justice Harlan F. Stone, dissenting:

I think the judgment below [enjoining the school board from demanding participation in the flag-salute ceremony] should be affirmed. . . .

The law which is [today] sustained is unique in the history of Anglo-American legislation. It does more than suppress freedom of speech and more than prohibit the free exercise of religion, which concededly are forbidden by the First Amendment and are violations of the liberty guaranteed by the Fourteenth. For by this law the state seeks to coerce these children to express a sentiment which, as they interpret it, they do not entertain, and which violates their deepest religious convictions.

Concededly the constitutional guarantees of personal liberty are not always absolutes. Government has a right to survive and powers conferred upon it are not necessarily set at naught by the express prohibitions of the Bill of Rights. It may make war and raise armies. To that end it may compel citizens to give military service and subject them to military training despite their religious objections. It may suppress religious practices dangerous to morals, and presumably those also which are inimical to public safety, health and good order. But it is a long step, and one which I am unable to take, to the position that government may, as a supposed educational measure and as a means of disciplining the young, compel public affirmations which violate their religious conscience.

The very fact that we have constitutional guaranties of civil liberties and the specificity of their command where freedom of speech and of religion are concerned require some accommodation of the powers which government normally exercises, when no question of civil liberty is involved, to the constitutional demand that those liberties be protected against the action of government itself. . . .

. . . [W]here there are competing demands of the interests of government and of liberty under the Constitution, and where the performance of governmental functions is brought into conflict with specific constitutional restrictions, there must, when that is possible, be reasonable accommodation between them so as to preserve the essentials of both and . . . it is the function of the courts to determine whether such accommodation is reasonably possible.[5] . . . [H]ere, even if we believe that such compulsions will contribute to national unity, there are other ways to teach loyalty and patriotism which are the sources of national unity, than by compelling the pupil to affirm that which he does not believe and by commanding a form of affirmance which violates his religious convictions. Without recourse to such compulsion, the state is free to compel attendance at school and require teaching by instruction and study of all in our history and in the structure and organization of our government, including the guaranties of civil liberty which tend to inspire patriotism and love of country. I cannot say that government here is deprived of any interest or function which it is entitled to maintain at the expense of the protection of civil liberties by requiring it to resort to the alternatives which do not coerce an affirmation of belief.

The guaranties of civil liberty are but guaranties of freedom of the human mind and spirit and of reasonable freedom and opportunity to express them. They presuppose the right of the individual to hold such opinions as he will and to give them reasonably free expression, and his freedom, and that of the state as well, to teach and persuade others by the communication of ideas. The very essence of the liberty which they guarantee is the freedom of the individual from compulsion as to

---

5. State "accommodation" of religious belief is a persistent theme in later religion-clause cases. Justice Stone appears to have been the first justice to use the term in a free-exercise context.

what he shall think and what he shall say, at least where the compulsion is to bear false witness to his religion. If these guaranties are to have any meaning they must, I think, be deemed to withhold from the state any authority to compel belief or the expression of it where that expression violates religious convictions, whatever may be the legislative view of the desirability of such compulsion.

History teaches us that there have been but few infringements of personal liberty by the state which have not been justified, as they are here, in the name of righteousness and the public good, and few which have not been directed, as they are now, at politically helpless minorities. The framers were not unaware that under the system which they created most governmental curtailments of personal liberty would have the support of a legislative judgment that the public interest would be better served by the curtailment of personal liberty than by its constitutional protection. I cannot conceive that in prescribing, as limitations upon the powers of government, the freedom of the mind and spirit secured by the explicit guaranties of freedom of speech and religion, they intended or rightly could have left any latitude for a legislative judgment that the compulsory expression of belief which violates religious convictions would better serve the public interest than their protection. The Constitution may well elicit expressions of loyalty to it and to the government which it created, but it does not command such expressions or otherwise give any indication that compulsory expressions of loyalty play any such part in our scheme of government as to override the constitutional protection of freedom of speech and religion. And while such expressions of loyalty, when voluntarily given, may promote national unity, it is quite another matter to say that their compulsory expression by children in violation of their own and their parents' religious convictions can be regarded as playing so important a part in our national unity as to leave school boards free to exact it despite the constitutional guaranty of freedom of religion. The very terms of the Bill of Rights preclude, it seems to me, any reconciliation of such compulsions with the constitutional guaranties by a legislative declaration that they are more important to the public welfare than the Bill of Rights.

But even if this view be rejected and it is considered that there is some scope for the determination by legislatures whether the citizen shall be compelled to give public expression of such sentiments contrary to his religion, I am not persuaded that we should refrain from passing upon the legislative judgment "as long as the remedial channels of the democratic process remain open and unobstructed." This seems to me no more than the surrender of the constitutional protection of the liberty of small minorities to the popular will. We have previously pointed to the importance of a searching judicial inquiry into the legislative judgment in situations where prejudice against discrete and insular minorities may tend to curtail the operation of those political processes ordinarily to be relied on to protect minorities. See *United States* v. *Carolene Products Co.*, 304 U.S. 144, 152, note 4.[6] And until now we have not hesitated similarly to scrutinize legislation restricting the civil liberty of racial and religious minorities although no political process was affected. Here we have such a small minority entertaining in good faith a religious belief, which is such a departure from the usual course of human conduct, that most persons are disposed to regard it with little toleration or concern. In such circumstances careful scrutiny of legislative efforts to secure conformity of belief and opinion by a compulsory affirmation of the desired belief, is especially needful if civil rights are to receive any protection. Tested by this standard, I am not prepared to say that the right of this small and helpless minority, including children having a strong religious conviction, whether they understand its nature or not, to refrain from a patriotic expression obnoxious to their religion, is to be overborne by the interest of the state in maintaining discipline in the schools.

The Constitution expresses more than the conviction of the people that democratic processes must be preserved at all costs. It is also an expression of faith and a command that freedom of mind and spirit must be preserved, which government must obey, if it is to adhere to that justice and moderation without which no free government can exist. For this reason it would seem that legislation which operates to repress the religious freedom of small minorities, which is admittedly within the scope of the protection of the Bill of Rights, must at least be subject to the same judicial scrutiny as legislation which we have recently held to infringe the constitutional liberty of religious and racial minorities.

---

6. Justice Stone was the author of the note here referred to in *Carolene Products*, a 1938 case. The note is one of the best known in the Court's history. "There may be," he wrote, "narrower scope for the operation of the presumption of constitutionality where legislation appears on its face to be within a specific prohibition of the Constitution, such as those of the first ten amendments, which are deemed equally specific when held to be embraced within the Fourteenth." Statutes, he said, "directed at particular religious . . . or national . . . or racial minorities" may call for "a more searching judicial inquiry." Stone's footnote expressed what soon became the Court's civil libertarian project, which included—though not in *Gobitis*, where it was rejected by Frankfurter—judicial protection of Jehovah's Witnesses who objected to state-mandated flag-salute ceremonies.

With such scrutiny I cannot say that the inconveniences which may attend some sensible adjustment of school discipline in order that the religious convictions of these children may be spared, presents a problem so momentous or pressing as to outweigh the freedom from compulsory violation of religious faith which has been thought worthy of constitutional protection.

Response

From **The Christian Century**, June 19, 1940, "The Flag Salute Case":

It was doubtless sheer coincidence that the Pennsylvania case of the children who had been expelled from school for refusal to salute the flag came up for final decision by the United States Supreme Court just at a time when the public mind was particularly inflamed by news of the war abroad and sensitive to suspicions of disloyalty at home. Not for a moment is it to be assumed that the decision of the court was influenced by the popular mood. Such a suggestion would be righteously resented even by those who, two or three years ago, were demanding that the highest court should be reorganized so that it would respond to the will of the people. The agreement between the decision and the current campaign against "fifth columnists" can also be set down as a coincidence. . . .

It is impossible not to view with respect an opinion written by the conspicuously liberal Justice Frankfurter and concurred in by so large a majority of the court. Yet it is permissible to believe that the decision was not a wise one. Perhaps the court was betrayed into making it in reaction against the respondent's brief, which was even less wise because it attempted to prove too much. That brief, if the argument were accepted in its entirety, would establish the absolute principle that the state must refrain from interfering with any action which the doer claims is in accordance with the will of God and from requiring any action which any citizen claims is contrary to the will of God. This is, as Justice Frankfurter pointed out, an impossible principle of government if it is conceived as an absolute, because there is a range of conduct in which the state has a legitimate concern but which may also fall within the scope of a religious motivation directed to an anti-social end.

In some corners of the world there are religious groups which practice human sacrifice in obedience to what they believe to be the will of God. They cannot operate freely in this country. The Bill of Rights and the tradition of religious liberty did not sustain the institution of polygamy in Utah, though it was supported by what many conscientiously believed to be a divine revelation. Now and then some individual refuses to pay taxes because he believes that human and secular government is contrary to the will of God; but he has to pay. Religious liberty must, of necessity, have some limits if any sort of social order is to be maintained, and without social order there is no liberty.

The principle of religious liberty which is embodied in the American tra-

37

dition is that there shall be complete freedom of conscience in all matters that do not manifestly and adversely affect the social order. That is a real principle, not merely a prudential arrangement. It distinguishes the American system from that which was in operation throughout Europe in the Middle Ages and which still exists vestigially wherever there is an established church. To grant complete freedom of conscience and equal treatment of all religions, subject only to the condition that no specific injury shall be done to society or to the rights of others, is something very different from assuming that any divergence from the religious opinions or practices of the majority is *ipso facto* an attack upon the stability of society.

Loyalty to the nation and to its government is important. Saluting the flag is merely an arbitrary piece of ritual which is one way of expressing and teaching loyalty. Many of us like it. We love the flag. . . . Still, it is quite conceivable that there may be those to whom saluting a symbol seems equivalent to worshipping an image. This is, in our judgment, a foolish idea. But it is of the essence of liberty that there be room for harmless foolish ideas—or harmless ideas that seem foolish to the majority. Willingness to salute the flag is no criterion of loyalty. To make this particular ceremony a test is to make the flag mean something quite different from what Justice Frankfurter says it means.

When William Tell refused to do obedience to Gessler's hat, he incurred a tyrant's displeasure for failure to salute a symbol of tyranny. It is bitterly ironical that a free government should inflict a penalty for refusal to salute a symbol of freedom. William Penn, a Quaker with conscientious scruples against removing his hat in the presence of royalty, scandalized the court of Charles II by remaining covered before the king. Charles, an arbitrary monarch in most respects, was wiser in this matter than his courtiers on Gessler or the Supreme Court. Wearing or not wearing a hat might be a question of conscience to Penn, but it was only a point of etiquette to the king. Let Penn have his own way about it, since he took it so seriously, if he would show his loyalty in things that mattered.

That lesson is one we need to learn in these tense and strident days, even if we have to learn it from a Stuart king. Within the past two weeks there have been half a dozen cases of mob violence against people who would not salute the flag. Two coal miners, described in the press reports as "religious zealots," quit their jobs rather than perform a compulsory salute to the flag. These people are not insidious enemies of the republic or secret agents of a foreign power. If they were, they would conform. They are conscientious but misguided zealots. Their refusal to go through the ritual of the salute is not half so dangerous to this country as the equally conscientious and equally misguided zeal of the patriots who, mistaking one formula of loyalty for the thing itself, are more anxious to have a symbol of liberty saluted than to have liberty maintained.

3

West Virginia State Board of Education v. Barnette

319 U.S. 624 (1943)

The Supreme Court here addressed, as it had three years earlier in *Minersville School District* v. *Gobitis* (Case 2), whether public school students may be required to join in a flag-salute ceremony; as in *Gobitis*, Jehovah's Witnesses objected on grounds of religious conscience. Because the Court changed its mind in this case, the case is often understood as overruling the free-exercise jurisprudence of *Gobitis*, a decision widely criticized by scholars and religious leaders. But *Barnette* did not do precisely that. The opinion for the Court written by Justice Robert Jackson did not embrace the argument put forth by Justice Harlan Stone in his dissent in *Gobitis*, namely, that those with religious objections should be exempted from otherwise valid law. Instead, the opinion took the broader First Amendment position that no one could be forced to salute the flag; at stake, as Jackson put it, was "the constitutional liberty of the individual."

For this reason *Barnette* is, strictly speaking, not a free-exercise case. It came to the Court as such, however, and was argued in those terms, and Justices Hugo Black and William Douglas, who joined in a separate opinion, and Justice Frank Murphy, who wrote a concurrence, saw the case at least in part as about a claim of religious liberty. So did Justice Felix Frankfurter, who filed a lengthy dissent reiterating what only three years earlier had been the opinion of the Court agreed to by all his then colleagues except Justice Stone. Frankfurter's dissent remains important for its powerful statement of the virtues of "judicial self-restraint." All four opinions are presented here. They are followed by editorial comments from *The Christian Century,* the (Washington) *Evening Star,* the *New York Times,* and the *Washington Post.*

The facts in *Barnette* were these: In the wake of the *Gobitis* decision in June 1940, the West Virginia legislature passed a law requiring all public schools to conduct courses in history and civics designed to foster national principles and ideals. The state board of education subsequently adopted a resolution that quoted from the Court's opinion in *Gobitis;* the resolution made saluting the flag a "regular part of the program of activities in the public schools." Expulsion was the penalty for anyone who refused, and parents of children expelled could be prosecuted under the state's criminal law. Walter Barnette and two other Jehovah's Witnesses objected, taking their complaint to the federal district court, which enjoined the state board of education from enforcing the resolution. The board then appealed to the Supreme Court, which affirmed the lower court's judgment.

Participating in *West Virginia State Board of Education* v. *Barnette,* decided June 14, 1943, were Chief Justice Harlan F. Stone and Associate Justices Hugo L. Black, William O. Douglas, Felix Frankfurter, Robert H. Jackson, Frank Murphy, Stanley F. Reed, Owen J. Roberts, and Wiley B. Rutledge.

Opinions

Justice Robert H. Jackson delivered the opinion of the Court:

This case calls upon us to reconsider a precedent decision [*Minersville School District* v. *Gobitis*, 1940], as the Court throughout its history often has been required to do. . . .

. . . The sole conflict [in this case] is between authority and rights of the individual. The State asserts power to condition access to public education on making a prescribed sign and profession and at the same time to coerce attendance by punishing both parent and child. . . .

There is no doubt that, in connection with the pledges, the flag salute is a form of utterance. Symbolism is a primitive but effective way of communicating ideas. The use of an emblem or flag to symbolize some system, idea, institution, or personality, is a short cut from mind to mind. Causes and nations, political parties, lodges and ecclesiastical groups seek to knit the loyalty of their followings to a flag or banner, a color or design. The State announces rank, function, and authority through crowns and maces, uniforms and black robes; the church speaks through the Cross, the Crucifix, the altar and shrine, and clerical raiment. Symbols of State often convey political ideas just as religious symbols come to convey theological ones. Associated with many of these symbols are appropriate gestures of acceptance or respect: a salute, a bowed or bared head, a bended knee. A person gets from a symbol the meaning he puts into it, and what is one man's comfort and inspiration is another's jest and scorn.

Over a decade ago Chief Justice Charles Evans Hughes led this Court in holding that the display of a red flag as a symbol of opposition by peaceful and legal means to organized government was protected by the free speech guaranties of the Constitution. *Stromberg* v. *California*, 283 U.S. 359 (1931). Here it is the State that employs a flag as a symbol of adherence to government as presently organized. It requires the individual to communicate by word and sign his acceptance of the political ideas it thus bespeaks. Objection to this form of communication when coerced is an old one, well known to the framers of the Bill of Rights.

41

It is also to be noted that the compulsory flag salute and pledge requires affirmation of a belief and an attitude of mind. It is not clear whether the regulation contemplates that pupils forgo any contrary convictions of their own and become unwilling converts to the prescribed ceremony or whether it will be acceptable if they simulate assent by words without belief and by a gesture barren of meaning. It is now a commonplace that censorship or suppression of expression of opinion is tolerated by our Constitution only when the expression presents a clear and present danger of action of a kind the State is empowered to prevent and punish. It would seem that involuntary affirmation could be commanded only on even more immediate and urgent grounds than silence. But here the power of compulsion is invoked without any allegation that remaining passive during a flag salute ritual creates a clear and present danger that would justify an effort even to muffle expression. To sustain the compulsory flag salute we are required to say that a Bill of Rights which guards the individual's right to speak his own mind, left it open to public authorities to compel him to utter what is not in his mind.

Whether the First Amendment to the Constitution will permit officials to order observance of ritual of this nature does not depend upon whether as a voluntary exercise we would think it to be good, bad, or merely innocuous. Any credo of nationalism is likely to include what some disapprove or to omit what others think essential, and to give off different overtones as it takes on different accents or interpretations. If official power exists to coerce acceptance of any patriotic creed, what it shall contain cannot be decided by courts, but must be largely discretionary with the ordaining authority, whose power to prescribe would no doubt include power to amend. Hence validity of the asserted power to force an American citizen publicly to profess any statement of belief or to engage in any ceremony of assent to one, presents questions of power that must be considered independently of any idea we may have as to the utility of the ceremony in question.

Nor does the issue as we see it turn on one's possession of particular religious views or the sincerity with which they are held. While religion supplies appellees' motive for enduring the discomforts of making the issue in this case, many citizens who do not share these religious views hold such a compulsory rite to infringe constitutional liberty of the individual. It is not necessary to inquire whether non-conformist beliefs will exempt from the duty to salute unless we first find power to make the salute a legal duty.[1]

---

1. *Barnette* thus did not expressly overrule *Gobitis* in respect to its free-exercise doc-

The *Gobitis* decision, however, *assumed*, as did the argument in that case and in this, that power exists in the State to impose the flag salute discipline upon school children in general. The Court only examined and rejected a claim based on religious beliefs of immunity from an unquestioned general rule. The question which underlies the flag salute controversy is whether such a ceremony so touching matters of opinion and political attitude may be imposed upon the individual by official authority under powers committed to any political organization under our Constitution. We examine rather than assume existence of this power and, against this broader definition of issues in this case, re-examine specific grounds assigned for the *Gobitis* decision.

1. It was said [in *Gobitis*] that the flag salute controversy confronted the Court with "the problem which Lincoln cast in memorable dilemma: 'Must a government of necessity be too *strong* for the liberties of its people, or too *weak* to maintain its own existence?' " and that the answer must be in favor of strength.

. . .

It may be doubted whether Mr. Lincoln would have thought that the strength of government to maintain itself would be impressively vindicated by our confirming power of the state to expel a handful of children from school. Such oversimplification, so handy in political debate, often lacks the precision necessary to postulates of judicial reasoning. If validly applied to this problem, the utterance cited would resolve every issue of power in favor of those in authority and would require us to override every liberty thought to weaken or delay execution of their policies.

Government of limited power need not be anemic government. Assurance that rights are secure tends to diminish fear and jealousy of strong government, and by making us feel safe to live under it makes for its better support. Without promise of a limiting Bill of Rights it is doubtful if our Constitution could have mustered enough strength to enable its ratification. To enforce those rights today is not to choose weak government over strong government. It is only to adhere as a means of strength to individual freedom of mind in preference to officially disciplined uniformity for which history indicates a disappointing and disastrous end.

The subject now before us exemplifies this principle. Free public education, if faithful to the ideal of secular instruction and political

---

trine. While *Barnette* is not a free-exercise case, it obviously could not have arisen absent the religious convictions of the appellees.

neutrality, will not be partisan or enemy of any class, creed, party or faction. If it is to impose any ideological discipline, however, each party or denomination must seek to control, or failing that, to weaken the influence of the educational system. Observance of the limitations of the Constitution will not weaken government in the field appropriate for its exercise.

2. It was also considered in *Gobitis* that functions of educational officers in states, counties, and school districts were such that to interfere with their authority "would in effect make us the school board for the country."

The Fourteenth Amendment, as now applied to the States, protects the citizen against the State itself and all of its creatures—Boards of Education not excepted. These have, of course, important, delicate, and highly discretionary functions, but none that they may not perform within the limits of the Bill of Rights. That they are educating the young for citizenship is reason for scrupulous protection of Constitutional freedoms of the individual, if we are not to strangle the free mind at its source and teach youth to discount important principles of our government as mere platitudes.

Such Boards are numerous and their territorial jurisdiction often small. But small and local authority may feel less sense of responsibility to the Constitution, and agencies of publicity may be less vigilant in calling it to account. The action of Congress in making flag observance voluntary and respecting the conscience of the objector in a matter so vital as raising the Army contrasts sharply with these local regulations in matters relatively trivial to the welfare of the nation. There are village tyrants as well as village Hampdens, but none who acts under color of law is beyond reach of the Constitution.

3. The *Gobitis* opinion reasoned that this is a field "where courts possess no marked and certainly no controlling competence," that it is committed to the legislatures as well as the courts to guard cherished liberties and that it is constitutionally appropriate to "fight out the wise use of legislative authority in the forum of public opinion and before legislative assemblies rather than to transfer such a contest to the judicial arena," since all the "effective means of inducing political changes are left free."

The very purpose of a Bill of Rights was to withdraw certain subjects from the vicissitudes of political controversy, to place them beyond the reach of majorities and officials and to establish them as legal principles to be applied by the courts. One's right to life, liberty, and property, to free speech, a free press, freedom of worship and assembly, and other fundamental rights may not be submitted to vote; they depend on the outcome of no elections.

. . . [W]hile it is the Fourteenth Amendment which bears directly upon the State, it is the more specific limiting principles of the First Amendment that finally govern this case.

Nor does our duty to apply the Bill of Rights to assertions of official authority depend upon our possession of marked competence in the field where the invasion of rights occurs. True, the task of translating the majestic generalities of the Bill of Rights, conceived as part of the pattern of liberal government in the eighteenth century, into concrete restraints on officials dealing with the problems of the twentieth century, is one to disturb self-confidence. These principles grew in soil which also produced a philosophy that the individual was the center of society, that his liberty was attainable through mere absence of governmental restraints, and that government should be entrusted with few controls and only the mildest supervision over men's affairs. We must transplant these rights to a soil in which the laissez-faire concept or principle of non-interference has withered at least as to economic affairs, and social advancements are increasingly sought through closer integration of society and through expanded and strengthened governmental controls. These changed conditions often deprive precedents of reliability and cast us more than we would choose upon our own judgment. But we act in these matters not by authority of our competence but force of our commissions. We cannot, because of modest estimates of our competence in such specialties as public education, withhold the judgment that history authenticates as the function of this Court when liberty is infringed.

4. Lastly, and this is the very heart of the *Gobitis* opinion, it reasons that "national unity is the basis of national security," that the authorities have "the right to select appropriate means for its attainment," and hence reaches the conclusion that such compulsory measures toward "national unity" are constitutional. Upon the verity of this assumption depends our answer in this case.

National unity as an end which officials may foster by persuasion and example is not in question. The problem is whether under our Constitution compulsion, as here employed, is a permissible means for its achievement.

Struggles to coerce uniformity of sentiment in support of some end thought essential to their time and country have been waged by many good as well as by evil men. Nationalism is a relatively recent phenomenon but at other times and places the ends have been racial or territorial security, support of a dynasty or regime, and particular plans for saving souls. As first and moderate methods to attain unity have failed, those bent on its accomplishment must report to an ever increasing severity. As governmental pressure toward unity becomes greater, so strife becomes more bitter as to whose unity it shall be. Probably no deeper division of our people could proceed from any provocation than from finding it necessary to choose what doctrine and whose program public educational officials shall compel youths to unite in embracing. Ultimate futility of such attempts to compel coherence is the lesson of every such effort from the Roman drive to stamp out Christianity as a disturber of its pagan unity, the Inquisition, as a means to religious and dynastic unity, the Siberian exiles as a means to Russian unity, down to the fast failing efforts of our present totalitarian enemies. Those who begin coercive elimination of dissent soon find themselves exterminating dissenters. Compulsory unification of opinion achieves only the unanimity of the graveyard.

It seems trite but necessary to say that the First Amendment to our Constitution was designed to avoid these ends by avoiding these beginnings. There is no mysticism in the American concept of the State or of the nature or origin of its authority. We set up government by consent of the governed, and the Bill of Rights denies those in power any legal opportunity to coerce that consent. Authority here is to be controlled by public opinion, not public opinion by authority.

The case is made difficult not because the principles of its decision are obscure but because the flag involved is our own. Nevertheless, we apply the limitations of the Constitution with no fear that freedom to be intellectually and spiritually diverse or even contrary will disintegrate the social organization. To believe that patriotism will not flourish if patriotic ceremonies are voluntary and spontaneous instead of a compulsory routine is to make an unflattering estimate of the appeal of our institutions to free minds. We can have intellectual individualism and the rich cultural diversities that we owe to exceptional minds only at the price of occasional eccentricity and abnormal attitudes. When they are so harmless to others or to the State as those we deal with here, the price is not too great. But freedom to differ is not limited to things that do not matter much. That would be a mere shadow of freedom. The test of its substance is the right to differ as to things that touch the heart of the existing order.

If there is any fixed star in our constitutional constellation, it is that no official, high or petty, can prescribe what shall be orthodox in politics, nationalism, religion, or other matters of opinion or force citizens to confess by word or act their faith therein. If there are any circumstances which permit an exception, they do not now occur to us.

We think the action of the local authorities in compelling the flag salute and pledge transcends constitutional limitations on their power and invades the sphere of intellect and spirit which it is the purpose of the First Amendment to our Constitution to reserve from all official control.

The decision of this Court in *Gobitis* . . . [is] overruled, and the judgment enjoining enforcement of the West Virginia Regulation is affirmed.

Justice Hugo L. Black and Justice William O. Douglas, concurring:

We are substantially in agreement with the opinion just read, but since we originally joined with the Court in *Gobitis*, it is appropriate that we make a brief statement of reasons for our change of view.

Reluctance to make the Federal Constitution a rigid bar against state regulation of conduct thought inimical to the public welfare was the controlling influence which moved us to consent to the *Gobitis* decision. Long reflection convinced us that although the principle is sound, its application in the particular case was wrong. *Jones v. Opelika*, 316 U.S. 584 (1942).[2] We believe that the statute before us fails to accord full scope to the freedom of religion secured to the appellees by the First and Fourteenth Amendments.

. . .

. . . Decision as to the constitutionality of particular laws which strike at the substance of religious tenets and practices must be made by this Court. The duty is a solemn one, and in meeting it we cannot say that a failure, because of religious scruples, to assume a particular physical position and to repeat the words of a patriotic formula creates a grave danger to the nation. Such a statutory exaction is a form of test oath, and the test oath has always been abhorrent in the United States.

. . .

Neither our domestic tranquility in peace nor our martial effort in war depend on compelling little children to participate in a ceremony

---

2. Justices Black, Douglas, and Frank Murphy dissented in *Jones* v. *Opelika*, which sustained the application of a non-discriminatory license fee to vendors of religious books and pamphlets. Eleven months later the Court vacated the decision and struck down such fees in *Jones* v. *Opelika*, 319 U.S. 103 (1943). In their dissent in the first *Opelika* case, the three understood *Gobitis* as sanctioning state action that suppresses or tends to suppress "the free exercise of a religion practiced by a minority group."

which ends in nothing for them but a fear of spiritual condemnation. If, as we think, their fears are groundless, time and reason are the proper antidotes for their errors. The ceremonial, when enforced against conscientious objectors, more likely to defeat than to serve its high purpose, is a handy implement for disguised religious persecution. As such, it is inconsistent with our Constitution's plan and purpose.

Justice Frank Murphy, concurring:

I agree with the opinion of the Court and join in it.
. . .

A reluctance to interfere with considered state action, the fact that the end sought is a desirable one, the emotion aroused by the flag as a symbol for which we have fought and are now fighting again—all of these are understandable. But there is before us the right of freedom to believe, freedom to worship one's Maker according to the dictates of one's conscience, a right which the Constitution specifically shelters. Reflection has convinced me that as a judge I have no loftier duty or responsibility than to uphold that spiritual freedom to its farthest reaches.

The right of freedom of thought and of religion as guaranteed by the Constitution against State action includes both the right to refrain from speaking at all, except in so far as essential operations of government may require it for the preservation of an orderly society, as in the case of compulsion to give evidence in court. Without wishing to disparage the purposes and intentions of those who hope to inculcate sentiments of loyalty and patriotism by requiring a declaration of allegiance as a feature of public education, or unduly belittle the benefits that may accrue therefrom, I am impelled to conclude that such a requirement is not essential to the maintenance of effective government and orderly society. . . .

I am unable to agree that the benefits that may accrue to society from the compulsory flag salute are sufficiently definite and tangible to justify the invasion of freedom and privacy that is entailed or to compensate for a restraint on the freedom of the individual to be vocal or silent according to his conscience or personal inclination.

Justice Felix Frankfurter, dissenting:

One who belongs to the most vilified and persecuted minority in history is not likely to be insensible to the freedoms guaranteed by our Constitution. Were my purely personal attitude relevant I should wholeheartedly associate myself with the general libertarian views in the Court's opinion, representing as they do the thought and action of a lifetime. But as judges we are neither Jew nor Gentile, neither Catholic nor agnostic. We owe equal attachment to the Constitution and are equally bound by our judicial obligations whether we derive our citizenship from the earliest or the latest immigrants to these shores. As a member of this Court I am not justified in writing my private notions of policy into the Constitution, no matter how deeply I may cherish them or how mischievous I may deem their disregard. The duty of a judge who must decide which of two claims before the Court shall prevail, that of a State to enact and enforce laws within its general competence or that of an individual to refuse obedience because of the demands of his conscience, is not that of the ordinary person. It can never be emphasized too much that one's own opinion about the wisdom or evil of a law should be excluded altogether when one is doing one's duty on the bench. The only opinion of our own even looking in that direction that is material is our opinion whether legislators could in reason have enacted such a law. In the light of all the circumstances, including the history of this question in this Court, it would require more daring than I possess to deny that reasonable legislators could have taken the action which is before us for review. Most unwillingly, therefore, I must differ from my brethren with regard to legislation like this. I cannot bring my mind to believe that the "liberty" secured by the Due Process Clause gives this Court authority to deny to the State of West Virginia the attainment of that which we all recognize as a legitimate legislative end, namely, the promotion of good citizenship, by employment of the means here chosen.

· · ·

The admonition that judicial self-restraint alone limits arbitrary exercise of our authority is relevant every time we are asked to nullify legislation. The Constitution does not give us greater veto power when dealing with one phase of "liberty" than with another. . . . Judicial self-restraint is . . . necessary whenever an exercise of political or legislative power is challenged. There is no warrant in the constitutional basis of this Court's authority for attributing different roles to it depending upon the nature of the challenge to the legislation. Our power does not vary according to the particular provision of the Bill of Rights which is invoked. The right not to have property taken without just compensation has, so far as the scope of judicial power is concerned, the same constitutional dignity as the right to be protected against unreasonable searches and seizures, and the latter has no less claim than freedom of the press or freedom of speech or religious freedom. In no instance is this Court the primary protector of the particular liberty that is invoked. . . .

When Justice Oliver Wendell Holmes wrote that "it must be remembered that legislatures are ultimate guardians of the liberties and welfare of the people in quite as great a degree as the courts," he went to the very essence of our constitutional system and the democratic conception of our society. He did not mean that for only some phases of civil government this Court was not to supplant legislatures and sit in judgment upon the right or wrong of a challenged measure. He was stating the comprehensive judicial duty and role of this Court in our constitutional scheme whenever legislation is sought to be nullified on any ground, namely, that responsibility for legislation lies with legislatures, answerable as they are directly to the people, and this Court's only and very narrow function is to determine whether within the broad grant of authority vested in legislatures they have exercised a judgment for which reasonable justification can be offered.

The framers of the federal Constitution might have chosen to assign an active share in the process of legislation to this Court. . . . But the framers of the Constitution denied such legislative powers to the federal judiciary. They chose instead to insulate the judiciary from the legislative function. They did not grant to this Court supervision over legislation.

The reason why from the beginning even the narrow judicial authority to nullify legislation has been viewed with a jealous eye is that it serves to prevent the full play of the democratic process. The fact that it may be an undemocratic aspect of our scheme of government does not call for its rejection or its disuse. But it is the best of reasons, as this Court has frequently recognized, for the greatest caution in its use.

. . . We have not before us any attempt by the State to punish disobedient children or visit penal consequences on their parents. All that is in question is the right of the State to compel participation in this exercise by those who choose to attend the public schools.

We are not reviewing merely the action of a local school board. The flag salute requirement in this case comes before us with the full authority of the State of West Virginia. We are in fact passing judgment on "the power of the State as a whole." Practically we are passing upon the political power of each of the forty-eight states. Moreover, since the First Amendment has been read into the Fourteenth, our problem is precisely the same as it would be if we had before us an Act of Con-

gress for the District of Columbia. To suggest that we are here concerned with the heedless action of some village tyrants is to distort the
augustness of the constitutional issue and the reach of the consequences of our decision.

Under our constitutional system the legislature is charged solely
with civil concerns of society. If the avowed or intrinsic legislative purpose is either to promote or to discourage some religious community
or creed, it is clearly within the constitutional restrictions imposed on
legislatures and cannot stand. But it by no means follows that legislative power is wanting whenever a general non-discriminatory civil regulation in fact touches conscientious scruples or religious beliefs of an
individual or a group. Regard for such scruples or beliefs undoubtedly
presents one of the most reasonable claims for the exertion of legislative accommodation. It is, of course, beyond our power to rewrite the
State's requirement, by providing exemptions for those who do not
wish to participate in the flag salute or by making some other accommodations to meet their scruples. . . . [T]he real question is, who is to
make such accommodations, the courts or the legislature?

This is no dry, technical matter. It cuts deep into one's conception
of the democratic process—it concerns no less the practical differences
between the means for making these accommodations that are open
to courts and to legislatures. A court can only strike down. It can only
say "This or that law is void." It cannot modify or qualify, it cannot
make exceptions to a general requirement. And it strikes down not
merely for a day. At least the finding of unconstitutionality ought not
to have ephemeral significance unless the Constitution is to be reduced
to the fugitive importance of mere legislation. . . . If the function of
this Court is to be essentially no different from that of a legislature, if
the considerations governing constitutional construction are to be
substantially those that underlie legislation, then indeed judges should
not have life tenure and they should be made directly responsible to
the electorate. . . .

. . .

. . . [T]he history out of which grew constitutional provisions for
religious equality and the writings of the great exponents of religious
freedom—Jefferson, Madison, John Adams, Benjamin Franklin—are
totally wanting in justification for a claim by dissidents of exceptional
immunity from civic measures of general applicability, measures not in
fact disguised assaults upon such dissident views. The great leaders of
the American Revolution were determined to remove political support
from every religious establishment. . . . Religious minorities were to be

equal in the eyes of the political state. But Jefferson and others also knew that minorities may disrupt society. It never would have occurred to them to write into the Constitution the subordination of the general civil authority of the state to sectarian scruples.

The constitutional protection of religious freedom terminated disabilities, it did not create new privileges. It gave religious equality, not civil immunity. Its essence is freedom from conformity to religious dogma, not freedom from conformity to law because of religious dogma. Religious loyalties may be exercised without hindrance from the state, not the state may not exercise that which except by leave of religious loyalties is within the domain of temporal power. Otherwise each individual could set up his own censor against obedience to laws conscientiously deemed for the public good by those whose business it is to make laws.

. . .

The essence of the religious freedom guaranteed by our Constitution is therefore this: no religion shall either receive the state's support or incur its hostility. Religion is outside the sphere of political government. This does not mean that all matters on which religious organizations or beliefs may pronounce are outside the sphere of government. Were this so, instead of the separation of church and state, there would be the subordination of the state on any matter deemed within the sovereignty of the religious conscience. Much that is the concern of temporal authority affects the spiritual interests of men. But it is not enough to strike down a non-discriminatory law that it may hurt or offend some dissident view. It would be too easy to cite numerous prohibitions and injunctions to which laws run counter if the variant interpretations of the Bible were made the tests of obedience to law. The validity of secular laws cannot be measured by their conformity to religious doctrines. It is only in a theocratic state that ecclesiastical doctrines measure legal right or wrong.

An act compelling profession of allegiance to a religion, no matter how subtly or tenuously promoted, is bad. But an act promoting good citizenship and national allegiance is within the domain of governmental authority and is therefore to be judged by the same considerations of power and of constitutionality as those involved in the many claims of immunity from civil obedience because of religious scruples.

That claims are pressed on behalf of sincere religious convictions does not of itself establish their constitutional validity. Nor does waving the banner of religious freedom relieve us from examining into the power we are asked to deny the states. Otherwise the doctrine of separation of church and state, so cardinal in the history of this nation and for the liberty of our people, would mean not the disestablishment of a state church but the establishment of all churches and of all religious groups.

. . .

Law is concerned with external behavior and not with the inner life of man. It rests in large measure upon compulsion. Socrates lives in history partly because he gave his life for the conviction that duty of obedience to secular law does not presuppose consent to its enactment or belief in its virtue. The consent upon which free government rests is the consent that comes from sharing in the process of making and unmaking laws. The state is not shut out from a domain because the individual conscience may deny the state's claim. The individual conscience may profess what faith it chooses. It may affirm and promote that faith—in the language of the Constitution, it may "exercise" it freely—but it cannot thereby restrict community action through political organs in matters of community concern, so long as the action is not asserted in a discriminatory way either openly or by stealth. One may have the right to practice one's religion and at the same time owe the duty of formal obedience to laws that run counter to one's beliefs. Compelling belief implies denial of opportunity to combat it and to assert dissident views. Such compulsion is one thing. Quite another matter is submission to conformity of action while denying its wisdom or virtue and with ample opportunity for seeking its change or abrogation.

. . .

. . . [I]f religious scruples afford immunity from civic obedience to laws, they may be invoked by the religious beliefs of any individual even though he holds no membership in any sect or organized denomination. Certainly this Court cannot be called upon to determine what claims of conscience should be recognized and what should be rejected as satisfying the "religion" which the Constitution protects. That would indeed resurrect the very discriminatory treatment of religion which the Constitution sought forever to forbid. . . .

Consider the controversial issue of compulsory Bible-reading in public schools. The educational policies of the states are in great conflict over this, and the state courts are divided in their decisions on the issue whether the requirement of Bible-reading offends constitutional provisions dealing with religious freedom. The requirement of Bible-reading has been justified by various state courts as an appropriate means of inculcating ethical precepts and familiarizing pupils with the most lasting expression of great English literature. Is this Court to overthrow such variant state educational policies by denying states the right to entertain such convictions in regard to their school systems, because of a belief that the King James version is in fact a sectarian text to which parents of the Catholic and Jewish faiths and of some Protestant persuasions may rightly object to having their children exposed? On the other hand the religious consciences of some parents may rebel at the absence of any Bible-reading in the schools. Or is this Court to enter the old controversy between science and religion by unduly defining the limits within which a state may experiment with its school curricula? The religious consciences of some parents may be offended by subjecting their children to the Biblical account of creation, while another state may offend parents by prohibiting a teaching of biology that contradicts such Biblical account. What of conscientious objections to what is devoutly felt by parents to be the poisoning of impressionable minds of children by chauvinistic teaching of history? This is very far from a fanciful suggestion for in the belief of many thoughtful people nationalism is the seed-bed of war.

There are other issues in the offing which admonish us of the difficulties and complexities that confront states in the duty of administering their local school systems. . . .

These questions assume increasing importance in view of the steady growth of parochial schools both in number and in population. I am not borrowing trouble by adumbrating these issues nor am I parading horrible examples of the consequences of today's decision. . . . Is it really a fair construction of such a fundamental concept as the right freely to exercise one's religion that a state cannot choose to require all children who attend public schools to make the same gesture of allegiance to the symbol of our national life because it may offend the conscience of some children, but that it may compel all children to attend public school to listen to the King James version although it may offend the consciences of their parents? And what of the larger issue of claiming immunity from obedience to a general civil regulation that has a reasonable relation to a public purpose within the general competence of the state? . . .

These questions are not lightly stirred. They touch the most delicate issues and their solution challenges the best wisdom of political and religious statesmen. But it presents awful possibilities to try to encase the solution of these problems within the rigid prohibitions of unconstitutionality. . . .

. . .

We are told that a flag salute is a doubtful substitute for adequate understanding of our institutions. The states that require such a school exercise do not have to justify it as the only means for promoting good citizenship in children, but merely as one of diverse means for accomplishing a worthy end. We may deem it a foolish measure, but the point is that this Court is not the organ of government to resolve doubts as to whether it will fulfill its purpose. . . .

. . .

One's conception of the Constitution cannot be severed from one's conception of a judge's function in applying it. The Court has no reason for existence if it merely reflects the pressures of the day. Our system is built on the faith that men set apart for this special function, freed from the influences of immediacy and from the deflections of worldly ambition, will become able to take a view of longer range than the period of responsibility entrusted to Congress and legislatures. We are dealing with matters as to which legislators and voters have conflicting views. Are we as judges to impose our strong convictions on where wisdom lies? That which three years ago had seemed to five successive Courts to lie within permissible areas of legislation is now outlawed by the deciding shift of opinion of two Justices. What reason is there to believe that they or their successors may not have another view a few years hence? Is that which was deemed to be of so fundamental a nature as to be written into the Constitution to endure for all times to be the sport of shifting winds of doctrine? Of course, judicial opinions, even as to questions of constitutionality, are not immutable. As has been true in the past, the Court will from time to time reverse its position. But I believe that never before these Jehovah's Witnesses cases (except for minor deviations subsequently retraced) has this Court overruled decisions so as to restrict the powers of democratic government. Always heretofore, it has withdrawn narrow views of legislative authority so as to authorize what formerly it had denied.

. . .

The uncontrollable power wielded by this Court brings it very close to the most sensitive areas of public affairs. As appeal from legislation to adjudication becomes more frequent, and its consequences more far-reaching, judicial self-restraint becomes more and not less important, lest we unwarrantably enter social and political domains wholly outside our concern. I think I appreciate fully the objections to the law before us. But to deny that it presents a question upon which men might reasonably differ appears to me to be intolerance. And since men may so reasonably differ, I deem it beyond my constitutional power to

assert my view of the wisdom of this law against the view of the State
of West Virginia.

. . .

. . . [P]atriotism cannot be enforced by the flag salute. But neither
can the liberal spirit be enforced by judicial invalidation of illiberal legislation. Our constant preoccupation with the constitutionality of legislation rather than with its wisdom tends to preoccupation of the
American mind with a false value. The tendency of focussing attention
on constitutionality is to make constitutionality synonymous with wisdom, to regard a law as all right if it is constitutional. Such an attitude
is a great enemy of liberalism. Particularly in legislation affecting freedom of thought and freedom of speech much which should offend a
free-spirited society is constitutional. Reliance for the most precious
interests of civilization, therefore, must be found outside of their vindication in courts of law. Only a persistent positive translation of the
faith of a free society into the convictions and habits and actions of a
community is the ultimate reliance against unabated temptations to
fetter the human spirit.

[Justices **Owen J. Roberts** and **Stanley F. Reed** adhered to the views
of the Court in *Gobitis* and thus voted to reverse the judgment of the
lower court; they did not write separately.]

Responses

From **The Christian Century,** June 23, 1943, "Court Upholds
Freedom of Conscience":

Appropriately, the Supreme Court chose Flag Day to hand down its decision enjoining the West Virginia board of education from requiring a flag salute of all pupils in the public schools of that state. . . . [T]he court did far more than to set right a legal blunder [*Minersville School District* v. *Gobitis*, 1940] which had far-reaching consequences for the freedom of conscience of Americans. In the decision, written by Justice Jackson, it incorporated at least one section which should become part of the "American scriptures," to be memorized and taken to heart by every patriot. "If there is any fixed star in our constitutional constellation," said the court, "it is that no official, high or petty, can prescribe what shall be orthodox in politics, nationalism, religion or other matters of opinion or force citizens to confess by word or act their faith therein. If there are any circumstances which permit an exception, they do not now occur to us."

By this flag salute decision the court has cleared up the whole range of cases involving freedom of conscience and freedom for the propagation of religious beliefs, all of them an outgrowth of the activities of Jehovah's Witnesses. The constitutional guarantees of religious liberty have been reaffirmed; the encroachments of the state in the realm of conscience have received a salutary check. But the sobering experience of the past three years should warn the churches that only their eternal vigilance will insure that the rights thus vindicated will be maintained.

From the (Washington) **Evening Star,** June 16, 1943, "The Flag
Salute Decision":

It is not difficult to agree with the thought of the majority that the tribute to the flag becomes an empty and meaningless gesture when forced on an unwilling participant as the price of public education. The religious scruples of a sect which views the ceremony as a violation of the doctrinal proscription against the worship of "images" also are due consideration. But, granting these things, there will be grave doubts as to the wisdom of the court's action in c erriding the judgment of the State Legislature to hold that compliance with a reasonable regulation, applied almost universally to promote good citizenship, depends on nothing more stable than the whim of the individual. By that logic the dissidents become the rule-makers and no regulation is safe.

From the **New York Times,** *June 19, 1943, "The Court on the Flag Salute":*

The layman may well be confused by the able reasoning on both sides of this case. If he has seen the [Jehovah's] Witnesses in action he may also be confused by an emotion of dislike. Yet the simple fact stands that a school child compelled to salute the flag, when he has been taught the flag is an "image" which the Bible forbids him to worship, is in effect made to say what he does not believe. It seems to be true, also, that real loyalty "to the flag of the United States of America and to the Republic for which it stands" is expressed by a willing salute, but neither expressed nor created by a reluctant one. The voluntary principle is the essence of civil rights as of common sense.

From the **Washington Post,** *June 16, 1943, "Religious Freedom":*

A majority of the justices decided, in effect, that the constitutional guarantee of religious freedom is unqualified.

No small share of credit for this judicial change of mind belongs to Chief Justice Stone. His dissenting voice was alone in protest against the *Gobitis* decision of 1940. Three of his associates, Justices Black, Douglas, and Murphy, who at that time had differed from him have now come to accept his view. This emergence of a dissenting opinion to majority acceptance is one of the real tests of judicial stature.

Justice Frankfurter, who had written the majority opinion in *Gobitis*, became spokesman for the minority. The diligence and sincerity with which he searched his mind and conscience on this issue is apparent in the reasoning he advanced. Yet one sentence of his carefully worded opinion cannot fail to evoke curiosity. "It is self delusive," he declared, "to believe that the liberal spirit can be enforced by judicial invalidation of illiberal legislation." Is it not, in fact, precisely the function of the Court on which Justice Frankfurter sits to guarantee protection to the liberal spirit as it is defined in the Constitution, against legislative acts which would undermine or corrupt it?

Laws are man-made. And in the Supreme Court's reversal of judgment we have just had fresh attestation of the fallibility of all men, even when they enjoy the Olympian detachment of the judiciary. It is as a safeguard against that fallibility that we preserve in the Constitution a set of basic principles which we permit neither men nor laws to violate. And for this reason we recognize that the apparent triviality of any violation cannot condone it or mitigate its ultimate threat to the liberal spirit.

4

Everson v. Board of Education

330 U.S. 1 (1947)

In this landmark case arising from the state of New Jersey, the Supreme Court upheld public funding of the transportation of pupils to and from both public and parochial schools. The policy had been challenged as a violation of the First Amendment's no-establishment provision, and for the Court to rule on the merits of the question, it had to agree that the provision binds the states as strictly as it does the federal government. Of course, the Court had indicated in *Cantwell v. Connecticut* (1940) that the religion clause applies to the states. But *Cantwell* involved only a free-exercise claim. If there was doubt as to whether the Court would also apply the establishment prohibition to the states, *Everson v. Board of Education* removed it.

Everson was the Court's first significant effort to interpret the religion clause. The opinion for the Court, written by Justice Hugo Black, declared that the term "no establishment" means that neither the federal government nor the states "can pass laws which aid one religion, aid all religions, or prefer one religion over another." "No tax in any amount, large or small," said the opinion, "can be levied to support any religious activities or institutions. . . . In the words of Jefferson [from his letter to the Danbury Baptists], the clause . . . was intended to erect 'a wall of separation between church and State.' "

The four dissenting justices agreed with this very broad interpretation but not with the majority's application of it to the facts in the case. While Justice Black concluded that New Jersey had not breached the wall separating church and state, Justices Harold Burton, Robert Jackson, Felix Frankfurter, and Wiley Rut-

59

ledge emphatically said otherwise. *Everson* generated three opinions—Justice Black's, for the Court, and dissents by Justices Jackson and Rutledge. All three are presented here. Following these opinions is a *Washington Post* editorial.

From the perspective of subsequent establishment cases, the 5-to-4 disagreement on the constitutionality of the New Jersey funding scheme is less important than the Court's agreement on not only the meaning of the no-establishment provision but also how that meaning is discerned. All nine justices drew on history, and all placed great weight upon the labors of Thomas Jefferson and especially James Madison in behalf of religious liberty in the Virginia of the 1770s and 1780s. Since *Everson*, some justices—most notably William Brennan in *Abington School District* v. *Schempp* (1963)—have been dubious about turning to history for guidance in interpreting the no-establishment provision. (See Case 9.) Others have argued that the justices in 1947 were right to look to history but got it wrong. For example, Justice William Rehnquist's lengthy dissent in the "moment of silence" case, *Wallace* v. *Jaffree* (1985), vigorously disputed the history informing the opinions in *Everson*, the pace-setting case for establishment jurisprudence. (See Case 21.) In *Lee* v. *Weisman* (1992), the graduation school-prayer case, Justice David Souter responded to Rehnquist's history by offering his view of the making of the ban. (See Case 25.)

Under New Jersey law authorizing local school boards to make rules and contracts for transporting children to and from schools, the board of education for the Township of Ewing approved reimbursement to parents of money they spent for the bus transportation of their children to schools, both public and Catholic. The fares amounted to about $40 a year. A township taxpayer challenged the reimbursement to parents of the parochial-school children as a violation of both state and federal constitutions. He won in the New Jersey Supreme Court, but the New Jersey Court of Errors and Appeals reversed. The federal questions were then appealed to the U.S. Supreme Court, which declined to strike down the funding arrangement.

Participating in *Everson* v. *Board of Education*, decided February 10, 1947, were Chief Justice Fred M. Vinson and Associate Justices Hugo L. Black, Harold H. Burton, William O. Douglas, Felix Frankfurter, Robert H. Jackson, Frank Murphy, Stanley F. Reed, and Wiley B. Rutledge.

Opinions

Justice Hugo L. Black delivered the opinion of the Court:

The New Jersey statute is challenged as a "law respecting an establishment of religion." The First Amendment, as made applicable to the states by the Fourteenth, commands that a state "shall make no law respecting an establishment of religion, or prohibiting the free exercise thereof." . . . [I]t is not inappropriate briefly to review the background and environment of the period in which that constitutional language was fashioned and adopted.[1]

A large proportion of the early settlers of this country came here from Europe to escape the bondage of laws which compelled them to support and attend government-favored churches. The centuries immediately before and contemporaneous with the colonization of America had been filled with turmoil, civil strife, and persecutions, generated in large part by established sects determined to maintain their absolute political and religious supremacy. With the power of government supporting them, at various times and places, Catholics had persecuted Protestants, Protestants had persecuted Catholics, Protestant sects had persecuted other Protestant sects, Catholics of one shade of belief had persecuted Catholics of another shade of belief, and all of these had from time to time persecuted Jews. . . .

These practices of the old world were transplanted to and began to thrive in the soil of the new America. The very charters granted by the English Crown to the individuals and companies designated to make the laws which would control the destinies of the colonials authorized these individuals and companies to erect religious establishments which all, whether believers or non-believers, would be required to

---

1. Note that Justice Black did not begin his interpretive effort by asking what the objective meaning of the First Amendment was at the time of its ratification. Arguably, such an inquiry would have required focusing more attention than he did on the actual framing of the religion clause in the First Congress. Justice Rutledge's dissenting opinion also was concerned with "the background and environment" of the period—i.e., with the Virginia experience and the work of Madison in securing religious liberty in that state. And his opinion also paid little attention to the actual framing of the relevant provisions.

61

support and attend. An exercise of this authority was accompanied by a repetition of many of the old-world practices and persecutions. Catholics found themselves hounded and proscribed because of their faith; Quakers who followed their conscience went to jail; Baptists were peculiarly obnoxious to certain dominant Protestant sects; men and women of varied faiths who happened to be in a minority in a particular locality were persecuted because they steadfastly persisted in worshipping God only as their own consciences dictated. And all of these dissenters were compelled to pay tithes and taxes to support government-sponsored churches whose ministers preached inflammatory sermons designed to strengthen and consolidate the established faith by generating a burning hatred against dissenters.

These practices became so commonplace as to shock the freedom-loving colonials into a feeling of abhorrence. The imposition of taxes to pay ministers' salaries and to build and maintain churches and church property aroused their indignation. It was these feelings which found expression in the First Amendment. No one locality and no one group throughout the Colonies can rightly be given entire credit for having aroused the sentiment that culminated in adoption of the Bill of Rights' provisions embracing religious liberty. But Virginia, where the established church had achieved a dominant influence in political affairs and where many excesses attracted wide public attention, provided a great stimulus and able leadership for the movement. The people there, as elsewhere, reached the conviction that individual religious liberty could be achieved best under a government which was stripped of all power to tax, to support, or otherwise to assist any or all religions, or to interfere with the beliefs of any religious individual or group.

The movement toward this end reached its dramatic climax in Virginia in 1785–86 when the Virginia legislative body was about to renew Virginia's tax levy for the support of the established church. Thomas Jefferson and James Madison led the fight against this tax. Madison wrote his great Memorial and Remonstrance against the law.[2]

---

2. Madison's "Memorial and Remonstrance" appeared to influence the First Amendment jurisprudence of all nine justices in *Everson*; Rutledge even appended the document to his opinion. John Courtney Murray observed soon after *Everson* that the members of the Court seemed oblivious to the fact that Madison's concept of church and state, as expressed in his "Remonstrance," was grounded in "a religious absolute, a sectarian idea of religion" ("Law or Prepossessions?" *Law and Contemporary Problems*, 14 [1949]: 30).

The Court's reliance on the "Remonstrance" raises at least two questions: First, was the Madison of the "Remonstrance" the complete Madison? Neither Black nor Rutledge mentioned that Madison was a member of the committee that recommended the chaplain system in the First Congress; ironically, under the strict-separationist view adopted by all the justices in *Everson*, it would seem that congressional chaplaincies must be

In it, he eloquently argued that a true religion did not need the support of law; that no person, either believer or non-believer, should be taxed to support a religious institution of any kind; that the best interest of a society required that the minds of men always be wholly free; and that cruel persecutions were the inevitable result of government-established religions. Madison's Remonstrance received strong support throughout Virginia, and the Assembly postponed consideration of the proposed tax measure until its next session. When the proposal came up for consideration at that session, it not only died in committee, but the Assembly enacted the famous "Virginia Bill for Religious Liberty" originally written by Thomas Jefferson. The preamble to that Bill states among other things that

Almighty God hath created the mind free; that all attempts to influence it by temporal punishments or burthens, or by civil incapacitations, tend only to beget habits of hypocrisy and meanness, and are a departure from the plan of the Holy author of our religion, who being Lord both of body and mind, yet chose not to propagate it by coercions on either . . . ; that to compel a man to furnish contributions of money for the propagation of opinions which he disbelieves, is sinful and tyrannical; that even the forcing him to support this or that teacher of his own religious persuasion, is depriving him of the comfortable liberty of giving his contributions to the particular pastor, whose morals he would make his pattern. . . .

And the statute itself enacted

That no man shall be compelled to frequent or support any religious worship, place, or ministry whatsoever, nor shall be enforced, restrained, molested, or burthened in his body or goods, nor shall otherwise suffer on account of his religious opinions or belief. . . .

The meaning and scope of the First Amendment preventing establishment of religion or prohibiting the free exercise thereof, in the light of its history and the evils it was designed forever to suppress, have been several times elaborated by the decisions of this Court prior to the application of the First Amendment to the states by the Fourteenth.[3] The broad meaning given the Amendment by these earlier

---

unconstitutional. (Faced with a challenge to the constitutionality of a state legislative chaplaincy almost two centuries after Madison did his First Amendment work, the Supreme Court rejected it in *Marsh* v. *Chambers* [1983]; see Case 19.) Second, did the First Amendment simply enact the "Remonstrance" (or at least the Court's view of it)? Many have disputed this, including Murray, in his 1949 essay, and, years later, justices of the Supreme Court.

3. Justice Black does not argue the case for applying the no-establishment provision to the states. Instead he cites precedents (listed in a footnote) for this proposition, and

cases has been accepted by this Court in its decisions concerning an individual's religious freedom rendered since the Fourteenth Amendment was interpreted to make the prohibitions of the First applicable to state action abridging religious freedom. There is every reason to give the same application and broad interpretation to the "establishment of religion" clause. . . .

The "establishment of religion" clause of the First Amendment means at least this:[4] Neither a state nor the Federal Government can set up a church.[5] Neither can pass laws which aid one religion, aid all religions, or prefer one religion over another.[6] Neither can force nor influence a person to go or to remain away from church against his will or force him to profess a belief or disbelief in any religion. No person can be punished for entertaining or professing religious beliefs or disbeliefs, for church attendance or non-attendance.[7] No tax in any

---

these are free-exercise cases. The first is *Cantwell* v. *Connecticut* (see Case 1), which itself did not explain why the free-exercise clause should bind the states; it merely cited a case in which the Court had asserted, but not argued for, the related proposition that the states are equally with Congress bound by the constraints of the First Amendment prohibition against abridging the freedom of speech. Akhil Amar of the Yale Law School comments that the ban on establishment was a guarantee to the states that the federal government would not establish religion. Thus the irony, according to Amar, is that "to apply the clause against a state government is precisely to eliminate its right to choose whether to establish a religion—a right explicitly confirmed by the establishment clause itself!" "The Fourteenth Amendment," Amar says, "might best be read as incorporating free exercise but not establishment principles against state governments" ("The Bill of Rights as a Constitution," *The Yale Law Journal*, 100 [1991]: 1158–59). Leonard Levy observes, no doubt correctly, that it is highly unrealistic to expect the Supreme Court to "disincorporate" the no-establishment provision; he also argues that the provision in fact protects an "individual freedom"—the freedom *from* an establishment of religion (*The Establishment Clause: Religion and the First Amendment* [New York: Macmillan, 1986], 166–68).

4. The words "at least" indicate that what follows is the minimal constitutional limitation imposed by the ban on establishment.

5. Assuming that the provision applies equally to the states, this statement of its substantive meaning is universally accepted. The no-establishment provision means *at least* this much: No government of any kind in the United States may set up a church.

6. What has proved controversial about this limitation is the words "aid all religions." All the justices in *Everson* agreed on this point, but later justices and indeed majorities in certain cases have not. Responding to Justice Black's statement that government may not "aid all religions," Robert L. Cord, for example, writes: "There is no historical evidence to suggest . . . that the Establishment Clause in any way constitutionally precludes non-discriminatory governmental aid to religion. In fact, the converse is confirmed historically" (*Separation of Church and State: Historical Fact and Current Fiction* [Grand Rapids: Baker Book House, 1988], 112). Cord cites, for example, the federal dollars given to missionaries of many Christian faiths to support their mission schools in Christianizing Indians. This practice was maintained during the nation's first 100 years. Leonard Levy disputes Cord's interpretation; see Levy, *The Establishment Clause*, 183.

7. This and the sentence preceding it express constitutional principles of religious liberty that no one disputes.

amount, large or small, can be levied to support any religious activities or institutions, whatever they may be called, or whatever form they may adopt to teach or practice religion.[8] Neither a state nor the Federal Government can, openly or secretly, participate in the affairs of any religious organizations or groups and *vice versa*.[9] In the words of Jefferson, the clause against establishment of religion by law was intended to erect "a wall of separation between church and State."[10]

We must consider the New Jersey statute in accordance with the foregoing limitations imposed by the First Amendment. But we must not strike that state statute down if it is within the State's constitutional power even though it approaches the verge of that power. . . .

. . . [W]e cannot say that the First Amendment prohibits New Jersey from spending tax-raised funds to pay the bus fares of parochial school pupils as a part of a general program under which it pays the fares of pupils attending public and other schools. It is undoubtedly true that children are helped to get to church schools. There is even a possibility that some of the children might not be sent to the church schools if the parents were compelled to pay their children's bus fares out of their own pockets when transportation to a public school would have been

---

8. Did Justice Black have in mind taxes specifically levied for the support of religious activities or institutions? Or did he also mean to proscribe the use of any tax monies (which would include general levies) to support religion? The tenor of his opinion suggests the latter, clearly absolute principle, although the specific holding in *Everson* indicates that Black himself was willing to find a way around it. The so-called Child Benefit Theory (see note 12) provided the way in this case.

9. The prohibition against government participation in the affairs of a religious group raises the question, unanswered by Justice Black, of just what "participation" might mean. Later cases have focused on this issue in terms of whether government is "excessively entangled" in religion. See *Lemon v. Kurtzman* (1971), Case 13.

10. Jefferson composed his famous metaphor in a letter he sent while president to the Danbury Connecticut Baptist Association on January 1, 1802. Here is the full paragraph containing the phrase: "Believing with you that religion is a matter which lies solely between man and his God, that he owes account to none other for his faith or his worship, that the legislative powers of government reach actions only, and not opinions, I contemplate with sovereign reverence that act of the whole American People which declared that their legislature should 'make no law respecting an establishment of religion, or prohibiting the free exercise thereof,' thus building *a wall of separation between church and State*. Adhering to this expression of the supreme will of the nation on behalf of the rights of conscience, I shall see with sincere satisfaction the progress of those sentiments which tend to restore to man all his natural rights, convinced he has no natural right in opposition to his social duties." Justices in later cases—though not in *Everson*—disputed the use of Jefferson's metaphor as a guide to interpreting the religion clause. Also, there is the historical question as to just what, to Jefferson's mind, the "wall" walled off. In 1803 President Jefferson made a treaty with the Kaskaskia Indians in which the federal government pledged money to build them a Roman Catholic church and to support their priest (Cord, *Separation of Church and State*, 115–16). None of the opinions in *Everson* discussed this treaty or Jefferson's request to Congress for an appropriation to meet the treaty obligations.

paid for by the State. The same possibility exists where the state requires a local transit company to provide reduced fares to school children including those attending parochial schools, or where a municipally owned transportation system undertakes to carry all school children free of charge. Moreover, state-paid policemen, detailed to protect children going to and from church schools from the very real hazards of traffic, would serve much the same purpose and accomplish much the same result as state provisions intended to guarantee free transportation of a kind which the state deems to be best for the school children's welfare. And parents might refuse to risk their children to the serious danger of traffic accidents going to and from parochial schools, the approaches to which were not protected by policemen. Similarly, parents might be reluctant to permit their children to attend schools which the state had cut off from such general government services as ordinary police and fire protection, connections for sewage disposal, public highways and sidewalks. Of course, cutting off church schools from these services, so separate and so indisputably marked off from the religious function, would make it far more difficult for the schools to operate. But such is obviously not the purpose of the First Amendment. That Amendment requires the state to be a neutral in its relations with groups of religious believers and non-believers; it does not require the state to be their adversary. State power is no more to be used so as to handicap religions than it is to favor them.

This Court has said that parents may, in the discharge of their duty under state compulsory education laws, send their children to a religious rather than a public school if the school meets the secular educational requirements which the state has power to impose.[11] It appears that these parochial schools meet New Jersey's requirements. The State contributes no money to the schools. It does not support them. Its legislation, as applied, does no more than provide a general program to help parents get their children, regardless of their religion, safely and expeditiously to and from accredited schools.[12]

The First Amendment has erected a wall between church and state.

---

11. Black here referred the reader to *Pierce* v. *Society of Sisters*, 268 U.S. 510 (1923), in which the Court voided a state law that would have, in effect, outlawed all private schools.

12. This part of Black's opinion drew upon the Child Benefit Theory articulated in a 1930 case, *Cochran* v. *Board of Education*, 281 U.S. 370, in which a Louisiana taxpayer had sued to stop the state board of education from spending funds to buy books for children attending parochial schools. The Supreme Court affirmed the judgment of the Louisiana Supreme Court, which had sustained the statute on grounds that the beneficiaries were not the parochial schools but the children themselves.

That wall must be kept high and impregnable. We could not approve the slightest breach. New Jersey has not breached it here.

Justice Robert H. Jackson, dissenting, joined by Justice Felix Frankfurter:

I find myself, contrary to first impressions, unable to join in this decision. I have a sympathy, though it is not ideological, with Catholic citizens who are compelled by law to pay taxes for public schools, and also feel constrained by conscience and discipline to support other schools for their own children. Such relief to them as this case involves is not in itself a serious burden to taxpayers and I had assumed it to be as little serious in principle. Study of this case convinces me otherwise. The Court's opinion marshals every argument in favor of state aid and puts the case in its most favorable light, but much of its reasoning confirms my conclusions that there are no good grounds upon which to support the present legislation. In fact, the undertones of the opinion, advocating complete and uncompromising separation of Church from State, seem utterly discordant with its conclusion yielding support to their commingling in educational matters. The case which irresistibly comes to mind as the most fitting precedent is that of Julia who, according to Byron's reports, "whispering 'I will ne'er consent,'—consented."

. . .

Whether the taxpayer constitutionally can be made to contribute aid to parents of students because of their attendance at parochial schools depends upon the nature of those schools and their relation to the Church. The Constitution says nothing of education. It lays no obligation on the states to provide schools and does not undertake to regulate state systems of education if they see fit to maintain them. But they cannot, through school policy any more than through other means, invade rights secured to citizens by the Constitution of the United States. *West Virginia State Board of Education* v. *Barnette* (1943).[13] One of our basic rights is to be free of taxation to support a transgression of the constitutional command that the authorities "shall make no law respecting an establishment of religion, or prohibiting the free exercise thereof."

. . .

It is no exaggeration to say that the whole historic conflict in temporal policy between the Catholic Church and non-Catholics comes

---

13. Justice Jackson wrote the Court's opinion in *Barnette*. See Case 3.

to a focus in their respective school policies. The Roman Catholic Church, counseled by experience in many ages and many lands and with all sorts and conditions of men, takes what, from the viewpoint of its own progress and the success of its mission, is a wise estimate of the importance of education to religion. It does not leave the individual to pick up religion by chance. It relies on early and indelible indoctrination in the faith and order of the Church by the word and example of persons consecrated to the task.

Our public school, if not a product of Protestantism, at least is more consistent with it than with the Catholic culture and scheme of values. It is a relatively recent development dating from about 1840. It is organized on the premise that secular education can be isolated from all religious teaching so that the school can inculcate all needed temporal knowledge and also maintain a strict and lofty neutrality as to religion. The assumption is that after the individual has been instructed in worldly wisdom he will be better fitted to choose his religion. Whether such a disjunction is possible, and if possible whether it is wise, are questions I need not try to answer.[14]

I should be surprised if any Catholic would deny that the parochial school is a vital, if not the most vital, part of the Roman Catholic Church. If put to the choice, that venerable institution, I should expect, would forego its whole service for mature persons before it would give up education of the young, and it would be a wise choice. Its growth and cohesion, discipline and loyalty, spring from its schools. Catholic education is the rock on which the whole structure rests, and to render tax aid to its Church school is indistinguishable to me from rendering the same aid to the Church itself.

. . .

It seems to me that the basic fallacy in the Court's reasoning, which accounts for its failure to apply the principles it avows, is in ignoring the essentially religious test by which beneficiaries of this expenditure are selected. A policeman protects a Catholic, of course—but not because he is a Catholic; it is because he is a man and a member of our society. The fireman protects the Church school—but not because it

---

14. Justice Jackson here touched on an important matter: the possibility and wisdom of disjoining the secular from the religious. Certainly many in the founding generation did not disjoin the two. The Massachusetts Constitution of 1780 said this about Harvard College: "[O]ur wise and pious ancestors . . . laid the foundation of Harvard College. . . . [E]ncouragement of arts and sciences, and all good literature, tends to the honor of God, the advantage of the Christian religion, and the great benefit of this and the other United States of America. . . ."

is a Church school; it is because it is property, part of the assets of our society. Neither the fireman nor the policeman has to ask before he renders aid "Is this man or building identified with the Catholic Church?" But before these school authorities draw a check to reimburse for a student's fare they must ask just that question, and if the school is a Catholic one they may render aid because it is such, while if it is of any other faith or is run for profit, the help must be withheld. To consider the converse of the Court's reasoning will best disclose its fallacy. That there is no parallel between police and fire protection and this plan of reimbursement is apparent from the incongruity of the limitation of this Act if applied to police and fire service. Could we sustain an Act that said the police shall protect pupils on the way to or from public schools and Catholic schools but not while going to and coming from other schools, and firemen shall extinguish a blaze in public or Catholic school buildings but shall not put out a blaze in Protestant Church schools or private schools operated for profit? That is the true analogy to the case we have before us and I should think it pretty plain that such a scheme would not be valid.

The Court's holding is that this taxpayer has no grievance because the state has decided to make the reimbursement a public purpose and therefore we are bound to regard it as such. I agree that this Court has left, and always should leave to each state, great latitude in deciding for itself, in the light of its own conditions, what shall be public purposes in its scheme of things. It may socialize utilities and economic enterprises and make taxpayers' business out of what conventionally had been private business. It may make public business of individual welfare, health, education, entertainment or security. But it cannot make public business of religious worship or instruction, or of attendance at religious institutions of any character. There is no answer to the proposition, more fully expounded by Justice Rutledge, that the effect of the religious freedom Amendment to our Constitution was to take every form of propagation of religion out of the realm of things which could directly or indirectly be made public business and thereby be supported in whole or in part at taxpayers' expense. That is a difference which the Constitution sets up between religion and almost every other subject matter of legislation, a difference which goes to the very root of religious freedom and which the Court is overlooking today. This freedom was first in the Bill of Rights because it was first in the forefathers' minds; it was set forth in absolute terms, and its strength is its rigidity. It was intended not only to keep the states' hands out of religion, but to keep religion's hands off the state, and, above all, to keep bitter religious controversy out of public life by denying to every denomination any advantage from getting control of public policy or the public purse. Those great ends I cannot but think are immeasurably compromised by today's decision.

This policy of our Federal Constitution has never been wholly pleasing to most religious groups. They all are quick to invoke its protections; they all are irked when they feel its restraints. This Court has gone a long way, if not an unreasonable way, to hold that public business of such paramount importance as maintenance of public order, protection of the privacy of the home, and taxation may not be pursued by a state in a way that even indirectly will interfere with religious proselyting.

But we cannot have it both ways. Religious teaching cannot be a private affair when the state seeks to impose regulations which infringe on it indirectly, and a public affair when it comes to taxing citizens of one faith to aid another, or those of no faith to aid all. If these principles seem harsh in prohibiting aid to Catholic education, it must not be forgotten that it is the same Constitution that alone assures Catholics the right to maintain these schools at all when predominant local sentiment would forbid them. Nor should I think that those who have done so well without this aid would want to see this separation between Church and State broken down. If the state may aid these religious schools, it may therefore regulate them. . . .

. . . I cannot read the history of the struggle to separate political from ecclesiastical affairs, well summarized in the opinion of Justice Rutledge in which I generally concur, without a conviction that the Court today is unconsciously giving the clock's hands a backward turn.

Justice Wiley B. Rutledge, dissenting, joined by Justices Felix Frankfurter, Robert H. Jackson, and Harold H. Burton:[15]

"Congress shall make no law respecting an establishment of religion, or prohibiting the free exercise thereof. . . ." U.S. Const., Amend. I.

"Well aware that Almighty God hath created the mind free; . . . that to compel a man to furnish contributions of money for the propagation of opinions which he disbelieves, is sinful and tyrannical; . . .

"We, the General Assembly, do enact, That no man shall be compelled

---

15. Justice William O. Douglas did not join this dissent although he apparently came to embrace it. In the landmark school-prayer case, *Engel* v. *Vitale* (1962), Douglas wrote that Rutledge's dissent expressed "durable First Amendment philosophy." See Case 8.

to frequent or support any religious worship, place, or ministry whatsoever, nor shall be enforced, restrained, molested, or burthened in his
body or goods, nor shall otherwise suffer, on account of his religious
opinions or belief. . . ."

I cannot believe that the great author of those words [Thomas Jefferson, "A Bill for Establishing Religious Freedom"], or the men who
made them law, could have joined in this decision. Neither so high nor
so impregnable today as yesterday is the wall raised between church
and state by Virginia's great statute of religious freedom and the First
Amendment, now made applicable to all the states by the Fourteenth.
New Jersey's statute sustained is the first, if indeed it is not the second
breach to be made by this Court's action. That a third, and a fourth,
and still others will be attempted, we may be sure. For just as *Cochran
v. Board of Education,* 281 U.S. 370 (1930), has opened the way by
oblique ruling for this decision, so will the two make wider the breach
for the third. Thus with time the most solid freedom steadily gives way
before continuing corrosive decision.

This case forces us to determine squarely for the first time what was
"an establishment of religion" in the First Amendment's conception;
and by that measure to decide whether New Jersey's action violates its
command. . . .

. . .

Not simply an established church, but any law respecting the establishment of religion is forbidden. The Amendment was broadly but not
loosely phrased. It is the compact and exact summation of its author's
views formed during his long struggle for religious freedom. In Madison's own words characterizing Jefferson's Bill for Establishing Religious Freedom, the guaranty he put in our national charter, like the
bill he piloted through the Virginia Assembly, was "a Model of technical precision, and perspicuous brevity." Madison could not have
confused "church" and "religion," or "an established church" and
"an establishment of religion."

The Amendment's purpose was not to strike merely at the official
establishment of a single sect, creed or religion, outlawing only a formal relation such as had prevailed in England and some of the colonies. Necessarily it was to uproot all such relationships. But the object
was broader than separating church and state in its narrow sense. It
was to create a complete and permanent separation of the spheres of
religious activity and civil authority by comprehensively forbidding
every form of public aid or support for religion. . . .[16]

---

16. Nothing in Madison's original draft of the religion clause, or in the clause itself

. . .

. . . The prohibition [against establishment] broadly forbids state support, financial or other, of religion in any guise, form or degree. It outlaws all use of public funds for religious purposes.

. . .

No provision of the Constitution is more closely tied to or given content by its generating history than the religion clause of the First Amendment. It is at once the refined product and the terse summation of that history. The history includes not only Madison's authorship and the proceedings before the First Congress, but also the long and intensive struggle for religious freedom in America, more especially in Virginia, of which the Amendment was the direct culmination. In the documents of the times, particularly of Madison, who was leader in the Virginia struggle before he became the Amendment's sponsor, but also in the writings of Jefferson and others and in the issues which engendered them is to be found irrefutable confirmation of the Amendment's sweeping content.

[Justice Rutledge here reviews the work of Madison in behalf of religious liberty. In particular, he discusses Madison's efforts in Virginia to enact Jefferson's Bill for Establishing Religious Freedom and to oppose the Assessment Bill under which Christian churches were to be supported through taxation; it was in successful opposition to the Assessment Bill that Madison delivered his historic "Memorial and Remonstrance," which Rutledge appended to his opinion.]

[The Memorial and Remonstrance] is Madison's complete . . . interpretation of religious liberty. It is a broadside attack upon all forms of "establishment" of religion, both general and particular, nondiscriminatory or selective. . . . [T]he Remonstrance is at once the most concise and the most accurate statement of the views of the First Amendment's author concerning what is "an establishment of religion."[17] . . .

The Remonstrance . . . killed the Assessment Bill. It collapsed in Committee shortly before Christmas, 1785. With this, the way was

---

as ratified as part of the First Amendment, refers to any comprehensive forbidding of every form of public aid or support for religion. His original draft, introduced on June 8, 1789, stated, "The civil rights of none shall be abridged on account of religious belief or worship, nor shall any national religion be established, nor shall the full and equal rights of Conscience be in any manner, or on any pretext, infringed."

17. Madison, of course, was not the only "author" of the First Amendment's religion clause. For an examination of the actual framing of the clause, see Michael Malbin, *Religion and Politics: The Intentions of the Authors of the First Amendment* (Washington, D.C.: American Enterprise Institute for Public Policy Research, 1978).

cleared at last for enactment of Jefferson's Bill for Establishing Religious Freedom [in 1786]. . . . This dual victory substantially ended the fight over establishments, settling the issue against them.

The next year Madison became a member of the Constitutional Convention. Its work done, he fought valiantly to secure the ratification of its great product in Virginia as elsewhere, and nowhere else more effectively. Madison was certain in his own mind that under the Constitution "there is not a shadow of right in the general government to intermeddle with religion" and that "this subject is, for the honor of America, perfectly free and unshackled. The government has no jurisdiction over it. . . ." Nevertheless, he pledged that he would work for a Bill of Rights, including a specific guaranty of religious freedom.
. . .

. . . [S]ent to the first Congress, [Madison] a little more than three years from his legislative victory at home . . . proposed and secured the submission and ratification of the First Amendment as the first article of our Bill of Rights.

All the great instruments of the Virginia struggle for religious liberty thus became warp and woof of our constitutional tradition, not simply by the course of history, but by the common unifying force of Madison's life, thought, and sponsorship. He epitomized the whole of that tradition in the Amendment's compact, but nonetheless comprehensive, phrasing.

As the Remonstrance discloses throughout, Madison opposed every form and degree of official relation between religion and civil authority. For him religion was a wholly private matter beyond the scope of civil power either to restrain or to support. Denial or abridgment of religious freedom was a violation of rights both of conscience and of natural equality. State aid was no less obnoxious or destructive to freedom and to religion itself than other forms of state interference. "Establishment" and "free exercise" were correlative and coextensive ideas, representing only different facets of the single great and fundamental freedom. . . . [Madison] sought to tear out the institution [of established religion] not partially but root and branch, and to bar its return forever.

In no phase was he more unrelentingly absolute than in opposing state support or aid by taxation. Not even "three pence" contribution was thus to be exacted from any citizen for such a purpose. Remonstrance, Par. 3. . . .

. . . [But Madison and his colleagues'] objection was not to small tithes. It was to any tithes whatsoever. Not the amount but "the principle of assessment was wrong." . . .

In view of this history no further proof is needed that the Amendment forbids any appropriation, large or small, from public funds to aid or support any and all religious exercises. But if more were called for, the debates in the First Congress . . . supply it.[18]

By contrast with the Virginia history, the congressional debates on consideration of the Amendment reveal only sparse discussion, reflecting the fact that the essential issues had been settled. Indeed, the matter had become so well understood as to have been taken for granted in all but formal phrasing. . . .

Compulsory attendance upon religious exercises went out early in the process of separating church and state, together with forced observance of religious forms and ceremonies. Test oaths and religious qualification for office followed later. These things none devoted to our great tradition of religious liberty would think of bringing back. Hence today, apart from efforts to inject religious training or exercises and sectarian issues into the public schools, the only serious surviving threat to maintaining that complete and permanent separation of religion and civil power which the First Amendment commands is through use of the taxing power to support religion, religious establishments, or establishments having a religious foundation whatever their form or special religious function.

Does New Jersey's action furnish support for religion by use of the taxing power? Certainly it does, if the test remains undiluted as Jefferson and Madison made it, that money taken by taxation from one is to be used or given to support another's religious training or belief, or indeed one's own. Today as then the furnishing of "contributions of money for the propagation of opinions which he disbelieves" is the forbidden exaction; and the prohibition is absolute for whatever measure brings that consequence and whatever amount may be sought or given to that end.

The funds used here were raised by taxation. The Court does not dispute, nor could it, that their use does in fact give aid and encouragement to religious instruction. It only concludes that this aid is not "support" in law. But Madison and Jefferson were concerned with aid and support in fact, not as a legal conclusion "entangled in precedents." Here parents pay money to send their children to parochial

---

18. Rutledge did not indicate which debates in the First Congress prove that the First Amendment forbids "any appropriation, large or small, from public funds to aid or support any and all religious exercises." Neither did he deal with evidence seemingly to the contrary, such as the First Congress's appropriation of public funds to pay for congressional chaplains.

schools and funds raised by taxation are used to reimburse them. This not only helps the children to get to school but also enables the parents to send them. It aids them in a substantial way to get the very thing which they are sent to the particular school to secure, namely, religious training and teaching.

Believers of all faiths, and others who do not express their feeling toward ultimate issues of existence in any creedal form, pay the New Jersey tax. When the money so raised is used to pay for transportation to religious schools, the Catholic taxpayer to the extent of his proportionate share pays for the transportation of Lutheran, Jewish, and otherwise religiously affiliated children to receive their non-Catholic religious instruction. Their parents likewise pay proportionately for the transportation of Catholic children to receive Catholic instruction. Each thus contributes to "the propagation of opinions which he disbelieves" in so far as their religions differ, as do others who accept no creed without regard to those differences. Each thus pays taxes also to support the teaching of his own religion, an exaction equally forbidden since it denies "the comfortable liberty" of giving one's contribution to the particular agency of instruction he approves.

New Jersey's action therefore exactly fits the type of exaction and the kind of evil at which Madison and Jefferson struck. Under the test they framed it cannot be said that the cost of transportation [roughly $40 a year, in 1947 dollars] is no part of the cost of education or of the religious instruction given. That it is a substantial and a necessary element is shown most plainly by the continuing and increasing demand for the state to assume it. Nor is there pretense that it relates only to the secular instruction given in religious schools or that any attempt is or could be made toward allocating proportional shares as between the secular and the religious instruction. . . . [T]he pupil . . . will receive not simply secular, but also and primarily religious, teaching and guidance.

Indeed the view is sincerely avowed by many of various faiths, that the basic purpose of all education is or should be religious, that the secular cannot be and should not be separated from the religious phase and emphasis. Hence the inadequacy of public or secular education and the necessity for sending the child to a school where religion is taught. But whatever may be the philosophy or its justification, there is undeniably an admixture of religious with secular teaching in all such institutions.

Yet this very admixture is what was disestablished when the First Amendment forbade "an establishment of religion." . . .

An appropriation from the public treasury to pay the cost of transportation to Sunday school, to weekday special classes at the church or parish house, or to the meetings of various young people's religious societies, . . . could not withstand constitutional attack. This would be true, whether or not secular activities were mixed with the religious. If such an appropriation could not stand, then it is hard to see how one becomes valid for the same thing upon the more extended scale of daily instruction. Surely constitutionality does not turn on where or how often the mixed teaching occurs.

. . .

For me . . . [it] is impossible to select so indispensable an item from the composite of total costs [of education], and characterize it as not aiding, contributing to, promoting or sustaining the propagation of beliefs which it is the very end of all to bring about. . . . Payment of transportation is no more, nor is it any the less essential to education, whether religious or secular, than payment for tuitions, for teachers' salaries, for buildings, equipment and necessary materials. Nor is it any the less directly related, in a school giving religious instruction, to the primary religious objective all those essential items of cost are intended to achieve. No rational line can be drawn between payment for such larger, but not more necessary, items and payment for transportation. The only line that can be so drawn is one between more dollars and less. Certainly in this realm such a line can be no valid constitutional measure. Now, as in Madison's time, not the amount but the principle of assessment is wrong.

But we are told that the New Jersey statute is valid in its present application because the appropriation is for a public, not a private purpose, namely, the promotion of education, and the majority accept this idea in the conclusion that all we have here is "public welfare legislation." If that is true . . . there could be no possible objection to more extensive support of religious education by New Jersey.

. . .

. . . The public function argument, by casting the issue in terms of promoting the general cause of education and the welfare of the individual, ignores the religious factor and its essential connection with the transportation, thereby leaving out the only vital element in the case. . . .

. . . To say that New Jersey's appropriation and her use of the power of taxation for raising the funds appropriated are not for public purposes but are for private ends, is to say that they are for the support of religion and religious teaching. Conversely, to say that they are for public purposes is to say that they are not for religious ones.

This is precisely for the reason that education which includes religious training and teaching, and its support, have been made matters of private right and function, not public, by the very terms of the First Amendment. . . .

. . .

Our constitutional policy . . . does not deny the value or the necessity for religious training, teaching, or observance. Rather it secures their free exercise. But to that end it does deny that the state can undertake or sustain them in any form or degree. For this reason the sphere of religious activity, as distinguished from the secular intellectual liberties, has been given the twofold protection and, as the state cannot forbid, neither can it perform or aid in performing the religious function. The dual prohibition makes that function altogether private. It cannot be made a public one by legislative act. This was the very heart of Madison's Remonstrance, as it is of the Amendment itself.

It is not because religious teaching does not promote the public or the individual's welfare, but because neither is furthered when the state promotes religious education, that the Constitution forbids it to do so. Both legislatures and courts are bound by that distinction. . . .

. . . Legislatures are free to make, and courts to sustain, appropriations only when it can be found that in fact they do not aid, promote, encourage, or sustain religious teaching or observances, be the amount large or small. No such finding has been or could be made in this case. The Amendment has removed this form of promoting the public welfare from legislative and judicial competence to make a public function. It is exclusively a private affair.

The reasons underlying the Amendment's policy have not vanished with time or diminished in force. . . . Public money devoted to payment of religious costs, educational or other, brings the quest for more. It brings too the struggle of sect against sect for the larger share or for any. Here one by numbers alone will benefit most, there another. That is precisely the history of societies which have had an established religion and dissident groups. It is the very thing Jefferson and Madison experienced and sought to guard against, whether in its blunt or in its more screened forms. The end of such strife cannot be other than to destroy the cherished liberty. The dominating group will achieve the dominant benefit; or all will embroil the state in their dissensions. . . .

Exactly such conflicts have centered of late around providing transportation to religious schools from public funds. . . .

In these conflicts wherever success has been obtained it has been upon the contention that by providing the transportation the general cause of education, the general welfare, and the welfare of the individual will be forwarded; hence that the matter lies within the realm of public function, for legislative determination. . . .

The majority here does not . . . deny that the individual or the school, or indeed both, are benefited directly and substantially. To do so would cut the ground from under the public function—social legislation thesis. On the contrary, the opinion concedes that the children are aided by being helped to get to the religious schooling. [And it implies] that the school is helped to reach the child with its religious teaching. The religious enterprise is common to both, as is the interest in having transportation for its religious purposes provided.

Notwithstanding [this] . . . the Court concludes that the aid so given is not "support" of religion. It is rather only support of education as such, without reference to its religious content, and thus becomes public welfare legislation. . . .

. . .

This is not . . . just a little case over bus fares. In paraphrase of Madison, distant as it may be in its present form from a complete establishment of religion, it differs from it only in degree; and is the first step in that direction. Today as in his time "the same authority which can force a citizen to contribute three pence only . . . for the support of any one [religious] establishment, may force him" to pay more; or "to conform to any other establishment in all cases whatsoever.". . .

The realm of religious training and belief remains, as the Amendment made it, the kingdom of the individual man and his God. It should be kept inviolately private, not "entangled . . . in precedents" or confounded with what legislatures legitimately may take over into the public domain.

No one conscious of religious values can be unsympathetic toward the burden which our constitutional separation puts on parents who desire religious instruction mixed with secular for their children. They pay taxes for others' children's education, at the same time the added cost of instruction for their own. Nor can one happily see benefits denied to children which others receive, because in conscience they or their parents for them desire a different kind of training others do not demand.

But if those feelings should prevail, there would be an end to our historic constitutional policy and command. No more unjust or discriminatory in fact is it to deny attendants at religious schools the cost of their transportation than it is to deny them tuitions, sustenance for their teachers, or any other educational expense which others receive at public cost. Hardship in fact there is which none can blink. But, for assuring to those who undergo it the greater, the most comprehensive freedom, it is one written by design and firm intent into our basic law.

. . .

Two great drives are constantly in motion to abridge, in the name of education, the complete division of religion and civil authority which our forefathers made. One is to introduce religious education and observances into the public schools. The other, to obtain public funds for the aid and support of various private religious schools. In my opinion, both avenues were closed by the Constitution. Neither should be opened by this Court. The matter is not one of quantity, to be measured by the amount of money expended. Now as in Madison's day it is one of principle, to keep separate the separate spheres as the First Amendment drew them; to prevent the first experiment upon our liberties; and to keep the question from becoming entangled in corrosive precedents. We should not be less strict to keep strong and untarnished the one side of the shield of religious freedom than we have been of the other.

Response

From the **Washington Post,** February 13, 1947, "Church and State":

Only a narrow gap divides the five Supreme Court justices who upheld the use of public funds for transportation of students to church schools from the four who took the opposite view. But that narrow gap runs to immense depth. For the principle at issue is one of the most fundamental in the American concept of government—the separation of church and state.

Speaking for the majority, Justice Black gave almost as much lip-service to the principles of religious freedom laid down by Jefferson and Madison as did the dissenters. He argued for a broad interpretation of the constitutional prohibition against enactment of any law "respecting the establishment of religion." . . . [H]e emphatically proclaimed the intention of Jefferson in his "Virginia Bill for Religious Liberty" and of the founding fathers in the first amendment to erect "a wall of separation between church and state."

Justice Black and his four colleagues also freely admitted that this "wall of separation" applies to the States through the fourteenth amendment. Yet they upheld New Jersey in paying for the transportation of students to Catholic schools on the ground that such payments promote the public welfare. Policemen are hired to guard children going to church schools, he said, and firemen to protect their property. Why should not tax funds also be used to help parents get their children to church schools as well as to other schools?

That superficial argument begins to fall apart as soon as one examines the facts that were before the court. The funds in question could not be used to pay for the transportation of children to all schools in the township, but only to public schools and Catholic schools. Surely, if public funds are to be used for this purpose, they must be distributed to all religious groups without discrimination. But the fundamental error lies in the court's assumption that the intrinsic merit of a private activity, such as financing transportation to church schools, may transform it into a public welfare function.

School children's bus fare is one of many items in our national bill of education. If citizens can be taxed to pay this expense, they can be taxed to pay the salaries of church school teachers and the cost of buildings for religious educational purposes. When and if this happens, the dominant group in any community will be in a position to dip into the public purse to propagate its own faith, and the separation of church and State, as we have known it in the past, will be nothing but a myth. The majority opinion carries strong sugges-

80

tions that the court would not go that far. But the court has destroyed the only basis on which a rational distinction can be made. Its resort to expediency in this instance will deprive it of an anchor to tie to when the larger issues are raised.

Justice Black's argument favoring this relatively small encroachment upon a constitutional principle reminds us of the young woman who tried to excuse her transgression of the moral law by saying that her illegitimate child was only a small one. It is the principle that is vital, as Justice Rutledge made clear in his powerful dissent, and not the amount of the assistance given. Taxes are wholly public. The religious function is wholly private. The two cannot be intermingled, in our opinion, without grave damage to both. We should think that every religious group interested in maintaining freedom in its relationship to the Deity would understand and appreciate this fact. For, as Justice Jackson wrote in his separate dissent, "If the State may aid these religious schools, it may therefore regulate them." In this sense, the court appears to have struck a blow at religious freedom as well as the separation of church and state, for the two are inextricably woven together.

5

Illinois ex rel. McCollum
v. *Board of Education*

333 U.S. 203 (1948)

A year after its decision in *Everson* v. *Board of Education* (1947) the Supreme Court acted under the principles of that case to invalidate, for the first time ever, a state practice on grounds that it established religion. An avowed atheist, Vashti McCollum, had challenged her local (Champaign, Illinois) school board's "released time" program under which teachers from all religious groups choosing to participate were allowed to offer religious instruction in the school for one hour once a week. Students in grades four to nine had the option of attending the religion class of their choice (as approved by parents) or else continuing their regular secular studies; the religion teachers were not paid by the state but were subject to the approval and supervision of the school superintendent. Mrs. McCollum asked that the board of education put an end to any kind of religious instruction in its public schools. She lost in the Illinois courts, but the Supreme Court ruled 8 to 1 that the "released time" program violated the ban on establishment.

The school board argued, contrary to *Everson*, that the no-establishment provision, properly interpreted, forbids only government preference of one religion over another. Writing for the Court as he had in *Everson*, Justice Black rejected this argument as well as the school board's request that the Court not follow or else overrule the part of *Everson* that applied the no-establishment provision to the states through the Fourteenth Amendment.

83

McCollum produced three opinions in addition to Justice Black's; all are presented here. Justice Felix Frankfurter, joined by Justices Robert Jackson, Wiley Rutledge, and Harold Burton, wrote to affirm what he called the "basic constitutional principle of absolute separation [of church and state]." Justice Jackson wrote a concurring opinion in which he nonetheless expressed reservations about the litigious path the Court seemed to be taking with its church-state jurisprudence. Guided by "no law but our own prepossessions," he said, the Court may prove incompetent to its new task of deciding "where the secular ends and the sectarian begins."

Finally, Justice Stanley Reed, in solitary dissent, became the first justice to criticize the Court's exegesis of the history of the no-establishment provision. Noting the Court's reliance on Thomas Jefferson's phrase in an 1802 letter regarding a "wall" separating church and state, Reed remarked that "a rule of law should not be drawn from a figure of speech."

The editorial responses to *McCollum* that are reprinted here are from the (Washington) *Evening Star* and *The Christian Century*.

Participating in *McCollum* v. *Board of Education*, decided March 8, 1948, were Chief Justice Fred M. Vinson and Associate Justices Hugo L. Black, Harold H. Burton, William O. Douglas, Felix Frankfurter, Robert H. Jackson, Frank Murphy, Stanley F. Reed, and Wiley B. Rutledge.

Opinions

Justice Hugo L. Black delivered the opinion of the Court:
The . . . facts [in this case] show the use of tax-supported property for religious instruction and the close cooperation between the school authorities and the religious council in promoting religious education. The operation of the state's compulsory education system thus assists and is integrated with the program of religious instruction carried on by separate religious sects. Pupils compelled by law to go to school for secular education are released in part from their legal duty upon the condition that they attend the religious classes. This is beyond all question a utilization of the tax-established and tax-supported public school system to aid religious groups to spread their faith. And it falls squarely under the ban of the First Amendment (made applicable to the States by the Fourteenth) as we interpreted it in *Everson* v. *Board of Education* (1947). . . . The majority in [that case] and the minority . . . agreed that the First Amendment's language, properly interpreted, had erected a wall of separation between Church and State.

Recognizing that the Illinois program is barred by the First and Fourteenth Amendments if we adhere to the views expressed both by the majority and the minority in the *Everson* Case, counsel for the respondents challenge those views as dicta and urge that we reconsider and repudiate them. They argue that historically the First Amendment was intended to forbid only government preference of one religion over another, not an impartial governmental assistance of all religions. In addition they ask that we distinguish or overrule our holding in the *Everson* Case that the Fourteenth Amendment made the "establishment of religion" clause of the First Amendment applicable as a prohibition against the States. After giving full consideration to the arguments presented we are unable to accept either of these contentions.

To hold that a state cannot consistently with the First and Fourteenth Amendments utilize its public school system to aid any or all religious faiths or sects in the dissemination of their doctrines and ideals does not, as counsel urge, manifest a governmental hostility to religion or religious teachings. A manifestation of such hostility would

85

be at war with our national tradition as embodied in the guaranty of the free exercise of religion. For the First Amendment rests upon the premise that both religion and government can best work to achieve their lofty aims if each is left free from the other within its respective sphere. Or, as we said in the *Everson* Case, the First Amendment has erected a wall between Church and State which must be kept high and impregnable.

Here not only are the state's tax-supported public school buildings used for the dissemination of religious doctrines. The State also affords sectarian groups an invaluable aid in that it helps to provide pupils for their religious classes through use of the state's compulsory public school machinery. This is not separation of Church and State.

The cause is reversed and remanded to the State Supreme Court for proceedings not inconsistent with this opinion.

Justice Felix Frankfurter, concurring, joined by Justices Robert H. Jackson, Wiley B. Rutledge, and Harold H. Burton:

We dissented in *Everson* because in our view the Constitutional principle requiring separation of Church and State compelled invalidation of the ordinance sustained by the majority. Illinois has here authorized the commingling of sectarian with secular instruction in the public schools. The Constitution of the United States forbids this.

This case . . . demonstrates anew that the mere formulation of a relevant Constitutional principle is the beginning of the solution of a problem, not its answer. This is so because the meaning of a spacious conception like that of the separation of Church from State is unfolded as appeal is made to the principle from case to case. We are all agreed that the First and Fourteenth Amendments have a secular reach far more penetrating in the conduct of Government than merely to forbid an "established church." But agreement, in the abstract, that the First Amendment was designed to erect a "wall of separation between Church and State," does not preclude a clash of views as to what the wall separates. Involved is not only the Constitutional principle but the implications of judicial review in its enforcement. Accommodation of legislative freedom and Constitutional limitations upon that freedom cannot be achieved by a mere phrase. We cannot illuminatingly apply the "wall-of-separation" metaphor until we have considered the relevant history of religious education in America, the place of the "release time" movement in that history, and its precise manifestation in the case before us.

. . . Traditionally, organized education in the Western world was

Church education. It could hardly be otherwise when the education of children was primarily study of the Word and the ways of God. Even in the Protestant countries, where there was a less close identification of Church and State, the basis of education was largely the Bible, and its chief purpose inculcation of piety. To the extent that the State intervened, it used its authority to further aims of the Church.

The emigrants who came to these shores brought this view of education with them. . . .

The evolution of colonial education, largely in the service of religion, into the public school system of today is the story of changing conceptions regarding the American democratic society, of the functions of State-maintained education in such a society and of the role therein of the free exercise of religion by the people. The modern public school derived from a philosophy of freedom reflected in the First Amendment. It is appropriate to recall that the Remonstrance of James Madison, an event basic in the history of religious liberty, was called forth by a proposal which involved support to religious education. As the momentum for popular education increased and in turn evoked strong claims for State support of religious education, contests not unlike that which in Virginia had produced Madison's Remonstrance appeared in various forms in other States. . . . The upshot of these controversies, often long and fierce, is fairly summarized by saying that long before the Fourteenth Amendment subjected the States to new limitations, the prohibition of furtherance by the State of religious instruction became the guiding principle, in law and feeling, of the American people. . . .

Separation in the field of education, then, was not imposed upon unwilling States by force of superior law. In this respect the Fourteenth Amendment merely reflected a principle then dominant in our national life. To the extent that the Constitution thus made it binding upon the States, the basis of the restriction is the whole experience of our people.[1] Zealous watchfulness against fusion of secular and religious activities by Government itself, through any of its instruments but especially through its educational agencies, was the democratic response of the American community to the particular needs of a young and growing nation unique in the composition of its people. . . .

It is pertinent to remind that the establishment of this principle of

---

1. Here, however belatedly in the opinions of the justices, was an explanation, albeit a very brief one, for the application of the religion clause to the states through the Fourteenth Amendment—"the whole experience of the people."

Separation in the field of education was not due to any decline in the religious beliefs of the people. Horace Mann was a devout Christian, and the deep religious feeling of James Madison is stamped upon the Remonstrance. The secular public school did not imply indifference to the basic role of religion in the life of the people, nor rejection of religious education as a means of fostering it. The claims of religion were not minimized by refusing to make the public schools agencies for their assertion. The non-sectarian or secular public school was the means of reconciling freedom in general with religious freedom. The sharp confinement of the public schools to secular education was a recognition of the need of a democratic society to educate its children, insofar as the State undertook to do so, in an atmosphere free from pressures in a realm in which pressures are most resisted and where conflicts are most easily and most bitterly engendered. Designed to serve as perhaps the most powerful agency for promoting cohesion among a heterogeneous democratic people, the public school must keep scrupulously free from entanglement in the strife of sects. The preservation of the community from divisive conflicts, of Government from irreconcilable pressures by religious groups, of religion from censorship and coercion however subtly exercised, requires strict confinement of the State to instruction other than religious, leaving to the individuals's church and home, indoctrination in the faith of his choice. . . .

. . .

Prohibition of the commingling of sectarian and secular instruction in the public school is of course only half the story. A religious people was naturally concerned about the part of the child's education entrusted "to the family altar, the church, and the private school." The promotion of religious education took many forms. Laboring under financial difficulties and exercising only persuasive authority, various denominations felt handicapped in their task of religious education. Abortive attempts were therefore frequently made to obtain public funds for religious schools. But the major efforts of religious inculcation were a recognition of the principle of Separation by the establishment of church schools privately supported. Parochial schools were maintained by various denominations. These, however, were often beset by serious handicaps, financial and otherwise, so that the religious aims which they represented found other directions. There were experiments with vacation schools, with Saturday as well as Sunday schools. They all fell short of their purpose. It was urged that by appearing to make religion a one-day-a-week matter, the Sunday school, which acquired national acceptance, tended to relegate the child's religious education, and thereby his religion, to a minor role not unlike the enforced piano lesson.

Out of these inadequate efforts evolved the week-day church school, held on one or more afternoons a week after the close of the public school. But children continued to be children; they wanted to play when school was out, particularly when other children were free to do so. Church leaders decided that if the week-day church school was to succeed, a way had to be found to give the child his religious education during what the child conceived to be his "business hours."

The initiation of the movement may fairly be attributed to Dr. George U. Wenner. The underlying assumption of his proposal made . . . in 1905 was that the public school unduly monopolized the child's time and that the churches were entitled to their share of it. This, the schools should "release." . . . This was to be carried out on church premises under church authority. Those not desiring to attend church schools would continue their normal classes. Lest these public school classes unfairly compete with the church education, it was requested that the school authorities refrain from scheduling courses or activities of compelling interest or importance.

The proposal aroused considerable opposition and it took another decade for a "released time" scheme to become part of a public school system. Gary, Indiana, inaugurated the movement [in 1914]. . . . The religious teaching was held on church premises and the public schools had no hand in the conduct of these church schools. They did not supervise the choice of instructors or the subject matter taught. Nor did they assume responsibility for the attendance, conduct or achievement of the child in a church school; and he received no credit for it. The period of attendance in the religious schools would otherwise have been a play period for the child, with the result that the arrangement did not cut into public school instruction or truly affect the activities or feelings of the children who did not attend the church schools.

From such a beginning "released time" has attained substantial proportions. In 1914–15, under the Gary program, 619 pupils left the public schools for church schools during one period a week. According to responsible figures almost 2,000,000 in some 2,200 communities participated in "released time" programs during 1947. A movement of such scope indicates the importance of the problem to which the "released time" programs are directed. But to the extent that aspects of these programs are open to Constitutional objection, the more extensively the movement operates, the more ominous the breaches in the wall of separation. . . .

. . . How does "released time" operate in Champaign? Public school teachers distribute to their pupils cards supplied by church groups, so that the parents may indicate whether they desire religious instruction for their children. For those desiring it, religious classes are conducted in the regular classrooms of the public schools by teachers of religion paid by the churches and appointed by them, but, as the State court found, "subject to the approval and supervision of the Superintendent." The courses do not profess to give secular instruction in subjects concerning religion. Their candid purpose is sectarian teaching. While a child can go to any of the religious classes offered, a particular sect wishing a teacher for its devotees requires the permission of the school superintendent "who in turn will determine whether or not it is practical for said group to teach in said school system." If no provision is made for religious instruction in the particular faith of a child, or if for other reasons the child is not enrolled in any of the offered classes, he is required to attend a regular school class, or a study period during which he is often left to his own devices. Reports of attendance in the religious classes are submitted by the religious instructor to the school authorities, and the child who fails to attend is presumably deemed a truant.

Religious education so conducted on school time and property is patently woven into the working scheme of the school. The Champaign arrangement thus presents powerful elements of inherent pressure by the school system in the interest of religious sects. The fact that this power has not been used to discriminate is beside the point. Separation is a requirement to abstain from fusing functions of Government and of religious sects, not merely to treat them all equally. That a child is offered an alternative may reduce the constraint; it does not eliminate the operation of influence by the school in matters sacred to conscience and outside the school's domain. The law of imitation operates, and non-conformity is not an outstanding characteristic of children. The result is an obvious pressure upon children to attend. Again, while the Champaign school population represents only a fraction of the more than two hundred and fifty sects of the nation, not even all the practicing sects in Champaign are willing or able to provide religious instruction. The children belonging to these non-participating sects will thus have inculcated in them a feeling of separatism when the school should be the training ground for habits of community, or they will have religious instruction in a faith which is not that of their parents. As a result, the public school system of Champaign actively furthers inculcation in the religious tenets of some faiths, and in the process sharpens the consciousness of religious differences at least among some of the children committed to its care. These are consequences not amenable to statistics. But they are precisely the consequences against which the Constitution was directed when it prohibited the Government common to all from becoming embroiled, however innocently, in the destructive religious conflicts of which the history of even this country records some dark pages.

· · ·

Separation means separation, not something less. Jefferson's metaphor in describing the relation between Church and State speaks of a "wall of separation," not of a fine line easily overstepped. The public school is at once the symbol of our democracy and the most pervasive means for promoting our common destiny. In no activity of the State is it more vital to keep out divisive forces than in its schools, to avoid confusing, not to say fusing, what the Constitution sought to keep strictly apart. . . .

We renew our conviction that "we have staked the very existence of our country on the faith that complete separation between the state and religion is best for the state and for religion." *Everson.* If nowhere else, in the relation between Church and State, "good fences make good neighbors."

Justice Robert H. Jackson, concurring:

I join the opinion of Mr. Justice Frankfurter, and concur in the result reached by the Court, but with these reservations: I think it is doubtful whether the facts of this case establish jurisdiction in this Court, but in any event that we should place some bounds on the demands for interference with local schools that we are empowered or willing to entertain. I make these reservations a matter of record in view of the number of litigations likely to be started as a result of this decision.

· · ·

If . . . jurisdiction is found to exist, it is important that we circumscribe our decision with some care. . . . The plaintiff, as she has every right to be, is an avowed atheist. What she has asked of the courts is that they not only end the "released time" plan but also ban every form of teaching which suggests or recognizes that there is a God. She would ban all teaching of the Scriptures. She especially mentions as an example of invasion of her rights "having pupils learn and recite such statements as 'The Lord is my Shepherd, I shall not want.' " And she objects to teaching that the King James version of the Bible "is called the Christian's Guide Book, the Holy Writ and the Word of God," and many other similar matters. This Court is directing the Illinois courts generally to sustain the plaintiff's complaint without exception of any of these grounds of complaint, without discriminating between them and without laying down any standards to define the limits of the effect of our decision.

To me, the sweep and detail of these complaints is a danger signal which warns of the kind of local controversy we will be required to arbitrate if we do not place appropriate limitation on our decision and exact strict compliance with jurisdictional requirements. Authorities list 256 separate and substantial religious bodies to exist in the continental United States. Each of them, through the suit of some discontented but unpenalized and untaxed representative, has as good a right as this plaintiff to demand that the courts compel the schools to sift out of their teaching everything inconsistent with its doctrines. If we are to eliminate everything that is objectionable to any of these warring sects or inconsistent with any of their doctrines, we will leave public education in shreds. Nothing but educational confusion and a discrediting of the public school system can result from subjecting it to constant law suits.

While we may and should end such formal and explicit instruction as the Champaign plan and can at all times prohibit teaching of creed and catechism and ceremonial and can forbid forthright proselyting in the schools, I think it remains to be demonstrated whether it is possible, even if desirable, to comply with such demands as plaintiff's completely to isolate and cast out of secular education all that some people may reasonably regard as religious instruction. Perhaps subjects such as mathematics, physics or chemistry are, or can be, completely secularized. But it would not seem practical to teach either practice or appreciation of the arts if we are to forbid exposure of youth to any religious influences. Music without sacred music, architecture minus the cathedral, or painting without the scriptural themes would be eccentric and incomplete, even from a secular point of view. Yet the inspirational appeal of religion in these guises is often stronger than in forthright sermon. Even such a "science" as biology raises the issue between evolution and creation as an explanation of our presence on this planet. Certainly a course in English literature that omitted the Bible and other powerful uses of our mother tongue for religious ends would be quite barren. And I should suppose it is a proper, if not an indispensable, part of preparation for a worldly life to know the roles that religion and religions have played in the tragic story of mankind. The fact is that, for good or for ill, nearly everything in our culture worth transmitting, everything which gives meaning to life, is saturated with religious influences, derived from paganism, Judaism, Christianity— both Catholic and Protestant—and other faiths accepted by a large part of the world's peoples. One can hardly respect a system of education that would leave the student wholly ignorant of the currents of religious thought that move the world society for a part in which he is being prepared.

But how one can teach, with satisfaction or even with justice to all faiths, such subjects as the story of the Reformation, the Inquisition, or even the New England effort to found "a Church without a Bishop and a State without a King," is more than I know. It is too much to expect that mortals will teach subjects about which their contemporaries have passionate controversies with the detachment they may summon to teaching about remote subjects such as Confucius or Mohammed. When instruction turns to proselyting and imparting knowledge becomes evangelism is, except in the crudest cases, a subtle inquiry.

. . . [P]ublic educational authorities have evolved a considerable variety of practices in dealing with the religious problem. Neighborhoods differ in racial, religious and cultural compositions. It must be expected that they will adopt different customs which will give emphasis to different values and will induce different experiments. And it must be expected that, no matter what practice prevails, there will be many discontented and possibly belligerent minorities. We must leave some flexibility to meet local conditions, some chance to progress by trial and error. While I agree that the religious classes involved here go beyond permissible limits, I also think the complaint demands more than plaintiff is entitled to have granted. So far as I can see this Court does not tell the State court where it may stop, nor does it set up any standards by which the State court may determine that question for itself.

The task of separating the secular from the religious in education is one of magnitude, intricacy and delicacy. To lay down a sweeping constitutional doctrine as demanded by complainant and apparently approved by the Court, applicable alike to all school boards of the nation, "to immediately adopt and enforce rules and regulations prohibiting all instruction in and teaching of religious education in all public schools," is to decree a uniform, rigid and, if we are consistent, an unchanging standard for countless school boards representing and serving highly localized groups which not only differ from each other but which themselves from time to time change attitudes. It seems to me that to do so is to allow zeal for our own ideas of what is good in public instruction to induce us to accept the role of a super board of education for every school district in the nation.

It is idle to pretend that this task is one for which we can find in the Constitution one word to help us as judges to decide where the secular ends and the sectarian begins in education. Nor can we find guidance in any other legal source. It is a matter on which we can find no law but our own prepossessions. If with no surer legal guidance we are to take up and decide every variation of this controversy, raised by persons not subject to penalty or tax but who are dissatisfied with the way schools are dealing with the problem, we are likely to have much business of the sort. And, more importantly, we are likely to make the legal "wall of separation between church and state" as winding as the famous serpentine wall designed by Mr. Jefferson for the University he founded.

Justice Stanley F. Reed, dissenting:

I find it difficult to extract from the opinions any conclusion as to what it is in the Champaign plan that is unconstitutional. Is it the use of school buildings for religious instruction; the release of pupils by the schools for religious instruction during school hours; the so-called assistance by teachers in handing out the request cards to pupils, in keeping lists of them for release and records of their attendance; or the action of the principals in arranging an opportunity for the classes and the appearance of the Council's instructors? None of the reversing opinions say whether the purpose of the Champaign plan for religious instruction during school hours is unconstitutional or whether it is some ingredient used in or omitted from the formula that makes the plan unconstitutional.

. . . From the holding and the language of the opinions, I can only deduce that religious instruction of public school children during school hours is prohibited. The history of American education is against such an interpretation of the First Amendment.

. . .

The phrase "an establishment of religion" may have been intended by Congress to be aimed only at a state church. . . . Passing years, however, have brought about the acceptance of a broader meaning, although never until today, I believe, has this Court widened its interpretation to any such degree as holding that recognition of the interest

of our nation in religion, through the granting, to qualified representatives of the principal faiths, of opportunity to present religion as an
optional, extracurricular subject during released school time in public
school buildings, was equivalent to an establishment of religion. A
reading of the general statements of eminent statesmen of former days,
referred to in the opinions in this case and in *Everson*, will show that
circumstances such as those in this case were far from the minds of
the authors. . . .

Mr. Jefferson, as one of the founders of the University of Virginia, a
school which from its establishment in 1819 has been wholly governed, managed and controlled by the State of Virginia, was faced with
the same problem that is before this Court today: the question of the
constitutional limitation upon religious education in public schools.
In his annual report as Rector, to the President and Directors of the
Literary Fund, dated October 7, 1822, approved by the Visitors of the
University of whom Mr. Madison was one, Mr. Jefferson set forth his
views at some length. These suggestions of Mr. Jefferson were adopted
and the Regulations of the University of October 4, 1824, provided
that:

"Should the religious sects of this State, or any of them, according
to the invitation held out to them, establish within, or adjacent to, the
precincts of the University, schools for instruction in the religion of
their sect, the students of the University will be free, and expected to
attend religious worship at the establishment of their respective sects,
in the morning, and in time to meet their school in the University at
its stated hour."

Thus, the "wall of separation between church and State" that Mr.
Jefferson built at the University which he founded did not exclude religious education from that school.[2] The difference between the generality of his statements on the separation of church and state and the
specificity of his conclusions on education is considerable. A rule of
law should not be drawn from a figure of speech.

Mr. Madison's Memorial and Remonstrance against Religious Assessments relied upon by the dissenting Justices in *Everson* is not applicable here. . . . It is clear from its historical setting and its language
that the Remonstrance was a protest against an effort by Virginia to
support Christian sects by taxation. Issues similar to those raised by
the instant case were not discussed. Thus, Mr. Madison's approval of

---

2. It appears that Mr. Jefferson's university also may have required attendance at
worship services, if "expected to attend" hints of coercion.

Mr. Jefferson's report as Rector gives, in my opinion, a clearer indication of his views on the constitutionality of religious education in public schools than his general statements on a different subject.

... The Court's opinion quotes the gist of the Court's reasoning in *Everson*. I agree as there stated that none of our governmental entities can "set up a church." I agree that they cannot "aid" all or any religions or prefer one "over another." But "aid" must be understood as a purposeful assistance directly to the church itself or to some religious group or organization doing religious work of such a character that it may fairly be said to be performing ecclesiastical functions. "Prefer" must give an advantage to one "over another." I agree that pupils cannot "be released in part from their legal duty" of school attendance upon condition that they attend religious classes. But as Illinois has held that it is within the discretion of the School Board to permit absence from school for religious instruction no legal duty of school attendance is violated. If the sentence in the Court's opinion, concerning the pupils' release from legal duty, is intended to mean that the Constitution forbids a school to excuse a pupil from secular control during school hours to attend voluntarily a class in religious education, whether in or out of school buildings, I disagree. Of course, no tax can be levied to support organizations intended "to teach or practice religion." I agree too that the state cannot influence one toward religion against his will or punish him for his beliefs. Champaign's religious education course does none of these things.

· · ·

The practices of the federal government offer many examples of ... "aid" by the state to religion. The Congress of the United States has a chaplain for each House who daily invokes divine blessings and guidance for the proceedings. The armed forces have commissioned chaplains from early days. They conduct the public services in accordance with the liturgical requirements of their respective faiths, ashore and afloat, employing for the purpose property belonging to the United States and dedicated to the services of religion. Under the Servicemen's Readjustment Act of 1944, eligible veterans may receive training at government expense for the ministry in denominational schools. The schools of the District of Columbia have opening exercises which "include a reading from the Bible without note or comment, and the Lord's prayer."

In the United States Naval Academy and the United States Military Academy, schools wholly supported and completely controlled by the federal government, there are a number of religious activities. Chaplains are attached to both schools. Attendance at church services on Sunday is compulsory at both the Military and Naval Academies.[3] At West Point the Protestant services are held in the Cadet Chapel, the Catholic in the Catholic Chapel, and the Jewish in the Old Cadet Chapel; at Annapolis only Protestant services are held on the reservation, midshipmen of other religious persuasions attend the churches of the city of Annapolis. These facts indicate that both schools since their earliest beginnings have maintained and enforced a pattern of participation in formal worship.

... [I]n the light of the meaning given to those words by the precedents, customs, and practices which I have detailed above, I cannot agree with the Court's conclusion that when pupils compelled by law to go to school for secular education are released from school so as to attend the religious classes, churches are unconstitutionally aided. Whatever may be the wisdom of the arrangement as to the use of the school buildings made with the Champaign Council of Religious Education, it is clear to me that past practice shows such cooperation between the schools and a non-ecclesiastical body is not forbidden by the First Amendment. When actual church services have always been permitted on government property, the mere use of the school buildings by a non-sectarian group for religious education ought not be condemned as an establishment of religion. For a non-sectarian organization to give the type of instruction here offered cannot be said to violate our rule as to the establishment of religion by the state. The prohibition of enactments respecting the establishment of religion do not bar every friendly gesture between church and state. It is not an absolute prohibition against every conceivable situation where the two may work together, any more than the other provisions of the First Amendment—free speech, free press—are absolutes. . . . This Court cannot be too cautious in upsetting practices embedded in our society by many years of experience. A state is entitled to have great leeway in its legislation when dealing with the important social problems of its population. A definite violation of legislative limits must be established. The Constitution should not be stretched to forbid national customs in the way courts act to reach arrangements to avoid federal taxation. Devotion to the great principle of religious liberty should not lead us into a rigid interpretation of the constitutional guarantee that

---

3. This policy was later changed. Today, attendance at church services at the academies is voluntary.

conflicts with accepted habits of our people. This is an instance where, for me, the history of past practices is determinative of the meaning of a constitutional clause, not a decorous introduction to the study of its text. The judgment should be affirmed.

Responses

From the (Washington) **Evening Star,** *March 11, 1948, "Church and State":*

On the face of the Supreme Court's latest interpretation, the doors of the public schools have been closed to any form of religious instruction. It would appear that the ban extends even to such a thing as the recitation of the Lord's Prayer. If this is true, if the court has gone to such an extreme in the enforced separation of church and state, then it is a matter which ought to be of the utmost concern in an age in which the old spiritual guides are crumbling under the impact of materialistic philosophy. . . .

These are the facts: Under the Champaign program, pupils are supplied by their teachers with cards on which parents may indicate whether or not they desire religious instruction to be given their children. It is entirely voluntary. There is no compulsion whatsoever. The program is interdenominational in character and is not supported by taxation, the salaries of the participating Protestant, Catholic, and Jewish instructors being paid by Champaign's Council on Religious Education. The program is informative in character, and is not of a proselytical nature. An atheist mother, complaining that her son was embarrassed because, at her direction, he did not attend the religious class, appealed to the courts. And the Supreme Court, on the basis of these facts, has decided that the program transgresses the constitutional ban on the "establishment of religion."

Justice Reed's dissent was strong and persuasive. "From the . . . language of the opinions," he said, "I can only deduce that religious instruction of public school children during the school hours is prohibited. The history of American education is against such an interpretation of the First Amendment." Justice Jackson joined the majority, but he had misgivings. Expressing regret that the court had not been more careful in circumscribing its decision, he pointed out that the effect of the ruling is not only to ban the particular program in Champaign, but also "to ban every form of teaching which suggests or recognizes that there is a God." Other disturbing questions arise. Is it now unconstitutional for children to sing Christmas carols at school plays? What about the chaplains in the military establishment, or the compulsory religious services at Annapolis and West Point? Must these things go, too?

From **The Christian Century,** *April 7, 1948, "The Champaign Case":*

This decision, following so closely after the *Everson* case, made explicit two specific doctrines found to be implicit in the constitutional separation of

99

church and state. These are: (1) that neither the federal government nor any state government can give aid to one church or to all churches, or give preferential treatment to one church over another; (2) that state or federal aid for religion is unconstitutional even if all sects are aided equally. Favoring one church over another would doubtless be a more flagrant breach, though in this case there was no occasion to argue that point. The essence of the doctrine which has now been twice affirmed by the highest court is that the Constitution forbids *any* governmental aid to *any* church. This sustains the contention, which *The Christian Century* has long supported, that the prohibition stated in the first amendment goes far beyond merely prohibiting the creation of an established church. . . .

[McCollum] leaves a great many points yet to be worked out if the total application of this principle is to be made consistent, and if the religious forces of the country are to have full freedom to perform their function in erecting a barrier against the advance of secularism.

One of the first things to be done is the formation of plans by which, if possible, the program of weekday religious education can be continued effectively without the employment of any of the practices which the court has held to be illegal. All "released time" is not necessarily under the ban. Use of public school buildings is. The wise leadership of the International Council of Religious Education and other experts and local organizations will be able to cope with this problem. If their eagerness to "get into the public schools" in order to reach the most children has led to a relationship that must be suspended, getting out of the public schools will give opportunity for more effective teaching of one of the most important lessons in the whole book of religious education—the meaning of separation of church and state as an essential of religious liberty.

The court's decision is obviously going to make it very difficult for Congress to pass a federal education bill giving a large subsidy to schools, including church schools nearly all of which are Roman Catholic; and more difficult still for the court itself, if such a law should be enacted, to uphold its constitutionality. To say that the wall between church and state was dangerously breached by the use of a couple of public school rooms in Champaign, Illinois, for classes in religion a few hours a week, but that a grant of millions of dollars of public funds for the support of Catholic schools is perfectly all right—that would be too preposterous.

There are still other school matters that will require readjustment, unless the court means to have the teeth of the First Amendment bite only innocent bystanders. There is the matter of those church schools which have been incorporated bodily into public school systems, bringing with them their curriculums, their textbooks, their teachers in the garb of their religious orders, and everything that enables them to discharge their main function of indoctrination. There is also the matter of the large federal appropriations currently being made for the maintenance of church schools for Indians.

But for a really embarrassing case of entangling alliance between church and state, the military and naval chaplaincy is conspicuous. Its features are too familiar to require description, and its functions have been too valuable to need praise. We know many of the chaplains, and like them. "Some of our best friends are" chaplains. We know all that can be said in defense of the present system, and it all boils down to this: it works. By the same argument St. Augustine defended the persecution of heretics; he had seen its blessed results in turning hotbeds of Donatism into solidly Catholic towns.

The army and navy want their men to have the ministrations of religion. The churches also want them to have it, but they are not willing to pay for it. Besides, the army and navy do not want the place cluttered up with civilians. They prefer to have their clergy in uniform and under orders. The "rank, pay, and allowances" are not displeasing to the chaplains. On the whole, the system works very well. No other has been seriously tried by this country. The only thing wrong is that it does seems to be flatly in violation of the Constitution. It is "an establishment of religion" as that phrase is now interpreted by the Supreme Court.

Mr. Justice Reed had some of these things in mind when, as the sole dissenter from the court's decision in the Champaign case, he reminded his colleagues that the complete withdrawal of the state from the last vestige of support for religion was a counsel of perfection impossible to attain in practice. While casting out the mote at Champaign, the government has left several beams in its own eye. They will require attention later, and will get it, one by one.

From **The Christian Century,** *April 28, 1948, "Public Schools Can Teach Religion!":*
While the court's decision forbids the church to enter the jurisdiction of the public school to give religious instruction, it does not prohibit the study of religion in the public schools. This question has never yet come before the court. No doubt a test case would come up if the practice were adopted. But it is hardly conceivable that the Supreme Court would find either in the Constitution or in its own precedents any ground for holding the inclusion of religious subject matter in the regular curriculum of the public school unconstitutional.

But if the subject matter of religion is included in the curriculum of public schools, two restrictive limitations are clear from the court's decision in the Champaign case. One is that the churches may not do the teaching. The other is that the school may not teach religion in a manner that tends toward the "establishment of religion," that is, toward a union of the state with any church or churches. There would be no violation of the "establishment of religion" clause of the first amendment should a public school or state university include religious subject matter as an integral part of its curriculum, provided that these limitations were adhered to.

But can the second limitation be adhered to? Can religion be taught on the same pedagogical basis as other subject matters? We believe that it can. The reason why it has not been included in the public school system does not lie in the Constitution, but in the community which supports and controls the public schools. The community is divided into many sectarian groups, and the assumption has long prevailed that no way could be found upon which a general consensus of the community could be reached for the inclusion of religion in the curriculum. This assumption has become a taboo. Time was when the assumption was probably true. But the time has now come to challenge it. And the challenge should come from the teaching profession, whose theory of its own vocation is stultified by the arbitrary refusal of the public school to recognize religion as a major social phenomenon and to impart to the youth of each generation a knowledge of its significance in history and in contemporary culture.

In order to see this as a practical possibility, it is necessary critically to examine what is meant by "teaching religion." The problem has been confused by an ambiguity in this concept. It may mean two different things. It may mean (1) the inculcation of religious attitudes and devotion together with the indoctrination of particular beliefs; in this sense religion is taught in parochial schools; in this sense also it was taught under released time. Such teaching of religion is generally known by the more thorough-going phrase, "religious education." Obviously, such religious teaching is constitutionally prohibited in the public schools and we should be grateful that it is. The political community of which the school is an instrument must keep its hands off the religious devotion of the people. This is a function of the home and the church — a church independent of the state and voluntarily supported by its members.

Or teaching of religion may mean (2) the imparting of knowledge concerning religion. Perhaps this can be more clearly stated from the point of view of the pupil instead of the teacher. "Teaching religion" would then be the *study* of religion. It would be absurd as well as entirely beyond constitutional bounds to prohibit the study of religion in the public schools. As Mr. Justice Jackson puts it in his separate but concurring opinion in the Champaign case, "If we are to eliminate everything [from the public schools] that is objectionable to any of these warring sects or inconsistent with any of their doctrines, we would leave public education in shreds." . . .

The one note lacking in [Justice Jackson's] fine statement is an appeal to the teaching profession to do what the distinguished justice in another paragraph confesses he is unable to do; namely, to show how it can be done. The teaching profession is the expert in this business. It is our belief that modern pedagogy could develop a subject matter and a method of instruction that would give religion the same status in public education which is now given to history, politics, economics, literature and art. . . .

[This] will . . . require the same kind of professional training that is now given to the pedagogy of other subject matters. And this training can be received only in the colleges where teachers receive their pedagogical training. The universities and teachers' colleges are now challenged by a great opportunity to make an advance in public education by creating departments in the pedagogy of religion, designed to develop a graded body of subject matter and to train teachers in a technique for its presentation.

Such departments might find it desirable to include in their faculties three broadly trained theological specialists—a Protestant, a Catholic and a Jew. These should be selected as individuals, without regard to any ecclesiastical action or appointment. That is, the project should be from beginning to end a pedagogical, not an ecclesiastical, project. It would express, primarily, the conscience of the teaching profession, whose theory of education is now distorted by a system which excludes this vast area of the communal culture from general education. Its motivation would derive from the pedagogical faith that this anomalous situation is unnecessary and should be rectified.

The project would have to begin at zero. Tentativeness and much experimentation would characterize its labors probably for some years. There would be skepticism among the clergy of all religious bodies, whose knowledge of the flexibility and resourcefulness of the teaching art is virtually nil. This, however, would not perturb or dissuade a university or teachers' college which once set its hand to this task. It is in the interest of the integrity of the teaching profession to take the leadership in abandoning the truncated kind of education which an irrational and thoroughly undemocratic tradition now compels them to offer.

It must be emphasized that such instruction in public schools as is possible under the Constitution cannot be a substitute for the direct inculcation of religious faith and the habits of devotion through direct instruction by the church itself. The imparting of knowledge of religion as a historical and social phenomenon is not to be equated with the more profound religious education which is a function of the church.

The church therefore has no ground to complain of the *irreligion* of the public school. It is the religious *illiteracy* of the youth-product of the public school that is rightly to be deplored. And it should be equally deplored in the name of democracy, of general culture, and of educational theory itself, as well as in the name of religion. The churches which deliver their children to the public school for their total systematic education may rightly demand that these children and youth be given sufficient knowledge about religion to create some intelligent respect for it as a social phenomenon and thus enable the churches to proceed with their own task without having to deal, as now, with a mental vacuum.

The released time decision should awaken in Protestantism a profound sense of its responsibility to re-examine its conventional religious education program and project it on a higher level of fruitfulness, adequacy and self-respect. A radical reorientation is necessary if the churches are to capitalize the conviction of which released time was a sound but misguided expression.

And it will be all the more necessary if the study of religion is eventually included in public education.

From the (Washington) Evening Star, March 15, 1948, "Church and State":

In these times, when the need for spiritual development is so self-evident, a program designed to serve that end should not be stricken down merely because of some far-fetched, fanciful fear that in the long run there is a possibility it might threaten a subordination of the state to the church. That is a danger which can and should be dealt with when it arises. Meanwhile, the overwhelming weight of the evidence supports the belief that religious instruction should be encouraged and supported in every reasonable manner.

6

Zorach v. Clauson

343 U.S. 306 (1952)

Four years after *McCollum v. Board of Education* (1948), the Supreme Court addressed the constitutionality of another "released time" program for public school students, this one in New York City. Taxpayers and residents whose children attended the city's public schools contended that the program was in essence not different from the one struck down in *McCollum*, even though in New York (unlike Illinois) the religious instruction was provided off campus, not on public school premises. This fact impressed Justice William O. Douglas, who wrote for the Court in affirming the judgment of the New York Court of Appeals that the released-time program was indeed constitutional.

Justice Douglas, who had voted with the majority in both *Everson v. Board of Education* (1947) and *McCollum*, declared that the First Amendment prohibitions are absolute "within the scope of [their] coverage" but that they do not command a "separation of church and state" in "every and all respects." His opinion included a sentence destined to become one of the most often cited from the Court's religion-clause cases: "We are a religious people whose institutions presuppose a Supreme Being."

Douglas's permissive or "accommodationist" view of the no-establishment provision, which he later recanted, did not satisfy Justices Hugo Black, Felix Frankfurter, and Robert Jackson, all three of whom filed strong dissents. Black, author of the Court's opinions in *Everson* and *McCollum*, said that while the New York City program did not make use of public school rooms for religious instruction, it nonetheless did employ "the State's compulsory public school machinery." Justices Frankfurter and Jackson saw the case in a similar light. For all the dissenters, the case turned on what they regarded as the released-time program's coercive nature. All four opinions are presented below, as are editorial responses to the decision from *The Christian Century*, the *New York Times*, and *Commonweal*.

Participating in *Zorach* v. *Clauson*, decided April 28, 1952, were Chief Justice Fred M. Vinson and Associate Justices Hugo L. Black, Harold H. Burton, Tom C. Clark, William O. Douglas, Felix Frankfurter, Robert H. Jackson, Sherman Minton, and Stanley F. Reed.

Opinions

Justice William O. Douglas delivered the opinion of the Court:

This "released time" program involves neither religious instruction in public school classrooms nor the expenditure of public funds. All costs, including the application blanks, are paid by the religious organizations. The case is therefore unlike *McCollum* v. *Board of Education* (1948). . . . In that case the classrooms were turned over to religious instructors. We accordingly held that the program violated the First Amendment. . . .

· · ·

There is a suggestion that the system involves the use of coercion to get public school students into religious classrooms. There is no evidence in the record before us that supports that conclusion. The present record indeed tells us that the school authorities are neutral in this regard and do no more than release students whose parents so request. If in fact coercion were used, if it were established that any one or more teachers were using their office to persuade or force students to take the religious instruction, a wholly different case would be presented. . . .

. . . [W]e do not see how New York by this type of "released time" program has made a law respecting an establishment of religion. . . . There cannot be the slightest doubt that the First Amendment reflects the philosophy that Church and State should be separated. And so far as interference with the "free exercise" of religion and an "establishment" of religion are concerned, the separation must be complete and unequivocal. The First Amendment within the scope of its coverage permits no exception; the prohibition is absolute. The First Amendment, however, does not say that in every and all respects there shall be a separation of Church and State. Rather, it studiously defines the manner, the specific ways, in which there shall be no concert or union or dependency one on the other. That is the common sense of the matter. Otherwise, the state and religion would be aliens to each other—hostile, suspicious, and even unfriendly. Churches could not be required to pay even property taxes. Municipalities would not be permitted to render police or fire protection to religious groups. Policemen who helped parishioners into their places of worship would violate the Constitution. Prayers in our legislative halls; the appeals to the Almighty in the messages of the Chief Executive; the proclamations making Thanksgiving Day a holiday; "so help me God" in our courtroom oaths—these and all other references to the Almighty that run through our laws, our public rituals, our ceremonies would be flouting the First Amendment. A fastidious atheist or agnostic could even object to the supplication with which the Court opens each session: "God save the United States and this Honorable Court."

We would have to press the concept of separation of Church and State to these extremes to condemn the present law on constitutional grounds. The nullification of this law would have wide and profound effects. A Catholic student applies to his teacher for permission to leave the school during hours on a Holy Day of Obligation to attend a mass. A Jewish student asks his teacher for permission to be excused for Yom Kippur. A Protestant wants the afternoon off for a baptismal ceremony. In each case the teacher requires parental consent in writing. In each case the teacher, in order to make sure the student is not a truant, goes further and requires a report from the priest, the rabbi, or the minister. The teacher in other words cooperates in a religious program to the extent of making it possible for her student to participate in it. Whether she does it occasionally for a few students, regularly for one, or pursuant to a systematized program designed to further the religious needs of all the students does not alter the character of the act.

We are a religious people whose institutions presuppose a Supreme Being. We guarantee the freedom to worship as one chooses. We make room for as wide a variety of beliefs and creeds as the spiritual needs of man deem necessary. We sponsor an attitude on the part of government that shows no partiality to any one group and that lets each flourish according to the zeal of its adherents and the appeal of its dogma. When the state encourages religious instruction or cooperates with religious authorities by adjusting the schedule of public events to sectarian needs, it follows the best of our traditions. For it then respects the religious nature of our people and accommodates the public service to their spiritual needs. To hold that it may not would be to find in the Constitution a requirement that the government show a callous indifference to religious groups. That would be preferring those who believe in no religion over those who do believe. Government may not finance religious groups nor undertake religious instruction nor blend secular and sectarian education nor use secular institutions to force one or some religion on any person. But we find no constitutional requirement which makes it necessary for government to be hostile to religion and to throw its weight against efforts to widen the effective scope of religious influence. The government must be neutral when it comes to competition between sects. It may not thrust any sect on any person. It may not make a religious observance compulsory. It may not coerce anyone to attend church, to observe a religious holiday, or to take religious instruction. But it can close its doors or suspend its operations as do those who want to repair to their religious sanctuary for worship or instruction. No more than that is undertaken here.

This program may be unwise and improvident from an educational or a community viewpoint. That appeal is made to us on a theory . . . that each case must be decided on the basis of "our own prepossessions." Our individual preferences, however, are not the constitutional standard. The constitutional standard is the separation of Church and State. The problem, like many problems in constitutional law, is one of degree.

In the *McCollum* case the classrooms were used for religious instruction and the force of the public school was used to promote that instruction. Here, as we have said, the public schools do no more than accommodate their schedules to a program of outside religious instruction. We follow the *McCollum* case. But we cannot expand it to cover the present released time program unless separation of Church and State means that public institutions can make no adjustments of their schedules to accommodate the religious needs of the people. We cannot read into the Bill of Rights such a philosophy of hostility to religion.

Justice Hugo L. Black, dissenting:

I see no significant difference between the invalid Illinois system and that of New York here sustained. Except for the use of the school buildings in Illinois, there is no difference between the systems which I consider even worthy of mention. In the New York program, as in that of Illinois, the school authorities release some of the children on the condition that they attend the religious classes, get reports on whether they attend, and hold the other children in the school building until the religious hour is over. As we attempted to make categorically clear, the *McCollum* decision would have been the same if the religious classes had not been held in the school buildings.

. . .

McCollum . . . held that Illinois could not constitutionally manipulate the compelled classroom hours of its compulsory school machinery so as to channel children into sectarian classes. Yet that is exactly what the Court holds New York can do.

I am aware that our *McCollum* decision on separation of Church and State has been subjected to a most searching examination throughout the country. Probably few opinions from this Court in recent years have attracted more attention or stirred wider debate. Our insistence on "a wall of separation between Church and State which must be kept high and impregnable" has seemed to some a correct exposition of the philosophy and a true interpretation of the language of the First Amendment to which we should strictly adhere. With equal conviction and sincerity, others have thought the *McCollum* decision fundamentally wrong and have pledged continuous warfare against it. The opinions in the court reflect these diverse viewpoints. In dissenting today, I mean to do more than give routine approval to our *McCollum* decision. I mean also to reaffirm my faith in the fundamental philosophy expressed in *McCollum* and *Everson* v. *Board of Education* (1947). . . .

. . . Here the sole question is whether New York can use its compulsory education laws to help religious sects get attendants presumably too unenthusiastic to go unless moved to do so by the pressure of this state machinery. That this is the plan, purpose, design and consequence of the New York program cannot be denied. The state thus makes religious sects beneficiaries of its power to compel children to attend secular schools. Any use of such coercive power by the state to help or hinder some religious sects or to prefer all religious sects over nonbelievers or vice versa is just what I think the First Amendment forbids. In considering whether a state has entered this forbidden field the question is not whether it has entered too far but whether it has entered at all. New York is manipulating its compulsory education laws to help religious sects get pupils. This is not separation but combination of Church and State.

The Court's validation of the New York system rests in part on its statement that Americans are "a religious people whose institutions presuppose a Supreme Being." This was at least as true when the First Amendment was adopted; and it was just as true when eight justices of this Court invalidated the released time system in *McCollum* on the premise that a state can no more "aid all religions" than it can aid one. It was precisely because Eighteenth Century Americans were a religious people divided into many fighting sects that we were given the

constitutional mandate to keep Church and State completely separate.
. . . Now as then, it is only by wholly isolating the state from the religious sphere and compelling it to be completely neutral, that the freedom of each and every denomination and of all nonbelievers can be maintained. It is this neutrality the Court abandons today when it treats New York's coercive system as a program which *merely* "encourages religious instruction or cooperates with religious authorities." The abandonment is all the more dangerous to liberty because of the Court's legal exaltation of the orthodox and its derogation of unbelievers.

Under our system of religious freedom, people have gone to their religious sanctuaries not because they feared the law but because they loved their God. The choice of all has been as free as the choice of those who answered the call to worship moved only by the music of the old Sunday morning church bells. The spiritual mind of man has thus been free to believe, disbelieve, or doubt, without repression, great or small, by the heavy hand of government. Statutes authorizing such repression have been stricken. Before today, our judicial opinions have refrained from drawing invidious distinctions between those who believe in no religion and those who do believe. The First Amendment has lost much if the religious followers and the atheist are no longer to be judicially regarded as entitled to equal justice under law.

State help to religion injects political and party prejudices into a holy field. It too often substitutes force for prayer, hate for love, and persecution for persuasion. Government should not be allowed, under cover of the soft euphemism of "co-operation," to steal into the sacred area of religious choice.

Justice Felix Frankfurter, dissenting:

The Court tells us that in the maintenance of its public schools, "[The State government][1] can close its doors or suspend its operations" so that its citizens may be free for religious devotions or instruction. If that were the issue, it would not rise to the dignity of a constitutional controversy. Of course a State may provide that the classes in its schools shall be dismissed, for any reason, or no reason, on fixed days, or for special occasions. The essence of this case is that the school system did not "close its doors" and did not "suspend its operations." There is all the difference in the world between letting the

---

1. Brackets are in original text.

children out of school and letting some of them out of school into religious classes. . . .

The pith of the case is that formalized religious instruction is substituted for other school activity which those who do not participate in the released-time program are compelled to attend. The school system is very much in operation during this kind of released time. . . .

Again, the Court relies upon the absence from the record of evidence of coercion in the operation of the system. . . . But the Court disregards the fact that as the case comes to us, there could be no proof of coercion, for the appellants were not allowed to make proof of it. Appellants alleged that "the operation of the released time program has resulted and inevitably results in the exercise of pressure and coercion upon parents and children to secure attendance by the children for religious instruction." This allegation . . . was denied by appellees. Thus were drawn issues of fact which cannot be determined, on any conceivable view of judicial notice, by judges out of their own knowledge or experience. Appellants sought an opportunity to adduce evidence in support of these allegations at an appropriate trial. . . . [But they] were denied that opportunity on the ground that such proof was irrelevant to the issue of constitutionality. . . .

When constitutional issues turn on facts, it is a strange procedure indeed not to permit the facts to be established. When such is the case, there are weighty considerations for us to require the State court to make its determination only after a thorough canvass of all the circumstances and not to bar them from consideration. If we are to decide this case on the present record, however, a strict adherence to the usage of courts in ruling on the sufficiency of pleadings would require us to take as admitted the facts pleaded in the appellants' complaint, including the fact of coercion, actual and inherent. Even on a more latitudinarian view, I cannot see how a finding that coercion was absent, deemed critical by this Court in sustaining the practice, can be made here, when appellants were prevented from making a timely showing of coercion because the courts below thought it irrelevant.

The result in *McCollum* was based on principles that received unanimous acceptance by this Court, barring only a single vote. I agree with Justice Black that those principles are disregarded in reaching the result in this case. Happily they are not disavowed by the Court. From this I draw the hope that in future variations of the problem which are bound to come here, these principles may again be honored in the observance.

Justice Robert H. Jackson, dissenting:

This released time program is founded upon a use of the State's power of coercion, which, for me, determines its unconstitutionality. Stripped to its essentials, the plan has two stages, first, that the State compel each student to yield a large part of his time for public secular education and, second, that some of it be "released" to him on condition that he devote it to sectarian religious purposes.

No one suggests that the Constitution would permit the State directly to require this "released" time to be spent "under the control of a duly constituted religious body." This program accomplishes that forbidden result by indirection. If public education were taking so much of the pupil's time as to injure the public or the students' welfare by encroaching upon their religious opportunity, simply shortening everyone's school day would facilitate voluntary and optional attendance at Church classes. But that suggestion is rejected upon the ground that if they are made free many students will not go to the Church. Hence, they must be deprived of freedom for this period, with Church attendance put to them as one of the two permissible ways of using it.

The greater effectiveness of this system over voluntary attendance after school hours is due to the truant officer who, if the youngster fails to go to the Church school, dogs him back to the public schoolroom. Here schooling is more or less suspended during the "released time" so the nonreligious attendants will not forge ahead of the churchgoing absentees. But it serves as a temporary jail for a pupil who will not go to Church. It takes more subtlety of mind than I possess to deny that this is governmental constraint in support of religion. It is as unconstitutional, in my view, when exerted by indirection as when exercised forthrightly.

As one whose children, as a matter of free choice, have been sent to privately supported Church schools, I may challenge the Court's suggestion that opposition to this plan can only be anti-religious, atheistic, or agnostic. My evangelistic brethren confuse an objection to compulsion with an objection to religion. It is possible to hold a faith with enough confidence to believe that what should be rendered to God does not need to be decided and collected by Caesar.

The day that this country ceases to be free for irreligion it will cease to be free for religion—except for the sect that can win political power. The same epithetical jurisprudence used by the Court today to beat down those who oppose pressuring children into some religion can devise as good epithets tomorrow against those who object to pressuring them into a favored religion. And, after all, if we concede to the State power and wisdom to single out "duly constituted religious" bodies as exclusive alternatives for compulsory secular instruction, it would be logical to also uphold the power and wisdom to choose the true faith among those "duly constituted." We start down a rough road when we begin to mix compulsory public education with compulsory godliness.

A number of Justices just short of a majority of the majority that promulgates today's passionate dialectics joined in answering them in *McCollum*. The distinction attempted between that case and this is trivial, almost to the point of cynicism, magnifying its nonessential details and disparaging compulsion which was the underlying reason for invalidity. A reading of the Court's opinion in that case along with its opinion in this case will show such difference of overtones and undertones as to make clear that *McCollum* has passed like a storm in a teacup. The wall which the Court was professing to erect between Church and State has become even more warped and twisted than I expected. Today's judgment will be more interesting to students of psychology and of the judicial processes than to students of constitutional law.

Responses

From **The Christian Century,** May 14, 1952, "The Court Concurs":

We believe that the terms in which Justice Douglas framed the court's decision will not clarify the church-and-state issue, but will produce much future litigation. To be sure, the verdict embodies a firm reaffirmation of the legal principle on which the court based its *Everson* and *McCollum* decisions. . . .

But the sweeping rhetorical generalities of Justice Douglas's decision— what Justice Jackson, in his dissent, calls the "passionate dialectics" and "epithetical jurisprudence" formulated by his "evangelistic brethren"—open the door to many differing views as to where the wall of separation runs. When the court says, "We are a religious people whose institutions presuppose a Supreme Being," and couples that with the assertion that "the First Amendment does not say that in every and all respects there shall be a separation of church and state," it is widening an area of doubt which the *Everson* and *McCollum* decisions had tried to narrow. . . .

Initial reaction by the churches . . . in most cases will probably be favorable. The churches are so disturbed by the growing secularization of our culture, and have been so indoctrinated with the idea that their efforts to offset this require some system of weekday religious instruction, that they have come to regard "released time" systems as their last chance to rear a religiously literate generation of American youth. We believe, however, that just as most Roman Catholic spokesmen first hailed the *Everson* verdict because it upheld public bus service for parochial school pupils and later sang a different tune when they reflected on the principles which underlay that verdict, so now a reflective appraisal will presently mute any hosannas.

The issues raised in the dissents in this New York case are of far-reaching importance. State coercion in behalf of religious programs or state discrimination between religious and nonreligious citizens can do infinite damage to the future stability of the American principle of church and state separation. Coercion involves intermingling of the functioning of the state with that of religious bodies. Discrimination brings inequality among citizens based on a religious test. Both are fundamentally repugnant to American constitutional principles and to our most precious national tradition. The only way to avoid such coercion and discrimination, if weekday religious classes are not to subvert the principles of the First Amendment, is, as Justice Frankfurter contends, to close the schools completely while these classes are in session and to give the dismissed students entire freedom to choose what they do in that time.

And when all is said and done, is the end which the churches seek by fighting these legal battles to sustain their released time systems worth the struggle? In the present instance they have won a court victory—at the cost of creating new and grave doubts regarding the extent to which church and state are in fact separate under the Constitution. Victory here may pave the way to calamitous later invasions of the separation principle. Yet the weekday religious instruction classes, as conducted, have in few instances produced results to substantiate the claims made for them. If the churches cannot carry out the educational program which they hold essential on Sunday or in hours when the public schools are not in session, would not their purposes and the purposes of all Americans who desire to see the separation of church and state maintained be better served if an effort were launched to close the schools for the period during which religious classes were being held, whether that closing involved a matter of an hour, or a half-day, or even a full day in every week?

From the New York Times, April 30, 1952, "Time Off for Religion":

The decision had been awaited with interest since a 1948 Supreme Court decision found that released time as practiced in Champaign, Ill., violated the Constitution. There the instruction was conducted within the schools, by religious instructors of various faiths who came into classrooms. In New York City religious instruction is not given on public school property. A student in the elementary schools whose parents ask that he be excused for religious teaching goes to church property; he omits the final hour of the school day, once a week. Of the 550,000 elementary school students here who could possibly be considered eligible last year (and this figure is subject to considerable reduction for various reasons) 105,467 took advantage of released time. In the decade since released time was first granted here the number released has increased greatly, but in recent years it has just about held steady.

Justice Douglas, writing for the majority, disposes of the constitutional question as follows: "We follow the *McCollum* case [from Champaign]. But we cannot expand it to cover the present released-time program [as practiced in New York City] unless separation of church and state means that public institutions can make no adjustments of their schedules to accommodate the religious needs of the people. We cannot read into the Bill of Rights such a philosophy of hostility to religion."

This view is indignantly rejected by the dissenters. One point made along the way by Justice Douglas deserves emphasis. "There is a suggestion," he writes, "that the system involves the use of coercion to get public school students into religious classrooms. If in fact coercion were used, if it were established that one or more teachers were using their office to persuade or force students to take the religious instruction, a wholly different case would be presented."

We find the majority opinion persuasive. At the same time we recognize the danger of abuses of released time, the possibility of divisiveness, of compulsion, of truancy, the danger that those left behind in the school classroom may suffer the waste of a purposeless hour. Despite the painstaking studies and evidence produced in this field by such organizations as the Public Education Association we lean hopefully to the view that the abuses can eventually be remedied or minimized.

In this time of so much moral bankruptcy, with the demonstrated need for religious and ethical training, we feel that the door cannot be closed to a program—shared by 2,000,000 or more young children over the nation each year—that offers promise of strengthening the religious and moral fiber of our youth. The fact that this is a minority does not preclude the fact that within this fairly small company some few may be touched by inspiration, in that time off for religion, to become spiritual leaders of tomorrow. If this hope is valid, then the challenge to our various faiths is to make the released-time program more vital, more meaningful, while avoiding such danger as admittedly surround an arms-length partnership—in separation between schools and religion.

From *Commonweal,* May 16, 1952, "A Matter of Tradition":

There remains an articulate group of American citizens who, for whatever reason, fear any formal public recognition that "we are a religious people whose institutions presume a Supreme Being."

It would be pleasant if all these fears were settled by the Supreme Court's authoritative pronouncement, if it dispelled their bitter antipathy to such questions as released time, federal aid to parochial school pupils, etc. But such antipathy and bitterness as sometimes get in print arise, one suspects, from feelings more deeply imbedded than a legal conviction or even loyalty to what is mistakenly believed to be an American "tradition." How to explain it?

Among the obvious elements is certainly a fear of clericalism—a hazy undefined fear of ecclesiastical power, which for many stands in direct opposition to all they have learned to revere as "progressive" and "enlightened." However dim the threat, it is very real to many people who were brought up on an idea of organized religion which was concocted almost exclusively of Inquisition horror stories and bloody sectarian wars.

Their one-sided picture of ecclesiastical influence on history reflects the very kind of limited secularist education which the released time program, among other things, may help to fill out.

Another important element is explained by those spiritually impoverished Americans who have exalted "democracy" into a kind of secularized religion. For these people the supreme value is something they call the "democratic" experience—the blurring or extinction of differences between Americans until uniformity brings about the broadest possible comity. Religious differences are a possible source of group tensions; therefore they would solve the problem by destroying religious differences, or at least by minimizing them, above all by refraining from any public act that calls attention to them. Even if religious values were not considered all-important by those who hold them and so not to be sacrificed with such ease, this solution would still be dubious. The genius of our democracy consists not in destroying diversity and imposing unity but of creating a political unity out of the widest diversity.

A third element looks upon religion itself as somewhat passé. These people will find Justice Douglas's dictum that "we are a religious people" an embarrassment. His insistence that the separation of Church and state in the U.S. is not absolute, will infuriate them. The plain fact of the matter is that the part of America's tradition which is religious is something they would like to forget about, for all their pious reverence for "tradition" where the separation of church and state is concerned.

But the present defeat for these sad attitudes should not be a source of smug contentment for religious-minded Americans. Rather, they should be a challenge to religious zeal. Holding them are men and women, fellow-Americans, who stand in as much need of religious influence as we. Beyond that, the presence of such attitudes among us should spur religious groups to avoid anything that might be honestly taken to conflict with the true tradition of church-state separation. Religious-minded Americans and their churches should be in the forefront to protect the notion of religious liberty. In the true American context, separation of church and state was set up to guarantee freedom *for* religion, however much misguided zealots have tried to make it look like freedom *from* religion. Let him who believes in the real tradition defend it.

7

Torcaso v. Watkins

367 U.S. 488 (1961)

A rticle VI of the Constitution states: "[N]o religious test shall ever be required as a qualification to any office or public trust under the United States." But may a *state* require a religious test? In *Torcaso* v. *Watkins* the Court emphatically said it may not.

Article 37 of the Declaration of Rights of the Maryland Constitution provided that "no religious test ought ever to be required as a qualification for any office of profit or trust in this state, other than a declaration of belief in the existence of God." Roy Torcaso, an appointee to the office of notary public in the state, was refused a commission to serve because he would not, as required by Article 37, declare his belief in the existence of God. He sued in state court, arguing that the state constitutional requirement violated the First and Fourteenth Amendments of the federal Constitution. The Maryland courts rejected his challenge, but on appeal the Supreme Court reversed.

Justice Hugo Black, writing for the Court, rested the decision on both the establishment and free-exercise provisions of the religion clause. "[N]either a State nor the Federal Government . . . can constitutionally pass laws or impose requirements which aid all religions as against nonbelievers," he wrote, in a paraphrase of a passage he had composed for the Court in *Everson* v. *Board of Education* (1947). Also, he continued, Maryland's oath requirement "unconstitutionally invades the appellant's freedom of belief and religion. . . ."

Justice Black expressed the view of seven members of the Court. The other two, Justices Felix Frankfurter and John M.

Harlan II, concurred in the result. No one other than Black wrote in *Torcaso*, which firmly established that the religion clause protects non-believers and believers alike.

Participating in *Torcaso* v. *Watkins*, decided June 19, 1961, were Chief Justice Earl Warren and Associate Justices Hugo L. Black, William J. Brennan, Jr., Tom C. Clark, William O. Douglas, Felix Frankfurter, John M. Harlan II, Potter Stewart, and Charles E. Whittaker.

Opinion

Justice Hugo L. Black delivered the opinion of the Court:

There is, and can be, no dispute about the purpose or effect of the Maryland Declaration of Rights requirement before us—it sets up a religious test which was designed to and, if valid, does bar every person who refuses to declare a belief in God from holding a public "office of profit or trust" in Maryland. The power and authority of the State of Maryland thus is put on the side of one particular sort of believers— those who are willing to say they believe in "the existence of God." It is true that there is much historical precedent for such laws. Indeed, it was largely to escape religious test oaths and declarations that a great many of the early colonists left Europe and came here hoping to worship in their own way. It soon developed, however, that many of those who had fled to escape religious test oaths turned out to be perfectly willing, when they had the power to do so, to force dissenters from their faith to take test oaths in conformity with that faith. This brought on a host of laws in the new Colonies imposing burdens and disabilities of various kinds upon varied beliefs depending largely upon what group happened to be politically strong enough to legislate in favor of its own beliefs. The effect of all this was the formal or practical "establishment" of particular religious faiths in most of the Colonies, with consequent burdens imposed on the free exercise of the faiths of non-favored believers.

There were, however, wise and far-seeing men in the Colonies—too many to mention—who spoke out against test oaths and all the philosophy of intolerance behind them. One of these, it so happens, was George Calvert (the first Lord Baltimore), who took a most important part in the original establishment of the Colony of Maryland. He was a Catholic and had, for this reason, felt compelled by his conscience to refuse to take the Oath of Supremacy in England at the cost of resigning om high governmental office. He again refused to take that oath when it was demanded by the Council of the Colony of Virginia, and as a result he was denied settlement in that Colony. A recent historian of the early period of Maryland's life has said that it was Calvert's hope

121

and purpose to establish in Maryland a colonial government free from the religious persecutions he had known—one "securely beyond the reach of oaths. . . ."[1]

When our Constitution was adopted, the desire to put the people "securely beyond the reach" of religious test oaths brought about the inclusion in Article 6 of that document of a provision that "no religious Test shall ever be required as a Qualification to any Office or public Trust under the United States." . . . Not satisfied, however, with Article 6 and other guarantees in the original Constitution, the First Congress proposed and the States very shortly thereafter adopted our Bill of Rights, including the First Amendment. That Amendment broke new constitutional ground in the protection it sought to afford to freedom of religion, speech, press, petition and assembly. Since prior cases in this Court have thoroughly explored and documented the history behind the First Amendment, the reasons for it, and the scope of the religious freedom it protects, we need not cover that ground again. What was said in our prior cases we think controls our decision here.

[Justice Black here cites passages from *Cantwell* v. *Connecticut* (1940) and *Everson* v. *Board of Education* (1947) that applied the religion clauses to the states and provided substantive interpretations of the clauses.]

While there were strong dissents in the *Everson* Case, they did not challenge the Court's interpretation of the First Amendment's coverage as being too broad, but thought the Court was applying that interpretation too narrowly to the facts of that case. Not long afterward, in *McCollum* v. *Board of Education* (1948), we were urged to repudiate as dicta the . . . *Everson* interpretation of the scope of the First Amendment's coverage. We declined to do this, but instead strongly reaffirmed what had been said in *Everson*, calling attention to the fact that both the majority and the minority in *Everson* had agreed on the principles declared in this part of the *Everson* opinion . . . .

The Maryland Court of Appeals thought, and it is argued here, that this Court's later holding and opinion in *Zorach* v. *Clauson* (1952) had in part repudiated the [rule of law stated] in . . . *Everson* . . . and previously reaffirmed in *McCollum*. But the Court's opinion in *Zorach* specifically stated: "We follow the *McCollum* case." Nothing decided or written in *Zorach* lends support to the idea that the Court there intended to open up the way for government, state or federal, to restore the historically and constitutionally discredited policy of probing reli-

---

1. A note here cites Hanley, *Their Rights and Liberties* (Newman Press, 1959), 65.

gious beliefs by test oaths or limiting public offices to persons who have, or perhaps more properly profess to have, a belief in some particular kind of religious concept.

We repeat and again reaffirm that neither a State nor the Federal Government can constitutionally force a person "to profess a belief or disbelief in any religion." Neither can constitutionally pass laws or impose requirements which aid all religions as against nonbelievers, and neither can aid those religions based on a belief in the existence of God as against those religions founded on different beliefs.[2]

In upholding the State's religious test for public office the highest court of Maryland said:

"The petitioner is not compelled to believe or disbelieve, under threat of punishment or other compulsion. True, unless he makes the declaration of belief he cannot hold public office in Maryland, but he is not compelled to hold office."

The fact, however, that a person is not compelled to hold public office cannot possibly be an excuse for barring him from office by state-imposed criteria forbidden by the Constitution. . . .

This Maryland religious test for public office unconstitutionally invades the appellant's freedom of belief and religion and therefore cannot be enforced against him.

---

2. This paragraph closely tracks Black's statement in *Everson* of the limitations imposed by the no-establishment provision: "Neither [a state nor the federal government] can pass laws which aid one religion, aid all religions, or prefer one religion over another. Neither can force nor influence a person to go or to remain away from church against his will or force him to profess a belief or disbelief in any religion."

Footnote eleven appears at this point in the opinion. It lists religions in the United States "which do not teach what would generally be considered a belief in the existence of God." These are: "Buddhism, Taoism, Ethical Culture, Secular Humanism and others."

8

Engel v. Vitale

370 U.S. 421 (1962)

Since their inception in the nineteenth century, public schools in most parts of the United States had sponsored prayers and other devotional exercises. Once the Supreme Court had applied the religion clause to the states, it was inevitable that the Court would be asked to decide the constitutionality of these state-sponsored religious activities. In fact, in 1952, in *Doremus* v. *Board of Education*, 342 U.S. 429, the Court in effect postponed consideration of this issue when it held that a taxpayer had no standing to challenge Bible reading in the public schools.

Ten years later, in *Engel* v. *Vitale*, the Court held that under the First Amendment a state may not sponsor prayers in its schools. No ruling in this area of constitutional law has provoked as much sustained public controversy.

The New York State Board of Regents composed and recommended for daily use in New York public schools a brief, nondenominational prayer: "Almighty God, we acknowledge our dependence upon Thee, and we beg Thy blessings upon us, our parents, our teachers and our Country." The officials justified the prayer as a part of a child's moral and spiritual training. Student participation was voluntary.

When the Board of Education of New Hyde Park, New York, directed its school principals to have the prayer recited daily, several parents sued, challenging the state action as a violation of the First Amendment. The New York courts were satisfied that the prayer was not an establishment of religion so long as the schools did not compel any student to join in the prayer over

125

his or his parents' objection. The Supreme Court disagreed. Writing for the Court, Justice Hugo Black said it was beside the point that students were not forced to participate; what offended the First Amendment, he said, was the fact that government had engaged in a religious activity by writing a prayer.

Polls showed that *Engel* and the related decision in 1963 in *Abington School District* v. *Schempp*, striking down Bible readings in public schools (see Case 9), were opposed by large majorities of the American people. Down through the years there have been various proposals to amend the Constitution so as to allow public school prayer and other devotional exercises. None has succeeded. Nor has the Court overruled these cases.

States have, however, enacted laws providing for a moment of silence during which public school students may pray. In 1985 the Supreme Court addressed the constitutionality of one such law in *Wallace* v. *Jaffree*; see Case 21. To clarify the circumstances in which public high school students may gather for religious purposes, including prayers, Congress in 1984 enacted the Equal Access Act, which provides student-led religious groups the same right of access to school facilities for their meetings as is enjoyed by student-led non-religious groups. In 1990 the law was upheld against constitutional challenge in *Board of Education* v. *Mergens*; see Case 24. The most recent addition to the law regarding school prayer came in 1992, when the Court, in *Lee* v. *Weisman*, struck down a public school's practice of having area clergy deliver prayers at junior and senior high school graduation ceremonies; see Case 25.

Engel generated three opinions: Justice Black, architect of the Court's establishment jurisprudence in *Everson* v. *Board of Education* (1947), wrote for the Court, expressing the views of five members; William O. Douglas also wrote separately, concurring in the judgment; and Justice Potter Stewart dissented. All three opinions are presented here. Justices Felix Frankfurter and Byron White did not participate in the case.

The editorial responses to the decision reprinted here are from the *New York Times*, the *Wall Street Journal*, the *Washington Post*, the (Washington) *Evening Star*, *Christianity and Crisis*, and *The New Republic*.

Participating in *Engel* v. *Vitale*, decided June 25, 1962, were Chief Justice Earl Warren and Associate Justices Hugo L. Black, William J. Brennan, Jr., Tom C. Clark, William O. Douglas, John M. Harlan II, and Potter Stewart.

Opinions

Justice Hugo L. Black delivered the opinion of the Court:

The petitioners contend among other things that the state laws requiring or permitting use of the Regents' prayer must be struck down as a violation of the Establishment Clause because that prayer was composed by governmental officials as a part of a governmental program to further religious beliefs. For this reason, petitioners argue, the State's use of the Regents' prayer in its public school system breaches the constitutional wall of separation between Church and State. We agree with that contention since we think that the constitutional prohibition against laws respecting an establishment of religion must at least mean that in this country it is no part of the business of government to compose official prayers for any group of the American people to recite as a part of a religious program carried on by government.

It is a matter of history that this very practice of establishing governmentally composed prayers for religious services was one of the reasons which caused many of our early colonists to leave England and seek religious freedom in America. The Book of Common Prayer, which was created under governmental direction and which was approved by Acts of Parliament in 1548 and 1549, set out in minute detail the accepted form and content of prayer and other religious ceremonies to be used in the established, tax-supported Church of England. The controversies over the Book and what should be its content repeatedly threatened to disrupt the peace of that country as the accepted forms of prayer in the established church changed with the views of the particular ruler that happened to be in control at the time. . . .

It is an unfortunate fact of history that when some of the very groups which had most strenuously opposed the established Church of England found themselves sufficiently in control of colonial governments in this country to write their own prayers into law, they passed laws making their own religion the official religion of their respective colonies. Indeed, as late as the time of the Revolutionary War, there were established churches in at least eight of the thirteen former colonies and established religions in at least four of the other five. But the

128

successful Revolution against English political domination was shortly followed by intense opposition to the practice of establishing religion by law. This opposition crystallized rapidly into an effective political force in Virginia where the minority religious groups such as Presbyterians, Lutherans, Quakers and Baptists had gained such strength that the adherents to the established Episcopal Church were actually a minority themselves. In 1785–1786, those opposed to the established Church, led by James Madison and Thomas Jefferson, who, though themselves not members of any of those dissenting religious groups, opposed all religious establishments by law on grounds of principle, obtained the enactment of the famous "Virginia Bill for Religious Liberty" by which all religious groups were placed on equal footing so far as the State was concerned. . . .

By the time of the adoption of the Constitution, our history shows that there was a widespread awareness among many Americans of the dangers of a union of Church and State. These people knew, some of them from bitter personal experience, that one of the greatest dangers to the freedom of the individual to worship in his own way lay in the Government's placing its official stamp of approval upon one particular kind of prayer or one particular form of religious services. They knew the anguish, hardship and bitter strife that could come when zealous religious groups struggled with one another to obtain the Government's stamp of approval from each King, Queen, or Protector that came to temporary power. The Constitution was intended to avert a part of this danger by leaving the government of this country in the hands of the people rather than in the hands of any monarch. But this safeguard was not enough. Our Founders were no more willing to let the content of their prayers and their privilege of praying whenever they pleased be influenced by the ballot box than they were to let these vital matters of personal conscience depend upon the succession of monarchs. The First Amendment was added to the Constitution to stand as a guarantee that neither the power nor the prestige of the Federal Government would be used to control, support or influence the kinds of prayer the American people can say—that the people's religions must not be subjected to the pressures of government for change each time a new political administration is elected to office. Under that Amendment's prohibition against governmental establishment of religion, as reinforced by the provisions of the Fourteenth Amendment, government in this country, be it state or federal, is without power to prescribe by law any particular form of prayer which is to be used as an official prayer in carrying on any program of governmentally sponsored religious activity.

There can be no doubt that New York's state prayer program officially establishes the religious beliefs embodied in the Regents' prayer. The respondents' argument to the contrary, which is largely based upon the contention that the Regents' prayer is "non-denominational" and the fact that the program, as modified and approved by state courts, does not require all pupils to recite the prayer but permits those who wish to do so to remain silent or be excused from the room, ignores the essential nature of the program's constitutional defects. Neither the fact that the prayer may be denominationally neutral nor the fact that its observance on the part of the students is voluntary can serve to free it from the limitations of the Establishment Clause, as it might from the Free Exercise Clause, of the First Amendment, both of which are operative against the States by virtue of the Fourteenth Amendment. Although these two clauses may in certain instances overlap, they forbid two quite different kinds of governmental encroachment upon religious freedom. The Establishment Clause, unlike the Free Exercise Clause, does not depend upon any showing of direct governmental compulsion and is violated by the enactment of laws which establish an official religion whether those laws operate directly to coerce nonobserving individuals or not. . . . The New York laws officially prescribing the Regents' prayer are inconsistent both with the purposes of the Establishment Clause and with the Establishment Clause itself.

It has been argued that to apply the Constitution in such a way as to prohibit state laws respecting an establishment of religious services in public schools is to indicate a hostility toward religion or toward prayer. Nothing, of course, could be more wrong. The history of man is inseparable from the history of religion. And perhaps it is not too much to say that since the beginning of that history many people have devoutly believed that "More things are wrought by prayer than this world dreams of." It was doubtless largely due to men who believed this that there grew up a sentiment that caused men to leave the crosscurrents of officially established state religions and religious persecution in Europe and come to this country filled with the hope that they could find a place in which they could pray when they pleased to the God of their faith in the language they chose. And there were men of this same faith in the power of prayer who led the fight for adoption of our Constitution and also for our Bill of Rights with the very guarantees of religious freedom that forbid the sort of governmental activity which New York has attempted here. These men knew that the First Amendment, which tried to put an end to governmental control of religion and of prayer, was not written to destroy either.[1] They knew rather that it was written to quiet well-justified fears which nearly all of them felt arising out of an awareness that governments of the past had shackled men's tongues to make them speak only the religious thoughts that government wanted them to speak and to pray only to the God that government wanted them to pray to. It is neither sacrilegious nor antireligious to say that each separate government in this country should stay out of the business of writing or sanctioning official prayers and leave that purely religious function to the people themselves and to those the people choose to look to for religious guidance.

It is true that New York's establishment of its Regents' prayer as an officially approved religious doctrine of that State does not amount to a total establishment of one particular religious sect to the exclusion of all others—that, indeed, the governmental endorsement of that prayer seems relatively insignificant when compared to the governmental encroachments upon religion which were commonplace 200 years ago. To those who may subscribe to the view that because the Regents' official prayer is so brief and general there can be no danger to religious freedom in its governmental establishment, however, it may be appropriate to say in the words of James Madison, the author of the First Amendment:[2]

> [I]t is proper to take alarm at the first experiment on our liberties. . . . Who does not see that the same authority which can establish Christianity, in exclusion of all other Religions, may establish with the same ease any particular sect of Christians, in exclusion of all other Sects? That the same authority which can force a citizen to contribute three pence only of his property for the support of any one establishment, may force him to conform to any other establishment in all cases whatsoever?

1. Justice Black did not speak to two historical facts of seeming relevance to his opinion. One is that the First Congress, which proposed the Bill of Rights, elected a chaplain of Congress who said prayers; the other is that the First Congress passed a resolution asking the President "to recommend to the people of the United States a day of public Thanksgiving and prayer, to be observed by acknowledging, with grateful hearts, the many signal favors of Almighty God."

2. The use of this statement, taken from Madison's "Memorial and Remonstrance," is further evidence of the tendency on Black's part, and indeed on the part of most of his colleagues, to understand the First Amendment as enacting certain views of Madison.

The judgment of the Court of Appeals of New York is reversed and the cause remanded for further proceedings not inconsistent with this opinion.

Justice William O. Douglas, concurring:

It is customary in deciding a constitutional question to treat it in its narrowest form. Yet at times the setting of the question gives it a form and content which no abstract treatment could give. The point for decision is whether the Government can constitutionally finance a religious exercise. Our system at the federal and state levels is presently honeycombed with such financing.[3] Nevertheless, I think it is an unconstitutional undertaking whatever form it takes.

First, a word as to what this case does not involve.

Plainly, our Bill of Rights would not permit a State or the Federal Government to adopt an official prayer and penalize anyone who would not utter it. This, however, is not that case, for there is no element of compulsion or coercion [here]. . . .

. . .

McCollum v. *Board of Education* (1948) does not decide this case. It involved the use of public school facilities for religious education of students. Students either had to attend religious instruction or "go to some other place in the school building for pursuit of their secular studies. . . . Reports of their presence or absence were to be made to their secular teachers." The influence of the teaching staff was therefore brought to bear on the student body, to support the instilling of religious principles. In the present case, school facilities are used to say the prayer and the teaching staff is employed to lead the pupils in it. There is, however, no effort at indoctrination and no attempt at exposition. Prayers of course may be so long and of such a character as to amount to an attempt at the religious instruction that was denied the public schools by the *McCollum* Case. But New York's prayer is of a character that does not involve any element of proselytizing.

The question presented by this case is therefore an extremely narrow one. It is whether New York oversteps the bounds when it finances a religious exercise.

---

3. Footnote one appears here in the opinion. It lists various "aids" to religion "at all levels of government." Among them are congressional and military chaplaincies, religious proclamations by Presidents, the use of the Bible to administer oaths of office, and the fact that religious organizations are exempt from federal income tax and have postal privileges. For Douglas, apparently, all these "aids to religion" are unconstitutional. Indeed, for him, it would seem, the very Congress that proposed the First Amendment actually violated it by providing for congressional and military chaplains.

What New York does on the opening of its public schools is what we do when we open court. Our Crier has from the beginning announced the convening of the Court and then added "God save the United States and this Honorable Court." That utterance is a supplication, a prayer in which we, the judges, are free to join, but which we need not recite any more than the student need recite the New York prayer.

What New York does on the opening of its public schools is what each House of Congress does at the opening of each day's business. . . .

In New York the teacher who leads in prayer is on the public payroll; and the time she takes seems minuscule as compared with the salaries appropriated by state legislatures and Congress for chaplains to conduct prayers in the legislative halls. Only a bare fraction of the teacher's time is given to reciting this short 22-word prayer, about the same amount of time that our Crier spends announcing the opening of our sessions and offering a prayer for this Court. Yet for me the principle is the same, no matter how briefly the prayer is said, for in each of the instances given the person praying is a public official on the public payroll, performing a religious exercise in a governmental institution. It is said that the element of coercion is inherent in the giving of this prayer. If that is true here, it is also true of the prayer with which this Court is convened, and of those that open the Congress. Few adults, let alone children, would leave our courtroom or the Senate or the House while those prayers are being given. Every such audience is in a sense a "captive" audience.

At the same time I cannot say that to authorize this prayer is to establish a religion in the strictly historic meaning of those words.[4] A religion is not established in the usual sense merely by letting those who choose to do so say the prayer that the public school teacher leads. Yet once government finances a religious exercise it inserts a divisive influence into our communities. The New York Court said that the prayer given does not conform to all of the tenets of the Jewish, Unitarian, and Ethical Cultural groups. One of the petitioners is an agnostic.

"We are a religious people whose institutions presuppose a Supreme Being." *Zorach* v. *Clauson* (1952). Under our Bill of Rights free play is given for making religion an active force in our lives. But . . . [b]y rea-

---

4. This statement suggests Douglas's belief that an interpretive effort focused on discerning the meaning of the no-establishment provision, at the time of its ratification as part of the First Amendment, would yield an understanding of the provision far different from Douglas's—or the Court's.

son of the First Amendment government is commanded "to have no interest in theology or ritual," for on those matters "government must be neutral." The First Amendment leaves the Government in a position not of hostility to religion but of neutrality. The philosophy is that the atheist or agnostic—the nonbeliever—is entitled to go his own way. The philosophy is that if government interferes in matters spiritual, it will be a divisive force. The First Amendment teaches that a government neutral in the field of religion better serves all religious interests.

My problem today would be uncomplicated but for *Everson* v. *Board of Education* (1947), which allowed taxpayers' money to be used to pay "the bus fares of parochial school pupils as a part of a general program under which" the fares of pupils attending public and other schools were also paid. The *Everson* Case seems in retrospect to be out of line with the First Amendment.[5] Its result is appealing, as it allows aid to be given to needy children. Yet by the same token, public funds could be used to satisfy other needs of children in parochial schools—lunches, books and tuition being obvious examples. Justice Rutledge stated in dissent what I think is durable First Amendment philosophy.

. . .

What New York does with this prayer is a break with that tradition. I therefore join the Court in reversing the judgment below.

Justice Potter Stewart, dissenting:

The Court does not hold, nor could it, that New York has interfered with the free exercise of anybody's religion. For the state courts have made clear that those who object to reciting the prayer must be entirely free of any compulsion to do so, including any "embarrassments and pressures." . . . But the Court says that in permitting school children to say this simple prayer, the New York authorities have established "an official religion."

With all respect, I think the Court has misapplied a great constitutional principle. I cannot see how an "official religion" is established by letting those who want to say a prayer say it.[6] On the contrary, I think that to deny the wish of these school children to join in reciting

---

5. Douglas, who joined the five-man majority in *Everson*, apparently changed his mind about that case. Had he voted differently in *Everson*, the reimbursement of parents for payment of bus fares for parochial school children would have been ruled in violation of the First Amendment.

6. David P. Currie has commented, "In this [Stewart] seemed to miss the point entirely; no one was arguing that the schools had a duty to prevent children from praying on their own" (*The Constitution in the Supreme Court: The Second Century, 1888–1986*, 412).

this prayer is to deny them the opportunity of sharing in the spiritual heritage of our Nation.

The Court's historical review of the quarrels over the Book of Common Prayer in England throws no light for me on the issue before us in this case. England had then and has now an established church. Equally unenlightening, I think, is the history of the early establishment and later rejection of an official church in our own States. For we deal here not with the establishment of a state church, which would, of course, be constitutionally impermissible, but with whether school children who want to begin their day by joining in prayer must be prohibited from doing so. Moreover, I think that the Court's task, in this as in all areas of constitutional adjudication, is not responsibly aided by the uncritical invocation of metaphors like the "wall of separation," a phrase nowhere to be found in the Constitution.[7] What is relevant to the issue here is . . . the history of the religious traditions of our people, reflected in countless practices of the institutions and officials of our government.

At the opening of each day's Session of this Court we stand, while one of our officials invokes the protection of God. Since the days of John Marshall our Crier has said, "God save the United States and this Honorable Court." Both the Senate and the House of Representatives open their daily Sessions with prayer. Each of our Presidents, from George Washington to John F. Kennedy, has upon assuming his office asked the protection and help of God.

The Court today says that the state and federal governments are without constitutional power to prescribe any particular form of words to be recited by any group of the American people on any subject touching religion. One of the stanzas of "The Star-Spangled Banner," made our National Anthem by Act of Congress in 1931, contains these verses:

> "Blest with victory and peace, may the heav'n rescued land
> Praise the Pow'r that hath made and preserved us a nation!
> Then conquer we must, when our cause it is just,
> And this be our motto 'In God is our Trust.' "

In 1954 Congress added a phrase to the Pledge of Allegiance to the Flag so that it now contains the words "one Nation *under God* indivisible, with liberty and justice for all." In 1952 Congress enacted legis-

---

7. Justice Stewart thus joined Justice Reed (in his dissent in *McCollum*) in questioning the validity of the Jeffersonian "wall" metaphor as a statement of constitutional principle.

lation calling upon the President each year to proclaim a National Day of Prayer. Since 1865 the words "In God We Trust" have been impressed on our coins.

Countless similar examples could be listed, but there is no need to belabor the obvious. It was all summed up by this Court just ten years ago in a single sentence: "We are a religious people whose institutions presuppose a Supreme Being." *Zorach.* I do not believe that this Court, or the Congress, or the President has by the actions and practices I have mentioned established an "official religion" in violation of the Constitution. And I do not believe the State of New York has done so in this case. What each has done has been to recognize and to follow the deeply entrenched and highly cherished spiritual traditions of our Nation—traditions which come down to us from those who almost two hundred years ago avowed their "firm Reliance on the Protection of divine Providence" when they proclaimed the freedom and independence of this brave new world.

I dissent.

Responses

*From the **New York Times**, June 27, 1962, "Prayer Is Personal":*

Few recent Supreme Court decisions have provoked so immediately critical a reaction as has the ruling that reading the Regents' prayer aloud in New York public schools violates the Constitution. In part the shock may be explained by the innocuous nature of the prayer. It invokes the blessing of God in neutral and non-denominational language, and most Americans would have difficulty understanding how its twenty-two words could offend anyone.

But there are persons who want to pray in their own way, or not at all. Doubtless those who oppose school prayers are a minority. But the Constitution was designed precisely to protect minorities; and the First Amendment bars the majority at any time from ordaining "an establishment of religion." The establishment clause is a keystone of American liberty; and if there is one thing that the establishment clause must mean, it is that government may not set up a religious norm from which one has to be excused—as was the case with the children in the New York school who did not wish to recite the prayer.

Some of the attacks on the decision are indeed far-fetched. References to the Deity at public occasions—mentioned by some critics—are not the same as a daily classroom prayer. The former are largely ceremonial, lacking the psychological elements of compulsion that are present when little children are asked to stand every morning and join their teacher—who is a symbol of wisdom and authority—in an officially composed prayer.

Nor is it remotely true, as one critic has said, that the decision amounts to "denying the privilege of prayer." To the contrary, everyone remains free to pray as he wishes; he simply cannot use official power to make others pray that way. And surely Mr. Justice Black was right when he said that prayer is peculiarly an individual matter—that how one prays is too personal and sacred a question to be decided by government officials or in fact by anyone but the individual without constraint.

There is a danger of the Supreme Court's becoming too doctrinaire in enforcing the separation of church and state. It is easy to imagine religious or quasi-religious elements in public activities that would not rise to the level of a constitutional violation. But nothing could be more divisive in this country than to mingle religion and government in the sensitive setting of the public schools, and under circumstances regarded by minorities as coercive. Our history counsels against that course, and the Supreme Court has wisely turned us from it.

137

*From the **Wall Street Journal,** June 27, 1962, "In the Name of Freedom":*

"Almighty God, we acknowledge our dependence upon thee, and we beg Thy blessings upon us, our parents, our teachers, and our country." This is the simple non-denominational prayer which the United States Supreme Court has now ruled an offense to the Constitution. . . . The Court decision is significant not only in itself but also as symptomatic of a broader move in the nation toward the rigid exclusion of all traces of religion in the public schools. We think this attitude bespeaks considerable confusion and no abundance of common sense. . . .

Now if it were true that the prayer constituted an establishment of religion, it would be a serious matter indeed. . . . But only a violent wrenching of language can produce the interpretation that the prayer establishes a religion. If one looks at its twenty-two innocuous words, it must be asked, What religion? Nor does it interfere with anyone's Constitutional right of free exercise of religion, including the right to practice no religion and believe in none. It is non-denominational; it is not mandatory in any school; no pupil is required to recite it.

It is simply one among innumerable official governmental references expressing what the Court itself said ten years ago, that by and large Americans are a religious people. As Justice Stewart observes in his dissent in the present case, "to deny the wish of these school children to join in reciting this prayer is to deny them the opportunity of sharing the spiritual heritage of our nation."

If the majority opinion prevails, however, it must logically require the excision of all those countless other official references to God—such as in the Declaration of Independence, the Pledge of Allegiance, the Star-Spangled Banner, the words used to inaugurate the President, open the Congress and convoke the Supreme Court itself. Justice Douglas, concurring with the majority, seems to say it does and should apply to these and all the other official instances.

And that is by no means all. If the majority doctrine stands, then anything that smacks of religious instruction or the subtle imparting of a religious viewpoint in the public schools becomes suspect. Do not suppose this to be a fanciful exaggeration. Already the Bible is banned from some schoolrooms. Already a Florida court decision has declared school observances at Easter and Christmas to be unconstitutional, and similar efforts are afoot elsewhere. (Poor kids, if they can't even sing Christmas carols.)

As for banning the Bible, with its magnificent poetry and philosophy, that is but the bare beginning, since so much of our culture is Biblical in derivation. In Matthew Arnold's phrase, the main streams of Western civilization are Hebraism and Hellenism, and by Hebraism is meant the whole Judeo-Christian tradition and ethic.

Shall we then uproot it? Out the window with everything from Dante to

Donne, from Milton to Dickens? Or how can public school teachers teach about Bach or Michelangelo, when the context is so inescapably religious? What is left of history?

Thus carried to its conclusion, the argument reduces itself to absurdity. That is why we would enter a plea for the exercise of a little common sense. Any actual attempt to establish a specific state religion is a danger that ought to be easily recognizable. But it is something entirely different to suppose that, short of unimaginable police tactics, teaching about religion can be divorced from the American education with which it is inextricably bound up as a central fact of our heritage.

Those who persist in such attempts had best take care lest, in the name of religious freedom, they do real damage to free institutions.

*From the **Washington Post**, June 28, 1962, "A Moment of Silence":*

Many citizens who are convinced of the United States Supreme Court's constitutional wisdom on the school prayer issue and of the sincerity and good faith of those who are profoundly disturbed and worried by that opinion will wish a way might be found to reconcile these opposing and deeply felt necessities.

And when the controversy has cooled a bit perhaps a way can be found. It is dangerous to venture at all into an area where so many hotly held convictions are involved, but it is dangerous as well to have rancor and ill will among persons of good motive.

Perhaps those not directly engaged or committed might suggest a point at which all minds might meet. Would it be possible and acceptable to those of varying views to have each school day commence with a quiet moment that would still the tumult of the playground and start a day of study? Couldn't this quiet moment be utilized for whatever silent purpose, religious or otherwise, that suits the inclination and discipline of each student? On each morning at the appointed hour at the signal of the teacher, could not each child turn silently to reflection, meditation or prayer, in conformity with the articles of his own faith or the instruction and wishes of his own parents? Surely such an interlude could give no offense to anyone, and it might give solace to many.

*From the (Washington) **Evening Star**, June 27, 1962, "Mr. Jefferson's 'Wall' ":*

In his majority opinion in the New York "prayer" case, Justice Black alluded to "the constitutional wall of separation between Church and State." This brought forth from dissenting Justice Stewart the following rather sharp comment: "Moreover, I think that the Court's task . . . is not responsibly aided by the uncritical invocation of metaphors like the 'wall of separation,' a phrase nowhere to be found in the Constitution."

Well, if not in the Constitution, where is this "wall of separation" to be found? It first cropped up, as far as we know, in a statement by Thomas Jefferson to the Danbury Baptist Association. An energetic supporter of the First Amendment, Mr. Jefferson told the Baptists:

> Believing with you that religion is a matter that lies solely between man and his God; that he owes account to none other for his faith or his worship; that the legislative powers of the Government reach actions only, and not opinions—I contemplate with sovereign reverence that act of the whole American people which declared that their legislature should "make no law respecting an establishment of religion or prohibiting the free exercise thereof," thus building a wall of separation between church and State.

Where does this leave us? The Supreme Court in 1879 said this statement by an "acknowledged leader" of the advocates of the First Amendment "may be accepted almost as an authoritative declaration of the scope and effect of the Amendment." But in that same opinion the court also held, despite the First Amendment, that Congress could lawfully make it a crime for a Mormon, pursuant to his religious beliefs, to practice polygamy. Many years earlier, Mr. Jefferson, founding the State-supported University of Virginia, strongly favored a thorough program of religious instruction at that institution.

What would Mr. Jefferson say if he were alive today? In the light of his views respecting the University of Virginia, would he think that his "wall of separation" barred the recital of a simple prayer in New York's public schools? Or would he be as bewitched and bewildered as are many of us today by the view which the Supreme Court takes of Mr. Jefferson's "wall"?

Whatever the answer, we think the school authorities in Washington should not act hastily to abandon religious exercises in the city's public schools. Presumably the Supreme Court will decide at its next term whether it is unconstitutional to recite the Lord's Prayer and to read without comment from the Bible. Meanwhile, we doubt that exposure to the Lord's Prayer and extracts from the Bible will destroy either the "wall of separation" or the school children of this city.

From *The Christian Century,* July 4, 1962, *"Prayer Still Legal in Public Schools":*

Nothing in the June 25 ruling by the Supreme Court prevents teachers or pupils in the public schools from engaging in prayer. Private prayer, the kind of prayer honored in Scripture and most often practiced by religious people, remains untouched. Nothing prevents parents or religious educators from teaching children to repeat to themselves at the opening of the school day and at any other time during the day: "Almighty God, we acknowledge our dependence upon Thee; we beg thy blessing upon us, our parents, our teachers and our country." The high court did rule, and rightly, that this or any other prayer might not be prescribed by New York school authorities or recited aloud by teachers and pupils in the public schools. . . . In our view the Supreme Court has rendered a service of the greatest importance to true religion as well as to the integrity of a democratic state. It has placed one more obstacle in the way of those who desire eventually to use the power of the state to enforce conformity to religious or political ideas. It is significant that Cardinal Spellman was "shocked and frightened," but Billy Graham was only "shocked and disappointed." The cardinal cannot tolerate the idea that our government is and must remain a government of limited powers, that the church is and must remain only a voluntary association, separate from the state. But neither the cardinal nor the evangelist is ready to accept the fact that under our Constitution the government is and must remain secular. It is not secularistic nor is it devoted to the teaching of secularism, but it is separated from any religious establishment, including establishment of religion-in-general.

From *Christianity and Crisis*, July 23, 1962, "The Regents' Prayer Decision":

The religious heritage of the nation does not depend upon the presence of this prayer in the opening exercises of the New York schoolroom. Yet the court decision holding the prayer to be in violation of the First Amendment to the Constitution has created a furor of positive and negative responses. This reaction reveals that symbols, rather than facts, were involved as they so frequently are in both religious and political controversies. The Regents' Prayer was a symbol of the religious life and tradition of the nation. The court decision symbolizes to some religious people the perils of secularization of our culture. Religious opinion on the decision was sharply divided. The most devastating criticism came from Cardinal Spellman, though his concern seemed in contradiction to the Roman Catholic criticism of the public schools as "godless." The religious champions of the separation of church and state, chiefly the Baptists, were not unanimous in their approval.

Actually the court decision was an instance of using a meat ax for solving a delicate problem that requires a scalpel. The problem is the religious pluralism of our American community, which includes an increasing number of people without religious convictions or practices. It was predominantly the latter group, rather than any one of the traditional faiths, that challenged the constitutionality of the prayer. The court upheld their challenge even though participation in the prayer was not compulsory. The prayer, which seemed to be a model of accommodation to the pluralistic nature of our society, could have offended only very sophisticated youngsters who regard all prayer as superstition.

The question that must be raised in the aftermath of the decisions is whether it will not work so consistently in the direction of a secularization of the school system as to amount to the suppression of religion and to give the impression that government must be anti-religion. This impression is certainly not consonant with the mood of either the Founding Fathers or our long tradition of separation of church and state, which is based on neutrality and not animosity.

In addition to these apprehensions, there is the important constitutional issue whether the court has not in fact assumed the legislative function in the guise of interpreting the Constitution. . . .

Justice Felix Frankfurter was not involved in the decision and he might well have voted with the majority. But it is worth noting his controversial, but salutary, doctrine of "judicial self-restraint," which the court might well have observed in this case. The doctrine asserts that the court should not legislate under the cover of interpreting old law. More specifically it means that it should not invalidate a law merely because it believes the law to be unwise. The states in a variegated and pluralistic national community may pass some laws that are deemed unwise. But they ought not to be invalidated by the court unless they are clearly in violation of the Constitution. . . .

In this case the court cuts through all the complicated adjustments by which a traditionally religious community with a large secular segment tries to adjust competing claims and interests, and establishes a rigid law for all sections of the nation. The result is a consistently secular education that the Founding Fathers certainly did not intend.

From *The New Republic*, *July 9, 1962, "Engel v. Vitale":*

The Justices of the Supreme Court confer in a setting of hallowed privacy. No law clerks or stenographers may be present when it is decided whether to hear or how to dispose of a case. If a message must be delivered to one of the Justices it is the convention that the most junior member of the Court goes to the door so the caller need not set foot within the Conference Room. Thus the Court places itself literally beyond the reach of rumor, and one can do no more than guess what might be in the mind of this or that Justice when the Court makes a critical judgment, as it did last December 4 in agreeing to hear the New York school prayer case.

Although the 6–1 ruling handed down in *Engel* v. *Vitale* last week has provided the occasion for the most savage controversy concerning the Court since the 1954 desegregation decision, the Justices, which is to say the four or more requisite for granting a writ of *certiorari*, took their determinative step seven months ago in deciding to hear the case at all. The act of agreeing to consider a case involves not only innumerable technical juridical considerations but often carries an implicit political judgment. For example, in its steadfast refusal to hear anti-miscegenation cases, the Court has advanced strained reasoning which leaves little doubt that its guiding preoccupation is the potential political impact of overturning the Southern statutes. It is a foregone conclusion among most lawyers and legal scholars that the Court would overturn them if it should ever hear such a case. But the Court cannot choose to remain above the battle indefinitely, and when a particular question presents itself repeatedly over a period of years this can become sufficient reason to grant a hearing. What appears remarkable to us in the prayer case is that there was no such insistent pressure.

Most authoritative observers believe that the practical consequences of *En-*

gel v. *Vitale* in our school system will be negligible; that the application of the decision by the lower courts will not be nearly so broad as the sweep of the majority opinion has led much of the lay public to suppose; and that consequently the Court might well have assumed in this instance that a reaffirmation of basic Constitutional principle would have relatively transitory political repercussions.

Clearly all the alarms about the "Star-Spangled Banner" and what the Court's crier has been in the habit of saying since the day of John Marshall are so many debating points. In 1948, the Court held in the *McCollum* decision that religious instruction on public school property, abetted by a "released time" program for pupils, was unconstitutional. About a decade later a study made in Illinois, the state in which the 1948 case had arisen, showed that while some modifications had been made in released time programs, the essential practice continued relatively unabated. It takes only a very minor prophet to predict that various forms of organized though non-denominational prayers will persist in our public schools.

By and large public schools have in recent years tried to be not only non-denominational but secular. But the absolute and sudden execution of the principle of scrupulous secularity would surely alienate great majorities in many of our communities. The great office of the American public school system in the past has been to serve as a unifying, egalitarian force in a vast and diverse society; one of the centripetal forces without which we would be in danger of being torn apart by our pluralistic stresses. School officials may in perfectly good faith conclude—in the present unsettled state of educational policy, and in light of other pressing needs of the school system—that the time and the problem call for accommodation and compromise. Though prayers indistinguishable from the New York one can, of course, no longer be used in equally indistinguishable circumstances, there are not likely to be many cases brought to local courts which are, in fact, indistinguishable from *Engel* v. *Vitale*, and there are not many judges who will go out of their way to invite further school prayer cases. To try now truly to cleanse the public schools of all religious or quasi-religious ceremonies of all sorts would be an undertaking of the magnitude and duration of the racial integration endeavor. And unlike integration, a judicial effort to such an end could not succeed in the immediately foreseeable future, for it would not command, over the country as a whole, like public and private support. Nor would the result, if accomplished, one might add, be remotely comparable in importance to desegregation.

Once having decided to hear *Engel* v. *Vitale* it is difficult to see how the Court could have reached a substantially different decision. The case posed the clear-cut issue of a prayer drafted by a state government and prescribed by certain local bodies. . . . The Supreme Court held that what is done in New York amounts to a religious ceremony, and that school boards may not constitutionally direct its performance. . . .

Mr. Justice Douglas concurring and Mr. Justice Stewart dissenting both thought—the one approvingly, the other with regret—that all sorts of invocations of the Deity associated with our public life are or will soon become unconstitutional. But the majority said nothing of the kind. The ruling does not, as former President Eisenhower has suggested, concern whether Americans are or are not "endowed by their Creator" with the rights set forth in the Declaration of Independence and the Constitution. It does not take the definitive and inflexible position attributed to it by Reinhold Niebuhr [that public schools must be "absolutely secular"]. . . . It does not preclude public school prayers which are in use as the result of custom or conventional practice by the consent of all groups in a community—a prayer drafted, let us say, by an inter-faith committee. What it does do is give recognition to the relatively recent phenomenon of a widespread secular humanism in the country which constitutes, as it were, a new religion of its own and which has coincided in its appearance with the militant revival of the old-time religion.

The record of the Court on church-state issues supports the belief that its intentions were limited. After its 1948 ruling holding the Illinois "released time" program unconstitutional, the Court proceeded in *Zorach* v. *Clauson* four years later to uphold a program that differed only in the sense that the questionable classes were held in separate buildings. "In the religious field," observes Anthony Lewis in the *New York Times*, "the Court has used strong language often, but its actual results have been wavering in the extreme."

To many, of course, the prudence of a Court decision to entertain a case is not even a legitimate issue. They see the law as an absolute, and the Court as its prophet. If a practice is unconstitutional, the Court must forbid it. Even if this may undermine the position of the Court, that is the risk that must be run. In cases where some substantial issue is at stake where the Court is protecting an unpopular minority from an angry majority, such absolutism is certainly in order. The Court is the conscience of the nation. If men are jailed unjustly, the Court must speak out for what it believes to be justice, no matter what the articulate public or Congress may say. But if the wrongs involve matters of principle lacking the urgency of palpable injustice on a wide scale, some see the imperatives less vividly. To make it awkward for a child to avoid being present when other children repeat a prayer is perhaps censorable. But it can hardly be maintained that it is a grave invasion of his rights, an abridgement of the Constitution which significantly threatens our personal liberties. To take a single illustration, such a requirement is far less objectionable than a requirement that children take courses indoctrinating them about the dangers of godless Communism.

. . . [I]t is possible that the Court has given life to quiescent forces which will do more damage to our free institutions than the prayer ever did. It is no disrespect to the Court to ponder the fact that *Engel* v. *Vitale* is likely to provide a rallying cry for the Radical Right with great evocative power among religious-minded people and, in particular, among those fundamentalist groups already attracted to the gospel according to John Birch. The fact that the practical consequences of the case will be negligible will not necessarily destroy its utility as a symbol.

Though the present agitation in Congress for a Constitutional Amendment has a phony quality, the emotional response and sense of alienation from Washington and its institutions apparent throughout the country in the wake of the decision seems to us a factor of authentic importance in the present national political climate. One must observe, too, that the chances for passage of federal school aid bills may suffer because of the impression that a sudden cold shower of uncompromising secularization has fallen on the public schools. No doubt, pressures for federal aid to private religious schools will be augmented, and many who have maintained opposition to such aid may be tempted to change sides, and save face with the argument that they had not known that God was to be forcibly driven out of the public schools by authority of the federal government. Finally it is obvious that the decision will strengthen the bitterness felt in the South, and among conservatives in both parties across the country, against the Supreme Court itself.

9

Abington School District
v. Schempp

374 U.S. 203 (1963)

The year after its unpopular decision in *Engel* v. *Vitale*, the Court reiterated the principles of that case in striking down state-sponsored Bible reading and recitation of the Lord's Prayer in public schools in two cases, arising from Pennsylvania and Maryland. In No. 142, a Pennsylvania statute required that at least ten Bible verses be read, without comment, at the start of each public school day; a child could be excused from the Bible reading upon the written request of his parents. In No. 119, a rule adopted by the Board of School Commissioners in Baltimore provided for devotions, also at the start of the school day, that consisted primarily of reading, without comment, a chapter from the Bible, or recitation of the Lord's Prayer, or both; the rule was later amended to permit children to be excused from the exercise upon parental request. Unitarians challenged the Pennsylvania statute, atheists the Baltimore rule. The Pennsylvania law was deemed unconstitutional in federal district court. The challenge to the Baltimore rule was dismissed by a Maryland trial court, a judgment then affirmed by the state's appeals court.

The Pennsylvania case was *Abington School District* v. *Schempp*, the Maryland case *Murray* v. *Curlett*. The two were combined in the Court's analysis and decision and are typically referred to as *Abington* v. *Schempp*.

The opinion of the Court, written by Justice Tom C. Clark, articulated two parts of what eight years later would become the three-part *Lemon* test for determining the constitutionality of a challenged government action: "[W]hat are the purpose and the primary effect of the enactment? If either is the advancement or inhibition of religion, then the enactment exceeds the scope of legislative power as circumscribed by the Constitution." (The third part was set forth in 1970 in *Walz* v. *Tax Commission*, Case 12.) As in the *Engel* case, Justice Potter Stewart found himself alone in dissent.

Schempp generated a lengthy concurrence by Justice William Brennan that is noteworthy for its comprehensive treatment of religious-liberty issues. It is presented here, as is Stewart's dissent. The editorial responses to *Schempp* are from the (Washington) *Evening Star*, the *New York Times*, and *The Christian Century*.

Participating in *Abington* v. *Schempp*, decided June 17, 1963, were Chief Justice Earl Warren and Associate Justices Hugo L. Black, William J. Brennan, Jr., Tom C. Clark, William O. Douglas, Arthur J. Goldberg, John M. Harlan II, Potter Stewart, and Byron R. White.

Opinions

Justice Tom C. Clark delivered the opinion of the Court:
In light of the First Amendment and of our cases interpreting and applying its requirements, we hold that the practices at issue and the laws requiring them are unconstitutional under the First Amendment, as applied to the states through the Fourteenth Amendment.

. . .

It is true that religion has been closely identified with our history and government. As we said in *Engel* v. *Vitale* (1962), "The history of man is inseparable from the history of religion. And . . . since the beginning of that history many people have devoutly believed that 'More things are wrought by prayer than this world dreams of.' " In *Zorach* v. *Clauson* (1952), we gave specific recognition to the proposition that "[w]e are a religious people whose institutions presuppose a Supreme Being." The fact that the Founding Fathers believed devotedly that there was a God and that the unalienable rights of man were rooted in Him is clearly evidenced in their writings, from the Mayflower Compact to the Constitution itself. This background is evidenced today in our public life through the continuance in our oaths of office from the Presidency to the Alderman of the final supplication, "So help me God." Likewise each House of Congress provides through its Chaplain an opening prayer, and the sessions of this Court are declared open by the crier in a short ceremony, the final phrase of which invokes the grace of God. Again, there are such manifestations in our military forces, where those of our citizens who are under the restrictions of military service wish to engage in voluntary worship. Indeed, only last year an official survey of the country indicated that 64 percent of our people have church membership, while less than 3 percent profess no religion whatever. It can be truly said, therefore, that today, as in the beginning, our national life reflects a religious people. . . .

This is not to say, however, that religion has been so identified with our history and government that religious freedom is not likewise as strongly imbedded in our public and private life. Nothing but the most telling of personal experiences in religious persecution suffered by our

149

forebears, see *Everson* v. *Board of Education* (1947), could have planted
our belief in liberty of religious opinion any more deeply in our heritage. It is true that this liberty frequently was not realized by the colonists, but this is readily accountable by their close ties to the Mother
Country. However, the views of Madison and Jefferson, preceded by
Roger Williams, came to be incorporated not only in the Federal Constitution but likewise in those of most of our States.[1] This freedom to
worship was indispensable in a country whose people came from the
four quarters of the earth and brought with them a diversity of religious opinion. Today authorities list 83 separate religious bodies, each
with membership exceeding 50,000, existing among our people, as
well as innumerable smaller groups. . . .

    . . .

    . . . [T]his Court has decisively settled that the First Amendment's
mandate that "Congress shall make no law respecting an establishment of religion, or prohibiting the free exercise thereof" has been
made wholly applicable to the States by the Fourteenth Amendment.
[Justice Clark here cites and quotes from *Cantwell* v. *Connecticut* (1940).]

    In a series of cases since *Cantwell* the Court has repeatedly reaf-
firmed that doctrine, and we do so now.

    . . . [T]his Court has rejected unequivocally the contention that the
Establishment Clause forbids only governmental preference of one religion over another. [Justice Clark here cites and quotes from *Everson*.]

    The same conclusion has been firmly maintained ever since [*Ever-
son*], and we reaffirm it now.

    While none of the parties to either of these cases has questioned
these basic conclusions of the Court, both of which have been long
established, recognized and consistently reaffirmed, others continue to
question their history, logic and efficacy. Such contentions, in the light
of the consistent interpretation in cases of this Court, seem entirely
untenable and of value only as academic exercises.[2]

[Justice Clark here reviews the Court's religion-clause jurisprudence, quoting *Cantwell, Everson, McCollum* v. *Board of Education* (1948),
Zorach, and other cases.]

---

    1. With its use of the word "incorporate," the Court here again stated its under-
standing—initially expressed in *Everson*—that the First Amendment constitutionalized
the views of Madison and Jefferson as the Court discerned those views in Virginia's
struggle for religious liberty.

    2. This remarkable statement indicated the Court's frustration with critics of its re-
ligion-clause decisions, *Engel* especially. While the *Schempp* Court seemed to be saying
that it was not receptive even to scholarly disagreement with its work in this area of the
law, it obviously could not bind its successors in this respect.

The wholesome "neutrality" of which this Court's cases speak thus stems from a recognition of the teachings of history that powerful sects or groups might bring about a fusion of governmental and religious functions or a concert or dependency of one upon the other to the end that official support of the State or Federal Government would be placed behind the tenets of one or of all orthodoxies. This the Establishment Clause prohibits. And a further reason for neutrality is found in the Free Exercise Clause, which recognizes the value of religious training, teaching, and observance and, more particularly, the right of every person to freely choose his own course with reference thereto, free of any compulsion from the state. This the Free Exercise Clause guarantees. Thus, as we have seen, the two clauses may overlap. As we have indicated, the Establishment Clause has been directly considered by this Court eight times in the past score of years and, with only one Justice dissenting on the point, it has consistently held that the clause withdrew all legislative power respecting religious belief or the expression thereof. The test may be stated as follows: what are the purpose and the primary effect of the enactment? If either is the advancement or inhibition of religion then the enactment exceeds the scope of legislative power as circumscribed by the Constitution. That is to say that to withstand the strictures of the Establishment Clause there must be a secular legislative purpose and a primary effect that neither advances nor inhibits religion. The Free Exercise Clause, likewise considered many times here, withdraws from legislative power, state and federal, the exertion of any restraint on the free exercise of religion. Its purpose is to secure religious liberty in the individual by prohibiting any invasions thereof by civil authority. Hence it is necessary in a free exercise case for one to show the coercive effect of the enactment as it operates against him in the practice of his religion. The distinction between the two clauses is apparent—a violation of the Free Exercise clause is predicated on coercion while the Establishment Clause violation need not be so attended.

Applying the Establishment Clause principles to [these] cases, we find that the States are requiring the selection and reading at the opening of the school day of verses from the Holy Bible and the recitation of the Lord's Prayer by the students in unison. These exercises are prescribed as part of the curricular activities of students who are required by law to attend school. They are held in the school buildings under the supervision and with the participation of teachers employed in those schools. None of these factors, other than compulsory school attendance, was present in the program upheld in *Zorach*. . . .

. . .

[I]n both cases the laws require religious exercises and such exercises are being conducted in direct violation of the rights of the appellees and petitioners. Nor are these required exercises mitigated by the fact that individual students may absent themselves upon parental request, for that fact furnishes no defense to a claim of unconstitutionality under the Establishment Clause. Further, it is no defense to urge that the religious practices here may be relatively minor encroachments on the First Amendment. The breach of neutrality that is today a trickling stream may all too soon became a raging torrent and, in the words of Madison, "it is proper to take alarm at the first experiment on our liberties."[3]

It is insisted that unless these religious exercises are permitted a "religion of secularism" is established in the schools. We agree of course that the State may not establish a "religion of secularism" in the sense of affirmatively opposing or showing hostility to religion, thus "preferring those who believe in no religion over those who do believe." *Zorach*. We do not agree, however, that this decision in any sense has that effect. In addition, it might well be said that one's education is not complete without a study of comparative religion or the history of religion and its relationship to the advancement of civilization. It certainly may be said that the Bible is worthy of study for its literary and historic qualities. Nothing we have said here indicates that such study of the Bible or of religion, when presented objectively as part of a secular program of education, may not be effected consistently with the First Amendment. But the exercises here do not fall into those categories. They are religious exercises, required by the States in violation of the command of the First Amendment that the Government maintain strict neutrality, neither aiding nor opposing religion.

Finally, we cannot accept that the concept of neutrality, which does not permit a State to require a religious exercise even with the consent of the majority of those affected, collides with the majority's right to free exercise of religion. While the Free Exercise Clause clearly prohibits the use of state action to deny the rights of free exercise to *anyone*, it has never meant that a majority could use the machinery of the State to practice its beliefs. . . .

. . .

---

3. These words of Madison, from his "Memorial and Remonstrance," were also quoted by the Court in its opinions in *Everson* and *Engel*.

The place of religion in our society is an exalted one, achieved through a long tradition of reliance on the home, the church and the inviolable citadel of the individual heart and mind. We have come to recognize through bitter experience that it is not within the power of government to invade that citadel, whether its purpose or effect be to aid or oppose, to advance or retard. In the relationship between man and religion, the State is firmly committed to a position of neutrality. Though the application of that rule requires interpretation of a delicate sort, the rule itself is clearly and concisely stated in the words of the First Amendment. Applying that rule to the facts of these cases, we affirm the judgment in No. 142 [the Abington case]. In No. 119 [the Baltimore case], the judgment is reversed and the cause remanded to the Maryland Court of Appeals for further proceedings consistent with this opinion.[4]

Justice William J. Brennan, Jr., concurring:[5]

It is true that the Framers' immediate concern was to prevent the setting up of an official federal church of the kind which England and some of the Colonies had long supported. But nothing in the text of the Establishment Clause supports the view that the prevention of the setting up of an official church was meant to be the full extent of the prohibitions against official involvements in religion. . . .

. . .

In sum, the history which our prior decisions have summoned to aid interpretation of the Establishment Clause permits little doubt that its prohibition was designed comprehensively to prevent those official involvements of religion which would tend to foster or discourage religious worship or belief.

But an awareness of history and an appreciation of the aims of the

---

4. The Court could have reached the same results on the narrower grounds that the practices at issue in No. 142 and No. 119 preferred the Jewish and Christian faiths over other religions.

5. Justice Brennan's concurrence in *Schempp*, totaling forty-four pages in *United States Reports*, is one of the longest opinions on religious liberty by a member of the Court. "The importance of the issue and the deep conviction with which views on both sides are held seem to me to justify detailing at some length my reasons for joining the Court's judgment and opinion." The opinion discusses the utility of history in determining the meaning of the First Amendment; analyzes the Court's opinions interpreting and applying it; addresses the absorption or incorporation of the guarantees of the First Amendment through the Fourteenth Amendment, with particular attention to which particular activities the no-establishment provision forbids the states to undertake; addresses the issues in the cases at hand, prefaced by a review of the "long history" of religious activities in American schools; and discusses which involvements of religion in public life are constitutional.

Founding Fathers do not always resolve concrete problems. The specific question before us has, for example, aroused vigorous dispute whether the architects of the First Amendment—James Madison and Thomas Jefferson particularly—understood the prohibition against any "law respecting an establishment of religion" to reach devotional exercises in the public schools. It may be that Jefferson and Madison would have held such exercises to be permissible. . . . But I doubt that their view, even if perfectly clear one way or the other, would supply a dispositive answer to the question presented by these cases. A more fruitful inquiry . . . is whether the practices here challenged threaten . . . to promote that type of interdependence between religion and state which the First Amendment was designed to prevent. Our task is to translate "the majestic generalities of the Bill of Rights, conceived as part of the pattern of liberal government in the eighteenth century, into concrete restraints on officials dealing with the problems of the twentieth century. . . ." *West Virginia State Board of Education* v. *Barnette* (1943).

A too literal quest for the advice of the Founding Fathers upon the issues of these cases seems to me futile and misdirected for several reasons:[6] First, on our precise problem the historical record is at best ambiguous, and statements can readily be found to support either side of the proposition. . . .

Second, the structure of American education has greatly changed since the First Amendment was adopted. In the context of our modern emphasis upon public education available to all citizens, any views of the eighteenth century as to whether the exercises at bar are an "establishment" offer little aid to decision. Education, as the Framers knew it, was in the main confined to private schools more often than not under strictly sectarian supervision. Only gradually did control of education pass largely to public officials. . . .

Third, our religious composition makes us a vastly more diverse people than were our forefathers. They knew differences chiefly among Protestant sects. Today the Nation is far more heterogeneous religiously, including as it does . . . those who worship according to no version of the Bible and those who worship no God at all. . . .

Whatever Jefferson and Madison would have thought of Bible reading or the recital of the Lord's Prayer in what few public schools existed

---

6. The members of the *Everson* Court had far greater confidence in the utility of history in determining the meaning of the First Amendment. Compare the opinion of the Court in *Everson* (Case 4) as well as Justice Wiley Rutledge's dissent.

in their day, our use of the history of their time must limit itself to broad purposes, not specific practices. By such a standard, I am persuaded, as is the Court, that the devotional exercises carried on in the Baltimore and Abington schools offend the First Amendment because they sufficiently threaten in our day those substantive evils the fear of which called forth the Establishment Clause of the First Amendment. . . .

Fourth, the American experiment in free public education available to all children has been guided in large measure by the dramatic evolution of the religious diversity among the population which our public schools serve. . . . It is implicit in the history and character of American public education that the public schools serve a uniquely *public* function: the training of American citizens in an atmosphere free of parochial, divisive, or separatist influences of any sort—an atmosphere in which children may assimilate a heritage common to all American groups and religions. This is a heritage neither theistic nor atheistic, but simply civic and patriotic.

Attendance at the public schools has never been compulsory; parents remain morally and constitutionally free to choose the academic environment in which they wish their children to be educated. . . . In my judgment the First Amendment forbids the State to inhibit that freedom of choice . . . by restricting the liberty of the private schools to inculcate whatever values they wish, or by jeopardizing the freedom of the public schools from private or sectarian pressures. The choice between these very different forms of education is one—very much like the choice of whether or not to worship—which our Constitution leaves to the individual parent. It is no proper function of the state or local government to influence or restrict that election. The lesson of history—drawn more from the experiences of other countries than from our own—is that a system of free public education forfeits its unique contribution to the growth of democratic citizenship when that choice ceases to be freely available to each parent.

· · ·

I turn now to the cases before us. The religious nature of the exercises here challenged seems plain. Unless *Engel* is to be overruled, or we are to engage in wholly disingenuous distinction, we cannot sustain these practices. Daily recital of the Lord's Prayer and the reading of passages of Scripture are quite as clearly breaches of the command of the Establishment Clause as was the daily use of the rather bland Regents' Prayer in the New York public schools. Indeed, I would suppose that, if anything, the Lord's Prayer and the Holy Bible are more clearly sectarian, and the present violations of the First Amendment consequently more serious. But the religious exercises challenged in these cases have a long history. . . .

. . .

The purposes underlying the adoption and perpetuation of these practices are somewhat complex. It is beyond question that the religious benefits and values realized from daily prayer and Bible reading have usually been considered paramount, and sufficient to justify the continuation of such practices. . . .

. . .

. . . [T]he understanding of educators [was] that the daily religious exercises in the schools served broader goals than compelling formal worship of God or fostering church attendance. The religious aims of the educators who adopted and retained such exercises were comprehensive, and in many cases quite devoid of sectarian bias—but the crucial fact is that they were nonetheless religious. While it has been suggested . . . that daily prayer and reading of scripture now serve secular goals as well, there can be no doubt that the origins of these practices were unambiguously religious, even where the educator's aim was not to win adherents to a particular creed or faith.

Almost from the beginning religious exercises in the public schools have been the subject of intense criticism, vigorous debate, and judicial or administrative prohibition. Significantly, educators and school boards early entertained doubts about both the legality and the soundness of opening the school day with compulsory prayer or Bible reading. Particularly in the large Eastern cities, where immigration had exposed the public schools to religious diversities and conflicts unknown to the homogeneous academies of the eighteenth century, local authorities found it necessary even before the Civil War to seek an accommodation. . . .

. . .

Particularly relevant for our purposes are the decisions of the state courts on questions of religion in the public schools. . . . The earliest of such decisions declined to review the propriety of actions taken by school authorities, so long as those actions were within the purview of the administrators' powers. . . .

The last quarter of the nineteenth century found the courts beginning to question the constitutionality of public school religious exercises. The legal context was still, of course, that of the state constitutions, since the First Amendment had not yet been held applicable to state action. And the state constitutional prohibitions against church-state cooperation or governmental aid to religion were generally less rigorous than the Establishment Clause of the First Amendment. It is therefore remarkable that the courts of a half dozen States found compulsory religious exercises in the public schools in violation of their respective state constitutions. These courts attributed much significance to the clearly religious origins and content of the challenged practices, and to the impossibility of avoiding sectarian controversy in their conduct. . . .

. . .

Even those state courts which have sustained devotional exercises under state law have usually recognized the primarily religious character of prayers and Bible readings. . . . Unlike the Sunday closing laws, these exercises appear neither to have been divorced from their religious origins nor deprived of their centrally religious character by the passage of time. On this distinction alone we might well rest a constitutional decision. But three further contentions have been pressed in the argument of these cases. These contentions deserve careful consideration, for if the position of the school authorities were correct in respect to any of them, we would be misapplying the principles of *Engel*.

First, it is argued that however clearly religious may have been the origins and early nature of daily prayer and Bible reading, these practices today serve so clearly secular educational purposes that their religious attributes may be overlooked. . . .

. . . The secular purposes which devotional exercises are said to serve fall into two categories—those which depend upon an immediately religious experience shared by the participating children; and those which appear sufficiently divorced from the religious content of the devotional material that they can be served equally by nonreligious materials. With respect to the first objective, much has been written about the moral and spiritual values of infusing some religious influence or instruction into the public school classroom. To the extent that only *religious* materials will serve this purpose, it seems to me that the purpose as well as the means is so plainly religious that the exercise is necessarily forbidden by the Establishment Clause. The fact that purely secular benefits may eventually result does not seem to me to justify the exercises, for similar indirect nonreligious benefits could no doubt have been claimed for the released time program invalidated in *McCollum*.

The second justification assumes that religious exercises at the start of the school day may directly serve solely secular ends—for example, by fostering harmony and tolerance among the pupils, enhancing the authority of the teacher, and inspiring better discipline. To the extent that such benefits result not from the content of the readings and recitation, but simply from the holding of such a solemn exercise at the opening assembly or the first class of the day, it would seem that less sensitive materials might equally well serve the same purpose. I have previously suggested that *Torcaso* v. *Watkins* (1961) and the Sunday Law Cases forbid the use of religious means to achieve secular ends where nonreligious means will suffice. That principle is readily applied to these cases. It has not been shown that readings from the speeches and messages of great Americans, for example, or from the documents of our heritage of liberty, daily recitation of the Pledge of Allegiance, or even the observance of a moment of reverent silence at the opening of a class, may not adequately serve the solely secular purposes of the devotional activities without jeopardizing either the religious liberties of any members of the community or the proper degree of separation between the spheres of religion and government.[7] Such substitutes would, I think, be unsatisfactory or inadequate only to the extent that the present activities do in fact serve religious goals. While I do not question the judgment of experienced educators that the challenged practices may well achieve valuable secular ends, it seems to me that the State acts unconstitutionally if it either sets about to attain even indirectly religious ends by religious means, or if it uses religious means to serve secular ends where secular means would suffice.

Second, it is argued that the particular practices involved in the two cases before us are unobjectionable because they prefer no particular sect or sects at the expense of others. Both the Baltimore and Abington procedures permit, for example, the reading of any of several versions of the Bible, and this flexibility is said to ensure neutrality sufficiently to avoid the constitutional prohibition. . . .

The argument contains . . . a . . . basic flaw. There are persons in every community—often deeply devout—to whom any version of the Judaeo-Christian Bible is offensive. There are others whose reverence for the Holy Scriptures demands private study or reflection and to whom public reading or recitation is sacrilegious, as one of the expert witnesses at the trial of the Schempp Case explained. To such persons it is not the fact of using the Bible in the public schools, nor the content of any particular version, that is offensive, but only the *manner* in

---

7. Twenty-two years later, in *Wallace* v. *Jaffree*, Justice Brennan did not vote to sustain a moment-of-silence statute. See Case 21.

which it is used. For such persons, the anathema of public communion is even more pronounced when prayer is involved. Many deeply devout persons have always regarded prayer as a necessarily private experience. . . . There is a similar problem with respect to comment upon the passages of Scripture which are to be read. . . .

· · ·

A third element . . . said to absolve the practices involved in these cases . . . is the provision to excuse or exempt students who wish not to participate. . . .

. . . [T]he short, and to me sufficient, answer is that the availability of excusal or exemption simply has no relevance to the establishment question, if it is once found that these practices are essentially religious exercises designed at least in part to achieve religious aims through the use of public school facilities during the school day.

The more difficult question, however, is whether the availability of excusal for the dissenting child serves to refute challenges to these practices under the Free Exercise Clause. . . . The answer is that the excusal procedure itself necessarily operates in such a way as to infringe the rights of free exercise of these children who wish to be excused. We have held in *Barnette* and *Torcaso*, respectively, that a State may require neither public school students nor candidates for an office of public trust to profess beliefs offensive to religious principles. By the same token the State could not constitutionally require a student to profess publicly his disbelief as the prerequisite to the exercise of his constitutional right of abstention. . . .

· · ·

To summarize my views concerning the merits of these two cases: The history, the purpose and the operation of the daily prayer recital and Bible reading leave no doubt that these practices standing by themselves constitute an impermissible breach of the Establishment Clause. Such devotional exercises may well serve legitimate nonreligious purposes. To the extent, however, that such purposes are really without religious significance, it has never been demonstrated that secular means would not suffice. Indeed, I would suggest that patriotic or other nonreligious materials might provide adequate substitutes—inadequate only to the extent that the purposes now served are indeed directly or indirectly religious. Under such circumstances, the States may not employ religious means to reach a secular goal unless secular means are wholly unavailing. I therefore agree with the Court that the judgment in *Schempp*, No. 142, must be affirmed, and that in *Murray*, No. 119, must be reversed.

These considerations bring me to a final contention of the school officials in these cases: that the invalidation of the exercises at bar permits this Court no alternative but to declare unconstitutional every vestige, however slight, of cooperation or accommodation between religion and government. I cannot accept that contention. While it is not, of course, appropriate for this Court to decide questions not presently before it, I venture to suggest that religious exercises in the public school present a unique problem. For not every involvement of religion in public life violates the Establishment Clause. Our decision in these cases does not clearly forecast anything about the constitutionality of other types of interdependence between religious and other public institutions.

Specifically, I believe that the line we must draw between the permissible and the impermissible is one which accords with history and faithfully reflects the understanding of the Founding Fathers. It is a line which the Court has consistently sought to mark in its decisions expounding the religious guarantees of the First Amendment. What the Framers meant to foreclose, and what our decisions under the Establishment Clause have forbidden, are those involvements of religious with secular institutions which (a) serve the essentially religious activities of religious institutions; (b) employ the organs of government for essentially religious purposes; or (c) use essentially religious means to serve governmental ends, where secular means would suffice. When the secular and religious institutions become involved in such a manner, there inhere in the relationship precisely those dangers—as much to church as to state—which the Framers feared would subvert religious liberty and the strength of a system of secular government. On the other hand, there may be myriad forms of involvements of government with religion which do not import such dangers and therefore should not, in my judgment, be deemed to violate the Establishment Clause. Nothing in the Constitution compels the organs of government to be blind to what everyone else perceives—that religious differences among Americans have important and pervasive implications for our society. Likewise nothing in the Establishment Clause forbids the application of legislation having purely secular ends in such a way as to alleviate burdens upon the free exercise of an individual's religious beliefs. Surely the Framers would never have understood that such a construction sanctions that involvement which violates the Establishment Clause. Such a conclusion can be reached, I would suggest, only by using the words of the First Amendment to defeat its very purpose.

. . . [A] brief survey of certain of these forms of accommodation will reveal that the First Amendment commands not official hostility toward religion, but only a strict neutrality in matters of religion. Moreover, it may serve to suggest that the scope of our holding today is to be measured by the special circumstances under which these cases have arisen, and by the particular dangers to church and state which religious exercises in the public schools present. It may be helpful for purposes of analysis to group these other practices and forms of accommodation into several rough categories.

A. *The Conflict Between Establishment and Free Exercise.* There are certain practices, conceivably violative of the Establishment Clause, the striking down of which might seriously interfere with certain religious liberties also protected by the First Amendment. Provisions for churches and chaplains at military establishments for those in the armed services may afford one such example. The like provision by state and federal governments for chaplains in penal institutions may afford another example. It is argued that such provisions may be assumed to contravene the Establishment Clause, yet be sustained on constitutional grounds as necessary to secure to the members of the Armed Forces and prisoners those rights of worship guaranteed under the Free Exercise Clause. Since government has deprived such persons of the opportunity to practice their faith at places of their choice, the argument runs, government may, in order to avoid infringing the free exercise guarantees, provide substitutes where it requires such persons to be. Such a principle might support, for example, the constitutionality of draft exemptions for ministers and divinity students; of the excusal of children from school on their respective religious holidays; and of the allowance by government of temporary use of public buildings by religious organizations when their own churches have become unavailable because of a disaster or emergency.

Such activities and practices seem distinguishable from the sponsorship of daily Bible reading and prayer recital. For one thing, there is no element of coercion present in the appointment of military or prison chaplains; the soldier or convict who declines the opportunities for worship would not ordinarily subject himself to the suspicion or obloquy of his peers. Of special significance to this distinction is the fact that we are here usually dealing with adults, not with impressionable children as in the public schools. Moreover, the school exercises are not designed to provide the pupils with general opportunities for worship denied them by the legal obligation to attend school. The student's compelled presence in school for five days a week in no way renders the regular religious facilities of the community less accessible to him than they are to others. The situation of the school child is therefore plainly unlike that of the isolated soldier or the prisoner.

The State must be steadfastly neutral in all matters of faith, and neither favor nor inhibit religion. In my view, government cannot sponsor religious exercises in the public schools without jeopardizing that neutrality. On the other hand, hostility, not neutrality, would characterize the refusal to provide chaplains and places of worship for prisoners and soldiers cut off by the State from all civilian opportunities for public communion, the withholding of draft exemptions for ministers and conscientious objectors, or the denial of the temporary use of an empty public building to a congregation whose place of worship has been destroyed by fire or flood. I do not say that government *must* provide chaplains or draft exemptions, or that the courts should intercede if it fails to do so.

B. *Establishment and Exercises in Legislative Bodies.* The saying of invocational prayers in legislative chambers, state or federal, and the appointment of legislative chaplains, might well represent no involvements of the kind prohibited by the Establishment Clause. Legislators, federal and state, are mature adults who may presumably absent themselves from such public and ceremonial exercises without incurring any penalty, direct or indirect. . . .

C. *Non-Devotional Use of the Bible in Public Schools.* The holding of the Court today plainly does not foreclose teaching *about* the Holy Scriptures or about the differences between religious sects in classes in literature or history. Indeed, whether or not the Bible is involved, it would be impossible to teach meaningfully many subjects in the social sciences or the humanities without some mention of religion. To what extent, and at what points in the curriculum, religious materials should be cited are matters which the courts ought to entrust very largely to the experienced officials who superintend our Nation's public schools. They are experts in such matters, and we are not. . . .

. . .

D. *Uniform Tax Exemptions Incidentally Available to Religious Institutions.* Nothing we hold today questions the propriety of certain tax deductions or exemptions which incidentally benefit churches and religious institutions, along with many secular charities and nonprofit organizations. If religious institutions benefit, it is in spite of rather than because of their religious character. For religious institutions simply share benefits which government makes generally available to educational, charitable, and eleemosynary groups. . . .

E. *Religious Considerations in Public Welfare Programs.* Since government may not support or directly aid religious *activities* without violating the Establishment Clause, there might be some doubt whether nondiscriminatory programs of governmental aid may constitutionally include *individuals* who become eligible wholly or partially for religious reasons. For example, it might be suggested that where a State provides unemployment compensation generally to those who are unable to find suitable work, it may not extend such benefits to persons who are unemployed by reason of religious beliefs or practices without thereby establishing the religion to which those persons belong. Therefore, the argument runs, the State may avoid an establishment only by singling out and excluding such persons on the ground that religious beliefs or practices have made them potential beneficiaries. Such a construction would, it seems to me, require government to impose religious discriminations and disabilities, thereby jeopardizing the free exercise of religion, in order to avoid what is thought to constitute an establishment.

The inescapable flaw in the argument, I suggest, is its quite unrealistic view of the aims of the Establishment Clause. The Framers were not concerned with the effects of certain incidental aids to individual worshippers which came about as by-products of general and nondiscriminatory welfare programs. If such benefits serve to make easier or less expensive the practice of a particular creed, or of all religions, it can hardly be said that the purpose of the program is in any way religious, or that the consequence of its nondiscriminatory application is to create the forbidden degree of interdependence between secular and sectarian institutions. I cannot therefore accept the suggestion, which seems to me implicit in the argument outlined here, that every judicial or administrative construction which is designed to prevent a public welfare program from abridging the free exercise of religious beliefs, is for that reason ipso facto an establishment of religion.

F. *Activities Which, Though Religious in Origin, Have Ceased to Have Religious Meaning.* As we noted in our Sunday Law decisions, nearly every criminal law in the books can be traced to some religious principle or inspiration. But that does not make the present enforcement of the criminal law in any sense an establishment of religion, simply because it accords with widely held religious principles. . . .

This general principle might also serve to insulate the various patriotic exercises and activities used in the public schools and elsewhere which, whatever may have been their origins, no longer have a religious purpose or meaning. The reference to divinity in the revised pledge of allegiance, for example, may merely recognize the historical fact that our Nation was believed to have been founded "under God."

The principles which we reaffirm and apply today can hardly be thought novel or radical. They are, in truth, as old as the Republic itself, and have always been as integral a part of the First Amendment as the very words of that charter of religious liberty. . . .

Justice Potter Stewart, dissenting:

I think the records in the two cases before us are so fundamentally deficient as to make impossible an informed or responsible determination of the constitutional issues presented. Specifically, I cannot agree that on these records we can say that the Establishment Clause has necessarily been violated. . . .

. . . It is, I think, a fallacious oversimplification to regard [the religion clauses] as establishing a single constitutional standard of "separation of church and state," which can be mechanically applied in every case to delineate the required boundaries between government and religion. We err in the first place if we do not recognize, as a matter of history and as a matter of the imperatives of our free society, that religion and government must necessarily interact in countless ways. Secondly, the fact is that while in many contexts the Establishment Clause and the Free Exercise Clause fully complement each other, there are areas in which a doctrinaire reading of the Establishment Clause leads to irreconcilable conflict with the Free Exercise Clause.

A single obvious example should suffice to make the point. Spending federal funds to employ chaplains for the armed forces might be said to violate the Establishment Clause. Yet a lonely soldier stationed at some faraway outpost could surely complain that a government which did *not* provide him the opportunity for pastoral guidance was affirmatively prohibiting the free exercise of his religion. . . .

As a matter of history, the First Amendment was adopted solely as a limitation upon the newly created National Government. The events leading to its adoption strongly suggest that the Establishment Clause was primarily an attempt to insure that Congress not only would be powerless to establish a national church, but would also be unable to interfere with existing state establishments. Each State was left free to go its own way and pursue its own policy with respect to religion. . . .

So matters stood until the adoption of the Fourteenth Amendment, or more accurately, until this Court's decision in *Cantwell*. . . .

I accept without question that the liberty guaranteed by the Fourteenth Amendment against impairment by the States embraces in full the right of free exercise of religion protected by the First Amendment. I accept too the proposition that the Fourteenth Amendment has somehow absorbed the Establishment Clause, although it is not without irony that a constitutional provision evidently designed to leave the States free to go their own way should now have become a restriction upon their autonomy. But I cannot agree with what seems to me the insensitive definition of the Establishment Clause contained in the Court's opinion, nor with the different but, I think, equally mechanistic definitions contained in the separate opinions which have been filed.

. . .

. . . [A] compulsory state educational system so structures a child's life that if religious exercises are held to be an impermissible activity in schools, religion is placed at an artificial and state-created disadvantage. Viewed in this light, permission of such exercises for those who want them is necessary if the schools are truly to be neutral in the matter of religion. And a refusal to permit religious exercises thus is seen, not as the realization of state neutrality, but rather as the establishment of a religion of secularism, or at the least, as government support of the beliefs of those who think that religious exercises should be conducted only in private.[8]

What seems to me to be of paramount importance, then, is recognition of the fact that the claim advanced here in favor of Bible reading is sufficiently substantial to make simple reference to the constitutional phrase "establishment of religion" as inadequate an analysis of the cases before us as the ritualistic invocation of the nonconstitutional phrase "separation of church and state." . . .

. . .

In the absence of evidence that the legislature or school board intended to prohibit local schools from substituting a different set of readings where parents requested such a change, we should not assume that the provisions before us—as actually administered—may not be construed simply as authorizing religious exercises, nor that the designations may not be treated simply as indications of the promulgating body's view as to the community's preference. We are under a duty to interpret these provisions so as to render them constitutional if reasonably possible. In the *Schempp* Case there is evidence which

---

8. This marked the first suggestion by a member of the Court that there is such a thing as "a religion of secularism" and that a refusal to permit religious exercises in the public schools might amount to an "establishment" of it.

indicates that variations were in fact permitted by the very school there involved, and that further variations were not introduced only because of the absence of requests from parents. And in the *Murray* Case the Baltimore rule itself contains a provision permitting another version of the Bible to be substituted for the King James version.

. . .

. . . [T]he records in both of the cases before us are wholly inadequate to support an informed or responsible decision. Both cases involve provisions which explicitly permit any student who wishes, to be excused from participation in the exercises. There is no evidence in either case as to whether there would exist any coercion of any kind upon a student who did not want to participate. . . .

What our Constitution indispensably protects is the freedom of each of us, be he Jew or Agnostic, Christian or Atheist, Buddhist or Free-thinker, to believe or disbelieve, to worship or not worship, to pray or keep silent, according to his own conscience, uncoerced and unrestrained by government. It is conceivable that these school boards, or even all school boards, might eventually find it impossible to administer a system of religious exercises during school hours in such a way as to meet this constitutional standard—in such a way as to completely free from any kind of official coercion those who do not affirmatively want to participate. But I think we must not assume that school boards so lack the qualities of inventiveness and good will as to make impossible the achievement of that goal.

I would remand both cases for further hearings.

Responses

From the (Washington) **Evening Star,** June 18, 1963, "The Court
Bars the Lord's Prayer":
The Supreme Court has spoken. Both the Lord's Prayer and Bible reading
have been barred from the public schools. This comes not as a surprise. But
in our view it is a shame.

It all seems so silly. Writing for the majority, Justice Clark conjured up
dreadful prospects if the court should allow a prayer to be said in a public
school. To permit such a thing, he argued, would depart from the concept of
a government that must be "neutral" to religious matters. And he went on to
say: "The breach of neutrality that is today a trickling stream may all too soon
become a raging torrent." Perhaps there is something to be said for this as
rhetoric. But it is nonsense when measured against the rise of secularism and
materialism in this country since the Founding Fathers drafted the
Amendment. . . .

Justice Stewart, the lone dissenter, stated his understanding of what is
meant by the First Amendment's guarantee of religious freedom. It is a forthright statement, and it appeals to us. "What our Constitution indispensably
protects," he said, "is the freedom of each of us, be he Jew or Agnostic, Christian or Atheist, Buddhist or Free-thinker, to believe or disbelieve, to worship
or not worship, to pray or to keep silent, according to his own conscience,
uncoerced and unrestrained by government." To us, this is quite different
from saying that the Constitution forbids one child, who may wish to do so,
to recite the Lord's Prayer in a public school merely because some other child,
who does not want to pray and who is not required to pray, objects. . . .

[W]e think the court's rulings in the area of religion, although certainly not
so intended, have already led to a climate of passive and perhaps even active
hostility to the religious. . . .

God and religion have all but been driven from the public schools. What
remains? Will the baccalaureate service and Christmas carols be the next to
go? Don't bet against it.

From the **New York Times,** June 19, 1963, "Freedom of Religion":
It is to protect freedom of worship that the Supreme Court once again has
ruled against official school prayers. That is the meaning of this week's decision that Bible reading and recitation of the Lord's Prayer in Maryland and
Pennsylvania public schools were unconstitutional. Last June the Court held

that reading the State Regents' prayer aloud in New York public schools violated the Constitution. These decisions together should now result in ending
religious exercises where practiced in many school districts across the
country. . . .

The First Amendment is a two-edged protection for freedom of worship. It
forbids the Government from establishing an official religion; it also forbids
the Government from prohibiting the free exercise of religion. These two aspects are indivisible and they insure for religion in this country both its indi-
viduality and its freedom. Freedom of religious practice can be observed in
homes and churches under family and self-chosen guidance.

The Supreme Court has outlawed neither God nor the Lord's Prayer; to
say it has is completely to distort the truth. Far from interfering with freedom
of religion, the Supreme Court decision helps guarantee it.

From *The Christian Century*, July 3, 1963, "The Court Decides Wisely":

[T]he court's ruling, while it favors neither religion nor irreligion directly,
protects religion from encroachments by the state. The power of the state to
coerce Bible reading and corporate prayer in public places is only a step removed from the state's power to prohibit Bible reading and corporate prayer
in all areas of common life. The corollary is that we cannot shatter the power
of the state to destroy religion without renouncing the power of the state to
aid the propagation of religion.

It is not the role of the Supreme Court to purify religion in part or in whole.
Nevertheless this decision indirectly does just that. The reading of ten verses
from the Bible—no more, no less—selected by one of the students at random,
the reading being unaccompanied by any comment, degenerates into incan-
tation. So to read the Bible is to turn it into a talisman which encourages
superstition or to make its recitation a meaningless rote. The decision delivers
public school children from such ritualistic, potentially harmful exposure to
an abuse of Holy Scripture. The decision is a good one, deeply rooted in the
spirit of the First Amendment and strongly supported by the court's previous
rulings. It deserves the careful and conscientious study of all Americans.

10

Sherbert v. Verner

374 U.S. 398 (1963)

Here for the first time the Supreme Court ruled that the free-exercise provision of the First Amendment requires exemption of religious believers from a non-discriminatory secular law. Adell Sherbert, a Seventh-day Adventist, was fired by her South Carolina employer because she refused to work on Saturday, the Sabbath day of her faith. Unable to find another job that did not require Saturday work, she filed a claim for unemployment compensation. The state rejected her claim on the grounds that by refusing to work on Saturday she had refused to accept suitable work and was therefore disqualified. Not surprisingly, given the Supreme Court's free-exercise decisions to this point, the South Carolina Supreme Court rejected Sherbert's contention that the state law abridged her First Amendment rights.

But, in a critical turning point for free-exercise jurisprudence, the Supreme Court reversed that judgment. Under *Reynolds* v. *United States*, 98 U.S. 145 (1879), government had authority to regulate religiously motivated action so long as it had a rational basis for doing so. The rational-basis burden was so easy to satisfy as to foreclose the possibility of constitutionally mandated exemptions from general law. In *Sherbert* v. *Verner*, the Court held that government may burden the free exercise of religion only if it has a *compelling* interest in doing so. South Carolina did not meet this new test.

In crafting a free-exercise exemption from general law, the Court, in an opinion written by Justice William Brennan, viewed the case differently from *Braunfeld* v. *Brown*, 366 U.S. 599 (1961),

169

which declined to recognize an exception for Sabbatarians from laws limiting work on Sunday. Writing separately, Justice Potter Stewart concurred in the judgment but thought the Court should have overruled *Braunfeld*. Justice John M. Harlan II, joined by Justice Byron White, in dissent, argued that the majority read the free-exercise provision too expansively and in fact did overrule *Braunfeld*. These three opinions are presented here. *Sherbert* v. *Verner* was handed down on the same day as *Abington School District* v. *Schempp*.

Participating in *Sherbert* v. *Verner*, decided June 17, 1963, were Chief Justice Earl Warren and Associate Justices Hugo L. Black, William J. Brennan, Jr., Tom C. Clark, William O. Douglas, Arthur J. Goldberg, John M. Harlan II, Potter Stewart, and Byron R. White.

Opinions

Justice William J. Brennan, Jr., delivered the opinion of the Court:

The door of the Free Exercise Clause stands tightly closed against any governmental regulation of religious *beliefs* as such, *Cantwell* v. *Connecticut* (1940). . . . On the other hand, the Court has rejected challenges under the Free Exercise Clause to governmental regulation of certain overt acts prompted by religious beliefs or principles, for "even when the action is in accord with one's religious convictions, [it] is not totally free from legislative restrictions." *Braunfeld* v. *Braun*, 366 U.S. 599 (1961).[1] The conduct or actions so regulated have invariably posed some substantial threat to public safety, peace or order.

Plainly enough, appellant's conscientious objection to Saturday work constitutes no conduct prompted by religious principles of a kind within the reach of state legislation. If, therefore, the decision of the South Carolina Supreme Court is to withstand appellant's constitutional challenge, it must be either because her disqualification as a beneficiary represents no infringement by the State of her constitutional rights of free exercise, or because any incidental burden on the free exercise of appellant's religion may be justified by a "compelling state interest in the regulation of a subject within the State's constitutional power to regulate. . . ." *NAACP* v. *Button*, 371 U.S. 415 (1963).

We turn first to the question whether the disqualification for benefits imposes any burden on the free exercise of appellant's religion. We think it is clear that it does. . . . [N]ot only is it apparent that appellant's declared ineligibility for benefits derives solely from the practice of her religion, but the pressure upon her to forgo that practice is unmistakable. The ruling forces her to choose between following the precepts of her religion and forfeiting benefits, on the one hand, and abandoning one of the precepts of her religion in order to accept work, on the

---

1. In *Braunfeld*, Orthodox Jews brought a free-exercise challenge to a Sunday closing law. Their faith required them to close their retail shops on Saturday; the law required that they close the shops on Sunday as well. Their lawsuit maintained that the law required them to violate a central tenet of their religion if they wanted to make a living. The Court refused to create a free-exercise exemption from the Sunday closing law.

171

other hand. Governmental imposition of such a choice puts the same kind of burden upon the free exercise of religion as would a fine imposed against appellant for her Saturday worship.

Nor may the South Carolina court's construction of the statute be saved from constitutional infirmity on the ground that unemployment compensation benefits are not appellant's "right" but merely a "privilege." It is too late in the day to doubt that the liberties of religion and expression may be infringed by the denial of or placing of conditions upon a benefit or privilege. . . . [T]o condition the availability of benefits upon this appellant's willingness to violate a cardinal principle of her religious faith effectively penalizes the free exercise of her constitutional liberties.

Significantly, South Carolina expressly saves the Sunday worshipper from having to make the kind of choice which we here hold infringes the Sabbatarian's religious liberty. When in times of "national emergency" the textile plants are authorized by the State Commissioner of Labor to operate on Sunday, "no employee shall be required to work on Sunday . . . who is conscientiously opposed to Sunday work; and if any employee should refuse to work on Sunday on account of conscientious . . . objections he or she shall not jeopardize his or her seniority by such refusal or be discriminated against in any other manner." No question of the disqualification of a Sunday worshipper for benefits is likely to arise, since we cannot suppose that an employer will discharge him in violation of this statute. The unconstitutionality of the disqualification of the Sabbatarian is thus compounded by the religious discrimination which South Carolina's general statutory scheme necessarily effects.

We must next consider whether some compelling state interest enforced in the eligibility provisions of the South Carolina statute justifies the substantial infringement of appellant's First Amendment right.[2] . . . The appellees suggest no more than a possibility that the filing of

---

2. The Court did not base its analysis here on a principle derived from the history of the free-exercise provision. Michael W. McConnell, after examining that history, concludes "that the modern doctrine of free-exercise exemptions is more consistent with the original understanding than is a position that leads only to the facial neutrality of legislation" ("The Origins and Historical Understanding of Free Exercise of Religion," *Harvard Law Review* 103 [1990]: 1512). Elsewhere McConnell has written, "While the historical evidence may not be unequivocal (it seldom is), it does, on balance, support *Sherbert*'s interpretation of the free-exercise clause" ("A Response to Professor Marshall, *University of Chicago Law Review* 58 [1991]: 329, n. 12). McConnell's originalist case for judicially crafted exemptions has been sharply criticized by Gerard V. Bradley in "Beguiled: Free Exercise Exemptions and the Siren Song of Liberalism" (*Hofstra Law Review* 20 [1991]: 245).

fraudulent claims by unscrupulous claimants feigning religious objections to Saturday work might not only dilute the unemployment compensation fund but also hinder the scheduling by employers of necessary Saturday work. But that possibility is not apposite here because no such objection appears to have been made before the South Carolina Supreme Court, and we are unwilling to assess the importance of an asserted state interest without the views of the state court. Nor, if the contention had been made below, would the record appear to sustain it; there is no proof whatever to warrant such fears of malingering or deceit as those which the respondents now advance. . . .

. . . [T]he state interest asserted in the present case is wholly dissimilar to the interests which were found to justify the less direct burden upon religious practices in *Braunfeld*. The Court recognized that the Sunday closing law which that decision sustained undoubtedly served "to make the practice of [the Orthodox Jewish merchants'] . . . religious beliefs more expensive." But the statute was nevertheless saved by a countervailing factor which finds no equivalent in the instant case—a strong state interest in providing one uniform day of rest for all workers. That secular objective could be achieved, the Court found, only by declaring Sunday to be that day of rest. Requiring exemptions for Sabbatarians, while theoretically possible, appeared to present an administrative problem of such magnitude, or to afford the exempted class so great a competitive advantage, that such a requirement would have rendered the entire statutory scheme unworkable. In the present case no such justifications underlie the determination of the state court that appellant's religion makes her ineligible to receive benefits.

In holding as we do, plainly we are not fostering the "establishment" of the Seventh-day Adventist religion in South Carolina, for the extension of unemployment benefits to Sabbatarians in common with Sunday worshippers reflects nothing more than the governmental obligation of neutrality in the face of religious differences, and does not represent that involvement of religious with secular institutions which it is the object of the Establishment Clause to forestall. Nor does the recognition of the appellant's right to unemployment benefits under the state statute serve to abridge any other person's religious liberties. Nor do we, by our decision today, declare the existence of a constitutional right to unemployment benefits on the part of all persons whose religious convictions are the cause of their unemployment. This is not a case in which an employee's religious convictions serve to make him a nonproductive member of society. Finally, nothing we say today constrains the States to adopt any particular form or scheme of unemployment compensation. Our holding today is only that South Carolina may not constitutionally apply the eligibility provisions so as to constrain a worker to abandon his religious convictions respecting the day of rest. This holding reaffirms a principle that we announced a decade and a half ago, namely that no State may "exclude individual Catholics, Lutherans, Mohammedans, Baptists, Jews, Methodists, Non-believers, Presbyterians, or the members of any other faith, *because of their faith, or lack of it,* from receiving the benefits of public welfare legislation." *Everson* v. *Board of Education* (1947).

. . .

The judgment of the South Carolina Supreme Court is reversed and the case is remanded for further proceedings not inconsistent with this opinion.

Justice Potter Stewart, concurring in the result:

Although fully agreeing with the result which the Court reaches in this case, I cannot join the Court's opinion. This case presents a double-barreled dilemma, which in all candor I think the Court's opinion has not succeeded in papering over. The dilemma ought to be resolved.[3]

. . .

I am convinced that no liberty is more essential to the continued vitality of the free society which our Constitution guarantees than is the religious liberty protected by the Free Exercise Clause explicit in the First Amendment and imbedded in the Fourteenth. And I regret that on occasion, and specifically in *Braunfeld*, the Court has shown what has seemed to me a distressing insensitivity to the appropriate demands of this constitutional guarantee. By contrast I think that the Court's approach to the Establishment Clause has on occasion, and specifically in [the school prayer-and-Bible-reading cases], been not only insensitive, but positively wooden, and that the Court has accorded to the Establishment Clause a meaning which neither the words, the history, nor the intention of the authors of that specific constitutional provision even remotely suggests.

But my views as to the correctness of the Court's decisions in these cases are beside the point here. The point is that the decisions are on the books. And the result is that there are many situations where legit-

---

3. David P. Currie has observed: "Stewart's way out of the dilemma was to repudiate the prayer cases, but in light of the purposes of the two clauses it is at least as plausible to conclude that it was *Sherbert* that was wrongly decided" (*The Constitution in the Supreme Court: The Second Century, 1888–1986,* 446).

imate claims under the Free Exercise Clause will run into head-on collision with the Court's insensitive and sterile construction of the Establishment Clause.[4] The controversy now before us is clearly such a case.

Because the appellant refuses to accept available jobs which would require her to work on Saturdays, South Carolina has declined to pay unemployment benefits to her. Her refusal to work on Saturdays is based on the tenets of her religious faith. The Court says that South Carolina cannot under these circumstances declare her to be not "available for work" within the meaning of its statute because to do so would violate her constitutional right to the free exercise of her religion.

Yet what this Court has said about the Establishment Clause must inevitably lead to a diametrically opposite result. If the appellant's refusal to work on Saturdays were based on indolence, or on a compulsive desire to watch the Saturday television programs, no one would say that South Carolina could not hold that she was not "available for work" within the meaning of its statute. That being so, the Establishment Clause as constructed by this court not only *permits* but affirmatively *requires* South Carolina equally to deny the appellant's claim for unemployment compensation when her refusal to work on Saturdays is based upon her religious creed. For, as said in *Everson*, the Establishment Clause bespeaks "a government . . . stripped of all power . . . to support, or otherwise to assist any or all religions . . . ," and no State "can pass laws which aid one religion. . . ." In Justice Rutledge's words [from his dissent in *Everson*], adopted by the Court today in *Abington* v. *Schempp*, the Establishment Clause forbids "every form of public aid or support for religion." In the words of the Court in *Engel* v. *Vitale* (1962), reaffirmed today in the *Schempp* case, the Establishment Clause forbids the "financial support of government" to be "placed behind a particular religious belief."

To require South Carolina to so administer its laws as to pay public money to the appellant under the circumstances of this case is thus clearly to require the State to violate the Establishment Clause as construed by this Court. This poses no problem for me, because I think the Court's mechanistic concept of the Establishment Clause is historically unsound and constitutionally wrong. I think the process of con-

---

4. Justice Stewart here supplied a footnote, number two in the text, chiding the Court: "The obvious potentiality of such collision has been studiously ignored by the Court, but has not escaped the perception of commentators."

stitutional decision in the area of the relationships between government and religion demands considerably more than the invocation of broad-brushed rhetoric of the kind I have quoted. And I think that the guarantee of religious liberty embodied in the Free Exercise Clause affirmatively requires government to create an atmosphere of hospitality and accommodation to individual belief or disbelief. In short, I think our Constitution commands the positive protection by government of religious freedom—not only for a minority, however small—not only for the majority, however large—but for each of us.

. . . [W]e do not have before us a situation where a State provides unemployment compensation generally, and singles out for disqualification only those persons who are unavailable for work on religious grounds. This is not, in short, a scheme which operates so as to discriminate against religion as such. But the Court nevertheless holds that the State must prefer a religious over a secular ground for being unavailable for work. . . .

Yet in cases decided under the Establishment Clause the Court has decreed otherwise. It has decreed that government must blind itself to the differing religious beliefs and traditions of the people. With all respect, I think it is the Court's duty to face up to the dilemma posed by the conflict between the Free Exercise Clause of the Constitution and the Establishment Clause as interpreted by the Court. . . . For so long as the resounding but fallacious fundamentalist rhetoric of some of our Establishment Clause opinions remains on our books, to be disregarded at will as in the present case, or to be undiscriminatingly invoked as in the *Schempp* Case, so long will the possibility of consistent and perceptive decision in this most difficult and delicate area of constitutional law be impeded and impaired. And so long, I fear, will the guarantee of true religious freedom in our pluralistic society be uncertain and insecure.

My second difference with the Court's opinion is that I cannot agree that today's decision can stand consistently with *Braunfeld*. The Court says that there was a "less direct burden upon religious practices" in that case than in this. With all respect, I think the Court is mistaken, simply as a matter of fact. The *Braunfeld* case involved a state *criminal* statute. The undisputed effect of that statute, as pointed out by Justice Brennan in his dissenting opinion in that case, was " . . . [to] put an individual to a choice between his business and his religion."

The impact upon the appellant's religious freedom in the present case is considerably less onerous. We deal here not with a criminal statute, but with the particularized administration of South Carolina's

Unemployment Compensation Act. Even upon the unlikely assumption that the appellant could not find suitable non-Saturday employment, the appellant at the worst would be denied a maximum of 22 weeks of compensation payments. I agree with the Court that the possibility of that denial is enough to infringe upon the appellant's constitutional right to the free exercise of her religion. But it is clear to me that in order to reach this conclusion the Court must explicitly reject the reasoning of *Braunfeld*. I think the *Braunfeld* Case was wrongly decided and should be overruled, and accordingly I concur in the result reached by the Court in the case before us.

Justice John M. Harlan II, dissenting, joined by Justice Byron R. White:

Today's decision is disturbing both in its rejection of existing precedent and in its implications for the future. The significance of the decision can best be understood after an examination of the state law applied in this case.

South Carolina's Unemployment Compensation Law was enacted in 1936 in response to the grave social and economic problems that arose during the depression of that period. . . .

. . . [T]he purpose of the legislation was to tide people over, and to avoid social and economic chaos, during periods when *work was unavailable*. But at the same time there was clearly no intent to provide relief for those who for purely personal reasons were or became *unavailable for work*. In accordance with this design, the legislature provided that "[a]n unemployed insured worker shall be eligible to receive benefits with respect to any week *only* if the Commission finds that . . . [h]e is able to work and is available for work. . . ."

The South Carolina Supreme Court has uniformly applied this law in conformity with its clearly expressed purpose. It has consistently held that one is not "available for work" if his unemployment has resulted not from the inability of industry to provide a job but rather from personal circumstances, no matter how compelling. The reference to "involuntary unemployment" in the legislative statement of policy, whatever a sociologist, philosopher, or theologian might say, has been interpreted not to embrace such personal circumstances.

In the present case all that the state court has done is to apply . . . accepted principles. Since virtually all of the mills in the Spartanburg area were operating on a six-day week, the appellant was "unavailable for work," and thus ineligible for benefits, when personal considerations prevented her from accepting employment on a full-time basis in the industry and locality in which she had worked. The fact that these personal considerations sprang from her religious convictions was wholly without relevance to the state court's application of the law. Thus in no proper sense can it be said that the State discriminated against the appellant on the basis of her religious beliefs or that she was denied benefits *because* she was a Seventh-day Adventist. She was denied benefits just as any other claimant would be denied benefits who was not "available for work" for personal reasons.

With this background, this Court's decision comes into clearer focus. What the Court is holding is that if the State chooses to condition unemployment compensation on the applicant's availability for work, it is constitutionally compelled to *carve out an exception*—and to provide benefits—for those whose unavailability is due to their religious convictions. Such a holding has particular significance in two respects.

First, despite the Court's protestations to the contrary, the decision necessarily overrules *Braunfeld*, which held that it did not offend the "Free Exercise" Clause of the Constitution for a State to forbid a Sabbatarian to do business on Sunday. The secular purpose of the statute before us today is even clearer than that involved in *Braunfeld*. And just as in *Braunfeld*, where exceptions to the Sunday closing laws for Sabbatarians would have been inconsistent with the purpose to achieve a uniform day of rest and would have required case-by-case inquiry into religious beliefs—so here, an exception to the rules of eligibility based on religious convictions would necessitate judicial examination of those convictions and would be at odds with the limited purpose of the statute to smooth out the economy during periods of industrial instability. Finally, the indirect financial burden of the present law is far less than that involved in *Braunfeld*. Forcing a store owner to close his business on Sunday may well have the effect of depriving him of a satisfactory livelihood if his religious convictions require him to close on Saturday as well. Here we are dealing only with temporary benefits. . . .

Second, the implications of the present decision are far more troublesome than its apparently narrow dimensions would indicate at first glance. The meaning of today's holding, as already noted, is that the State must furnish unemployment benefits to one who is unavailable for work if the unavailability stems from the exercise of religious convictions. The State, in other words, must *single out* for financial assistance those whose behavior is religiously motivated, even though it denies such assistance to others whose identical behavior (in this case, inability to work on Saturdays) is not religiously motivated.

. . . My own view . . . is that at least under the circumstances of this case it would be a permissible accommodation of religion for the State, if it *chose* to do so, to create an exception to its eligibility requirements for persons like the appellant. The constitutional obligation of "neutrality" is not so narrow a channel that the slightest deviation from an absolutely straight course leads to condemnation. There are too many instances in which no such course can be charted, too many areas in which the pervasive activities of the State justify some special provision for religion to prevent it from being submerged by an all-embracing secularism. The State violates its obligation of neutrality when, for example, it mandates a daily religious exercise in its public schools, with all the attendant pressures on the school children that such an exercise entails. But there is, I believe, enough flexibility in the Constitution to permit a legislative judgment accommodating an unemployment compensation law to the exercise of religious beliefs such as appellant's.

For very much the same reasons, however, I cannot subscribe to the conclusion that the State is constitutionally *compelled* to carve out an exception to its general rule of eligibility in the present case. Those situations in which the Constitution may require special treatment on account of religion are, in my view, few and far between. . . . Such compulsion in the present case is particularly inappropriate in light of the indirect, remote, and insubstantial effect of the decision below on the exercise of appellant's religion and in light of the direct financial assistance to religion that today's decision requires.

11

Board of Education v. Allen

392 U.S. 236 (1968)

The landmark case of *Everson* v. *Board of Education* (1947) concerned the constitutionality of state aid to church-related schools. Twenty-one years passed before another such case found its way to the Supreme Court. *Board of Education* v. *Allen* then proved to be the first in a series of cases in which the Court attempted to say which forms of state aid to church-related schools might be permissible under the First Amendment.

In *Allen*, the Court sustained a New York state law requiring local schools to lend textbooks free of charge to students in grades 7 to 12, including those attending religious schools. Members of a local school board had succeeded in persuading the trial court that the statute violated the First Amendment. This decision was reversed on appeal, however, and the Supreme Court declined to upset that judgment.

Allen produced five opinions, four of which are presented here. (A concurrence by Justice John Harlan is omitted.) Justice Byron White wrote for the Court, expressing the views of six members. Justice Hugo Black, who wrote for the Court in the landmark *Everson* case, here delivered his final religion-clause opinion, and he now wrote in dissent. Like Justice William O. Douglas, another dissenter, Justice Black believed the Court had not adhered to the teachings of *Everson*. Justice Abe Fortas wrote a dissent also.

Allen drew immediate comment in the secular and religious press. Presented here are editorials from *The Christian Century*, the *Wall Street Journal*, and *America*.

Participating in *Board of Education* v. *Allen*, decided June 10,

181

1968, were Chief Justice Earl Warren and Associate Justices Hugo L. Black, William J. Brennan, Jr., William O. Douglas, Abe Fortas, John M. Harlan II, Thurgood Marshall, Potter Stewart, and Byron R. White.

Opinions

Justice Byron R. White delivered the opinion of the Court:

Everson v. *Board of Education* (1947) and later cases have shown that the line between state neutrality to religion and state support of religion is not easy to locate. . . . Based on *Everson* . . . and other cases, *Abington* v. *Schempp* (1963) fashioned a test subscribed to by eight Justices for distinguishing between forbidden involvements of the State with religion and those contacts which the Establishment clause permits:

> The test may be stated as follows: what are the purpose and the primary effect of the enactment? If either is the advancement or inhibition of religion then the enactment exceeds the scope of legislative power as circumscribed by the Constitution. That is to say that to withstand the strictures of the Establishment Clause there must be a secular legislative purpose and a primary effect that neither advances nor inhibits religion. *Everson.*

This test is not easy to apply, but the citation of *Everson* by the *Schempp* Court to support its general standard made clear how the *Schempp* rule would be applied to the facts of *Everson*. The statute upheld in *Everson* would be considered a law having "a secular legislative purpose and a primary effect that neither advances nor inhibits religion." We reach the same result with respect to the New York law requiring school books to be loaned free of charge to all students in specified grades. The express purpose of [the law] was stated by the New York Legislature to be furtherance of the educational opportunities available to the young. Appellants have shown us nothing about the necessary effects of the statute that is contrary to its stated purpose. The law merely makes available to all children the benefits of a general program to lend school books free of charge. Books are furnished at the request of the pupil and ownership remains, at least technically, in the State. Thus no funds or books are furnished to parochial schools, and the financial benefit is to parents and children, not to schools. Perhaps free books make it more likely that some children choose to attend a sectarian school, but that was true of the state-paid bus fares in *Everson* and does not alone demonstrate an unconstitutional degree of support for a religious institution.

Of course books are different from buses. Most bus rides have no inherent religious significance, while religious books are common. However, the language of [the law] does not authorize the loan of religious books, and the State claims no right to distribute religious literature. Although the books loaned are those required by the parochial school for use in specific courses, each book loaned must be approved by the public school authorities; only secular books may receive approval. The law was construed by the Court of Appeals of New York as "merely making available secular textbooks at the request of the individual student," and the record contains no suggestion that religious books have been loaned. Absent evidence, we cannot assume that school authorities, who constantly face the same problem in selecting textbooks for use in the public schools, are unable to distinguish between secular and religious books or that they will not honestly discharge their duties under the law. In judging the validity of the statute on this record we must proceed on the assumption that books loaned to students are books that are not unsuitable for use in the public schools because of religious content.

The major reason offered by appellants for distinguishing free textbooks from free bus fares is that books, but not buses, are critical to the teaching process, and in a sectarian school that process is employed to teach religion. However this Court has long recognized that religious schools pursue two goals, religious instruction and secular education. . . . [A] substantial body of case law has confirmed the power of the States to insist that attendance at private schools, if it is to satisfy state compulsory-attendance laws, be at institutions which provide minimum hours of instruction, employ teachers of specified training, and cover prescribed subjects of instruction. . . .

Underlying [our] cases, and underlying also the legislative judgments that have preceded the court decisions, has been a recognition that private education has played and is playing a significant and valuable role in raising national levels of knowledge, competence, and experience. Americans care about the quality of the secular education available to their children. They have considered high quality education to be an indispensable ingredient for achieving the kind of nation, and the kind of citizenry, that they have desired to create. Considering this attitude, the continued willingness to rely on private school systems, including parochial systems, strongly suggests that a wide segment of informed opinion, legislative and otherwise, has found that those schools do an acceptable job of providing secular education to their students. This judgment is further evidence that parochial schools are performing, in addition to their sectarian function, the task of secular education.

Against this background of judgment and experience, unchallenged in the meager record before us in this case, we cannot agree with appellants either that all teaching in a sectarian school is religious or that the processes of secular and religious training are so intertwined that secular textbooks furnished to students by the public are in fact instrumental in the teaching of religion. . . . We are unable to hold, based solely on judicial notice, that this statute results in unconstitutional involvement of the State with religious instruction or that [the law], for this or the other reasons urged, is a law respecting the establishment of religion.

Justice Hugo L. Black, dissenting:

I believe the New York law held valid is a flat, flagrant, open violation of the First and Fourteenth Amendments which together forbid Congress or state legislatures to enact any law "respecting an establishment of religion." . . .

. . .

The *Everson* and *McCollum* cases plainly interpret the First and Fourteenth Amendments as protecting the taxpayers of a State from being compelled to pay taxes to their government to support the agencies of private religious organizations the taxpayers oppose. To authorize a State to tax its residents for such church purposes is to put the State squarely in the religious activities of certain religious groups that happen to be strong enough politically to write their own religious preferences and prejudices into the laws. This links state and churches together in controlling the lives and destinies of our citizenship—a citizenship composed of people of myriad religious faiths, some of them bitterly hostile to and completely intolerant of the others. It was to escape laws precisely like this that a large part of the Nation's early immigrants fled to this country. It was also to escape such laws and such consequences that the First Amendment was written in language strong and clear barring passage of any law "respecting an establishment of religion."

It is true, of course, that the New York law does not as yet formally adopt or establish a state religion. But it takes a great stride in that direction and coming events cast their shadows before them. The same powerful sectarian religious propagandists who have succeeded in se-

curing passage of the present law to help religious schools carry on
their sectarian religious purposes can and doubtless will continue their
propaganda, looking toward complete domination and supremacy of
their particular brand of religion. And it nearly always is by insidious
approaches that the citadels of liberty are most successfully attacked.

I know of no prior opinion of this Court upon which the majority
here can rightfully rely to support its holding. . . . In saying this, I am
not unmindful of the fact that the New York Court of Appeals purported to follow *Everson*, in which this Court, in an opinion written by
me, upheld a New Jersey law authorizing reimbursement to parents for
the transportation of children attending sectarian schools. That law
did not attempt to deny the benefit of its general terms to children of
any faith going to any legally authorized school. Thus, it was treated in
the same way as a general law paying the streetcar fare *of all school children*, or a law providing midday lunches for all children or all school
children, or a law to provide police protection for children going to
and from school, or general laws to provide police and fire protection
for buildings, including, of course, churches and church school buildings as well as others.

As my Brother Douglas so forcefully shows, in an argument with
which I fully agree, upholding a State's power to pay bus or streetcar
fares for school children cannot provide support for the validity of a
state law using tax-raised funds to buy school books for a religious
school. . . . Books are the most essential tool of education since they
contain the resources of knowledge which the educational process is
designed to exploit. In this sense it is not difficult to distinguish books,
which are the heart of any school, from bus fares, which provide a
convenient and helpful general public transportation service. With respect to the former, state financial support actively and directly assists
the teaching and propagation of sectarian religious viewpoints in clear
conflict with the First Amendment's establishment bar; with respect to
the latter, the State merely provides a general and nondiscriminatory
transportation service in no way related to substantive religious views
and beliefs. . . . It requires no prophet to foresee that on the argument
used to support this law others could be upheld providing for state or
federal government funds to buy property on which to erect religious
school buildings or to erect the buildings themselves, to pay the salaries of the religious school teachers, and finally to have the sectarian
religious groups cease to rely on voluntary contributions of members
of their sects while waiting for the Government to pick up all the bills
for the religious schools.

I still subscribe to the belief that tax-raised funds cannot constitutionally be used to support religious schools, buy their school books, erect their buildings, pay their teachers, or pay any other of their maintenance expenses, even to the extent of one penny. . . . And I still believe that the only way to protect minority religious groups from majority groups in this country is to keep the wall of separation between church and state high and impregnable as the First and Fourteenth Amendments provide. The Court's affirmance here bodes nothing but evil to religious peace in this country.

Justice William O. Douglas, dissenting:

. . . [T]he statutory system provides that the parochial school will ask for the books that it wants. Can there be the slightest doubt that the head of the parochial school will select the book or books that best promote its sectarian creed?

If the board of education supinely submits by approving and supplying the sectarian or sectarian-oriented textbooks, the struggle to keep church and state separate has been lost. If the board resists, then the battle line between church and state will have been drawn and the contest will be on to keep the school board independent or to put it under church domination and control.

Whatever may be said of *Everson*, there is nothing ideological about a bus. There is nothing ideological about a school lunch, or a public nurse, or a scholarship. The constitutionality of such public aid to students in parochial schools turns on considerations not present in this textbook case. The textbook goes to the very heart of education in a parochial school. It is the chief, although not solitary, instrumentality for propagating a particular religious creed or faith. How can we possibly approve such state aid to a religion? A parochial school textbook may contain many, many more seeds of creed and dogma than a prayer. Yet we struck down in *Engel* v. *Vitale* an official New York prayer for its public schools, even though it was not plainly denominational. For we emphasized the violence done the Establishment Clause when the power was given religious-political groups "to write their own prayers into law." That risk is compounded here by giving parochial schools the initiative in selecting the textbooks they desire to be furnished at public expense.

· · ·

. . . Now that "secular" textbooks will pour into religious schools, we can rest assured that a contest will be on to provide those books for religious schools which the dominant religious group concludes best reflect the theocentric or other philosophy of the particular church.

Justice Abe Fortas, dissenting:

The majority opinion of the Court upholds the New York statute by ignoring a vital aspect of it. Public funds are used to buy, for students in sectarian schools, textbooks which are selected and prescribed by the sectarian schools themselves. As my Brother Douglas points out, despite the transparent camouflage that the books are furnished to students, the reality is that they are selected and their use is prescribed by the sectarian authorities. The child must use the prescribed book. He cannot use a different book prescribed for use in the public schools. The State cannot choose the book to be used. It is true that the public school boards must "approve" the book selected by the sectarian authorities; but this has no real significance. The purpose of these provisions is to hold out promise that the books will be "secular" . . . but the fact remains that the books are chosen by and for the sectarian schools.

It is misleading to say, as the majority opinion does, that the New York "law merely makes available to all children the benefits of a general program to lend school books free of charge." This is not a "general" program. It is a specific program to use state funds to buy books prescribed by sectarian schools which, in New York, are primarily Catholic, Jewish, and Lutheran sponsored schools. It could be called a "general" program only if the school books made available to all children were precisely the same—the books selected for and used in the public schools. But this program is not one in which all children are treated alike, regardless of where they go to school. This program, in its unconstitutional features, is hand-tailored to satisfy the specific needs of sectarian schools. Children attending such schools are given *special* books—books selected by the sectarian authorities. How can this be other than the use of public money to aid those sectarian establishments?

It is also beside the point, in my opinion, to "assume," as the majority opinion does, that "books loaned to students are books that are not unsuitable for use in the public schools because of religious content." The point is that the books furnished to students of sectarian schools are selected by the religious authorities and are prescribed by them.

This case is not within the principle of *Everson*. Apart from the differences between textbooks and bus rides, the present statute does not call for extending to children attending sectarian schools the same service or facility extended to children in public schools. This statute calls for furnishing special, separate, and particular books, specially, separately, and particularly chosen by religious sects or their representatives for use in their sectarian schools. This is the infirmity, in my opinion. This is the feature that makes it impossible, in my view, to reach any conclusion other than that this statute is an unconstitutional use of public funds to support an establishment of religion.

Responses

From **The Christian Century**, July 17, 1968, "The Court Concludes a Term":

Not surprisingly, Msgr. George A. Kelly, education secretary for the Roman Catholic archdiocese of New York, lauded the textbook-loan ruling as "a Magna Carta for the parents of nonpublic school children." Justice White strongly stressed that federal aid may be allocated only to those aspects of parochial education which are secular. But if this "secular" argument were to be extended with any consistency, the general public could end up paying for just about everything involved in parochial education—everything down to chalk and erasers, everything except materials for catechism classes and the salaries of teaching nuns.

A writer for the Jesuit magazine *America* touted Justice White's language as "remarkably clean" and "carefully chiseled"; this may be true of his language, but his *reasoning* strikes us as specious, even devious, relying as it does on the legal fiction of "child benefit" to effect indirectly what is forbidden directly. In the words of Justice Fortas's dissent, "This statute calls for furnishing special, separate, and particular books, specially, separately, and particularly chosen by religious sects or their representatives for use in their sectarian schools." The dissent of Justice Hugo Black was much more vehement, so much so that it could be interpreted as anti-Catholic. Labeling the New York law a "flat, flagrant, open violation" of the First and 14th amendments, the justice went on to say: "The same powerful sectarian religious propagandists who have succeeded in securing passage of the present law to help religious schools carry on their sectarian religious purposes can and doubtless will continue their propaganda, looking toward complete domination and supremacy of their particular brand of religion." Black summed up with a dire prediction: "The Court's affirmance here bodes nothing but evil to religious peace in this country."

Our fear is not as great as Justice Black's (perhaps he has not heard about the ameliorating effects of ecumenism—though admittedly the school-aid issue has thus far proved largely unamenable to ecumenical resolution). Furthermore, we are fully aware of the tremendous financial burden of parochial schools and of the necessity for finding a "way out" if such schools are to impart education of quality. But we are also concerned about the state of the public schools and what is likely to follow upon further expansion of the child-benefit concept. If that concept is carried to its logical conclusion, writes Sam-

190

uel Rabinove, director of the American Jewish Committee's legal division, "the same amount spent by government for each child in public schools must also be spent for each child in non-public schools." And:

> This would result in a proliferation of divisive private schools, religious and otherwise, and ultimately in the public schools becoming no more than trash heaps for society's rejects who, for whatever reason, were denied admission to private schools. Such a development would also deal a death blow to the urgent national goal of racially integrated public schools, affording equal educational opportunity to all. Hence, government should furnish no inducement to encourage citizens to desert the public schools and thus further fragmentize American education.

It seems that this nation is far from being out of the woods in regard to the complex and vexatious issue of federal aid to parochial education. Further consideration of the issue seems inevitable as litigants bring [new] challenges.

From the *Wall Street Journal*, June 14, 1968, "The Establishment of Confusion":

"Congress should make no law respecting an establishment of religion, or prohibiting the free exercise thereof," the amendment says. The statement is simply a strong affirmation of religious tolerance, a tolerance that would be unlikely if the Government recognized the Catholic, Episcopal or any other church as the state church. A few years ago, however, the Supreme Court decided that the amendment meant more than that. To be precise, it meant that it was unconstitutional for public schools to provide for Bible readings or even secularized "prayers" in the classrooms. If the words are indeed that amazingly elastic, how much further will they stretch?

Many people have been quick to provide their own answers. Some of them argue that strict separation of the state and religion, which seems to be implied by the school prayer decision, ought to rule out tax exemption for churches. The exemptions, after all, amount to a state subsidy to religious organizations.

Other groups and individuals have attacked the growing state and Federal subsidies to religiously affiliated schools. While governments have tried to sidestep Constitutional problems by claiming the aid goes to the pupils, not the schools, it would be silly to contend the institutions do not benefit. . . .

In the end the courts may or may not rule out Federal aid to parochial and other private schools. But it's significant that the Supreme Court . . . found it was perfectly all right for New York State to require public school systems to lend textbooks to children in private schools.

If the Federal aid is finally approved, it will be hard to label the result either "right" or "wrong." In this area, as in others, ethical absolutes may be indefinable.

Those who argue that public funds should not go to private schools may be right when they say that the payments will weaken public schools, which already have troubles enough. But that will be true only if the public refuses to supply the financing needed by all the schools.

Proponents of rigid religion-state separation also maintain that governmental subsidies to religious organizations and their activities are a threat to religious freedom. Since it is true that subsidies can lead to a measure of control, that argument is one that surely should be considered, especially by those institutions that receive the help.

If, however, the public then decides that it still wants to offer help to private schools it should be able to do so. Moreover, if the public through its elected representatives wants to continue tax exemption of religious organizations, that should be its privilege.

Whether school prayers "established" a religion or not, the Supreme Court in ruling them out has established a great deal of confusion. Religion, in the general sense and not in the sense of a specific church, is and always has been deeply imbedded in the fabric of our society. Those who attempt to segregate completely its institutions from those of pervasive government are trying what seems sure to be impossible.

*From **America**, June 22, 1968, "The Constitution and American Education":*

In 1925, the [Supreme Court] ruled that Catholic and other private schools that meet State standards have the right to exist. Just twenty-two years later it held that States may constitutionally provide free transportation to school children, including those attending Catholic and other private schools. Another twenty-one years later, the Court has now ruled that States may provide secular textbooks as well as transportation. It will not be surprising if it takes twenty years more to resolve the deep questions raised by the rulings in the textbooks and taxpayer-standing case.

Complicated as these questions are, they cannot dim the clarity of three propositions that emerge from Mr. Justice White's opinion for a solid majority of the Court. Religious schools pursue two goals: religious instruction and secular education. The State has the right and the duty to foster this secular education, but without destroying the religious instruction. The fact that churches operate the schools for religious as well as secular purposes does not erect a wall of separation between the State and the children in the schools.

The court emphasized that it intended to adhere to the separation of Church and State as the constitutional standard. Such separation, however, does not mean that otherwise valid Federal programs are automatically invalidated by any degree of benefit to religious organizations, no matter how small, unintended or unavoidable the benefit may be. "The problem, like many problems in constitutional law, is one of degree."

The "No Aid, Nohow, No Matter What" dogma of certain liberals and fundamentalists is constitutionally dead. The Supreme Court, of course, is not going to give a blank check to students in Church-related schools. It would be fatuous, however, for anyone to fail to recognize what the court has given: a generous definitive endorsement of the place of Catholic and other Church-related schools in American education.

12

Walz v. Tax Commission

397 U.S. 664 (1970)

In this first religion-clause case decided during the tenure of
Chief Justice Warren E. Burger, the Supreme Court upheld
the practice—dating to the American founding—of granting tax
exemptions "to religious organizations for religious property
used for religious purposes." Frederick Walz, a New York City
property owner, sued to enjoin the city tax commission from
granting tax exemptions to religious organizations for property
they used solely for religious purposes. The complaint failed in
the state courts. On appeal the Supreme Court held that such
tax exemptions do not violate the First Amendment.

In economic terms, *Walz* v. *Tax Commission* was obviously important. Had the Court sided with Frederick Walz, churches
across America would have been faced with the prospect of paying large tax bills. *Walz* also proved legally significant because of
its articulation of what soon became (in *Lemon* v. *Kurtzman*,
1971) the third element of the three-part test for determining
whether a government action violates the no-establishment provision: whether the challenged action creates an "excessive government entanglement" with religion. Here the Court held that
granting property-tax exemptions to religious groups does not
do that.

Chief Justice Burger's predecessor, Earl Warren, wrote no important religion-clause opinions either for the Court or separately. Burger, however, wrote several of major importance (notably in *Lemon*, Case 13). Here he wrote the opinion of the
Court, expressing the views of five members. Justices William
Brennan and John Harlan, while concurring in the result, wrote

195

separate opinions. Only Justice William Douglas dissented; for him, a tax exemption "is a subsidy." All four opinions aré presented here. They are followed by editorials from the *Washington Post* and *America*.

Participating in *Walz* v. *Tax Commission*, decided May 4, 1970, were Chief Justice Warren E. Burger and Associate Justices Hugo L. Black, William J. Brennan, Jr., William O. Douglas, John M. Harlan II, Thurgood Marshall, Potter Stewart, and Byron R. White. Only eight justices participated; when *Walz* was argued, President Nixon had been unable to fill the seat of Associate Justice Abe Fortas, who had resigned in May 1969.

Opinions

Chief Justice Warren E. Burger delivered the opinion of the Court:

The Establishment and Free Exercise Clauses of the First Amendment are not the most precisely drawn portions of the Constitution. The sweep of the absolute prohibitions in the Religion Clauses may have been calculated; but the purpose was to state an objective, not to write a statute. In attempting to articulate the scope of the two Religion Clauses, the Court's opinions reflect the limitations inherent in formulating general principles on a case-by-case basis. The considerable internal inconsistency in the opinions of the Court derives from what, in retrospect, may have been too sweeping utterances on aspects of these clauses that seemed clear in relation to the particular cases but have limited meaning as general principles.[1]

The Court has struggled to find a neutral course between the two Religion Clauses, both of which are cast in absolute terms, and either of which, if expanded to a logical extreme, would tend to clash with the other. . . .

. . .

The course of constitutional neutrality in this area cannot be an absolutely straight line; rigidity could well defeat the basic purpose of these provisions, which is to insure that no religion be sponsored or favored, none commanded, and none inhibited. The general principle deducible from the First Amendment and all that has been said by the Court is this: that we will not tolerate either governmentally established religion or governmental interference with religion. Short of those expressly proscribed governmental acts there is room for play in the joints productive of a benevolent neutrality which will permit religious exercise to exist without sponsorship and without interference.[2]

Each value judgment under the Religion Clauses must therefore turn on whether particular acts in question are intended to establish

---

1. Note that Chief Justice Burger was less impressed with the Court's religion-clause precedents than were most members of the Vinson and Warren courts.

2. With the possible exception of *Zorach* v. *Clauson* (1952), no previous opinion for the Court in an establishment case had evinced such friendliness toward religion in public life.

or interfere with religious beliefs and practices or have the effect of doing so. Adherence to the policy of neutrality that derives from an accommodation of the Establishment and Free Exercise Clauses has prevented the kind of involvement that would tip the balance toward government control of churches or governmental restraint on religious practice.

. . . No perfect or absolute separation is really possible; the very existence of the Religion Clauses is an involvement of sorts—one that seeks to mark boundaries to avoid excessive entanglement.

. . .

. . . In *Everson* v. *Board of Education* (1947) the Court declined to construe the Religion Clauses with a literalness that would undermine the ultimate constitutional objective as illuminated by history. Surely, bus transportation and police protection to pupils who receive religious instruction "aid" that particular religion to maintain schools that plainly tend to assure future adherents to a particular faith by having control of their total education at an early age. No religious body that maintains schools would deny this as an affirmative if not dominant policy of church schools. But if as in *Everson* buses can be provided to carry and policemen to protect church school pupils, we fail to see how a broader range of police and fire protection given equally to all churches, along with nonprofit hospitals, art galleries, and libraries receiving the same tax exemption, is different for purposes of the Religion Clauses.

Similarly, making textbooks available to pupils in parochial schools in common with public schools was surely an "aid" to the sponsoring churches because it relieved those churches of an enormous aggregate cost for those books. Supplying of costly teaching materials was not seen either as manifesting a legislative purpose to aid or as having a primary effect of aid contravening the First Amendment. *Board of Education* v. *Allen* (1968). In so holding the Court was heeding both its own prior decisions and our religious tradition. Justice Douglas, in *Zorach* v. *Clauson* (1952), after recalling that we "are a religious people whose institutions presuppose a Supreme Being," went on to say:

We make room for as wide a variety of beliefs and creeds as the spiritual needs of man deem necessary. . . . *When the state encourages religious instruction it follows the best of our traditions.* For it then respects the religious nature of our people and accommodates the public service to their spiritual needs. (Emphasis added.)

With all the risks inherent in programs that bring about administrative relationships between public education bodies and church-sponsored schools, we have been able to chart a course that preserved the autonomy and freedom of religious bodies while avoiding any semblance of established religion. This is a "tight rope" and one we have successfully traversed.

The legislative purpose of a property tax exemption is neither the advancement nor the inhibition of religion; it is neither sponsorship nor hostility. New York, in common with the other States, has determined that certain entities that exist in a harmonious relationship to the community at large, and that foster its "moral or mental improvement," should not be inhibited in their activities by property taxation or the hazard of loss of those properties for nonpayment of taxes. It has not singled out one particular church or religious group or even churches as such; rather, it has granted exemption to all houses of religious worship within a broad class of property owned by nonprofit, quasi-public corporations which include hospitals, libraries, playgrounds, scientific, professional, historical, and patriotic groups. The State has an affirmative policy that considers these groups as beneficial and stabilizing influences in community life and finds this classification useful, desirable, and in the public interest. . . .

Governments have not always been tolerant of religious activity, and hostility toward religion has taken many shapes and forms—economic, political, and sometimes harshly oppressive. Grants of exemption historically reflect the concern of authors of constitutions and statutes as to the latent dangers inherent in the imposition of property taxes; exemption constitutes a reasonable and balanced attempt to guard against those dangers. The limits of permissible state accommodation to religion are by no means co-extensive with the noninterference mandated by the Free Exercise Clause. To equate the two would be to deny a national heritage with roots in the Revolution itself. We cannot read New York's statute as attempting to establish religion; it is simply sparing the exercise of religion from the burden of property taxation levied on private profit institutions.

. . .

Determining that the legislative purpose of tax exemption is not aimed at establishing, sponsoring, or supporting religion does not end the inquiry. . . . We must also be sure that the end result—the effect—is not an excessive government entanglement with religion. The test is inescapably one of degree. Either course, taxation of churches or exemption, occasions some degree of involvement with religion. Elimination of exemption would tend to expand the involvement of government by giving rise to tax valuation of church property, tax liens, tax foreclosures, and the direct confrontations and conflicts that follow in the train of those legal processes.

Granting tax exemptions to churches necessarily operates to afford an indirect economic benefit and also gives rise to some, but yet a lesser, involvement than taxing them. In analyzing either alternative the questions are whether the involvement is excessive, and whether it is a continuing one calling for official and continuing surveillance leading to an impermissible degree of entanglement. Obviously a direct money subsidy would be a relationship pregnant with involvement and, as with most governmental grant programs, could encompass sustained and detailed administrative relationships for enforcement of statutory or administrative standards, but that is not this case. The hazards of churches supporting government are hardly less in their potential than the hazards of government supporting churches; each relationship carries some involvement rather than the desired insulation and separation. We cannot ignore the instances in history when church support of government led to the kind of involvement we seek to avoid.

The grant of a tax exemption is not sponsorship since the government does not transfer part of its revenue to churches but simply abstains from demanding that the church support the state. No one has ever suggested that tax exemption has converted libraries, art galleries, or hospitals into arms of the state or put employees "on the public payroll." There is no genuine nexus between tax exemption and establishment of religion. . . . The exemption creates only a minimal and remote involvement between church and state and far less than taxation of churches. It restricts the fiscal relationship between church and state, and tends to complement and reinforce the desired separation insulating each from the other.

Separation in this context cannot mean absence of all contact; the complexities of modern life inevitably produce some contact and the fire and police protection received by houses of religious worship are no more than incidental benefits accorded all persons or institutions within a State's boundaries, along with many other exempt organizations. . . .

All of the fifty States provide for tax exemption of places of worship, most of them doing so by constitutional guarantees. For so long as federal income taxes have had any potential impact on churches—over seventy-five years—religious organizations have been expressly exempt from the tax. Such treatment is an "aid" to churches no more and no less in principle than the real estate tax exemption granted by States.

Few concepts are more deeply embedded in the fabric of our national life, beginning with pre-Revolutionary colonial times, than for the government to exercise at the very least this kind of benevolent neutrality toward churches and religious exercise generally so long as none was favored over others and none suffered interference.

. . .

. . . [N]o one acquires a vested or protected right in violation of the Constitution by long use, even when that span of time covers our entire national existence and indeed predates it. Yet an unbroken practice of according the exemption to churches, openly and by affirmative state action, not covertly or by state inaction, is not something to be lightly cast aside. . . .

Nothing in this national attitude toward religious tolerance and two centuries of uninterrupted freedom from taxation has given the remotest sign of leading to an established church or religion and on the contrary it has operated affirmatively to help guarantee the free exercise of all forms of religious belief. Thus, it is hardly useful to suggest that tax exemption is but the "foot in the door" or the "nose of the camel in the tent" leading to an established church. If tax exemption can be seen as this first step toward "establishment" of religion, as Mr. Justice Douglas fears, the second step has been long in coming. Any move that realistically "establishes" a church or tends to do so can be dealt with "while this Court sits."

. . .

The argument that making "fine distinctions" between what is and what is not absolute under the Constitution is to render us a government of men, not laws, gives too little weight to the fact that it is an essential part of adjudication to draw distinctions, including fine ones, in the process of interpreting the Constitution. We must frequently decide, for example, what are "reasonable" searches and seizures under the Fourth Amendment. Determining what acts of government tend to establish or interfere with religion falls well within what courts have long been called upon to do in sensitive areas.

. . .

It appears that at least up to 1885 this Court, reflecting more than a century of our history and uninterrupted practice, accepted without discussion the proposition that federal or state grants of tax exemption to churches were not a violation of the Religion Clauses of the First Amendment. As to the New York statute, we now confirm that view.

Justice William J. Brennan, Jr., concurring:

The existence from the beginning of the Nation's life of a practice, such as tax exemptions for religious organizations, is not conclusive of its constitutionality. But such practice is a fact of considerable import in the interpretation of abstract constitutional language. On its face, the Establishment Clause is reasonably susceptible of different interpretations regarding the exemptions. This Court's interpretation of the clause, accordingly, is appropriately influenced by the reading it has received in the practices of the Nation. . . . The more longstanding and widely accepted a practice, the greater its impact upon constitutional interpretation. History is particularly compelling in the present case because of the undeviating acceptance given religious tax exemptions from our earliest days as a Nation. Rarely if ever has this Court considered the constitutionality of a practice for which the historical support is so overwhelming.

The Establishment Clause, along with the other provisions of the Bill of Rights, was ratified by the States in 1791. Religious tax exemptions were not an issue in the petitions calling for the Bill of Rights, in the pertinent congressional debates, or in the debates preceding ratification by the States. The absence of concern about the exemptions could not have resulted from failure to foresee the possibility of their existence, for they were widespread during colonial days. Rather, it seems clear that the exemptions were not among the evils that the Framers and Ratifiers of the Establishment Clause sought to avoid. Significantly, within a decade after ratification, at least four States passed statutes exempting the property of religious organizations from taxation.

. . .

The exemptions have continued uninterrupted to the present day. They are in force in all fifty states. No judicial decision, state or federal, has ever held that they violate the Establishment Clause. . . .

. . .

Government has two basic secular purposes for granting real property tax exemptions to religious organizations. First, these organizations are exempted because they, among a range of other private, nonprofit organizations contribute to the well-being of the community in a variety of nonreligious ways, and thereby bear burdens that would otherwise either have to be met by general taxation, or be left undone to the detriment of the community. . . .

Appellant seeks to avoid the force of this secular purpose of the exemptions by limiting his challenge to "exemptions from real property taxation to religious organizations on real property used exclusively for religious purposes." Appellant assumes, apparently, that church-owned property is used for exclusively religious purposes if it does not house a hospital, orphanage, weekday school, or the like. Any assumption that a church building itself is used for exclusively religious activities, however, rests on a simplistic view of ordinary church operations. As the appellee's brief cogently observes, "the public welfare activities and the sectarian activities of religious institutions are . . . intertwined. . . . Often a particular church will use the same personnel, facilities and source of funds to carry out both its secular and religious activities." Thus, the same people who gather in church facilities for religious worship and study may return to these facilities to participate in Boy Scout activities, to promote antipoverty causes, to discuss public issues, or to listen to chamber music. Accordingly, the funds used to maintain the facilities as a place for religious worship and study also maintain them as a place for secular activities beneficial to the community as a whole. Even during formal worship services, churches frequently collect the funds used to finance their secular operations and make decisions regarding their nature.

Second, government grants exemptions to religious organizations because they uniquely contribute to the pluralism of American society by their religious activities. Government may properly include religious institutions among the variety of private, nonprofit groups that receive tax exemptions, for each group contributes to the diversity of association, viewpoint, and enterprise essential to a vigorous, pluralistic society. . . . To this end, New York extends its exemptions not only to religious and social service organizations but also to scientific, literary, bar, library, patriotic, and historical groups, and generally to institutions "organized exclusively for the moral or mental improvement of men and women." . . .

Although governmental purposes for granting religious exemptions may be wholly secular, exemptions can nonetheless violate the Establishment Clause if they result in extensive state involvement with religion. Accordingly, those who urge the exemptions' unconstitutionality argue that exemptions are the equivalent of governmental subsidy of churches. General subsidies of religious activities would of course, constitute impermissible state involvement with religion.

Tax exemptions and general subsidies, however, are qualitatively different. Though both provide economic assistance, they do so in fundamentally different ways. A subsidy involves the direct transfer of public monies to the subsidized enterprise and uses resources exacted from taxpayers as a whole. An exemption, on the other hand, involves no such transfer. It assists the exempted enterprise only passively, by relieving a privately funded venture of the burden of paying taxes. . . .

. . .

. . . I must conclude that the exemptions do not "serve the essentially religious activities of religious institutions." Their principal effect is to carry out secular purposes—the encouragement of public service activities and of a pluralistic society. During their ordinary operations, most churches engage in activities of a secular nature that benefit the community; and all churches by their existence contribute to the diversity of association, viewpoint, and enterprise. . . .

Nor do I find that the exemptions "employ the organs of government for essentially religious purposes." To the extent that the exemptions further secular ends, they do not advance "essentially religious purposes." To the extent that purely religious activities are benefitted by the exemptions, the benefit is passive. Government does not affirmatively foster these activities by exempting religious organizations from taxes, as it would were it to subsidize them. The exemption simply leaves untouched that which adherents of the organization bring into being and maintain.

Finally, I do not think that the exemptions "use essentially religious means to serve governmental ends, where secular means would suffice." The means churches use to carry on their public service activities are not "essentially religious" in nature. They are the same means used by any purely secular organization—money, human time and skills, physical facilities. It is true that each church contributes to the pluralism of our society through its purely religious activities, but the state encourages these activities not because it champions religion per se but because it values religion among a variety of private, non-profit enterprises that contribute to the diversity of the Nation. Viewed in this light, there is no nonreligious substitute for religion as an element in our societal mosaic, just as there is no nonliterary substitute for literary groups.

Justice John M. Harlan II, concurring in the result:

I think it relevant to face up to the fact that it is far easier to agree on the purpose that underlies the First Amendment's Establishment and Free Exercise Clauses than to obtain agreement on the standards that should govern their application. What is at stake as a matter of policy is preventing that kind and degree of government involvement in religious life that, as history teaches us, is apt to lead to strife and frequently strain a political system to the breaking point.

Two requirements frequently articulated and applied in our cases for achieving this goal are "neutrality" and "voluntarism." These related and mutually reinforcing concepts are short-form for saying that the Government must neither legislate to accord benefits that favor religion over nonreligion, nor sponsor a particular sect, nor try to encourage participation in or abnegation of religion. . . . In the vast majority of cases the inquiry, albeit an elusive one, can end at this point. Neutrality and voluntarism stand as barriers against the most egregious and hence divisive kinds of state involvement in religious matters.

While these concepts are at the "core" of the Religion Clauses, they may not suffice by themselves to achieve in all cases the purposes of the First Amendment. As Professor [Paul] Freund has only recently pointed out in "Public Aid to Parochial Schools," 82 *Harvard Law Review* 1680 (1969), governmental involvement, while neutral, may be so direct or in such degree as to engender a risk of politicizing religion. Thus, as the opinion of the Chief Justice notes, religious groups inevitably represent certain points of view and not infrequently assert them in the political arena, as evidenced by the continuing debate respecting birth control and abortion laws. Yet history cautions that political fragmentation on sectarian lines must be guarded against. Although the very fact of neutrality may limit the intensity of involvement, government participation in certain programs, whose very nature is apt to entangle the state in details of administration and planning, may escalate to the point of inviting undue fragmentation.

This legislation neither encourages nor discourages participation in religious life and thus satisfies the voluntarism requirement of the First Amendment. Unlike the instances of school prayers or "released time" programs, the State is not "utilizing the prestige, power, and influence" of a public institution to bring religion into the lives of citizens.

The statute also satisfies the requirement of neutrality. Neutrality in its application requires an equal protection mode of analysis. The Court must survey meticulously the circumstances of governmental categories to eliminate, as it were, religious gerrymanders. In any particular case the critical question is whether the circumference of legislation encircles a class so broad that it can be fairly concluded that religious institutions could be thought to fall within the natural perimeter.

The statute that implements New York's constitutional provision for tax exemptions to religious organizations has defined a class of nontaxable entities whose common denominator is their nonprofit pursuit of activities devoted to cultural and moral improvement and the doing of "good works" by performing certain social services in the community that might otherwise have to be assumed by government. . . .

. . .

Whether the present exemption entails that degree of involvement with government that presents a threat of fragmentation along religious lines involves, for me, a more subtle question than deciding simply whether neutrality has been violated. Unlike the subsidy that my Brother Douglas foresees as the next step down the road, tax exemptions to nonprofit organizations are an institution in themselves, so much so that they are, as The Chief Justice points out, expected and accepted as a matter of course. In the instant case noninvolvement is further assured by the neutrality and breadth of the exemption. In the context of an exemption so sweeping as the one before us here its administration need not entangle government in difficult classifications of what is or is not religious, for any organization—although not religious in a customary sense—would qualify under the pervasive rubric of a group dedicated to the moral and cultural improvement of men. . . .

I agree with my Brother Douglas that exemptions do not differ from subsidies as an economic matter. Aside from the longstanding tradition behind exemptions there are other differences, however. Subsidies, unlike exemptions, must be passed on periodically and thus invite more political controversy than exemptions. Moreover, subsidies or direct aid, as a general rule, are granted on the basis of enumerated and more complicated qualifications and frequently involve the state in administration to a higher degree. . . .

Whether direct or subsidies aid entail that degree of involvement that is prohibited by the Constitution is a question that must be reserved for a later case upon a record that fully develops all the pertinent considerations such as the significance and character of subsidies in our political system and the role of the government in administering the subsidy in relation to the particular program aided. It may also be that the States, while bound to observe strict neutrality, should be freer to experiment with involvement—on a neutral basis—than the Federal Government.[3]

I recognize that for those who seek inflexible solutions this tripartite analysis provides little comfort. It is always possible to shrink from a

---

3. Justice Harlan believed that in certain areas—and "experiments" involving religion were one—the states should have greater latitude than the federal government. Harlan stated this view in his separate opinion in *Roth* v. *United States*, 354 U.S. 476 (1957).

first step lest the momentum will plunge the law into pitfalls that lie in the trail ahead. I, for one, however, do not believe that a "slippery slope" is necessarily without a constitutional toehold. Like The Chief Justice, I am of the view that it is the task of this tribunal to "draw distinctions, including fine ones, in the process of interpreting the Constitution." The prospect of difficult questions of judgment in constitutional law should not be the basis for prohibiting legislative action that is constitu⋅ionally permissible. I think this one is.

Justice William O. Douglas, dissenting:

There is a line between what a State may do in encouraging "religious" activities and what a State may not do by using its resources to promote "religious" activities, or bestowing benefits because of them. Yet that line may not always be clear. Closing public schools on Sunday is in the former category; subsidizing churches, in my view, is in the latter. Indeed I would suppose that in common understanding one of the best ways to "establish" one or more religions is to subsidize them, which a tax exemption does. . . .

In affirming this judgment the Court largely overlooks the revolution initiated by the adoption of the Fourteenth Amendment. That revolution involved the imposition of new and far-reaching constitutional restraints on the States. Nationalization of many civil liberties has been the consequence of the Fourteenth Amendment. . . .

[Justice Douglas discusses the "steady" process of "selective incorporation of various provisions of the Bill of Rights into the Fourteenth Amendment." He observes that judicial decisions pursuant to the application of the religion clauses to the states, such as Engel v. Vitale (1962), have had "unsettling effects"—effects that he does not consider objectionable.]

Hence the question in the present case makes irrelevant the "two centuries of uninterrupted freedom from taxation," referred to by the Court. If history be our guide, then tax exemption of church property in this country is indeed highly suspect, as it arose in the early days when the church was an agency of the state. . . .

With all due respect the governing principle is not controlled by Everson. Everson involved the use of public funds to bus children to parochial as well as to public schools. Parochial schools teach religion; yet they are also educational institutions offering courses competitive with public schools. They prepare students for the professions and for activities in all walks of life. Education in the secular sense was combined with religious indoctrination at the parochial schools involved in *Everson*. Even so, the *Everson* decision was five to four and, though one of the five, I have since had grave doubts about it, because I have become convinced that grants to institutions teaching a sectarian creed violate the Establishment Clause.[4]

This case, however, is quite different. Education is not involved. The financial support rendered here is to the church, the place of worship. A tax exemption is a subsidy. . . .

The problem takes us back where Madison was in 1784 and 1785 when he battled the *Assessment Bill* in Virginia. That bill levied a tax for the support of Christian churches, leaving to each taxpayer the choice as to "what society of Christians" he wanted the tax paid; and absent such designation, the tax was to go for education. Even so, Madison was unrelenting in his opposition. . . .

[Madison's] *Remonstrance* stirred up such a storm of popular protest that the Assessment Bill was defeated.

The *Remonstrance* covers some aspects of the present subsidy, including Madison's protest in paragraph three to a requirement that any person be compelled to contribute even "three pence" to support a church. All men, he maintained in paragraph four, enter society "on equal conditions," including the right to free exercise of religion. . . .

Madison's assault on the *Assessment Bill* was in fact an assault based on both the concepts of "free exercise" and "establishment" of religion later embodied in the First Amendment. Madison, whom we recently called "the leading architect of the religion clauses of the First Amendment" (*Flast* v. *Cohen*, 392 U.S. 83 [1968]), was indeed their author and chief promoter. . . .

. . .

State aid to places of worship, whether in the form of direct grants or tax exemption, takes us back to the *Assessment Bill* and the *Remonstrance*. The church *qua* church would not be entitled to that support from believers and from nonbelievers alike. Yet the church *qua* nonprofit, charitable institution is one of many that receive a form of subsidy through tax exemption. To be sure, the New York statute does not single out the church for grant or favor. It includes churches in a long list of nonprofit organizations. . . . While the beneficiaries cover a wide range, "atheistic," "agnostic," or "antitheological" groups do not seem to be included.

Churches perform some functions that a State would constitution-

---

4. Justice Douglas here cites his concurrence in *Engel*, where he expressed "grave doubts" about the holding in *Everson*.

ally be empowered to perform. I refer to nonsectarian social welfare operations such as the care of orphaned children and the destitute and people who are sick. A tax exemption to agencies performing those functions would therefore be as constitutionally proper as the grant of direct subsidies to them. Under the First Amendment a State may not, however, provide worship if private groups fail to do so. . . .

. . .

The exemptions provided here insofar as welfare projects are concerned may have the ring of neutrality. But subsidies either through direct grant or tax exemption for sectarian causes, whether carried on by church *qua* church or by church *qua* welfare agency, must be treated differently, lest we in time allow the church *qua* church to be on the public payroll, which, I fear, is imminent.

. . .

The religiously used real estate of the churches today constitutes a vast domain. . . . Their assets total over $141 billion and their annual income at least $22 billion. And the extent to which they are feeding from the public trough in a variety of forms is alarming.

We are advised that since 1968 at least five States have undertaken to give subsidies to parochial and other private schools—Pennsylvania, Ohio, New York, Connecticut, and Rhode Island. And it is reported that under two federal Acts, the Elementary and Secondary Education Act of 1965 and the Higher Education Act of 1965, *billions of dollars* have been granted to parochial and other private schools.

. . .

If believers are entitled to public financial support, so are nonbelievers. A believer and nonbeliever under the present law are treated differently because of the articles of their faith. Believers are doubtless comforted that the cause of religion is being fostered by this legislation. Yet one of the mandates of the First Amendment is to promote a viable, pluralistic society and to keep government neutral, not only between sects, but also between believers and nonbelievers. The present involvement of government in religion may seem *de minimis*. But it is, I fear, a long step down the Establishment path. Perhaps I have been misinformed. But as I have read the Constitution and its philosophy, I gathered that independence was the price of liberty.

I conclude that this tax exemption is unconstitutional.

[Justice Douglas appended to his opinion copies of the Assessment Bill and the "Memorial and Remonstrance" as appended to Justice Wiley Rutledge's dissent in *Everson* v. *Board of Education*.]

Responses

From the **Washington Post,** May 11, 1970, "The Supreme Court and the Churches":

· The Supreme Court's decision upholding tax-exemption for churches is significant largely because the Court had previously seemed to look in the other direction. Actually freedom of religion from taxes has been an established policy throughout our history. All of the fifty states give the churches exemption, and the same policy has been written into the federal income tax laws for seventy-five years. "Few concepts are more deeply embedded in the fabric of our national life, beginning with pre-Revolutionary colonial times," Chief Justice Burger wrote in his opinion for the Court, "than for the government to exercise at the very least this kind of benevolent neutrality toward churches and religious exercises generally so long as none was favored over others and none suffered interference."

But Justice Black had written in his *Everson* opinion (1947) that "Neither a state nor the Federal Government can . . . pass laws which aid one religion, *aid all religions,* or prefer one religion over another." The Court has now eaten the three troublesome words in that sentence, with Justice Black's concurrence, while clinging to the principle of general separation of church and state and to the necessity of treating all religious organizations alike. Perhaps, however, the shift of ground is more apparent than real. It has often been noted that the result of the *Everson* decision was to validate benefits which New Jersey conferred upon the churches by allowing use of tax funds to pay the bus fares of children attending parochial schools. In any event, the Court has now cleared away the confusion that flowed from Justice Black's sweeping *obiter dicta.*

The new statement to which the Court adheres is an admirable generality: "that we will not tolerate either governmentally established religion or governmental interference with religion." This recognizes that no absolute separation of church and state is possible, but that each must be kept in its proper sphere, with the Supreme Court in the role of final arbiter. . . .

Fortunately, there was no pretense on the part of the Court that tax exemption does not aid religion. Obviously it is a privilege of enormous value. Yet, the Chief Justice insisted, "the exemption creates only a minimal and remote involvement between church and state and far less than taxation of churches." This decision has gone a long way toward clearing away the confusion resulting from the "too sweeping utterances" in some related opinions of the past.

210

*From **Charles M. Whelan**, "The Walz Case," in **America**,*
May 16, 1970:

In the long run the *Walz* decision may be remembered more for the fresh air it has breathed into church-state discussions than for its vindication of church tax exemptions. . . .

Chief Justice Burger's opinion for the court is remarkable for its candor and vigor. The Chief Justice speaks plainly of the "considerable internal inconsistency" of the court's earlier church-state decisions. He admits that there is a serious problem in reconciling the demands of the Free Exercise and No Establishment clauses of the First Amendment. He insists that making "fine distinctions" between what is and what is not absolute under the Constitution is an essential part of constitutional adjudication.

From a technical, legal point of view, the most interesting problem in *Walz* was how the Supreme Court would relate its decision to the constitutional test it had announced in the *Schempp* case of 1963 and reaffirmed in the *Allen* case of 1968. Under that test, for a statute to avoid conflict with the No Establishment clause of the First Amendment, the statute had to have "a secular legislative purpose and a primary effect that neither advances nor inhibits religion."

In *Schempp* the Supreme Court applied this test and struck down the practice of reciting the Lord's Prayer or reading verses from the Bible at the beginning of the public school day. In *Allen* the court again applied the test and sustained the inclusion of parochial school children in a New York textbook-lending for all school children in grades seven to twelve.

In view of this recent reliance and emphasis by the Supreme Court on the *Schempp* test, it is striking that Chief Justice Burger's opinion for the court in *Walz* does not even mention the *Schempp* case. The Chief Justice does mention the *Allen* case, with strong approval of its holding, but he does not base his argument for the constitutionality of church tax exemptions squarely on the *Schempp-Allen* test.

What the Chief Justice does, instead, is to rewrite the basic approach of the Supreme Court to church-state questions. He lays to rest (forever, I hope) the key argument of Leo Pfeffer and the American Civil Liberties Union that the *Everson* decision of 1947 means that any governmental program that results in aid to religion is unconstitutional.

The Chief Justice praises the "eminently sensible and realistic application" of the First Amendment by the Court in the *Everson* case—an application that upheld the constitutionality of including parochial school children in a transportation program for all school children. But the Chief Justice also points out that the reasoning in the *Everson* opinion gives good grounds for the perplexity and abundantly illustrates "the hazards of placing too much weight on a few words or phrases of the court."

Although the Chief Justice, in the tradition of many of his predecessors, never says flatly that he is announcing a new church-state philosophy for the Supreme Court, he leaves no room for doubt that the Court, in its long deliberation on the *Walz* case, has come to recognize and admit the shortcomings of its earlier types of reasoning. . . .

What, then, is the new approach of the Supreme Court? It is an approach of "benevolent neutrality," a concept that will undoubtedly occupy, if not perplex, church-state students for some time to come. . . .

The emphasis by the court on the concept of "excessive entanglement" is one of the new notes struck in the *Walz* opinion. The court has spoken of the dangers of entanglement before, but never with such reliance on them as a constitutional touchstone. In effect, the court has held that proof that a statute with a secular purpose does not result in undue entanglement of the government in church affairs will substitute for the *Schempp* requirement that a statute must have "a primary [secular] effect that neither advances nor inhibits religion."

The Chief Justice's opinion enjoyed the full support of Justices Black, Stewart, White and Marshall and the "basic agreement" of Justice Harlan. Justice Brennan concurred in the result but preferred to abide by the line of reasoning he first explained in his concurring opinion in the *Schempp* case of 1963. Although this line of reasoning differs in some important particulars from that announced by the Chief Justice for the court in the *Walz* case, the thrust of Justice Brennan's reasoning is generally similar.

It is beyond doubt, therefore, that *Walz* is the tombstone of the type of No Establishment reasoning used by the court in the *Everson* case of 1947. Henceforth, lower federal and state courts will not have to wrestle with arguments based on an absolutist interpretation of the "no tax, no aid" language of *Everson*.

It by no means follows, however, that the defenders of the constitutionality of the inclusion of church-related schools in governmental aid-to-education programs can now rest easy. The *Walz* decision will be of great assistance to them, especially in dealing with the "no aid" language of *Everson*. But it must always be remembered that Mr. Justice Black, who joined with the Chief Justice's opinion in *Walz*, voted against the constitutionality of including parochial school children in the textbook program in *Allen*. There could be no clearer proof that *Walz* can be read both ways on the school aid question.

13

Lemon v. *Kurtzman*

403 U.S. 602 (1971)

B y the end of the sixties it appeared that under the Supreme
Court's First Amendment jurisprudence a state might be
free to assist secular education in parochial schools provided
none of the state money supported instruction in religion. In
1971, the Court explicitly addressed this question in *Tilton* v.
Richardson (403 U.S. 672) and *Lemon* v. *Kurtzman*, cases distinguished from each other primarily by the fact that in *Tilton* the
state aid went to higher education, while in *Lemon* it went to precollege education.

This distinction proved critical to the Court as it decided the
two cases. In *Tilton* the Court sustained federal grants to
church-related colleges and universities for the construction of
buildings used for secular purposes, but in *Lemon* it struck down
state laws of Pennsylvania (No. 89) and Rhode Island (Nos. 569
and 570) that supported instructors engaged in teaching secular
subjects in church-related elementary and secondary schools.
Lemon actually consisted of three separate cases decided together.

In *Tilton*, decided the same day as *Lemon*, no opinion was written for the Court. *Lemon* is the case with major doctrinal significance, for here the Court majority announced for the first time
a three-part test for determining whether a challenged governmental action passes constitutional muster. Applying the *Lemon*
test in subsequent cases involving state aid to religious schools,
the Court handed down a series of decisions that seemed contradictory. In the eighties, the Court grew skeptical about the
utility of the *Lemon* test, refusing to apply it in 1983 in *Marsh* v.

Chambers, when it upheld a legislative chaplaincy against constitutional challenge; see Case 19. The Court, however, rejected invitations to scrap the test, which has attracted substantial scholarly discussion. Few critics have been entirely satisfied with it. For a brief summary of the scholarly literature on the test, see the entry "Lemon Test" in Kermit L. Hall, ed., *The Oxford Companion to the Supreme Court of the United States* (New York: Oxford University Press, 1992).

Chief Justice Warren Burger wrote for the Court in *Lemon*, expressing the views of seven (on Nos. 569 and 570) and six (on No. 89) members. There were three other opinions, two of which are presented here, as are editorial responses from the *Washington Post, The New Republic*, and *Christianity and Crisis*.

Participating in the two cases from Rhode Island, Nos. 569 and 570, were Chief Justice Warren E. Burger and Associate Justices Hugo L. Black, Harry A. Blackmun, William J. Brennan, Jr., William O. Douglas, John M. Harlan II, Thurgood Marshall, Potter Stewart, and Byron R. White. All but Justice Marshall participated in the case from Pennsylvania, No. 89. The decisions were handed down on June 28, 1971.

Opinions

Chief Justice Warren E. Burger delivered the opinion of the
Court:

In _Everson_ v. _Board of Education_ (1947), this Court upheld a state statute that reimbursed the parents of parochial school children for bus transportation expenses. There Justice Black, writing for the majority, suggested that the decision carried to "the verge" of forbidden territory under the Religion Clauses. Candor compels acknowledgment, moreover, that we can only dimly perceive the lines of demarcation in this extraordinarily sensitive area of constitutional law.

The language of the Religion Clauses of the First Amendment is at best opaque, particularly when compared with other portions of the Amendment. Its authors did not simply prohibit the establishment of a state church or a state religion, an area history shows they regarded as very important and fraught with great dangers. Instead they commanded that there should be "no law _respecting_ an establishment of religion." A law may be one "respecting" the forbidden objective while falling short of its total realization. A law "respecting" the proscribed result, that is, the establishment of religion, is not always easily identifiable as one violative of the Clause. A given law might not _establish_ a state religion but nevertheless be one "respecting" that end in the sense of being a step that could lead to such establishment and hence offend the First Amendment.

In the absence of precisely stated constitutional prohibitions, we must draw lines with reference to the three main evils against which the Establishment Clause was intended to afford protection: "sponsorship, financial support, and active involvement of the sovereign in religious activity." _Walz_ v. _Tax Commission_ (1970).

Every analysis in this area must begin with consideration of the cumulative criteria developed by the Court over many years. Three such tests may be gleaned from our cases. First, the statute must have a secular legislative purpose; second, its principal or primary effect must be one that neither advances nor inhibits religion, _Board of Education_ v.

215

Allen (1968); finally, the statute must not foster "an excessive government entanglement with religion." *Walz*.[1]

Inquiry into the legislative purposes of the Pennsylvania and Rhode Island statutes affords no basis for a conclusion that the legislative intent was to advance religion. On the contrary, the statutes themselves clearly state that they are intended to enhance the quality of the secular education in all schools covered by the compulsory attendance laws. There is no reason to believe the legislatures meant anything else. A State always has a legitimate concern for maintaining minimum standards in all·schools it allows to operate. As in *Allen*, we find nothing here that undermines the stated legislative intent; it must therefore be accorded appropriate deference.

In *Allen*, the Court acknowledged that secular and religious teachings were not necessarily so intertwined that secular textbooks furnished to students by the State were in fact instrumental in the teaching of religion. The legislatures of Rhode Island and Pennsylvania have concluded that secular and religious education are identifiable and separable. In the abstract we have no quarrel with this conclusion.

The two legislatures, however, have also recognized that church-related elementary and secondary schools have a significant religious mission and that a substantial portion of their activities is religiously oriented. They have therefore sought to create statutory restrictions designed to guarantee the separation between secular and religious educational functions and to ensure that State financial aid supports only the former. All these provisions are precautions taken in candid recognition that these programs approached, even if they did not intrude upon, the forbidden areas under the Religion Clauses. We need not decide whether these legislative precautions restrict the principal or primary effect of the programs to the point where they do not offend the Religion Clauses, for we conclude that the cumulative impact of the entire relationship arising under the statutes in each State involves excessive entanglement between government and religion.

---

1. These criteria soon became known as the *Lemon* test. The first and second parts of the test, drawing on doctrine dating from *Everson*, were first stated by Justice Tom C. Clark in his opinion for the Court in *Abington School District* v. *Schempp* (1963) and subsequently articulated by the Court in *Allen*. They amount to a rephrasing of the Child Benefit Theory of *Everson*. The third part of the test was first stated by the Court in *Walz*. Under *Lemon*, failure to pass any of the three parts is apparently enough to condemn a government action as unconstitutional.

Cases since *Lemon* have falsified the Court's statement that "every analysis in this area must begin with consideration" of the three-part test. See, for example, *Marsh* v. *Chambers* (1983), Case 19, in which the Court, dispensing with the *Lemon* test, held that a state legislative chaplaincy does not violate the First Amendment.

In *Walz*, the Court upheld state tax exemptions for real property owned by religious organizations and used for religious worship. That holding, however, tended to confine rather than enlarge the area of permissible state involvement with religious institutions by calling for close scrutiny of the degree of entanglement involved in the relationship. The objective is to prevent, as far as possible, the intrusion of either into the precincts of the other.

Our prior holdings do not call for total separation between church and state; total separation is not possible in an absolute sense. Some relationship between government and religious organizations is inevitable. Fire inspections, building and zoning regulations, and state requirements under compulsory school-attendance laws are examples of necessary and permissible contacts. . . . Judicial caveats against entanglement must recognize that the line of separation, far from being a "wall," is a blurred, indistinct, and variable barrier depending on all the circumstances of a particular relationship.

. . .

In order to determine whether the government entanglement with religion is excessive, we must examine the character and purposes of the institutions that are benefited, the nature of the aid that the State provides, and the resulting relationship between the government and the religious authority. . . .

The Rhode Island Program

The District Court made extensive findings on the grave potential for excessive entanglement that inheres in the religious character and purpose of the Roman Catholic elementary schools of Rhode Island, to date the sole beneficiaries of the Rhode Island Salary Supplement Act.

The church schools involved in the program are located close to parish churches. This understandably permits convenient access for religious exercises since instruction in faith and morals is part of the total educational process. The school buildings contain identifying religious symbols such as crosses on the exterior and crucifixes . . . religious paintings and statues either in the classrooms or hallways. Although only approximately thirty minutes a day are devoted to direct religious instruction, there are religiously oriented extracurricular activities. Approximately two-thirds of the teachers in these schools are nuns of various religious orders. Their dedicated efforts provide an atmosphere in which religious instruction and religious vocations are natural and proper parts of life in such schools. Indeed, as the District Court found, the role of teaching nuns in enhancing the religious atmosphere has led the parochial school authorities to attempt to maintain a one-to-one ratio between nuns and lay teachers in all schools rather than to permit some to be staffed almost entirely by lay teachers.

On the basis of these findings the District Court concluded that the parochial schools constituted "an integral part of the religious mission of the Catholic Church." The various characteristics of the schools make them "a powerful vehicle for transmitting the Catholic faith to the next generation." This process of inculcating religious doctrine is, of course, enhanced by the impressionable age of the pupils, in primary schools particularly. In short, parochial schools involve substantial religious activity and purpose.

The substantial religious character of these church-related schools gives rise to entangling church-state relationships of the kind the Religion Clauses sought to avoid. Although the District Court found that concern for religious values did not inevitably or necessarily intrude into the content of secular subjects, the considerable religious activities of these schools led the legislature to provide for careful governmental controls and surveillance by state authorities in order to ensure that state aid supports only secular education.

The dangers and corresponding entanglements are enhanced by the particular form of aid that the Rhode Island Act provides. Our decisions from *Everson* to *Allen* have permitted the States to provide church-related schools with secular, neutral, or nonideological services, facilities, or materials. Bus transportation, school lunches, public health services, and secular textbooks supplied in common to all students were not thought to offend the Establishment Clause. . . .

In *Allen* the Court refused to make assumptions, on a meager record, about the religious content of the textbooks that the State would be asked to provide. We cannot, however, refuse here to recognize that teachers have a substantially different ideological character from books. In terms of potential for involving some aspect of faith or morals in secular subjects, a textbook's content is ascertainable, but a teacher's handling of a subject is not. We cannot ignore the danger that a teacher under religious control and discipline poses to the separation of the religious from the purely secular aspects of precollege education. The conflict of functions inheres in the situation.

In our view the record shows these dangers are present to a substantial degree. The Rhode Island Roman Catholic elementary schools are under the general supervision of the Bishop of Providence and his appointed representative, the Diocesan Superintendent of Schools. In most cases, each individual parish, however, assumes the ultimate financial responsibility for the school, with the parish priest authorizing the allocation of parish funds. With only two exceptions, school principals are nuns appointed either by the Superintendent or the Mother Provincial of the order whose members staff the school. By 1969, lay teachers constituted more than a third of all teachers in the parochial elementary schools, and their number is growing. They are first interviewed by the superintendent's office and then by the school principal. The contracts are signed by the parish priest, and he retains some discretion in negotiating salary levels. Religious authority necessarily pervades the school system.

The schools are governed by the standards set forth in a "Handbook of School Regulations," which has the force of synodal law in the diocese. It emphasizes the role and importance of the teacher in parochial schools: "The prime factor for the success or the failure of the school is the spirit and personality, as well as the professional competency, of the teacher. . . ." The Handbook also states that "Religious formation is not confined to formal courses; nor is it restricted to a single subject area." Finally, the Handbook advises teachers to stimulate interest in religious vocations and missionary work. Given the mission of the church school, these instructions are consistent and logical.

. . .

. . . [A] dedicated religious person, teaching in a school affiliated with his or her faith and operated to inculcate its tenets, will inevitably experience great difficulty in remaining religiously neutral. . . . With the best of intentions such a teacher would find it hard to make a total separation between secular teaching and religious doctrine. What would appear to some to be essential to good citizenship might well for others border on or constitute instruction in religion. Further difficulties are inherent in the combination of religious discipline and the possibility of disagreement between teacher and religious authorities over the meaning of the statutory restrictions.

We do not assume, however, that parochial school teachers will be unsuccessful in their attempts to segregate their religious beliefs from their secular educational responsibilities. But the potential for impermissible fostering of religion is present. The Rhode Island Legislature has not, and could not, provide state aid on the basis of a mere assumption that secular teachers under religious discipline can avoid conflicts. The State must be certain, given the Religion Clauses, that subsidized teachers do not inculcate religion—indeed the State here has undertaken to do so. To ensure that no trespass occurs, the State has therefore carefully conditioned its aid with pervasive restrictions. An eligible recipient must teach only those courses that are offered in the public schools and use only those texts and materials that are found in the public schools. In addition the teacher must not engage in teaching any course in religion.

A comprehensive, discriminating, and continuing state surveillance will inevitably be required to ensure that these restrictions are obeyed and the First Amendment otherwise respected. Unlike a book, a teacher cannot be inspected once so as to determine the extent and intent of his or her personal beliefs and subjective acceptance of the limitations imposed by the First Amendment. These prophylactic contacts will involve excessive and enduring entanglement between state and church.

. . . The statute excludes teachers employed by non-public schools whose average per-pupil expenditures on secular education equal or exceed the comparable figures for public schools. In the event that the total expenditures of an otherwise eligible school exceed this norm, the program requires the government to examine the school's records in order to determine how much of the total expenditures is attributable to secular eduction and how much to religious activity. This kind of state inspection and evaluation of the religious content of a religious organization is fraught with . . . entanglement that the Constitution forbids. . . .

The Pennsylvania Program

The Pennsylvania statute also provides state aid to church-related schools for teachers' salaries. The complaint describes an educational system that is very similar to the one existing in Rhode Island. According to the allegations, the church-related elementary and secondary schools are controlled by religious organizations, have the purpose of propagating and promoting a particular religious faith, and conduct their operations to fulfill that purpose. Since this complaint was dismissed for failure to state a claim for relief, we must accept these allegations as true for purposes of our review.

As we noted earlier, the very restrictions and surveillance necessary to ensure that teachers play a strictly nonideological role give rise to entanglements between church and state. The Pennsylvania statute, like that of Rhode Island, fosters this kind of relationship. Reimbursement is not only limited to courses offered in the public schools and materials approved by state officials, but the statute excludes "any subject matter expressing religious teaching, or the morals or forms of worship of any sect." In addition, schools seeking reimbursement must maintain accounting procedures that require the State to establish the cost of the secular as distinguished from the religious instruction.

The Pennsylvania statute, moreover, has the further defect of providing state financial aid directly to the church-related school. This factor distinguishes both *Everson* and *Allen*, for in both those cases the Court was careful to point out that state aid was provided to the student and his parents—not to the church-related school. . . . The history of government grants of a continuing cash subsidy indicates that such programs have almost always been accompanied by varying measures of control and surveillance. The government cash grants before us now provide no basis for predicting that comprehensive measures of surveillance and controls will not follow. In particular the government's post-audit power to inspect and evaluate a church-related school's financial records and to determine which expenditures are religious and which are secular creates an intimate and continuing relationship between church and state.

A broader base of entanglement of yet a different character is presented by the divisive political potential of these state programs. In a community where such a large number of pupils are served by church-related schools, it can be assumed that state assistance will entail considerable political activity. Partisans of parochial schools, understandably concerned with rising costs and sincerely dedicated to both the religious and secular educational missions of their schools, will inevitably champion this cause and promote political action to achieve their goals. Those who oppose state aid, whether for constitutional, religious, or fiscal reasons, will inevitably respond and employ all of the usual political campaign techniques to prevail. Candidates will be forced to declare and voters to choose. It would be unrealistic to ignore the fact that many people confronted with issues of this kind will find their votes aligned with their faith.

Ordinarily political debate and division, however vigorous or even partisan, are normal and healthy manifestations of our democratic system of government, but political division along religious lines was one of the principal evils against which the First Amendment was intended to protect. The potential divisiveness of such conflict is a threat to the normal political process.[2] To have States or communities divide on the

---

2. What is the "normal" political process? The Court offered no answer other than

issues presented by state aid to parochial schools would tend to confuse and obscure other issues of great urgency. We have an expanding array of vexing issues, local and national, domestic and international, to debate and divide on. It conflicts with our whole history and tradition to permit questions of the Religion Clauses to assume such importance in our legislatures and in our elections that they could divert attention from the myriad issues and problems that confront every level of government. The highways of church and state relationships are not likely to be one-way streets, and the Constitution's authors sought to protect religious worship from the pervasive power of government. The history of many countries attests to the hazards of religion's intruding into political power or of political power intruding into the legitimate and free exercise of religious belief.

. . .

The potential for political divisiveness related to religious belief and practice is aggravated in these two statutory programs by the need for continuing annual appropriations and the likelihood of larger and larger demands as costs and populations grow. . . .

. . .

. . . [N]othing we have said can be construed to disparage the role of church-related elementary and secondary schools in our national life. Their contribution has been and is enormous. Nor do we ignore their economic plight in a period of rising costs and expanding need. Taxpayers generally have been spared vast sums by the maintenance of these educational institutions by religious organizations, largely by the gifts of faithful adherents.

The merit and benefits of these schools, however, are not the issue before us in these cases. The sole question is whether state aid to these schools can be squared with the dictates of the Religion Clauses. Under our system the choice has been made that government is to be entirely excluded from the area of religious instruction and churches excluded from the affairs of government. The Constitution decrees that religion must be a private matter for the individual, the family, and the institutions of private choice, and that while some involvement and entanglement are inevitable, lines must be drawn.

---

to suggest that political division along religious lines is *not* normal. Yet it seems clear that a society can be, as many commentators argue ours now is, divided along cultural lines informed by religious and philosophical beliefs. (See James Davison Hunter, *Culture Wars: The Struggle to Define America* [New York: Basic Books, 1991].) The division over abortion is a case in point. This state of affairs hardly seems "abnormal" for a society with a history of cultural-religious division over such issues as slavery and temperance.

The judgment of the Rhode Island District Court in No. 569 and No. 570 is affirmed. The judgment of the Pennsylvania District Court in No. 89 is reversed, and the case is remanded for further proceedings consistent with this opinion.

Justice William O. Douglas, concurring, joined by Justice Hugo L. Black:

There is in my view . . . an entanglement here. The surveillance or supervision of the States needed to police grants involved in these three cases, if performed, puts a public investigator into every class-room and entails a pervasive monitoring of these church agencies by the secular authorities. Yet if that surveillance or supervision does not occur the zeal of religious proselytizers promises to carry the day and make a shambles of the Establishment Clause. Moreover, when tax-payers of many faiths are required to contribute money for the propagation of one faith, the Free Exercise Clause is infringed.

The analyses of the constitutional objections to these two state systems of grants to parochial or sectarian schools must start with the admitted and obvious fact that the *raison d'être* of parochial schools is the propagation of a religious faith. They also teach secular subjects; but they came into existence in this country because Protestant groups were perverting the public schools by using them to propagate their faith. The Catholics naturally rebelled. . . . Hence the advent of parochial schools.

. . .

The story of the conflict and dissension is long and well known. The result was a state of so-called equilibrium where religious instruction was eliminated from public schools and the use of public funds to support religious schools was deemed to be banned.

But the hydraulic pressures created by political forces and by economic stress were great and they began to change the situation. Laws were passed—state and federal—that dispensed public funds to sustain religious schools and the plea was always in the educational frame of reference: education in all sectors was needed, from languages to calculus to nuclear physics. And it was forcefully argued that a linguist or mathematician or physicist trained in religious schools was just as competent as one trained in secular schools.

And so we have gradually edged into a situation where vast amounts of public funds are supplied each year to sectarian schools.

And the argument is made that the private parochial school system takes about $9 billion a year off the back of government—as if that were enough to justify violating the Establishment Clause.

. . .

. . . [W]e have never faced, until recently, the problem of policing sectarian schools. Any surveillance to date has been minor and has related only to the consistently unchallenged matters of accreditation of the sectarian school in the State's school system.

. . .

When Madison in his Remonstrance attacked a taxing measure to support religious activities, he advanced a series of reasons for opposing it. One that is extremely relevant here was phrased as follows: "[It] will destroy that moderation and harmony which the forbearance of our laws to intermeddle with Religion, has produced amongst its several sects." Intermeddling, to use Madison's word, or "entanglement," to use what was said in *Walz*, has two aspects. The intrusion of government into religious schools through grants, supervision, or surveillance may result in establishment of religion in the constitutional sense when what the State does enthrones a particular sect for overt or subtle propagation of its faith. Those activities of the State may also intrude on the Free Exercise Clause by depriving a teacher, under threats of reprisals, of the right to give sectarian construction or interpretation of, say, history and literature, or to use the teaching of such subjects to inculcate a religious creed or dogma.

Under these laws there will be vast governmental suppression, surveillance, or meddling in church affairs. . . . [S]chool prayers, the daily routine of parochial schools, must go if our decision in *Engel* is honored. If it is not honored, then the state has established a religious sect. Elimination of prayers is only part of the problem. The curriculum presents subtle and difficult problems. The constitutional mandate can in part be carried out by censoring the curricula. What is palpably a sectarian course can be marked for deletion. But the problem only starts there.

Sectarian instruction, in which, of course, a State may not indulge, can take place in a course on Shakespeare or in one on mathematics. No matter what the curriculum offers, the question is, what is *taught*? We deal not with evil teachers but with zealous ones who may use any opportunity to indoctrinate a class.

. . .

One can imagine what a religious zealot, as contrasted to a civil libertarian, can do with the Reformation or with the Inquisition. Much history can be given the gloss of a particular religion. I would think that policing these grants to detect sectarian instruction would be insufferable to religious partisans and would breed division and dissension between the church and state.

· · ·

Lemon involves a state statute that prescribes that courses in mathematics, modern foreign languages, physical science, and physical education "shall not include any subject matter expressing religious teaching, or the morals or forms of worship of any sect." The subtleties involved in applying this standard are obvious. It places the State astride a sectarian school and gives it power to dictate what is or is not secular, what is or is not religious. I can think of no more disrupting influence apt to promote rancor and ill-will between church and state than this kind of surveillance and control. They are the very opposite of the "moderation and harmony" between church and state which Madison thought was the aim and purpose of the Establishment Clause.

· · ·

The *DiCenso* cases [Nos. 569 and 570] have all the vices which are in *Lemon*, because the supplementary salary payable to the teacher is conditioned on his or her not teaching "a course in religion."

· · ·

If the government closed its eyes to the manner in which these grants are actually used it would be allowing public funds to promote sectarian education. If it did not close its eyes but undertook the surveillance needed, it would, I fear, intermeddle in parochial affairs in a way that would breed only rancor and dissension.

· · ·

In my view the taxpayers' forced contribution to the parochial schools in the present cases violates the First Amendment.

[Justice Thurgood Marshall, "while intimating no view as to the continuing vitality of *Everson*," concurred in Justice William O. Douglas's opinion covering Nos. 569 and 570. He did not take part in the consideration of No. 89.]

Justice William J. Brennan, Jr.:[3]

The common feature of all three statutes [Pennsylvania, Rhode Island, and U.S.] before us is the provision of a direct subsidy from pub-

---

3. Justice Brennan's opinion also applied to No. 153, *Tilton* v. *Richardson*, decided the same day as *Lemon*.

lic funds for activities carried on by sectarian educational institutions. We have sustained the reimbursement of parents for bus fares of students under a scheme applicable to both public and nonpublic schools, *Everson*. We have also sustained the loan of textbooks in secular subjects to students of both public and nonpublic schools, *Allen*.

The statutory schemes before us, however, have features not present in either the *Everson* or *Allen* schemes. For example, the reimbursement or the loan of books ended government involvement in *Everson* and *Allen*. In contrast each of the schemes here exacts a promise in some form that the subsidy will not be used to finance courses in religious subjects—promises that must be and are policed to assure compliance. Again, although the federal subsidy, similar to the *Everson* and *Allen* subsidies, is available to both public and nonpublic colleges and universities, the Rhode Island and Pennsylvania subsidies are restricted to nonpublic schools, and for practical purposes to Roman Catholic parochial schools. These and other features I shall mention mean for me that *Everson* and *Allen* do not control these cases. Rather, the history of public subsidy of sectarian schools, and the purposes and operation of these particular statutes must be examined to determine whether the statutes breach the Establishment Clause.

In sharp contrast to the "undeviating acceptance given religious tax exemptions from our earliest days as a Nation," *Walz*, subsidy of sectarian educational institutions became embroiled in bitter controversies very soon after the Nation was formed. Public education was, of course, virtually nonexistent when the Constitution was adopted. . . . Education in the Colonies was overwhelmingly a private enterprise, usually carried on as a denominational activity by the dominant Protestant sects. In point of fact, government generally looked to the church to provide education, and often contributed support through donations of land and money.

Nor was there substantial change in the years immediately following ratification of the Constitution and the Bill of Rights. Schools continued to be local and, in the main, denominational institutions. But the demand for public education soon emerged. The evolution of the struggle in New York City is illustrative. In 1786, the first New York State Legislature ordered that one section in each township be set aside for the "gospel and schools." With no public schools, various private agencies and churches operated "charity schools" for the poor of New York City and received money from the state common school fund. The forerunner of the city's public schools was organized in 1805 when DeWitt Clinton founded "The Society for Establishment of a Free School in the City of New York for the Education of such poor Children as do not belong to or are not provided for by any Religious Society." The State and city aided the society, and it built many schools. Gradually, however, competition and bickering among the Free School Society and the various church schools developed over the apportionment of state school funds. As a result, in 1825, the legislature transferred to the city council the responsibility for distributing New York City's share of the state funds. The council stopped funding religious societies which operated sixteen sectarian schools but continued supporting schools connected with the Protestant Orphan Asylum Society. Thereafter, in 1831, the Catholic Orphan Asylum Society demanded and received public funds to operate its schools but a request of Methodists for funds for the same purpose was denied. Nine years later, the Catholics enlarged their request for public monies to include all parochial schools, contending that the council was subsidizing sectarian books and instruction of the Public School Society, which Clinton's Free School Society had become. The city's Scotch Presbyterian and Jewish communities immediately followed with requests for funds to finance their schools. Although the Public School Society undertook to revise its texts to meet the objections, in 1842, the state legislature closed the bitter controversy by enacting a law that established a City Board of Education to set up free public schools, prohibited the distribution of public funds to sectarian schools, and prohibited the teaching of sectarian doctrine in any public school.

The Nation's rapidly developing religious heterogeneity, the tide of Jacksonian democracy, and growing urbanization soon led to widespread demands throughout the States for secular public education. At the same time strong opposition developed to use of the States' taxing powers to support private sectarian schools. Although the controversy over religious exercises in the public schools continued into this century, the opponents of subsidy to sectarian schools had largely won their fight by 1900. In fact, after 1840, no efforts of sectarian schools to obtain a share of public school funds succeeded. Between 1840 and 1875, nineteen States had added provisions to their constitutions prohibiting the use of public school funds to aid sectarian schools, and by 1900, sixteen more states had added similar provisions. In fact, no State admitted to the Union after 1858, except West Virginia, omitted such provision from its first constitution. Today fewer than a half-dozen States omit such provisions from their constitutions.

· · ·

Thus for more than a century, the consensus, enforced by legislatures and courts with substantial consistency, has been that public subsidy of sectarian schools constitutes an impermissible involvement of secular with religious institutions. If this history is not itself compelling against the validity of the three subsidy statutes . . . other forms of governmental involvement that each of the three statutes requires tip the scales in my view against the validity of each of them. . . . All three of these statutes require "too close a proximity" of government to the subsidized sectarian institutions and in my view create real dangers of "the secularization of a creed."

. . .

. . . I do not believe that elimination of these aspects of "too close a proximity" would save these three statutes. I expressed the view in *Walz* that "[g]eneral subsidies of religious activities would, of course, constitute impermissible state involvement with religion." I do not think the subsidies under these statutes fall outside "[g]eneral subsidies of religious activities" merely because they are restricted to support of the teaching of secular subjects. . . .

. . .

. . . I do not read *Pierce* v. *Society of Sisters*, 268 U.S. 510 (1925), or *Allen* as supporting the proposition that public subsidy of sectarian institutions' secular training is permissible state involvement. I read them as supporting the proposition that as an identifiable set of skills and an identifiable quantum of knowledge, secular education may be effectively provided either in the religious context of parochial schools, or outside the context of religion in public schools. . . .

. . .

Allen, in my view, simply sustained a statute in which the State was "neutral in its relations with groups of religious believers and nonbelievers." The only context in which the Court in *Allen* employed the distinction between secular and religious in a parochial school was to reach its conclusion that the textbooks that the State was providing could and would be secular. The present cases, however, involve direct subsidies of tax monies to the schools themselves and we cannot blink the fact that the secular eduction those schools provide goes hand in hand with the religious mission that is the only reason for the schools' existence. . . .

. . .

The common ingredient of the three prongs of the test set forth at the outset of this opinion is whether the statutes involve government in the "essentially religious activities" of religious institutions. My analysis of the operation, purposes, and effects of these statutes leads me inescapably to the conclusion that they do impermissibly involve the States and the Federal Government with the "essentially religious activities" of sectarian educational institutions. More specifically, for the reasons stated, I think each government uses "essentially religious means to serve governmental ends, where secular means would suffice." This Nation long ago committed itself to primary reliance upon publicly supported public education to serve its important goals in secular education. Our religious diversity gave strong impetus to that commitment.

Responses

From the **Washington Post,** June 30, 1971, "*Safeguarding Religious Freedom*":

The Supreme Court's decisions forbidding state financial support of church-related parochial schools should be recognized for what they really are—a strengthening of the traditional wall of separation which shields religion in America from governmental intrusion. No doubt these decisions will seem disappointing and perhaps even hostile to many conscientious Catholics who sincerely believe that the valuable contribution their parochial schools have made to public education in this country deserves recompense; no doubt these decisions will be painful to Catholics who believe that their extensive school system will be doomed if state and federal tax money is not made available to sustain it. Nevertheless, the decisions serve the cause of church independence and of the freedom of men of every faith to worship as they wish.

Catholics need only ask themselves why they want their children in parish schools separate from the community's public schools in order to understand why the use of public money to pay their teachers or to support their courses involves what the Chief Justice called an "excessive entanglement between government and religion." The reason they want their children in parish schools is simply that they want their children to have a religiously oriented education; they want schools in which prayer will play a part and in which the doctrines of the church will be stressed. These are entirely legitimate aims; and the right to pursue them is indisputable. But there is simply no gainsaying the truth of Mr. Justice Douglas's observation that "the *raison d'être* of parochial schools is the propagation of a religious faith." That is precisely the kind of propagation which the First Amendment was designed to prohibit government from undertaking.

The English experience, from which so many of the authors of the Constitution drew their knowledge and inspiration, was an experience in which Protestants were persecuted when a Catholic monarch was on the throne and Catholics were persecuted in turn when Henry VIII and his successors established a national church over which they ruled. The Crown was forever meddling in modes of worship, in the designation of religious orthodoxy and in the preferment of clerics. The aim of the First Amendment was to keep Americans free from that kind of interference.

If parochial schools were to receive public funds, a rigorous auditing of their accounts and an extensive supervision of their classroom practices would

230

be necessary; indeed, there was provision for these in the Rhode Island and Pennsylvania laws which came under the court's scrutiny. . . .

Independence is costly. But it is the fundamental condition of religious liberty. In denying the Catholic Church a government subsidy, the court has assured it unrestricted control over its own destiny.

From *The New Republic, July 10, 1971, "Parochial School Aid"*:

Parochial, like other elementary and secondary schools, have been in a financial crisis of late, with the consequence that some thirty-six states have taken various measures to aid them. By no means have all these measures been declared even presumptively unconstitutional. But an ominous cloud now does overhang them as a consequence of the July 28 decisions of the Supreme Court, rendered by Chief Justice Burger for eight-man majorities, with Justice Byron White alone taking a different view.

The Court's test, a recently developed one, of the validity of public aid to church-connected schools turns on the question of whether the form of the aid results in "an excessive government entanglement with religion." Rhode Island and Pennsylvania programs for supplementing the salaries of teachers of strictly secular subjects in parochial schools were held unconstitutional, because the Court found that they did entangle government with religion. The *Lemon* decision struck down state laws in Pennsylvania and Rhode Island that supported instructors who taught secular subjects in church-related elementary and secondary schools. The states would have to exercise surveillance to make sure that public monies were put to the strictly secular use intended by these programs, the Court held, and besides, all teaching in a parochial school, secular or not, necessarily tends to be part of the process of religious formation, which is the chief mission of such schools. So, the Court thought, the state gets entangled in trying to separate the inseparable, and having got entangled, it fails—a double fault. Federal grants for construction of secular facilities in church-connected universities, however, were held constitutional because each grant is a one-time, non-entangling involvement of government with secular aspects of a religious institution.

Justice White, characterizing the Court's reasoning, with not a little justification, as "a curious and mystifying blend," feared that the Court had created "an insoluble paradox for the state and the parochial school." That is probably an exaggeration, since the now reigning "entanglement" test is a porous one. It does not follow from these decisions that aid channeled to the pupil by way of scholarships rather than directly to the parochial school will be held unconstitutional. And construction grants are apparently all right. These and other variables are likely to come to judgment before long, since the parochial school problem will not go away. Twenty-five per cent of Rhode Island's elementary school pupils are in private schools, 95 per cent of which, in turn, are parochial. In Pennsylvania, the respective percentages are 20 and 98. These figures are high, but not unique in the industrial states. Pennsylvania and Rhode Island have spent a few million dollars annually—five in Pennsylvania—supporting parochial schools and helping them stay open. Should the parochial schools close, the flood of pupils would overwhelm the public schools. Hence, the states may be expected to keep trying.

From **Waldo Beach,** *"The Court's Church-State Confusion," in* **Christianity and Crisis,** *August 9, 1971:*

A great deal was at stake in these decisions, not only for economic security of many church-related colleges and Catholic parochial schools facing a bleak fiscal future, but also for the shape of church-state relations in American education in the decades ahead. . . .

The texts of the decisions are wondrous exercises in legal logic. To a layman in the law, the distinctions on which the apparently self-contradictory decisions were made—one apparently favoring federal support of church colleges, the other precluding state support of church schools—appear fine distinctions indeed (according to Justice White's opinion, "a curious and mystifying blend").

As all parties to the decisions agreed, no point can be fixed between the poles of complete establishment and total separation that can do justice to the dynamics of necessary church-state relationships in the area of education. . . .

What tipped the decision in favor of the Catholic colleges and turned it almost unanimously against aid to the Catholic parochial schools was that in the former case [*Tilton* v. *Richardson*], the funds for building construction are consonant with the "secular" purpose of the law, while in the latter cases [*Lemon* v. *Kurtzmann, Robinson* v. *DiCenso*], the support of parochial school teachers, albeit for the teaching of secular subjects, in effect constitutes more direct aid to the church and is conducive to an "excessive entanglement between government and religion."

Unschooled in the niceties of constitutional law, we hesitate to pass judgment on the scruples of the Supreme Court in its conscientious interpretations. In essence, we applaud the decision of the Court in the *Tilton* case, but by the same token we question the parochial school verdicts, though for somewhat different reasons than the Court.

Though the Court carefully avoided theological or religious judgments, there are theological issues unavoidably submerged in the argument. What constitutes the parameters of the "secular" or "religious"? What defines "sectarian" or "indoctrination" or "proselytize"? Value judgments haunt legal reasons. "Excessive entanglements" between government and religion are to be shunned. The word "entanglements" in this setting has a sinister ring, though in other settings (such as the East Room of the White House) the mutual support of government and religion is celebrated and encouraged.

The reasoning that finds the buildings constructed on the Catholic campuses safely "secular" but the parochial teachers' salary supplement dangerously "sectarian" seems precarious indeed. As the dissent of Justice Douglas complains, can religious and secular purposes be so neatly delineated? Two of the college buildings are libraries, another a music and arts center. The Bibles or theological works studied in the former presumably have some religious impact on the minds of the students. Certainly a performance of the B Minor Mass in the latter would exercise a more powerful religious influence than that of a grammar or driver-education teacher in a parochial school.

The Court made a further dubious distinction between the teaching and learning processes at the college level. There thought control and proselytizing are less apt to take place than at the lower levels since "college students are less impressionable and less susceptible to religious indoctrination" and "college and post-graduate courses tend to limit the opportunities for sectarian influence by virtue of their own internal discipline." Anyone close to the core of a university is well aware of sectarian proselytizing for the religions of Scientism, Freudian psychology, or the New Consciousness among highly impressionable students. The judgment that primary and secondary schools are more loaded religiously and higher education more neutral religiously can hardly stand.

No, the case for the use of tax funds for religious purposes in education might more clearly be supported on the rather different grounds represented in the theory of "free cooperation" between church and state. This position breaks through the wall that separates the "religious" and "secular" spheres. Its premise is the inevitably "religious" aspect of all but the most technical forms of education at the primary, secondary, and university level. On this basis it would affirm that responsible education, public and private, should include, rather than avoid, the critical assessment of the variety of religious traditions of the West (and now of the East as well).

Direct and indirect teaching would of course proceed from a partial point of view, as in all fields. But why should that be feared any more than the radically secular point of view, which in fact is the establishment today? The increasingly ecumenical spirit of Roman Catholic, Protestant, and Jewish educational leadership should be trusted to set policy that can assure the exposure to the rich religious pluralism of culture that is indispensable to a liberal education.

It should be remembered that the framers of the First Amendment did not fear *religion* but *sectarianism*. Permissive and positive state support of church-related education, instanced in the *Tilton* decision, fosters the "free exercise" of religion in public life while at the same time safeguarding the public from the sectarian favoritism or ecclesiastical control that the framers of the First Amendment rightly feared.

14

Wisconsin v. Yoder

406 U.S. 205 (1972)

In 1879 the Supreme Court held in *Reynolds* v. *U.S.*, 98 U.S. 145, that religiously motivated conduct created no claim to exemption from otherwise valid law. The Court followed this principle in 1940 in *Minersville* v. *Gobitis*. In overruling *Gobitis* three years later in *West Virginia State Board of Education* v. *Barnette*, the Court did not explicitly repudiate its reasoning in that case or in *Reynolds*. Not until 1963, in *Sherbert* v. *Verner*, did the Court prove willing to say that the Constitution can require an exemption for conduct grounded in religious belief from otherwise valid law. Yet *Sherbert* was the sole exception to the Court's jurisprudence in this area—until *Wisconsin* v. *Yoder*. In this case the Court relied on *Sherbert* to rule that the state may not require Amish parents to send their children to school beyond the eighth grade. The Court articulated a "balancing" approach in deciding the case: "[A] State's interest in universal education . . . is not totally free from a balancing process when it impinges on fundamental rights. . . ."

Wisconsin state law required parents of all children to send them to private or public schools until they reached age 16. Some Amish parents, however, refused to send their children, ages 14 and 15, to public school after they completed the eighth grade. The parents were convicted of violating the compulsory-attendance law. The Wisconsin Supreme Court reversed their convictions on free-exercise grounds.

Yoder produced four opinions. Chief Justice Warren Burger wrote for the Court, expressing the views of six members. Justice Potter Stewart and Justice Byron White wrote separate concurring opinions. Justices Lewis Powell and William Rehnquist did not participate in the case. Only Justice William O. Douglas dissented, and his was a partial dissent. His opinion and Chief Justice Burger's opinion for the Court are presented here.

Participating in *Wisconsin* v. *Yoder*, decided May 15, 1972, were Chief Justice Warren E. Burger and Associate Justices William J. Brennan, Jr., Harry A. Blackmun, William O. Douglas, Thurgood Marshall, Potter Stewart, and Byron R. White.

Opinions

Chief Justice Warren E. Burger delivered the opinion of the Court:

There is no doubt as to the power of a State, having a high responsibility for education of its citizens, to impose reasonable regulations for the control and duration of basic education. See, e.g., *Pierce v. Society of Sisters*, 268 U.S. 510, 534 (1925).[1] Providing public schools ranks at the very apex of the function of a State. Yet even this paramount responsibility was, in *Pierce*, made to yield to the right of parents to provide an equivalent education in a privately operated system. There the Court held that Oregon's statute compelling attendance in a public school from age eight to age 16 unreasonably interfered with the interests of parents in directing the rearing of their offspring, including their education in church-operated schools. As that case suggests, the values of parental direction of the religious upbringing and education of their children in their early and formative years have a high place in our society. Thus, a State's interest in universal education, however highly we rank it, is not totally free from a balancing process when it impinges on fundamental rights and interests, such as those specifically protected by the Free Exercise Clause of the First

---

1. In *Pierce* the Supreme Court applied the principle of *Meyer v. Nebraska*, 262 U.S. 390 (1923), to strike down an Oregon statute that effectively banned private schools. In *Meyer* the Court had set aside a conviction for teaching German to a child who had not finished the eighth grade. Both *Meyer* and *Pierce* are substantive due-process cases. The Court believed that at stake in each was a liberty—in *Meyer* the right to teach a foreign language and the right to engage a language instructor, in *Pierce* the right of parents and guardians to direct the upbringing and education of children—that deserved protection under the due-process clause of the Fourteenth Amendment. Of course, prior to *Meyer* the Court had committed substantive due process in behalf of certain *economic* liberties; the leading case is *Lochner v. New York*, 198 U.S. 45 (1905), in which the Court reversed the conviction of a baker who worked more than sixty hours a week in violation of a statute limiting employment to those hours. The significance of *Meyer*, as David P. Currie has written, is that substantive due process was "for the first time drawn upon to protect an intellectual freedom dear to the modern observer against a ham-handed measure most would now find seriously misguided." *Meyer* and *Pierce* are generally applauded today—although more for the outcomes in the cases than for the reasoning. "[T]he doctrinal basis for *Meyer* [and thus for *Pierce*]," Currie comments, "is as shaky as that of *Lochner* itself, for it is the very same" (*The Constitution in the Supreme Court*, 154).

237

Amendment, and the traditional interest of parents with respect to the religious upbringing of their children so long as they, in the words of *Pierce*, "prepare [them] for additional obligations."[2]

It follows that in order for Wisconsin to compel school attendance beyond the eighth grade against a claim that such attendance interferes with the practice of a legitimate religious belief, it must appear either that the State does not deny the free exercise of religious belief by its requirement, or that there is a state interest of sufficient magnitude to override the interest claiming protection under the Free Exercise Clause. Long before there was general acknowledgement of the need for universal formal education, the Religion Clauses had specifically and firmly fixed the right to free exercise of religious beliefs, and buttressing this fundamental right was an equally firm, even if less explicit, prohibition against the establishment of any religion by government. The values underlying these two provisions relating to religion have been zealously protected, sometimes even at the expense of other interests of admittedly high social importance. The invalidation of financial aid to parochial schools by government grants for a salary subsidy for teachers is but one example of the extent to which courts have gone in this regard, notwithstanding that such aid programs were legislatively determined to be in the public interest and the service of sound educational policy by States and by Congress. *Lemon* v. *Kurtzman* (1971).

The essence of all that has been said and written on the subject is that only those interests of the highest order and those not otherwise served can overbalance legitimate claims to the free exercise of religion. . . .

We come then to the quality of the claims of the respondents concerning the alleged encroachment of Wisconsin's compulsory school-attendance statute on their rights and the rights of their children to the free exercise of [their] religious beliefs. . . . [W]e must be careful to determine whether the Amish religious faith and their mode of life are, as they claim, inseparable and interdependent. A way of life, however virtuous and admirable, may not be interposed as a barrier to reasonable state regulation of education if it is based on purely secular considerations; to have the protection of the Religion Clauses, the claims must be rooted in religious belief. Although a determination of what is

---

2. The Court's "balancing" approach in free-exercise cases was challenged by Justice Antonin Scalia and defended by Justice Sandra Day O'Connor in *Employment Division* v. *Smith* (1990); see Case 23.

a "religious" belief or practice entitled to constitutional protection may present a most delicate question, the very concept of ordered liberty precludes allowing every person to make his own standard on matters of conduct in which society as a whole has important interests. Thus, if the Amish asserted their claims because of their subjective evaluation and rejection of the contemporary secular values accepted by the majority, much as Thoreau rejected the social values of his time and isolated himself at Walden Pond, their claims would not rest on a religious basis. Thoreau's choice was philosophical and personal rather than religious, and such belief does not rise to the demands of the Religion Clauses.[3]

Giving no weight to such secular considerations, however, we see that the record in this case abundantly supports the claim that the traditional way of life of the Amish is not merely a matter of personal preference, but one of deep religious conviction, shared by an organized group, and intimately related to daily living. That the Old Order Amish daily life and religious practice stem from their faith is shown by the fact that it is in response to their literal interpretation of the Biblical injunction from the Epistle of Paul to the Romans, "be not conformed to this world. . . ." This command is fundamental to the Amish faith. Moreover, for the Old Order Amish, religion is not simply a matter of theocratic belief. As the expert witness explained, the Old Order Amish religion pervades and determines virtually their entire way of life, regulating it with the detail of the Talmudic diet through the strictly enforced rules of the church community.

. . .

As the society around the Amish has become more populous, urban, industrialized, and complex, particularly in this century, government regulation of human affairs has correspondingly become more detailed and pervasive. The Amish mode of life has thus come into conflict increasingly with requirements of contemporary society exerting a hydraulic insistence on conformity to majoritarian standards. So long as compulsory education laws were confined to eight grades of elementary basic education imparted in a nearby rural schoolhouse,

---

3. The Court's distinction, for purposes of determining whether a claim may be protected under the free-exercise provision, between Thoreau-like claims rooted in philosophical and personal beliefs and claims like those of the Amish that are grounded in religious beliefs was challenged by Justice William O. Douglas in dissent and has not always been embraced by the Court. In *Torcaso* v. *Watkins* (1961), the Court seemed to say that secular humanism was a religion whose free exercise deserves protection under the religion clause.

with a large proportion of students of the Amish faith, the Old Order Amish had little basis to fear that school attendance would expose their children to the worldly influence they reject. But modern compulsory secondary education in rural areas is now largely carried on in a consolidated school, often remote from the student's home and alien to his daily home life. As the record so strongly shows, the values and programs of the modern secondary school are in sharp conflict with the fundamental mode of life mandated by the Amish religion; modern laws requiring compulsory secondary education have accordingly engendered great concern and conflict. The conclusion is inescapable that secondary schooling, by exposing Amish children to worldly influences in terms of attitudes, goals, and values contrary to beliefs, and by substantially interfering with the religious development of the Amish child and his integration into the way of life of the Amish faith community at the crucial adolescent stage of development, contravenes the basic religious tenets and practice of the Amish faith, both as to the parent and the child.

The impact of the compulsory-attendance law on respondents' practice of the Amish religion is not only severe, but inescapable, for the Wisconsin law affirmatively compels them, under threat of criminal sanction, to perform acts undeniably at odds with fundamental tenets of their religious beliefs. Nor is the impact of the compulsory-attendance law confined to grave interference with important Amish religious tenets from a subjective point of view. It carries with it precisely the kind of objective danger to the free exercise of religion that the First Amendment was designed to prevent. As the record shows, compulsory school attendance to age 16 for Amish children carries with it a very real threat of undermining the Amish community and religious practice as they exist today; they must either abandon belief and be assimilated into society at large, or be forced to migrate to some other and more tolerant region.

. . . [E]nforcement of the State's requirement of compulsory formal education after the eighth grade would gravely endanger if not destroy the free exercise of respondent's religious beliefs.

Neither the findings of the trial court nor the Amish claims as to the nature of their faith are challenged in this Court by the State of Wisconsin. Its position is that the State's interest in universal compulsory formal secondary education to age 16 is so great that it is paramount to the undisputed claims of respondents that their mode of preparing their youth for Amish life, after the traditional elementary education, is an essential part of their religious belief and practice. Nor does the State undertake to meet the claim that the Amish mode of life and education is inseparable from and a part of the basic tenets of their religion—indeed, as much a part of their religious belief and practices as baptism, the confessional, or a sabbath may be for others.

Wisconsin concedes that under the Religion Clauses religious beliefs are absolutely free from the State's control, but it argues that "actions," even though religiously grounded, are outside the protection of the First Amendment. But our decisions have rejected the idea that religiously grounded conduct is always outside the protection of the Free Exercise Clause. It is true that activities of individuals, even when religiously based, are often subject to regulation by the States in the exercise of their undoubted power to promote the health, safety, and general welfare, or the Federal Government in the exercise of its delegated powers. But to agree that religiously grounded conduct must often be subject to the broad police power of the State is not to deny that there are areas of conduct protected by the Free Exercise Clause of the First Amendment and thus beyond the power of the State to control, even under regulations of general applicability. This case, therefore, does not become easier because respondents were convicted for their "actions" in refusing to send their children to the public high school; in this context belief and action cannot be neatly confined in logic-tight compartments.

Nor can this case be disposed of on the grounds that Wisconsin's requirement for school attendance to age 16 applies uniformly to all citizens of the State and does not, on its face, discriminate against religions or a particular religion, or that it is motivated by legitimate secular concerns. A regulation neutral on its face may, in its application, nonetheless offend the constitutional requirement for governmental neutrality if it unduly burdens the free exercise of religion. *Sherbert* v. *Verner* (1963). The Court must not ignore the danger that an exception from a general obligation of citizenship on religious grounds may run afoul of the Establishment Clause, but that danger cannot be allowed to prevent any exception no matter how vital it may be to the protection of values promoted by the right of free exercise. By preserving doctrinal flexibility and recognizing the need for a sensible and realistic application of the Religion Clauses "we have been able to chart a course that preserved the autonomy and freedom of religious bodies while avoiding any semblance of established religion. This is a 'tight rope' and one we have successfully traversed." *Walz* v. *Tax Commission* (1970).

We turn, then, to the State's broader contention that its interest in its system of compulsory education is so compelling that even the established religious practices of the Amish must give way. Where fundamental claims of religious freedom are at stake, however, we cannot accept such a sweeping claim; despite its admitted validity in the generality of cases, we must searchingly examine the interests that the State seeks to promote by its requirement for compulsory education to age 16, and the impediment to those objectives that would flow from recognizing the claimed Amish exemption.

The State advances two primary arguments in support of its system of compulsory education. It notes, as Thomas Jefferson pointed out early in our history, that some degree of education is necessary to prepare citizens to participate effectively and intelligently in our open political system if we are to preserve freedom and independence. Further, education prepares individuals to be self-reliant and self-sufficient participants in society. We accept these propositions.

However, the evidence adduced by the Amish in this case is persuasively to the effect that an additional one or two years of formal high school for Amish children in place of their long-established program of informal vocational education would do little to serve those interests. . . .

The State attacks respondents' position as one fostering "ignorance" from which the child must be protected by the State. No one can question the State's duty to protect children from ignorance but this argument does not square with the facts disclosed in the record. Whatever their idiosyncrasies as seen by the majority, this record strongly shows that the Amish community has been a highly successful social unit within our society, even if apart from the conventional "mainstream." . . .

It is neither fair not correct to suggest that the Amish are opposed to education beyond the eighth grade level. What this record shows is that they are opposed to conventional formal education of the type provided by a certified high school because it comes at the child's crucial adolescent period of religious development. . . .

We must not forget that in the Middle Ages important values of the civilization of the Western World were preserved by members of religious orders who isolated themselves from all worldly influences against great obstacles. There can be no assumption that today's majority is "right" and the Amish and others like them are "wrong." A way of life that is odd or even erratic but interferes with no rights or interests of others is not to be condemned because it is different.

The State . . . argues that if Amish children leave their church they should not be in the position of making their way in the world without the education available in the one or two additional years the State requires. However, on this record, that argument is highly speculative. There is no specific evidence of the loss of Amish adherents by attrition, nor is there any showing that upon leaving the Amish community Amish children, with their practical agricultural training and habits of industry and self-reliance, would become burdens on society because of educational shortcomings. . . .

There is nothing in this record to suggest that the Amish qualities of reliability, self-reliance, and dedication to work would fail to find ready markets in today's society. Absent some contrary evidence supporting the State's position, we are unwilling to assume that persons possessing such valuable vocational skills and habits are doomed to become burdens on society should they determine to leave the Amish faith, nor is there any basis in the record to warrant a finding that an additional one or two years of formal school education beyond the eighth grade would serve to eliminate any such problem that might exist.

Insofar as the State's claim rests on the view that a brief additional period of formal education is imperative to enable the Amish to participate effectively and intelligently in our democratic process, it must fall. The Amish alternative to formal secondary school education has enabled them to function effectively in their day-to-day life under self-imposed limitations on relations with the world, and to survive and prosper in contemporary society as a separate, sharply identifiable and highly self-sufficient community for more than 200 years in this country. In itself this is strong evidence that they are capable of fulfilling the social and political responsibilities of citizenship without compelled attendance beyond the eighth grade at the price of jeopardizing their free exercise of religious belief. . . .

. . .

Finally, the State, on authority of *Prince* v. *Massachusetts*, 321 U.S. 158 (1944), argues that a decision exempting Amish children from the State's requirement fails to recognize the substantive right of the Amish child to a secondary education, and fails to give due regard to the power of the State as *parens patriae* to extend the benefit of secondary education to children regardless of the wishes of their parents.[4] Taken at its broadest sweep, the Court's language in *Prince* might be

---

4. In *Prince* the Supreme Court upheld application of child-labor laws to the proselytizing activities of Jehovah's Witnesses.

read to give support to the State's position. However, the Court was not confronted in *Prince* with a situation comparable to that of the Amish as revealed in this record; this is shown by the Court's severe characterization of the evils that it thought the legislature could legitimately associate with child labor, even when performed in the company of an adult. The Court later took great care to confine *Prince* to a narrow scope in *Sherbert*. . . .

This case, of course, is not one in which any harm to the physical or mental health of the child or to the public safety, peace, order, or welfare has been demonstrated or may be properly inferred. The record is to the contrary, and any reliance on that theory would find no support in the evidence.

Contrary to the suggestion of the dissenting opinion of Justice Douglas, our holding today in no degree depends on the assertion of the religious interest of the child as contrasted with that of the parents. It is the parents who are subject to prosecution here for failing to cause their children to attend school, and it is their right of free exercise, not that of their children, that must determine Wisconsin's power to impose criminal penalties on the parent. The dissent argues that a child who expresses a desire to attend public high school in conflict with the wishes of his parents should not be prevented from doing so. There is no reason for the Court to consider that point since it is not an issue in the case. The children are not parties to this litigation. The State has at no point tried this case on the theory that respondents were preventing their children from attending school against their expressed desires, and indeed the record is to the contrary. The State's position from the outset has been that it is empowered to apply its compulsory attendance law to Amish parents in the same manner as to other parents—that is, without regard to the wishes of the child. That is the claim we reject today.

The State's argument proceeds without reliance on any actual conflict between the wishes of parents and children. It appears to rest on the potential that exemption of Amish parents from the requirements of the compulsory-education law might allow some parents to act contrary to the best interests of their children by foreclosing their opportunity to make an intelligent choice between the Amish way of life and that of the outside world. The same argument could, of course, be made with respect to all church schools short of college. There is nothing in the record or in the ordinary course of human experience to suggest that non-Amish parents generally consult with children of ages 14–16 if they are placed in a church school of the parents' faith.

Indeed it seems clear that if the State is empowered, as *parens patriae*, to "save" a child from himself or his Amish parents by requiring an additional two years of compulsory formal high school education, the State will in large measure influence, if not determine, the religious future of the child. Even more markedly than in *Prince*, therefore, this case involves the fundamental interest of parents, as contrasted with that of the State, to guide the religious future and education of their children. The history and culture of Western civilization reflect a strong tradition of parental concern for the nurture and upbringing of their children. This primary role of the parents in the upbringing of their children is now established beyond debate as an enduring American tradition. If not the first, perhaps the most significant statements of the Court in this area are found in *Pierce*, in which the Court observed:

> Under the doctrine of *Meyer* v. *Nebraska*, 262 U.S. 390 (1923), we think it entirely plain that the Act of 1922 unreasonably interferes with the liberty of parents and guardians to direct the upbringing and education of children under their control. As often heretofore pointed out, rights guaranteed by the Constitution may not be abridged by legislation which has no reasonable relation to some purpose within the competency of the State. The fundamental theory of liberty upon which all governments in this Union repose excludes any general power of the State to standardize its children by forcing them to accept instruction from public teachers only. The child is not the mere creature of the State; those who nurture him and direct his destiny have the right, coupled with the high duty, to recognize and prepare him for additional obligations.

The duty to prepare the child for "additional obligations" . . . must be read to include the inculcation of moral standards, religious beliefs, and elements of good citizenship. *Pierce*, of course, recognized that where nothing more than the general interest of the parent in the nurture and education of his children is involved, it is beyond dispute that the State acts "reasonably" and constitutionally in requiring education to age 16 in some public or private school meeting the standards prescribed by the State.

However read, the Court's holding in *Pierce* stands as a charter of the rights of parents to direct the religious upbringing of their children. And, when the interests of parenthood are combined with a free exercise claim of the nature revealed by this record, more than merely a "reasonable relation to some purpose within the competency of the State" is required to sustain the validity of the State's requirement under the First Amendment. To be sure, the power of the parent, even when linked to a free exercise claim, may be subject to limitation under *Prince* if it appears that parental decisions will jeopardize the health or safety of the child, or have a potential for significant social burdens. But in this case, the Amish have introduced persuasive evidence undermining the arguments the State has advanced to support its claims in terms of the welfare of the child and society as a whole. The record strongly indicates that accommodating the religious objections of the Amish by forgoing one, or at most two, additional years of compulsory education will not impair the physical or mental health of the child, or result in an inability to be self-supporting or to discharge the duties and responsibilities of citizenship, or in any other way materially detract from the welfare of society.

In the face of our consistent emphasis on the central values underlying the Religion Clauses in our constitutional scheme of government, we cannot accept a *parens patriae* claim of such all-encompassing scope and with such sweeping potential for broad and unforeseeable application as that urged by the State.

For the reasons stated we hold, with the Supreme Court of Wisconsin, that the First and Fourteenth Amendments prevent the State from compelling respondents to cause their children to attend formal high school to age 16.[5] Our disposition of this case, however, in no way alters our recognition of the obvious fact that courts are not school boards or legislatures, and are ill-equipped to determine the "necessity" of discrete aspects of a State's program of compulsory education. This should suggest that courts must move with great circumspection in performing the sensitive and delicate task of weighing a State's legitimate social concern when faced with religious claims for exemption from generally applicable educational requirements. It cannot be overemphasized that we are not dealing with a way of life and mode of education by a group claiming to have recently discovered some "pro-

---

5. [Footnote twenty-two in the text of the opinion.] What we have said should meet the suggestion that the decision of the Wisconsin Supreme Court recognizing an exemption for the Amish from the State's system of compulsory education constituted an impermissible establishment of religion. . . . Accommodating the religious beliefs of the Amish can hardly be characterized as sponsorship or active involvement. The purpose and effect of such an exemption are not to support, favor, advance, or assist the Amish, but to allow their centuries-old religious society, here long before the advent of any compulsory educating, to survive free from the heavy impediment compliance with the Wisconsin compulsory-education law would impose. Such an accommodation "reflects nothing more than the governmental obligation of neutrality in the face of religious differences, and does not represent that involvement of religious with secular institutions which it is the object of the Establishment Clause to forestall." *Sherbert.*

gressive" or more enlightened process for rearing children for modern life.

. . .

Nothing we hold is intended to undermine the general applicability of the State's compulsory school-attendance statutes or to limit the power of the State to promulgate reasonable standards that, while not impairing the free exercise of religion, provide for continuing agricultural vocational education under parental and church guidance by the Old Order Amish or others similarly situated. The States have had a long history of amicable and effective relationships with church-sponsored schools, and there is no basis for assuming that, in this related context, reasonable standards cannot be established concerning the content of the continuing vocational education of Amish children under parental guidance, provided always that state regulations are not inconsistent with what we have said in this opinion.

Justice William O. Douglas, dissenting in part:

I agree with the Court that the religious scruples of the Amish are opposed to the education of their children beyond the grade schools, yet I disagree with the Court's conclusion that the matter is within the dispensation of the parents alone. The Court's analysis assumes that the only interests at stake in the case are those of the Amish parents on the one hand, and those of the State on the other. The difficulty with this approach is that, despite the Court's claim, the parents are seeking to vindicate not only their free exercise claims, but also those of the high-school-age children.

It is argued that the right of the Amish children to religious freedom is not presented by the facts of the case. . . .

First, respondents' motion to dismiss in the trial court expressly asserts, not only the religious liberty of the adults, but also that of the children, as a defense to the prosecutions. It is, of course, beyond question that the parents have standing as defendants in a criminal prosecution to assert the religious interests of their children as a defense. Although the lower courts and a majority of this Court assume an identity of interest between parent and child, it is clear that they have treated the religious interest of the child as a factor in the analysis.

Second, it is essential to reach the question to decide the case, not only because the question was squarely raised in the motion to dismiss, but also because no analysis of religious-liberty claims can take place in a vacuum. If the parents in this case are allowed a religious exemption, the inevitable effect is to impose the parents' notions of religious duty upon their children. Where the child is mature enough to express potentially conflicting desires, it would be an invasion of the child's rights to permit such an imposition without canvassing his views. . . . As the child has no other effective forum, it is in this litigation that his rights should be considered. And, if an Amish child desires to attend high school, and is mature enough to have that desire respected, the State may well be able to override the parents' religiously motivated objections.

Religion is an individual experience. It is not necessary, nor even appropriate, for every Amish child to express his views on the subject in a prosecution of a single adult. Crucial, however, are the views of the child whose parent is the subject of the suit. Frieda Yoder has in fact testified that her own religious views are opposed to high-school education. I therefore join the judgment of the Court as to respondent Jonas Yoder. But [his daughter] Frieda Yoder's views may not be those of Vernon Yutzy or Barbara Miller [the children of other prosecuted parents]. I must dissent, therefore, as to respondents Adin Yutzy and Wallace Miller as their motion to dismiss also raised the question of their children's religious liberty.

This issue has never been squarely presented before today. . . . Recent cases, however, have clearly held that the children themselves have constitutionally protectible interests.

These children are "persons" within the meaning of the Bill of Rights. We have so held over and over again. . . .

. . .

On this important and vital matter of education, I think the children should be entitled to be heard. While the parents, absent dissent, normally speak for the entire family, the education of the child is a matter on which the child will often have decided views. He may want to be a pianist or an astronaut or an oceanographer. To do so he will have to break from the Amish tradition.

It is the future of the student, not the future of the parents, that is imperiled by today's decision. If a parent keeps his child out of school beyond the grade school, then the child will be forever barred from entry into the new and amazing world of diversity that we have today. The child may decide that is the preferred course, or he may rebel. It is the student's judgment, not his parents', that is essential if we are to give full meaning to what we have said about the Bill of Rights and of the right of students to be masters of their own destiny. If he is harnessed to the Amish way of life by those in authority over him and if his education is truncated, his entire life may be stunted and deformed.

The child, therefore, should be given an opportunity to be heard before the State gives the exemption which we honor today.

. . .

The Court rightly rejects the notion that actions, even though religiously grounded, are always outside the protection of the Free Exercise Clause. . . .

. . . [But] what we do today . . . opens the way to give organized religion a broader base than it has ever enjoyed; and it even promises that in time *Reynolds* v. *United States*, 98 U.S. 145 (1879), will be overruled.[6]

In another way, however, the Court retreats when in reference to Henry Thoreau it says his "choice was philosophical and personal rather than religious, and such belief does not rise to the demands of the Religion Clauses." That is contrary to what we held in *U.S.* v. *Seeger*, 380 U.S. 163 (1965), where we were concerned with the meaning of the words "religious training and belief" in the Selective Service Act, which were the basis of many conscientious objector claims. We said:

> Within that phrase would come all sincere religious beliefs which are based upon a power or being, or upon a faith, to which all else is subordinate or upon which all else is ultimately dependent. The test might be stated in these words: A sincere and meaningful belief, which occupies in the life of its possessor a place parallel to that filled by the God of those admittedly qualifying for the exemption, comes within the statutory definition. This construction avoids imputing to Congress an intent to classify different religious beliefs, exempting some and excluding others, and is in accord with the well-established congressional policy of equal treatment for those whose opposition to service is grounded in their religious tenets.

Welsh v. *U.S.*, 398 U.S. 333 (1970), was in the same vein. . . .

The essence of Welsh's philosophy, on the basis of which we held he was entitled to an exemption, was in these words:

> I believe that human life is valuable in and of itself; in its living; therefore I will not injure or kill another human being. This belief (and the corresponding "duty" to abstain from violence toward another person) is not "superior to those arising from any human relation." On the contrary: *it is essential to every human relation*. I cannot, therefore, conscientiously comply with the Government's insistence that I assume duties which I feel are immoral and totally repugnant.

---

6. In *Reynolds* v. *U.S.*, the Court upheld the conviction of a Mormon for violating an anti-polygamy statute.

I adhere to these exacted views of "religion" and see no acceptable alternative to them now that we have become a Nation of many religions and sects, representing all of the diversities of the human race.

15

Stone v. Graham

449 U.S. 39 (1980)

The Ten Commandments are as central as any document to the history of the West, and indeed of mankind. But may a state require its public schools to post a copy of the Decalogue? In 1980 the Supreme Court declined to hear arguments in a case challenging the constitutionality of a Kentucky law to that effect. Instead, it issued a *per curiam* opinion (one issued "by the court" instead of by an individual justice) in which it said that under the three-part *Lemon* test the law violated the ban on establishment.

The Kentucky trial court had upheld the statute on grounds that its legislative purpose was "secular and not religious" and that it would "neither advance nor inhibit any religion or religious group," nor involve the state excessively in religious matters. The state supreme court affirmed.

Stone v. *Graham* is included in this volume because it illustrates the sharp division among the justices over the Court's establishment jurisprudence. The opinion was signed by Justices William Brennan, Thurgood Marshall, Lewis Powell, John Paul Stevens, and Byron White. Chief Justice Warren Burger and Justice Harry Blackmun, who dissented, would have taken the case and heard argument. Dissenting on grounds that the courts of Kentucky appeared to have applied correct constitutional criteria in reaching their decisions, Justice Potter Stewart voted not to take the case at all. And Justice William Rehnquist also dissented, arguing that it was wrong for the Court summarily to reject the secular purpose articulated by the Kentucky legislature and affirmed by that state's trial court. (Under the so-called Rule of

Four, the Court does not review the merits of a case unless at least four justices vote to do so.) The *per curiam* opinion and Justice Rehnquist's dissent are presented here.

Participating in *Stone* v. *Graham*, decided November 17, 1980, were Chief Justice Warren E. Burger and Associate Justices Harry A. Blackmun, William J. Brennan, Jr., Thurgood Marshall, Lewis F. Powell, Jr., William H. Rehnquist, John Paul Stevens, Potter Stewart, and Byron R. White.

Opinions

Per Curiam.

This Court has announced a three-part test for determining whether a challenged state statute is permissible under the Establishment Clause. . . . *Lemon* v. *Kurtzman* (1971). If a statute violates any of these three principles, it must be struck down. . . . We conclude that Kentucky's statute requiring the posting of the Ten Commandments in public school rooms has no secular legislative purpose, and is therefore unconstitutional.

The Commonwealth insists that the statute in question serves a secular legislative purpose, observing that the legislature required the following notation in small print at the bottom of each display of the Ten Commandments: "The secular application of the Ten Commandments is clearly seen in its adoption as the fundamental legal code of Western Civilization and the Common Law of the United States."

The trial court found the "avowed" purpose of the statute to be secular, even as it labeled the statutory declaration "self-serving." Under this Court's rulings, however, such an "avowed" secular purpose is not sufficient to avoid conflict with the First Amendment. In *Abington* v. *Schempp* (1963), this Court held unconstitutional the daily reading of Bible verses and the Lord's Prayer in the public schools, despite the school district's assertion of such secular purposes as "the promotion of moral values, the contradiction to the materialistic trends of our times, the perpetuation of our institutions and the teaching of literature."

The pre-eminent purpose for posting the Ten Commandments on schoolroom walls is plainly religious in nature. The Ten Commandments are undeniably a sacred text in the Jewish and Christian faiths, and no legislative recitation of a supposed secular purpose can blind us to that fact. The Commandments do not confine themselves to arguably secular matters, such as honoring one's parents, killing or murder, adultery, stealing, false witness, and covetousness. See Exodus 20:12–17; Deuteronomy 5:16–21. Rather, the first part of the Commandments concerns the religious duties of believers; worshipping the

253

Lord God alone, avoiding idolatry, not using the Lord's name in vain, and observing the Sabbath Day. See Exodus 20:1–11; Deuteronomy 5:6–15.

This is not a case in which the Ten Commandments are integrated into the school curriculum, where the Bible may constitutionally be used in an appropriate study of history, civilization, ethics, comparative religion, or the like. Posting of religious texts on the wall serves no such educational function. If the posted copies of the Ten Commandments are to have any effect at all, it will be to induce the schoolchildren to read, meditate upon, perhaps to venerate and obey, the Commandments. However desirable this might be as a matter of private devotion, it is not a permissible state objective under the Establishment Clause.

It does not matter that the posted copies of the Ten Commandments are financed by voluntary private contributions, for the mere posting of the copies under the auspices of the legislature provides the "official support of the State . . . Government" that the Establishment Clause prohibits. *Schempp*. Nor is it significant that the Bible verses involved in this case are merely posted on the wall, rather than read aloud as in *Schempp* and *Engel* v. *Vitale* (1962), for "it is no defense to urge that the religious practices here may be relatively minor encroachments on the First Amendment." *Schempp*. We conclude that [the statute] violates the first part of the *Lemon* test, and thus the Establishment Clause of the Constitution.

Justice William H. Rehnquist, dissenting:

With no support beyond its own *ipse dixit*, the Court concludes that the Kentucky statute involved in this case "has *no* secular legislative purpose," and that "[t]he pre-eminent purpose for posting the Ten Commandments on schoolroom walls is plainly religious in nature." This even though, as the trial court found, "[t]he General Assembly thought the statute had a secular legislative purpose and specifically said so." The Court's summary rejection of a secular purpose articulated by the legislature and confirmed by the state court is without precedent in Establishment Clause jurisprudence. This Court regularly looks to legislative articulations of a statute's purpose in Establishment Clause cases and accords such pronouncements the deference they are due. . . . The fact that the asserted secular purpose may overlap with what some may see as a religious objective does not render it unconstitutional. As this Court stated in *McGowan* v. *Maryland*, 366 U.S. 420 (1961), in upholding the validity of Sunday closing laws, "the present purpose and effect of most of [these laws] is to provide a uniform day of rest for all citizens; the fact that this day is Sunday, a day of particular significance for the dominant Christian sects, does not bar the state from achieving its secular goals."

Schempp, repeatedly cited by the Court, is not to the contrary. No statutory findings of secular purpose supported the challenged enactments in that case. In one of the two cases considered in *Schempp* the trial court had determined that the challenged exercises were intended by the State to be religious exercises. A contrary finding is presented here. In the other case no specific finding had been made, and "the religious character of the exercise was admitted by the State."

The Court rejects the secular purpose articulated by the State because the Decalogue is "undeniably a sacred text." It is equally undeniable, however, as the elected representative of Kentucky determined, that the Ten Commandments have had a significant impact on the development of secular legal codes of the Western World. The trial court concluded that evidence submitted substantiated this determination. . . . Certainly the State was permitted to conclude that a document with such secular significance should be placed before its students with an appropriate statement of the document's secular import. . . .

The Establishment Clause does not require that the public sector be insulated from all things which may have a religious significance or origin. This Court has recognized that "religion has been closely identified with our history and government," *Schempp*, and that "[t]he history of man is inseparable from the history of religion," *Engel*. Kentucky has decided to make students aware of this fact by demonstrating the secular impact of the Ten Commandments. The words of Justice Jackson, concurring in *McCollum* v. *Board of Education* (1948), merit quotation at length:

> I think it remains to be demonstrated whether it is possible, even if desirable, to comply with such demands as plaintiff's completely to isolate and cast out of secular education all that some people may reasonably regard as religious instruction. Perhaps subjects such as mathematics, physics or chemistry are, or can be, completely secularized. But it would not seem practical to teach either practice or appreciation of the arts if we are to forbid exposure of youth to any religious influences. Music without sacred music, architecture minus the cathedral, or painting without the scriptural themes would be eccentric and incomplete, even from a secular point of view. . . . I should suppose it is a proper, if not an indispensable, part of preparation for a worldly life to know the roles that religion and religions

have played in the tragic story of mankind. The fact is that, for good or for ill, nearly everything in our culture worth transmitting, everything which gives meaning to life, is saturated with religious influences, derived from paganism, Judaism, Christianity—both Catholic and Protestant—and other faiths accepted by a large part of the world's peoples. One can hardly respect the system of education that would leave the student wholly ignorant of the currents of religious thought that move the world society for a part in which he is being prepared.

I therefore dissent from what I cannot refrain from describing as a cavalier summary reversal, without benefit of oral argument or briefs on the merits, of the highest court of Kentucky.

16

Thomas v. Review Board

450 U.S. 707 (1981)

In this case the Supreme Court held that the denial of unemployment compensation to a Jehovah's Witness who voluntarily left his job for religious reasons violated the free-exercise provision. The Court decided the case in light of *Sherbert* v. *Verner* (1963).

Eddie Thomas had worked for an Indiana foundry and machinery company for a year when the sheet-steel-making part closed and he was transferred to a department that produced turrets for military tanks. He claimed, and Indiana authorities reviewing his case agreed, that his religious beliefs prevented him from taking part in the production of war machines, and he quit. Indiana law conditioned unemployment compensation upon job termination based upon a "good cause" arising in connection with an employee's work. The reviewing authorities held that Thomas's religious reason for quitting did not qualify him for benefits. The Indiana Court of Appeals reversed this conclusion, holding that the Indiana Employment Security Act burdened his right to the free exercise of religion. The state supreme court disagreed.

Thomas generated two opinions. Chief Justice Burger wrote the opinion of the Court, expressing the views of seven members (an eighth, Justice Harry Blackmun, concurred in part). Justice William Rehnquist filed the only dissent. Both are presented here.

Participating in *Thomas* v. *Review Board*, decided April 6, 1981, were Chief Justice Warren E. Burger and Associate Justices Harry A. Blackmun, William J. Brennan, Jr., Thurgood Marshall, Lewis F. Powell, Jr., William H. Rehnquist, John Paul Stevens, Potter Stewart, and Byron R. White.

257

Opinions

Chief Justice Warren E. Burger delivered the opinion of the Court:

The judgment under review must be examined in light of our prior decisions, particularly *Sherbert* v. *Verner* (1963).

Only beliefs rooted in religion are protected by the Free Exercise Clause, which, by its terms, gives special protection to the exercise of religion. *Sherbert, Wisconsin* v. *Yoder* (1972). The determination of what is a "religious" belief or practice is more often than not a difficult and delicate task. . . . However, the resolution of that question is not to turn upon a judicial perception of the particular belief or practice in question; religious beliefs need not be acceptable, logical, consistent, or comprehensible to others to merit First Amendment protection.

In support of his claim for benefits, Thomas testified:

Q. And then when it comes to actually producing the tank itself, hammering it out; that you will not do. . . .
"A. That's right, that's right when . . . I'm daily faced with the knowledge that these are tanks. . . .
"A. I really could not, you know, conscientiously continue to work with armaments. It would be against all of the e.g. . . . religious principles that . . . I have come to learn. . . ."

Based upon this and other testimony, the referee held that Thomas "quit due to his religious convictions." The Review Board adopted that finding, and the finding is not challenged in this Court.

The Indiana Supreme Court apparently took a different view of the record. It concluded that "although the claimant's reasons for quitting were described as religious, it was unclear what his belief was, and what the religious basis of his belief was." In that court's views, Thomas had made a merely "personal philosophical choice rather than a religious choice."

In reaching its conclusion, the Indiana court seems to have placed considerable reliance on the facts that Thomas was "struggling" with his beliefs and that he was not able to "articulate" his belief precisely. . . . But, Thomas' statements reveal no more than that he found work in the roll foundry sufficiently insulated from producing weapons of war. We see, therefore, that Thomas drew a line, and it is not for us to say that the line he drew was an unreasonable one. Courts should not undertake to dissect religious beliefs because the believer admits that he is "struggling" with his position or because his beliefs are not articulated with the clarity and precision that a more sophisticated person might employ.

The Indiana court also appears to have given significant weight to the fact that another Jehovah's Witness had no scruples about working on tank turrets; for that other Witness, at least, such work was "scripturally" acceptable. Intrafaith differences of that kind are not uncommon among followers of a particular creed, and the judicial process is singularly ill equipped to resolve such differences in relation to the Religion Clauses. One can, of course, imagine an asserted claim so bizarre, so clearly nonreligious in motivation, as not to be entitled to protection under the Free Exercise Clause; but that is not the case here, and the guarantee of free exercise is not limited to beliefs which are shared by all of the members of a religious sect. Particularly in this sensitive area, it is not within the judicial function and judicial competence to inquire whether the petitioner or his fellow worker more correctly perceived the command of their common faith. Courts are not arbiters of scriptural interpretation.

The narrow function of a reviewing court in this context is to determine whether there was an appropriate finding that petitioner terminated his work because of an honest conviction that such work was forbidden by his religion. Not surprisingly, the record before the referee and the Review Board was not made with an eye to the microscopic examination often exercised in appellate judicial review. However, judicial review is confined to the facts as found and conclusions drawn. On this record, it is clear that Thomas terminated his employment for religious reasons.

More than thirty years ago [in *Everson* v. *Board of Education*, 1947], the Court held that a person may not be compelled to choose between the exercise of a First Amendment right and participation in an otherwise available public program. . . .

Later, in *Sherbert* the Court examined South Carolina's attempt to deny unemployment compensation benefits to a Sabbatarian who declined to work on Saturday. . . .

The respondent Review Board argues, and the Indiana Supreme Court held, that the burden of proof upon religion here is only the indirect consequence of public welfare legislation that the State clearly has authority to enact. . . . Indiana requires applicants for unemployment compensation to show that they left work for "good cause in connection with the work."

A similar argument was made and rejected in *Sherbert*, however. It is true that, as in *Sherbert*, the Indiana law does not *compel* a violation of conscience. But, "this is only the beginning, not the end, of our inquiry." In a variety of ways we have said that "[a] regulation neutral on its face may, in its application, nonetheless offend the constitutional requirement for governmental neutrality if it unduly burdens the free exercise of religion." *Yoder*.

Here, as in *Sherbert*, the employee was put to a choice between fidelity to religious belief or cessation of work; the coercive impact on Thomas is indistinguishable from Sherbert. . . . Where the state conditions receipt of an important benefit upon conduct proscribed by a religious faith, or where it denies such a benefit because of conduct mandated by religious belief, thereby putting substantial pressure on an adherent to modify his behavior and to violate his beliefs, a burden upon religion exists. While the compulsion may be indirect, the infringement upon free exercise is nonetheless substantial.

. . .

The mere fact that the petitioner's religious practice is burdened by a governmental program does not mean that an exemption accommodating his practice must be granted. The state may justify an inroad on religious liberty by showing that it is the least restrictive means of achieving some compelling state interest. However, it is still true that "[t]he essence of all that has been said and written on the subject is that only those interests of the highest order . . . can overbalance legitimate claims to the free exercise of religion." *Yoder*.

The purposes urged to sustain the disqualifying provision of the Indiana unemployment compensation scheme are twofold: (1) to avoid widespread unemployment and the consequent burden on the fund resulting if people were permitted to leave jobs for "personal" reasons; and (2) to avoid a detailed probing by employers into job applicants' religious beliefs. . . .

There is no evidence in the record to indicate that the number of people who find themselves in the predicament of choosing between benefits and religious beliefs is large enough to create "widespread unemployment," or even to seriously affect unemployment—and no such claim was advanced by the Review Board. Similarly, although detailed inquiry by employers into applicants' religious beliefs is undesirable, there is no evidence in the record to indicate that such inquiries will occur in Indiana, or that they have occurred in any of the states that extend benefits to people in the petitioner's position. Nor is there any reason to believe that the number of people terminating employment for religious reasons will be so great as to motivate employers to make such inquiries.

Neither of the interests advanced is sufficiently compelling to justify the burden upon Thomas' religious liberty. Accordingly, Thomas is entitled to receive benefits unless, as the respondents contend and the Indiana court held, such payment would violate the Establishment Clause.

The respondents contend that to compel benefit payments to Thomas involves the State in fostering a religious faith. There is, in a sense, a "benefit" to Thomas deriving from his religious beliefs, but this manifests no more than the tension between the two Religious Clauses resolved in *Sherbert*. . . .

Unless we are prepared to overrule *Sherbert*, Thomas cannot be denied the benefits due him on the basis of the findings of the referee, the Review Board, and the Indiana Court of Appeals that he terminated his employment because of his religious convictions.

Justice William H. Rehnquist, dissenting:

The Court today holds that the State of Indiana is constitutionally required to provide direct financial assistance to a person solely on the basis of his religious beliefs. Because I believe that the decision today adds mud to the already muddied waters of First Amendment jurisprudence, I dissent.

The Court correctly acknowledges that there is a "tension" between the Free Exercise and Establishment Clauses of the First Amendment of the United States Constitution. Although the relationship of the two Clauses has been the subject of much commentary, the "tension" is of fairly recent vintage, unknown at the time of the framing and adoption of the First Amendment. The causes of tension, it seems to me, are threefold. First, the growth of social welfare legislation during the latter part of the twentieth century has greatly magnified the potential for conflict between the two Clauses, since such legislation touches the individual at so many points in his life. Second, the decision by this Court that the First Amendment was "incorporated" into the Fourteenth Amendment and thereby made applicable against the States . . . similarly multiplied the number of instances in which the "tension" might arise. The third, and perhaps the most important, cause of the tension is our overly expansive interpretation of *both* Clauses. By broadly construing both Clauses, the Court has constantly narrowed the channel between the Scylla and Charybdis through which any state or federal action must pass in order to survive constitutional scrutiny.

None of these developments could have been foreseen by those who framed and adopted the First Amendment. The First Amendment was adopted well before the growth of much social welfare legislation and at a time when the Federal Government was in a real sense considered a government of limited delegated powers. Indeed, the principal argument against adopting the Constitution *without* a "Bill of Rights" was not that such an enactment would be *undesirable*, but that it would be *unnecessary* because of the limited nature of the Federal Government. So long as the Government enacts little social welfare legislation, as was the case in 1791, there are few occasions in which the two Clauses may conflict. Moreover, as originally enacted, the First Amendment applied only to the Federal Government, not the government of the States. *Barron* v. *Baltimore*, 7 Pet. 243 (1833).[1] The Framers could hardly anticipate *Barron* being superseded by the "selective incorporation" doctrine adopted by the Court, a decision which greatly expanded the number of statutes which would be subject to challenge under the First Amendment. Because those who drafted and adopted the First Amendment could not have foreseen either the growth of social welfare legislation or the incorporation of the First Amendment into the Fourteenth Amendment, we simply do not know how they would view the scope to the two Clauses.

The decision today illustrates how far astray the Court has gone in interpreting the Free Exercise and Establishment Clauses of the First Amendment. Although the Court holds that a State is constitutionally required to provide direct financial assistance to persons solely on the basis of their religious beliefs and recognizes the "tension" between the two Clauses, it does little to help resolve that tension or to offer meaningful guidance to other courts which must decide cases like this on a day-by-day basis. Instead, it simply asserts that there is no Establishment Clause violation here and leaves the tension between the two Religion Clauses to be resolved on a case-by-case basis. As suggested above, however, I believe that the "tension" is largely of this Court's own making, and would diminish almost to the vanishing point if the Clauses were properly interpreted.

Just as it did in *Sherbert*, the Court today reads the Free Exercise

---

1. In *Barron*, the Court refused to apply a provision of the Fifth Amendment to the states.

Clause more broadly than is warranted. As to the proper interpretation of the Free Exercise Clause, I would accept the decision of *Braunfeld* v. *Brown*, 366 U.S. 599 (1961), and the dissent in *Sherbert*. In *Braunfeld*, we held that Sunday closing laws do not violate the First Amendment rights of Sabbatarians. Chief Justice Warren explained that the statute did not make unlawful any religious practices of appellants; it simply made the practice of their religious beliefs more expensive. We concluded that "[t]o strike down, without the most critical scrutiny, legislation which imposes only an indirect burden on the exercise of religion, i.e., legislation which does not make unlawful the religious practice itself, would radically restrict the operating latitude of the legislature." Likewise in this case, it cannot be said that the State discriminated against Thomas on the basis of his religious beliefs or that he was denied benefits *because* he was a Jehovah's Witness. Where, as here, a State has enacted a general statute, the purpose and effect of which is to advance the State's secular goals, the Free Exercise Clause does not in my view require the State to conform that statute to the dictates of religious conscience of any group. As Justice Harlan recognized in his dissent in *Sherbert*, "Those situations in which the Constitution may require special treatment on account of religion are . . . few and far between." Like him I believe that although a State could choose to grant exemptions to religious persons from state unemployment regulations, a State is not constitutionally compelled to do so.[2]

The Court's treatment of the Establishment Clause issue is equally unsatisfying. Although today's decision requires a State to provide direct financial assistance to persons solely on the basis of their religious

---

2. [The following appears as footnote two in Justice Rehnquist's opinion.] To the extent *Sherbert* was correctly decided, it might be argued that cases such as *McCollum* v. *Board of Education* (1948), *Engel* v. *Vitale* (1962), *Abington School District* v. *Schempp* (1963), *Lemon* v. *Kurtzman* (1971), and *Committee for Public Education* v. *Nyquist*, 413 U.S. 756 (1973) were wrongly decided. The "aid" rendered to religion in these latter cases may not be significantly different, in kind or degree, from the "aid" afforded Mrs. Sherbert or Thomas. For example, if the State in *Sherbert* could not deny compensation to someone refusing work for religious reasons, it might be argued that a State may not deny reimbursement to students who choose for religious reasons to attend parochial schools. The argument would be that although a State need not allocate any funds to education, once it has done so, it may not require any person to sacrifice his religious beliefs in order to obtain an equal education. There can be little doubt that to the extent secular education provides answers to important moral questions without references to religion or teaches that there are no answers, a person in one sense sacrifices his religious belief by attending secular schools. And even if such "aid" were not constitutionally compelled by the Free Exercise Clause, Justice John M. Harlan II may well have been right in *Sherbert* when he found sufficient flexibility in the Establishment Clause to permit the States to voluntarily choose to grant such benefits to individuals.

beliefs, the Court nonetheless blandly assures us, just as it did in *Sherbert*, that its decision "plainly" does not foster the "establishment" of religion. I would agree that the Establishment Clause, properly interpreted, would not be violated if Indiana voluntarily chose to grant unemployment benefits to those persons who left their jobs for religious reasons. But I also believe that the decision below is inconsistent with many of our prior Establishment Clause cases. Those cases, if faithfully applied, would require us to hold that such voluntary action by a State *did* violate the Establishment Clause.

Justice Stewart noted this point in his concurring opinion in *Sherbert*. He observed that decisions like *Sherbert*, and the one rendered today, squarely conflict with the more extreme language of many of our prior Establishment Clause cases. In *Everson*, the Court stated that the Establishment Clause bespeaks a "government . . . stripped of all power . . . to support, or otherwise to assist any or all religion . . . ," and no State "can pass laws which aid one religion . . . [or] all religions." In *Torcaso* v. *Watkins* (1961), the Court asserted that the government cannot "constitutionally pass laws or impose requirements which aid all religions as against non-believers." And in *Abington School District* v. *Schempp* (1963), the Court adopted Justice Rutledge's words in *Everson* that the Establishment Clause forbids "every form of public aid or support for religion."

In recent years the Court has moved away from the mechanistic "no-aid-to-religion" approach to the Establishment Clause and has stated a three-part test to determine the constitutionality of governmental aid to religion. See *Lemon* v. *Kurtzman* (1971); *Committee for Public Education* v. *Nyquist*, 413 U.S. 756 (1973).[3] . . .

It is not surprising that the Court today makes no attempt to apply those principles to the facts of this case. If Indiana were to legislate what the Court today requires—an unemployment compensation law which permitted benefits to be granted to those persons who quit their jobs for religious reasons—the statute would "plainly" violate the Establishment Clause as interpreted in such cases as *Lemon* and *Nyquist*. First, although the unemployment statute as a whole would be enacted

---

3. In *Nyquist* the Court struck down a state law whose "effect" under the *Lemon* test was to advance religion. The statute had three elements. One provided grants to private schools for maintenance and repair of school facilities: another provided reimbursement of 50 percent of private school tuition to parents making less than $5,000 a year; the third allowed taxpayers who had paid at least $50 in private school tuition to deduct varying amounts depending on their income level, with a maximum tax reduction of $50.

to serve a secular legislative purpose, the proviso would clearly serve only a religious purpose. It would grant financial benefits for the sole purpose of accommodating religious beliefs. Second, there can be little doubt that the primary effect of the proviso would be to "advance" religion by facilitating the exercise of religious belief. Third, any statute including such a proviso would surely "entangle" the State in religion far more than the mere grant of tax exemptions, as in *Walz*, or the award of tuition grants and tax credits, as in *Nyquist*. By granting financial benefits to persons solely on the basis of their religious beliefs, the State must necessarily inquire whether the claimant's belief is "religious" and whether it is sincerely held. Otherwise any dissatisfied employee may leave his job without cause and claim that he did so because his own particular beliefs required it.

It is unclear from the Court's opinion whether it has temporarily retreated from its expansive view of the Establishment Clause, or wholly abandoned it. I would welcome the latter. Just as I think that Justice Harlan in *Sherbert* correctly stated the proper approach to free exercise questions, I believe that Justice Stewart, dissenting in *Schempp*, accurately stated the reach of the Establishment Clause. He explained that the Establishment Clause is limited to "government support of proselytizing activities of religious sects by throwing the weight of secular authorit[ies] behind the dissemination of religious tenets." Conversely, governmental assistance which does not have the effect of "inducing" religious belief, but instead merely "accommodates" or implements an independent religious choice does not impermissibly involve the government in religious choices and therefore does not violate the Establishment Clause of the First Amendment. I would think that in this case, as in *Sherbert*, had the State voluntarily chosen to pay unemployment compensation benefits to persons who left their jobs for religious reasons, such aid would be constitutionally permissible because it redounds directly to the benefit of the individual.

In sum, my difficulty with today's decision is that it reads the Free Exercise Clause too broadly and it fails to squarely acknowledge that such a reading conflicts with many of our Establishment Clause cases. As such, the decision simply exacerbates the "tension" between the two Clauses. If the Court were to construe the Free Exercise Clause as it did in *Braunfeld* and the Establishment Clause as Justice Stewart did in *Schempp*, the circumstances in which there would be a conflict between the two Clauses would be few and far between. Although I heartily agree with the Court's tacit abandonment of much of our rhetoric about the Establishment Clause, I regret that the Court cannot see its way clear to restore what was surely intended to have been a greater degree of flexibility to the Federal and State Governments in legislating consistently with the Free Exercise Clause. Accordingly, I would affirm the judgment of the Indiana Supreme Court.

17

Widmar v. Vincent

454 U.S. 263 (1981)

The Supreme Court here turned to a question of "equal access": May a state university refuse to grant a student religious group access to facilities generally open to other student groups? The Court's answer was no. Three years earlier, in *McDaniel* v. *Paty*, 435 U.S. 612, the Court had held that a minister could not be disqualified on grounds of his religious faith from serving as a delegate to a state constitutional convention. In both cases the Court rejected the argument that the no-establishment provision requires the state to discriminate against religion.

Because the Court in *Widmar* based its decision on the constitutional protection for freedom of expression, it is not, strictly speaking, a free-exercise case. But it arose in part in terms of the free exercise of religion, and religious liberty surely was affected by the ruling. Moreover, the case had a clear establishment component.

The University of Missouri at Kansas City routinely made its facilities available to student organizations registered with the school, more than one hundred in all. From 1973 to 1977 a registered group of Christians called Cornerstone regularly sought and received permission to hold its meetings in university facilities. But in 1977 the university, acting upon a regulation prohibiting the use of school buildings or grounds "for purposes of religious worship or religious teaching," told Cornerstone it could no longer meet on campus. Eleven student members of Cornerstone sued, alleging violation of their rights to the free exercise of religion, equal protection, and freedom of speech. The university regulation was upheld in federal district court, which also found that the regulation was in fact required by the establishment prohibition. The U.S. Court of Appeals for the Eighth Circuit reversed.

Widmar generated three opinions. The opinion of the Court—written by Justice Lewis Powell and expressing the views of seven members—and the lone dissent by Justice Byron White are presented here. Justice John Paul Stevens concurred in the judgment but wrote separately.

Participating in *Widmar* v. *Vincent*, decided December 8, 1981, were Chief Justice Warren E. Burger and Associate Justices Harry A. Blackmun, William J. Brennan, Jr., Thurgood Marshall, Lewis F. Powell, Jr., William H. Rehnquist, John Paul Stevens, Potter Stewart, and Byron R. White.

Opinions

Justice Lewis F. Powell, Jr., delivered the opinion of the Court:

Through its policy of accommodating their meetings, the University has created a forum generally open for use by student groups. Having done so, the University has assumed an obligation to justify its discriminations and exclusions under applicable constitutional norms. The Constitution forbids a State to enforce certain exclusions from a forum generally open to the public, even if it was not required to create the forum in the first place. . . .

The University's institutional mission, which it describes as providing a *"secular education"* to its students, does not exempt its actions from constitutional scrutiny. With respect to persons entitled to be there, our cases leave no doubt that the First Amendment rights of speech and association extend to the campuses of state universities.

Here the University of Missouri at Kansas City has discriminated against student groups and speakers based on their desire to use a generally open forum to engage in religious worship and discussion. These are forms of speech and association protected by the First Amendment.[1] In order to justify discriminatory exclusion from a pub-

---

1. [This appears as footnote six in the text of the opinion.] The dissent argues that "religious worship" is not speech generally protected by the "free speech" guarantee of the First Amendment and the "equal protection" guarantee of the Fourteenth Amendment. If "religious worship" were protected "speech," the dissent reasons, "the Religion Clauses would be emptied of any independent meaning in circumstances in which religious practice took the form of speech." This is a novel argument. The dissent does not deny that speech *about* religion is speech entitled to the general protections of the First Amendment. It does not argue that descriptions of religious experiences fail to qualify as "speech." Nor does it repudiate last term's decision in *Hefron* v. *International Society for Krishna Consciousness, Inc.*, 452 U.S. 640 (1981), which assumed that religious appeals to nonbelievers constituted protected "speech." Rather, the dissent seems to attempt a distinction between the kinds of religious speech explicitly protected by our cases and a new class of religious "speech act[s]," constituting "worship." There are at least three difficulties with this distinction.

First, the dissent fails to establish that the distinction has intelligible content. There is no indication when "singing hymns, reading scripture, and teaching biblical principles" cease to be "singing, teaching, and reading"—all apparently forms of "speech," despite their religious subject matter—and become unprotected "worship."

Second, even if the distinction drew an arguably principled line, it is highly doubtful that it would lie within the judicial competence to administer. Merely to draw the dis-

lic forum based on the religious content of a group's intended speech, the University must therefore satisfy the standard of review appropriate to content-based exclusions. It must show that its regulation is necessary to serve a compelling state interest and that it is narrowly drawn to achieve that end.

In this case the University claims a compelling interest in maintaining strict separation of church and State. It derives this interest from the "Establishment Clause" of both the Federal and Missouri Constitutions.

The University first argues that it cannot offer its facilities to religious groups and speakers on the terms available to other groups without violating the Establishment Clause of the Constitution of the United States. We agree that the interest of the University in complying with its constitutional obligations may be characterized as compelling. It does not follow, however, that an "equal access" policy would be incompatible with this Court's Establishment Clause cases. Those cases hold that a policy will not offend the Establishment Clause if it can pass a three-pronged test. . . . *Lemon* v. *Kurtzman* (1971).

In this case two prongs of the test are clearly met. Both the District Court and the Court of Appeals held that an open-forum policy, including nondiscrimination against religious speech,[2] would have a secular purpose and would avoid entanglement with religion. But the District Court concluded, and the University argues here, that allowing

---

tinction would require the university—and ultimately the courts—to inquire into the significance of words and practices to different religious faiths, and in varying circumstances by the same faith. Such inquiries would tend inevitably to entangle the State with religion in a manner forbidden by our cases. E.g., *Walz* v. *Tax Commission* (1970).

Finally, the dissent fails to establish the *relevance* of the distinction on which it seeks to rely. The dissent apparently wishes to preserve the vitality of the Establishment Clause. But it gives no reason why the Establishment Clause, or any other provision of the Constitution, would require different treatment for religious speech designed to win religious converts . . . than for religious worship by persons already converted. It is far from clear that the State gives greater support in the latter case than in the former.

2. [The following appears as footnote nine in the text of the opinion.] As the dissent emphasizes, the Establishment Clause requires the State to distinguish between "religious" speech—speech, undertaken or approved by the State, the primary effect of which is to support an establishment of religion—and "nonreligious" speech—speech, undertaken or approved by the State, the primary effect of which is not to support an establishment of religion. This distinction is required by the plain text of the Constitution. It is followed in our cases. E.g., *Stone* v. *Graham* (1980). The dissent attempts to equate this distinction with its view of an alleged constitutional difference between religious "speech" and religious "worship." We think that the distinction advanced by the dissent lacks a foundation in either the Constitution or in our cases, and that it is judicially unmanageable.

religious groups to share the limited public forum would have the "primary effect" of advancing religion.

The University's argument misconceives the nature of this case. The question is not whether the creation of a religious forum would violate the Establishment Clause. The University has opened its facilities for use by student groups, and the question is whether it can now exclude groups because of the content of their speech. In this context we are unpersuaded that the primary effect of the public forum, open to all forms of discourse, would be to advance religion.

We are not oblivious to the range of an open forum's likely effects. It is possible—perhaps even foreseeable—that religious groups will benefit from access to University facilities. But this Court has explained that a religious organization's enjoyment of merely "incidental" benefits does not violate the prohibition against the "primary advancement" of religion. . . .

We are satisfied that any religious benefits of an open forum at UMKC would be "incidental" within the meaning of our cases. Two factors are especially relevant.

First, an open forum in a public university does not confer any imprimatur of State approval on religious sects or practices. As the Court of Appeals quite aptly stated, such a policy "would no more commit the University . . . to religious goals," than it is "now committed to the goals of the Students for a Democratic Society, the Young Socialist Alliance," or any other group eligible to use its facilities.[3]

Second, the forum is available to a broad class of nonreligious as well as religious speakers; there are over 100 recognized student groups at UMKC. The provision of benefits to so broad a spectrum of groups is an important index of secular effect. If the Establishment Clause barred the extension of general benefits to religious groups, "a church could not be protected by the police and fire departments, or have its public sidewalk kept in repair." *Roemer* v. *Maryland Board of Public Works*, 426 U.S. 736 (1976).[4] At least in the absence of empirical evidence that religious groups will dominate UMKC's open forum, we

---

3. [The following is from footnote fourteen in the text of the opinion.] University students are, of course, young adults. They are less impressionable than younger students and should be able to appreciate that the University's policy is one of neutrality toward religion. . . .

4. In *Roemer*, a case involving public aid to higher education, the Court upheld general subsidies for nonsectarian uses. "[R]eligious institutions need not be quarantined from public benefits that are neutrally available to all," wrote Justice Harry Blackmun in his opinion.

agree with the Court of Appeals that the advancement of religion would not be the forum's "primary effect."

Arguing that the State of Missouri has gone further than the federal Constitution in proscribing indirect state support for religion, the University claims a compelling interest in complying with the applicable provisions of the Missouri Constitution.

The Missouri courts have not ruled whether a general policy of accommodating student groups, applied equally to those wishing to gather to engage in religious and nonreligious speech, would offend the State Constitution. We need not, however, determine how the Missouri courts would decide this issue. It is also unnecessary for us to decide whether, under the Supremacy Clause, a state interest, derived from its own constitution, could ever outweigh free speech interests protected by the First Amendment. We limit our holding to the case before us.

On one hand, respondents' First Amendment rights are entitled to special constitutional solicitude. Our cases have required the most exacting scrutiny in cases in which a State undertakes to regulate speech on the basis of its content. On the other hand, the state interest asserted here—in achieving greater separation of church and State than is already ensured under the Establishment Clause of the Federal constitution—is limited by the Free Exercise Clause and in this case by the Free Speech clause as well. In this constitutional context, we are unable to recognize the State's interest as sufficiently "compelling" to justify content-based discrimination against respondents' religious speech.

Our holding in this case in no way undermines the capacity of the University to establish reasonable time, place, and manner regulations. Nor do we question the right of the University to make academic judgments as to how best to allocate scarce resources. . . . Finally, we affirm the continuing validity of cases that recognize a university's right to exclude even First Amendment activities that violate reasonable campus rules or substantially interfere with the opportunity of other students to obtain an education.

The basis for our decision is narrow. Having created a forum generally open to student groups, the University seeks to enforce a content-based exclusion of religious speech. Its exclusionary policy violates the fundamental principle that a state regulation of speech should be content-neutral, and the University is unable to justify this violation under applicable constitutional standards.

Justice Byron R. White, dissenting:

In affirming the decision of the Court of Appeals, the majority rejects petitioners' argument that the Establishment Clause of the Constitution prohibits the use of university buildings for religious purposes. A state university may permit its property to be used for purely religious services without violating the First and Fourteenth amendments. With this I agree. The Establishment Clause, however, sets limits only on what the State may do with respect to religious organizations; it does not establish what the State is *required* to do. I have long argued that Establishment Clause limits on state action which incidentally aids religion are not as strict as the Court has held. The step from the permissible to the necessary, however, is a long one. In my view, just as there is room under the Religion Clauses for state policies that may have some beneficial effect on religion, there is also room for state policies that may incidentally burden religion. In other words, I believe the States to be a good deal freer to formulate policies that affect religion in divergent ways than does the majority. The majority's position will inevitably lead to those contradictions and tension between the Establishment and Free Exercise Clauses warned against by Justice Stewart in *Sherbert* v. *Verner* (1963).

. . . The issue here is only whether the University regulation as applied and interpreted in this case is impermissible under the Federal Constitution. If it is impermissible, it is because it runs afoul of either the Free Speech or the Free Exercise Clause of the First Amendment.

A large part of respondents' argument, accepted by the court below and accepted by the majority, is founded on the proposition that because religious worship uses speech, it is protected by the Free Speech Clause of the First Amendment. Not only is it protected, they argue, but religious worship *qua* speech is not different from any other variety of protected speech as a matter of constitutional principle. I believe that this proposition is plainly wrong. Were it right, the Religion Clauses would be emptied of any independent meaning in circumstances in which religious practice took the form of speech.

Although the majority describes this argument as "novel," I believe it to be clearly supported by our previous cases. Just last Term, the Court found it sufficiently obvious that the Establishment Clause prohibited a State from posting a copy of the Ten Commandments on the classroom wall that a statute requiring such a posting was summarily struck down. *Stone* v. *Graham* (1980). That case necessarily presumed that the State could not ignore the religious content of the written message, nor was it permitted to treat that content as it would, or must, treat, other—secular—messages under the First Amendment's protection of speech. Similarly, the Court's decisions prohibiting prayer in the public schools rest on a content-based distinction between varieties of speech: as a speech act, apart from its content, a prayer is indistinguishable from a biology lesson. Operation of the Free Exercise Clause is equally dependent, in certain circumstances, on recognition of a content-based distinction between religious and secular speech. Thus, in *Torcaso* v. *Watkins* (1961), the Court struck down, as violative of the Free Exercise Clause, a state requirement that made a declaration of belief in God a condition of state employment. A declaration is again a speech act, but it was the content of the speech that brought the case within the scope of the Free Exercise Clause.

If the majority were right that no distinction may be drawn between verbal acts of worship and other verbal acts, all of these cases would have to be reconsidered. Although I agree that the line may be difficult to draw in many cases, surely the majority cannot seriously suggest that no line may ever be drawn.[5] If that were the case, the majority would have to uphold the University's right to offer a class entitled "Sunday Mass." Under the majority's view, such a class would be—as a matter of constitutional principle—indistinguishable from a class entitled "The History of the Catholic Church."

There may be instances in which a State's attempt to disentangle itself from religious worship would intrude upon secular speech about religion. In such a case, the State's action would be subject to challenge under the Free Speech Clause of the First Amendment. This is not such a case. This case involves religious worship only; the fact that worship is accomplished through speech does not add anything to respondents' argument. That argument must rely upon the claim that the State's action impermissibly interferes with the free exercise of respondents' religious practices. Although this is a close question, I conclude that it does not.

Plausible analogies on either side suggest themselves. Respondents argue, and the majority agrees, that by permitting any student group to use its facilities for communicative purposes other than religious worship, the University has created a "public forum." With ample

---

5. [The following appears as footnote three in the text of the opinion.] Indeed, while footnote 6 of the majority opinion [see, above, n. 1] suggests that no intelligible distinction may be drawn between worship and other forms of speech, footnote 9 [see, above, n. 2] recognizes that the Establishment Clause "requires" that such a line be drawn. The majority does not adequately explain why the State is "required" to observe a line in one context, but prohibited from voluntarily recognizing it in another context.

support, they argue that the State may not make content-based distinctions as to what groups may use, or what messages may be conveyed in, such a forum. The right of the religious to nondiscriminatory access to the public forum is well established. Moreover, it is clear that there are bounds beyond which the University could not go in enforcing its regulation: I don't suppose it could prevent students from saying grace before meals in the school cafeteria, or prevent distribution of religious literature on campus.

Petitioners, on the other hand, argue that allowing use of their facilities for religious worship is constitutionally indistinguishable from directly subsidizing such religious services. . . . They argue that the fact that secular student groups are entitled to the in-kind subsidy at issue here does not establish that a religious group is entitled to the same subsidy. They could convincingly argue, for example, that a state university that pays for basketballs for the basketball team is not thereby required to pay for Bibles for a group like Cornerstone.

A third analogy suggests itself, one that falls between these two extremes. There are a variety of state policies which incidentally benefit religion that this Court has upheld without implying that they were constitutionally required of the State. Provision of university facilities on a uniform basis of all student groups is not very different from provision of textbooks [*Board of Education* v. *Allen*, 1968] or transportation [*Everson* v. *Board of Education*, 1947]. From this perspective the issue is not whether the state must, or must not, open its facilities to religious worship; rather, it is whether the State may choose not to do so.

Each of these analogies is persuasive. Because they lead to different results, however, they are of limited help in reaching a decision here. They also demonstrate the difficulty in reconciling the various interests expressed in the Religion Clauses. In my view, therefore, resolution of this case is best achieved by returning to first principles. This requires an assessment of the burden on respondents' ability freely to exercise their religious beliefs and practices and of the State's interest in enforcing its regulation.

Respondents complain that compliance with the regulation would require them to meet "about a block and a half" from campus under conditions less comfortable than those previously available on campus. I view this burden on free exercise as minimal. Because the burden is minimal, the State need do no more than demonstrate that the regulation furthers some permissible state end. The State's interest in avoiding claims that it is financing or otherwise supporting religious worship—in maintaining a definitive separation between church and

State—is such an end. That the State truly does mean to act toward this end is amply supported by the treatment of religion in the State Constitution. Thus, I believe the interest of the State is sufficiently strong to justify the imposition of the minimum burden on respondents' ability freely to exercise their religious beliefs.

On these facts, therefore, I cannot find that the application of the regulation to prevent Cornerstone from holding religious worship services in University facilities violates the First and Fourteenth Amendments. I would not hold as the majority does that if a university permits students and others to use its property for secular purposes, it must also furnish facilities to religious groups for the purposes of worship and the practice of their religion. Accordingly, I would reverse the judgment of the Court of Appeals.

18

Mueller v. Allen

463 U.S. 388 (1983)

R eturning to the vexed issue of public aid to church-related
schools, the Supreme Court in *Mueller* v. *Allen* upheld a
Minnesota law allowing deduction of school tuition costs
against income taxes. The deduction was available to all parents
of school-age children, regardless of the nature of the schools
the children attended—public or private, church-related or secular. Minnesota taxpayers had challenged the law on grounds
that it provided financial help to sectarian institutions, and in
fact almost all the deductions taken were claimed by parents of
children in church-related schools. But the federal district court
held that the statute did not violate the ban on establishment,
and the U.S. Court of Appeals for the Eighth Circuit affirmed,
maintaining that the law benefited a broad class of the state's
citizens.

Mueller v. *Allen* produced two opinions. Justice William Rehnquist wrote for the Court, reflecting the views of five members,
and Justice Thurgood Marshall filed a dissent joined by Justices
Harry Blackmun, William Brennan, and John Paul Stevens.
Both opinions are presented here, followed by editorial responses from the *Washington Post* and the *Wall Street Journal.*

Participating in *Mueller* v. *Allen,* decided June 29, 1983, were
Chief Justice Warren E. Burger and Associate Justices Harry A.
Blackmun, William J. Brennan, Jr., Thurgood Marshall, Sandra
Day O'Connor, Lewis F. Powell, Jr., William H. Rehnquist, John
Paul Stevens, and Byron R. White.

Opinions

Justice William H. Rehnquist delivered the opinion of the Court:

Today's case is no exception to our oft-repeated statement that the Establishment Clause presents especially difficult questions of interpretation and application. It is easy enough to quote the few words constituting that Clause—"Congress shall make no law respecting an establishment of religion." It is not at all easy, however, to apply this Court's various decisions construing the Clause to governmental programs of financial assistance to sectarian schools and the parents of children attending those schools. Indeed, in many of these decisions we have expressly or implicitly acknowledged that "we can only dimly perceive the lines of demarcation in this extraordinarily sensitive area of constitutional law." *Lemon* v. *Kurtzmann* (1971).[1]

One fixed principle in this field is our consistent rejection of the argument that "any program which in some manner aids an institution with a religious affiliation" violates the Establishment Clause. *Hunt* v. *McNair*, 413 U.S. 734 (1973).[2] For example, it is now well established that a State may reimburse parents for expenses incurred in transporting their children to school, *Everson* v. *Board of Education* (1947), and that it may loan secular textbooks to all schoolchildren within the State, *Board of Education* v. *Allen* (1968).

Notwithstanding the repeated approval given programs such as those in *Allen* and *Everson*, our decisions also have struck down arrangements resembling, in many respects, these forms of assistance. See, e.g., *Lemon*; *Levitt* v. *Committee for Public Education*, 413 U.S. 472 (1973); *Meek* v. *Pittenger*, 421 U.S. 349 (1975); *Wolman* v. *Walter*, 433 U.S. 229 (1977).[3] In this case we are asked to decide whether Minne-

---

1. The tone of this paragraph is consistent with that in other opinions by Justice Rehnquist on the religion clause; it is the decisional law on the two provisions of the clause, not their text or history, that he finds problematic.

2. In *McNair*, the Court upheld against constitutional challenge the issuance of state revenue bonds for the construction, on college campuses, including church-related ones, of buildings used for secular purposes.

3. In *Lemon* the Court struck down state reimbursement of non-public schools for the cost of teachers' salaries, textbooks, and instructional materials, and the state's pay-

278

sota's tax deduction bears greater resemblance to those types of assistance to parochial schools we have approved, or to those we have struck down. Petitioners place particular reliance on our decision in *Committee for Public Education* v. *Nyquist*, 413 U.S. 756 (1973), where we held invalid a New York statute providing public funds for the maintenance and repair of the physical facilities of private schools and granting thinly disguised "tax benefits," actually amounting to tuition grants, to the parents of children attending private schools. As explained below, we conclude that bears less resemblance to the arrangement struck down in *Nyquist* than it does to assistance programs upheld in our prior decisions and those discussed with approval in *Nyquist*.

The general nature of our inquiry in this area has been guided, since the decision in *Lemon*, by the "three-part" test laid down in that case. . . . While this principle is well settled, our cases have also emphasized that it provides "no more than [a] helpful signpos[t]" in dealing with Establishment Clause challenges. *McNair*. With this caveat in mind, we turn to the specific challenges raised against [the Minnesota statute] under the Lemon framework.

Little time need be spent on the question of whether the Minnesota tax deduction has a secular purpose. Under our prior decisions, governmental assistance programs have consistently survived this inquiry even when they have run afoul of other aspects of the *Lemon* framework. This reflects, at least in part, our reluctance to attribute unconstitutional motives to the States, particularly when a plausible secular purpose for the State's program may be discerned from the face of the statute.

A State's decision to defray the costs of educational expenses incurred by parents—regardless of the type of schools their children attend—evidences a purpose that is both secular and understandable. An educated populace is essential to the political and economic health of any community, and a State's efforts to assist parents in meeting the rising cost of educational expenses plainly serves this secular purpose of ensuring that the State's citizenry is well educated. Similarly, Minnesota, like other States, could conclude that there is a strong public interest in assuring the continued financial health of private schools,

---

ment of a salary supplement to teachers in non-public schools. In *Levitt* the Court struck down a state program reimbursing non-public schools for the cost of teacher-prepared examinations. In *Meek* and *Wolman* the Court held unconstitutional a direct loan of instructional materials to non-public schools while upholding the loan of textbooks to individual students.

both sectarian and nonsectarian. By educating a substantial number of students such schools relieve public schools of a correspondingly great burden—to the benefit of all taxpayers. . . .

We turn . . . to the more difficult but related question whether the Minnesota statute has "the primary effect of advancing the sectarian aims of the nonpublic schools." *Committee for Public Education* v. *Regan* 444 U.S. 646 (1980). In concluding that it does not, we find several features of the Minnesota tax deduction particularly significant. First, an essential feature of Minnesota's arrangement is the fact that [the deduction] is only one among many deductions—such as those for medical expenses, and charitable contributions—available under the Minnesota tax laws. Our decisions consistently have recognized that traditionally "[l]egislatures have especially broad latitude in creating classifications and distinctions in tax statutes," in part because the "familiarity with local conditions" enjoyed by legislators especially enables them to "achieve an equitable distribution of the tax burden." Under our prior decisions, the Minnesota Legislature's judgment that a deduction for educational expenses fairly equalizes the tax burden of its citizens and encourages desirable expenditures for educational purposes is entitled to substantial deference.

Other characteristics of [the statute] argue equally strongly for [its] constitutionality. Most importantly, the deduction is available for educational expenses incurred by all parents, including those whose children attend public schools and those whose children attend nonsectarian private schools or sectarian private schools. Just as in *Widmar* v. *Vincent* (1981), where we concluded that the State's provision of a forum neutrally "available to a broad class of non-religious as well as religious speakers" does not "confer any imprimatur of state approval," so here: "[t]he provision of benefits to so broad a spectrum of groups is an important index of secular effect."

In this respect, as well as others, this case is vitally different from the scheme struck down in *Nyquist*. There, public assistance amounting to tuition grants was provided only to parents of children in *nonpublic* schools. This fact had considerable bearing on our decision striking down the New York statute at issue; we explicitly distinguished both *Allen* and *Everson* on the grounds that "[i]n both cases the class of beneficiaries included *all* schoolchildren, those in public as well as those in private schools." Moreover, we intimated that "public assistance (e.g., scholarships) made available generally without regard to the sectarian-nonsectarian, or public-nonpublic nature of the institution benefitted," might not offend the Establishment Clause. We think the tax deduction adopted by Minnesota is more similar to this latter type of program than it is to the arrangement struck down in *Nyquist*. Unlike the assistance at issue in *Nyquist*, [the Minnesota statute] permits *all* parents—whether their children attend public school or private—to deduct their children's educational expenses. [A] program that neutrally provides state assistance to a broad spectrum of citizens is not readily subject to challenge under the Establishment Clause.

We also agree with the Court of Appeals that, by channeling whatever assistance it may provide to parochial schools through individual parents, Minnesota has reduced the Establishment Clause objections to which its action is subject. It is true, of course, that financial assistance provided to parents ultimately has an economic effect comparable to that of aid given directly to the school attended by their children. It is also true, however, that under Minnesota's arrangement public funds became available only as a result of numerous, private choices of individual parents of school-age children. For these reasons, we recognized in *Nyquist* that the means by which state assistance flows to private schools is of some importance: we said that "the fact that aid is disbursed to parents rather than to . . . schools" is a material consideration in Establishment Clause analysis, albeit "only one among many factors to be considered." It is noteworthy that all but one of our recent cases invalidating state aid to parochial schools have involved the direct transmission of assistance from the State to the schools themselves. The exception, of course, was *Nyquist*, which, as discussed previously, is distinguishable from this case on other grounds. Where, as here, aid to parochial schools is available only as a result of decisions of individual parents no "imprimatur of state approval" can be deemed to have been conferred on any particular religion, or on religion generally.

We find it useful, in the light of the foregoing characteristics of [the Minnesota statute], to compare the attenuated financial benefits flowing to parochial schools from the section to the evils against which the Establishment Clause was designed to protect. . . . The Establishment Clause of course extends beyond prohibition of a state church or payment of state funds to one or more churches. We do not think, however, that its prohibition extends to the type of tax deduction established by Minnesota. The historic purposes of the Clause simply do not encompass the sort of attenuated financial benefit, ultimately controlled by the private choices of individual parents, that eventually flows to parochial schools from the neutrally available tax benefit at issue in this case.

Petitioners argue that . . . the statute primarily benefits religious institutions. [They] rely . . . on a statistical analysis of the type of persons claiming the tax deduction. They contend that most parents of public school children incur no tuition expenses, and that other expenses deductible under [the statute] are negligible in value; moreover, they claim that 96% of the children in private schools in 1978–1979 attended religiously affiliated institutions. Because of all this, they reason, the bulk of deductions taken under [the statute] will be claimed by parents of children in sectarian schools. Respondents reply that petitioners have failed to consider the impact of deductions for items such as transportation, summer school tuition, tuition paid by parents whose children attended schools outside the school districts in which they resided, rental or purchase costs for a variety of equipment, and tuition for certain types of instruction not ordinarily provided in public schools.

We need not consider these contentions in detail. We would be loath to adopt a rule grounding the constitutionality of a facially neutral law on annual reports reciting the extent to which various classes of private citizens claimed benefits under the law. Such an approach would scarcely provide the certainty that this field stands in need of, nor can we perceive principled standards by which such statistical evidence might be evaluated. . . .

. . .

. . . [W]e hold that the Minnesota tax deduction for educational expenses satisfies the primary effect inquiry of our Establishment Clause cases.

Turning to the third part of the *Lemon* inquiry, we have no difficulty in concluding that the Minnesota statute does not "excessively entangle" the State in religion. The only plausible source of the "comprehensive, discriminating, and continuing state surveillance" necessary to run afoul of this standard would lie in the fact that state officials must determine whether particular textbooks qualify for a deduction. In making this decision, state officials must disallow deductions taken for "instructional books and materials used in the teaching of religious tenets, doctrines or worship, the purpose of which is to inculcate such tenets, doctrines or worship." Making decisions such as this does not differ substantially from making the types of decisions approved in earlier opinions of this Court. In *Allen*, for example, the Court upheld the loan of secular textbooks to parents or children attending nonpublic schools; though state officials were required to determine whether particular books were or were not secular, the system was held not to violate the Establishment Clause. . . . The same result follows in this case.[4]

Justice Thurgood Marshall, dissenting, joined by Justices William J. Brennan, Jr., Harry A. Blackmun, and John Paul Stevens:

The majority today does not question the continuing vitality of this Court's decision in *Nyquist*. That decision established that a State may not support religious education either through direct grants to parochial schools or through financial aid to parents of parochial school students. *Nyquist* also established that financial aid to parents of students attending parochial schools is no more permissible if it is provided in the form of a tax credit than if provided in the form of cash payments. Notwithstanding these accepted principles, the Court today upholds a statute that provides a tax deduction for the tuition charged by religious schools. The Court concludes that the Minnesota statute is "vitally different" from the New York statute at issue in *Nyquist*. [T]here is no significant difference between the two schemes. The Minnesota tax statute violates the Establishment Clause for precisely the same reason as the statute struck down in *Nyquist*: it has a direct and immediate effect of advancing religion.

In calculating their net income for state income tax purposes, Minnesota residents are permitted to deduct the cost of their children's tuition, subject to a ceiling of $500 or $700 per child. By taking this deduction, a taxpayer reduces his tax bill by a sum equal to the amount of tuition multiplied by his rate of tax. Although this tax benefit is available to any parents whose children attend schools which charge tuition, the vast majority of the taxpayers who are eligible to receive the benefit are parents whose children attend religious schools. In the 1978–1979 school year, 90,000 students were enrolled in nonpublic schools charging tuition; over 95% of those students attended sectarian schools. Although the statute also allows a deduction for the tuition expenses of children attending public schools, Minnesota public schools are generally prohibited by law from charging tuition. Public schools may assess tuition charges only for students accepted from

---

4. David P. Currie has observed that the difference between *Lemon* and *Mueller* is striking: "*Lemon* had forbidden the state to support even secular instruction; *Mueller* allowed it to support religious instruction as well" (*The Constitution in the Second Century*, 534). At the level of principle, however, *Mueller* was consistent with *Everson* v. *Board of Education*, according to Currie, because "when the state affords benefits to the public generally, it need not discriminate against religious activities."

outside the district. In the 1978–1979 school year, only 79 public school students fell into this category. The parents of the remaining 815,000 students who attended public schools were ineligible to receive this tax benefit.

Like the law involved in *Nyquist*, the Minnesota law can be said to serve a secular purpose: promoting pluralism and diversity among the State's public and nonpublic schools. But the Establishment Clause requires more than that legislation have a secular purpose. . . .

As we recognized in *Nyquist*, direct government subsidization of parochial school tuition is impermissible because "the effect of the aid is unmistakably to provide desired financial support for nonpublic, sectarian institutions." "[A]id to the educational function of [parochial] schools . . . necessarily results in aid to the sectarian school enterprise as a whole" because "[t]he very purpose of many of those schools is to provide an integrated secular and religious education." *Meek*. For this reason, aid to sectarian schools must be restricted to ensure that it may not be used to further the religious mission of those schools. See, e.g., *Wolman*. While "services such as police and fire protection, sewage disposal, highways, and sidewalks," may be provided to parochial schools in common with other institutions, because this type of assistance is clearly " 'marked off from the religious function' " of those schools, *Nyquist*, quoting *Everson*, unrestricted financial assistance, such as grants for the maintenance and construction of parochial schools, may not be provided. *Nyquist*. . . .

Indirect assistance in the form of financial aid to parents for tuition payments is similarly impermissible because it is not "subject to . . . restrictions" which " 'guarantee the separation between secular and religious educational functions and . . . ensure that State financial aid supports only the former.' " *Nyquist*. By ensuring that parents will be reimbursed for tuition payments they make, the Minnesota statute requires that taxpayers in general pay for the cost of parochial education and extends a financial "incentive to parents to send their children to sectarian schools." *Nyquist*. . . .

That parents receive a reduction of their tax liability, rather than a direct reimbursement, is of no greater significance here than it was in *Nyquist*. . . . It is equally irrelevant whether a reduction in taxes takes the form of a tax "credit," a tax "modification," or a tax "deduction." What is of controlling significance is not the form but the "substantive impact" of the financial aid.

The majority attempts to distinguish *Nyquist* by pointing to two differences between the Minnesota tuition-assistance program and the program struck down in *Nyquist*. Neither of these distinctions can withstand scrutiny.

The majority first attempts to distinguish *Nyquist* on the ground that Minnesota makes all parents eligible to deduct up to $500 or $700 for each dependent, whereas the New York law allowed a deduction only for parents whose children attended nonpublic schools. Although Minnesota taxpayers who send their children to local public schools may not deduct tuition expenses because they incur none, they may deduct other expenses, such as the cost of gym clothes, pencils, and notebooks, which are shared by all parents of school-age children. This, in the majority's view, distinguishes the Minnesota scheme from the law at issue in *Nyquist*.

That the Minnesota statute makes some small benefit available to all parents cannot alter the fact that the most substantial benefit provided by the statute is available only to those parents who send their children to schools that charge tuition. It is simply undeniable that the single largest expense that may be deducted under the Minnesota statute is tuition. The statute is little more than a subsidy of tuition masquerading as a subsidy of general educational expenses. The other deductible expenses are *de minimis* in comparison to tuition expenses.

Contrary to the majority's suggestion, the bulk of the tax benefits afforded by the Minnesota scheme are enjoyed by parents of parochial school children not because parents of public school children fail to claim deductions to which they are entitled, but because the latter are simply *unable* to claim the largest tax deduction that Minnesota authorizes. Fewer than 100 of more than 900,000 school-age children in Minnesota attend public schools that charge a general tuition. Of the total number of taxpayers who are eligible for the tuition deduction, approximately 96% send their children to religious schools. Parents who send their children to free public schools are simply ineligible to obtain the full benefit of the deduction except in the unlikely event that they buy $700 worth of pencils, notebooks, and bus rides for their school-age children. Yet parents who pay at least $700 in tuition to nonpublic, sectarian schools can claim the full deduction even if they incur no other educational expenses.

That this deduction has a primary effect of promoting religion can easily be determined without any resort to the type of "statistical evidence" that the majority fears would lead to constitutional uncertainty. The only factual inquiry necessary is the same as that employed in *Nyquist*: whether the deduction permitted for tuition expenses primarily benefits those who send their children to religious schools. In *Ny-*

quist we unequivocally rejected any suggestion that, in determining the effect of a tax statute, this Court should look exclusively to what the statute on its face purports to do and ignore the actual operation of the challenged provision. In determining the effect of the New York statute, we emphasized that "virtually all" of the schools receiving direct grants for maintenance and repair were Roman Catholic schools, that reimbursements were given to parents "who send their children to nonpublic schools, the bulk of which is concededly sectarian in orientation," that "it is precisely the function of New York's law to provide assistance to private schools, the great majority of which are sectarian," and that "tax deductions authorized by this law flow primarily to the parents of children attending sectarian, nonpublic schools.". . .

In this case, it is undisputed that well over 90% of the children attending tuition-charged schools in Minnesota are enrolled in sectarian schools. History and experience likewise instruct us that any generally available financial assistance for elementary and secondary school tuition expenses mainly will further religious education because the majority of the schools which charge tuition are sectarian. Because Minnesota, like every other State, is committed to providing free public education, tax assistance for tuition payments inevitably redounds to the benefit of nonpublic, sectarian schools and parents who send their children to those schools.

The majority also asserts that the Minnesota statute is distinguishable from the statute struck down in *Nyquist* in another respect: the tax benefit available under Minnesota law is a "genuine tax deduction," whereas the New York law provided a benefit which, while nominally a deduction, also had features of a "tax credit.". . .

This is a distinction without a difference. Our prior decisions have rejected the relevance of the majority's formalistic distinction between tax deductions and the tax benefit at issue in *Nyquist*. The deduction afforded by Minnesota law was "designed to yield a [tax benefit] in exchange for performing a specific act which the State desires to encourage." *Nyquist*. Like the tax benefit held impermissible in *Nyquist*, the tax deduction at issue here concededly was designed to "encourag[e] desirable expenditures for educational purposes." Of equal importance, as the majority also concedes, the "economic consequenc[e]" of these programs is the same, for in each the "financial assistance provided to parents ultimately has an economic effect comparable to that of aid given directly to the schools." It was precisely the substantive impact of the financial support, and not its particular form, that rendered the program in *Nyquist* unconstitutional.

The majority incorrectly asserts that Minnesota's tax deduction for tuition expenses "bears less resemblance to the arrangement stuck down in *Nyquist* than it does to assistance programs upheld in our prior decisions and those discussed with approval in *Nyquist*." One might as well say that a tangerine bears less resemblance to an orange than to an apple. The two cases relied on by the majority are inapposite today for precisely the same reasons that they were inapposite in *Nyquist*.

The Minnesota tuition tax deduction is not available to *all* parents, but only to parents whose children attend schools that charge tuition, which are comprised almost entirely of sectarian schools. More importantly, the assistance that flows to parochial schools as a result of the tax benefit is not restricted, and cannot be restricted, to the secular functions of those schools.

In my view, Minnesota's tax deduction for the cost of textbooks and other instructional materials is also constitutionally infirm. The majority is simply mistaken in concluding that a tax deduction, unlike a tax credit or a direct grant to parents, promotes religious education in a manner that is only "attenuated." A tax deduction has a primary effect that advances religion if it is provided to offset expenditures which are not restricted to the secular activities of parochial schools.

. . .

. . . Secular textbooks, like other secular instructional materials, contribute to the religious mission of the parochial schools that use those books. Although this Court upheld the loan of secular textbooks to religious schools in *Allen*, the Court believed at that time that it lacked sufficient experience to determine "based solely on judicial notice" that "the processes of secular and religious training are so intertwined that secular textbooks furnished to students by the public [will always be] instrumental in the teaching of religion." This basis for distinguishing secular instructional materials and secular textbooks is simply untenable, and is inconsistent with many of our more recent decisions concerning state aid to parochial schools. . . .

In any event, the Court's assumption in *Allen* that the textbooks at issue there might be used only for secular education was based on the fact that those very books had been chosen by the State for use in the public schools. In contrast, the Minnesota statute does not limit the tax deduction to those books that are chosen by the parochial schools. Rather, it permits a deduction for books that are chosen by the parochial schools themselves. Indeed, under the Minnesota statutory scheme, textbooks chosen by parochial schools but not used by public schools are likely to be precisely the ones purchased by parents for their children's use. . . .

There can be little doubt that the State of Minnesota intended to provide, and has provided, "[s]ubstantial aid to the educational function of [church-related] schools," and that the tax deduction for tuition and other educational expenses "necessarily results in aid to the sectarian school enterprise as a whole." *Meek.* It is beside the point that the State may have legitimate secular reasons for providing such aid. In focusing upon the contributions made by church-related schools, the majority has lost sight of the issue before us in this case.

> The sole question is whether state aid to these schools can be squared with the dictates of the Religion Clauses. Under our system the choice has been made that government is to be entirely excluded from the area of religious instruction. . . . The Constitution decrees that religion must be a private matter for the individual, the family, and the institutions of private choice, and that while some involvement and entanglement are inevitable, lines must be drawn. *Lemon.*

In my view, the lines drawn in *Nyquist* were drawn on a reasoned basis with appropriate regard for the principles of neutrality embodied by the Establishment Clause. I do not believe that the same can be said of the lines drawn by the majority today. For the first time, the Court has upheld financial support for religious schools without any reason at all to assume that the support will be restricted to the secular functions of those schools and will not be used to support religious instruction. This result is flatly at odds with the fundamental principle that a State may provide no financial support whatsoever to promote religion. As the Court stated in *Everson,* and has often repeated:

> No tax in any amount, large or small, can be levied to support any religious activities or institutions, whatever they may be called, or whatever form they may adopt to teach or practice religion.

I dissent.

Responses

*From the **Washington Post**, June 30, 1983, "The Court, Education, and Religion"*:

·The Supreme Court's decision to uphold, 5 to 4, Minnesota's tuition tax deduction is a poorly reasoned and unpersuasive interpretation of the constitutional separation of church and state. Minnesota's state income tax allows parents to deduct their children's school tuition and fees up to $700 a year. That provides, indirectly but very effectively, a state subsidy to private schools.

Justice Rehnquist's majority opinion reads like a result in search of a rationalization. It will encourage a proliferation of tax expenditures to finance private schools—and how about college tuition?

On the legal points, it is difficult to decide when a government tax or spending policy stops being broad support for religious activities. But the majority's effort to distinguish earlier cases striking down various grant and tax schemes doesn't work. They argue that the Minnesota law applies neutrally to both public and private schools. But the apparent neutrality ignores the actual effect: 95 percent of Minnesota's private schoolchildren *are* in sectarian schools, and deductible costs at free public schools are negligible. Although the purpose of the statute may be secular—support for education—the *effect* is to direct these tax dollars overwhelmingly toward religious institutions. Once they are there, the commingling of religious and nonreligious activities is unavoidable.

The court also says that Minnesota has used a "genuine tax deduction" similar to other credit and deduction provisions and that such legislative choices about tax burden are entitled to judicial deference. But this is *not* a complicated policy choice among different classes of corporate taxpayers or different kinds of tax shelters. The majority's further argument that Minnesota's financial support is indirect and only as a result of parental choices about schooling is a fair distinction from outright grants to religious institutions, but it hardly balances the reality: rather than mere "attenuated financial benefits," religious schools stand to profit handsomely from schemes modeled after Minnesota's.

The court's constitutional decision does not change the merits of the policy arguments. Tax benefits for private school tuition represent a threat to public education, not healthy competition. Public education had been and remains a crucial community institution and a vital aid to social and economic advancement for the great majority of families. It is unfortunate that just when the

289

country seemed on the brink of a major new commitment to public education, the court has encouraged a divisive diversion.

From the **Wall Street Journal**, *July 1, 1983, "School Rule":*

The Supreme Court has just ruled that government plans to give parents tax credits for their children's private school tuition are not necessarily unconstitutional. Educators have been fighting over this issue for years, and each team has some good arguments going for it. But the court has now removed the major bottleneck to putting the idea into action.

Tuition tax credit advocates have always contended that our public schools are falling partly because they suffer from an advanced case of inflamed government monopolitis. The rich have always had the money to send their kids to private school and buy an escape from substandard teaching. But poorer parents have had nowhere else to put their children. These parents have watched helplessly while classroom standards declined, schools became physically unsafe and powerful unions protected teachers from accountability and allowed them to rot the kiddies' brains with the latest fashionable ideas.

The advocates say you aren't going to get much improvement until you find some concrete way to hold the public schools' feet to the fire. Giving parents the money to opt for private schools will do the trick.

The opponents of tax credits have answers, some of them respectable. They warn that if you let the middle-class kids buy out, you'll turn the public schools into neglected holding pens for the children of the poor. You will also ensure that the schools can no longer play their traditional and necessary role of initiating children of all classes into the democratic American ethos.

The opponents have also shaken their fingers and pointed out that a tuition tax credit plan will cost governments a pretty penny in lost revenue. These opponents have been very considerate to call attention to this undoubted danger. Their concern would be more persuasive if they weren't often the same types who are usually willing to spend the federal government right into the mud.

And, finally, the opponents have rested heavily on the Constitution. Most of the private schools that would benefit from tax credit plans are parochial. Thus any such plan would involve the state with religion, and until now it has seemed that the courts would always declare this involvement unconstitutional. Public school champions, who under other circumstances have been happy enough to see religion involve itself in politics, are now, on this issue, arguing high-mindedly for the sanitary separation of church and state.

Well, in a surprising move the Supreme Court has now kicked over part of the opponents' argument. The Minnesota tuition tax credit plan that the court has just ruled on gave tax credits to parents with children in all types of schools, public and private. Parochial schools happened to get the main economic benefits of the plan. But the court's majority said this circumstance by itself did not invalidate the law, because the clear purpose of the statute was to help all parents neutrally. The way is now clear for governments to put permissible plans in place.

There is no doubt that the court was softer on religion in this ruling than it has been in the past, and people who worry about the separation of church and state are going to be unhappy with what they see as the change in standards. These guardians might note the fact that a clean and simple notion of church-state separation does not take account of the large and complex secular role that parochial schools have assumed in the educational life of the nation.

The guardians might also ask themselves why so many Americans are adamantly demanding a way to get their children into parochial school, even one with a denomination different from their children's. The reason, of course, is that for many parents the public schools have become insupportable; if the church-state distinction stands in the way of escape, these parents will insist that the church-state distinction must bend. Those who are most interested in preserving this distinction in American life are perhaps most responsible for seeing to it that the public schools are good enough to offer an acceptable alternative.

19

Marsh v. Chambers

463 U.S. 783 (1983)

Whether a state-sponsored legislative chaplaincy could survive First Amendment challenge was a question the Supreme Court was bound to consider once the two provisions of the religion clause had been applied to the states, and in 1983 such a case made its way to the Court. In *Marsh* v. *Chambers* the Court affirmed the constitutionality of the legislative chaplaincy sponsored and paid for by the state of Nebraska.

Chief Justice Warren Burger, author of the three-part *Lemon* test for determining the constitutionality of a challenged government action, did not examine the Nebraska chaplaincy in those terms in his opinion for the Court. Indeed, except in his summary of the facts in the case, which required him to refer to the *Lemon* test because the federal court of appeals had used it in striking down the chaplaincy, Burger did not mention the three-part test or even *Lemon* itself. Instead he argued from the "unambiguous and unbroken history of more than 200 years"—a history including both federal and state chaplaincies—in order to sustain the Nebraska practice.

Justice William Brennan, who in *Abington School District* v. *Schempp* (1963) had said such practices might be constitutional, was now convinced they were not and argued in a dissent that the Nebraska chaplaincy violated all three parts of the *Lemon* test. Justice John Paul Stevens also wrote in dissent. All three opinions are presented here.

The Court's opinion cast doubt upon the notion that the no-establishment provision prohibits government promotion of religion—a principle as old as its first articulation in *Everson* v.

293

Board of Education (1947)—and, in turn, upon the durability of the school-prayer and Bible-reading cases. After all, if the state may sponsor prayer for its legislators, why may it not do so for those attending its public schools? Perhaps the answer lay in the Court's arguments about the "impressionability" of minors. On the other hand—and the Court's subsequent decisions seem to bear this out—it may be that *Marsh* was only an aberration from establishment doctrine, not the beginning of a new direction, and certainly not one fraught with the kind of implications that would compel the Court to overrule *Engel* v. *Vitale* (1962) and *Schempp*.

The Nebraska legislature began each of its sessions with a prayer offered by a chaplain chosen by a council appointed for the task and paid with public funds. Robert E. Palmer, a Presbyterian minister, had served as chaplain since 1965. A member of the legislature, Ernest Chambers, sued, challenging the chaplaincy as an unconstitutional establishment of religion. The U.S. Court of Appeals for the Eighth Circuit held that the chaplaincy violated the *Lemon* test. The U.S. Supreme Court then reversed.

Participating in *Marsh* v. *Chambers*, decided July 5, 1983, were Chief Justice Warren E. Burger and Associate Justices Harry A. Blackmun, William J. Brennan, Jr., Thurgood Marshall, Sandra Day O'Connor, Lewis F. Powell, Jr., William H. Rehnquist, John Paul Stevens, and Byron R. White.

Opinions

Chief Justice Warren E. Burger delivered the opinion of the Court:

The opening of sessions of legislative and other deliberative public bodies with prayer is deeply embedded in the history and tradition of this country. From colonial times through the founding of the Republic and ever since, the practice of legislative prayer has coexisted with the principles of disestablishment and religious freedom. In the very courtrooms in which the United States District Judge and later three Circuit Judges heard and decided this case, the proceedings opened with an announcement that concluded, "God save the United States and this Honorable Court." The same invocation occurs at all sessions of this Court.

The tradition in many of the Colonies was, of course, linked to an established church, but the Continental Congress, beginning in 1774, adopted the traditional procedure of opening its sessions with a prayer offered by a paid chaplain. Although prayers were not offered during the Constitutional Convention, the First Congress . . . adopted the policy of selecting a chaplain to open each session with prayer. . . .

On September 25, 1789, three days after Congress authorized the appointment of paid chaplains, final agreement was reached on the language of the Bill of Rights. Clearly the men who wrote the First Amendment Religion Clauses did not view paid legislative chaplains and opening prayers as a violation of that Amendment, for the practice of opening sessions with prayer has continued without interruption ever since that early session of Congress. It has also been followed consistently in most of the states, including Nebraska, where the institution of opening legislative sessions with prayer was adopted even before the State attained statehood.

Standing alone, historical patterns cannot justify contemporary violations of constitutional guarantees, but there is far more here than simply historical patterns. In this context, historical evidence sheds light not only on what the draftsmen intended the Establishment Clause to mean, but also on how they thought that Clause applied to

295

the practice authorized by the First Congress—their actions reveal their intent. . . . In *Walz* v. *Tax Commission* (1970), we considered the weight to be accorded to history:

> It is obviously correct that no one acquires a vested or protected right in violation of Constitution by long use, even when that span of time covers our entire national existence and indeed predates it. Yet an unbroken practice . . . is not something to be lightly cast aside.

No more is Nebraska's practice of over a century, consistent with two centuries of national practice, to be cast aside. It can hardly be thought that in the same week Members of the First Congress voted to appoint and to pay a chaplain for each House and also voted to approve the draft of the First Amendment for submission to the states, they intended the Establishment Clause of the Amendment to forbid what they had just declared acceptable. In applying the First Amendment to the states through the Fourteenth Amendment, *Cantwell* v. *Connecticut* (1940), it would be incongruous to interpret that Clause as imposing more stringent First Amendment limits on the states than the draftsmen imposed on the Federal Government.

This unique history leads us to accept the interpretation of the First Amendment draftsmen who saw no real threat to the Establishment Clause arising from a practice of prayer similar to that now challenged. We conclude that legislative prayer presents no more potential for establishment than the provision of school transportation, *Everson* v. *Board of Education* (1947), beneficial grants for higher education, *Tilton* v. *Richardson*, 403 U.S. 672 (1971), or tax exemptions for religious organizations, *Walz*.

. . .

In light of the unambiguous and unbroken history of more than 200 years, there can be no doubt that the practice of opening legislative sessions with prayer has become part of the fabric of our society. To invoke Divine guidance on a public body entrusted with making the laws is not, in these circumstances, an "establishment" of religion or a step toward establishment; it is simply a tolerable acknowledgment of beliefs widely held among the people of this country. As Justice Douglas observed, "[w]e are a religious people whose institutions presuppose a Supreme Being." *Zorach* v. *Clauson* (1952).

We turn then to the question of whether any features of the Nebraska practice violate the Establishment Clause. Beyond the bare fact that a prayer is offered, three points have been made: first, that a clergyman of only one denomination—Presbyterian—has been selected for sixteen years; second, that the chaplain is paid at public expense; and third, that the prayers are in the Judeo-Christian tradition. Weighed against the historical background, these factors do not serve to invalidate Nebraska's practice.

The Court of Appeals was concerned that Palmer's long tenure has the effect of giving preference to his religious views. We cannot, any more than Members of the Congresses of this century, perceive any suggestion that choosing a clergyman of one denomination advances the beliefs of a particular church. To the contrary, the evidence indicates that Palmer was reappointed because his performance and personal qualities were acceptable to the body appointing him. Palmer was not the only clergyman heard by the legislature; guest chaplains have officiated at the request of various legislators and as substitutes during Palmer's absences. Absent proof that the chaplain's reappointment stemmed from an impermissible motive, we conclude that his long tenure does not in itself conflict with the Establishment Clause.

Nor is the compensation of the chaplain from public funds a reason to invalidate the Nebraska Legislature's chaplaincy; remuneration is grounded in historic practice initiated, as we noted earlier, by the same Congress that drafted the Establishment Clause of the First Amendment. The Continental Congress paid its chaplain, as did some of the states. Currently, many state legislatures and the United States Congress provide compensation for their chaplains. Nebraska has paid its chaplain for well over a century. The content of the prayer is not of concern to judges where, as here, there is no indication that the prayer opportunity has been exploited to proselytize or advance any one, or to disparage any other, faith or belief. That being so, it is not for us to embark on a sensitive evaluation or to parse the content of a particular prayer.

We do not doubt the sincerity of those who, like respondent, believe that to have prayer in this context risks the beginning of the establishment the Founding Fathers feared. But this concern is not well founded. . . . The unbroken practice for two centuries in the National Congress, for more than a century in Nebraska and in many other states, gives abundant assurance that there is no real threat "while the Court sits."

Justice William J. Brennan, Jr., dissenting, joined by Justice Thurgood Marshall:

The Court today has written a narrow and, on the whole, careful opinion. In effect, the Court holds that officially sponsored legislative prayer, primarily on account of its "unique history," is generally exempted from the First Amendment's prohibition against "an establishment of religion." The Court's opinion is consistent with dictum in at least one of our prior decisions [*Zorach*], and its limited rationale should pose little threat to the overall fate of the Establishment Clause. Moreover, disagreement with the Court requires that I confront the fact that some twenty years ago, in a concurring opinion in one of the cases striking down official prayer and ceremonial Bible reading in the public schools, I came very close to endorsing essentially the result reached by the Court today.[1] Nevertheless, after much reflection, I have come to the conclusion that I was wrong then and that the Court is wrong today. I now believe that the practice of official invocational prayer, as it exists in Nebraska and most other state legislatures, is unconstitutional. It is contrary to the doctrine as well as the underlying purposes of the Establishment Clause, and it is not saved either by its history or by any of the other considerations suggested in the Court's opinion.

I respectfully dissent.

The Court makes no pretense of subjecting Nebraska's practice of legislative prayer to any of the formal "tests" that have traditionally structured our inquiry under the Establishment Clause. That it fails to do so is, in a sense, a good thing, for it simply confirms that the Court is carving out an exception to the Establishment Clause rather than reshaping Establishment Clause doctrine to accommodate legislative prayer. For my purposes, however, I must begin by demonstrating what should be obvious: that, if the Court were to judge legislative prayer through the unsentimental eye of our settled doctrine, it would have to strike it down as a clear violation of the Establishment Clause.

The most commonly cited formulation of prevailing Establishment Clause doctrine is found in *Lemon.* . . .

That the "purpose" of legislative prayer is pre-eminently religious rather than secular seems to me to be self-evident. "To invoke Divine guidance on a public body entrusted with making the laws" [a quotation from the majority opinion] is nothing but a religious act. . . .

The "primary effect" of legislative prayer is also clearly religious. As we said in the context of officially sponsored prayers in the public schools, "prescribing a particular form of religious worship," even if

---

1. In *Schempp*, Justice Brennan wrote that "[t]he saying of invocational prayers in legislative chambers, state or federal, and the appointment of legislative chaplains, might well represent no involvements of the kind prohibited by the Establishment Clause."

the individuals involved have the choice not to participate, places "indirect coercive pressure upon religious minorities to conform to the prevailing officially approved religion. . . . " *Engel*. More importantly, invocations in Nebraska's legislative halls explicitly link religious belief and observance to the power and the prestige of the State. . . . Finally, there can be no doubt that the practice of legislative prayer leads to excessive "entanglement" between the State and religion. *Lemon* pointed out that "entanglement" can take two forms: First, a state statute or program might involve the state impermissibly in monitoring and overseeing religious affairs. In the case of legislative prayer, the process of choosing a "suitable" chaplain, whether on a permanent or rotating basis, and insuring that the chaplain limits himself or herself to "suitable" prayers, involves precisely the sort of supervision that agencies of government should if at all possible avoid.

Second, excessive "entanglement" might arise out of "the divisive political potential" of a state statute or program. . . . In this case, this second aspect of entanglement is also clear. The controversy between Senator Chambers and his colleagues, which had reached the stage of difficulty and rancor long before this lawsuit was brought, has split the Nebraska Legislature precisely on issues of religion and religious conformity. The record in this case also reports a series of instances, involving legislators other than Senator Chambers, in which invocations by Reverend Palmer and others led to controversy along religious lines. And in general, the history of legislative prayer has been far more eventful—and divisive—than a hasty reading of the Court's opinion might indicate.

In sum, I have no doubt that, if any group of law students were asked to apply the principles of *Lemon* to the question of legislative prayer, they would nearly unanimously find the practice to be unconstitutional.

The path of formal doctrine, however, can only imperfectly capture the nature and importance of the issues at stake in this case. A more adequate analysis must therefore take into account the underlying function of the Establishment Clause, and the forces that have shaped its doctrine.

. . . The Establishment Clause . . . is, to its core, nothing less and nothing more than a statement about the proper role of *government* in the society that we have shaped for ourselves in this land.

The Establishment Clause embodies a judgment, born of a long and turbulent history, that, in our society, religion "must be a private matter for the individual, the family, and the institutions of private choice . . . ." *Lemon*. . . .

The principles of "separation" and "neutrality" implicit in the Establishment Clause serve many purposes. Four of these are particularly relevant here.

The first . . . [is] to guarantee the individual right to conscience. The right to conscience, in the religious sphere, is not only implicated when the government engages in direct or indirect coercion. It is also implicated when the government requires individuals to support the practices of a faith with which they do not agree. . . .

The second purpose of separation and neutrality is to keep the state from interfering in the essential autonomy of religious life, either by taking upon itself the decision of religious issues, or by unduly involving itself in the supervision of religious institutions or officials.

The third purpose of separation and neutrality is to prevent the trivialization and degradation of religion by too close an attachment to the organs of government. . . .

Finally, the principles of separation and neutrality help assure that essentially religious issues, precisely because of their importance and sensitivity, not become the occasion for battle in the political arena. . . . With regard to most issues, the government may be influenced by partisan argument and may act as a partisan itself. In each case, there will be winners and losers in the political battle, and the losers' most common recourse is the right to dissent and the right to fight the battle again another day. With regard to matters that are essentially religious, however, the Establishment Clause seeks that there should be no political battles, and that no American should at any point feel alienated from his government because that government has declared or acted upon some "official" or "authorized" point of view on a matter of religion.

The imperatives of separation and neutrality are not limited to the relationship of government to religious institutions or denominations, but extend as well to the relationship of government to religious beliefs and practices. In *Torcaso* v. *Watkins* (1961), for example, we struck down a state provision requiring a religious oath as a qualification to hold office, not only because it violated principles of free exercise of religion, but also because it violated the principles of nonestablishment of religion. And, of course, in the pair of cases that hang over this one like a reproachful set of parents, we held that official prayer and prescribed Bible reading in the public schools represent a serious encroachment on the Establishment Clause. *Schempp, Engel*. . . .

. . .

Legislative prayer clearly violates the principles of neutrality and separation that are embedded within the Establishment Clause. It is contrary to the fundamental message of *Engel* and *Schempp*. It intrudes on the right to conscience by forcing some legislators either to participate in a "prayer opportunity" with which they are in basic disagreement, or to make their disagreement a matter of public comment by declining to participate. It forces all residents of the State to support a religious exercise that may be contrary to their own beliefs. It requires the State to commit itself on fundamental theological issues. It has the potential for degrading religion by allowing a religious call to worship to be intermeshed with a secular call to order. And it injects religion into the political sphere by creating the potential that each and every selection of a chaplain, or consideration of a particular prayer, or even reconsideration of the practice itself, will provoke a political battle along religious lines and ultimately alienate some religiously identified group of citizens.

One response to the foregoing account, of course, is that "neutrality" and "separation" do not exhaust the full meaning of the Establishment Clause as it has developed in our cases. It is indeed true that there are certain tensions inherent in the First Amendment itself, or inherent in the role of religion and religious belief in any free society, that have shaped the doctrine of the Establishment Clause, and required us to deviate from an absolute adherence to separation and neutrality. Nevertheless, these considerations, although very important, are also quite specific, and where none of them is present, the Establishment Clause gives us no warrant simply to look the other way and treat an unconstitutional practice as if it were constitutional. Because the Court occasionally suggests that some of these considerations might apply here, it becomes important that I briefly identify the most prominent of them and explain why they do not in fact have any relevance to legislative prayer.

A number of our cases have recognized that religious institutions and religious practices may, in certain contexts, receive the benefit of government programs and policies generally available, on the basis of some secular criterion, to a wide class of similarly situated nonreligious beneficiaries, and the precise cataloging of those contexts is not necessarily an easy task. I need not tarry long here, however, because the provision for a daily official invocation by a nonmember officer of a legislative body could by no stretch of the imagination appear anywhere in that catalog.

Conversely, our cases have recognized that religion can encompass a broad, if not total, spectrum of concerns, overlapping considerably with the range of secular concerns, and that not every governmental act which coincides with or conflicts with a particular religious belief is for that reason an establishment of religion. See e.g., *McGowan* v. *Maryland*, 366 U.S. 420 (1961) (Sunday laws); *Harris* v. *McRae*, 448 U.S. 297 (1980) (abortion restrictions). The Court seems to suggest at one point that the practice of legislative prayer may be excused on this ground, but I cannot really believe that it takes this position seriously. The practice of legislative prayer is nothing like the statute we considered in *McGowan* and *McRae*; prayer is not merely "conduct whose . . . effect . . . harmonize[s] with the tenets of some or all other religions," *McGowan*; prayer is fundamentally and necessarily religious. . . .

We have also recognized that government cannot, without adopting a decidedly *anti*-religious point of view, be forbidden to recognize the religious beliefs and practices of the American people as an aspect of our history and culture. Certainly, *bona fide* classes in comparative religion can be offered in the public schools. And certainly, the text of Abraham Lincoln's Second Inaugural Address which is inscribed on a wall of the Lincoln Memorial need not be purged of its profound theological content. The practice of offering invocations at legislative sessions cannot, however, simply be dismissed as "a tolerable *acknowledgment of beliefs* widely held among the people of this country." . . . Reverend Palmer and other members of the clergy who offer invocations at legislative sessions are not museum pieces, put on display once a day for the edification of the legislature. Rather, they are engaged by the legislature to lead it—as a body—in an act of religious worship. If upholding the practice requires denial of this act, I suspect that many supporters of legislative prayer would feel that they had been handed a pyrrhic victory.

Our cases have recognized that the purposes of the Establishment Clause can sometimes conflict. For example, in *Walz*, we upheld tax exemptions for religious institutions in part because subjecting those institutions to taxation might even foster serious administrative entanglement. Here, however, no such tension exists; the State can vindicate *all* the purposes of the Establishment Clause by abolishing legislative prayer.

Finally, our cases recognize that, in one important respect, the Constitution is *not* neutral on the subject of religion: Under the Free Exercise Clause, religiously motivated claims of conscience may give rise to constitutional rights that other strongly held beliefs do not. Moreover, even when the government is not compelled to do so by the Free Exercise Clause, it may to some extent act to facilitate the opportunities of individuals to practice their religion. This is not, however, a case in which a State is accommodating individual religious interests. We are not faced here with the right of the legislature to allow its members to offer prayers during the course of general legislative debate. We are certainly not faced with the right of legislators to form voluntary groups for prayer or worship. We are not even faced with the right of the State to employ members of the clergy to minister to the private religious needs of individual legislators. Rather, we are faced here with the regularized practice of conducting official prayers, on behalf of the entire legislature, as part of the order of business constituting the formal opening of every single session of the legislative term. If this is Free Exercise, the Establishment Clause has no meaning whatsoever.

With the exception of the few lapses I have already noted, each of which is commendably qualified so as to be limited to the facts of this case, the Court says almost nothing contrary to the above analysis.[2] Instead it holds that "the practice of opening legislative sessions with prayer has become part of the fabric of our society," and chooses not to interfere. I sympathize with the Court's reluctance to strike down a practice so prevalent and so ingrained as legislative prayer. I am, however, unconvinced by the Court's arguments. . . .

The Court's main argument for carving out an exception sustaining legislative prayer is historical. The Court cannot—and does not—purport to find a pattern of "undeviating acceptance" of legislative prayer. It also disclaims exclusive reliance on the mere longevity of legislative prayer. The Court does, however, point out that, only three days before the First Congress reached agreement on the final wording of the Bill of Rights, it authorized the appointment of paid chaplains for its own proceedings, and the Court argues that in light of this "unique history," the actions of Congress reveal its intent as to the meaning of the Establishment Clause. I agree that historical practice is "of considerable import in the interpretation of abstract constitutional language." This is a case, however, in which—absent the Court's invocation of history—there would be no question that the practice at issue is unconstitutional. And despite the surface appeal of the Court's argument, there are at least three reasons why specific historical practice should not in this case override that clear constitutional imperative.

---

2. Justice Brennan's view that *Marsh* represents an aberration from established doctrine, and not the first step in a new direction, was borne out by the Court's decisions in later establishment cases.

First, it is significant that the Court's historical argument does not rely on the legislative history of the Establishment Clause itself. Indeed, that formal history is profoundly unilluminating on this and most other subjects. Rather, the Court assumes that the Framers of the Establishment Clause would not have themselves authorized a practice that they thought violated the guarantees contained in the Clause. This assumption, however, is questionable. Legislators, influenced by the passions and exigencies of the moment, the pressure of constituents and colleagues, and the press of business, do not always pass sober constitutional judgment on every piece of legislation they enact, and this must be assumed to be as true of the Members of the First Congress as any other. Indeed, the fact that James Madison, who voted for the bill authorizing the payment of the first congressional chaplains, later expressed the view that the practice was unconstitutional, is instructive on precisely this point. Madison's later views may not have represented so much a change of *mind* as a change of *role*, from a Member of Congress engaged in the hurley-burley of legislative activity to a detached observer engaged in unpressured reflection. Since the latter role is precisely the one with which this Court is charged, I am not at all sure that Madison's later writings should be any less influential in our deliberations than his earlier vote.

Second, the Court's analysis treats the First Amendment simply as an Act of Congress, as to whose meaning the intent of Congress is the single touchstone. Both the Constitution and its Amendments, however, became supreme law only by virtue of their ratification by the States, and the understanding of the States should be as relevant to our analysis as the understanding of Congress. . . . This observation is especially compelling in considering the meaning of the Bill of Rights. The first ten Amendments were not enacted because the Members of the First Congress came up with a bright idea one morning; rather, their enactment was forced upon Congress by a number of the States as a condition for their ratification of the original Constitution. To treat any practice authorized by the First Congress as presumptively consistent with the Bill of Rights is therefore somewhat akin to treating any action of a party to a contract as presumptively consistent with the terms of the contract. The latter proposition, if it were accepted, would of course resolve many of the heretofore perplexing issues in contract law.

Finally, and most importantly, the argument tendered by the Court is misguided because the Constitution is not a static document whose meaning on every detail is fixed for all time by the life experience of the

Framers. We have recognized in a wide variety of constitutional contexts that the practices that were in place at the time any particular guarantee was enacted into the Constitution do not necessarily fix forever the meaning of that guarantee. . . .

The inherent adaptability of the Constitution and its amendments is particularly important with respect to the Establishment Clause. . . . President John Adams issued during his Presidency a number of official proclamations calling on all Americans to engage in Christian prayer. Justice Story, in his treatise on the Constitution, contended that the "real object" of the First Amendment "was, not to countenance, much less to advance Mahometanism, or Judaism, or infidelity, by prostrating Christianity; but to exclude all rivalry among Christian sects. . . ." Whatever deference Adams' actions and Story's views might once have deserved in this Court, the Establishment Clause must now be read in a very different light. Similarly, the Members of the First Congress should be treated, not as sacred figures whose every action must be emulated, but as the authors of a document meant to last for the ages. Indeed, a proper respect for the Framers themselves forbids us to give so static and lifeless a meaning to their work. To my mind, the Court's focus here on a narrow piece of history is, in a fundamental sense, a betrayal of the lessons of history.

. . .

. . . There is another theme which, although implicit, also pervades the Court's opinion. . . . Simply put, the Court seems to regard legislative prayer as at most a *de minimis* violation, somehow unworthy of our attention. I frankly do not know what should be the proper disposition of features of our public life such as "God save the United States and this Honorable Court," "In God We Trust," "One Nation Under God," and the like. I might well adhere to the view expressed in *Schempp*[3] that such mottos are consistent with the Establishment Clause, not because their import is *de minimis*, but because they have lost any true religious significance. Legislative invocations, however, are very different.

. . . [A]s Justice Stevens' dissent so effectively highlights, legislative prayer, unlike mottos with fixed wordings, can easily turn narrowly and obviously sectarian. . . .

The argument is made occasionally that a strict separation of religion and state robs the Nation of its spiritual identity. I believe quite the contrary. . . . If the Court had struck down legislative prayer today,

---

3. In Justice Brennan's own opinion.

it would likely have stimulated a furious reaction. But it would also, I am convinced, have invigorated both the "spirit of religion" and the "spirit of freedom."

Justice John Paul Stevens, dissenting:

In a democratically elected legislature, the religious beliefs of the chaplain tend to reflect the faith of the majority of the lawmakers' constituents. Prayers may be said by a Catholic priest in the Massachusetts Legislature and by a Presbyterian minister in the Nebraska Legislature, but I would not expect to find a Jehovah's Witness or a disciple of Mary Baker Eddy or the Reverend Moon serving as the official chaplain in any state legislature. Regardless of the motivation of the majority that exercises the power to appoint the chaplain, it seems plain to me that the designation of a member of one religious faith to serve as the sole official chaplain of a state legislature for a period of sixteen years constitutes the preference of one faith over another in violation of the Establishment Clause of the First Amendment.

The Court declines to "embark on a sensitive evaluation or to parse the content of a particular prayer." Perhaps it does so because it would be unable to explain away the clearly sectarian content of some of the prayers given by Nebraska's chaplain. Or perhaps the Court is unwilling to acknowledge that the tenure of the chaplain must inevitably be conditioned on the acceptability of that content to the silent majority.

I would affirm the judgment of the Court of Appeals.

20

Lynch v. Donnelly

465 U.S. 668 (1984)

Is it constitutional for a city to include a Nativity scene in its annual Christmas display? Yes, said the Supreme Court in *Lynch* v. *Donnelly*. The Court did not justify its decision on what would have been the broad and, indeed, precedent-shattering ground that the government may support religion. Instead, applying the three-part *Lemon* test, it found a legitimate secular purpose for the crèche: "to celebrate," as Chief Justice Warren Burger wrote in his opinion for the Court, "the Holiday and to depict the origins of that Holiday." This non-religious view of the crèche was vigorously disputed by Justices William Brennan and Harry Blackmun.

The city of Pawtucket, Rhode Island, erected a Christmas display as part of its observance of the holiday season. Among the items in the display, all owned by the city, were a Santa Claus house, reindeer pulling Santa's sleigh, a Christmas tree, and a clown, as well as a crèche consisting of the Infant Jesus, Mary and Joseph, angels, shepherds and kings, and animals. The display was located in a park owned by a nonprofit organization. Some residents of the city who were members of the American Civil Liberties Union, along with the ACLU itself, challenged the display as an establishment of religion. The district court agreed, and the U.S. Court of Appeals for the First Circuit affirmed. In a 5–4 decision, the Supreme Court reversed that judgment.

Lynch produced three opinions in addition to the majority opinion written by the Chief Justice and expressing the views of five justices. Justice Sandra Day O'Connor joined the Court's opinion but also wrote separately. Justice William Brennan, joined by Justices Thurgood Marshall, Harry Blackmun, and John Paul Stevens, wrote in dissent; Justice Blackmun also dissented separately, joined by Justice Stevens. The four opinions in the case are presented here, followed by an editorial from the *Wall Street Journal*.

Five years after *Lynch*, in *Allegheny County v. ACLU, Greater Pittsburgh Chapter*, 492 U.S. 573, the Court found unconstitutional the display of a crèche in a public building; this crèche was not surrounded by other, more secular holiday decorations. In the same case the Court also refused to declare unconstitutional the public display of a menorah; the menorah survived constitutional challenge because it was flanked by secular symbols.

Participating in *Lynch v. Donnelly*, decided March 5, 1984, were Chief Justice Warren E. Burger and Associate Justices Harry A. Blackmun, William J. Brennan, Jr., Thurgood Marshall, Sandra Day O'Connor, Lewis F. Powell, Jr., William H. Rehnquist, John Paul Stevens, and Byron R. White.

Opinions

Chief Justice Warren E. Burger delivered the opinion of the Court:

This Court has explained that the purpose of the Establishment and Free Exercise Clauses of the First Amendment is "to prevent, as far as possible, the intrusion of either [the church or the state] into the precincts of the other." *Lemon* v. *Kurtzman* (1971). At the same time, however, the Court has recognized that "total separation is not possible in an absolute sense. Some relationship between government and religious organizations is inevitable." *Lemon*. In every Establishment Clause case, we must reconcile the inescapable tension between the objective of preventing unnecessary intrusion of either the church or the state upon the other, and the reality that, as the Court has so often noted, total separation of the two is not possible.

The Court has sometimes described the Religion Clauses as erecting a "wall" between church and state. See, e.g., *Everson* v. *Board of Education* (1947). The metaphor has served as a reminder that the Establishment Clause forbids an established church or anything approaching it. But the metaphor itself is not a wholly accurate description of the practical aspects of the relationship that in fact exists between church and state.

No significant segment of our society and no institution within it can exist in a vacuum or in total or absolute isolation from all other parts, much less from government. . . . Nor does the Constitution require complete separation of church and state; it affirmatively mandates accommodation, not merely tolerance, of all religions, and forbids hostility toward any. See, e.g., *Zorach* v. *Clauson* (1952), *McCollum* v. *Board of Education* (1948). Anything less would require the "callous indifference" we have said was never intended by the Establishment Clause. *Zorach*. Indeed, we have observed, such hostility would bring us into "war with our national traditions as embodied in the First Amendment's guaranty of the free exercise of religion." *McCollum*.

The Court's interpretation of the Establishment Clause has comported with what history reveals was the contemporaneous understanding of its guarantees. A significant example of the contemporaneous understanding of that Clause is found in the events of the first week of the First Session of the First Congress in 1789. In the very week that Congress approved the Establishment Clause as part of the Bill of Rights for submission to the states, it enacted legislation providing for paid chaplains for the House and Senate. In *Marsh* v. *Chambers* (1983), we noted that seventeen Members of that First Congress had been Delegates to the Constitutional Convention where freedom of speech, press, and religion and antagonism toward an established church were subjects of frequent discussion. We saw no conflict with the Establishment Clause when Nebraska employed members of the clergy as official legislative Chaplains to give opening prayers at sessions of the state legislature.

. . . It is clear that neither the seventeen draftsmen of the Constitution who were Members of the First Congress, nor the Congress of 1789, saw any establishment problem in the employment of congressional Chaplains to offer daily prayers in the Congress, a practice that has continued for nearly two centuries. It would be difficult to identify a more striking example of the accommodation of religious belief intended by the Framers.

There is an unbroken history of official acknowledgment by all three branches of government of the role of religion in American life from at least 1789. . . .

Our history is replete with official references to the value and invocation of Divine guidance in deliberations and pronouncements of the Founding Fathers and contemporary leaders. Beginning in the early colonial period long before Independence, a day of Thanksgiving was celebrated as a religious holiday to give thanks for the bounties of Nature as gifts from God. President Washington and his successors proclaimed Thanksgiving, with all its religious overtones, a day of national celebration and Congress made it a National Holiday more than a century ago. That holiday has not lost its theme of expressing thanks for Divine aid any more than has Christmas lost its religious significance.

Executive Orders and other official announcements of Presidents and of the Congress have proclaimed both Christmas and Thanksgiving National Holidays in religious terms. And, by Acts of Congress, it has long been the practice that federal employees are released from duties on these National Holidays, while being paid from the same public revenues that provide the compensation of the Chaplains of the Senate and the House and the military services. Thus, it is clear that

Government has long recognized—indeed it has subsidized—holidays with religious significance.

Other examples of reference to our religious heritage are found in the statutorily prescribed national motto "In God We Trust," which Congress and the President mandated for our currency, and in the language "One nation under God," as part of the Pledge of Allegiance to the American flag. . . .

Art galleries supported by public revenues display religious paintings of the fifteenth and sixteenth centuries, predominantly inspired by one religious faith. The National Gallery in Washington, maintained with Government support, for example, has long exhibited masterpieces with religious messages, notably the Last Supper, and paintings depicting the Birth of Christ, the Crucifixion, and the Resurrection, among many others with explicit Christian themes and messages. The very chamber in which oral arguments on this case were heard is decorated with a notable and permanent—not seasonal—symbol of religion: Moses with the Ten Commandments. Congress has long provided chapels in the Capitol for religious worship and meditation.

There are countless other illustrations of the Government's acknowledgment of our religious heritage and governmental sponsorship of graphic manifestations of that heritage. Congress has directed the President to proclaim a National Day of Prayer each year "on which [day] the people of the United States may turn to God in prayer and meditation at churches, in groups, and as individuals." Our Presidents have repeatedly issued such Proclamations. Presidential Proclamations and messages have also been issued to commemorate Jewish Heritage Week and the Jewish High Holy Days. . . . [P]ervasive is the evidence of accommodation of all faiths and all forms of religious expression, and hostility toward none. . . .

This history may help explain why the Court consistently has declined to take a rigid, absolutist view of the Establishment Clause. We have refused "to construe the Religion Clauses with a literalness that would undermine the ultimate constitutional objective as *illuminated by history*." *Walz* v. *Tax Commission* (1970) (emphasis added). . . .

Rather than mechanically invalidating all governmental conduct or statutes that confer benefits or give special recognition to religion in general or to one faith—as an absolutist approach would dictate—the Court has scrutinized challenged legislation or official conduct to determine whether, in reality, it establishes a religion or religious faith, or tends to do so. See *Walz*.

In the line-drawing process we have often found it useful to . . .
[follow the three-part *Lemon* test]. But, we have repeatedly emphasized
our unwillingness to be confined to any single test or criterion in this
sensitive area. . . . In two cases, the Court did not even apply the *Lemon*
"test." We did not , for example, consider that analysis relevant in
Marsh. Nor did we find *Lemon* useful in *Larson* v. *Valente*, 456 U.S. 228
(1982), where there was substantial evidence of overt discrimination
against a particular church.[1]

In this case, the focus of our inquiry must be on the crèche in the
context of the Christmas season. . . . In *Stone* v. *Graham* (1980) . . . we
invalidated a state statute requiring the posting of a copy of the Ten
Commandments on public classroom walls. But the Court carefully
pointed out that the Commandments were posted purely as a religious
admonition, not "integrated into the school curriculum, where the Bible may constitutionally be used in an appropriate study of history,
civilization, ethics, comparative religion, or the like." Similarly, in *Abington* v. *Schempp* (1963), although the Court struck down the practices
in two States requiring daily Bible readings in public schools, it specifically noted that nothing in the Court's holding was intended to "in-
dicat[e] that such study of the Bible or of religion, when presented
objectively as part of a secular program of education, may not be effected consistently with the First Amendment." Focus exclusively on
the religious component of any activity would inevitably lead to its invalidation under the Establishment Clause.

The Court has invalidated legislation or governmental action on the
ground that a secular purpose was lacking, but only when it has concluded there was no question that the statute or activity was motivated
wholly by religious considerations. See, e.g., *Stone*, *Epperson* v. *Arkansas*,
393 U.S. 97 (1968),[2] *Schempp*, *Engel* v. *Vitale* (1962). Even where the
benefits to religion were substantial, as in *Everson*, *Allen*, [and] *Walz*, . . .
we saw a secular purpose and no conflict with the Establishment
Clause. . . .

The District Court inferred from the religious nature of the crèche
that the city has no secular purpose for the display. In so doing, it
rejected the city's claim that its reasons for including the crèche are

---

1. In *Larson*, the Court held that a statute or practice that plainly embodies an intentional discrimination among religions must be closely fitted to a compelling state purpose in order to survive constitutional challenge.

2. In *Epperson*, the Court struck down a state law forbidding the teaching of evolution. "No suggestion has been made that Arkansas' law may be justified by considerations of state policy other than the religious views of some of its citizens," said the Court.

essentially the same as its reasons for sponsoring the display as a whole. The District Court plainly erred by focusing almost exclusively on the crèche. When viewed in the proper context of the Christmas Holiday season, it is apparent that, on this record, there is insufficient evidence to establish that the inclusion of the crèche is a purposeful or surreptitious effort to express some kind of subtle governmental advocacy of a particular religious message. In a pluralistic society a variety of motives and purposes are implicated. The city, like the Congresses and Presidents, however, has principally taken note of a significant historical religious event long celebrated in the Western World. The crèche in the display depicts the historical origins of this traditional event long recognized as a National Holiday.

The narrow question is whether there is a secular purpose for Pawtucket's display of the crèche. The display is sponsored by the city to celebrate the Holiday and to depict the origins of that Holiday. These are legitimate secular purposes. The District Court's inference, drawn from the religious nature of the crèche, that the city has no secular purpose was, on this record, clearly erroneous.

The District Court found that the primary effect of including the crèche is to confer a substantial and impermissible benefit on religion in general and on the Christian faith in particular. Comparisons of the relative benefits to religion of different forms of governmental support are elusive and difficult to make. But to conclude that the primary effect of including the crèche is to advance religion in violation of the Establishment Clause would require that we view it as more beneficial to and more an endorsement of religion, for example, than expenditure of large sums of public money for textbooks supplied throughout the country to students attending church-sponsored schools, *Allen*; expenditure of public funds for transportation of students to church-sponsored schools, *Everson*; federal grants for college buildings of church-sponsored institutions of higher education combining secular and religious education, *Tilton* v. *Richardson*, 403 U.S. 672 (1971); noncategorical grants to church-sponsored colleges and universities, *Roemer* v. *Maryland Board of Public Works*, 426 U.S. 736 (1976); and the tax exemptions for church properties sanctioned in *Walz*. It would also require that we view it as more of an endorsement of religion than the Sunday Closing Laws upheld in *McGowan* v. *Maryland*, 366 U.S. 420 (19 .); the release time program for religious training in *Zorach*; and the legislative prayers upheld in *Marsh*.

We are unable to discern a greater aid to religion deriving from inclusion of the crèche than from these benefits and endorsements previously held not violative of the Establishment Clause. What was said about the legislative prayers in *Marsh* and implied about the Sunday Closing Laws in *McGowan* is true of the city's inclusion of the crèche: its "reason or effect merely happens to coincide or harmonize with the tenets of some . . . religions." . . .

This case differs significantly from *Larkin* v. *Grendel's Den, Inc.*, 459 U.S. 116 (1982), and *McCollum*, where religion was substantially aided. In *Grendel's Den*, important governmental power—a licensing veto authority—had been vested in churches.[3] In *McCollum*, government had made religious instruction available in public school classrooms; the State had not only used the public school buildings for the teaching of religion, it had "afford[ed] sectarian groups an invaluable aid . . . [by] provid[ing] pupils for their religious classes through use of the State's compulsory public school machinery." No comparable benefit to religion is discernible here.

The dissent asserts some observers may perceive that the city has aligned itself with the Christian faith by including a Christian symbol in its display and that this serves to advance religion. We can assume, *arguendo*, that the display advances religion in a sense; but our precedents plainly contemplate that on occasion some advancement of religion will result from governmental action. The Court has made it abundantly clear, however, that "not every law that confers an 'indirect,' 'remote,' or 'incidental' benefit upon [religion] is, for that reason alone, constitutionally invalid." *Nyquist*. Here, whatever benefit to one faith or religion or to all religions, is indirect, remote, and incidental; display of the crèche is no more an advancement or endorsement of religion than the Congressional and Executive recognition of the origins of the Holiday itself as "Christ's Mass," or the exhibition of literally hundreds of religious paintings in governmentally supported museums.

The District Court found that there had been no administrative entanglement between religion and state resulting from the city's ownership and use of the crèche. But it went on to hold that some political divisiveness was engendered by this litigation. Coupled with its finding of an impermissible sectarian purpose and effect, this persuaded the court that there was "excessive entanglement." The Court of Appeals expressly declined to accept the District Court's finding that inclusion of the crèche has caused political divisiveness along religious lines, and

---

3. In *Grendel's Den*, the Court struck down a provision that gave only churches and schools a veto over the grant of liquor licenses on neighboring premises.

noted that this Court has never held that political divisiveness alone was sufficient to invalidate government conduct.

Entanglement is a question of kind and degree. In this case, however, there is no reason to disturb the District Court's finding on the absence of administrative entanglement. There is no evidence of contact with church authorities concerning the content or design of the exhibit prior to or since Pawtucket's purchase of the crèche. No expenditures for maintenance of the crèche have been necessary; and since the city owns the crèche, now valued at $200, the tangible material it contributes is *de minimis*. . . .

The Court of Appeals correctly observed that this Court has not held that political divisiveness alone can serve to invalidate otherwise permissible conduct. And we decline to so hold today. This case does not involve a direct subsidy to church-sponsored schools or colleges, or other religious institutions, and hence no inquiry into potential political divisiveness is even called for, *Mueller* v. *Allen* (1983). In any event, apart from this litigation there is no evidence of political friction or divisiveness over the crèche in the forty-year history of Pawtucket's Christmas celebration. The District Court stated that the inclusion of the crèche for the forty years has been "marked by no apparent dissension" and that the display has had a "calm history." Curiously, it went on to hold that the political divisiveness engendered by this lawsuit was evidence of excessive entanglement. A litigant cannot, by the very act of commencing a lawsuit, however, create the appearance of divisiveness and then exploit it as evidence of entanglement.

We are satisfied that the city has a secular purpose for including the crèche, that the city has not impermissibly advanced religion, and that including the crèche does not create excessive entanglement between religion and government.

Justice Brennan describes the crèche as a "re-creation of an event that lies at the heart of Christian faith." The crèche, like a painting, is passive; admittedly it is a reminder of the origins of Christmas. Even the traditional, purely secular displays extant at Christmas, with or without the crèche, would inevitably recall the religious nature of the Holiday. The display engenders a friendly community spirit of goodwill in keeping with the season. The crèche may well have special meaning to those whose faith includes the celebration of religious Masses, but none who sense the origins of the Christmas celebration would fail to be aware of its religious implications. That the display brings people into the central city, and serves commercial interests and benefits merchants and their employees, does not, as the dissent points out, determine the character of the display. That a prayer invoking Divine guidance in Congress is preceded and followed by debate and partisan conflict over taxes, budgets, national defense, and myriad mundane subjects, for example, has never been thought to demean or taint the sacredness of the invocation.

Of course the crèche is identified with one religious faith but no more so than the examples we have set out from prior cases in which we found no conflict with the Establishment Clause. . . . It would be ironic, however, if the inclusion of a single symbol of a particular historic religious event, as part of a celebration acknowledged in the Western World for twenty centuries, and in this country by the people, by the Executive Branch, by the Congress, and the courts for two centuries, would so "taint" the city's exhibit as to render it violative of the Establishment Clause. To forbid the use of this one passive symbol—the crèche—at the very time people are taking note of the season with Christmas hymns and carols in public schools and other public places, and while the Congress and legislatures open sessions with prayers by paid chaplains, would be a stilted overreaction contrary to our history and to our holdings. If the presence of the crèche in this display violates the Establishment Clause, a host of other forms of taking official note of Christmas, and of our religious heritage, are equally offensive to the Constitution.

. . .

We hold that, notwithstanding the religious significance of the crèche, the city of Pawtucket has not violated the Establishment Clause of the First Amendment. Accordingly, the judgment of the Court of Appeals is reversed.

Justice Sandra Day O'Connor, concurring:

I concur in the opinion of the Court. I write separately to suggest a clarification of our Establishment Clause doctrine. The suggested approach leads to the same result in this case as that taken by the Court, and the Court's opinion, as I read it, is consistent with my analysis.

The Establishment Clause prohibits government from making adherence to a religion relevant in any way to a person's standing in the political community. Government can run afoul of that prohibition in two principal ways. One is excessive entanglement with religious institutions, which may interfere with the independence of the institutions, give the institutions access to government or governmental powers not fully shared by nonadherents of the religion, and foster the creation of political constituencies defined along religious lines. The second and more direct infringement is government endorsement or disapproval of religion. Endorsement sends a message to nonadherents that they are outsiders, not full members of the political community. Disapproval sends the opposite message.

Our prior cases have used the three-part test articulated in *Lemon* as a guide to detecting these two forms of unconstitutional government action. It has never been entirely clear, however, how the three parts of the test relate to the principles enshrined in the Establishment Clause. Focusing on institutional entanglement and on endorsement or disapproval of religion clarifies the *Lemon* test as an analytical device.

In this case, as even the District Court found, there is no institutional entanglement. Nevertheless, the respondents contend that the political divisiveness caused by Pawtucket's display of its crèche violates the excessive-entanglement prong of the *Lemon* test. The Court's opinion follows the suggestion in *Mueller* and concludes that "no inquiry into potential political divisiveness is even called for" in this case. In my view, political divisiveness along religious lines should not be an independent test of constitutionality.

· · ·

The central issue in this case is whether Pawtucket has endorsed Christianity by its display of the crèche. To answer that question, we must examine both what Pawtucket intended to communicate in displaying the crèche and what message the city's display actually conveyed. The purpose and effect prongs of the *Lemon* test represent these two aspects of the meaning of the city's action.

The meaning of a statement to its audience depends both on the intention of the speaker and on the "objective" meaning of the statement in the community. Some listeners need not rely solely on the words themselves in discerning the speaker's intent: they can judge the intent by, for example, examining the context of the statement or asking questions of the speaker. Other listeners do not have or will not seek access to such evidence of intent. They will rely instead on the words themselves; for them the message actually conveyed may be something not actually intended. If the audience is large, as it always is when government "speaks" by word or deed, some portion of the audience will inevitably receive a message determined by the "objective" content of the statement, and some portion will inevitably receive the intended message. Examination of both the subjective and the objective components of the message communicated by a government action is therefore necessary to determine whether the action carries a forbidden meaning.

The purpose prong of the *Lemon* test asks whether government's actual purpose is to endorse or disapprove of religion. The effect prong asks whether, irrespective of government's actual purpose, the practice under review in fact conveys a message of endorsement or disapproval. An affirmative answer to either question should render the challenged practice invalid.

The purpose prong of the *Lemon* test requires that a government activity have a secular purpose. That requirement is not satisfied, however, by the mere existence of some secular purpose, however dominated by religious purposes. In *Stone* v. *Graham* (1980), for example, the Court held that posting copies of the Ten Commandments in schools violated the purpose prong of the *Lemon* test, yet the State plainly had some secular objectives, such as instilling most of the values of the Ten Commandments and illustrating their connection to our legal system. The proper inquiry under the purpose prong of *Lemon*, I submit, is whether the government intends to convey a message of endorsement or disapproval of religion.

Applying that formulation to this case, I would find that Pawtucket did not intend to convey any message of endorsement of Christianity or disapproval of non-Christian religions. The evident purpose of including the crèche in the larger display was not promotion of the religious content of the crèche but celebration of the public holiday through its traditional symbols. Celebration of public holidays, which have cultural significance even if they also have religious aspects, is a legitimate secular purpose.

. . .

Focusing on the evil of government endorsement or disapproval of religion makes clear that the effect prong of the *Lemon* test is properly interpreted not to require invalidation of a government practice merely because it in fact causes, even as a primary effect, advancement or inhibition of religion. . . . What is crucial is that a government practice not have the effect of communicating a message of government endorsement or disapproval of religion. It is only practices having that effect, whether intentionally or unintentionally, that make religion relevant, in reality or public perception, to status in the political community.

Pawtucket's display of its crèche, I believe, does not communicate a message that the government intends to endorse the Christian beliefs represented by the crèche. Although the religious and indeed sectarian significance of the crèche, as the District Court found, is not neutralized by the setting, the overall holiday setting changes what viewers may fairly understand to be the purpose of the display—as a typical museum setting, though not neutralizing the religious content of a religious painting, negates any message of endorsement of that content. The display celebrates a public holiday, and no one contends that declaration of that holiday is understood to be an endorsement of religion. The holiday itself has very strong secular components and traditions. Government celebration of the holiday, which is extremely common, generally is not understood to endorse the religious content of the holiday, just as government celebration of Thanksgiving is not so understood. The crèche is a traditional symbol of the holiday that is very commonly displayed along with purely secular symbols, as it was in Pawtucket.

These features combine to make the government's display of the crèche in this particular physical setting no more an endorsement of religion than such governmental "acknowledgments" of religion as legislative prayers of the type approved in *Marsh*, government declaration of Thanksgiving as a public holiday, printing of "In God We Trust" on coins, and opening court sessions with "God save the United States and this honorable court." Those government acknowledgments of religion serve, in the only ways reasonably possible in our culture, the legitimate secular purposes of solemnizing public occasions, expressing confidence in the future, and encouraging the recognition of what is worthy of appreciation in society. For that reason, and because of their history and ubiquity, those practices are not understood as conveying government approval of particular religious beliefs. The display of the crèche likewise serves a secular purpose—celebration of a public holiday with traditional symbols. It cannot fairly be understood to convey a message of government endorsement of religion. It is significant in this regard that the crèche display apparently caused no political divisiveness prior to the filing of this lawsuit. For these reasons, I conclude that Pawtucket's display of the crèche does not have the effect of communicating endorsement of Christianity.

Justice William J. Brennan, Jr., dissenting, joined by Justices Thurgood Marshall, Harry A. Blackmun, and John Paul Stevens:

Last Term, I expressed the hope that the Court's decision in *Marsh* would prove to be only a single, aberrant departure from our settled method of analyzing Establishment Clause cases. That the Court today returns to the settled analysis of our prior cases gratifies that hope. At the same time, the Court's less-than-vigorous application of the *Lemon* test suggests that its commitment to those standards may only be superficial. After reviewing the Court's opinion, I am convinced that this case appears hard not because the principles of decision are obscure, but because the Christmas holiday seems so familiar and agreeable. Although the Court's reluctance to disturb a community's chosen method of celebrating such an agreeable holiday is understandable, that cannot justify the Court's departure from controlling precedent. In my view, Pawtucket's maintenance and display at public expense of a symbol as distinctively sectarian as a crèche simply cannot be squared with our prior cases. And it is plainly contrary to the purposes and values of the Establishment Clause to pretend, as the Court does, that the otherwise secular setting of Pawtucket's nativity scene dilutes in some fashion the crèche's singular religiosity, or that the city's annual display reflects nothing more than an "acknowledgment" of our shared national heritage. Neither the character of the Christmas holiday itself, nor our heritage of religious expression supports this result. Indeed, our remarkable and precious religious diversity as a Nation, which the Establishment Clause seeks to protect, runs directly counter to today's decision.

. . .

Applying the three-part [*Lemon*] test to Pawtucket's crèche, I am persuaded that the city's inclusion of the crèche in its Christmas display simply does not reflect a "clearly . . . secular purpose." [H]ere we have no explicit statement of purpose by Pawtucket's municipal government accompanying its decisions to purchase, display, and maintain the crèche. Governmental purpose may nevertheless be inferred. . . . In the present case, the city claims that its purposes were exclusively secular. Pawtucket sought, according to this view, only to participate in the celebration of a national holiday and to attract people to the downtown area in order to promote pre-Christmas retail sales and to help engender the spirit of goodwill and neighborliness commonly associated with the Christmas season.

Despite these assertions, two compelling aspects of this case indicate that our generally prudent "reluctance to attribute unconstitutional motives" to a governmental body, *Mueller*, should be overcome. First, as was true in *Larkin*, all of Pawtucket's "valid secular objectives can be readily accomplished by other means." Plainly, the city's interest in celebrating the holiday and in promoting both retail sales and goodwill are fully served by the elaborate display of Santa Claus, reindeer, and wishing wells that are already a part of Pawtucket's annual

Christmas display. More importantly, the nativity scene, unlike every other element of the Hodgson Park display, reflects a sectarian exclusivity that the avowed purposes of celebrating the holiday season and promoting retail commerce simply do not encompass. To be found constitutional, Pawtucket's seasonal celebration must at least be non-denominational and not serve to promote religion. The inclusion of a distinctively religious element like the crèche, however, demonstrates that a narrower sectarian purpose lay behind the decision to include a nativity scene. That the crèche retained this religious character for the people and municipal government of Pawtucket is suggested by the Mayor's testimony at trial in which he stated that for him, as well as others in the city, the effort to eliminate the nativity scene from Pawtucket's Christmas celebration "is a step towards establishing another religion, non-religion that it may be." Plainly, the city and its leaders understood that the inclusion of the crèche in its display would serve the wholly religious purpose of "keep[ing] 'Christ in Christmas.'" From this record, therefore, it is impossible to say with the kind of confidence that was possible in *McGowan* that a wholly secular goal predominates.

The "primary effect" of including a nativity scene in the city's display is, as the District Court found, to place the government's imprimatur of approval on the particular religious beliefs exemplified by the crèche. Those who believe in the message of the nativity receive the unique and exclusive benefit of public recognition and approval of their views. . . . The effect on minority religious groups, as well as on those who may reject all religion, is to convey the message that their views are not similarly worthy of public recognition nor entitled to public support. It was precisely this sort of religious chauvinism that the Establishment Clause was intended forever to prohibit. . . . Pawtucket itself owns the crèche and instead of extending similar attention to a "broad spectrum" of religious and secular groups, it has singled out Christianity for special treatment.

Finally, it is evident that Pawtucket's inclusion of a crèche as part of its annual Christmas display does pose a significant threat of fostering "excessive entanglement." As the Court notes, the District Court found no administrative entanglement in this case, primarily because the city had been able to administer the annual display without extensive consultation with religious officials. Of course, there is no reason to disturb that finding, but it is worth noting that after today's decision, administrative entanglements may well develop. Jews and other non-Christian groups, prompted perhaps by the Mayor's remark that he will include a Menorah in future displays, can be expected to press government for inclusion of their symbols, and faced with such requests, government will have to become involved in accommodating the various demands. More importantly, although no political divisiveness was apparent in Pawtucket prior to the filing of respondents' lawsuit, that act, as the District Court found, unleashed powerful emotional reactions which divided the city along religious lines. The fact that calm had prevailed prior to this suit does not immediately suggest the absence of any division on the point for, as the District Court observed, the quiescence of those opposed to the crèche may have reflected nothing more than their sense of futility in opposing the majority. . . . [T]he Court should not blind itself to the fact that because communities differ in religious composition, the controversy over whether local governments may adopt religious symbols will continue to fester. In many communities, non-Christian groups can be expected to combat practices similar to Pawtucket's; this will be so especially in areas where there are substantial non-Christian minorities.

· · ·

The Court advances two principal arguments to support its conclusion that the Pawtucket crèche satisfies the *Lemon* test. Neither is persuasive.

First. The Court, by focusing on the holiday "context" in which the nativity scene appeared, seeks to explain away the clear religious import of the crèche and the findings of the District Court that most observers understood the crèche as both a symbol of Christian beliefs and a symbol of the city's support for those beliefs. . . . Thus, although the Court concedes that the city's inclusion of the nativity scene plainly serves to "depict the origins" of Christmas as a "significant historical religious event," and that the crèche "is identified with one religious faith," we are nevertheless expected to believe that Pawtucket's use of the crèche does not signal the city's support for the sectarian symbolism that the nativity scene evokes. The effect of the crèche, of course, must be gauged not only by its inherent religious significance but also by the overall setting in which it appears. But it blinks reality to claim, as the Court does, that by including such a distinctively religious object as the crèche in its Christmas display, Pawtucket has done no more than make use of a "traditional" symbol of the holiday, and has thereby purged the crèche of its religious content and conferred only an "incidental and indirect" benefit on religion.

The Court's struggle to ignore the clear religious effect of the crèche seems to me misguided for several reasons. In the first place, the city has positioned the crèche in a central and highly visible location within the Hodgson Park display. . . .

Moreover, the city has done nothing to disclaim government approval of the religious significance of the crèche, to suggest that the crèche represents only one religious symbol among many others that might be included in a seasonal display truly aimed at providing a wide catalog of ethnic and religious celebrations, or to disassociate itself from the religious content of the crèche. . . .

Third, we have consistently acknowledged that an otherwise secular setting alone does not suffice to justify a governmental practice that has the effect of aiding religion. . . .

Finally, and most importantly, even in the context of Pawtucket's seasonal celebration, the crèche retains a specifically Christian religious meaning. I refuse to accept the notion implicit in today's decision that non-Christians would find that the religious content of the crèche is eliminated by the fact that it appears as part of the city's otherwise secular celebration of the Christmas holiday. The nativity scene is clearly distinct in its purpose and effect from the rest of the Hodgson Park display for the simple reason that it is the only one rooted in a biblical account of Christ's birth. It is the chief symbol of the characteristically Christian belief that a divine Savior was brought into the world and that the purpose of this miraculous birth was to illuminate a path toward salvation and redemption. For Christians, that path is exclusive, precious, and holy. But for those who do not share these beliefs, the symbolic reenactment of the birth of a divine being who has miraculously incarnated as a man stands as a dramatic reminder of their differences with Christian faith. . . . To be so excluded on religious grounds by one's elected government is an insult and an injury that, until today, could not be countenanced by the Establishment Clause.

Second. The Court also attempts to justify the crèche by entertaining a beguilingly simple, yet faulty syllogism. The Court begins by noting that government may recognize Christmas Day as a public holiday; the Court then asserts that the crèche is nothing more than a traditional element of Christmas celebrations; and it concludes that the inclusion of a crèche as part of a government's annual Christmas celebration is constitutionally permissible. . . . The Court apparently believes that once it finds that the designation of Christmas as a public holiday is constitutionally acceptable, it is then free to conclude that virtually every form of governmental association with the celebration of the holiday is also constitutional. The vice of this dangerously superficial argument is that it overlooks the fact that the Christmas holiday in our national culture contains both secular and sectarian elements. To say that government may recognize the holiday's traditional, secular elements of gift-giving, public festivities, and community spirit, does not mean that government may indiscriminately embrace the distinctively sectarian aspects of the holiday. Indeed, in its eagerness to approve the crèche, the Court has advanced a rationale so simplistic that it would appear to allow the Mayor of Pawtucket to participate in the celebration of a Christmas Mass, since this would be just another unobjectionable way for the city to "celebrate the holiday." . . . [T]he Court's logic is fundamentally flawed both because it obscures the reason why public designation of Christmas Day as a holiday is constitutionally acceptable, and blurs the distinction between the secular aspects of Christmas and its distinctively religious character, as exemplified by the crèche.

When government decides to recognize Christmas Day as a public holiday, it does no more than accommodate the calendar of public activities to the plain fact that many Americans will expect on that day to spend time visiting with their families, attending religious services, and perhaps enjoying some respite from preholiday activities. The Free Exercise Clause, of course, does not necessarily compel the government to provide this accommodation, but neither is the Establishment Clause offended by such a step. Because it is clear that the celebration of Christmas has both secular and sectarian elements, it may well be that by taking note of the holiday, the government is simply seeking to serve the same kinds of wholly secular goals—for instance, promoting goodwill and a common day of rest—that were found to justify Sunday Closing Laws in *McGowan*. If public officials go further and participate in the *secular* celebration of Christmas—by for example, decorating public places with such secular images as wreaths, garlands, of Santa Claus figures—they move closer to the limits of their constitutional power but nevertheless remain within the boundaries set by the Establishment Clause. But when those officials participate in or appear to endorse the distinctively religious elements of this otherwise secular event, they encroach upon First Amendment freedoms. For it is at that point that the government brings to the forefront the theological content of the holiday, and places the prestige, power, and financial support of a civil authority in the service of a particular faith.

The inclusion of a crèche in Pawtucket's otherwise secular celebration of Christmas clearly violates these principles. Unlike such secular figures as Santa Claus, reindeer, and carolers, a nativity scene represents far more than a mere "traditional" symbol of Christmas. The essence of the crèche's symbolic purpose and effect is to prompt the observer to experience a sense of simple awe and wonder appropriate to the contemplation of one of the central elements of Christian dogma—that God sent His Son into the world to be a Messiah. Contrary to the Court's suggestion, the crèche is far from a mere representation of a "particular historic religious event." It is, instead, best understood as a mystical re-creation of an event that lies at the heart of Christian faith. To suggest, as the Court does, that such a symbol is merely "traditional" and therefore no different from Santa's house or reindeer is not only offensive to those for whom the crèche has profound significance, but insulting to those who insist for religious or personal reasons that the story of Christ is in no sense a part of "history" nor an unavoidable element in our national "heritage."

For these reasons, the crèche in this context simply cannot be viewed as playing the same role that an ordinary museum display does. . . .

. . . In the absence of any other religious symbols or of any neutral disclaimer, the inescapable effect of the crèche will be to remind the average observer of the religious roots of the celebration he is witnessing and to call to mind the scriptural message that the nativity symbolizes. The fact that Pawtucket has gone to the trouble of making such an elaborate public celebration and of including a crèche in that otherwise secular setting inevitably serves to reinforce the sense that the city means to express solidarity with the Christian message of the crèche and to dismiss other faiths as unworthy of similar attention and support.

. . . The Court's opinion . . . sounds a broader and more troubling theme. Invoking the celebration of Thanksgiving as a public holiday, the legend "In God We Trust" on our coins, and the proclamation "God save the United States and this Honorable Court" at the opening of judicial sessions, the Court asserts, without explanation, that Pawtucket's inclusion of a crèche in its annual Christmas display poses no more of a threat to Establishment Clause values than these other official "acknowledgments" of religion.

Intuition tells us that some official "acknowledgment" is inevitable in a religious society if government is not to adopt a stilted indifference to the religious life of the people. It is equally true, however, that if government is to remain scrupulously neutral in matters of religious conscience, as our Constitution requires, then it must avoid those overly broad acknowledgments of religious practices that may imply governmental favoritism toward one set of religious beliefs. This does not mean, of course, that public officials may not take account, when necessary, of the separate existence and significance of the religious institutions and practices in the society they govern. Should government choose to incorporate some arguably religious element into its public ceremonies, that acknowledgment must be impartial; it must not tend to promote one faith or handicap another; and it should not sponsor religion generally over nonreligion. . . .

Despite this body of case law, the Court has never comprehensively addressed the extent to which government may acknowledge religion by, for example, incorporating religious references into public ceremonies and proclamations, and I do not presume to offer a comprehensive approach. Nevertheless, it appears from our prior decisions that at least three principles—tracing the narrow channels which government acknowledgments must follow to satisfy the Establishment Clause—may be identified.

First, although the government may not be compelled to do so by the Free Exercise Clause, it may, consistently with the Establishment Clause, act to accommodate to some extent the opportunities of individuals to practice their religion. . . . And for me that principle would justify government's decision to declare December 25th a public holiday.

Second, our cases recognize that while a particular governmental practice may have derived from religious motivations and retain certain religious connotations, it is nonetheless permissible for the government to pursue the practice when it is continued today solely for secular reasons. . . . Thanksgiving Day, in my view, fits easily within this principle, for despite its religious antecedents, the current practice of celebrating Thanksgiving is unquestionably secular and patriotic. . . .

Finally, we have noted that government cannot be completely prohibited from recognizing in its public actions the religious beliefs and practices of the American people as an aspect of our national history and culture. While I remain uncertain about these questions, I would suggest that such practices as the designation of "In God We Trust" as our national motto, or the references to God contained in the Pledge of Allegiance can best be understood . . . as a form of "ceremonial deism," protected from Establishment Clause scrutiny chiefly because they have lost through rote repetition any significant religious content. Moreover, these references are uniquely suited to serve such wholly secular purposes as solemnizing public occasions, or inspiring commitment to meet some national challenge in a manner that simply could not be fully served in our culture if government were limited to purely nonreligious phrases. The practices by which the government has long acknowledged religion are therefore probably necessary to serve certain secular functions, and that necessity, coupled with their long history, gives those practices an essentially secular meaning.

The crèche fits none of these categories. . . . [Its] message . . . begins and ends with reverence for a particular image of the divine.

. . .

The American historical experience concerning the public celebration of Christmas, if carefully examined, provides no support for the Court's decision. The opening sections of the Court's opinion, while seeking to rely on historical evidence, do no more than recognize the obvious: because of the strong religious currents that run through our history, an unflexible or absolutistic enforcement of the Establishment Clause would be both imprudent and impossible. This observation is at once uncontroversial and unilluminating. . . .

Indeed, the Court's approach suggests a fundamental misapprehension of the proper uses of history in constitutional interpretation. . . . [H]istorical acceptance of a particular practice alone is never sufficient to justify a challenged governmental action. . . . Attention to the details of history should not blind us to the cardinal purposes of the Establishment Clause, nor limit our central inquiry in these cases—whether the challenged practices "threaten those consequences which the Framers deeply feared." In recognition of this fact, the Court has, until today, consistently limited its historical inquiry to the particular practice under review.

. . .

Although invoking [*McGowan*, *Walz*, and *Marsh*] in support of its result, the Court wholly fails to discuss the history of the public celebration of Christmas or the use of publicly displayed nativity scenes. The Court, instead, simply asserts, without any historical analysis or support whatsoever, that the now familiar celebration of Christmas springs from an unbroken history of acknowledgment "by the people, by the Executive Branch, by the Congress, and the courts for two centuries. . . ." The Court's complete failure to offer any explanation of its assertion is perhaps understandable, however, because the historical record points in precisely the opposite direction. Two features of this history are worth noting. First, at the time of the adoption of the Constitution and the Bill of Rights, there was no settled pattern of celebrating Christmas, either as a purely religious holiday or as a public event. Second, the historical evidence, such as it is, offers no uniform pattern of widespread acceptance of the holiday and indeed suggests that the development of Christmas as a public holiday is a comparatively recent phenomenon.

The intent of the Framers with respect to the public display of nativity scenes is virtually impossible to discern primarily because the widespread celebration of Christmas did not emerge in its present form until well into the nineteenth century. Carrying a well-defined Puritan hostility to the celebration of Christ's birth with them to the New World, the founders of the Massachusetts Bay Colony pursued a vigilant policy of opposition to any public celebration of the holiday. To the Puritans, the celebration of Christmas represented a "Popish" practice lacking any foundation in Scripture. This opposition took legal form in 1659 when the Massachusetts Bay Colony made the observance of Christmas Day, "by abstinence from labor, feasting, or any other way," an offense punishable by fine. Although the Colony eventually repealed this ban in 1681, the Puritan objection remained firm.

During the eighteenth century, sectarian division over the celebration of the holiday continued. . . .

. . .

. . . It was not until 1836 that a State first granted legal recognition to Christmas as a public holiday. This was followed, in the period between 1845 and 1865, by twenty-eight jurisdictions which included Christmas Day as a legal holiday. Congress did not follow the States' lead until 1870 when it established December 25th, along with the Fourth of July, New Year's Day, and Thanksgiving, as a legal holiday in the District of Columbia. This pattern of legal recognition tells us only that public acceptance of the holiday was gradual and that the practice—in stark contrast to the record presented in either *Walz* or *Marsh*—did not take on the character of a widely recognized holiday until the middle of the nineteenth century.

The historical evidence with respect to public financing and support for governmental displays of nativity scenes is even more difficult to gauge. . . .

In sum, there is no evidence whatsoever that the Framers would have expressly approved a federal celebration of the Christmas holiday including public displays of a nativity scene; accordingly, the Court's repeated invocation of the decision in *Marsh* is not only baffling, it is utterly irrelevant. Nor is there any suggestion that publicly financed and supported displays of Christmas crèches are supported by a record of widespread, undeviating acceptance that extends throughout our history. Therefore, our prior decisions which relied upon concrete, specific historical evidence to support a particular practice simply have no bearing on the question presented in this case. Contrary to today's careless decision, those prior cases have all recognized that the "illumination" provided by history must always be focused on the particular practice at issue in a given case. Without that guiding principle and the intellectual discipline it imposes, the Court is at sea, free to select random elements of America's varied history solely to suit the views of five Members of this Court.

. . . [T]he City's action should be recognized for what it is: a coercive, though perhaps small, step toward establishing the sectarian preferences of the majority, at the expense of the minority, accomplished by placing public facilities and funds in support of the religious symbolism and theological tidings that the crèche conveys. . . .

I dissent.

Justice Harry A. Blackmun, dissenting, joined by Justice John Paul Stevens:

Not only does the Court's resolution of this controversy make light of our precedents, but also, ironically, the majority does an injustice to the crèche and the message it manifests. While certain persons, including the Mayor of Pawtucket, undertook a crusade to "keep 'Christ' in Christmas," the Court today has declared that presence virtually irrelevant. . . . The crèche has been relegated to the role of a neutral harbinger of the holiday season, useful for commercial purposes, but devoid of any inherent meaning and incapable of enhancing the religious tenor of a display of which it is an integral part. The city has its victory—but it is a Pyrrhic one indeed.

The import of the Court's decision is to encourage use of the creche in a municipally sponsored display, a setting where Christians feel constrained in acknowledging its symbolic meaning and non-Christians feel alienated by its presence. Surely, this is a misuse of a sacred symbol. Because I cannot join the Court in denying either the force of our precedents or the sacred message that is at the core of the crèche, I dissent and join Justice Brennan's opinion.

Response

From the **Wall Street Journal,** March 7, 1984, "*Trivial Pursuits*":

One of the court's tasks is to apply a test of reasonableness to divisive issues and hence derail tendencies toward absolutism. But while reasonable people have every right to wonder how a simple Nativity display became a *cause célèbre*, the broad issue of church-state separation has never been a trivial matter in America. Religious beliefs do not lend themselves to trivialization.

As the Supreme Court was deciding the Pawtucket case, the United States Senate was debating a constitutional amendment to ameliorate a 1962 Supreme Court decision that had cut the opposite way, outlawing official school prayer. The proposed amendment seeks to accommodate the existing constitutional ban on establishment of religion by saying schools can have prayers but the state cannot compose a prayer or make prayer mandatory. The amendment, like the Pawtucket case, is mainly an exercise in symbolism, a bow to that considerable number of Americans who believe that the public schools have become overly secularized with the result that students are deprived of the character-shaping benefits of religious values and spiritual experience. To say that such symbolism is unimportant would be to deny the heat of the Senate debate and the important role Ronald Reagan's support of school prayer is likely to play in the coming presidential campaign. Indeed, Mr. Reagan just yesterday delivered a thumping speech in Columbus, Ohio, to the National Association of Evangelicals on behalf of the school-prayer amendment and laws that would permit classrooms to be used by student religious groups.

Since the beginning of this republic, courts and legislatures have faced the ticklish task of balancing religious commitment with religious tolerance. The need was seen by the authors of the Constitution, who even then knew they must accommodate religious pluralism and try to avoid the rigidities that had existed in the Massachusetts theocracy. When you compare the vigor of religion in America today with that of, say, the "established" Church of England or the state "protected" (that is to say suppressed) religions in communist countries, it is easy to see that the main benefits of religious liberty have been to religion itself.

But what of the fear that public institutions, and particularly the schools, have become overly secularized? It is disquieting to see the U.S. Supreme Court gnawing on whether or not a Nativity scene serves a secular purpose—like promoting the Christmas sales of Pawtucket merchants—in judging

330

whether it is constitutionally permissible. Chief Justice Burger dealt with that rather summarily by saying that engendering seasonal good will is sufficiently secular. Justice Brennan, author of the minority opinion, replied that Santa Clauses and reindeer can engender the Christmas spirit without resort to religious symbols. Such barren arguments suggest it was about time for the court to swing away from the absolutism that has characterized some of its past interpretations of the establishment clause.

That over-secularization in public institutions has contributed to a breakdown in public morality was argued at some length by Mr. Reagan yesterday. This belief carries considerable weight. It has fostered a birth of religious education as an alternative to public education. It has brought demands in some states for at least requiring ethical studies in secondary school curricula. It has been a main tenet of that political force we know as The New Right.

The only thing that can be said for sure is that there is plenty of evidence all around of a decline in what were once broadly accepted standards of public morality. Movie houses and magazine stands offer sufficient testimony. A new generation might argue that the old morality has been exposed for its hypocrisy and replaced with a new, more honest, morality. That is at least worthy of debate, but it doesn't satisfy a substantial segment of the American polity. The dissatisfaction was expressed in the election of Ronald Reagan.

The Supreme Court, in the Pawtucket case, has followed the hallowed court tradition of keeping one eye on the ballot box. If our friends are correct that its finding is unexceptionable, it suggests that the Court is in tune with the times.

21

Wallace v. Jaffree

472 U.S. 38 (1985)

U nder *Engel* v. *Vitale* (1962), a state may not sponsor public
school prayer. But may a state authorize public schools to
set aside a moment of silence in which students can meditate—
or pray? In *Wallace* v. *Jaffree*, the Supreme Court said no. The
case did not promise to be the last word on "moment of silence"
laws, enacted by numerous states; the opinions in the case in
fact suggested that a majority of the Court would have approved
such a law had the one under inspection—Alabama's—been
crafted differently. The doctrinal importance of *Jaffree* lay in the
fact that the Court now seemed to put an end to the precedent-
shattering suggestion in *Marsh* v. *Chambers* (1983) that government might support religion after all.

Ishmael Jaffree of Mobile County, Alabama, sued on behalf of
his three children, all in public schools, challenging the constitutionality of three Alabama statutes: §16-1-20, enacted in
1978, which authorized a one-minute period of silence in all
public schools "for meditation"; §16-1-20.1, enacted in 1981,
which authorized a period of silence "for meditation or voluntary prayer"; and §16-1-20.2, enacted in 1982, which authorized teachers to lead "willing students" in a prescribed prayer to
"Almighty God . . . the Creator and Supreme Judge of the
world." The federal district court concluded that, because the
ban on establishment did not apply to the states, Alabama had
the power to establish religion.

This was a remarkable judgment. Lower courts almost always
adhere to the decisions of the U.S. Supreme Court, but in this
instance the district court had declared, in effect, that it was not

to be bound by *Cantwell* v. *Connecticut* (1940) and *Everson* v. *Board of Education* (1947), the two cases applying the religion clause to the states. Indeed, the district judge challenged *Everson*, declaring that the Court had "erred in its reading of history." The U.S. Court of Appeals for the Eleventh Circuit reversed the lower court on the issue of Alabama's power to establish religion (thus reaffirming *Everson*) and held that 16-1-20.1 and 16-1-20.2 were unconstitutional. In 1984 the Supreme Court affirmed the appeals court's ruling in respect to 16-1-20.2, limiting argument to 16-1-20.1, the "moment of silence" statute. It is this law that the Court, by a 6-to-3 vote, deemed unconstitutional in *Jaffree*.

Polls taken since the Court's school-prayer decision in *Engel* v. *Vitale* (1962) had produced consistently large majorities favoring the reintroduction of formal prayer in the public schools, and numerous state legislatures, like Alabama's, had passed laws aiding religious practices and schools. The 1980 election of Ronald Reagan and the development of a litigating capability on the part of cultural conservatives did not bode well for the strict "separationist" position. Indeed, by 1985 the new administration had won from the Supreme Court more "accommodationist" decisions in *Mueller* v. *Allen* (1983), *Marsh* v. *Chambers* (1983), and *Lynch* v. *Donnelly* (1984). In *Jaffree*, the original school prayer and Bible-reading cases seemed vulnerable. But the decision disappointed those who hoped the Court would alter its establishment jurisprudence by lowering *Everson*'s famous "wall" separating church and state.

The case produced six opinions, all of which are presented here. Justice John Paul Stevens wrote for the Court, expressing the views of five members. Justice Lewis Powell, concurring in the judgment and the opinion, and Justice Sandra Day O'Connor, concurring in the judgment, also wrote separately. Chief Justice Warren Burger, Justice Byron White, and Justice William Rehnquist each filed dissents. The opinions are followed by commentary from *The Christian Century*, the *Wall Street Journal*, and a syndicated column by George Will.

Stevens's opinion for the the Court advanced the usual separationist arguments. The most notable opinion in the case was Rehnquist's dissent, the first opinion by any justice since *Everson* to challenge *Everson*'s history, which Rehnquist said was "totally incorrect." Upon examination of the original First Amendment history, Rehnquist advanced the "no preference" understanding of the establishment prohibition. His opinion provoked scholarly discussion in law reviews and, in *Lee* v. *Weisman* (1992), a lengthy response in an opinion by Justice David Souter (see Case 25).

Participating in *Wallace* v. *Jaffree*, decided June 4, 1985, were Chief Justice Warren E. Burger and Associate Justices Harry A. Blackmun, William J. Brennan, Jr., Thurgood Marshall, Sandra Day O'Connor, Lewis F. Powell, Jr., William H. Rehnquist, John Paul Stevens, and Byron R. White.

Opinions

Justice John Paul Stevens delivered the opinion of the Court:

Our unanimous affirmance of the Court of Appeals' judgment concerning §16-1-20.2 makes it unnecessary to comment at length on the District Court's remarkable conclusion that the Federal Constitution imposes no obstacle to Alabama's establishment of a state religion. Before analyzing the precise issue that is presented to us, it is nevertheless appropriate to recall how firmly embedded in our constitutional jurisprudence is the proposition that the several States have no greater power to restrain the individual freedoms protected by the First Amendment than does the Congress of the United States.

As is plain from its text, the First Amendment was adopted to curtail the power of Congress to interfere with the individual's freedom to believe, to worship, and to express himself in accordance with the dictates of his own conscience. Until the Fourteenth Amendment was added to the Constitution, the First Amendment's restraints on the exercise of federal power simply did not apply to the States. But when the Constitution was amended to prohibit any State from depriving any person of liberty without due process of law, that Amendment imposed the same substantive limitations on the States' power to legislate that the First Amendment had always imposed on the Congress' power.[1] This Court has confirmed and endorsed this elementary proposition of law time and time again.

· · ·

Just as the right to speak and the right to refrain from speaking are complementary components of a broader concept of individual freedom of mind, so also the individual's freedom to choose his own creed is the counterpart of his right to refrain from accepting the creed established by the majority. At one time it was thought that this right

---

1. Justice Stevens evidently believed that as originally understood the Fourteenth Amendment imposed "the same substantive limitations" on the states. Other justices have disagreed, believing that the application of the First Amendment's religion provisions to the states was a matter of judicial decree, not framers' intent. In his dissent in this case, Justice Rehnquist simply assumes that states are limited by the demands of the no-establishment provision, without stating how this came about.

336

merely proscribed the preference of one Christian sect over another, but would not require equal respect for the conscience of the infidel, the atheist, or the adherent of a non-Christian faith such as Islam or Judaism. But when the underlying principle has been examined in the crucible of litigation, the Court has unambiguously concluded that the individual freedom of conscience protected by the First Amendment embraces the right to select any religious faith or none at all.[2] This conclusion derives support not only from the interest in respecting the individual's freedom of conscience, but also from the conviction that religious beliefs worthy of respect are the product of free and voluntary choice by the faithful,[3] and from recognition of the fact that the political interest in forestalling intolerance extends beyond intolerance among Christian sects—or even intolerance among "religions"—to encompass intolerance of the disbeliever and the uncertain. . . . As Justice Jackson eloquently stated in *West Virginia State Board of Education* v. *Barnette* (1943): "If there is any fixed star in our constitutional constellation, it is that no official, high or petty, can prescribe what shall be orthodox in politics, nationalism, religion, or other matters of opinion or force citizens to confess by word or act their faith therein."

The State of Alabama, no less than the Congress of the United States, must respect that basic truth.

When the Court has been called upon to construe the breadth of the Establishment Clause, it has examined the criteria developed [in litigation] over a period of many years. . . .

In applying the purpose test [from *Lemon* v. *Kurtzman*, 1971], it is appropriate to ask "whether government's actual purpose is to endorse or disapprove of religion." In this case, the answer to that question is dispositive. For the record not only provides us with an unambiguous affirmative answer, but it also reveals that the enactment of [the statute] was not motivated by any clearly secular purpose—indeed, the statute had *no* secular purpose.

---

2. See Justice Rehnquist's comment on "the crucible of litigation" in his dissent, pp. 360, 363.

3. Michael Sandel has identified this as "the clearest statement of the voluntarist conception of religious liberty." It is this conception that undergirds the jurisprudence of government neutrality toward religion, and, as Sandel points out, it presupposes a liberal theory of persons as "free and independent selves, capable of choosing their religious convictions for themselves." The question this theory raises is whether it can do justice to religious liberty, because not all religious beliefs or actions can be described simply as matters of free choice. ("Freedom of Conscience or Freedom of Choice?" in James Davison Hunter and Os Guinness, ed., *Articles of Faith, Articles of Peace: The Religious Liberty Clauses and the American Public Philosophy* [Washington, D.C.: Brookings Institution, 1990], pp. 85–87.) Sandel's article is excerpted in Part Two of this volume.

The sponsor of the bill that became [the statute], Senator Donald Holmes, inserted into the legislative record—apparently without dissent—a statement indicating that the legislation was an "effort to return voluntary prayer" to the public schools. Later Senator Holmes confirmed this purpose before the District Court.[4] In response to the question whether he had any purpose for the legislation other than returning voluntary prayer to public schools, he stated: "No, I did not have no other purpose in mind." The State did not present evidence of *any* secular purpose.

The unrebutted evidence of legislative intent contained in the legislative record and in the testimony of the sponsor of §16-1-20.1 is confirmed by a consideration of the relationship between this statute and the two other measures that were considered in this case. The District Court found that the 1981 statute and its 1982 sequel had a common, nonsecular purpose. The wholly religious character of the later enactment is plainly evident from its text. When the differences between §16-1-20.1 and its 1978 predecessor, §16-1-20, are examined, it is equally clear that the 1981 statute has the same wholly religious character.

There are only three textual differences between §16-1-20.1 and §16-1-20: (1) the earlier statute applies only to grades one through six, whereas §16-1-20.1 applies to all grades; (2) the earlier statute uses the word "shall" whereas §16-1-20.1 uses the word "may"; (3) the earlier statute refers only to "meditation" whereas §16-1-20.1 refers to "meditation or voluntary prayer." The first difference is of no relevance in this litigation because the minor appellees were in kindergarten or second grade during the 1981-1982 academic year. The second difference would also have no impact on this litigation because the mandatory language of §16-1-20 continued to apply to grades one through six. Thus the only significant textual difference is the addition of the words "or voluntary prayer."

The legislative intent to return prayer to the public schools is, of course, quite different from merely protecting every student's right to engage in voluntary prayer during an appropriate moment of silence during the school day. The 1978 statute already protected that right, containing nothing that prevented any student from engaging in voluntary prayer during a silent minute of meditation. Appellants have

---

4. David P. Currie notes that "it was most unusual for the Court . . . to look beyond the text of the legislation and the absence of any conceivable legitimate purpose in searching for improper legislative motivation" (*The Constitution in the Supreme Court*, 537).

not identified any secular purpose that was not fully served by §16-1-20 before the enactment of §16-1-20.1. Thus, only two conclusions are consistent with the text of §16-1-20.1: (1) the statute was enacted to convey a message of State endorsement and promotion of prayer; or (2) the statute was enacted for no purpose. No one suggests that the statute was nothing but a meaningless or irrational act.

We must, therefore, conclude that the Alabama Legislature intended to change existing law and that it was motivated by the same purpose that the Governor's answer to the second amended complaint expressly admitted; that the statement inserted in the legislative history revealed; and that Senator Holmes' testimony frankly described. The legislature enacted §16-1-20.1, despite the existence of §16-1-20 for the sole purpose of expressing the State's endorsement of prayer activities for one minute at the beginning of each schoolday. The addition of "or voluntary prayer" indicates that the State intended to characterize prayer as a favored practice. Such an endorsement is not consistent with the established principle that the government must pursue a course of complete neutrality toward religion.

The importance of that principle does not permit us to treat this as an inconsequential case involving nothing more than a few words of symbolic speech on behalf of the political majority. For whenever the State itself speaks on a religious subject, one of the questions that we must ask is "whether the government intends to convey a message of endorsement or disapproval of religion." The well-supported concurrent findings of the District Court and the Court of Appeals—that §16-1-20.1 was intended to convey a message of state approval of prayer activities in the public schools—make it unnecessary, and indeed inappropriate, to evaluate the practical significance of the addition of the words "or voluntary prayer" to the statute. Keeping in mind, as we must, "both the fundamental place held by the Establishment Clause in our constitutional scheme and the myriad, subtle ways in which Establishment Clause values can be eroded,"[5] we conclude that §16-1-20.1 violates the First Amendment.

Justice Lewis F. Powell, Jr., concurring:

My concurrence is prompted by Alabama's persistence in attempting to institute state-sponsored prayer in the public schools by enacting three successive statutes. I agree fully with Justice O'Connor's as-

---

5. Justice Stevens here quotes Justice Sandra Day O'Connor's concurring opinion in Case 20, *Lynch* v. *Donnelly* (1984).

sertion that some moment-of-silence statutes may be constitutional, a suggestion set forth in the Court's opinion as well.

I write separately to express additional views and to respond to criticism of the three-pronged *Lemon* test. *Lemon* identifies standards that have proved useful in analyzing case after case both in our decisions and in those of other courts. It is the only coherent test a majority of the Court has ever adopted. . . . *Lemon* has not been overruled or its test modified. Yet, continued criticism of it could encourage other courts to feel free to decide Establishment Clause cases on an ad hoc basis.

The first inquiry under *Lemon* is whether the challenged statute has a "secular legislative purpose." As Justice O'Connor recognizes, this secular purpose must be "sincere"; a law will not pass constitutional muster if the secular purpose articulated by the legislature is merely a "sham." . . .

The record before us, however, makes clear that Alabama's purpose was solely religious in character. Senator Donald Holmes, the sponsor of the bill that became Alabama Code §16-1-20.1, freely acknowledged that the purpose of this statute was "to return voluntary prayer" to the public schools. I agree with Justice O'Connor that a single legislator's statement, particularly if made following enactment, is not necessarily sufficient to establish purpose. But, as noted in the Court's opinion, the religious purpose of §16-1-20.1 is manifested in other evidence, including the sequence and history of the three Alabama statutes.

. . .

I would vote to uphold the Alabama statute if it also had a clear secular purpose. . . . Nothing in the record before us, however, identifies a clear secular purpose, and the State also has failed to identify any nonreligious reason for the statute's enactment. Under these circumstances, the Court is required by our precedents to hold that the statute fails the first prong of the *Lemon* test and therefore violates the Establishment Clause.[6]

Justice Sandra Day O'Connor, concurring in the judgment:

The religion clauses of the First Amendment, coupled with the Fourteenth Amendment's guarantee of ordered liberty, preclude both the Nation and the States from making any law respecting an establish-

---

6. Compare Justice Rehnquist's view of precedent when it conflicts with the original meaning of the Constitution, as found in his dissent. Compare as well Justice Powell's defense of the precedent at issue here—*Lemon*—with Justice O'Connor's criticism of *Lemon* in her concurring opinion.

ment of religion or prohibiting the free exercise thereof. Although a distinct jurisprudence has enveloped each of these Clauses, their common purpose is to secure religious liberty. On these principles the Court has been and remains unanimous.

As these cases once again demonstrate, however, "it is far easier to agree on the purpose that underlies the First Amendment's Establishment and Free Exercise Clauses than to obtain agreement on the standards that should govern their application." *Walz* v. *Tax Commission* (1970) (opinion of Justice John M. Harlan II). It once appeared that the Court had developed a workable standard by which to identify impermissible government establishments of religion. See *Lemon*. Under the now familiar *Lemon* test, statutes must have both a secular legislative purpose and a principal or primary effect that neither advances nor inhibits religion, and in addition they must not foster excessive government entanglement with religion. Despite its initial promise, the *Lemon* test has proven problematic. The required inquiry into "entanglement" has been modified and questioned, see *Mueller* v. *Allen* (1983), and in one case we have upheld state action against an Establishment Clause challenge without applying the *Lemon* test at all. *Marsh* v. *Chambers* (1983). The author of *Lemon* himself apparently questions the test's general applicability. See *Lynch* v. *Donnelly* (1984). Justice Rehnquist today suggests that we abandon *Lemon* entirely, and in the process limit the reach of the Establishment Clause to state discrimination between sects and government designation of a particular church as a "state" or "national" one.

Perhaps because I am new to the struggle, I am not ready to abandon all aspects of the *Lemon* test. I do believe, however, that the standards announced in *Lemon* should be reexamined and refined in order to make them more useful in achieving the underlying purpose of the First Amendment. . . . Last Term [in *Lynch*], I proposed a refinement of the *Lemon* test. . . .

[My] *Lynch* concurrence suggested that the religious liberty protected by the Establishment Clause is infringed when the government makes adherence to religion relevant to a person's standing in the political community. Direct government action endorsing religion or a particular religious practice is invalid under this approach because it "sends a message to nonadherents that they are outsiders, not full members of the political community, and an accompanying message to adherents that they are insiders, favored members of the political community." Under this view, *Lemon*'s inquiry as to the purpose and effect of a statute requires courts to examine whether government's purpose is to endorse religion and whether the statute actually conveys a message of endorsement.

The endorsement test is useful because of the analytic content it gives to the *Lemon*-mandated inquiry into legislative purpose and effect. In this country, church and state must necessarily operate within the same community. Because of this coexistence, it is inevitable that the secular interests of government and the religious interests of various sects and their adherents will frequently intersect, conflict, and combine. A statute that ostensibly promotes a secular interest often has an incidental or even a primary effect of helping or hindering a sectarian belief. Chaos would ensue if every such statute were invalid under the Establishment Clause. For example, the State could not criminalize murder for fear that it would thereby promote the Biblical command against killing. The task for the Court is to sort out those statutes and government practices whose purpose and effect go against the grain of religious liberty protected by the First Amendment.

The endorsement test does not preclude government from acknowledging religion or from taking religion into account in making law and policy. It does preclude government from conveying or attempting to convey a message that religion or a particular religious belief is favored or preferred. . . . At issue today is whether state moment of silence statutes in general, and Alabama's moment of silence statute in particular, embody an impermissible endorsement of prayer in public schools.

Twenty-five states permit or require public school teachers to have students observe a moment of silence in their classrooms. A few statutes provide that the moment of silence is for the purpose of meditation alone. . . . The typical statute, however, calls for a moment of silence at the beginning of the schoolday during which students may meditate, pray, or reflect on the activities of the day. . . . Federal trial courts have divided on the constitutionality of these moment of silence laws. . . . Relying on this Court's decisions disapproving vocal prayer and Bible reading in the public schools, . . . the courts that have struck down the moment of silence statutes generally conclude that their purpose and effect are to encourage prayer in public schools.

Engel v. *Vitale* (1962) and *Abington* v. *Schempp* (1963) are not dispositive on the constitutionality of moment of silence laws. In those cases, public school teachers and students led their classes in devotional exercises. In *Engel*, a New York statute required teachers to lead their classes in a vocal prayer. The Court concluded that "it is no part of the business of government to compose official prayers for any group of the American people to recite as part of a religious program carried on by the government." In *Abington*, the Court addressed Pennsylvania and Maryland statutes that authorized morning Bible readings in public schools. The Court reviewed the purpose and effect of the statutes, concluded that they required religious exercises, and therefore found them to violate the Establishment Clause. Under all of these statutes, a student who did not share the religious beliefs expressed in the course of the exercise was left with the choice of participating, thereby compromising the nonadherent's beliefs, or withdrawing, thereby calling attention to his or her nonconformity. The decisions acknowledged the coercion implicit under the statutory schemes, but they expressly turned only on the fact that the government was sponsoring a manifestly religious exercise.

A state-sponsored moment of silence in the public schools is different from state-sponsored vocal prayer or Bible reading. First, a moment of silence is not inherently religious. Silence, unlike prayer or Bible reading, need not be associated with a religious exercise. Second, a pupil who participates in a moment of silence need not compromise his or her beliefs. During a moment of silence, a student who objects to prayer is left to his or her own thoughts, and is not compelled to listen to the prayers or thoughts of others. For these simple reasons, a moment of silence statute does not stand or fall under the Establishment Clause according to how the Court regards vocal prayer or Bible reading. . . .

By mandating a moment of silence, a State does not necessarily endorse any activity that might occur during the period. Even if a statute specifies that a student may choose to pray silently during a quiet moment, the State has not thereby encouraged prayer over other specified alternatives. Nonetheless, it is also possible that a moment of silence statute, either as drafted or as actually implemented, could effectively favor the child who prays over the child who does not. For example, the message of endorsement would seem inescapable if the teacher exhorts children to use the designated time to pray. Similarly, the face of the statute or its legislative history may clearly establish that it seeks to encourage or promote voluntary prayer over other alternatives, rather than merely provide a quiet moment that may be dedicated to prayer by those so inclined. The crucial question is whether the State has conveyed or attempted to convey the message that children should use the moment of silence for prayer. This question cannot be answered in the abstract, but instead requires courts to examine the history, language, and administration of a particular statute to determine whether it operates as an endorsement of religion.

Before reviewing Alabama's moment of silence law to determine whether it endorses prayer, some general observations on the proper scope of the inquiry are in order. First, the inquiry into the purpose of the legislature in enacting a moment of silence law should be deferential and limited. In determining whether the government intends a moment of silence statute to convey a message of endorsement or disapproval of religion, a court has no license to psychoanalyze the legislators. If a legislature expresses a plausible secular purpose for a moment of silence statute in either the text or the legislative history, or if the statute disclaims an intent to encourage prayer over alternatives during a moment of silence, then courts should generally defer to that stated intent. It is particularly troublesome to denigrate an expressed secular purpose due to postenactment testimony by particular legislators or by interested persons who witnessed the drafting of the statute. Even if the text and official history of a statute express no secular purpose, the statute should be held to have an improper purpose only if it is beyond purview that endorsement of religion or religious belief "was and is the law's reason for existence." *Epperson v. Arkansas*, 393 U.S. 97 (1968).[7] Since there is arguably a secular pedagogical value to a moment of silence in public schools, courts should find an improper purpose behind such a statute only if the statute on its face, in its official legislative history, or in its interpretation by a responsible administrative agency suggests it has the primary purpose of endorsing prayer.

Justice Rehnquist suggests that this sort of deferential inquiry into legislative purpose "means little," because "it only requires the legislature to express any secular purpose and omit all sectarian references." It is not a trivial matter, however, to require that the legislature manifest a secular purpose and omit all sectarian endorsements from its laws. That requirement is precisely tailored to the Establishment Clause's purpose of assuring that government not intentionally endorse religion or a religious practice. . . . While the secular purpose requirement alone may rarely be determinative in striking down a statute, it nevertheless serves an important function. It reminds government that when it acts it should do so without endorsing a particular religious belief or practice that all citizens do not share. . . .

Second, the *Lynch* concurrence suggested that the effect of a mo-

---

7. In *Epperson* the Court struck down an Arkansas law forbidding the teaching of evolution on grounds that it advanced religion.

ment of silence law is not entirely a question of fact. . . . The relevant issue is whether an objective observer, acquainted with the text, legislative history, and implementation of the statute, would perceive it as a state endorsement of prayer in public schools. A moment of silence law that is clearly drafted and implemented so as to permit prayer, meditation, and reflection within the prescribed period, without endorsing one alternative over the others, should pass this test.

The analysis above suggests that moment of silence laws in many States should pass Establishment Clause scrutiny because they do not favor the child who chooses to pray during a moment of silence over the child who chooses to meditate or reflect. Alabama Code §16-1-20.1 does not stand on the same footing. However deferentially one examines its text and legislative history, however objectively one views the message attempted to be conveyed to the public, the conclusion is unavoidable that the purpose of the statute is to endorse prayer in public schools.

[Justice O'Connor states that, "for the reasons expressed above," she would give "little, if any, weight" to the testimony of State Senator Holmes as evidence of legislative intent. She says she would give weight, however, to other facts as evidence of legislative intent: that Alabama already had a moment of silence statute before it enacted the law at issue, and that the sole purpose reflected in the official legislative history was "to return voluntary prayer to our public schools." She concludes that the statute "sponsors a religious exercise."]

In his dissenting opinion, Justice Rehnquist reviews the text and history of the First Amendment Religion Clauses. His opinion suggests that a long line of this Court's decisions are inconsistent with the intent of the drafters of the Bill of Rights. He urges the Court to correct the historical inaccuracies in its past decisions by embracing a far more restricted interpretation of the Establishment Clause, an interpretation that presumably would permit vocal group prayer in public schools.

The United States, in an *amicus* brief, suggests a less sweeping modification of Establishment Clause principles. In the Federal Government's view, a state-sponsored moment of silence is merely an "accommodation" of the desire of some public school children to practice their religion by praying silently. Such an accommodation is contemplated by the First Amendment's guarantee that the Government will not prohibit the free exercise of religion. Because the moment of silence implicates free exercise values, the United States suggests that the *Lemon*-mandated inquiry into purpose and effect should be modified.

There is an element of truth and much helpful analysis in each of these suggestions. . . .

. . .

. . . The primary issue raised by Justice Rehnquist's dissent is whether the historical fact that our Presidents have long called for public prayers of Thanks should be dispositive on the constitutionality of prayer in public schools. I think not. At the very least, Presidential Proclamations are distinguishable from school prayer in that they are received in a non-coercive setting and are primarily directed at adults, who presumably are not readily susceptible to unwilling religious indoctrination. This Court's decisions have recognized a distinction when government-sponsored religious exercises are directed at impressionable children who are required to attend school, for then government endorsement is much more likely to result in coerced religious beliefs. Although history provides a touchstone for constitutional problems, the Establishment Clause concern for religious liberty is dispositive here.

The element of truth in the United States' arguments, I believe, lies in the suggestion that Establishment Clause analysis must comport with the mandate of the Free Exercise Clause that government make no law prohibiting the free exercise of religion. Our cases have interpreted the Free Exercise Clause to compel the government to exempt persons from some generally applicable government requirements so as to permit those persons to freely exercise their religion. See, e.g., *Thomas* v. *Review Board* (1981); *Wisconsin* v. *Yoder* (1972); *Sherbert* v. *Verner* (1963). Even where the Free Exercise Clause does not compel the government to grant an exemption, the Court has suggested that the government in some circumstances may voluntarily choose to exempt religious observers without violating the Establishment Clause. The challenge posed by the United States' argument is how to define the proper Establishment Clause limits on voluntary government efforts to facilitate the free exercise of religion. On the one hand, a rigid application of the *Lemon* test would invalidate legislation exempting religious observers from generally applicable government obligations. By definition, such legislation has a religious purpose and effect in promoting the free exercise of religion. On the other hand, judicial deference to all legislation that purports to facilitate the free exercise of religion would completely vitiate the Establishment Clause. Any statute pertaining to religion can be viewed as an "accommodation" of free exercise rights. Indeed, the statute at issue in *Lemon*, which provided salary supplements, textbooks, and instructional materials to Pennsylvania parochial schools, can be viewed as an accommodation of the religious beliefs of parents who choose to send their children to religious schools.

It is obvious that either of the two Religion Clauses, "if expanded to a logical extreme, would tend to clash with the other." *Walz*. The Court has long exacerbated the conflict by calling for government "neutrality" toward religion. See, e.g., *Committee for Public Education* v. *Nyquist*, 413 U.S. 756 (1973), *Board of Education* v. *Allen* (1968). It is difficult to square any notion of "complete neutrality" with the mandate of the Free Exercise Clause that government must sometimes exempt a religious observer from an otherwise generally applicable obligation. A government that confers a benefit on an explicitly religious basis is not neutral toward religion.

The solution to the conflict between the Religion Clauses lies not in "neutrality," but rather in identifying workable limits to the government's license to promote the free exercise of religion. The text of the Free Exercise Clause speaks of laws that prohibit the free exercise of religion. On its face, the Clause is directed at government interference with free exercise. Given that concern, one can plausibly assert that government pursues Free Exercise Clause values when it lifts a government-imposed burden on the free exercise of religion. If a statute falls within this category, then the standard Establishment Clause test should be modified accordingly. It is disingenuous to look for a purely secular purpose when the manifest objective of a statute is to facilitate the free exercise of religion by lifting a government-imposed burden. Instead, the Court should simply acknowledge that the religious purpose of such a statute is legitimated by the Free Exercise Clause. I would also go further. In assessing the effect of such a statute—that is, in determining whether the statute conveys the message of endorsement of religion or a particular religious belief—courts should assume that the "objective observer" is acquainted with the Free Exercise Clause and the values it promotes. Thus individual perceptions, or resentment that a religious observer is exempted from a particular government requirement, would be entitled to little weight if the Free Exercise Clause strongly supported the exemption.

While this "accommodation" analysis would help reconcile our Free Exercise and Free Establishment Clause standards, it would not save Alabama's moment of silence law. If we assume that the religious activity that Alabama seeks to protect is silent prayer, then it is difficult to discern any state-imposed burden on that activity that is lifted by Alabama Code §16-1-20.1. No law prevents a student who is so inclined from praying silently in public schools. Moreover, state law already provided a moment of silence to these appellees irrespective of §16-1-20.1. Of course, the State might argue that §16-1-20.1 protects not silent prayer, but rather group silent prayer under state sponsorship. Phrased in these terms, the burden lifted by the statute is not one imposed by the State of Alabama, but by the Establishment Clause as interpreted in *Engel* and *Schempp*. In my view, it is beyond the authority of the State of Alabama to remove burdens imposed by the Constitution itself. I conclude that the Alabama statute at issue today lifts no state-imposed burden on the free exercise of religion, and accordingly cannot properly be viewed as an accommodation statute.

The Court does not hold that the Establishment Clause is so hostile to religion that it precludes the States from affording schoolchildren an opportunity for voluntary silent prayer. To the contrary, the moment of silence statutes of many States should satisfy the Establishment Clause standard we have here applied. The Court holds only that Alabama has intentionally crossed the line between creating a quiet moment during which those so inclined may pray, and affirmatively endorsing the particular religious practice of prayer. This line may be a fine one, but our precedents and the principles of religious liberty require that we draw it.

Chief Justice Warren E. Burger, dissenting:

Some who trouble to read the opinions in these cases will find it ironic—perhaps even bizarre—that on the very day we heard arguments in the cases, the Court's session opened with an invocation for Divine protection. Across the park a few hundred yards away, the House of Representatives and the Senate regularly open each session with a prayer. These legislative prayers are not just one minute in duration, but are extended, thoughtful invocations and prayers for Divine guidance. They are given, as they have been since 1789, by clergy appointed as official chaplains and paid from the Treasury of the United States. Congress has also provided chapels in the Capitol, at public expense, where Members and others may pause for prayer, meditation—or a moment of silence.

Inevitably some wag is bound to say that the Court's holding today reflects a belief that the historic practice of the Congress and this Court is justified because members of the Judiciary and Congress are more in need of Divine guidance than are schoolchildren. Still others will say that all this controversy is "much ado about nothing," since no power on earth—including this Court and Congress—can stop any teacher from opening the school day with a moment of silence for pupils to meditate, to plan their day—or to pray if they voluntarily elect to do so.

I make several points about today's curious holding.

(a) It makes no sense to say that Alabama has "endorsed prayer" by merely enacting a new statute "to specify expressly that voluntary prayer is *one* of the authorized activities during a moment of silence" (O'Connor, J., concurring in judgment) (emphasis added). To suggest that a moment-of-silence statute that includes the word "prayer" unconstitutionally endorses religion, while one that simply provides for a moment of silence does not, manifests not neutrality but hostility toward religion. For decades our opinions have stated that hostility toward any religion or toward all religions is as much forbidden by the Constitution as is an official establishment of religion. The Alabama Legislature has no more "endorsed" religion than a state or the Congress does when it provides for legislative chaplains, or than this Court does when it opens each session with an invocation to God. . . .

(b) The inexplicable aspect of the foregoing opinions, however, is what they advance as support for the holding concerning the purpose of the Alabama Legislature. Rather than determining legislative purpose from the face of the statute as a whole, the opinions rely on three factors in concluding that the Alabama Legislature had a "wholly religious" purpose for enacting the statute under review: (i) statements of the statute's sponsor, (ii) admissions in Governor James' answer to the second amended complaint, and (iii) the difference between §16-1-20.1 and its predecessor statute.

Curiously, the opinions do not mention that *all* of the sponsor's statements relied upon—including the statement "inserted" into the Senate Journal—were made *after* the legislature had passed the statute; indeed, the testimony that the Court finds critical was given well over a year after the statute was enacted. As even the appellees concede, there is not a shred of evidence that the legislature as a whole shared the sponsor's motive or that a majority in either house was even aware of the sponsor's view of the bill when it was passed. The sole relevance of the sponsor's statements, therefore, is that they reflect the personal, subjective motives of a single legislator. No case in the 195-year history of this Court supports the disconcerting idea that post-enactment statements by individual legislators are relevant in determining the constitutionality of legislation.

Even if an individual legislator's after-the-fact statements could rationally be considered relevant, all of the opinions fail to mention that the sponsor also testified that one of his purposes in drafting and sponsoring the moment-of-silence bill was to clear up a widespread misunderstanding that a school-child is legally *prohibited* from engaging in silent, individual prayer once he steps inside a public school building. That testimony is at least as important as the statements the Court relies upon, and surely that testimony manifests a permissible purpose.

The Court also relies on the admissions of Governor James' answer to the second amended complaint. Strangely, however, the Court neglects to mention that there was no trial bearing on the constitutionality of the Alabama statutes; trial became unnecessary when the District Court held that the Establishment Clause does not apply to the states. The absence of a trial on the issue of the constitutionality of §16-1-20.1 is significant because the answer filed by the State Board and Superintendent of Education did not make the same admissions that the Governor's answer made. The Court cannot know whether, if these cases had been tried, those state officials would have offered evidence to contravene appellees' allegations concerning legislative purpose. Thus, it is completely inappropriate to accord any relevance to the admissions in the Governor's answer.

The several preceding opinions conclude that the principal difference between §16-1-20.1 and its predecessor statute proves that the sole purposes behind the inclusion of the phrase "or voluntary prayer" in §16-1-20.1 was to endorse and promote prayer. This reasoning is simply a subtle way of focusing exclusively on the religious component of the statute rather than examining the statute as a whole. Such logic—if it can be called that—would lead the Court to hold, for example, that a state may enact a statute that provides reimbursement for bus transportation to the parents of all schoolchildren, but may not *add* parents of parochial school students to an existing program providing reimbursement for parents of public school students. Congress amended the statutory Pledge of Allegiance 31 years ago to add the words "under God." Do the several opinions in support of the judgment today render the Pledge unconstitutional? That would be the consequence of their method of focusing on the difference between §16-1-20.1 and its predecessor statute rather than examining §16-1-20.1 as a whole. . . .

(c) The Court's extended treatment of the [*Lemon*] "test" . . . suggests a naive pre-occupation with an easy, bright-line approach for addressing constitutional issues. . . . [O]ur responsibility is not to apply tidy formulas by rote; our duty is to determine whether the statute or practice at issue is a step toward establishing a state religion. Given today's decision, however, perhaps it is understandable that the opinions in support of the judgment all but ignore the Establishment Clause itself and the concerns that underlie it.

(d) The notion that the Alabama statute is a step toward creating an established church borders on, if it does not trespass into, the ridiculous. The statute does not remotely threaten religious liberty; it affirmatively furthers the values of religious freedom and tolerance that the Establishment Clause was designed to protect. Without pressuring those who do not wish to pray, the statute simply creates an opportunity to think, to plan, or to pray if one wishes—as Congress does by providing chaplains and chapels. It accommodates the purely private, voluntary religious choices of the individual pupils who wish to pray. . . . The statute "endorses" only the view that the religious observances of others should be tolerated and, where possible, accommodated. If the government may not accommodate religious needs when it does so in a wholly neutral and noncoercive manner, the "benevolent neutrality" that we have long considered the correct constitutional standard will quickly translate into the "callous indifference" that the Court has consistently held the Establishment Clause does not require.

. . . Justice O'Connor paradoxically acknowledges: "It is difficult to discern a serious threat to religious liberty from a room of silent, thoughtful schoolchildren." I would add to that, "even if they choose to pray."

The mountains have labored and brought forth a mouse.

Justice Byron R. White, dissenting:

For the most part agreeing with the opinion of The Chief Justice, I dissent from the Court's judgment invalidating Alabama Code §16-1-20.1. Because I do, it is apparent that in my view the First Amendment does not proscribe either (1) statutes authorizing or requiring in so many words a moment of silence before classes begin or (2) a statute that provides, when it is initially passed, for a moment of silence for meditation or prayer. As I read the filed opinions, a majority of the Court would approve statutes that provided for a moment of silence but did not mention prayer. . . .

I appreciate Justice Rehnquist's explication of the history of the Religion Clauses of the First Amendment. Against that history, it would be quite understandable if we undertook to reassess our cases dealing with these Clauses, particularly those dealing with the Establishment Clause. Of course, I have been out of step with many of the Court's decisions dealing with this subject matter, and it is thus not surprising that I would support a basic reconsideration of our precedents.

Justice William H. Rehnquist, dissenting:

Thirty-eight years ago this Court, in *Everson*, summarized its exegesis of Establishment Clause doctrine thus: "In the words of Jefferson, the clause against establishment of religion by law was intended to erect 'a wall of separation between church and State.' " *Reynolds* v. *United States*, 98 U.S. 145 (1879). This language from *Reynolds*, a case involving the Free Exercise Clause of the First Amendment rather than the Establishment Clause, quoted from Thomas Jefferson's letter to the Danbury Baptist Association the phrase "I contemplate with sovereign reverence that act of the whole American people which declared that their legislature should 'make no law respecting an establishment of religion, or prohibiting the free exercise thereof,' thus building a wall of separation between church and State."

It is impossible to build sound constitutional doctrine upon a mistaken understanding of constitutional history, but unfortunately the Establishment Clause has been expressly freighted with Jefferson's misleading metaphor for nearly forty years. Thomas Jefferson was of course in France at the time the constitutional Amendments known as the Bill of Rights were passed by Congress and ratified by the States. His letter to the Danbury Baptist Association was a short note of courtesy, written fourteen years after the Amendments were passed by Congress. He would seem to any detached observer as a less than ideal source of contemporary history as to the meaning of Religion Clauses of the First Amendment.

Jefferson's fellow Virginian, James Madison, with whom he was joined in the battle for the enactment of the Virginia Statute of Religious Liberty of 1786, did play as large a part as anyone in the drafting of the Bill of Rights. He had two advantages over Jefferson in this regard: he was present in the United States, and he was a leading member of the First Congress. But when we turn to the record of the proceedings in the First Congress leading up to the adoption of the Establishment Clause of the Constitution, including Madison's significant contributions thereto, we see a far different picture of its purpose than the highly simplified "wall of separation between church and State."

During the debates in the Thirteen Colonies over ratification of the Constitution, one of the arguments frequently used by opponents of ratification was that without a Bill of Rights guaranteeing individual liberty the new general Government carried with it a potential for tyranny. The typical response to this argument on the part of those who favored ratification was that the general Government established by the Constitution had only delegated powers, and that these delegated powers were so limited that the Government would have no occasion to violate individual liberties. This response satisfied some, but not others, and of the eleven Colonies which ratified the Constitution by early 1789, five proposed one or another amendments guaranteeing individual liberty. Three—New Hampshire, New York, and Virginia—included in one form or another a declaration of religious freedom. Rhode Island and North Carolina flatly refused to ratify the Constitution in the absence of amendments in the nature of a Bill of Rights. . . . Virginia and North Carolina proposed identical guarantees of religious freedom:

> [A]ll men have an equal, natural and unalienable right to the free exercise of religion, according to the dictates of conscience, and that no particular religious sect or society ought to be favored or established, by law, in preference to others.

On June 8, 1789, James Madison rose in the House of Representatives and "reminded the House that this was the day that he had heretofore named for bringing forward amendments to the Constitution." Madison's subsequent remarks in urging the House to adopt his drafts of the proposed amendments were less those of a dedicated advocate of the wisdom of such measures than those of a prudent statesman seeking the enactment of measures sought by a number of his fellow citizens which could surely do no harm and might do a great deal of good. . . .

The language Madison proposed for what ultimately became the Religion Clauses of the First Amendment was this:

> The civil rights of none shall be abridged on account of religious belief or worship, nor shall any national religion be established, nor shall the full and equal rights of conscience be in any manner, or on any pretext, infringed.

On the same day that Madison proposed them, the amendments which formed the basis for the Bill of Rights were referred by the House to a Committee of the Whole, and after several weeks' delay were then referred to a Select Committee consisting of Madison and ten others. The Committee revised Madison's proposal regarding the establishment of religion to read:

[N]o religion shall be established by law, nor shall the equal rights of conscience be infringed.

The Committee's proposed revisions were debated in the House on August 15, 1789. The entire debate on the Religion Clauses is contained in two full columns of the "Annals," and does not seem particularly illuminating. Representative Peter Sylvester of New York expressed his dislike for the revised version, because it might have a tendency "to abolish religion altogether." Representative John Vining suggested that the two parts of the sentence be transposed; Representative Elbridge Gerry thought the language should be changed to read "that no religious doctrine shall be established by law." Roger Sherman of Connecticut had the traditional reason for opposing provisions of a Bill of Rights—that Congress had no delegated authority to "make religious establishments"—and therefore he opposed the adoption of the amendment. Representative Daniel Carroll of Maryland thought it desirable to adopt the words proposed, saying "[h]e would not contend with gentlemen about the phraseology, his object was to secure the substance in such a manner as to satisfy the wishes of the honest part of the community."

Madison then spoke, and said that "he apprehended the meaning of the words to be, that Congress should not establish a religion, and enforce the legal observation of it by law, nor compel men to worship God in any manner contrary to their conscience." He said that some of the state conventions had thought that Congress might rely on the Necessary and Proper Clause to infringe the rights of conscience or to establish a national religion, and "to prevent these effects he presumed the amendment was intended, and he thought it as well expressed as the nature of the language would admit."

Representative Benjamin Huntington then expressed the view that the Committee's language might "be taken in such latitude as to be extremely hurtful to the cause of religion. He understood the amendment to mean what had been expressed by the gentleman from Virginia; but others might find it convenient to put another construction upon it." Huntington, from Connecticut, was concerned that in the New England States, where state established religions were the rule rather than the exception, the federal courts might not be able to entertain claims based upon an obligation under the bylaws of a religious organization to contribute to the support of a minister or the building of a place of worship. He hoped that "the amendment would be made in such a way as to secure the rights of conscience, and a free exercise of the rights of religion, but not to patronise those who professed no religion at all."

Madison responded that the insertion of the word "national" before the word "religion" in the Committee version should satisfy the minds of those who had criticized the language. "He believed that the people feared one sect might obtain a preeminence, or two combine together, and establish a religion to which they would compel others to conform. He thought that if the word 'national' was introduced, it would point the amendment directly to the object it was intended to prevent." Representative Samuel Livermore expressed himself as dissatisfied with Madison's proposed amendment, and thought it would be better if the Committee language were altered to read that "Congress shall make no laws touching religion, or infringing the rights of conscience."

Representative Gerry spoke in opposition to the use of the word "national" because of strong feelings expressed during the ratification debates that a federal government, not a national government, was created by the Constitution. Madison thereby withdrew his proposal but insisted that his reference to a "national religion" only referred to a national establishment and did not mean that the Government was a national one. The question was taken on Representative Livermore's motion, which passed by a vote of 31 for and 20 against.

The following week, without any apparent debate, the House voted to alter the language of the Religion Clause to read "Congress shall make no law establishing religion, or to prevent the free exercise thereof, or to infringe the rights of conscience." The floor debates in the Senate were secret, and therefore not reported in the Annals. The Senate on September 3, 1789, considered several different forms of the Religion Amendment, and reported this language back to the House:

> Congress shall make no law establishing articles of faith or a mode of worship, or prohibiting the free exercise of religion.

The House refused to accept the Senate's changes in the Bill of Rights and asked for a conference; the version which emerged from the conference was that which ultimately found its way into the Constitution as a part of the First Amendment.[8]

> Congress shall make no law respecting an establishment of religion, or prohibiting the free exercise thereof.

---

8. Justice Rehnquist, in the preceding paragraphs, thus became the first member of the Court ever to analyze the congressional debates over the adoption of the religion clause.

On the basis of the record of these proceedings in the House of Representatives, James Madison was undoubtedly the most important architect among the Members of the House of the Amendments which became the Bill of Rights, but it was James Madison speaking as an advocate of sensible legislative compromise, not as an advocate of incorporating the Virginia Statute of Religious Liberty into the United States Constitution. During the ratification debate in the Virginia Convention, Madison had actually opposed the idea of any Bill of Rights. His sponsorship of the Amendments in the House was obviously not that of a zealous believer in the necessity of the Religion Clauses, but one who felt it might do some good, could do no harm, and would satisfy those who had ratified the Constitution on the condition that Congress propose a Bill of Rights. His original language "nor shall any national religion be established" obviously does not conform to the "wall of separation" between church and State idea which latter-day commentators have ascribed to him. His explanation on the floor of the meaning of his language—"that Congress should not establish a religion, and enforce the legal observation of it by law" is of the same ilk. When he replied to Huntington in the debate over the proposal which came from the Select Committee of the House, he urged that the language "no religion shall be established by law" should be amended by inserting the word "national" in front of the word "religion."

It seems indisputable from these glimpses of Madison's thinking, as reflected by actions on the floor of the House in 1789, that he saw the Amendment as designed to prohibit the establishment of a national religion, and perhaps to prevent discrimination among sects. He did not see it as requiring neutrality on the part of government between religion and irreligion. Thus the Court's opinion in *Everson*—while correct in bracketing Madison and Jefferson together in their exertions in their home State leading to the enactment of the Virginia Statute of Religious Liberty—is totally incorrect in suggesting that Madison carried these views onto the floor of the United States House of Representatives when he proposed the language which would ultimately become the Bill of Rights.

The repetition of this error in the Court's opinion in *McCollum* v. *Board of Education* (1948), and, inter alia, *Engel*, does not make it any sounder historically. Finally, in *Schempp*, the Court made the truly remarkable statement that "the views of Madison and Jefferson, preceded by Roger Williams, came to be incorporated not only in the Federal Constitution but likewise in those of most of our States." On the basis of what evidence we have, this statement is demonstrably incorrect as a matter of history. And its repetition in varying forms in succeeding opinions of the court can give it no more authority than it possesses as a matter of fact; *stare decisis* may bind courts as to matters of law, but it cannot bind them as to matters of history.

None of the other Members of Congress who spoke during the August 15th debate expressed the slightest indication that they thought the language before them from the Select Committee, or the evil to be aimed at, would require that the Government be absolutely neutral as between religion and irreligion. The evil to be aimed at, so far as those who spoke were concerned, appears to have been the establishment of a national church, and perhaps the preference of one religious sect over another; but it was definitely not concern about whether the Government might aid all religions evenhandedly. If one were to follow the advice of Justice Brennan, concurring in *Schempp*, and construe the Amendment in the light of what particular "practices . . . challenged threaten those consequences which the Framers deeply feared; whether, in short, they tend to promote that type of interdependence between religion and state which the First Amendment was designed to prevent," one would have to say that the First Amendment Establishment Clause should be read no more broadly than to prevent the establishment of a national religion or the governmental preference of one religious sect over another.

The actions of the First Congress, which reenacted the Northwest Ordinance for the governance of the Northwest Territory in 1789, confirm the view that Congress did not mean that the Government should be neutral between religion and irreligion. The House of Representatives took up the Northwest Ordinance on the same day as Madison introduced his proposed amendments which became the Bill of Rights; while at the time the Federal Government was of course not bound by draft amendments to the Constitution which had not yet been proposed by Congress, say nothing of ratified by the States, it seems highly unlikely that the House of Representatives would simultaneously consider proposed amendments to the Constitution and enact an important piece of territorial legislation which conflicted with the intent of those proposals. The Northwest Ordinance re-enacted the Northwest Ordinance of 1787 and provided that "[r]eligion, morality, and knowledge, being necessary to good government and the happiness of mankind, schools and the means of education shall forever be encouraged." Land grants for schools in the Northwest Territory were not limited to public schools. It was not until 1845 that Congress limited land grants in the new States and Territories to nonsectarian schools.

On the day after the House of Representatives voted to adopt the form of the First Amendment Religion Clause which was ultimately proposed and ratified, Representative Elias Boudinot proposed a resolution asking President George Washington to issue a Thanksgiving Day proclamation. Boudinot said he "could not think of letting the session pass over without offering an opportunity to all the citizens of the United States of joining with one voice, in returning to Almighty God their sincere thanks for the many blessings he had poured down upon them." Representative Aedanas Burke objected to the resolution because he did not like "this mimicking of European customs"; Representative Thomas Tucker objected that whether or not the people had reason to be satisfied with the Constitution was something that the States knew better than the Congress, and in any event "it is a religious matter, and, as such, is proscribed to us." Representative Sherman supported the resolution "not only as a laudable one in itself, but as warranted by a number of precedents in Holy Writ: for instance, the solemn thanksgivings and rejoicings which took place in the time of Solomon, after the building of the temple, was a case in point. This example, he thought, worthy of Christian imitation on the present occasion. . . ."

Boudinot's resolution was carried in the affirmative on September 25, 1789. Boudinot and Sherman, who favored the Thanksgiving proclamation, voted in favor of the adoption of the proposed amendments to the Constitution, including the Religion Clause; Tucker, who opposed the Thanksgiving proclamation, voted against the adoption of the amendments which became the Bill of Rights.

Within two weeks of this action by the House, George Washington responded to the Joint Resolution which by now had been changed to include the language that the President "recommend to the people of the United States a day of public thanksgiving and prayer, to be observed by acknowledging with grateful hearts the many and signal favors of Almighty God, especially by affording them an opportunity peaceably to establish a form of government for their safety and happiness." . . .

George Washington, John Adams, and James Madison all issued Thanksgiving Proclamations; Thomas Jefferson did not. . . .

As the United States moved from the eighteenth into the nineteenth century, Congress appropriated time and again public monies in support of sectarian Indian education carried on by religious organizations. Typical of these was Jefferson's treaty with the Kaskaskia Indians, which provided annual cash support for the Tribe's Roman Catholic priest and church. It was not until 1897, when aid to sectarian education for Indians had reached $500,000 annually, that Congress decided thereafter to cease appropriating money for education in sectarian schools. See generally R. Cord, *Separation of Church and State* 61–82 (1982).[9] This history shows the fallacy of the notion found in *Everson* that "no tax in any amount" may be levied for religious activities in any form.

· · ·

It would seem from this evidence that the Establishment Clause of the First Amendment had acquired a well-accepted meaning: it forbade establishment of a national religion, and forbade preference among religious sects or denominations. Indeed, the first American dictionary defined the word "establishment" as "the act of establishing, founding, ratifying or ordaining," such as in "[t]he episcopal form of religion, so called, in England." The Establishment Clause did not require government neutrality between religion and irreligion nor did it prohibit the Federal Government from providing nondiscriminatory aid to religion. There is simply no historical foundation for the proposition that the Framers intended to build the "wall of separation" that was constitutionalized in *Everson*.

Notwithstanding the absence of a historical basis for this theory of rigid separation, the wall idea might well have served as a useful albeit misguided analytical concept, had it led this Court to unified and principled results in Establishment Clause cases. The opposite, unfortunately, has been true; in the thirty-eight years since *Everson* our Establishment Clause cases have been neither principled nor unified. Our recent opinions, many of them hopelessly divided pluralities, have with embarrassing candor conceded that the "wall of separation" is merely a "blurred, indistinct, and variable barrier," which "is not wholly accurate" and can only be "dimly perceived." *Lemon*; *Tilton* v. *Richardson*, 403 U.S. 672 (1971); *Wolman* v. *Walter*, 433 U.S. 229 (1977); *Lynch* v. *Donnelly* (1984).

Whether due to its lack of historical support or its practical unworkability, the *Everson* "wall" has proved all but useless as a guide to sound constitutional adjudication. . . .

---

9. Robert Cord's book expresses many of the same views of both history and legal precedent as are here articulated by Justice Rehnquist. The book was republished in 1988 by Baker Book House (Grand Rapids, Michigan).

But the greatest injury of the "wall" notion is its mischievous diversion of judges from the actual intentions of the drafters of the Bill of Rights. The "crucible of litigation" [referred to by Justice Stevens in his opinion for the Court] is well adapted to adjudicating factual disputes on the basis of testimony presented in court, but no amount of repetition of historical errors in judicial opinions can make the errors true. The "wall of separation between church and State" is a metaphor based on bad history, a metaphor which has proved useless as a guide to judging. It should be frankly and explicitly abandoned.

The Court has more recently attempted to add some mortar to *Everson*'s wall through the three-part test of *Lemon*, which served at first to offer a more useful test for purposes of the Establishment Clause than did the "wall" metaphor. Generally stated, the *Lemon* test proscribes state action that has a sectarian purpose or effect, or causes an impermissible governmental entanglement with religion.

Lemon cited *Allen* as the source of the "purpose" and "effect" prongs of the three-part test. The *Allen* opinion explains, however, how it inherited the purpose and effect elements from *Schempp* and *Everson*, both of which contain the historical errors described above. . . . Thus the purpose and effect prongs have the same historical deficiencies as the wall concept itself: they are in no way based on either the language or intent of the drafters.

The secular purpose prong has proven mercurial in application because it has never been fully defined, and we have never fully stated how the test is to operate. If the purpose prong is intended to void those aids to sectarian institutions accompanied by a stated legislative purpose to aid religion, the prong will condemn nothing so long as the legislature utters a secular purpose and says nothing about aiding religion. Thus the constitutionality of a statute may depend upon what the legislators put into the legislative history and, more importantly, what they leave out. The purpose prong means little if it only requires the legislature to express any secular purpose and omit all sectarian references, because legislators might do just that. Faced with a valid legislative secular purpose, we could not properly ignore that purpose without a factual basis for doing do.

However, if the purpose prong is aimed to void all statutes enacted with the intent to aid sectarian institutions, whether stated or not, then most statutes providing any aid, such as textbooks or bus rides for sectarian schoolchildren, will fail because one of the purposes behind every statute, whether stated or not, is to aid the target of its largesse. In other words, if the purpose prong requires an absence of *any* intent to aid sectarian institutions, whether or not expressed, few state laws in this area could pass the test, and we would be required to void some state aids to religion which we have already upheld. E.g. *Allen*.

The entanglement prong of the *Lemon* test came from *Walz*. *Walz* involved a constitutional challenge to New York's time-honored practice of providing state property tax exemptions to church property used in worship. The *Walz* opinion refused to "undermine the ultimate constitutional objective [of the Establishment Clause] as illuminated by history," and upheld the tax exemption. The Court examined the historical relationship between the State and church when church property was in issue, and determined that the challenged tax exemption did not so entangle New York with the church as to cause an intrusion or interference with religion. Interferences with religion should arguably be dealt with under the Free Exercise Clause, but the entanglement inquiry in *Walz* was consistent with that case's broad survey of the relationship between state taxation and religious property.

We have not always followed *Walz'* reflective inquiry into entanglement, however. E.g., *Wolman*. One of the difficulties with the entanglement prong is that, when divorced from the logic of *Walz*, it creates an "insoluble paradox" in school aid cases: we have required aid to parochial schools to be closely watched lest it be put to sectarian use, yet this close supervision itself will create an entanglement. *Roemer* v. *Maryland Board of Public Works*, 426 U.S. 736 (1976). For example, in *Wolman*, the Court in part struck the State's nondiscriminatory provision of buses for parochial school field trips, because the state supervision of sectarian officials in charge of field trips would be too onerous. This type of self-defeating result is certainly not required to ensure that States do not establish religions.

The entanglement test as applied in cases like *Wolman* also ignores the myriad state administrative regulations properly placed upon sectarian institutions such as curriculum, attendance, and certification requirements for sectarian schools, or fire and safety regulations for churches. Avoiding entanglement between church and State may be an important consideration in a case like *Walz*, but if the entanglement prong were applied to all state and church relations in the automatic manner in which it has been applied to school aid cases, the State could hardly require anything of church-related institutions as a condition for receipt of financial assistance.

These difficulties arise because the *Lemon* test has no more grounding in the history of the First Amendment than does the wall theory upon which it rests. The three-part test represents a determined effort to craft a workable rule from a historically faulty doctrine; but the rule can only be as sound as the doctrine it attempts to service. The three-part test has simply not provided adequate standards for deciding Establishment Clause cases, as this Court has slowly come to realize. Even worse, the *Lemon* test has caused this Court to fracture into unworkable plurality opinions, depending upon how each of the three factors applies to a certain state action. The results from our school services cases show the difficulty we have encountered in making the *Lemon* test yield principled results.

For example, a State may lend to parochial schoolchildren geography textbooks that contain maps of the United States [*Allen*], but the State may not lend maps of the United States for use in geography class [*Meek*]. A State may lend textbooks on American colonial history, but it may not lend a film on George Washington, or a film projector to show it in history class. A State may lend classroom workbooks, but may not lend workbooks in which the parochial schoolchildren write, thus rendering them nonreusable [*Meek*]. A State may pay for bus transportation to religious schools [*Everson*] but may not pay for bus transportation from the parochial school to the public zoo or natural history museum for a field trip [*Wolman*]. A State may pay for diagnostic services conducted in the parochial school but therapeutic services must be given in a different building; speech and hearing "services" conducted by the State inside the sectarian school are forbidden [*Meek*], but the State may conduct speech and hearing diagnostic testing inside the sectarian school [*Wolman*]. Exceptional parochial school students may receive counseling, but it must take place outside of the parochial school [*Wolman, Meek*], such as in a trailer parked down the street. A State may give cash to a parochial school to pay for the administration of state-written tests and state-ordered reporting services [*Committee for Public Education and Religious Liberty* v. *Regan*, 444 U.S. 646 (1980)], but it may not provide funds for teacher-prepared tests on secular subjects [*Levitt* v. *Committee for Public Education and Religious Liberty*, 413 U.S. 472 (1973)]. Religious instruction may not be given in public school [*McCollum*], but the public school may release students during the day for religion classes elsewhere, and may enforce attendance at those classes with its truancy laws [*Zorach*].

These results violate the historically sound principle "that the Establishment Clause does not forbid governments . . . to [provide] general welfare under which benefits are distributed to private individuals, even though many of those individuals may elect to use those benefits in ways that 'aid' religious instruction or worship." *Nyquist*. It is not surprising in the light of this record that our most recent opinions have expressed doubt on the usefulness of the *Lemon* test.

Although the test initially provided helpful assistance, e.g., *Tilton*, we soon began describing the test as only a "guideline," *Nyquist*, and lately we have described it as "no more than [a] useful signpos[t]." *Mueller*, citing *Hunt* v. *McNair*, 413 U.S. 734 (1973); *Larkin* v. *Grendel's Den, Inc.*, 459 U.S. 116 (1982). We have noted that the *Lemon* test is "not easily applied," *Meek*, and as Justice White noted in *Regan*, under the *Lemon* test we have "sacrifice[d] clarity and predictability for flexibility." In *Lynch*, we reiterated that the *Lemon* test has never been binding on the Court, and we cited two cases where we had declined to apply it. *Marsh*, *Larson* v. *Valente*, 456 U.S. 228 (1982).

If a constitutional theory has no basis in the history of the amendment it seeks to interpret, is difficult to apply and yields unprincipled results, I see little use in it. The "crucible of litigation" has produced only consistent unpredictability, and today's effort is just a continuation of "the sisyphean task of trying to patch together the 'blurred, indistinct and variable barrier' described in *Lemon*."[10] We have done much straining since 1947, but still we admit that we can only "dimly perceive" the *Everson* wall. *Tilton*. Our perception has been clouded not by the Constitution but by the mists of an unnecessary metaphor.

The true meaning of the Establishment Clause can only be seen in its history.[11] . . . As drafters of our Bill of Rights, the Framers inscribed the principles that control today. Any deviation from their intention frustrates the permanence of that Charter and will only lead to the type of unprincipled decision-making that has plagued our Establishment Clause cases since *Everson*.

The Framers intended the Establishment Clause to prohibit the designation of any church as a "national" one. The Clause was also designed to stop the Federal Government from asserting a preference

---

10. The phrase "crucible of litigation" comes from the opinion for the Court in this case by Justice Stevens, who also wrote about "the sisyphean task" in *Lemon*, thus becoming a foil for the dissenting Rehnquist.

11. Justice Rehnquist's opinion rested upon a method of constitutional interpretation that requires judges to inquire into the original meaning of the provision at issue. *His* history has been challenged by Douglas Laycock, " 'Nonpreferential' Aid to Religion: A False Claim About Original Intent," *William & Mary Law Review* 27 (1986): 875, and defended by John S. Baker, Jr., "The Establishment Clause as Intended: No Preference among Sects and Pluralism in a Large Commercial Republic," in Eugene W. Hickok, Jr., ed. *The Bill of Rights: Original Meaning and Current Understanding* (Charlottesville: University Press of Virginia, 1991), 41–53.

for one religious denomination or sect over others. Given the "incorporation" of the Establishment Clause as against the States via the Fourteenth Amendment in *Everson*, States are prohibited as well from establishing a religion or discriminating between sects. As its history abundantly shows, however, nothing in the Establishment Clause requires government to be strictly neutral between religion and irreligion, nor does that Clause prohibit Congress or the States from pursuing legitimate secular ends through nondiscriminatory sectarian means.

The Court strikes down the Alabama statute because the State wished to "characterize prayer as a favored practice." It would come as much of a shock to those who drafted the Bill of Rights as it will to a large number of thoughtful Americans today to learn that the Constitution, as construed by the majority, prohibits the Alabama Legislature from "endorsing" prayer. George Washington himself, at the request of the very Congress which passed the Bill of Rights, proclaimed a day of "public thanksgiving and prayer, to be observed by acknowledging with grateful hearts the many and signal favors of Almighty God." History must judge whether it was the Father of his Country in 1789, or a majority of the Court today, which has strayed from the meaning of the Establishment Clause.

The State has a secular interest in regulating the manner in which the public schools are conducted. Nothing in the Establishment Clause of the First Amendment, properly understood, prohibits any such generalized "endorsement" of prayer.

Responses

From **Donald L. Drakeman**, *"New Ruling on School Prayer," in*
The Christian Century, June 19–25, 1985:

The Supreme Court has struck down Alabama's law setting aside a minute of silence at the beginning of the public school day for "meditation or voluntary prayer." As is usual in church-state cases, the court has left many questions unanswered. . . .

Although the court has reached the correct decision in this case, it missed the point by singling out legislative purpose as the law's sole defect. First, the court's approach makes this case irredeemably inconsistent with *Marsh* v. *Chambers*, in which the court allowed the state of Nebraska to appoint and pay· a legislative chaplain. If a secular purpose is a constitutional requirement, how can the court allow legislative chaplains to pray publicly and yet not permit a minute of silent prayer or meditation in the schools? What secular purpose supports legislative chaplains that does not apply equally to moments of silence? This kind of inconsistency not only creates havoc for lawyers; it also sheds a bad light on a judicial system theoretically committed to providing some uniformity and consistency in the interpretation of the Constitution.

Second, the Court's reliance on legislative purpose will only encourage state lawmakers to achieve their unconstitutional goals through less explicit statutes. In invalidating New Mexico's moment-of-silence law, a federal district court judge showed more sensitivity to this problem than did the Supreme Court. Not only did he strike down the law but he also enjoined any similar program, saying: "[The legislators] would be more careful to disguise their purpose the next time. With a wink and a nod, they could discuss the secular purposes . . . and prohibit any mention of the school prayer issue. Having avoided the factors which lead the Court to rule against them in this case, they could reinstitute the moment of silence."

The major problem with the moment-of-silence law is its effect on schoolchildren. Cast in the mold of the daily devotionals that took place for decades in our public schools (and still continue in parts of the country), the moment of silence provides an opportunity for the state to get involved in telling children when, where and how to pray. Whatever its purpose, it is the law's effect that we should question.

In light of the Supreme Court's decision, the courts may now have to deal with all twenty-five moment-of-silence laws in other states. If they continue to focus on legislative purpose, we may find identical statutes permitted in some states yet disallowed in others where lawmakers were less discrete. Our over-burdened courts scarcely need this kind of work.

This case, taken together with other recent church-state cases (which have tended to go the other direction, toward government accommodation of religion), gives the lie to the court's periodic attempts to say that it makes constitutional decisions by simply discerning the unchanging intent of the Framers. In fact, the religion clauses have been chameleons, changing colors with each new case as the justices scrambled to reach a consensus. The perplexing result is that the Court invariably starts with whatever result is favored by the majority and then works backward to some sort of constitutional rationale. Our church-state jurisprudence will remain confusing until that process is turned around.

From **Peter J. Ferrara**, *"Reading Between the Lines of the School-Prayer Decision,"* in the **Wall Street Journal**, *June 11, 1985:*

Liberals would be wrong to claim last week's Supreme Court school prayer ruling in *Wallace v. Jaffree* as one for their cause. For though the case was indeed disappointing to social conservatives, in terms of practical effect, the substance of the decision actually favored advocates of school prayer. Moreover, doctrinally the court's written opinions in the case further indicate that sweeping changes are under way in the court's interpretation of the Constitution's ban on governmental establishment of religion.

Every justice agreed in *Jaffree* that a state could require by law that schools set aside a moment of silence during which students may pray. Indeed, an Alabama law providing for a "moment of meditation" was expressly left standing by the court, with all nine justices agreeing that it was constitutional. Moreover, though the decision is not entirely clear on this point, it appears that the government can even state in the statute that students may use the time for prayer among other listed alternatives, such as meditation or contemplation or just thinking quietly.

What is prohibited by the majority is any indication by the government that it would prefer that students use the moment to pray. The majority found such a preference in the legislative history of a second Alabama statute requiring a moment of silence for "meditation or voluntary prayer," and held that statute unconstitutional.

The fact that a moment of silence is inherently neutral between prayer and other forms of meditation or contemplation should have been sufficient for the court to uphold the Alabama law. The majority's suggestion that students would somehow be bullied into praying by the history of the Alabama statute or the expressed hope by some legislators that students would use the time to pray, surpasses fantasy.

But if the court means what it says, the substantive bottom line is that a required moment of silence at the start of a school day, during which students may pray, is constitutional, regardless of whether or exactly how the government can affirmatively indicate that students may use the time to pray.

Doctrinally, Justice William Rehnquist won a major conservative victory, albeit in dissent, when he reviewed and correctly rejected as phony the historical foundation of prevailing Establishment Clause doctrine since the late 1940's. He suggested that the court return to the correct historical view that the Constitution only prohibits a government preference for one religious sect over another. The uncompromising determination expressed by Justice Rehnquist, the depth of the historical scholarship supporting him, and indications by three other justices that they agreed with his reading of history suggest that any workable consensus on the court concerning the historical foundation of prior Establishment Clause doctrines has been irretrievably shattered.

Even the majority opinion evidenced a subtle but potentially powerful shift in the law. The majority seemed to adopt a formulation first advocated by Justice Sandra Day O'Connor in a previous case, saying that the Constitution prohibits the government from pursuing a policy with the purpose or effect of "endorsing" religion. But the strict orthodoxy previously held that government may not "aid" or "benefit" religion. A broad range of government activities can aid or benefit religion without endorsing it, and this shift in doctrine can consequently herald a sharp narrowing of Establishment Clause prohibitions.

The problem with the orthodox view of the Establishment Clause stems from the notion that any aid or benefit to religion from government action is prohibited. For merely allowing religion to participate in the public sector and government programs and activities on the same terms as everyone else can be seen, and often has been by the courts, as aiding or benefiting religion. Even enforcing the same rights of expression and conduct in the public sector for the religious as for others can be construed, and sometimes has been, as an impermissible aid or benefit.

As the public sector grows, such a strict no aid view sharply reduces the presence and scope of religion in our daily lives, and the freedom of individuals to engage in religious activity. Moreover, this formerly prevailing doctrine radically departs from the concept of an establishment of religion. How can merely allowing religion to participate in the public sector, in government programs, institutions and activities, on the same terms and with the same rights as everyone else, involve an establishment of religion? The very essence of "establishment" suggests some special preference or consideration, not equal rights and participation. Merely applying the same rules to the religious as to everyone else cannot possibly violate the Establishment Clause.

The Supreme Court must uphold such equal rights and participation for the religious. A religious organization, activity or individual should be allowed to participate in and receive the benefits of general government programs and activities on the same terms and conditions as everyone else. For example, education vouchers or tuition tax credits that could be used at any school, public or private, would clearly be constitutional under such a principle.

With regard to school prayer, such a doctrine of equal rights would mean that public school students should be allowed to pray, silently or vocally, individually or in groups in any circumstance in which they are otherwise allowed to express themselves voluntarily. This would include lunch periods and other free time, during moments of silence, and in school newspapers, assemblies or other open student forums.

Such a view should in fact be supported by consistent civil libertarians not overwhelmed by an earnest cultural distaste for religion. Such support would help hasten the court's journey.

From *George Will,* syndicated column for June 9, 1985:

Last week the Court chewed yet again on the First Amendment's Establishment Clause, that simple injunction ("Congress shall make no law respecting an establishment of religion. . .") which the Court has contrived to make absurdly complicated. . . .

The Establishment Clause, reasonably read, is devoid of complexity. It means government must not be partial to a particular religion or sect. But last week a litigious Alabaman persuaded six justices . . . to rule that Alabama ravished the Constitution with a law authorizing a minute of silence in public schools "for meditation or voluntary prayer."

A moral, although not a constitutional, objection to "voluntary spoken prayer" in schools is that it can be neither really prayer not truly voluntary. It must be thin liturgical gruel to give no offense to any sect, and children will feel coercive peer pressure to participate. But what injury does a moment of silence do, even if the legislature hopes children will use it for prayer? The only "injury" is to a few litigious adults — self-appointed thought police — whose injury is the annoyance they feel about what might be in a child's mind, or a legislature's hopes.

Had Alabama deleted the last three words in the phrase "meditation or voluntary prayer," the Court probably would have said the law passed constitutional muster. Indeed, the man who brought this frivolous suit . . . said he only did so because he detected a suggestion that prayer is the "preferred activity" during the silent minute.

The justices could devote even more time to complaining about their case load if they would just use Will's Generic Opinion. It is a one-sentence opinion applicable in 99.99 percent of all contemporary cases arising from government action touching religion: "The practice in question does not do what the Establishment Clause was intended to prevent—impose an official creed, or significantly enhance or hinder a sect—so the practice is constitutional and the complaining parties should buzz off."

But in 1971, the Court decided, contrary to the clear evidence of the Framers' intentions, that the Establishment Clause requires government to be punctiliously neutral, not between religious sects but between religion and secularism. So the Court devised a rococo three-part test: Government action touching religion is presumptively unconstitutional unless it has a secular purpose, and its primary effect neither advances nor inhibits religion, and it does not foster excessive entanglement of government with religion. Given that formula, the outcome of the Alabama case was, perhaps, predictable.

Still, Justice Stevens, writing for the majority, took twenty-three pages to explain that Alabama's purpose was not pristinely secular and hence the law violates the convoluted misconstruction with which the Court had replaced the unambiguous concision of the Framers' Establishment Clause. Now, what of the twenty-four other states that have "moment of silence" laws? The Court can put each law, complete with each law's legislative history, under its moral microscope.

22

Grand Rapids School District v. Ball

473 U.S. 373 (1985)

Aguilar v. Felton

473 U.S. 402 (1985)

I n this pair of cases decided together on July 1, 1985, the Supreme Court struck down state and federal programs under
which public school teachers were sent into church-related
schools to teach secular subjects. Justice William Brennan wrote
for a sharply divided Court in both cases.

In the first, the school district of Grand Rapids, Michigan,
adopted two programs in which classes for non-public school
students were financed by the public school system, taught by
teachers hired by the public school system, and conducted in
classrooms in the non-public schools. The Shared Time program supplemented the core curriculum by providing "remedial" and "enrichment" courses in reading, art, music, physical
education, and other subjects. The Community Education program provided instruction in such areas as arts and crafts, home
economics, and Spanish, for both adults and children, after the
regular school day. The Shared Time teachers were full-time
employees, and the Community Education teachers part-time
employees, of the public schools. Virtually all the non-public
schools taking advantage of the programs were religious in
character.

Six taxpayers sued the school district, charging that the programs violated the no-establishment provision. The district
court agreed with their complaint, and the U.S. Court of Ap-

peals for the Sixth Circuit affirmed. The Supreme Court sustained that ruling in *Grand Rapids School District* v. *Ball*.

In the second case, *Aguilar* v. *Felton*: Title I of the Elementary and Secondary Education Act of 1965 authorized the Secretary of Education to fund local educational institutions so as to meet the needs of educationally deprived children from low-income families. Since 1966 the city of New York had used Title I money to provide instructional services for parochial school students on the premises of their schools. Students were taught remedial reading, reading skills, remedial mathematics, and English as a second language. Those administering the programs were employees of the public schools who had volunteered to teach in the parochial schools. The city made teacher assignments, and the teachers were supervised by field personnel who paid unannounced visits at least once a month; the program required that the classrooms in which the instruction took place be cleared of all religious symbols.

As in the *Grand Rapids* case, six taxpayers sued, alleging that the Title I program as administered by New York was unconstitutional. The district court granted a summary judgment in favor of the city, but the U.S. Court of Appeals for the Second Circuit reversed that decision. The Supreme Court then affirmed.

In both cases the same five justices—William Brennan, Thurgood Marshall, Harry Blackmun, Lewis Powell, and John Paul Stevens—agreed on the result and the reasoning as articulated in the opinions of the Court written by Justice Brennan. *Grand Rapids* generated four additional opinions, *Aguilar* five. Presented here are three opinions from *Grand Rapids* and four from *Aguilar*.

Participating in both cases were Chief Justice Warren E. Burger and Associate Justices Harry A. Blackmun, William J. Brennan, Jr., Thurgood Marshall, Sandra Day O'Connor, Lewis F. Powell, Jr., William H. Rehnquist, John Paul Stevens, and Byron R. White.

Opinions: Grand Rapids v. Ball

Justice William J. Brennan, Jr., delivered the opinion of the Court:

Since *Everson* v. *Board of Education* (1947) made clear that the guarantees of the Establishment Clause apply to the States, we have often grappled with the problem of state aid to nonpublic, religious schools. In all of these cases, our goal has been to give meaning to the sparse language and broad purposes of the Clause, while not unduly infringing on the ability of the States to provide for the welfare of their people in accordance with their own particular circumstances. Providing for the education of schoolchildren is surely a praiseworthy purpose. But our cases have consistently recognized that even such a praiseworthy, secular purpose cannot validate government aid to parochial schools when the aid has the effect of promoting a single religion or religion generally or when the aid unduly entangles the government in matters religious. For just as religion throughout history has provided spiritual comfort, guidance, and inspiration to many, it can also serve powerfully to divide societies and to exclude those whose beliefs are not in accord with particular religions or sects that have from time to time achieved dominance. The solution to this problem adopted by the Framers and consistently recognized by this Court is jealously to guard the right of every individual to worship according to the dictates of conscience while requiring the government to maintain a course of neutrality among religions, and between religion and non-religion. . . .

We have noted that the three-part test first articulated in *Lemon* v. *Kurtzman* (1971) guides "[t]he general nature of our inquiry in this area," *Mueller* v. *Allen* (1983). . . . These tests "must not be viewed as setting the precise limits to the necessary constitutional inquiry, but serve only as guidelines with which to identify instances in which the objectives of the Establishment Clause have been impaired." *Meek* v. *Pittenger*, 421 U.S. 349 (1975).[1] We have particularly relied on *Lemon* in

---

1. In *Meek*, the Court affirmed that parochial students might be provided with secular books but forbade provision of such items as maps and laboratory equipment to the schools themselves.

every case involving the sensitive relationship between government and religion in the education of our children. The government's activities in this area can have a magnified impact on impressionable young minds, and the occasional rivalry of parallel public and private school systems offers an all-too-ready opportunity for divisive rifts along religious lines in the body politic. . . . The *Lemon* test concentrates attention on the issues—purposes, effect, entanglement—that determine whether a particular state action is an improper "law respecting an establishment of religion." We therefore reaffirm that state action alleged to violate the Establishment Clause should be measured against the *Lemon* criteria.

As has often been true in school aid cases, there is no dispute as to the first test. Both the District Court and the Court of Appeals found that the purpose of the Community Education and Shared Time programs was "manifestly secular." We find no reason to disagree with this holding, and therefore go on to consider whether the primary or principal effect of the challenged programs is to advance or inhibit religion.

Our inquiry must begin with a consideration of the nature of the institutions in which the programs operate. Of the forty-one private schools where these "part-time public schools" have operated, forty are identifiably religious schools. . . .

Given that forty of the forty-one schools in this case are thus "pervasively sectarian," the challenged public-school programs operating in the religious schools may impermissibly advance religion in three different ways. First, the teachers participating in the programs may become involved in intentionally or inadvertently inculcating particular religious tenets or beliefs. Second, the programs may provide a crucial symbolic link between government and religion, thereby enlisting—at least in the eyes of impressionable youngsters—the powers of government to the support of the religious denomination operating the school. Third, the programs may have the effect of directly promoting religion by impermissibly providing a subsidy to the primary religious mission of the institutions affected.

Although Establishment Clause jurisprudence is characterized by few absolutes, the Clause does absolutely prohibit government-financed or government-sponsored indoctrination into the beliefs of a particular religious faith. . . . Such indoctrination, if permitted to occur, would have devastating effects on the right of each individual voluntarily to determine what to believe (and what not to believe) free of any coercive pressures from the State, while at the same time tainting the resulting religious beliefs with a corrosive secularism.

In *Meek*, the Court invalidated a statute providing for the loan of state-paid professional staff—including teachers—to nonpublic schools to provide remedial and accelerated instruction, guidance counseling and testing, and other services on the premises of the nonpublic schools. . . . The program in *Meek*, if not sufficiently monitored, would simply have entailed too great a risk of state-sponsored indoctrination.

The programs before us today share the defect that we identified in *Meek*. With respect to the Community Education Program, the District Court found that "virtually every Community Education course conducted on facilities leased from nonpublic schools has an instructor otherwise employed full time by the same nonpublic school." These instructors, many of whom no doubt teach in the religious schools because they are adherents of the controlling denomination and want to serve their religious community zealously, are expected during the regular school day to inculcate their students with the tenets and beliefs of their particular religious faiths. Yet the premise of the program is that those instructors can put aside their religious convictions and engage in entirely secular Community Education instruction as soon as the school day is over. Moreover, they are expected to do so before the same religious-school students and in the same religious-school classrooms that they employed to advance religious purposes during the "official" school day. Nonetheless, as petitioners themselves asserted, Community Education classes are not specifically monitored for religious content.

We do not question that the dedicated and professional religious school teachers employed by the Community Education program will attempt in good faith to perform their secular mission conscientiously. . . . Nonetheless, there is a substantial risk that, overtly or subtly, the religious message they are expected to convey during the regular school day will infuse the supposedly secular classes they teach after school. . . .

The Shared Time program, though structured somewhat differently, nonetheless also poses a substantial risk of state-sponsored indoctrination. The most important difference between the programs is that most of the instructors in the Shared Time program are full-time teachers hired by the public schools. Moreover, although "virtually every" Community Education instructor is a full-time religious school teacher, only "[a] significant portion" of the Shared Time instructors previously worked in the religious school. Nonetheless, as with Community Education program, no attempt is made to monitor the Shared Time courses for religious content.

Thus, despite these differences between the two programs, our holding in *Meek* controls the inquiry with respect to Shared Time, as well as Community Education. Shared Time instructors are teaching academic subjects in religious schools in courses virtually indistinguishable from the other courses offered during the regular religious-school day. The teachers in this program, even more than their Community Education colleagues, are "performing important educational services in schools in which education is an integral part of the dominant sectarian mission and in which an atmosphere dedicated to the advancement of religious belief is constantly maintained." *Meek*. Teachers in such an atmosphere may well subtly (or overtly) conform their instruction to the environment in which they teach, while students will perceive the instruction provided in the context of the dominantly religious message of the institution, thus reinforcing the indoctrinating effect. . . .

The Court of Appeals of course recognized that respondents adduced no evidence of specific incidents of religious indoctrination in this case. But the absence of proof of specific incidents is not dispositive. When conducting a supposedly secular class in the pervasively sectarian environment of a religious school, a teacher may knowingly or unwillingly tailor the content of the course to fit the school's announced goals. If so, there is no reason to believe that this kind of ideological influence would be detected or reported by students, by their parents, or by the school system itself. . . .

Our cases have recognized that the Establishment Clause guards against more than direct, state-funded efforts to indoctrinate youngsters in specific religious beliefs. Government promotes religion as effectively when it fosters a close identification of its powers and responsibilities with those of any—or all—religious denominations as when it attempts to inculcate specific religious doctrines. If this identification conveys a message of government endorsement or disapproval of religion, a core purpose of the Establishment Clause is violated. . . .

It follows that an important concern of the effects test is whether the symbolic union of church and state effected by the challenged governmental action is sufficiently likely to be perceived by adherents of the controlling denominations as an endorsement, and by the non-adherents as a disapproval, of their individual religious choices. The inquiry into this kind of effect must be conducted with particular care when many of the citizens perceiving the governmental message are children in their formative years. . . . The symbolism of a union between church and state is most likely to influence children of tender years, whose experience is limited and whose beliefs consequently are the function of environment as much as of free and voluntary choice.

Our school-aid cases have recognized a sensitivity to the symbolic impact of the union of church and state. Grappling with problems in many ways parallel to those we face today, *McCollum* v. *Board of Education* (1948) held that a public school may not permit part-time religious instruction on its premises as a part of the school program, even if participation in that instruction is entirely voluntary and even if the instruction itself is conducted only by nonpublic-school personnel. Yet in *Zorach* v. *Clauson* (1952), the Court held that a similar program conducted off the premises of the public school passed constitutional muster. The difference in symbolic impact helps to explain the difference between the cases. The symbolic connection of church and state in the *McCollum* program presented the students with a graphic symbol of the "concert or union or dependency" of church and state. . . . This very symbolic union was conspicuously absent in the *Zorach* program.

In the programs challenged in this case, the religious school students spend their typical school day moving between religious-school and "public-school" classes. Both types of classes take place in the same religious-school building and both are largely composed of students who are adherents of the same denomination. In this environment, the students would be unlikely to discern the crucial difference between the religious-school classes and the "public-school" classes, even if the latter were successfully kept free of religious indoctrination. . . . Consequently, even the student who notices the "public school" sign temporarily posted would have before him a powerful symbol of state endorsement and encouragement of the religious beliefs taught in the same class at some other time during the day. . . .

. . .

In *Everson* the Court stated that "[n]o tax in any amount, large or small, can be levied to support any religious activities or institutions, whatever they may be called, or whatever form they may adopt to teach or practice religion." With but one exception, our subsequent cases have struck down attempts by States to make payments out of public tax dollars directly to primary or secondary religious educational institutions. . . .[2]

---

2. Justice Brennan's one exception was *Committee for Public Education* v. *Regan*, 444 U.S. 646 (1980), which permitted public subsidy for certain routinized record-keeping and testing services performed by non-public schools but required by state law.

Aside from cash payments, the Court has distinguished between two categories of programs in which public funds are used to finance secular activities that religious schools would otherwise fund from their own resources. In the first category, the Court has noted that it is "well established . . . that not every law that confers an 'indirect,' 'remote', or 'incidental' benefit upon religious institutions is, for that reason alone, constitutionally invalid." In such "indirect" aid cases, the government has used primarily secular means to accomplish a primarily secular end, and no "primary effect" of advancing religion has thus been found. On this rationale, the Court has upheld programs providing for loans of secular textbooks to nonpublic school students and programs providing bus transportation for nonpublic school children.

In the second category of cases, the Court has relied on the Establishment Clause prohibition of forms of aid that provide "direct and substantial advancement of the sectarian enterprise." *Wolman* v. *Walter*, 433 U.S. 229 (1977).[3] In such "direct aid" cases, the government, although acting for a secular purpose, has done so by directly supporting a religious institution. Under this rationale, the Court has struck down state schemes providing for tuition grants and tax benefits for parents whose children attend religious school . . . and programs providing for "loan" of instructional materials to be used in religious schools. . . .

Thus, the Court has never accepted the mere possibility of subsidization, as the above cases demonstrate, as sufficient to invalidate an aid program. On the other hand, this effect is not wholly unimportant for Establishment Clause purposes. If it were, the public schools could gradually take on themselves the entire responsibility for teaching secular subjects on religious school premises. The question in each case must be whether the effect of the proffered aid is "direct and substantial" (*Nyquist*), or indirect and incidental. "The problem, like many problems in constitutional law, is one of degree." *Zorach*.

. . . The programs challenged here, which provide teachers in addition to the instructional equipment and materials, have [the] forbidden . . . effect of advancing religion. This kind of direct aid to the educational function of the religious school is indistinguishable from the provision of a direct cash subsidy to the religious school that is most clearly prohibited under the Establishment Clause.

Petitioners claim that the aid . . . flows primarily to the students, not

---

3. In *Wolman*, the Court held that pupils in church-related schools could be provided with diagnostic and remedial services and standardized tests as well as books but not with other instructional materials of the sort involved in *Meek*.

to the religious schools. Of course, all aid to religious schools ultimately "flows to" the students, and petitioners' argument if accepted would validate all forms of nonideological aid to religious schools, including those explicitly rejected in our prior cases. Yet in *Meek*, we held unconstitutional the loan of instructional materials to religious schools and in *Wolman*, we rejected the fiction that a similar program could be saved by masking it as aid to individual students. It follows *a fortiori* that the aid here, which includes not only instructional materials but also the provision of instructional services by teachers in the parochial school building, "inescapably [has] the primary effect of providing a direct and substantial advancement of the sectarian enterprise." *Wolman*. . . .

Petitioners also argue that this "subsidy" effect is not significant in this case, because the Community Education and Shared Time programs supplemented the curriculum with courses not previously offered in the religious schools and not required by school rule or state regulation. Of course, this fails to distinguish the programs here from those found unconstitutional in *Meek*. . . . As in *Meek*, we do not find that this feature of the program is controlling. First, there is no way of knowing whether the religious schools would have offered some or all of these courses if the public school system had not offered them first. . . . Second, although the precise courses offered in these programs may have been new to the participating religious schools, their general subject matter—reading, math, etc.—was surely a part of the curriculum in the past, and the concerns of the Establishment Clause may thus be triggered despite the "supplemental" nature of the courses. . . . Third, and most important, petitioners' argument would permit the public schools gradually to take over the entire secular curriculum of the religious school, for the latter could surely discontinue existing courses so that they might be replaced a year or two later by a Community Education or Shared Time course with the same content. The average religious school student, for instance, now spends 10 percent of the school day in Shared Time classes. But there is no principled basis on which this Court can impose a limit on the percentage of the religious-school day that can be subsidized by the public school. To let the genie out of the bottle in this case would be to permit ever larger segments of the religious school curriculum to be turned over to the public school system, thus violating the cardinal principle that the State may not in effect become the prime supporter of the religious school system.

We conclude that the challenged programs have the effect of promoting religion in three ways. The state-paid instructors, influenced by the pervasively sectarian nature of the religious schools in which they work, may subtly or overtly indoctrinate the students in particular religious tenets at public expense. The symbolic union of church and state inherent in the provision of secular, state-provided instruction in the religious school buildings threatens to convey a message of state support for religion to students and to the general public. Finally, the programs in effect subsidize the religious functions of the parochial schools by taking over a substantial portion of their responsibility for teaching secular subjects. For these reasons, the conclusion is inescapable that the Community Education and Shared Time programs have the "primary or principal" effect of advancing religion, and therefore violate the dictates of the Establishment Clause of the First Amendment.

[In a brief paragraph, **Chief Justice Warren E. Burger** concurred in the judgment in part and dissented in part. In his view, the Grand Rapids Community Education program violated the no-establishment principles as stated in *Lemon*, but the Shared Time program was constitutional, for reasons he states in his dissent in *Aguilar* v. *Felton* (see p. 386). In a short opinion, **Justice Sandra Day O'Connor** also concurred in the judgment in part and dissented in part. Like Burger, she thought the Community Education program was not constitutional but would have upheld the Shared Time program.]

Justice Byron R. White, dissenting:

As evidenced by my dissenting opinions in *Lemon* and *Nyquist*, I have long disagreed with the Court's interpretation and application of the Establishment Clause in the context of state aid to private schools. For the reasons stated in those dissents, I am firmly of the belief that the Court's decisions in these cases, like its decisions in *Lemon* and *Nyquist*, are "not required by the First Amendment and [are] contrary to the long-range interests of the country." For those same reasons, I am satisfied that what the States have sought to do in these cases [*Grand Rapids* and *Aguilar*] is well within their authority and is not forbidden by the Establishment Clause. Hence, I dissent and would reverse the judgment in each of these cases.

Justice William H. Rehnquist, dissenting:

I dissent for the reasons stated in my dissenting opinion in *Wallace* v. *Jaffree* (1985). In *Grand Rapids*, the Court relies heavily on the principles of *Everson* and *McCollum* but declines to discuss the faulty "wall" premise upon which those cases rest. In doing so the Court blinds itself to the first 150 years' history of the Establishment Clause.

The Court today attempts to give content to the "effects" prong of the *Lemon* test by holding that a "symbolic link between government and religion" creates an impermissible effect. But one wonders how the teaching of "Math Topics," "Spanish," and "Gymnastics" which is struck down today, creates a greater "symbolic link" than the municipal crèche upheld in *Lynch* v. *Donnelly* (1984) or the legislative chaplain upheld in *Marsh*. A most unfortunate result of *Grand Rapids* is that to support its holding the Court, despite its disclaimers, impugns the integrity of public school teachers. Contrary to the law and the teachers' promises, they are assumed to be eager inculcators of religious dogma requiring, in the Court's words, "ongoing supervision." Not one instance of attempted religious inculcation exists in the records of the school aid cases decided today, even though both the Grand Rapids and New York programs have been in operation for a number of years. I would reverse.

Opinions: Aguilar v. Felton

Justice William J. Brennan, Jr., delivered the opinion of the Court:

The New York City programs challenged in this case are very similar to the programs we examined in *Grand Rapids*. In both cases, publicly funded instructors teach classes composed exclusively of private school students in private school buildings. In both cases, an overwhelming number of the participating private schools are religiously affiliated. In both cases, the publicly funded programs provide not only professional personnel, but also all materials and supplies necessary for the operation of the programs. Finally, the instructors in both cases are told that they are public school employees under the sole control of the public school system.

The appellants attempt to distinguish this case on the ground that the City of New York, unlike the Grand Rapids Public School District, has adopted a system for monitoring the religious content of publicly funded Title I classes in the religious schools. At best, the supervision in this case would assist in preventing the Title I program from being used, intentionally or unwittingly, to inculcate the religious beliefs of the surrounding parochial school. But appellants' argument fails in any event, because the supervisory system established by the City of New York inevitably results in the excessive entanglement of church and state, an Establishment Clause concern distinct from that addressed by the effects doctrine. Even where state aid to parochial institutions does not have the primary effect of advancing religion, the provision of such aid may nonetheless violate the Establishment Clause owing to the nature of the interaction of church and state in the administration of that aid.

The principle that the state should not become too closely entangled with the church in the administration of assistance is rooted in two concerns. When the state becomes enmeshed with a given denomination in matters of religious significance, the freedom of religious belief of those who are not adherents of the denomination suffers, even when the governmental purpose underlying the involvement is largely

382

secular. In addition, the freedom of even the adherents of the denomination is limited by the governmental intrusion into sacred matters. . . .

. . .

As the Court of Appeals recognized, the elementary and secondary schools here are far different from the colleges at issue in *Roemer* v. *Maryland Board of Public Works*, 426 U.S. 736 (1976), *Hunt* v. *McNair*, 413 U.S. 734 (1973), and *Tilton* v. *Richardson*, 403 U.S. 672 (1971). Unlike the colleges, which were found to be "pervasively sectarian," many of the schools involved in this case are the same sectarian schools which had " 'as a substantial purpose the inculcation of religious values' " in *Nyquist*. Moreover, our holding in *Meek* invalidating the instructional services much like those at issue in this case rested on the ground that the publicly funded teachers were "performing important educational services in schools in which education is an integral part of the dominant sectarian mission and in which an atmosphere dedicated to the advancement of religious belief is constantly maintained." The court below found that the schools involved in this case were "well within this characterization." Unlike the schools in *Roemer* many of the schools here receive funds and report back to their affiliated church, require attendance at church religious exercises, begin the schoolday or class period with prayer, and grant preference in admission to members of the sponsoring denominations. In addition, the Catholic schools at issue here, which constitute the vast majority of the aided schools, are under the general supervision and control of the local parish.

The critical elements of the entanglement proscribed in *Lemon* and *Meek* are thus present in this case. First, as noted above, the aid is provided in a pervasively sectarian environment. Second, because assistance is provided in the form of teachers, ongoing inspection is required to ensure the absence of a religious message. . . . In short, the scope and duration of New York City's Title I program would require a permanent and pervasive state presence in the sectarian schools receiving aid.

This pervasive monitoring by public authorities in the sectarian schools infringes precisely those Establishment Clause values at the root of the prohibition of excessive entanglement. Agents of the city must visit and inspect the religious school regularly, alert for the subtle or over presence of religious matter in Title I classes. . . . In addition, the religious school must obey these same agents when they make determinations as to what is and what is not a "religious symbol" and thus off limits in a Title I classroom. . . . In short, the religious school, which has as a primary purpose the advancement and preservation of a particular religion, must endure the ongoing presence of state personnel whose primary purpose is to monitor teachers and students in an attempt to guard against the infiltration of religious thought.

The administrative cooperation that is required to maintain the educational program at issue here entangles church and state in still another way that infringes interests at the heart of the Establishment Clause. Administrative personnel of the public and parochial school systems must work together in resolving matters related to schedules, classroom assignments, problems that arise in the implementation of the program, requests for additional services, and the dissemination of information regarding the program. Furthermore, the program necessitates "frequent contacts between the regular and the remedial teachers (or other professionals), in which each side reports on individual student needs, problems encountered, and results achieved."

We have long recognized that underlying the Establishment Clause is "the objective . . . to prevent, as far as possible, the intrusion of either [church or state] into the precincts of the other." *Lemon.* . . . The numerous judgments that must be made by agents of the city concern matters that may be subtle and controversial, yet may be of deep religious significance to the controlling denominations. As government agents must make these judgments, the dangers of political divisiveness along religious lines increase. At the same time, "[t]he picture of state inspectors prowling the halls of parochial schools and auditing classroom instruction surely raises more than an imagined specter of governmental 'secularization of a creed,' " *Lemon.*

Despite the well-intentioned efforts taken by the City of New York, the program remains constitutionally flawed owing to the nature of the aid, to the institution receiving the aid, and to the constitutional principles that they implicate—that neither the State nor Federal Government shall promote or hinder a particular faith or faith generally through the advancement of benefits or through the excessive entanglement of church and state in the administration of those benefits.

Justice Lewis F. Powell, Jr., concurring:[4]

I concur in the Court's opinions and judgments today in this case and in *Grand Rapids*, holding that the aid to parochial schools involved in those cases violates the Establishment Clause of the First Amend-

---

4. This opinion also applies to *Grand Rapids*.

ment. I write to emphasize additional reasons why precedents of this Court require us to invalidate these two educational programs that concededly have "done so much good and little, if any detectable harm.". . .

I agree with the Court that in this case the Establishment Clause is violated because there is too great a risk of government entanglement in the administration of the religious schools; the same is true in *Grand Rapids*. As beneficial as the Title I program appears to be in accomplishing its secular goal of supplementing the education of deprived children, its elaborate structure, the participation of public school teachers, and the government surveillance required to ensure that public funds are used for secular purposes inevitably present a serious risk of excessive entanglement. Our cases have noted that " '[t]he State must be *certain*, given the Religion Clauses, that subsidized teachers do not inculcate religion.' " *Meek*. This is true whether the subsidized teachers are religious school teachers, as in *Lemon*, or public school teachers teaching secular subjects to parochial school children at the parochial schools. . . .

The risk of entanglement is compounded by the additional risk of political divisiveness stemming from the aid to religion at issue here. I do not suggest that at this point in our history the Title I program or similar parochial aid plans could result in the establishment of a state religion. There likewise is a small chance that these programs would result in significant religious or denominational control over our democratic processes. Nonetheless, there remains a considerable risk of continuing political strife over the propriety of direct aid to religious schools and the proper allocation of limited governmental resources. As this Court has repeatedly recognized, there is a likelihood whenever direct governmental aid is extended to some groups that there will be competition and strife among them and others to gain, maintain, or increase the financial support of government. In States such as New York that have large and varied sectarian populations, one can be assured that politics will enter into any state decision to aid parochial schools. Public schools, as well as private schools, are under increasing financial pressure to meet real and perceived needs. Thus, any proposal to extend direct governmental aid to parochial schools alone is likely to spark political disagreement from taxpayers who support the public schools, as well as from nonrecipient sectarian groups, who may fear that needed funds are being diverted from them. . . . Although the Court's opinion does not discuss it at length, the potential for such divisiveness is a strong additional reason for holding that the Title I and Grand Rapids programs are invalid on entanglement grounds.

The Title I program at issue in this case also would be invalid under the "effects" prong of the test adopted in *Lemon*. . . . [T]he type of aid provided in New York by the Title I program amounts to a state subsidy of the parochial schools by relieving those schools of the duty to provide the remedial and supplemental education their children require. This is not the type of "indirect and incidental effect beneficial to [the] religious institutions" that we suggested in *Nyquist* would survive Establishment Clause scrutiny. . . .

I recognize the difficult dilemma in which governments are placed by the interaction of the "effects" and entanglement prongs of the *Lemon* test. Our decisions require governments extending aid to parochial schools to tread an extremely narrow line between being certain that the "principal or primary effect" of the aid is not to advance religion, *Lemon*, and avoiding excessive entanglement. Nonetheless, the Court has never foreclosed the possibility that some types of aid to parochial schools could be valid under the Establishment Clause, *Mueller*. Our cases have upheld evenhanded secular assistance to both parochial and public school children in some areas. e.g., *Mueller* (tax deductions for educational expenses); *Board of Education* v. *Allen* (1968) (provision of secular textbooks); *Everson* (1947) (reimbursements for bus fare to school). I do not read the Court's opinion as precluding these types of indirect aid to parochial schools. In the cases cited, the assistance programs made funds available equally to public and nonpublic schools without entanglement. The constitutional defect in the Title I program, as indicated above, is that it provides a direct financial subsidy to be administered in significant part by public school teachers within parochial schools—resulting in both the advancement of religion and forbidden entanglement. If, for example, Congress could fashion a program of evenhanded financial assistance to both public and private schools that could be administered, without governmental supervision in the private schools, so as to prevent the diversion of the aid from secular purposes, we would be presented with a different question.

Chief Justice Warren E. Burger, dissenting:

Under the guise of protecting Americans from the evils of an Established Church such as those of the eighteenth century and earlier times, today's decision will deny countless schoolchildren desperately needed remedial teaching services funded under Title I. The program at issue covers remedial reading, reading skills, remedial mathematics, English as a second language, and assistance for children needing special help in the learning process. The "remedial reading" portion of this program, for example, reaches children who suffer from dyslexia, a disease known to be difficult to diagnose and treat. Many of these children now will not receive the special training they need, simply because their parents desire that they attend religiously affiliated schools.

What is disconcerting about the result reached today is that, in the face of the human cost entailed by this decision, the Court does not even attempt to identify any threat to religious liberty posed by the operation of Title I. I share Justice White's concern that the Court's obsession with the criteria identified in *Lemon* has led to results that are "contrary to the long-range interests of the country." As I wrote in *Wallace*, "our responsibility is not to apply tidy formulas by rote; our duty is to determine whether the statute or practice at issue is a step toward establishing a state religion." Federal programs designed to prevent a generation of children from growing up without being able to read effectively are not remotely steps in that direction. . . .

. . . We have frequently recognized that some interaction between church and state is unavoidable, and that an attempt to eliminate all contact between the two would be both futile and undesirable. . . . The Court today fails to demonstrate how the interaction occasioned by the program at issue presents any threat to the values underlying the Establishment Clause.

. . . The notion that denying these services to students in religious schools is a neutral act to protect us from an Established Church has no support in logic, experience, or history. Rather than showing the neutrality the Court boasts of, it exhibits nothing less than hostility toward religion and the children who attend church-sponsored schools.

Justice William H. Rehnquist, dissenting:

I dissent for the reasons stated in my dissenting opinion in *Wallace*. In this case the Court takes advantage of the "Catch-22" paradox of its own creation . . . whereby aid must be supervised to ensure no entanglement but the supervision itself is held to cause an entanglement. The Court today strikes down nondiscriminatory nonsectarian aid to educationally deprived children from low-income families. The Establishment Clause does not prohibit such sorely needed assistance; we have indeed traveled far afield from the concerns which prompted the adoption of the First Amendment when we rely on gossamer abstractions to invalidate a law which obviously meets an entirely secular need. I would reverse.

Justice Sandra Day O'Connor, dissenting, joined in Parts II and III by Justice William H. Rehnquist:

Today the Court affirms the holding of the Court of Appeals that public school teachers can offer remedial instruction to disadvantaged students who attend religious schools "only if such instruction . . . [is] afforded at a neutral site off the premises of the religious school." This holding rests on the theory, enunciated in . . . *Meek*, that public school teachers who set foot on parochial school premises are likely to bring religion into their classes, and that the supervision necessary to prevent religious teaching would unduly entangle church and state. Even if this theory were valid in the abstract, it cannot validly be applied to New York City's nineteen-year-old Title I program. The Court greatly exaggerates the degree of supervision necessary to prevent public school teachers from inculcating religion, and thereby demonstrates the flaws of a test that condemns benign cooperation between church and state. I would uphold Congress' efforts to afford remedial instruction to disadvantaged schoolchildren in both public and parochial schools.

I

As in *Wallace*, and *Thornton* v. *Caldor*, 472 U.S. 703 (1985), the Court in this litigation adheres to the three-part Establishment Clause test enunciated in *Lemon*. Under *Lemon* and its progeny, direct state aid to parochial schools that has the purpose or effect of furthering the religious mission of the schools is unconstitutional. I agree with that principle. According to the Court, however, the New York Title I program is defective not because of any improper purpose or effect, but rather because it fails the third part of the *Lemon* test: the Title I program allegedly fosters excessive government entanglement with religion. I disagree with the Court's analysis of entanglement, and I question the utility of entanglement as a separate Establishment Clause standard in most cases. . . .

The purpose of Title I is to provide special educational assistance to disadvantaged children who would not otherwise receive it. . . .

After reviewing the text of the statute and its legislative history, the

District Court concluded that Title I serves a secular purpose of aiding needy children regardless of where they attend school. The Court of Appeals did not dispute this finding, and no party in this Court contends that the purpose of the statute or of the New York City Title I program is to advance or endorse religion. Indeed, the record demonstrates that New York City public school teachers offer Title I classes on the premises of parochial schools solely because alternative means to reach the disadvantaged parochial school students—such as instruction for parochial school students at the nearest public school, either after or during regular school hours—were unsuccessful. Whether one looks to the face of the statute or to its implementation, the Title I program is undeniably animated by a legitimate secular purpose.

The Court's discussion of the effect of the New York City Title I program is even more perfunctory than its analysis of the program's purpose. . . .

One need not delve too deeply in the record to understand why the Court does not belabor the effect of the Title I program. The abstract theories explaining why on-premises instruction might possibly advance religion dissolve in the face of experience in New York City. . . . [I]n nineteen years there has never been a single incident in which a Title I instructor "subtly or overtly" attempted to "indoctrinate the students in particular religious tenets at public expense."

Common sense suggests a plausible explanation for this unblemished record. New York City's public Title I instructors are professional educators who can and do follow instructions not to inculcate religion in their classes. They are unlikely to be influenced by the sectarian nature of the parochial school where they teach, not only because they are carefully supervised by public officials, but also because the vast majority of them visit several different schools each week and are not of the same religion as their parochial students. In light of the ample record, an objective observer of the implementation of Title I program in New York City would hardly view it as endorsing the tenets of the participating parochial schools. To the contrary, the actual and perceived effect of the program is precisely the effect intended by Congress: impoverished schoolchildren are being helped to overcome learning deficits, improving their test scores, and receiving a significant boost in their struggle to obtain both a thorough education and the opportunities that flow from it.

The only type of impermissible effect that arguably could carry over from the *Grand Rapids* decision to this litigation, then, is the effect of subsidizing "the religious functions of the parochial schools by taking over a substantial portion of their responsibility for teaching secular subjects." That effect is tenuous, however, in light of the statutory directive that Title I funds may be used only to provide services that otherwise would not be available to the participating students. . . .

Even if we were to assume that Title I remedial classes in New York City may have duplicated to some extent instruction parochial schools would have offered in the absence of Title I, the Court's delineation of this third type of effect proscribed by the Establishment Clause would be seriously flawed. Our Establishment Clause decisions have not barred remedial assistance to parochial school children, but rather remedial assistance *on the premises of the parochial school*. . . .

II

Recognizing the weakness of any claim of an improper purpose or effect, the Court today relies entirely on the entanglement prong of *Lemon* to invalidate the New York City Title I program. The Court holds that the occasional presence of peripatetic public school teachers on parochial school grounds threatens undue entanglement of church and state because (1) the remedial instruction is afforded in a pervasively sectarian environment; (2) ongoing supervision is required to assure that the public school teachers do not attempt to inculcate religion; (3) the administrative personnel of the parochial and public school systems must work together in resolving administrative and scheduling problems; and (4) the instruction is likely to result in political divisiveness over the propriety of direct aid.

This analysis of entanglement, I acknowledge, finds support in some of this Court's precedents. In *Meek* the Court asserted that it could not rely "on the good faith and professionalism of the secular teachers and counselors functioning in church-related schools to ensure that a strictly nonideological posture is maintained." Because "a teacher remains a teacher," the Court stated, there remains a risk that teachers will intertwine religious doctrine with secular instruction. The continuing state surveillance necessary to prevent this from occurring would produce undue entanglement of church and state. The Court's opinion in *Meek* further asserted that public instruction on parochial school premises creates a serious risk of divisive political conflict over the issue of aid to religion. *Meek's* analysis of entanglement was reaffirmed in *Wolman* two Terms later.

I would accord these decisions the appropriate deference commanded by the doctrine of *stare decisis* if I could discern logical support for their analysis. But experience has demonstrated that the analysis in . . . the *Meek* opinion is flawed. At the time *Meek* was decided, thoughtful dissents pointed out the absence of any record support for the notion that public school teachers would attempt to inculcate religion simply because they temporarily occupied a parochial school classroom, or that such instruction would produce political divisiveness. Experience has given greater force to the arguments of the dissenting opinions in *Meek*. It is not intuitively obvious that a dedicated public school teacher will tend to disobey instructions and commence proselytizing students at public expense merely because the classroom is within a parochial school. *Meek* is correct in asserting that a teacher of remedial reading "remains a teacher," but surely it is significant that the teacher involved is a professional, full-time public school employee who is unaccustomed to bringing religion into the classroom. Given that not a single incident of religious indoctrination has been identified as occurring in the thousands of classes offered in Grand Rapids and New York City over the past two decades, it is time to acknowledge that the risk identified in *Meek* was greatly exaggerated.

Just as the risk that public school teachers in parochial classrooms will inculcate religion has been exaggerated, so has the degree of supervision required to manage that risk. In this respect the New York City Title I program is instructive. What supervision has been necessary in New York City to enable public school teachers to help disadvantaged children for nineteen years without once proselytizing? Public officials have prepared careful instructions warning public school teachers of their exclusively secular mission, and have required Title I teachers to study and observe them. Under the rules, Title I teachers are not accountable to parochial or private school officials; they have sole responsibility for selecting the students who participate in their class, must administer their own tests for determining eligibility, cannot engage in team teaching or cooperative activities with parochial school teachers, must make sure that all materials and equipment they use are not otherwise used by the parochial school, and must not participate in religious activities in the schools or introduce any religious matter into their teaching. To ensure compliance with the rules, a field supervisor and a program coordinator, who are full-time public school employees, make unannounced visits to each teacher's classroom at least once a month.

The Court concludes that this degree of supervision of public school employees by other public school employees constitutes excessive entanglement of church and state. I cannot agree. The supervision that occurs in New York City's Title I program does not differ significantly from the supervision any public school teacher receives, regardless of the location of the classroom. Justice Powell suggests that the required supervision is extensive because the State must be *certain* that public school teachers do not inculcate religion. That reasoning would require us to close our public schools, for there is always some chance that a public school teacher will bring religion into the classroom, regardless of its location. . . . Even if I remained confident of the usefulness of entanglement as an Establishment Clause test, I would conclude that New York City's efforts to prevent religious indoctrination in Title I classes have been adequate and have not caused excessive institutional entanglement of church and state.

The Court's reliance on the potential for political divisiveness as evidence of undue entanglement is also unpersuasive. There is little record support for the proposition that New York City's admirable Title I program has ignited any controversy other than this litigation. . . .

I adhere to the doubts about the entanglement test that were expressed in *Lynch*. It is curious indeed to base our interpretation of the Constitution on speculation as to the likelihood of a phenomenon which the parties may create merely by prosecuting a lawsuit. My reservations about the entanglement test, however, have come to encompass its institutional aspects as well. As Justice Rehnquist has pointed out [in *Wallace*], many of the inconsistencies in our Establishment Clause decisions can be ascribed to our insistence that parochial aid programs with a valid purpose and effect may still be invalid by virtue of undue entanglement. . . .

If a statute lacks a purpose or effect of advancing or endorsing religion, I would not invalidate it merely because it requires some ongoing cooperation between church and state or some state supervision to ensure that state funds do not advance religion.

III

Today's ruling does not spell the end of the Title I program of remedial education for disadvantaged children. Children attending public schools may still obtain the benefits of the program. Impoverished children who attend parochial schools may also continue to benefit from Title I programs offered off the premises of their schools—possibly in portable classrooms just over the edge of school property. The only disadvantaged children who lose under the Court's holding are those in cities where it is not economically and logistically feasible to provide public facilities for remedial education adjacent to the parochial school. But this subset is significant, for it includes more than 20,000 New York City schoolchildren and uncounted others elsewhere in the country.

For these children, the Court's decision is tragic. The Court deprives them of a program that offers a meaningful chance at success in life, and it does so on the untenable theory that public school teachers (most of whom are of different faiths than their students) are likely to start teaching religion merely because they have walked across the threshold of a parochial school. I reject this theory and the analysis in *Meek* on which it is based. I cannot close my eyes to the fact that, over almost two decades, New York City's public school teachers have helped thousands of impoverished parochial school children to overcome educational disadvantages without once attempting to inculcate religion. Their praiseworthy efforts have not eroded and do not threaten the religious liberty assured by the Establishment Clause. The contrary judgment of the Court of Appeals should be reversed.

I respectfully dissent.

23

Employment Division v. Smith

485 U.S. 660 (1990)

A state may deny unemployment benefits to persons dismissed from their jobs on account of illegal drug use, even if the use of the drug is religiously based. So said the Supreme Court in its highly controversial *Smith* decision. Not since *Minersville* v. *Gobitis* (1940) had a free-exercise decision drawn as much negative commentary in the press and the academy, and a major legislative effort was soon mounted to change it. In *Smith*, the Court, with Justice Antonin Scalia writing, limited the implications of *Sherbert* v. *Verner* (1963), which exempted religious believers from a non-discriminatory secular law that inhibited the exercise of their religious beliefs, and seemed to some observers to revive *Gobitis*. The *Smith* case, taken together with *Board of Education* v. *Mergens* (see Case 24), also decided in 1990, suggested the Court's willingness (short-lived, in light of its decision two years later in *Lee* v. *Weisman*, Case 25) to defer to the political process on questions of church and state.

Oregon law prohibited the knowing or intentional possession of a "controlled substance" unless it had been medically prescribed. Anyone violating the law was guilty of a felony. Alfred Smith and Galen Black were fired from their jobs with a private drug-rehabilitation organization because they ingested the hallucinogenic drug peyote, used for sacramental purposes at a ceremony of the Native American Church. When they applied to the state Employment Division for unemployment compensation, they were judged ineligible for benefits because they had been fired for work-related "misconduct"—i.e., their use of a

395

"controlled substance" that could not be lawfully possessed in Oregon.

Smith and Galen challenged the decision on free-exercise grounds. The case went through the Oregon courts, with its supreme court deciding that the petitioners were entitled to unemployment benefits. When the case first came to the U.S. Supreme Court, it was sent back to Oregon so that state courts could decide whether sacramental use of peyote was in fact proscribed by the state's controlled-substance law—a matter disputed by the parties. The Oregon Supreme Court held that the petitioners' apparently religiously inspired use of peyote did indeed fall within the prohibition of the Oregon statute, which "makes no exception for the sacramental use" of the drug. That court then concluded that this prohibition violated the free-exercise provision, and that the petitioners were therefore entitled to unemployment compensation. On appeal, the U.S. Supreme Court reversed this judgment: "[A]n individual's religious beliefs [do not] excuse him from compliance with an otherwise valid law prohibiting conduct that the State is free to regulate." (A year later the Oregon legislature voted to change the law so that such persons as Alfred Smith and Galen Black *would* be eligible for unemployment benefits; see note 8 in the opinions.)

The case produced three opinions—Scalia's, for the Court, expressing the views of five members; Justice Sandra Day O'Connor's, concurring in the judgment but disagreeing with the Court's jurisprudence; and Justice Harry Blackmun's, in dissent. All three are presented here.

The decision in *Smith* was sharply criticized by groups and individuals ordinarily on opposite sides of the theological and political spectrum. Both religious liberals (the National Council of Churches) and religious conservatives (including Richard John Neuhaus, editor of *First Things*) faulted Scalia's opinion, as did both the American Jewish Committee, sponsor of *Commentary*, and the liberal American Jewish Congress. The American Civil Liberties Union, People for the American Way, and the American Humanist Association denounced the decision. Joining them were constitutional lawyers normally not aligned with their positions, such as Michael McConnell of the University of

Chicago Law School. For negative evaluations of *Smith*, see Edward McGlynn Gaffney, Douglas Laycock, and Michael W. McConnell, "An Open Letter to the Religious Community," *First Things*, March 1991. For a view substantially in agreement with Justice Scalia's opinion, see Gerard V. Bradley, "Beguiled: Free Exercise Exemptions and the Siren Song of Liberalism," *Hofstra Law Review* 20 (1991): 245. By the spring of 1993, legislation to restore the conduct exemption to free-exercise jurisprudence seemed a strong possibility. Also in 1993, the Court explicitly reaffirmed the *Smith* decision in *Church of the Lukumi* v. *Hialeah*.

Participating in *Employment Division* v. *Smith*, decided April 17, 1990, were Chief Justice William H. Rehnquist and Associate Justices Harry A. Blackmun, William J. Brennan, Jr., Thurgood Marshall, Sandra Day O'Connor, Lewis F. Powell, Jr., Antonin Scalia, John Paul Stevens, and Byron R. White.

Opinions

Justice Antonin Scalia delivered the opinion of the Court:

Respondents' claim for relief rests on our decisions in *Sherbert* v. *Verner* (1963), *Thomas* v. *Review Board* (1981), and *Hobbie* v. *Unemployment Appeals Commission*, 480 U.S. 136 (1987), in which we held that a State could not condition the availability of unemployment insurance on an individual's willingness to forgo conduct required by his religion. As we observed in *Smith* I (1988),[1] however, the conduct at issue in those cases was not prohibited by law. We held that distinction to be critical, for "if Oregon does prohibit the religious use of peyote, and if that prohibition is consistent with the Federal Constitution, there is no federal right to engage in that conduct in Oregon," and "the State is free to withhold unemployment compensation from respondents for engaging in work-related misconduct, despite its religious motivation." Now that the Oregon Supreme Court has confirmed that Oregon does prohibit the religious use of peyote, we proceed to consider whether that prohibition is permissible under the Free Exercise Clause.

. . . The free exercise of religion means, first and foremost, the right to believe and profess whatever religious doctrine one desires. Thus, the First Amendment obviously excludes all "governmental regulation of religious *beliefs* as such." *Sherbert*. The government may not compel affirmation of religious belief, punish the expression of religious doctrines it believes to be false, impose special disabilities on the basis of religious views or religious status, or lend its power to one or the other side in controversies over religious authority or dogma.[2]

---

1. *Employment Division* v. *Smith*, 485 U.S. 660 (1988).
2. Although known as an "originalist," Justice Scalia did not repair to the history of the free-exercise provision in order to determine its meaning. The most thorough originalist inquiry into the meaning of the free-exercise provision is by a leading critic of Scalia's *Smith* opinion, Michael McConnell. See his "The Origins and Historical Understanding of Free Exercise of Religion," *Harvard Law Review* 103 (1990): 1409. A briefer treatment is his "Free Exercise as the Framers Understood It," in Eugene W. Hickok, ed., *The Bill of Rights: Original Meaning and Current Understanding* (Charlottesville: University of Virginia Press, 1991), 54–69. For a response to McConnell by a scholar who is also an originalist, see Gerard V. Bradley, "Beguiled: Free Exercise Exemptions and the Siren Song of Liberalism," *Hofstra Law Review* 20 (1991): 245.

But the "exercise of religion" often involves not only belief and profession but the performance of (or abstention from) physical acts:. assembling with others for a worship service, participating in sacramental use of bread and wine, proselytizing, abstaining from certain foods or certain modes of transportation. It would be true, we think (though no case of ours has involved the point), that a state would be "prohibiting the free exercise [of religion]" if it sought to ban such acts or abstentions only when they are engaged in for religious reasons, or only because of the religious belief that they display. It would doubtless be unconstitutional, for example, to ban the casting of "statues that are to be used for worship purposes," or to prohibit bowing down before a golden calf.

Respondents in the present case, however, seek to carry the meaning of "prohibiting the free exercise [of religion]" one large step further. They contend that their religious motivation for using peyote places them beyond the reach of a criminal law that is not specifically directed at their religious practice, and that is concededly constitutional as applied to those who use the drug for other reasons. They assert, in other words, that "prohibiting the free exercise [of religion]" includes requiring any individual to observe a generally applicable law that requires (or forbids) the performance of an act his religious belief forbids (or requires). As a textual matter, we do not think the words must be given that meaning. It is no more necessary to regard the collection of a general tax, for example, as "prohibiting the free exercise [of religion]" by those citizens who believe support of organized government to be sinful, than it is to regard the same tax as "abridging the freedom . . . of the press" of those publishing companies that must pay the tax as a condition of staying in business. It is a permissible reading of the text, in the one case as in the other, to say that if prohibiting the exercise of religion (or burdening the activity of printing) is not the object of the tax but merely the incidental effect of a generally applicable and otherwise valid provision, the First Amendment has not been offended. Our decisions reveal that the latter reading is the correct one. We have never held that an individual's religious beliefs excuse him from compliance with an otherwise valid law prohibiting conduct that the State is free to regulate. On the contrary, the record of more than a century of our free exercise jurisprudence contradicts that proposition. As described succinctly by Justice Frankfurter in *Minersville* v. *Gobitis* (1940): "Conscientious scruples have not, in the course of the long struggle for religious toleration, relieved the individual from obedience to a general law not aimed at the promotion or restriction of religious beliefs. The mere possession of religious convictions which contradict the relevant concerns of a political society does not relieve the citizen from the discharge of political responsibilities."[3] We first had occasion to assert that principle in *Reynolds* v. *U.S.*, 98 U.S. 145 (1879), where we rejected the claim that criminal laws against polygamy could not be constitutionally applied to those whose religion commanded the practice. "Laws," we said, "are made for the government of actions, and while they cannot interfere with mere religious belief and opinions, they may with practices. . . . Can a man excuse his practices to the contrary because of his religious belief? To permit this would be to make the professed doctrines of religious belief superior to the law of the land, and in effect to permit every citizen to become a law unto himself."

Subsequent decisions have consistently held that the right of free exercise does not relieve an individual of the obligation to comply with a "valid and neutral law of general applicability on the ground that the law proscribes (or prescribes) conduct that his religion prescribes (or proscribes)." In *Prince* v. *Massachusetts*, 321 U.S. 158 (1944), we held that a mother could be prosecuted under the child labor laws for using her children to dispense literature in the streets, her religious motivation notwithstanding. We found no constitutional infirmity in "excluding [these children] from doing there what no other children may do." In *Braunfeld* v. *Brown*, 366 U.S. 599 (1961) (plurality opinion), we upheld Sunday-closing laws against the claim that they burdened the religious practices of persons whose religions compelled them to refrain from work on other days. In *Gillette* v. *U.S.*, 401 U.S. 437 (1971), we sustained the military selective service system against the claim that it violated free exercise by conscripting persons who opposed a particular war on religious grounds.

Our most recent decision involving a neutral, generally applicable regulatory law that compelled activity forbidden by an individual's religion was *United States* v. *Lee*, 455 U.S. 252 (1982). There, an Amish employer, on behalf of himself and his employees, sought exemption from collection and payment of Social Security taxes on the ground that the Amish faith prohibited participation in governmental support programs. We rejected the claim that an exemption was constitutionally required. There would be no way, we observed, to distinguish the

---

3. Compare Scalia's treatment of *Gobitis* with Justice O'Connor's view, expressed in her dissent, that *Gobitis* was overruled by *West Virginia State Board of Education* v. *Barnette* (1943).

Amish believer's objection to Social Security taxes from the religious objections that others might have to the collection or use of other taxes. "If, for example, a religious adherent believes war is a sin, and if a certain percentage of the federal budget can be identified as devoted to war-related activities, such individuals would have a similarly valid claim to be exempt from paying that percentage of the income tax. The tax system could not function if denominations were allowed to challenge the tax system because tax payments were spent in a manner that violates their religious belief."

The only decisions in which we have held that the First Amendment bars application of a neutral, generally applicable law to religiously motivated action have involved not the Free Exercise Clause alone, but the Free Exercise Clause in conjunction with other constitutional protections, such as freedom of speech and of the press, see *Cantwell* v. *Connecticut* (1940) (invalidating a licensing system for religious and charitable solicitations under which the administrator had discretion to deny a license to any cause he deemed nonreligious); *Murdock* v. *Pennsylvania*, 319 U.S. 105 (1943) (invalidating a flat tax on solicitation as applied to the dissemination of religious ideas); *Follett* v. *McCormick*, 321 U.S. 573 (1944) (same); or the right of parents, acknowledged in *Pierce* v. *Society of Sisters*, 268 U.S. 510 (1925), to direct the education of their children, see *Wisconsin* v. *Yoder* (1972) (invalidating compulsory school-attendance laws as applied to Amish parents who refused on religious grounds to send their children to school). Some of our cases prohibiting compelled expression, decided exclusively upon free speech grounds, have also involved freedom of religion, cf. *Wooley* v. *Maynard*, 430 U.S. 705 (1977) (invalidating compelled display of a license plate slogan that offended individual religious beliefs); *Barnette* (invalidating compulsory flag salute statute challenged by religious objectors).

The present case does not present such a hybrid situation, but a free exercise claim unconnected with any communicative activity or parental right. Respondents urge us to hold, quite simply, that when otherwise prohibitable conduct is accompanied by religious convictions, not only the convictions but the conduct itself must be free from governmental regulation. We have never held that, and decline to do so now. There being no contention that Oregon's drug law represents an attempt to regulate religious beliefs, the communication of religious beliefs, or the raising of one's children in those beliefs, the rule to which we have adhered ever since *Reynolds* plainly controls. . . .

Respondents argue that even though exemption from generally applicable criminal laws need not automatically be extended to religiously motivated actors, at least the claim for a religious exemption must be evaluated under the balancing test set forth in *Sherbert*. Under the *Sherbert* test, governmental actions that substantially burden a religious practice must be justified by a compelling governmental interest. Applying that test we have, on three occasions, invalidated state unemployment compensation rules that conditioned the availability of benefits upon an applicant's willingness to work under conditions forbidden by his religion. See *Sherbert*; *Thomas*; *Hobbie*. We have never invalidated any governmental action on the basis of the *Sherbert* test except the denial of unemployment compensation. Although we have sometimes purported to apply the *Sherbert* test in contexts other than that, we have always found that test satisfied, see *Lee*, *Gillette*. In recent years we have abstained from applying the *Sherbert* test (outside the unemployment compensation field) at all. In *Bowen* v. *Roy*, 476 U.S. 693 (1986), we declined to apply *Sherbert* analysis to a federal statutory scheme that required benefit applicants and recipients to provide their Social Security numbers. The plaintiffs in that case asserted that it would violate their religious beliefs to obtain and provide a Social Security number for their daughter. We held the statute's application to the plaintiffs valid regardless of whether it was necessary to effectuate a compelling interest. In *Lyng* v. *Northwest Indian Cemetery Protective Assn.*, 485 U.S. 439 (1988), we declined to apply *Sherbert* analysis to the Government's logging and road construction activities on lands used for religious purposes by several Native American Tribes, even though it was undisputed that the activities "could have devastating effects on traditional Indian religious practices." In *Goldman* v. *Weinberger*, 475 U.S. 503 (1986), we rejected application of the *Sherbert* test to military dress regulations that forbade the wearing of yarmulkes. In *O'Lone* v. *Estate of Shabazz*, 482 U.S. 342 (1987), we sustained, without mentioning the *Sherbert* test, a prison's refusal to excuse inmates from work requirements to attend worship services.

Even if we were inclined to breathe into *Sherbert* some life beyond the unemployment compensation field, we would not apply it to require exemptions from a generally applicable criminal law. The *Sherbert* test, it must be recalled, was developed in a context that lent itself to individualized governmental assessment of the reasons for the relevant conduct. As a plurality of the Court noted in *Roy*, a distinctive feature of unemployment compensation programs is that their eligibility criteria invite consideration of the particular circumstances behind an applicant's unemployment: "The statutory conditions [in *Sherbert* and

Thomas] provided that a person was not eligible for unemployment compensation benefits if, 'without good cause,' he had quit work or refused available work. The 'good cause' standard created a mechanism for individualized exemptions." As the plurality pointed out in *Roy*, our decisions in the unemployment cases stand for the proposition that where the State has in place a system of individual exemptions, it may not refuse to extend that system to cases of "religious hardship" without compelling reason.

Whether or not the decisions are that limited, they at least have nothing to do with an across-the-board criminal prohibition on a particular form of conduct. Although, as noted earlier, we have sometimes used the *Sherbert* test to analyze free exercise challenges to such laws, see *Lee, Gillette*, we have never applied the test to invalidate one. We conclude today that the sounder approach, and the approach in accord with the vast majority of our precedents, is to hold the test inapplicable to such challenges.[4] The government's ability to enforce generally applicable prohibitions of socially harmful conduct, like its ability to carry out other aspects of public policy, "cannot depend on measuring the effects of a governmental action on a religious objector's spiritual development." *Lyng*. To make an individual's obligation to obey such a law contingent upon the law's coincidence with his religious beliefs, except where the State's interest is "compelling"—permitting him, by virtue of his beliefs, "to become a law unto himself," *Reynolds*—contradicts both constitutional tradition and common sense.[5]

The "compelling government interest" requirement seems benign, because it is familiar from other fields. But using it as the standard that must be met before the government may accord different treatment on the basis of race or before the government may regulate the content of speech is not remotely comparable to using it for the purpose asserted

4. *Sherbert* thus is made, apparently, a limited precedent.

5. [The following appears as footnote two in Scalia's opinion.] Justice O'Connor seeks to distinguish *Lyng* and *Bowen* on the ground that those cases involved the government's conduct of "its own internal affairs," which is different because, as Justice Douglas said in *Sherbert*, " 'the Free Exercise Clause is written in terms of what the government cannot do to the individual, not in terms of what the individual can exact from the government.' " But since Justice Douglas voted with the majority in *Sherbert*, that quote obviously envisioned that what "the government cannot do to the individual" includes not just the prohibition of an individual's freedom of action through criminal laws but also the running of its programs (in *Sherbert*, state unemployment compensation) in such fashion as to harm the individual's religious interests. Moreover, it is hard to see any reason in principle or practicality why the government should have to tailor its health and safety laws to conform to the diversity of religious belief, but should not have to tailor its management of public lands, *Lyng*, or its administration of welfare programs, *Roy*.

here. What it produces in those other fields—equality of treatment, and an unrestricted flow of contending speech—are constitutional norms; what it would produce here—a private right to ignore generally applicable laws—is a constitutional anomaly.[6]

Nor is it possible to limit the impact of respondents' proposal by requiring a "compelling state interest" only when the conduct prohibited is "central" to the individual's religion. It is no more appropriate for judges to determine the "centrality" of religious beliefs before applying a "compelling interest" test in the free exercise field, than it would be for them to determine the "importance" of ideas before applying the "compelling interest" test in the free speech field. What principle of law or logic can be brought to bear to contradict a believer's assertion that a particular act is "central" to his personal faith? . . .

If the "compelling interest" test is to be applied at all, then, it must be applied across the board, to all actions thought to be religiously commanded. Moreover, if "compelling interest" really means what it says (and watering it down here would subvert its rigor in the other fields where it is applied), many laws will not meet the test. Any society adopting such a system would be courting anarchy, but that danger increases in direct proportion to the society's diversity of religious beliefs, and its determination to coerce or suppress none of them. Precisely because "we are a cosmopolitan nation made up of people of almost every conceivable religious preference," *Braunfeld*, and precisely because we value and protect that religious divergence, we cannot afford the luxury of deeming *presumptively invalid*, as applied to the religious objector, every regulation of conduct that does not protect an

---

6. [The following appears as footnote three in Scalia's opinion.] Justice O'Connor suggests that "[t]here is nothing talismanic about neutral laws of general applicability," and that all laws burdening religious practices should be subject to compelling-interest scrutiny because "the First Amendment unequivocally makes freedom of religion, like freedom from race discrimination and freedom of speech, a 'constitutional norm,' not an 'anomaly.'" But this comparison with other fields supports, rather than undermines, the conclusion we draw today. Just as we subject to the most exacting scrutiny laws that make classifications based on race or the content of speech, so too we strictly scrutinize governmental classifications based on religion, see *McDaniel* v. *Paty*, 435 U.S. 618 (1987); see also *Torcaso* v. *Watkins* (1961). But we have held that race-neutral laws that have the effect of disproportionately disadvantaging a particular racial group do not thereby become subject to compelling-interest analysis under the Equal Protection Clause; and we have held that generally applicable laws unconcerned with regulating speech that have the effect of interfering with speech do not thereby become subject to compelling-interest analysis under the First Amendment. Our conclusion that generally applicable, religion-neutral laws that have the effect of burdening a particular religious practice need not be justified by a compelling governmental interest is the only approach compatible with these precedents.

interest of the highest order. The rule respondents favor would open the prospect of constitutionally required religious exemptions from civic obligations of almost every conceivable kind—ranging from compulsory military service to the payment of taxes, to health and safety regulation such as manslaughter and child neglect laws, compulsory vaccination laws, drug laws, and traffic laws, to social welfare legislation such as minimum wage laws, child labor laws, animal cruelty laws, environmental protection laws, and laws providing for equality of opportunity for the races. The First Amendment's protection of religious liberty does not require this.[7]

Values that are protected against government interference through enshrinement in the Bill of Rights are not thereby banished from the political process. Just as a society that believes in the negative protection accorded to the press by the First Amendment is likely to enact laws that affirmatively foster the dissemination of the printed word, so also a society that believes in the negative protection accorded to religious belief can be expected to be solicitous of that value in its legislation as well. It is therefore not surprising that a number of States have made an exception to their drug laws for sacramental peyote use. [Arizona in 1989, Colorado in 1985, New Mexico in 1989.] But to say that a nondiscriminatory religious-practice exemption is permitted, or even that it is desirable, is not to say that it is constitutionally required, and that the appropriate occasions for its creation can be discerned by the courts. It may fairly be said that leaving accommodation to the political process will place at a relative disadvantage those religious practices that are not widely engaged in; but that unavoidable consequence of democratic government must be preferred to a system in which each conscience is a law unto itself or in which judges weigh the social importance of all laws against the centrality of all religious beliefs.[8]

---

7. [The following appears as footnote five in Scalia's opinion.] Justice O'Connor contends that the "parade of horribles" in the text only "demonstrates . . . that courts have been quite capable of strik[ing] sensible balances between religious liberty and competing state interests." But the cases we cite have struck "sensible balances" only because they have all applied the general laws, despite the claims for religious exemption. In any event, Justice O'Connor mistakes the purpose of our parade: it is not to suggest that courts would necessarily permit harmful exemptions from these laws (though they might), but to suggest that courts would constantly be in the business of determining whether the "severe impact" of various laws on religious practice (to use Justice Blackmun's terminology) or the "constitutiona[l] significan[ce]" of the "burden on the particular plaintiffs" (to use Justice O'Connor's terminology) suffices to permit us to confer an exemption. It is a parade of horribles because it is horrible to contemplate that federal judges will regularly balance against the importance of general laws the significance of religious practice.

8. Gerard V. Bradley of the Notre Dame Law School has asked whether the plaintiffs in the case were in fact members of the Native American Church or merely guests at the

Because respondents' ingestion of peyote was prohibited under Oregon law, and because that prohibition is constitutional, Oregon may, consistent with the Free Exercise Clause, deny respondents unemployment compensation when their dismissal results from use of the drug. The decision of the Oregon Supreme Court is accordingly reversed.

Justice Sandra Day O'Connor, concurring in the judgment, joined in Parts I and II by Justices William J. Brennan, Jr., Thurgood Marshall, and Harry A. Blackmun:[9]

Although I agree with the result the Court reaches in this case, I cannot join its opinion. In my view, today's holding dramatically departs from well-settled First Amendment jurisprudence, appears unnecessary to resolve the question presented, and is incompatible with our Nation's fundamental commitment to individual religious liberty.

[Part I concludes that the constitutional question presented and addressed is properly before the Court.]

II

The Court today extracts from our long history of free exercise precedents the single categorical rule that "if prohibiting the exercise of

church's ceremony; a *New York Times* article of July 9, 1991, reporting interviews with the two plaintiffs and their lawyers, suggests they were not members. This apparent fact is relevant to Bradley's criticism of the conduct exemption, which he says is not a doctrine of religious liberty but "one aspect of the post–World War II takeover of our civil liberties corpus by the political morality of liberal individualism" ("Beguiled," 248). This morality maintains that "government ought to be 'neutral' among conceptions of what is good or right for individuals to do, and possesses no right to coerce or to discourage conduct unless the conduct 'harms' persons who have not consented to engage in it" (308). Bradley argues that the conduct exemption "does not need to know if Black and Smith believe anything at all, much less if they believe in Native American spirituality," that "[s]omeone without a scintilla of religious conviction could, right now, attend a Native American ritual and ingest peyote to see what it was like" and if "some legally cognizable harm" resulted, "he is a conduct exemption plaintiff" (315). "The purpose of [the conduct exemption]—promotion of ideal conditions for unencumbered self-choice—does not require that live, religious commitments of this plaintiff actually be distressed; just that someone's might be" (315).

In 1991 the Oregon legislature voted to make an exception to its drug law for sacramental peyote use. Oregon thus accommodated the free exercise of religion, and it would appear that Justice Scalia's faith in the political process was vindicated. Regarding Scalia's view of the role of the judiciary, compare his opinion for the Court here with Justice Frankfurter's opinion for the Court in *Gobitis* (Case 2) and in dissent in *Barnette* (Case 3).

9. Justices Brennan, Marshall, and Blackmun did not concur in the judgment.

religion . . . is . . . merely the incidental effect of a generally applicable and otherwise valid provision, the First Amendment has not been offended." Indeed, the Court holds that where the law is a generally applicable criminal prohibition, our usual free exercise jurisprudence does not even apply. To reach this sweeping result, however, the Court must not only give a strained reading of the First Amendment but must also disregard our consistent application of free exercise doctrine to cases involving generally applicable regulations that burden religious conduct.

. . . Because the First Amendment does not distinguish between religious belief and religious conduct, conduct motivated by sincere religious belief, like the belief itself, must therefore be at least presumptively protected by the Free Exercise Clause.

The Court today, however, interprets the Clause to permit the government to prohibit, without justification, conduct mandated by an individual's religious beliefs, so long as that prohibition is generally applicable. But a law that prohibits certain conduct—conduct that happens to be an act of worship for someone—manifestly does prohibit that person's free exercise of his religion. A person who is barred from engaging in religiously motivated conduct is barred from freely exercising his religion. Moreover, that person is barred from freely exercising his religion regardless of whether the law prohibits the conduct only when engaged in for religious reasons, only by members of that religion, or by all persons. It is difficult to deny that a law that prohibits religiously motivated conduct, even if the law is generally applicable, does not at least implicate First Amendment concerns.

The Court responds that generally applicable laws are "one large step" removed from laws aimed at specific religious practices. The First Amendment, however, does not distinguish between laws that are generally applicable and laws that target particular religious practices. Indeed, few States would be so naive as to enact a law directly prohibiting or burdening a religious practice as such. Our free exercise cases have all concerned generally applicable laws that had the effect of significantly burdening a religious practice. If the First Amendment is to have any vitality, it ought not be construed to cover only the extreme and hypothetical situation in which a State directly targets a religious practice. . . .

To say that a person's right to free exercise has been burdened, of course, does not mean that he has an absolute right to engage in the conduct. Under our established First Amendment jurisprudence, we have recognized that the freedom to act, unlike the freedom to believe, cannot be absolute. Instead, we have respected both the First Amendment's express textual mandate and the governmental interest in regulation of conduct by requiring the Government to justify any substantial burden on religiously motivated conduct by a compelling state interest and by means narrowly tailored to achieve that interest. The compelling interest test effectuates the First Amendment's command that religious liberty is an independent liberty, that it occupies a preferred position, and that the Court will not permit encroachments upon this liberty, whether direct or indirect, unless required by clear and compelling governmental interests "of the highest order," *Yoder*. . . .

The Court attempts to support its narrow reading of the Clause by claiming that "[w]e have never held that an individual's religious beliefs excuse him from compliance with an otherwise valid law prohibiting conduct that the State is free to regulate." But as the Court later notes, as it must, in cases such as *Cantwell* and *Yoder* we have in fact interpreted the Free Exercise Clause to forbid application of a generally applicable prohibition to religiously motivated conduct. Indeed, in *Yoder* we expressly rejected the interpretation the Court now adopts. . . . The Court endeavors to escape from our decisions in *Cantwell* and *Yoder* by labeling them "hybrid" decisions, but there is no denying that both cases expressly relied on the Free Exercise Clause, and that we have consistently regarded those cases as part of the mainstream of our free exercise jurisprudence. Moreover, in each of the other cases cited by the Court to support its categorical rule, we rejected the particular constitutional claims before us only after carefully weighing the competing interests. . . . That we rejected the free exercise claims in those cases hardly calls into question the applicability of First Amendment doctrine in the first place. Indeed, it is surely unusual to judge the vitality of a constitutional doctrine by looking to the win-loss record of the plaintiffs who happen to come before us.

Respondents, of course, do not contend that their conduct is automatically immune from all governmental regulation simply because it is motivated by their sincere religious beliefs. The Court's rejection of that argument might therefore be regarded as merely harmless dictum. Rather, respondents invoke our traditional compelling interest test to argue that the Free Exercise Clause requires that the State grant them a limited exemption from its general criminal prohibition against the possession of peyote. The Court today, however, denies them even the opportunity to make that argument, concluding that "the sounder approach, and the approach in accord with the vast majority of our precedents, is to hold the [compelling interest] test inapplicable to" challenges to general criminal prohibitions.

In my view, however, the essence of a free exercise claim is relief from a burden imposed by government on religious practices or beliefs, whether the burden is imposed directly through laws that prohibit or compel specific religious practices or indirectly through lawsuits that, in effect, make abandonment of one's own religion or conformity to the religious beliefs of others the price of an equal place in the civil community. . . . A State that makes criminal an individual's religiously motivated conduct burdens that individual's free exercise of religion in the severest manner possible, for it "results in the choice to the individual of either abandoning his religious principle or facing criminal prosecution." *Braunfeld*. I would have thought it beyond argument that such laws implicate free exercise concerns.

Indeed, we have never distinguished between cases in which a State conditions receipt of a benefit on conduct prohibited by religious beliefs and cases in which a State affirmatively prohibits such conduct. The *Sherbert* compelling interest test applies in both kinds of cases. . . . [A] neutral criminal law prohibiting conduct that a State may legitimately regulate is, if anything, *more* burdensome than a neutral civil statute placing legitimate conditions on the award of a state benefit.

Legislatures, of course, have always been "left free to reach actions which were in violation of social duties or subversive of good order." *Reynolds*. Yet because of the close relationship between conduct and religious belief, "[i]n every case the power to regulate must be so exercised as not, in attaining a permissible end, unduly to infringe the protected freedom." *Cantwell*. Once it has been shown that a government regulation or criminal prohibition burdens the free exercise of religion, we have consistently asked the Government to demonstrate that unbending application of its regulation to the religious objector "is essential to accomplish an overriding governmental interest," *Lee*, or represents "the least restrictive means of achieving some compelling state interest," *Thomas*. To me, the sounder approach—the approach more consistent with our role as judges to decide each case on its individual merits—is to apply this test in each case to determine whether the burden on the specific plaintiffs before us is constitutionally significant and whether the particular criminal interest asserted by the State before us is compelling. Even if, as an empirical matter, a government's criminal laws might usually serve a compelling interest in health, safety, or public order, the First Amendment at least requires a case-by-case determination of the question, sensitive to the facts of each particular claim. Given the range of conduct that a State might legitimately make criminal, we cannot assume, merely because a law carries criminal sanctions and is generally applicable, that the First Amendment *never* requires the State to grant a limited exemption for religiously motivated conduct.

Moreover, we have not "rejected" or "declined to apply" the compelling interest test in our recent cases. Recent cases have instead affirmed that test as a fundamental part of our First Amendment doctrine. See, e.g., . . . *Hobbie*. The cases cited by the Court signal no retreat from our consistent adherence to the compelling interest test. In both *Roy* and *Lyng*, for example, we expressly distinguished *Sherbert* on the ground that the First Amendment does not "require the Government *itself* to behave in ways that the individual believes will further his or her spiritual development. . . . The Free Exercise Clause simply cannot be understood to require the Government to conduct its own internal affairs in ways that comport with the religious beliefs of particular citizens." *Roy*. This distinction makes sense because "the Free Exercise Clause is written in terms of what the government cannot do to the individual, not in terms of what the individual can exact from the government." *Sherbert* (Douglas, J., concurring). Because the case *sub judice*, like the other cases in which we have applied *Sherbert*, plainly falls into the former category, I would apply those established precedents to the facts of this case.

Similarly, the other cases cited by the Court for the proposition that we have rejected application of the *Sherbert* test outside the unemployment compensation field are distinguishable because they arose in the narrow, specialized contexts in which we have not traditionally required the government to justify a burden on religious conduct by articulating a compelling interest. That we did not apply the compelling interest test in these cases says nothing about whether the test should continue to apply in paradigm free exercise cases such as the one presented here.

The Court today gives no convincing reason to depart from settled First Amendment jurisprudence. There is nothing talismanic about neutral laws of general applicability or general criminal prohibitions, for laws neutral toward religion can coerce a person to violate his religious conscience or intrude upon his religious duties just as effectively as laws aimed at religion. Although the Court suggests that the compelling interest test, as applied to generally applicable laws, would result in a "constitutional anomaly," the First Amendment unequivocally makes freedom of religion, like freedom from race discrimination and freedom of speech, a "constitutional nor[m]," not an "anomaly." Nor would application of our established free exercise doctrine to this case necessarily be incompatible with our equal protection cases. We have in any event recognized that the Free Exercise Clause protects values distinct from those protected by the Equal Protection Clause. As the language of the Clause itself makes clear, an individual's free exercise of religion is a preferred constitutional activity. A law that makes criminal such an activity therefore triggers constitutional concern—and heightened judicial scrutiny—even if it does not target the particular religious conduct at issue. Our free speech cases similarly recognize that neutral regulations that affect free speech values are subject to a balancing, rather than categorical, approach. The Court's parade of horribles not only fails as a reason for discarding the compelling interest test, it instead demonstrates just the opposite: that the courts have been quite capable of applying our free exercise jurisprudence to strike sensible balances between religious liberty and competing state interests.

Finally, the Court today suggests that the disfavoring of minority religions is an "unavoidable consequence" under our system of government and that accommodation of such religions must be left to the political process. In my view, however, the First Amendment was enacted precisely to protect the rights of those whose religious practices are not shared by the majority and may be viewed with hostility. The history of our free exercise doctrine amply demonstrates the harsh impact majoritarian rule has had on unpopular or emerging religious groups such as the Jehovah's Witnesses and the Amish. Indeed, the words of Justice Jackson in *Barnette* (overruling *Gobitis*, [1940]) are apt:

> The very purpose of a Bill of Rights was to withdraw certain subjects from the vicissitudes of political controversy, to place them beyond the reach of majorities and officials and to establish them as legal principles to be applied to the courts. One's right to life, liberty, and property, to free speech, a free press, freedom of worship and assembly, and other fundamental rights may not be submitted to vote: they depend on the outcome of no elections.

The compelling interest test reflects the First Amendment's mandate of preserving religious liberty to the fullest extent possible in a pluralistic society. For the Court to deem this command a "luxury" is to denigrate "[t]he very purpose of a Bill of Rights."

III

The Court's holding today not only misreads settled First Amendment precedent; it appears to be unnecessary to this case. I would reach the same result applying our established free exercise jurisprudence.

There is no dispute that Oregon's criminal prohibition of peyote places a severe burden on the ability of respondents to freely exercise their religion. Peyote is a sacrament of the Native American Church and is regarded as vital to respondents' ability to practice their religion. ... Under Oregon law, as construed by the State's highest court, members of the Native American Church must choose between carrying out the ritual embodying their religious beliefs and avoidance of criminal prosecution. That choice is, in my view, more than sufficient to trigger First Amendment scrutiny.

There is also no dispute that Oregon has a significant interest in enforcing laws that control the possession and use of controlled substances by its citizens. As we recently noted, drug abuse is "one of the greatest problems affecting the health and welfare of our population" and thus "one of the most serious problems confronting our society today." Indeed, under federal law (incorporated by Oregon law in relevant part), peyote is specifically regulated as a Schedule I controlled substance, which means that Congress has found that it has a high potential for abuse, that there is no currently accepted medical use, and that there is a lack of accepted safety for use of the drug under medical supervision. . . . [R]espondents do not seriously dispute that Oregon has a compelling interest in prohibiting the possession of peyote by its citizens.

Thus, the critical question in this case is whether exempting respondents from the State's general criminal prohibition "will unduly interfere with fulfillment of the governmental interest." *Lee*. Although the question is close, I would conclude that uniform application of Oregon's criminal prohibition is "essential to accomplish," *Lee*, its overriding interest in preventing the physical harm caused by the use of a Schedule I controlled substance. Oregon's criminal prohibition represents that State's judgment that the possession and use of controlled substances, even by only one person, is inherently harmful and dangerous. Because the health effects caused by the use of controlled substances exist regardless of the motivation of the user, the use of such substances, even for religious purposes, violates the very purpose of the laws that prohibit them. Moreover, in view of the societal interest in preventing trafficking in controlled substances, uniform application of the criminal prohibition at issue is essential to the effectiveness of Oregon's stated interest in preventing any possession of peyote.

For these reasons, I believe that granting a selective exemption in this case would seriously impair Oregon's compelling interest in prohibiting possession of peyote by its citizens. Under such circumstances, the Free Exercise Clause does not require the State to accommodate respondents' religiously motivated conduct. . . .

Respondents contend that any incompatibility is belied by the fact that the Federal Government and several States provide exemptions for the religious use of peyote. But other governments may surely choose to grant an exemption without Oregon, with its specific asserted interest in uniform application of its drug laws, being *required* to do so by the First Amendment. . . . [O]ur determination of the constitutionality of Oregon's general criminal prohibition cannot, and should not, turn on the centrality of the particular religious practice at issue. . . .

I would therefore adhere to our established free exercise jurisprudence and hold that the State in this case has a compelling interest in regulating peyote use by its citizens and that accommodating respondents' religiously motivated conduct "will unduly interfere with fulfillment of the governmental interest." Accordingly, I concur in the judgment of the Court.

Justice Harry A. Blackmun, dissenting, joined by Justices William J. Brennan, Jr., and Thurgood Marshall:

This Court over the years painstakingly has developed a consistent and exacting standard to test the constitutionality of a state statute that burdens the free exercise of religion. Such a statute may stand only if the law in general, and the State's refusal to allow a religious exemption in particular, are justified by a compelling interest that cannot be served by less restrictive means.

Until today, I thought this was a settled and inviolate principle of this Court's First Amendment jurisprudence. The majority, however, perfunctorily dismisses it as a "constitutional anomaly." As carefully detailed in Justice O'Connor's concurring opinion, the majority is able to arrive at this view only by mischaracterizing this Court's precedents. The Court discards leading free exercise cases such as *Cantwell* and *Yoder* as "hybrid." The Court views traditional free exercise analysis as somehow inapplicable to criminal prohibitions (as opposed to conditions on the receipt of benefits), and to state laws of general applicability (as opposed, presumably, to laws that expressly single out religious practices). The Court cites cases in which, due to various exceptional circumstances, we found strict scrutiny inapposite, to hint that the Court has repudiated that standard altogether. In short, it effectuates a wholesale overturning of settled law concerning the Religion Clauses of our Constitution. One hopes that the Court is aware of the consequences, and that its result is not a product of overreaction to the serious problems the country's drug crisis has generated.

The distorted view of our precedents leads the majority to conclude that strict scrutiny of a state law burdening the free exercise of religion is a "luxury" that a well-ordered society cannot afford and that the repression of minority religions is an "unavoidable consequence of democratic government." I do not believe the Founders thought their dearly bought freedom from religious persecution a "luxury," but an essential element of liberty—and they could not have thought religious intolerance "unavoidable," for they drafted the Religion Clauses precisely in order to avoid that intolerance.

For these reasons, I agree with Justice O'Connor's analysis of the applicable free exercise doctrine, and I join Parts I and II of her opinion. As she points out, "the critical question in this case is whether exempting respondents from the State's general criminal prohibition 'will unduly interfere with fulfillment of the governmental interest.' " I do disagree, however, with her specific answer to that question.

In weighing respondents' clear interest in the free exercise of their religion against Oregon's asserted interest in enforcing its drug laws, it is important to articulate in precise terms the state interest involved. It is not the State's broad interest in fighting the critical "war on drugs" that must be weighed against respondents' claim, but the State's narrow interest in refusing to make an exception for the religious ceremonial use of peyote. Failure to reduce the competing interests to the same plane of generality tends to distort the weighing process in the State's favor. . . .

The State's interest in enforcing its prohibition, in order to be sufficiently compelling to outweigh a free exercise claim, cannot be merely abstract or symbolic. The State cannot plausibly assert that unbending application of a criminal prohibition is essential to fulfill any compelling interest, if it does not, in fact, attempt to enforce that prohibition. In this case, the State actually has not evinced any concrete interest in enforcing its drug laws against religious users of peyote. Oregon has never sought to prosecute respondents, and does not claim that it has made significant enforcement efforts against other religious users of peyote. The State's asserted interest thus amounts only to the symbolic preservation of an unenforced prohibition. [This] . . . cannot suffice to abrogate the constitutional rights of individuals.

Similarly, this Court's prior decisions have not allowed a government to rely on mere speculation about potential harms, but have demanded evidentiary support for a refusal to allow a religious exception. See *Thomas, Yoder, Sherbert.* In this case, the State's justification for refusing to recognize an exception to its criminal laws for religious peyote use is entirely speculative.

The State proclaims an interest in protecting the health and safety of its citizens from the dangers of unlawful drugs. It offers, however, no evidence that the religious use of peyote had ever harmed anyone. The factual findings of other courts cast doubt on the State's assumption that religious use of peyote is harmful.

The fact that peyote is classified as a Schedule I controlled substance does not, by itself, show that any and all uses of peyote, in any circumstance, are inherently harmful and dangerous. The Federal Government, which created the classifications of unlawful drugs from which Oregon's drug laws are derived, apparently does not find peyote so dangerous as to preclude an exemption for religious use. Moreover, other Schedule I drugs have lawful uses.

The carefully circumscribed ritual context in which respondents used peyote is far removed from the irresponsible and unrestricted recreational use of unlawful drugs. The Native American Church's internal restrictions on, and supervision of, its members' use of peyote substantially obviate the State's health and safety concerns.

Moreover, just as in *Yoder,* the values and interests of those seeking a religious exemption in this case are congruent, to a great degree, with those the State seeks to promote through its drug laws. Not only does the Church's doctrine forbid nonreligious use of peyote; it is also generally advocates self-reliance, familial responsibility, and abstinence from alcohol. There is considerable evidence that the spiritual and social support provided by the Church has been effective in combating the tragic effects of alcoholism on the Native American population. . . . Far from promoting the lawless and irresponsible use of drugs, Native American Church members' spiritual code exemplifies values that Oregon's drug laws are presumably intended to foster.

The State also seeks to support its refusal to make an exception for religious use of peyote by invoking its interest in abolishing drug trafficking. There is, however, practically no illegal traffic in peyote. . . .

Finally, the State argues that granting an exception for religious peyote use would erode its interest in the uniform, fair, and certain enforcement of its drug laws. The State fears that, if it grants an exemption for religious peyote use, a flood of other claims to religious exemptions will follow. It would then be placed in a dilemma, it says, between allowing a patchwork of exemptions that would hinder its law enforcement efforts, and risking a violation of the Establishment Clause by arbitrarily limiting its religious exemptions. This argument, however, could be made in almost any free exercise case. This Court . . . consistently has rejected similar arguments in past free exercise cases, and it should do so here as well.

The State's apprehension of a flood of other religious claims is purely speculative. Almost half the States, and the Federal Government, have maintained an exemption for religious peyote use for many years, and apparently have not found themselves overwhelmed by claims to other religious exemptions. Allowing an exemption for religious peyote use would not necessarily oblige the State to grant a similar exemption to other religious groups. . . .

· · ·

Respondents believe, and their sincerity has *never* been at issue, that the peyote plant embodies their deity, and eating it is an act of worship and communion. Without peyote, they could not enact the essential ritual of their religion. . . .

If Oregon can constitutionally prosecute them for this act of worship, they, like the Amish, may be "forced to migrate to some other and more tolerant region." *Yoder.* This potentially devastating impact must be viewed in light of the federal policy—reached in reaction to many years of religious persecution and intolerance—of protecting the religious freedom of Native Americans.

· · ·

For these reasons, I conclude that Oregon's interest in enforcing its drug laws against religious use of peyote is not sufficiently compelling to outweigh respondents' right to the free exercise of their religion. Since the State could not constitutionally enforce its criminal prohibition against respondents, the interests underlying the State's drug laws cannot justify its denial of unemployment benefits. Absent such justification, the State's regulatory interest in denying benefits for religiously motivated "misconduct" is indistinguishable from the state interests this Court has rejected in . . . *Hobbie, Thomas,* and *Sherbert.* The State of Oregon cannot, consistently with the Free Exercise Clause, deny respondents unemployment benefits.

24

Board of Education v. Mergens

496 U.S. 226 (1990)

The political argument over public school prayer triggered by the Supreme Court's 1962 decision in *Engel* v. *Vitale* led in 1984 to passage of the Equal Access Act. In 1990 the Supreme Court ruled that the law does not violate the First Amendment.

The Equal Access Act prohibits public secondary schools that receive federal funds and that maintain a "limited open forum" (i.e., "one or more noncurriculum related student groups" are allowed to meet on school premises before or after classes) from denying "equal access" to student groups on the basis of the "religious, political, philosophical, or other content" of the speech at their meetings. In 1985 Bridget Mergens, a student at Westside High School in Omaha, Nebraska, asked permission to form a Christian club that would have the same privileges and meet on the same terms as other Westside student groups, except that it would not have a faculty sponsor. The members would read and discuss the Bible and pray. The club would be open to all students regardless of religious affiliation. Mergens's request was denied on the grounds that school policy required all student clubs to have faculty sponsors, and that a religious club would violate the ban on establishment. She sued, charging Westside with violating the Equal Access Act. The school responded that the Act did not apply to Westside and that, even if it did apply, it constituted an establishment of religion.

The district court held that the Act did not apply because Westside did not have a "limited open forum" as the Act specifies. The U.S. Court of Appeals for the Eighth Circuit reversed, holding that Westside did have such a forum and therefore could not discriminate against Bridget Mergens and other members of the proposed club. The appeals court then ruled that the Equal Access Act did not violate the Constitution. On appeal, the Supreme Court affirmed.

Board of Education v. *Mergens* produced four opinions. Justice Sandra Day O'Connor wrote for the Court; five justices joined Parts I and II of her opinion, but two of the five did not join Part III. Those two, Justice Anthony Kennedy and Justice Thurgood Marshall, concurred in the judgment; each wrote separately, joined by another justice. Justice John Paul Stevens dissented. The Court's opinion and the two concurring opinions are presented here, followed by editorial responses from the *Washington Post* and the *New York Times*.

Participating in *Board of Education* v. *Mergens*, decided June 4, 1990, were Chief Justice William H. Rehnquist and Associate Justices Harry A. Blackmun, William J. Brennan, Jr., Anthony M. Kennedy, Thurgood Marshall, Sandra Day O'Connor, Antonin Scalia, John Paul Stevens, and Byron R. White.

Opinions

***Justice Sandra Day O'Connor delivered the opinion of the
Court, except as to Part III:***

[In Part I Justice O'Connor reviewed the facts of the case. Part II
begins here.] In *Widmar* v. *Vincent* (1981) we invalidated, on free speech
grounds, a state university regulation that prohibited student use of
school facilities " 'for purposes of religious worship or religious teaching.' " In doing so, we held that an "equal access" policy would not
violate the Establishment Clause under our decision in *Lemon* v. *Kurtzman* (1971). In particular, we held that such a policy would have a secular purpose, would not have the primary effect of advancing religion,
and would not result in excessive entanglement between government
and religion. We noted, however, that "[u]niversity students are, of
course, young adults. They are less impressionable than younger students and should be able to appreciate that the University's policy is
one of neutrality toward religion."

In 1984, Congress extended the reasoning of *Widmar* to public secondary schools. Under the Equal Access Act, a public secondary
school with a "limited open forum" is prohibited from discriminating
against students who wish to conduct a meeting within that forum on
the basis of the "religious, political, philosophical, or other content of
the speech at such meetings." Specifically, the Act provides:

> It shall be unlawful for any public secondary school which receives
> Federal financial assistance and which has a limited open forum to
> deny equal access or a fair opportunity to, or discriminate against,
> any students who wish to conduct a meeting within that limited
> open forum on the basis of the religious, political, philosophical, or
> other content of the speech at such meetings.

A "limited open forum" exists whenever a public secondary school
"grants an offering to or opportunity for one or more noncurriculum
related student groups to meet on school premises during noninstructional time." "Meeting" is defined to include "those activities of student groups which are permitted under a school's limited open forum
and are not directly related to the school curriculum." "Noninstruc-

419

tional time" is defined to mean "time set aside by the school before actual classroom instruction begins or after actual classroom instruction ends." Thus, even if a public secondary school allows only one "noncurriculum related student group" to meet, the Act's obligations are triggered, and the school may not deny other clubs, on the basis of the content of their speech, equal access to school premises during noninstructional time.

The Act further specifies that "[s]chools shall be deemed to offer a fair opportunity to students who wish to conduct a meeting within its limited open forum" if the school uniformly provides that the meetings are voluntary and student-initiated; are not sponsored by the school, the government, or its agents or employees; do not materially and substantially interfere with the orderly conduct of educational activities within the school; and are not directed, controlled, conducted, or regularly attended by "nonschool persons." "Sponsorship" is defined to mean "the act of promoting, leading, or participating in a meeting. The assignment of a teacher, administrator, or other school employee to a meeting for custodial purposes does not constitute sponsorship of the meeting." If the meetings are religious, employees or agents of the school or government may attend only in a "nonparticipatory capacity." Moreover, a State may not influence the form of any religious activity, require any person to participate in such activity, or compel any school agent or employee to attend a meeting if the content of the speech at the meeting is contrary to that person's beliefs.

Finally, the Act does not "authorize the United States to deny or withhold Federal financial assistance to any school," or "limit the authority of the school, its agents or employees, to maintain order and discipline on school premises, to protect the well-being of students and faculty, and to assure that attendance of students at the meetings is voluntary."

The parties agree that Westside High School receives federal financial assistance and is a public secondary school within the meaning of the Act. The Act's obligation to grant equal access to student groups is therefore triggered if Westside maintains a "limited open forum"— i.e., if it permits one or more "noncurriculum related student groups" to meet on campus before or after classes.

Unfortunately, the Act does not define the crucial phrase "noncurriculum related student group." Our immediate task is therefore one of statutory interpretation. We begin, of course, with the language of the statute. The common meaning of the term "curriculum" is "the whole body of courses offered by an educational institution or one of its branches." *Webster's Third New International Dictionary* 557 (1976). Any sensible interpretation of "noncurriculum related student group" must therefore be anchored in the notion that such student groups are those that are not related to the body of courses offered by the school. The difficult question is the degree of "unrelatedness to the curriculum" required for a group to be considered "noncurriculum related."

The Act's definition of the sort of "meeting[s]" that must be accommodated under the statute sheds some light on this question. "[T]he term 'meeting' includes those activities of student groups which are . . . not *directly related* to the school curriculum" (emphasis added). Congress' use of the phrase "directly related" implies that student groups directly related to the subject matter of courses offered by the school do not fall within the "noncurriculum related" category and would therefore be considered "curriculum related."

The logic of the Act also supports this view, namely, that a curriculum-related student group is one that has more than just a tangential or attenuated relationship to courses offered by the school. Because the purpose of granting equal access is to prohibit discrimination between religious or political clubs on the one hand and other noncurriculum-related student groups on the other, the Act is premised on the notion that a religious or political club is itself likely to be a non-curriculum-related student group. It follows, then, that a student group that is "curriculum related" must at least have a more direct relationship to the curriculum than a religious or political club would have.

Although the phrase "noncurriculum related student group" nevertheless remains sufficiently ambiguous that we might normally resort to legislative history, we find the legislative history on this issue less than helpful. Because the bill that led to the Act was extensively rewritten in a series of multilateral negotiations after it was passed by the House and reported out of committee by the Senate, the committee reports shed no light on the language actually adopted. During congressional debate on the subject, legislators referred to a number of different definitions, and thus both petitioners and respondents can cite to legislative history favoring their interpretation of the phrase. . . .

We think it significant, however, that the Act, which was passed by wide, bipartisan majorities in both the House and the Senate, reflects at least some consensus on a broad legislative purpose. The committee reports indicate that the Act was intended to address perceived widespread discrimination against religious speech in public schools. . . .

The committee reports also show that the Act was enacted in part in response to two federal appellate court decisions holding that student religious groups could not, consistent with the Establishment Clause, meet on school premises during noninstructional time.[1] A broad reading of the Act would be consistent with the views of those who sought to end discrimination by allowing students to meet and discuss religion before and after classes.[2]

In light of this legislative purpose, we think that the term "noncurriculum related student group" is best interpreted broadly to mean any student group that does not *directly* relate to the body of courses offered by the school. In our view, a student group directly relates to a school's curriculum if the subject matter of the group is actually taught, or will soon be taught, in a regularly offered course; if the subject matter of the group concerns the body of courses as a whole; if participation in the group is required for a particular course; or if participation results in academic credit. We think this limited definition of groups that directly relate to the curriculum is a commonsense interpretation of the Act that is consistent with Congress' intent to provide a low threshold for triggering the Act's requirements.

For example, a French club would directly relate to the curriculum if a school taught French in a regularly offered course or planned to teach the subject in the near future. A school's student government would generally relate directly to the curriculum to the extent that it addresses concerns, solicits opinions, and formulates proposals pertaining to the body of courses offered by the school. If participation in a school's band or orchestra were required for the band or orchestra classes, or resulted in academic credit, then those groups would also directly relate to the curriculum. The existence of such groups at a school would not trigger the Act's obligations.

On the other hand, unless a school could show that groups such as a chess club, a stamp collecting club, or a community service club fell within our description of groups that directly relate to the curriculum, such groups would be "noncurriculum related student groups" for purposes of the Act. The existence of such groups would create a "lim-

---

1. The two cases are *Lubbock Civil Liberties Union* v. *Lubbock Independent School Dist.*, 669 F. 2d 1038 (CA5 1982), cert. denied, 459 U.S. 1155–56 (1983), and *Brandon* v. *Guilderland Bd. of Ed.*, 635 F. 2d 971 (CA2 1980), cert. denied, 454 U.S. 1123 (1981).

2. The Equal Access Act partly resolved the more than two-decades-long debate over public school prayer and devotional exercises touched off by the Court's decisions in *Engel* v. *Vitale* (1962) and *Abington School District* v. *Schempp* (1963). It did so in the form of a compromise: Government may accommodate the voluntary religious activities of high school students.

ited open forum" under the Act and would prohibit the school from denying equal access to any other student group on the basis of the content of that group's speech. Whether a specific student group is a "noncurriculum related student group" will therefore depend on a particular school's curriculum, but such determinations would be subject to factual findings well within the competence of trial courts to make.

Petitioners contend that our reading of the Act unduly hinders local control over schools and school activities, but we think that schools and school districts nevertheless retain a significant measure of authority over the type of officially recognized activities in which their students participate. . . .

The dissent suggests that "an extracurricular student organization is 'noncurriculum related' if it has as its purpose (or as part of its purpose) the advocacy of partisan theological, political, or ethical views." This interpretation of the Act, we are told, is mandated by Congress' intention to "track our own Free Speech Clause jurisprudence," by incorporating *Widmar*'s notion of a "limited public forum" into the language of the Act.

This suggestion is flawed for at least two reasons. First, the Act itself neither uses the phrase "limited public forum" nor so much as hints that that doctrine is somehow "incorporated" into the words of the statute. The operative language of the statute, of course, refers to a "limited open forum," a term that is specifically defined in the next subsection. Congress was presumably aware that "limited public forum," as used by the Court, is a term of art, and had it intended to import that concept into the Act, one would suppose that it would have done so explicitly. Indeed, Congress' deliberate choice to use a different term—and to define that term—can only mean that it intended to establish a standard different from the one established by our free speech cases. . . .

Second, and more significant, the dissent's reliance on the legislative history to support its interpretation of the Act shows just how treacherous that task can be. The dissent appears to agree with our view that the legislative history of the Act, even if relevant, is highly unreliable, yet the interpretation it suggests rests solely on a few passing, general references by legislators to our decision in *Widmar*. We think that reliance on legislative history is hazardous at best, but where " 'not even the sponsors of the bill knew what it meant,' " such reliance cannot form a reasonable basis on which to interpret the text of a statute. . . .

The parties in this case focus their dispute on ten of Westside's approximately thirty voluntary student clubs: Interact (a service club related to Rotary International); Chess; Subsurfers (a club for students interested in scuba diving); National Honor Society; Photography; Welcome to Westside (a club to introduce new students to the school); Future Business Leaders of America; Zonta (a female counterpart to Interact); Student Advisory Board (student government). Petitioners contend that all of these student activities are curriculum-related because they further the goals of particular aspects of the school's curriculum. . . .

To the extent that petitioners contend that "curriculum related" means anything remotely related to abstract educational goals, however, we reject that argument. To define "curriculum related" in a way that results in almost no schools having limited open fora, or in a way that permits schools to evade the Act by strategically describing existing student groups, would render the Act merely hortatory. . . .

Rather, we think it clear that Westside's existing student groups include one or more "noncurriculum related student groups." Although Westside's physical education classes apparently include swimming, counsel stated at oral argument that scuba diving is not taught in any regularly offered course at the school. Based on Westside's own description of the group, Subsurfers does not directly relate to the curriculum as a whole in the same way that a student government or similar group might. Moreover, participation in Subsurfers is not required by any course at the school and does not result in extra academic credit. Thus, Subsurfers is a "noncurriculum related student group" for purposes of the Act. . . . The record therefore supports a finding that Westside has maintained a limited open forum under the Act.

Although our definition of "noncurriculum related student activities" looks to a school's actual practice rather than its stated policy, we note that our conclusion is also supported by the school's own description of its student activities. . . . We therefore conclude that Westside permits "one or more noncurriculum related student groups to meet on school premises during noninstructional time." Because Westside maintains a "limited open forum" under the Act, it is prohibited from discriminating, based on the content of the students' speech, against students who wish to meet on school premises during noninstructional time.

The remaining statutory question is whether petitioners' denial of respondents' request to form a religious group constitutes a denial of "equal access" to the school's limited open forum. Although the school apparently permits respondents to meet informally after school, respondents seek equal access in the form of official recognition by the school. Official recognition allows student clubs to be part of the student activities program and carries with it access to the school newspaper, bulletin boards, the public address system, and the annual Club Fair. Given that the Act explicitly prohibits denial of "equal access . . . to . . . any students who wish to conduct a meeting within [the school's] limited open forum" on the basis of the religious content of the speech at such meetings, we hold that Westside's denial of respondents' request to form a Christian club denies them "equal access" under the Act.

Because we rest our conclusion on statutory grounds, we need not decide—and therefore express no opinion on—whether the First Amendment requires the same result.

III

Petitioners contend that even if Westside has created a limited open forum within the meaning of the Act, its denial of official recognition to the proposed Christian club must nevertheless stand because the Act violates the Establishment Clause of the First Amendment. . . . Specifically, petitioners maintain that because the school's recognized student activities are an integral part of its educational mission, official recognition of respondents' proposed club would effectively incorporate religious activities into the school's official program, endorse participation in the religious club, and provide the club with an official platform to proselytize other students.

We disagree. In *Widmar*, we applied the three-part *Lemon* test to hold that an "equal access" policy, at the university level, does not violate the Establishment Clause. We concluded that "an open-forum policy, including nondiscrimination against religious speech, would have a secular purpose," and would in fact *avoid* entanglement with religion. We also found that although incidental benefits accrued to religious groups who used university facilities, this result did not amount to an establishment of religion. . . .

We think the logic of *Widmar* applies with equal force to the Equal Access Act. As an initial matter, the Act's prohibition of discrimination on the basis of "political, philosophical, or other" speech as well as religious speech is a sufficient basis for meeting the secular purpose prong of the *Lemon* test. Congress' avowed purpose—to prevent discrimination against religious and other types of speech—is undeniably secular. Even if some legislators were motivated by a conviction that religious speech in particular was valuable and worthy of protection, that alone would not invalidate the Act, because what is relevant is the legislative *purpose* of the statute, not the possibly religious *motives* of the legislators who enacted the law. Because the Act on its face grants equal access to both secular and religious speech, we think it clear that the Act's purpose was not to " 'endorse or disapprove of religion.' "

Petitioners' principal contention is that the Act has the primary effect of advancing religion. Specifically, petitioners urge that, because the student religious meetings are held under school aegis, and because the state's compulsory attendance laws bring the students together (and thereby provide a ready-made audience for student evangelists), an objective observer in the position of a secondary school student will perceive official school support for such religious meetings.

We disagree. First, although we have invalidated the use of public funds to pay for teaching state-required subjects at parochial schools, in part because of the risk of creating "a crucial symbolic link between government and religion, thereby enlisting—at least in the eyes of impressionable youngsters—the powers of government to the support of the religious denomination operating the school," *Grand Rapids* v. *Ball* (1985), there is a crucial difference between *government* speech endorsing religion, which the Establishment Clause forbids, and *private* speech endorsing religion, which the Free Speech and Free Exercise Clauses protect. We think that secondary school students are mature enough and are likely to understand that a school does not endorse or support student speech that it merely permits on a nondiscriminatory basis. The proposition that schools do not endorse everything they fail to censor is not complicated.

Indeed, we note that Congress specifically rejected the argument that high school students are likely to confuse an equal access policy with state sponsorship of religion. . . . [W]e do not lightly second-guess such legislative judgments, particularly where the judgments are based in part on empirical determinations.

Second, we note that the Act expressly limits participation by school officials at meetings of student religious groups, and that any such meetings must be held during "noninstructional time." The Act therefore avoids the problems of "the students' emulation of teachers as role models" and "mandatory attendance requirements." To be sure, the possibility of *student* peer pressure remains, but there is little if any risk of official state endorsement or coercion where no formal classroom activities are involved and no school officials actively participate.

Moreover, petitioners' fear of a mistaken inference of endorsement is largely self-imposed, because the school itself has control over any impressions it gives its students. To the extent a school makes clear that its recognition of respondents' proposed club is not an endorsement of the views of the club's participants, students will reasonably understand that the school's official recognition of the club evinces neutrality toward, rather than endorsement of, religious speech.

Third, the broad spectrum of officially recognized student clubs at Westside, and the fact that Westside students are free to initiate and organize additional student clubs, counteract any possible message of official endorsement of or preference for religion or a particular religious belief. Although a school may not itself lead or direct a religious club, a school that permits a student-initiated and student-led religious club to meet after school, just as it permits any other student group to do, does not convey a message of state approval or endorsement of the particular religion. Under the Act, a school with a limited open forum may not lawfully deny access to a Jewish students' club, a Young Democrats club, or a philosophy club devoted to the study of Nietzsche. To the extent that a religious club is merely one of many different student-initiated voluntary clubs, students should perceive no message of government endorsement of religion. Thus, we conclude that the Act does not, at least on its face and as applied to Westside, have the primary effect of advancing religion.

Petitioners' final argument is that by complying with the Act's requirement, the school risks excessive entanglement between government and religion. The proposed club, petitioners urge, would be required to have a faculty sponsor who would be charged with actively directing the activities of the group, guiding its leaders, and ensuring balance in the presentation of controversial ideas. Petitioners claim that this influence over the club's religious program would entangle the government in day-to-day surveillance of religion of the type forbidden by the Establishment Clause.

Under the Act, however, faculty monitors may not participate in any religious meetings, and nonschool persons may not direct, control, or regularly attend activities of student groups. Moreover, the Act prohibits school "sponsorship" of any religious meetings, which means that school officials may not promote, lead, or participate in any such meeting. Although the Act permits "[t]he assignment of a teacher, administrator, or other school employee to the meeting for custodial purposes," such custodial oversight of the student-initiated religious group, merely to ensure order and good behavior, does not impermis-

sibly entangle government in the day-to-day surveillance or administration of religious activities. . . .

Accordingly, we hold that the Equal Access Act does not on its face
contravene the Establishment Clause. Because we hold that petitioners
have violated the Act, we do not decide respondents' claims under the
Free Speech and Free Exercise Clauses.

Justice Anthony M. Kennedy, concurring in part and concurring in the judgment, joined by Justice Antonin Scalia:

The Court's interpretation of the statutory term "noncurriculum
related groups" is proper and correct, in my view, and I join in Parts I
and II of the Court's opinion. I further agree that the Act does not
violate the Establishment Clause, and so I concur in the judgment; but
my view of the analytic premise that controls the establishment question differs from that employed by the plurality. I write to explain
why I cannot join all that is said in Part III of Justice O'Connor's
opinion.

A brief initial comment on the statutory issue is in order. The student clubs recognized by Westside school officials are a far cry from
the groups given official recognition by university officials in *Widmar*.
As Justice Stevens points out in dissent, one of the consequences of
the statute, as we now interpret it, is that clubs of a most controversial
character might have access to the student life of high schools that in
the past have given official recognition only to clubs of a more conventional kind.

It must be apparent to all that the Act has made a matter once left
to the discretion of local school officials the subject of comprehensive
regulation by federal law.[3] This decision, however, was for Congress to
make, subject to constitutional limitations. Congress having decided
in favor of legislative intervention, it faced the task of formulating general statutory standards against the background protections of the Free
Speech Clause, as well as the Establishment and Free Exercise Clauses.
Given the complexities of our own jurisprudence in these areas, there
is no doubt that the congressional task was a difficult one. While I can
not pretend that the language Congress used in the Act is free from

3. It again bears emphasis that the religion clause as originally enacted did not apply
to the states. Decisions made possible only by the application of the clause to the states —
for example, *Engel* v. *Vitale* (1962) — created the public debate that led to enactment of
the federal legislation under review in this case. Ironically, this legislation further reduced local school-board discretion.

ambiguity in some of its vital provisions, the Court's interpretation of the phrase "noncurriculum related" seems to me to be the most rational and indeed the most plausible interpretation available, given the words and structure of the Act and the constitutional implications of the subject it addresses.

. . .

I agree with the plurality that a school complying with the statute . . . does not violate the Establishment Clause. The accommodation of religion mandated by the Act is a neutral one, and in the context of this case it suffices to inquire whether the Act violates either one of two principles. The first is that the government cannot "give direct benefits to religion in such a degree that it in fact 'establishes a [state] religion or religious faith, or tends to do so.' " *County of Allegheny* v. *American Civil Liberties Union*, 492 U.S. 573 (1989) (Kennedy, J., concurring in judgment in part and dissenting in part) (quoting *Lynch*). Any incidental benefits that accompany official recognition of a religious club under the criteria set forth in the [statute] do not lead to the establishment of religion under this standard. The second principle controlling the case now before us, in my view, is that the government cannot coerce any student to participate in a religious activity. The Act is consistent with this standard as well. Nothing on the face of the Act or in the facts of the case as here presented demonstrate that enforcement of the statute will result in the coercion of any student to participate in a religious activity. . . .

The plurality uses a different test, one which asks whether school officials, by complying with the Act, have endorsed religion. It is true that when government gives impermissible assistance to a religion it can be said to have "endorsed" religion; but endorsement cannot be the test. The word endorsement has insufficient content to be dispositive. And . . . its literal application may result in neutrality in name but hostility in fact when the question is the government's proper relation to those who express some religious preference.

I should think it inevitable that a public high school "endorses" a religious club, in a common-sense use of the term, if the club happens to be one of many activities that the school permits students to choose in order to further the development of their intellect and character in an extracurricular setting. But no constitutional violation occurs if the school's action is based upon a recognition of the fact that membership in a religious club is one of many permissible ways for a student to further his or her own personal enrichment. The inquiry with respect to coercion must be whether the government imposes pressure upon a student to participate in a religious activity. This inquiry, of course, must be undertaken with sensitivity to the special circumstances that exist in a secondary school where the line between voluntary and coerced participation may be difficult to draw. No such coercion, however, has been shown to exist as a necessary result of this statute, either on its face or as respondents seek to invoke it on the facts of this case.

Justice Thurgood Marshall, concurring in the judgment, joined by Justice William J. Brennan, Jr.:

I agree with the majority that "noncurriculum" must be construed broadly to "prohibit schools from discriminating on the basis of the content of a student group's speech." As the majority demonstrates, such a construction "is consistent with Congress' intent to provide a low threshold for triggering the Act's requirements." In addition, to the extent that Congress intended the Act to track this Court's free speech jurisprudence, as the dissent argues, the majority's construction is faithful to our commitment to nondiscriminatory access to open fora in public schools. *Widmar*. . . . [T]he Act as construed by the majority simply codifies in statute what is already constitutionally mandated: schools may not discriminate among student-initiated groups that seek access to school facilities for expressive purposes not directly related to the school's curriculum.

. . . [A]lthough I agree with the plurality that the Act as applied to Westside *could* withstand Establishment Clause scrutiny, I write separately to emphasize the steps Westside must take to avoid appearing to endorse the Christian Club's goals. The plurality's Establishment Clause analysis pays inadequate attention to the differences between this case and *Widmar* and dismisses too lightly the distinctive pressures created by Westside's highly structured environment.

This case involves the intersection of two First Amendment guarantees—the Free Speech Clause and the Establishment Clause. We have long regarded free and open debate over matters of controversy as necessary to the functioning of our constitutional system. That the Constitution requires toleration of speech over its suppression is not less true in our Nation's schools.

But the Constitution also demands that the State not take action that has the primary effect of advancing religion. The introduction of religious speech into the public schools reveals the tension between these two constitutional commitments, because the failure of a school to stand apart from religious speech can convey a message that the school endorses rather than merely tolerates that speech. Recognizing the potential dangers of school-endorsed religious practice, we have shown particular "vigilan[ce] in monitoring compliance with the Establishment Clause in elementary and secondary schools." *Edwards* v. *Aguillard*, 482 U.S. 578 (1987).[4] This vigilance must extend to our monitoring of the actual effects of an "equal access" policy. If public schools are perceived as conferring the imprimatur of the State on religious doctrine or practice as a result of such policy, the nominally "neutral" character of the policy will not save it from running afoul of the Establishment Clause.

We addressed at length the potential conflict between toleration and endorsement of religious speech in *Widmar*. There, a religious study group sought the same access to university facilities that the university afforded to over 100 officially recognized student groups, including many political organizations. In those circumstances, we concluded that granting religious organizations similar access to the public forum would have neither the purpose nor the primary effect of advancing religion. The plurality suggests that our conclusion in *Widmar* controls this case. But the plurality fails to recognize that the wide-open and independent character of the student forum in *Widmar* differs substantially from the forum at Westside.

Westside currently does not recognize any student club that advocates a controversial viewpoint. Indeed, the clubs at Westside that trigger the Act involve scuba diving, chess, and counseling for special education students. As a matter of school policy, Westside encourages student participation in clubs based on a broad conception of its educational mission. That mission comports with the Court's acknowledgment "that public schools are vitally important 'in the preparation of individuals for participation as citizens,' and as vehicles for 'inculcating fundamental values necessary to the maintenance of a democratic political system.' " Given the nature and function of student clubs at Westside, the school makes no effort to disassociate itself from the activities and goals of its student clubs.

The entry of religious clubs into such a realm poses a real danger that those clubs will be viewed as part of the school's effort to inculcate fundamental values. The school's message with respect to its existing clubs is not one of toleration but one of endorsement. As the majority concedes, the program is part of the "district's commitment to teach-

---

4. In *Aguillard*, the Court struck down a Louisiana statute that required the teaching of creationism in that state's public schools.

ing academic, physical, civic, and personal skills and values." But although a school may permissibly encourage its students to become well-rounded as student-athletes, student-musicians, and student-tutors, the Constitution forbids schools to encourage students to become well-rounded as student-worshippers. Neutrality toward religion, as required by the Constitution, is not advanced by requiring a school that endorses the goals of some noncontroversial secular organizations to endorse the goals of religious organizations as well.

The fact that the Act, when triggered, provides access to political as well as religious speech does not ameliorate the potential threat of endorsement. The breadth of beneficiaries under the Act does suggest that the Act may satisfy the "secular purpose" requirement of the Establishment Clause inquiry we identified in *Lemon*. But the crucial question is how the Act affects each school. If a school already houses numerous ideological organizations, then the addition of a religion club will most likely not violate the Establishment Clause because the risk that students will erroneously attribute the views of the religion club to the school is minimal. To the extent a school tolerates speech by a wide range of ideological clubs, students cannot reasonably understand the school to endorse all of the groups' divergent and contradictory views. But if the religion club is the sole advocacy-oriented group in the forum, or one of a very limited number, and the school continues to promote its student-club program as instrumental to citizenship, then the school's failure to disassociate itself from the religious activity will reasonably be understood as an endorsement of that activity. That political and other advocacy-oriented groups are permitted to participate in a forum that, through school support and encouragement, is devoted to fostering a student's civic identity does not ameliorate the appearance of school endorsement unless the invitation is accepted and the forum is transformed into a forum like that in *Widmar*.

For this reason, the plurality's reliance on *Widmar* is misplaced. The University of Missouri took concrete steps to ensure "that the University's name will not 'be identified in any way with the aims, policies, programs, products, or opinions of any organization or its members.' " Westside, in contrast, explicitly promotes its student clubs "as a vital part of the total education program [and] as a means of developing citizenship.". . .

The different approaches to student clubs embodied in these policies reflect a significant difference, for Establishment Clause purposes, between the respective roles that Westside High School and the

University of Missouri attempt to play in their students' lives. To the extent that a school emphasizes the autonomy of its students, as does the University of Missouri, there is a corresponding decrease in the likelihood that student speech will be regarded as school speech. Conversely, where a school such as Westside regards its student clubs as a mechanism for defining and transmitting fundamental values, the inclusion of a religious club in the school's program will almost certainly signal school endorsement of the religious practice.

Thus, the underlying difference between this case and *Widmar* is not that college and high school students have varying capacities to perceive the subtle differences between toleration and endorsement, but rather that the University of Missouri and Westside actually choose to define their respective missions in different ways. That high schools tend to emphasize student autonomy less than universities may suggest that high school administrators tend to perceive a difference in the maturity of secondary and university students. But the school's behavior, not the purported immaturity of high school students, is dispositive. If Westside stood apart from its club program and expressed the view, endorsed by Congress through its passage of the Act, that high school students are capable of engaging in wide-ranging discussion of sensitive and controversial speech, the inclusion of religious groups in Westside's forum would confirm the school's commitment to nondiscrimination. Here, though, the Act requires the school to permit religious speech in a forum explicitly designed to advance the school's interest in shaping the character of its students.

. . . If a school has a variety of ideological clubs, as in *Widmar*, I agree with the plurality that a student is likely to understand that "a school does not endorse or support student speech that it merely permits on a nondiscriminatory basis." When a school has a religion club but no other political or ideological organizations, however, that relatively fine distinction may be lost.

Moreover, in the absence of a truly robust forum that includes the participation of more than one advocacy-oriented group, the presence of a religious club could provide a fertile ground for peer pressure, especially if the club commanded support from a substantial portion of the student body. Indeed, it is precisely in a school without such a forum that intolerance for different religious and other views would be most dangerous and that a student who does not share the religious beliefs of his classmates would perceive "that religion or a particular religious belief is favored or preferred."

The plurality concedes that there is a "possibility of *student* peer pressure," but maintains that this does not amount to "official state endorsement." This dismissal is too facile. . . . When the government, through mandatory attendance laws, brings students together in a highly controlled environment every day for the better part of their waking hours and regulates virtually every aspect of their existence during that time, we should not be so quick to dismiss the problem of peer pressure as if the school environment had nothing to do with creating and fostering it. The State has structured an environment in which students holding mainstream views may be able to coerce adherents of minority religions to attend club meetings or to adhere to club beliefs. Thus, the State cannot disclaim its responsibility for those resulting pressures.

Given these substantial risks posed by the inclusion of the proposed Christian Club within Westside's present forum, Westside must redefine its relationship to its club program. The plurality recognizes that such redefinition is necessary to avoid the risk of endorsement and construes the Act accordingly. . . .

Westside . . . must do more than merely prohibit faculty members from actively participating in the Christian Club's meetings. It must fully disassociate itself from the Club's religious speech and avoid appearing to sponsor or endorse the Club's goals.

[**Justice John Paul Stevens** dissented from the Court's interpretation of the Equal Access Act, arguing that Congress intended to recognize a much narrower forum than "the Court has legislated into existence today." Thus Westside did not violate the Act. Stevens's understanding of the statute made it unnecessary for him to reach the constitutional question.]

Responses

*From the **Washington Post**, June 6, 1990, "Religious Meetings in Schools":*

While we have never been happy about the idea of mixing religious meetings and public schools, the majority opinion on the constitutionality of the statute is not unreasonable. We do, however, share the misgivings of Justice Stevens, who was the sole dissenter, and Justices Marshall and Brennan, who concurred. All three focused on the specific situation in Omaha, where the religious meeting group was the only club organized for a sectarian, political or philosophical purpose and was therefore more likely to be thought to have official approval than would be the case if there were a host of such clubs. With the concurring justices, we hope that as the statute is implemented across the country, school officials will be careful to emphasize that allowing religious meetings is not the same as endorsing them, to address the real possibility of peer pressure and to encourage the establishment of a variety of such groups so that students will not infer that any one organization is preferred.

*From the **New York Times**, June 6, 1990, "Of Bible Groups and Scuba Clubs":*

The Equal Access Act of 1984 was a sop to those in Congress who wanted to say something politically appealing about the role of religion in school. Unable to pass a school prayer amendment to the Constitution, they eventually settled for a law requiring public schools to allow religious and political clubs to meet on the same basis as other extracurricular organizations. The Supreme Court has now upheld that law by an 8-to-1 vote. As a few justices noted, the laws is a strange departure from principles of local educational control. But it doesn't violate the Constitution's ban on the establishment of religion. As construed by the Court, it can't do much harm. And if carefully enforced, it may even bring some calm to church-state storms and persuade Congress to stop roiling the issue. . . .

Applying the equal access rule will not be simple. Administrators who are already required to observe official neutrality on religious matters must now confront another layer of subtlety.

Justice John Paul Stevens's dissent warns that when schools are asked to deal with applications for, say, a Ku Klux Klan chapter, they may be forced to sacrifice desirable extracurricular programs in order to close the doors to undesirable ones. That would be regrettable, but it wouldn't be the first challenge

435

to the ingenuity of schools officials eager to hold students' interest and en- hance their education.

From *Edwin M. Yoder, Jr.*, *"Religion and Absurdity in the Schools,"* in the *Washington Post*, *June 9, 1990*:

The substance of a Supreme Court decision is occasionally less revealing than what it says implicitly about the state of the national dialogue. And a good example is the decision in the case of the after-hours "Christian club" at an Omaha high school. It offers dismal witness to what years of violent contro- versy have done to the Establishment Clause, and to religion and learning. . . .

The notion that a student Bible-study club that is not officially sponsored and is entirely voluntary might somehow be an illicit "establishment of reli- gion" is farfetched. It springs from a gross but common misreading of what the court has said over the years about prayer and Bible reading in the schools.

It was not study, it was official prescription of prayer and Bible reading in devotional settings, that the court sought to check; and properly so. Other- wise, and as properly, the court has never attempted to dictate rules for the study of religion, even in the classroom, let alone after hours. Indeed, in the school prayer decision, the court went out of its way to note that it was not attempting to expunge religious or scriptural study.

But that disclaimer, along with other subtleties, soon was lost sight of. And no wonder. The shrill criticism that followed the prayer decision had an explo- sive theme: The court was "taking God out of the schools" or "secularizing" them. These misconceived and mischievous charges took their toll. They con- fused school boards and administrators, textbook publishers, parents and stu- dents, and even an occasional lower-court judge. Religion became too hot to handle, too controversial to be dealt with in a sane and balanced way. The easy alternative was to pretend it was nonexistent or unimportant. Hence the ab- surdities multiplied.

People for the American Way, for instance, discovered not long ago that in their usual mousy fashion, certain textbook publishers had laundered the re- ligious factor right out of American history. It was "Hamlet" without the ghost. It was as if Massachusetts Bay or Rhode Island had begun as overseas health resorts for the seventeenth century equivalent of the English jet set. And what odd contortions were resorted to in the teaching of literature. What might be said, for instance, about Milton's "Paradise Lost"—on the premise that the inspirations of religion were an unmentionable subject—could only be imagined.

The court's internal argument in the Omaha case reflects the same reti- cence, the same fear of grappling incisively with the central issue. Eight of the nine justices agreed that the "equal access" law does not conflict with the First Amendment, but the varied explanations commanded no single majority. Meanwhile, the great question of how the vital protections of the Establish- ment Clause may be reconciled with a sensible acknowledgment of the centrality of religious tradition in our history or in Western culture went unaddressed. One could only imagine, rather wistfully, what use a Felix Frankfurter or a Robert Jackson would have made of such an invitation to reflection.

No, the Court's rather dreary argument mainly had to do with the meaning of the term "noncurricular," with the dangers that "peer pressure" might drive students against their will into the Christian club, and the like. But why is it so hard to distinguish between worship or indoctrination in the schools (which are out of place) and the study of religion (which is not)? Why can't we agree to keep sectarian rituals out of the classroom without making religion into a bugaboo?

The Court is a great teaching, as well as adjudicating, institution. But on this subject, it has turned the classroom over to the dunces and zealots. And with the results you might expect.

25

Lee v. *Weisman*

112 Sup. Ct. 2649 (1992)

The Supreme Court addressed questions of school prayer for the first time in 1962, holding in *Engel* v. *Vitale* that a state-sponsored prayer used in public schools violated the Constitution. Thirty years later, in *Lee* v. *Weisman*, the Court extended the principle of Engel to hold that a state may not sponsor prayers at middle and high school graduation ceremonies.

The case arose from Providence, Rhode Island, whose middle and high school principals invited members of the clergy from around the city to give invocation and benediction prayers as part of their schools' graduation ceremonies. Robert E. Lee, principal of Nathan Bishop Middle School, invited Rabbi Leslie Gutterman of Temple Beth El to offer the prayers at his school's 1989 graduation ceremony. Principal Lee gave Rabbi Gutterman a pamphlet containing guidelines for the composition of the prayers and advised him that the invocation and benediction should be nonsectarian. The prayers that the rabbi said at the ceremony, which took place on school premises on June 29, 1989, were of that nature.

Four days before the ceremony Daniel Weisman, whose daughter Deborah was in the graduating class, sought in her behalf a temporary restraining order in federal district court to prohibit school officials from including a prayer in the graduation ceremony. The motion was denied, but in July 1989 Daniel Weisman amended his complaint, seeking a permanent injunction against including prayers in Providence's middle and high school graduation ceremonies. The district court held that the graduation-ceremony prayers were unconstitutional, and the U.S. Court of Appeals for the First Circuit affirmed.

Daniel Weisman prevailed in the Supreme Court by a 5-to-4 vote. Justice Anthony Kennedy, joined by Justices Harry Blackmun, John Paul Stevens, Sandra Day O'Connor, and David Souter, wrote for the Court. The case produced three other opinions: a concurrence by Justice Blackmun, a concurrence by Justice Souter, and a dissent by Justice Antonin Scalia. Justice Kennedy's opinion for the Court, Justice Souter's concurrence, and Justice Scalia's dissent are presented here. They are followed by editorial responses from the *Washington Post* and the *Dallas Morning News*.

It was widely expected that the Court would use the *Lee* case to reconsider its approach, laid down in *Lemon* v. *Kurtzman*, to establishment questions. That did not happen. Of interest, however, is not only the argument that took place between Justices Kennedy and Scalia, in their opinions, but also the inquiry into the original meaning of the no-establishment provision undertaken by Justice Souter in his opinion, which seeks to answer (then Associate) Justice William Rehnquist's lengthy dissent in *Wallace* v. *Jaffree* (1985).

Participating in *Lee* v. *Weisman*, decided June 24, 1992, were Chief Justice William H. Rehnquist and Associate Justices Harry A. Blackmun, Anthony M. Kennedy, Sandra Day O'Connor, Antonin Scalia, David H. Souter, John Paul Stevens, Clarence Thomas, and Byron R. White.

Opinions

Justice Anthony M. Kennedy delivered the opinion of the Court:

These dominant facts mark and control our decision: State officials direct the performance of a formal religious exercise at promotional and graduation ceremonies for secondary schools. Even for those students who object to the religious exercise, their attendance and participation in the state-sponsored religious activity are in a fair and real sense obligatory, though the school district does not require attendance as a condition for receipt of the diploma.

This case does not require us to revisit the difficult questions dividing us in recent cases, questions of the definition and full scope of the principles governing the extent of permitted accommodation by the State for the religious beliefs and practices of many of its citizens. See *Allegheny County* v. *Greater Pittsburgh ACLU*, 492 U.S. 573 (1989);[1] *Wallace* v. *Jaffree* (1985); *Lynch* v. *Donnelly* (1984). For without reference to those principles in other contexts, the controlling precedents as they relate to prayer and religious exercise in primary and secondary public schools compel the holding here that the policy of the city of Providence is an unconstitutional one. We can decide the case without reconsidering the general constitutional framework by which public schools' efforts to accommodate religion are measured. Thus we do not accept the invitation of petitioners and *amicus* the United States to reconsider our decision in *Lemon* v. *Kurtzman* (1971). The government involvement with religious activity in this case is pervasive, to the point of creating a state-sponsored and state-directed religious exercise in a public school. Conducting this formal religious observance conflicts with settled rules pertaining to prayer exercises for students, and that suffices to determine the question before us.

---

1. In *Allegheny County* the Court held (1) that a crèche depicting the Christian Nativity scene, which was donated by a Roman Catholic group and located on the grand staircase of the Allegheny County Courthouse, violated the First Amendment; and (2) that a Chanukah menorah, owned by a Jewish group and placed just outside the City-County Building next to the city of Pittsburgh's forty-five-foot decorated Christmas tree, did *not* violate the First Amendment.

441

The principle that government may accommodate the free exercise of religion does not supersede the fundamental limitation imposed by the Establishment Clause. It is beyond dispute that, at a minimum, the Constitution guarantees that government may not coerce anyone to support or participate in religion or its exercise, or otherwise act in a way which "establishes a [state] religion or religious faith, or tends to do so." *Lynch.* The State's involvement in the school prayers challenged today violates these central principles.

That involvement is as troubling as it is undenied. A school official, the principal, decided that an invocation and a benediction should be given; this is a choice attributable to the State, and from a constitutional perspective it is as if a state statute decreed that the prayers must occur. The principal chose the religious participant, here a rabbi, and that choice is also attributable to the State. The reason for the choice of a rabbi is not disclosed by the record, but the potential for divisiveness over the choice of a particular member of the clergy to conduct the ceremony is apparent.

Divisiveness, of course, can attend any state decision respecting religions, and neither its existence nor its potential necessarily invalidates the State's attempts to accommodate religion in all cases. The potential for divisiveness is of particular relevance here though, because it centers around an overt religious exercise in a secondary school environment where, as we discuss below, subtle coercive pressures exist and where the student had no real alternative which would have allowed her to avoid the fact or appearance of participation.

The State's role did not end with the decision to include a prayer and with the choice of clergyman. Principal Lee provided Rabbi Gutterman with a copy of the "Guidelines for Civic Occasions," and advised him that his prayers should be nonsectarian. Through these means the principal directed and controlled the content of the prayer. Even if the only sanction for ignoring the instructions were that the rabbi would not be invited back, we think no religious representative who valued his or her continued reputation and effectiveness in the community would incur the State's displeasure in this regard. It is a cornerstone principle of our Establishment Clause jurisprudence that "it is no part of the business of government to compose official prayers for any group of the American people to recite as a part of a religious program carried on by the government," *Engel* v. *Vitale* (1962), and that is what the school officials attempted to do.

Petitioners argue, and we find nothing in the case to refute it, that the directions for the content of the prayers were a good-faith attempt by the school to ensure that the sectarianism which is so often the flashpoint for religious animosity be removed from the graduation ceremony. The concern is understandable, as a prayer which uses ideas or images identified with a particular religion may foster a different sort of sectarian rivalry than an invocation or benediction in terms more neutral. The school's explanation, however, does not resolve the dilemma caused by its participation. The question is not the good faith of the school in attempting to make the prayer acceptable to most persons, but the legitimacy of its undertaking that enterprise at all when the object is to produce a prayer to be used in a formal religious exercise which students, for all practical purposes, are obliged to attend.

We are asked to recognize the existence of a practice of nonsectarian prayer, prayer within the embrace of what is known as the Judeo-Christian tradition, prayer which is more acceptable than one which, for example, makes explicit references to the God of Israel, or to Jesus Christ, or to a patron saint. . . . But though the First Amendment does not allow the government to stifle prayers which aspire to these ends, neither does it permit the government to undertake that task for itself.

The First Amendment's Religion Clauses mean that religious beliefs and religious expression are too precious to be either proscribed or prescribed by the State. The design of the Constitution is that preservation and transmission of religious beliefs and worship is a responsibility and a choice committed to the private sphere, which itself is promised freedom to pursue that mission. It must not be forgotten then, that while concern must be given to define the protection granted to an objector or a dissenting non-believer, these same Clauses exist to protect religion from government interference. . . .

These concerns have particular application in the case of school officials, whose effort to monitor prayer will be perceived by the students as inducing a participation they might otherwise reject. Though the efforts of the school officials in this case to find common ground appear to have been a good-faith attempt to recognize the common aspects of religions and not the divisive ones, our precedents do not permit school officials to assist in composing prayers as an incident to a formal exercise for their students. *Engel.* And these same precedents caution us to measure the idea of a civic religion against the central meaning of the Religion Clauses of the First Amendment, which is that all creeds must be tolerated and none favored. The suggestion that government may establish an official or civic religion as a means of avoiding the establishment of a religion with more specific creeds strikes us as a contradiction that cannot be accepted.

The degree of school involvement here made it clear that the graduation prayers bore the imprint of the State and thus put school-age children who objected in an untenable position. We turn our attention now to consider the position of the students, both those who desired the prayer and she who did not.

To endure the speech of false ideas or offensive content and then to counter it is part of learning how to live in a pluralistic society, a society which insists upon open discourse towards the end of a tolerant citizenry. And tolerance presupposes some mutuality of obligation. It is argued that our constitutional vision of a free society requires confidence in our own ability to accept or reject ideas of which we do not approve, and that prayer at a high school graduation does nothing more than offer a choice. By the time they are seniors, high school students no doubt have been required to attend classes and assemblies and to complete assignments exposing them to ideas they find distasteful or immoral or absurd or all of these. Against this background, students may consider it an odd measure of justice to be subjected during the course of their educations to ideas deemed offensive and irreligious, but to be denied a brief, formal prayer ceremony that the school offers in return. This argument cannot prevail, however. It overlooks a fundamental dynamic of the Constitution.

The First Amendment protects speech and religion by quite different mechanisms. Speech is protected by insuring its full expression even when the government participates, for the very object of some of our most important speech is to persuade the government to adopt an idea as its own. The method for protecting freedom of worship and freedom of conscience in religious matters is quite the reverse. In religious debate or expression the government is not a prime participant, for the Framers deemed religious establishment antithetical to the freedom of all. The Free Exercise Clause embraces a freedom of conscience and worship that has close parallels in the speech provisions of the First Amendment, but the Establishment Clause is a specific prohibition on forms of state intervention in religious affairs with no precise counterpart in the speech provision. The explanation is in the lesson of history that was and is the inspiration for the Establishment Clause, the lesson that in the hands of government what might begin as a tolerant expression of religious views may end in a policy to indoctrinate and coerce. A state-created orthodoxy puts at grave risk that freedom of belief and conscience which are the sole assurance that religious faith is real, not imposed.

The lessons of the First Amendment are as urgent in the modern world as in the Eighteenth Century when it was written. One timeless lesson is that if citizens are subjected to state-sponsored religious exercises, the State disavows its own duty to guard and respect that sphere of inviolable conscience and belief which is the mark of a free people. To compromise that principle today would be to deny our own tradition and forfeit our standing to urge others to secure the protections of that tradition for themselves.

As we have observed before, there are heightened concerns with protecting freedom of conscience from subtle coercive pressure in the elementary and secondary public schools. Our decisions in *Engel* and *Abington* v. *Schempp* (1963) recognize, among other things, that prayer exercises in public schools carry a particular risk of indirect coercion. The concern may not be limited to the context of schools, but it is most pronounced there. . . . What to most believers may seem nothing more than a reasonable request that the nonbeliever respect their religious practices, in a school context may appear to the nonbeliever or dissenter to be an attempt to employ the machinery of the State to enforce a religious orthodoxy.

We need not look beyond the circumstances of this case to see the phenomenon at work. The undeniable fact is that the school district's supervision and control of a high school graduation ceremony places public pressure, as well as peer pressure, on attending students to stand as a group or, at least, maintain respectful silence during the Invocation and Benediction. This pressure, though subtle and indirect, can be as real as any overt compulsion. Of course, in our culture standing or remaining silent can signify adherence to a view or simple respect for the views of others. And no doubt some persons who have no desire to join a prayer have little objection to standing as a sign of respect for those who do. But for the dissenter of high school age, who has a reasonable perception that she is being forced by the State to pray in a manner her conscience will not allow, the injury is no less real. There can be no doubt that for many, if not most, of the students at the graduation, the act of standing or remaining silent was an expression of participation in the Rabbi's prayer. That was the very point of the religious exercise. It is of little comfort to a dissenter, then, to be told that for her the act of standing or remaining in silence signifies mere respect, rather than participation. What matters is that, given our social conventions, a reasonable dissenter in this milieu could believe that the group exercise signified her own participation or approval of it.

Finding no violation under these circumstances would place objectors in the dilemma of participating, with all that implies, or protesting. We do not address whether that choice is acceptable if the affected citizens are mature adults, but we think the State may not, consistent with the Establishment Clause, place primary and secondary school children in this position. Research in psychology supports the common assumption that adolescents are often susceptible to pressure from their peers towards conformity, and that the influence is strongest in matters of social convention. . . .

The injury caused by the government's action, and the reason why Daniel and Deborah Weisman object to it, is that the State, in a school setting, in effect required participation in a religious exercise. It is, we concede, a brief exercise during which the individual can concentrate on joining its message, meditate on her own religion, or let the mind wander. But the embarrassment and the intrusion of the religious exercise cannot be refuted by arguing that these prayers, and similar ones to be said in the future, are of a *de minimis* character. To do so would be an affront to the Rabbi who offered them and to all those for whom the prayers were an essential and profound recognition of divine authority. And for the same reason, we think that the intrusion is greater than the two minutes or so of time consumed for prayers like these. Assuming, as we must, that the prayers were offensive to the student and the parent who now object, the intrusion was both real and, in the context of a secondary school, a violation of the objectors' rights. That the intrusion was in the course of promulgating religion that sought to be civic or nonsectarian rather than pertaining to one sect does not lessen the offense or isolation to the objectors. At best it narrows their number, at worse increases their sense of isolation and affront.

. . . Petitioners and the United States, as *amicus*, . . . argu[ed] that the option of not attending the graduation excuses any inducement or coercion in the ceremony itself. The argument lacks all persuasion. Law reaches past formalism. And to say a teenage student has a real choice not to attend her high school graduation is formalistic in the extreme. True, Deborah could elect not to attend commencement without renouncing her diploma; but we shall not allow the case to turn on this point. Everyone knows that in our society and in our culture high school graduation is one of life's most significant occasions. A school rule which excuses attendance is beside the point. Attendance may not be required by official decree, yet it is apparent that a student is not free to absent herself from the graduation exercise in any real sense of the term "voluntary," for absence would require forfeiture of those intangible benefits which have motivated the student through youth and all her high school years. . . .

The importance of the event is the point the school district and the United States rely upon to argue that a formal prayer ought to be permitted, but it becomes one of the principal reasons why their argument must fail. Their contention, one of considerable force were it not for the constitutional constraints applied to state action, is that the prayers are an essential part of these ceremonies because for many persons an occasion of this significance lacks meaning if there is no recognition, however brief, that human achievements cannot be understood apart from their spiritual essence. We think the Government's position that this interest suffices to force students to choose between compliance or forfeiture demonstrates fundamental inconsistency in its argumentation. It fails to acknowledge that what for many of Deborah's classmates and their parents was a spiritual imperative was for Daniel and Deborah Weisman religious conformance compelled by the State. While in some societies the wishes of the majority might prevail, the Establishment Clause of the First Amendment is addressed to this contingency and rejects the balance urged upon us. The Constitution forbids the State to exact religious conformity from a student as the price of attending her own high school graduation. This is the calculus the Constitution commands.

The Government's argument gives insufficient recognition to the real conflict of conscience faced by the young student. The essence of the Government's position is that with regard to a civic, social occasion of this importance it is the objector, not the majority, who must take unilateral and private action to avoid compromising religious scruples, here by electing to miss the graduation exercise. This turns conventional First Amendment analysis on its head. It is a tenet of the First Amendment that the State cannot require one of its citizens to forfeit his or her rights and benefits as the price of resisting conformance to state-sponsored religious practice. To say that a student must remain apart from the ceremony at the opening invocation and closing benediction is to risk compelling conformity in an environment analogous to the classroom setting, where we have said the risk of compulsion is especially high. . . .

Inherent differences between the public school system and a session of a State Legislature distinguish this case from *Marsh* v. *Chambers* (1983). . . . The atmosphere at the opening of a session of a state legislature where adults are free to enter and leave with little comment and for any number of reasons cannot compare with the constraining potential of the one school event most important for the student to attend. The influence and force of a formal exercise in a school graduation are far greater than the prayer exercise we condoned in *Marsh*. The *Marsh* majority in fact gave specific recognition to this distinction and placed particular reliance on it in upholding the prayers at issue there. Today's case is different. At a high school graduation, teachers and principals must and do retain a high degree of control over the precise contents of the program, the speeches, the timing, the movements, the dress, and the decorum of the students. In this atmosphere the state-imposed character of an invocation and benediction by clergy selected by the school combine to make the prayer a state-sanctioned religious exercise in which the student was left with no alternative but to submit. This is different from *Marsh* and suffices to make the religious exercise a First Amendment violation. Our Establishment Clause jurisprudence remains a delicate and fact-sensitive one, and we cannot accept the parallel relied upon by petitioners and the United States between the facts of *Marsh* and the case now before us. . . .

We do not hold that every state action implicating religion is invalid if one or a few citizens find it offensive. People may take offense at all manner of religious as well as nonreligious messages, but offense alone does not in every case show a violation. We know too that sometimes to endure social isolation or even anger may be the price of conscience or nonconformity. But, by any reading of our cases, the conformity required of the student in this case was too high an exaction to withstand the test of the Establishment Clause. The prayer exercises in this case are especially improper because the State has in every practical sense compelled attendance and participation in an explicit religious exercise at an event of singular importance to every student, one the objecting student had no real alternative to avoid.

Our jurisprudence in this area is of necessity one of line-drawing, of determining at what point a dissenter's rights of religious freedom are infringed by the State. . . .

Our society would be less than true to its heritage if it lacked abiding concern for the values of its young people, and we acknowledge the profound belief of adherents to many faiths that there must be a place in the student's life for precepts of a morality higher even than the law we today enforce. We express no hostility to those aspirations, nor would our oath permit us to do so. A relentless and all-pervasive attempt to exclude religion from every aspect of public life could itself become inconsistent with the Constitution. . . . We recognize that, at graduation time and throughout the course of the educational process, there will be instances when religious values, religious practices, and religious persons will have some interaction with the public schools and their students. See *Westside Community Board of Education* v. *Mergens* (1990). But these matters, often questions of accommodation of religion, are not before us. The sole question presented is whether a religious exercise may be conducted at a graduation ceremony in circumstances where, as we have found, young graduates who object are induced to conform. No holding by this Court suggests that a school can persuade or compel a student to participate in a religious exercise. That is being done here, and it is forbidden by the Establishment Clause of the First Amendment.

Justice David H. Souter, concurring, joined by Justice John Paul Stevens and Justice Sandra Day O'Connor:

I write separately . . . on two issues of Establishment Clause analysis that underlie my independent resolution of this case: whether the Clause applies to governmental practices that do not favor one religion or denomination over others, and whether state coercion of religious conformity, over and above state endorsement of religious exercise or belief, is a necessary element of an Establishment Clause violation.

Forty-five years ago, this Court announced a basic principle of constitutional law from which it has not strayed: the Establishment Clause forbids not only state practices that "aid one religion . . . or prefer one religion over another," but also those that "aid all religions." *Everson* v. *Board of Education* (1947). Today we reaffirm that principle, holding that the Establishment Clause forbids state-sponsored prayers in public school settings no matter how nondenominational the prayers may be. In barring the State from sponsoring generically Theistic prayers where it could not sponsor sectarian ones, we hold true to a line of precedent from which there is no adequate historical case to depart.

Since *Everson*, we have consistently held the Clause applicable no less to governmental acts favoring religion generally than to acts favoring one religion over others. Thus in *Engel* we held that the public schools may not subject their students to readings of any prayer, however "denominationally neutral." More recently, in *Jaffree*, we held that an Alabama moment-of-silence statute passed for the sole purpose of "returning voluntary prayer to public schools" violated the Establishment Clause even though it did not encourage students to pray to any particular deity. . . .

Likewise, in *Texas Monthly, Inc.* v. *Bullock*, 489 U.S. 1 (1989), we struck down a state tax exemption benefiting only religious periodicals;

even though the statute in question worked no discrimination among sects, a majority of the Court found that its preference for religious publications over all other kinds "effectively endorses religious belief." And in *Torcaso* v. *Watkins* (1961), we struck down a provision of the Maryland Constitution requiring public officials to declare a " 'belief in the existence of God,' " reasoning that, under the Religion Clauses of the First Amendment, "neither a State nor the Federal Government . . . can constitutionally pass laws or impose requirements which aid all religions as against non-believers. . . ."

Such is the settled law. Here, as elsewhere, we should stick to it absent some compelling reason to discard it. . . .

Some have challenged this precedent by reading the Establishment Clause to permit "nonpreferential" state promotion of religion. The challengers argue that, as originally understood by the Framers, "[t]he Establishment Clause did not require government neutrality between religion and irreligion nor did it prohibit the Federal Government from providing nondiscriminatory aid to religion." *Jaffree* (Rehnquist, J., dissenting); see also R. Cord, *Separation of Church and State: Historical Fact and Current Fiction* (1988). While a case has been made for this position, it is not so convincing as to warrant reconsideration of our settled law; indeed, I find in the history of the Clause's textual development a more powerful argument supporting the Court's jurisprudence following *Everson*.

When James Madison arrived at the First Congress with a series of proposals to amend the National Constitution, one of the provisions read that "[t]he civil rights of none shall be abridged on account of religious belief or worship, nor shall any national religion be established, nor shall the full and equal rights of conscience be in any manner, or on any pretext, infringed." Madison's language did not last long. It was sent to a Select Committee of the House, which, without explanation, changed it to read that "no religion shall be established by law, nor shall the equal rights of conscience be infringed." Thence the proposal went to the Committee of the Whole, which was in turn dissatisfied with the Select Committee's language and adopted an alternative proposed by Samuel Livermore of New Hampshire: "Congress shall make no laws touching religion, or infringing the rights of conscience." Livermore's proposal would have forbidden laws having anything to do with religion and was thus not only far broader than Madison's version, but broader even than the scope of the Establishment Clause as we now understand it. . . .

The House rewrote the amendment once more before sending it to the Senate, this time adopting, without recorded debate, language derived from a proposal by Fisher Ames of Massachusetts: "Congress shall make no law establishing Religion, or prohibiting the free exercise thereof, nor shall the rights of conscience be infringed." Perhaps, on further reflection, the Representatives had thought Livermore's proposal too expansive, or perhaps, as one historian has suggested, they had simply worried that his language would not "satisfy the demands of those who wanted something said specifically against establishments of religion." L. Levy, *The Establishment Clause* (1986), p. 81. We do not know; what we do know is that the House rejected the Select Committee's version, which arguably ensured only that "no religion" enjoyed an official preference over others, and deliberately chose instead a prohibition extending to laws establishing "religion" in general.

The sequence of the Senate's treatment of this House proposal, and the House's response to the Senate, confirm that the Framers meant the Establishment Clause's prohibition to encompass nonpreferential aid to religion. In September 1789, the Senate considered a number of provisions that would have permitted such aid, and ultimately it adopted one of them. First, it briefly entertained this language: "Congress shall make no law establishing One Religious Sect or Society in preference to others, nor shall the rights of conscience be infringed." After rejecting two amendments to that proposal, the Senate dropped it altogether and chose a provision identical to the House's proposal, but without the clause protecting the "rights of conscience." With no record of the Senate debates, we cannot know what prompted these changes, but the record does tell us that, six days later, the Senate went half circle and adopted its narrowest language yet: "Congress shall make no law establishing articles of faith or a mode of worship, or prohibiting the free exercise of religion." The Senate sent this proposal to the House along with its versions of the other constitutional amendments proposed.

Though it accepted much of the Senate's work on the Bill of Rights, the House rejected the Senate's version of the Establishment Clause and called for a joint conference committee, to which the Senate agreed. The House conferees ultimately won out, persuading the Senate to accept this as the final text of the Religion Clauses: "Congress shall make no law respecting an establishment of religion, or prohibiting the free exercise thereof." What is remarkable is that, unlike the earliest House drafts or the final Senate proposal, the prevailing language is not limited to laws respecting an establishment of "a religion," "a national religion," "one religious sect," or specific "articles of faith." The Framers repeatedly considered and deliberately rejected such narrow language and instead extended their prohibition to state support for "religion" in general.

Implicit in their choice is the distinction between preferential and nonpreferential establishments, which the weight of evidence suggests the Framers appreciated.[2] . . . Of particular note, the Framers were vividly familiar with efforts in the colonies and, later, the States to impose general, nondenominational assessments and other incidents of ostensibly ecumenical establishments. The Virginia Statute for Religious Freedom, written by Jefferson and sponsored by Madison, captured the separationist response to such measures. Condemning all establishments, however nonpreferentialist, the Statute broadly guaranteed that "no man shall be compelled to frequent or support any religious worship, place, or ministry whatsoever," including his own. . . .

What we thus know of the Framers' experience underscores the observation of one prominent commentator, that confining the Establishment Clause to a prohibition on preferential aid "requires a premise that the Framers were extraordinarily bad drafters—that they believed one thing but adopted language that said something substantially different, and that they did so after repeatedly attending to the choice of language."[3] We must presume, since there is no conclusive evidence to the contrary, that the Framers embraced the significance of their textual judgment.[4] Thus, on balance, history neither contradicts nor warrants reconsideration of the settled principle that the Es-

---

2. Justice Souter here directs readers to Douglas Laycock, " 'Nonpreferential' Aid to Religion: A False Claim About Original Intent," *William & Mary Law Review* 27 (1986): 875, and Leonard Levy, *The Establishment Clause* (1986). Both Laycock and Levy criticize Rehnquist's "no preference" argument in his *Jaffree* dissent. Souter's opinion appears to draw heavily on the work of these two scholars.

3. Souter again refers the reader to Laycock, " 'Nonpreferential' Aid" (882–83).

4. [Footnote three in the text of the opinion.] In his dissent in *Wallace*, the Chief Justice rested his nonpreferentialist interpretation partly on the post-ratification actions of the early national government. Aside from the willingness of some (but not all) early Presidents to issue ceremonial religious proclamations, which were at worst trivial breaches of the Establishment Clause, he cited such seemingly preferential aid as a treaty provision, signed by Jefferson, authorizing federal subsidization of a Roman Catholic priest and church for the Kaskaskia Indians. But this proves too much, for if the Establishment Clause permits a special appropriation of tax money for the religious activities of a particular sect, it forbids virtually nothing. See Laycock, " 'Nonpreferential' Aid," 915. Although evidence of historical practice can indeed furnish valuable aid in the interpretation of contemporary language, acts like the one in question prove only that public officials, no matter when they serve, can turn a blind eye to constitutional principle.

tablishment Clause forbids support for religion in general no less than support for one religion or some.

While these considerations are, for me, sufficient to reject the non-preferentialist position, one further concern animates my judgment. In many contexts, including this one, nonpreferentialism requires some distinction between "sectarian" religious practices and those that would be, by some measure, ecumenical enough to pass Establishment Clause muster. Simply by requiring the enquiry, nonpreferentialists invite the courts to engage in comparative theology. I can hardly imagine a subject less amenable to the competence of the federal judiciary, or more deliberately to be avoided where possible.

This case is nicely in point. Since the nonpreferentiality of a prayer must be judged by its text, Justice Blackmun pertinently observes [in his concurring opinion] that Rabbi Gutterman drew his exhortation "[t]o do justly, to love mercy, to walk humbly" straight from the King James version of Micah, ch. 6, v. 8. At some undefinable point, the similarities between a state-sponsored prayer and the sacred text of a specific religion would so closely identify the former with the latter that even a nonpreferentialist would have to concede a breach of the Establishment Clause. And even if Micah's thought is sufficiently generic for most believers, it still embodies a straightforwardly Theistic premise, and so does the Rabbi's prayer. Many Americans who consider themselves religious are not Theistic; some, like several of the Framers, are Deists who would question Rabbi Gutterman's plea for divine advancement of the country's political and moral good. Thus, a nonpreferentialist who would condemn subjecting public school graduates to, say, the Anglican liturgy would still need to explain why the government's preference for Theistic over non-Theistic religion is constitutional.

Nor does it solve the problem to say that the State should promote a "diversity" of religious views; that position would necessarily compel the government and, inevitably, the courts to make wholly inappropriate judgments about the number of religions the State should sponsor and the relative frequency with which it should sponsor each. . . . [T]he judiciary should not willingly enter the political arena to battle the centripetal force leading from religious pluralism to official preference for the faith with the most votes.

Petitioners rest most of their argument on a theory that, whether or not the Establishment Clause permits extensive nonsectarian support for religion, it does not forbid the state to sponsor affirmations of religious belief nor participation in religious observance. I appreciate the force of some of the arguments supporting a "coercion" analysis of the Clause.[5] . . . But we could not adopt that reading without abandoning our settled law, a course that, in my view, the text of the Clause would not readily permit. Nor does the extratextual evidence of original meaning stand so unequivocally at odds with the textual premise inherent in existing precedent that we should fundamentally reconsider our course. . . .

. . .

Like the provisions about "due" process and "unreasonable" searches and seizures, the constitutional language forbidding laws "respecting an establishment of religion" is not pellucid. But virtually everyone acknowledges that the Clause bans more than formal establishments of religion in the traditional sense, that is, massive state support for religion through, among other means, comprehensive schemes of taxation. . . . This much follows from the Framers' explicit rejection of simpler provisions prohibiting either the establishment of a religion or laws "establishing religion" in favor of the broader ban on laws "respecting an establishment of religion."

While some argue that the Framers added the word "respecting" simply to foreclose federal interference with State establishments of religion, . . . the language sweeps more broadly than that. In Madison's words, the Clause in its final form forbids "everything like" a national religious establishment, . . . and, after incorporation, it forbids "everything like" a State religious establishment. . . .

While petitioners insist that the prohibition extends only to the "coercive" features and incidents of establishment, they cannot easily square that claim with the constitutional text. The First Amendment forbids not just laws "respecting an establishment of religion," but also those "prohibiting the free exercise thereof." Yet laws that coerce nonadherents to "support or participate in any religion or its exercise," *Allegheny County* (opinion of Justice Kennedy), would virtually by definition violate their right to religious free exercise. See *Employment Division v. Smith* (1990). . . . Thus, a literal application of the coercion test would render the Establishment Clause a virtual nullity, as petitioners' counsel essentially conceded at oral argument.

Our cases presuppose as much; as we said in *Abington*, "[t]he dis-

---

5. Here Justice Souter refers the reader to Justice Kennedy's dissent in *Allegheny County v. ACLU* (1989), 492 U.S. 573. Under a coercion (or "noncoercion") analysis, government may aid or endorse all religion or particular religions so long as it does not force anyone to practice or believe in a religion. In *Allegheny County*, Justice Kennedy added to coercion analysis the requirement that government refrain from proselytizing.

tinction between the two clauses is apparent—a violation of the Free
Exercise Clause is predicated on coercion while the Establishment
Clause violation need not be so attended." . . . While one may argue
that the Framers meant the Establishment Clause simply to ornament
the First Amendment, cf. T. Curry, *The First Freedoms* (1986), 216–17,
that must be a reading of last resort. Without compelling evidence to
the contrary, we should presume that the Framers meant the Clause to
stand for something more than petitioners attribute to it.

Petitioners argue from the political setting in which the Establishment Clause was framed, and from the Framers' own political practices
following ratification, that government may constitutionally endorse
religion so long as it does not coerce religious conformity. The setting
and the practices warrant canvassing, but while they yield some evidence for petitioners' argument, they do not reveal the degree of consensus in early constitutional thought that would raise a threat to *stare
decisis* by challenging the presumption that the Establishment Clause
adds something to the Free Exercise Clause that follows it.

The Framers adopted the Religion Clauses in response to a long
tradition of coercive state support for religion, particularly in the form
of tax assessments, but their special antipathy to religious coercion did
not exhaust their hostility to the features and incidents of establishment. Indeed, Jefferson and Madison opposed any political appropriation of religion. . . .

Petitioners contend that because the early Presidents included religious messages in their inaugural and Thanksgiving Day addresses,
the Framers could not have meant the Establishment Clause to forbid
noncoercive state endorsement of religion. The argument ignores the
fact, however, that Americans today find such proclamations less controversial than did the founding generation, whose published thoughts
on the matter belie petitioners' claim. President Jefferson, for example,
steadfastly refused to issue Thanksgiving proclamations of any kind,
in part because he thought they violated the Religion Clauses. . . .

During his first three years in office, James Madison also refused to
call for days of thanksgiving and prayer, though later, amid the political
turmoil of the War of 1812, he did so on four separate occasions. . . .

Madison's failure to keep pace with his principles in the face of congressional pressure cannot erase the principles. He admitted to back-
sliding, and explained that he had made the content of his wartime
proclamations inconsequential enough to mitigate much of their
impropriety. . . .

To be sure, the leaders of the young Republic engaged in some of the practices that separationists like Jefferson and Madison criticized. The First Congress did hire institutional chaplains, and Presidents Washington and Adams unapologetically marked days of "public thanksgiving and prayer," see R. Cord, *Separation of Church and State* (1988), 53. Yet in the face of the separationist dissent, those practices prove, at best, that the Framers simply did not share a common understanding of the Establishment Clause, and, at worst, that they, like other politicians, could raise constitutional ideals one day and turn their backs on them the next. . . .

While we may be unable to know for certain what the Framers meant by the Clause, we do know that, around the time of its ratification, a respectable body of opinion supported a considerably broader reading than petitioners urge upon us. This consistency with the textual considerations is enough to preclude fundamentally reexamining our settled law. . . .

. . .

That government must remain neutral in matters of religion does not foreclose it from ever taking religion into account. The State may "accommodate" the free exercise of religion by relieving people from generally applicable rules that interfere with their religious callings. . . .

. . .

Whatever else may define the scope of accommodation permissible under the Establishment Clause, one requirement is clear: accommodation must lift a discernible burden on the free exercise of religion. Concern for the position of religious individuals in the modern regulatory state cannot justify official solicitude for a religious practice unburdened by general rules; such gratuitous largesse would effectively favor religion over disbelief. By these lights one easily sees that, in sponsoring the graduation prayers at issue here, the State has crossed the line from permissible accommodation to unconstitutional establishment.

Justice Antonin Scalia, dissenting, joined by Chief Justice William H. Rehnquist, Justice Byron R. White, and Justice Clarence Thomas:

Three Terms ago, I joined an opinion recognizing that the Establishment Clause must be construed in light of the "[g]overnment policies of accommodation, acknowledgment, and support for religion [that] are an accepted part of our political and cultural heritage." That opinion affirmed that "the meaning of the Clause is to be determined by reference to historical practices and understandings." It said that "[a] test for implementing the protections of the Establishment Clause that, if applied with consistency, would invalidate longstanding traditions cannot be a proper reading of the Clause." *Allegheny County* (Kennedy, J., concurring in judgment in part and dissenting in part).

These views of course prevent me from joining today's opinion, which is conspicuously bereft of any reference to history. In holding that the Establishment Clause prohibits invocations and benedictions at public-school graduation ceremonies, the Court—with nary a mention that it is doing so—lays waste a tradition that is as old as public-school graduation ceremonies themselves, and that is a component of an even more longstanding American tradition of nonsectarian prayer to God at public celebrations generally. As its instrument of destruction, the bulldozer of its social engineering, the Court invents a boundless, and boundlessly manipulable, test of psychological coercion. . . . Today's opinion shows more forcefully than volumes of argumentation why our Nation's protection, that fortress which is our Constitution, cannot possibly rest upon the changeable philosophical predilections of the Justices of this Court, but must have deep foundations in the historic practices of our people.

. . .

The history and tradition of our Nation are replete with public ceremonies featuring prayers of thanksgiving and petition. Illustrations of this point have been amply provided in our prior opinions, but since the Court is so oblivious to our history as to suggest that the Constitution restricts "preservation and transmission of religious beliefs . . . to the private sphere," it appears necessary to provide another brief account.

From our Nation's origin, prayer has been a prominent part of governmental ceremonies and proclamations. The Declaration of Independence, the document marking our birth as a separate people, "appeal[ed] to the Supreme Judge of the world for the rectitude of our intentions" and avowed "a firm reliance on the protection of divine Providence." In his first inaugural address, after swearing his oath of office on a Bible, George Washington deliberately made a prayer a part of his first official act as President:

> it would be peculiarly improper to omit in this first official act my fervent supplications to that Almighty Being who rules over the universe, who presides in the councils of nations, and whose providential aids can supply every human defect, that His benediction may consecrate to the liberties and happiness of the people of the United

States a Government instituted by themselves for these essential purposes.

Such supplications have been a characteristic feature of inaugural addresses ever since. . . .

Our national celebration of Thanksgiving likewise dates back to President Washington. . . . This tradition of Thanksgiving Proclamations—with their religious theme of prayerful gratitude to God—has been adhered to by almost every President.

The other two branches of the Federal Government also have a long-established practice of prayer at public events. As we detailed in *Marsh*, Congressional sessions have opened with a chaplain's prayer ever since the First Congress. And this Court's own sessions have opened with the invocation "God save the United States and this Honorable Court" since the days of Chief Justice Marshall.

In addition to this general tradition of prayer at public ceremonies, there exists a more specific tradition of invocations and benedictions at public-school graduation exercises. By one account, the first public-high-school graduation ceremony took place in Connecticut in July 1868—the very month, as it happens, that the Fourteenth Amendment (the vehicle by which the Establishment Cause has been applied against the States) was ratified—when "15 seniors from the Norwich Free Academy marched in their best Sunday suits and dresses into a church hall and waited through majestic music and long prayers." As the Court obliquely acknowledges in describing the "customary features" of high school graduations, and as respondents do not contest, the invocation and benediction have long been recognized to be [as one commentator has written] "as traditional as any other parts of the [school] graduation program and are widely established."

The Court presumably would separate graduation invocations and benedictions from other instances of public "preservation and transmission of religious beliefs" on the ground that they involve "psychological coercion." I find it a sufficient embarrassment that our Establishment Clause jurisprudence regarding holiday displays has come to "requir[e] scrutiny more commonly associated with interior decorators than with the judiciary." *American Jewish Congress* v. *Chicago*, 827 F. 2d 120, 129 (Easterbrook, J., dissenting). But interior decorating is a rock-hard science compared to psychology practiced by amateurs. A few citations of "[r]esearch in psychology" that have no particular bearing upon the precise issue here cannot disguise the fact that the Court has gone beyond the realm where judges know what they are doing. The

Court's argument that state officials have "coerced" students to take part in the invocation and benediction at graduation ceremonies is, not to put too fine a point on it, incoherent.

The Court identifies two "dominant facts" that it says dictate its ruling that invocations and benedictions at public-school graduation ceremonies violate the Establishment Clause. Neither of them is in any relevant sense true.

The Court declares that students' "attendance and participation in the [invocation and benediction] are in a fair and real sense obligatory." But what exactly is this "fair and real sense"? According to the Court, students at graduation who want "to avoid the fact or appearance of participation" in the invocation and benediction are *psychologically* obligated by "public pressure, as well as peer pressure, . . . to stand as a group or, at least, maintain respectful silence" during those prayers. This assertion—*the very linchpin of the Court's opinion*—is almost as intriguing for what it does not say as for what it says. It does not say, for example, that students are psychologically coerced to bow their heads, place their hands in a Dürer-like prayer position, pay attention to the prayers, utter "Amen," or in fact pray. (Perhaps further intensive psychological research remains to be done on these matters.) It claims only that students are psychologically coerced "to stand . . . or, at least, maintain respectful silence" (emphasis added). Both halves of this disjunctive (*both* of which must amount to the fact or appearance of participation in prayer if the Court's analysis is to survive on its own terms) merit particular attention.

To begin with the latter: The Court's notion that a student who simply *sits* in "respectful silence" during the invocation and benediction (when all others are standing) has somehow joined—or would somehow be perceived as having joined—in the prayers is nothing short of ludicrous. We indeed live in a vulgar age. But surely "our social conventions" have not coarsened to the point that anyone who does not stand on his chair and shout obscenities can reasonably be deemed to have assented to everything said in his presence. Since the Court does not dispute that students exposed to prayer at graduation ceremonies retain (despite "subtle coercive pressures") the free will to sit, there is absolutely no basis for the Court's decision. It is fanciful enough to say that "a reasonable dissenter," standing head erect in a class of bowed heads, "could believe that the group exercise signified her own participation or approval of it." It is beyond the absurd to say that she could entertain such a belief while pointedly declining to rise.

But let us assume the very worst, that the nonparticipating graduate is "subtly coerced" . . . to stand! [Ellipsis in text.] Even that half of the disjunctive does not remotely establish a "participation" (or an "appearance of participation") in a religious exercise. The Court acknowledges that "in our culture standing . . . can signify adherence to a view or simple respect for the views of others." (Much more often the latter than the former, I think, except perhaps in the proverbial town meeting, where one votes by standing.) But if it is a permissible inference that one who is standing is doing so simply out of respect for the prayers of others that are in progress, then how can it possibly be said that a "reasonable dissenter . . . could believe that the group exercise signified her own participation or approval"? Quite obviously, it cannot. I may add, moreover, that maintaining respect for the religious observances of others is a fundamental civic virtue that government (including the public schools) can and should cultivate—so that even if it were the case that the displaying of such respect might be mistaken for taking part in the prayer, I would deny that the dissenter's interest in avoiding *even the false appearance of participation* constitutionally trumps the government's interest in fostering respect for religion generally.

The opinion manifests that the Court itself has not given careful consideration to its test of psychological coercion. For if it had, how could it observe, with no hint of concern or disapproval, that students stood for the Pledge of Allegiance, which immediately preceded Rabbi Gutterman's invocation? The government can, of course, no more coerce political orthodoxy than religious orthodoxy. *West Virginia Board of Education* v. *Barnette* (1943). Moreover, since the Pledge of Allegiance has been revised since *Barnette* to include the phrase "under God," recital of the Pledge would appear to raise the same Establishment Clause issue as the invocation and benediction. If students were psychologically coerced to remain standing during the invocation, they must also have been psychologically coerced, moments before, to stand for (and thereby, in the Court's view, take part in or appear to take part in) the Pledge. Must the Pledge therefore be barred from the public schools (both from graduation ceremonies and from the classroom)? In *Barnette* we held that a public-school student could not be compelled to *recite* the Pledge; we did not even hint that she could not be compelled to reserve respectful silence—indeed, even to *stand* in respectful silence—when those who wished to recite it did so. Logically, that ought to be the next project for the Court's bulldozer.

. . .

The other "dominant fac[t]" identified by the Court is that "[s]tate officials direct the performance of a formal religious exercise" at school graduation ceremonies. "Direct[ing] the performance of a formal religious exercise" has a sound of liturgy to it, summoning up images of the principal directing acolytes where to carry the cross, or showing the rabbi where to unroll the Torah. A Court professing to be engaged in a "delicate and fact-sensitive" line-drawing would better describe what it means as "prescribing the content of an invocation and benediction." But even that would be false. All the record shows is that principals of the Providence public schools, acting within their delegated authority, have invited clergy to deliver invocations and benedictions at graduations; and that Principal Lee invited Rabbi Gutterman, provided him a two-page flyer, prepared by the National Conference of Christians and Jews, giving general advice on inclusive prayer for civic occasions, and advised him that his prayers at graduation should be nonsectarian. How these facts can fairly be transformed into the charges that Principal Lee "directed and controlled the content of [Rabbi Gutterman's] prayer," that school officials "monitor prayer" and attempted to " 'compose official prayers,' " and that the "government involvement with religious activity in this case is pervasive," is difficult to fathom. The Court identifies nothing in the record remotely suggesting that school officials have ever drafted, edited, screened or censored graduation prayers, or that Rabbi Gutterman was a mouthpiece of the school officials.

These distortions of the record are, of course, not harmless error: without them the Court's solemn assertion that the school officials could reasonably be perceived to be "enforc[ing] a religious orthodoxy" would ring as hollow as it ought.

The deeper flaw in the Court's opinion does not lie in its wrong answer to the question whether there was state-induced "peer-pressure" coercion; it lies, rather, in the Court's making violation of the Establishment Clause hinge on such a precious question. The coercion that was a hallmark of historical establishments of religion was coercion of religious orthodoxy and of financial support *by force of law and threat of penalty*. Typically, attendance at the state church was required; only clergy of the official church could lawfully perform sacraments; and dissenters, if tolerated, faced an array of civil disabilities. L. Levy, *The Establishment Clause* (1986), 4. Thus, for example, in the colony of Virginia, where the Church of England had been established, ministers were required by law to conform to the doctrine and rites of the Church of England; and all persons were required to attend church and observe the Sabbath, were tithed for the public support of Anglican ministers, and were taxed for the costs of building and repairing churches.

The Establishment Clause was adopted to prohibit such an establishment of religion at the federal level (and to protect state establishments of religion from federal interference). I will further acknowledge for the sake of argument that, as some scholars have argued, by 1790 the term "establishment" had acquired an additional meaning— "financial support of religion generally, by public taxation"—that reflected the development of "general or multiple" establishments, not limited to a single church. But that would still be an establishment coerced *by force of law*. And I will further concede that our constitutional tradition, from the Declaration of Independence and the first inaugural address of Washington, quoted earlier, down to the present day, has, with a few aberrations, ruled out of order government-sponsored endorsement of religion—even when no legal coercion is present, and indeed even when no ersatz, "peer-pressure" psycho-coercion is present—where the endorsement is sectarian, in the sense of specifying details upon which men and women who believe in a benevolent, omnipotent Creator and Ruler of the world, are known to differ (for example, the divinity of Christ). But there is simply no support for the proposition that the officially sponsored nondenominational invocation and benediction read by Rabbi Gutterman—with no one legally coerced to recite them—violated the Constitution of the United States. To the contrary, they are so characteristically American they could have come from the pen of George Washington or Abraham Lincoln himself.

Thus, while I have no quarrel with the Court's general proposition that the Establishment Cause "guarantees that government may not coerce anyone to support or participate in religion or its exercise," I see no warrant for expanding the concept of coercion beyond acts backed by threat of penalty—a brand of coercion that, happily, is readily discernible to those of us who have made a career of reading the disciples of Blackstone rather than of Freud. The Framers were indeed opposed to coercion of religious worship by the National Government; but, as their own sponsorship of nonsectarian prayer in public events demonstrates, they understood that "[s]peech is not coercive; the listener may do as he likes." *American Jewish Congress* v. *Chicago*, 827 F. 2d, at 132 (Easterbrook, J., dissenting).

This historical discussion places in revealing perspective the Court's extravagant claim that the State has "for all practical purposes," and "in every practical sense," compelled students to participate in prayers at graduation. Beyond the fact, stipulated to by the parties, that attendance at graduation is voluntary, there is nothing in the record to indicate that failure of attending students to take part in the invocation or benediction was subject to any penalty or discipline. Contrast this with, for example, the facts of *Barnette*: Schoolchildren were required by law to recite the Pledge of Allegiance; failure to do so resulted in expulsion, threatened the expelled child with the prospect of being sent to a reformatory for criminally inclined juveniles, and subjected his parents to prosecution (and incarceration) for causing delinquency. To characterize the "subtle coercive pressures" allegedly present here as the "practical" equivalent of the legal sanctions in *Barnette* is . . . well, let me just say it is not a "delicate and fact-sensitive" analysis.

The Court relies on our "school prayer" cases, *Engel* and *Schempp*. But whatever the merit of those cases, they do not support, much less compel, the Court's psycho-journey. In the first place, *Engel* and *Schempp* do not constitute an exception to the rule, distilled from historical practice, that public ceremonies may include prayer; rather, they simply do not fall within the scope of the rule (for the obvious reason that school instruction is not a public ceremony). Second, we have made clear our understanding that school prayer occurs within a framework in which legal coercion to attend school (*i.e.*, coercion under threat of penalty) provides the ultimate backdrop. In *Schempp*, for example, we emphasized that the prayers were "prescribed as part of the curricular activities of students who are *required by law* to attend school" (emphasis added). *Engel*'s suggestion that the school-prayer program at issue there—which permitted students "to remain silent or be excused from the room"—involved "indirect coercive pressure" should be understood against this backdrop of legal coercion. The question whether the opt-out procedure in *Engel* sufficed to dispel the coercion resulting from the mandatory attendance requirement is quite different from the question whether forbidden coercion exists in an environment *utterly devoid of legal compulsion*. And finally, our school-prayer cases turn in part on the fact that the classroom is inherently an instructional setting, and daily prayer there . . . might be thought to raise special concerns regarding state interference with the liberty of parents to direct the religious upbringing of their children. . . . Voluntary prayer at graduation—a one-time ceremony at which parents, friends and relatives are present—can hardly be thought to raise the same concerns.

Our religion-clause jurisprudence has become bedeviled (so to speak) by reliance on formulaic abstractions that are not derived from,

but positively conflict with, our long-accepted constitutional traditions. Foremost among these has been the so-called *Lemon* test, which
has received well-earned criticism from many members of this Court.
See, *e.g.*, *Allegheny County* (opinion of Kennedy, J.); *Edwards* v. *Aguillard*,
482 U.S. 578 (1987) (Scalia, J., dissenting); *Jaffree* (Rehnquist, J., dissenting); *Aguilar* v. *Felton* (1985) (O'Connor, J., dissenting); *Roemer* v.
Maryland Board of Public Works, 426 U.S. 736 (1976) (White, J., concurring in judgment). The Court today demonstrates the irrelevance of
Lemon by essentially ignoring it, and the interment of that case may be
the one happy byproduct of the Court's otherwise lamentable decision.
Unfortunately, however, the Court has replaced *Lemon* with its psycho-
coercion test, which suffers the double disability of having no roots
whatever in our people's historic practice, and being as infinitely ex-
pandable as the reasons for psychotherapy itself.

Another happy aspect of the case is that it is only a jurisprudential
disaster and not a practical one. Given the odd basis for the Court's
decision, invocations and benedictions will be able to be given at public-school graduations next June, as they have for the past century and
a half, so long as school authorities make clear that anyone who abstains from screaming in protest does not necessarily participate in the
prayers. All that is seemingly needed is an announcement, or perhaps
a written insertion at the beginning of the graduation Program, to the
effect that, while all are asked to rise for the invocation and benediction, none is compelled to join in them, nor will be assumed, by rising,
to have done so. That obvious fact recited, the graduates and their
parents may proceed to thank God, as Americans have always done,
for the blessings He has generously bestowed on them and on their
country.

The reader has been told much in this case about the personal interest of Mr. Weisman and his daughter, and very little about the personal interests on the other side. They are not inconsequential.
Church and state would not be such a difficult subject if religion were,
as the Court apparently thinks it to be, some purely personal avocation
that can be indulged entirely in secret, like pornography, in the privacy
of one's room. For most believers it is *not* that, and has never been.
Religious men and women of almost all denominations have felt it necessary to acknowledge and beseech the blessing of God as a people,
and not just as individuals, because they believe in the "protection of
divine Providence," as the Declaration of Independence put it, not just
for individuals but for societies; because they believe God to be, as
Washington's first Thanksgiving Proclamation put it, the "Great Lord

and Ruler of Nations." One can believe in the effectiveness of such public worship, or one can deprecate and deride it. But the longstanding American tradition of prayer at official ceremonies displays with unmistakable clarity that the Establishment Clause does not forbid the government to accommodate it.

The narrow context of the present case involves a community's celebration of one of the milestones in its young citizens' lives, and it is a bold step for this Court to seek to banish from that occasion, and from thousands of similar celebrations throughout this land, the expression of gratitude to God that a majority of the community wishes to make. The issue before us today is not the abstract philosophical question whether the alternative of frustrating this desire of a religious majority is to be preferred over the alternative of imposing "psychological coercion," or a feeling of exclusion, upon nonbelievers. Rather, the question is *whether a mandatory choice in favor of the former has been imposed by the United States Constitution.* As the age-old practices of our people show, the answer to that question is not at all in doubt.

I must add one final observation: The founders of our Republic knew the fearsome potential of sectarian religious belief to generate civil dissension and civil strife. And they also knew that nothing, absolutely nothing, is so inclined to foster among religious believers of various faiths a toleration—no, an affection—for one another than voluntarily joining in prayer together, to the God whom they all worship and seek. Needless to say, no one should be compelled to do that, but it is a shame to deprive our public culture of the opportunity, and indeed the encouragement for people to do it voluntarily. The Baptist or Catholic who heard and joined in the simple and inspiring prayers of Rabbi Gutterman on this official and patriotic occasion was inoculated from religious bigotry and prejudice in a manner that can not be replicated. To deprive our society of that important unifying mechanism, in order to spare the nonbeliever what seems to me the minimal inconvenience of standing or even sitting in respectful nonparticipation, is as senseless in policy as it is unsupported in law.

For the foregoing reasons, I dissent.

Responses

From the **Washington Post**, June 25, 1992, "Graduation Prayers":

Rabbi Leslie Gutterman prepared a prayer for the 1989 graduation ceremonies at Nathan Bishop Middle School in Providence, R.I. Using guidelines published by the National Conference of Christians and Jews, his prayer was both nondenominational and generally religious, stressing thanks for the virtues of country, school and family and asking for blessings on all those in attendance. It was nevertheless a prayer at a public school ceremony, and yesterday the U.S. Supreme Court ruled that the practice was unconstitutional.

The decision came as a surprise, since many legal scholars had predicted that the court would relax its long-standing ban on religious activities in schools. Specifically, the Providence school system, supported by the Bush administration, had asked the justices to abandon the traditional test used in church-state cases and adopt a far more flexible one. Since 1971, when it decided a case called *Lemon* v. *Kurtzman*, the court has found that a law or a government practice is unconstitutional if it does not have a secular purpose, if its primary effect is to promote religion or if it fosters excessive government entanglement with religion. Using this standard, a variety of school practices, including holiday observances, the posting of the Ten Commandments in classroom and compulsory moments of silence for meditation, have been evaluated. Providence officials, however, argued that the test ought to be simply coercion. As long as the government is not enforcing its view of religious orthodoxy, they maintained, ceremonial prayers of this kind should be allowed. In addition, and coldly it seems to us, they pointed out that no coercion is involved in this case because students do not have to go to their own graduation.

The justices are closely divided on the law of church and state, and only five elected to preserve the *Lemon* test. They are right, of course. Measuring coercion is an impossible task, especially if the practice at issue involves schoolchildren, as this one does. Justice Kennedy, who wrote the majority opinion, stressed that this ruling is not meant to diminish the importance of religion in American life. But for thirty years, since the original school prayer ruling that for a time was so controversial, Americans have accepted the distinction between the promotion of religious values and practice in the home and the government's attempts to promote its version of piety in public life. A graduation prayer, no matter how carefully nondenominational, is as constitutionally invalid as the long-banned morning ritual in the classroom. In nei-

466

that case may the government put schoolchildren in a position in which they have to choose between participation and protest.

From the *Dallas Morning News,* June 26, 1992, "School Prayer":

The Supreme Court, after taking a fresh look at the constitutional boundary between church and state, decided to leave well enough alone at least for the time being. By ruling that public school graduation ceremonies may not include prayers, the high court left intact a legal precedent that has served the nation well for three decades.

The government's attorneys had tried to persuade the justices to permit public schools to offer prayers at commencement without unraveling the legal precedent that has prohibited organized prayer in public school classrooms since 1962. But Justice Anthony Kennedy, author of the court's majority opinion, did not accept that reasoning.

"Everyone knows that . . . high school graduation is one of life's most significant occasions," he wrote. Including a prayer in such a ceremony, he explained, constituted "pervasive" government involvement in a religious activity that left students no real choice but to participate. As such, it violated the Constitution.

As controversial as the court's decision may be, it was the right one to make. Justices, both liberal and conservative, have recognized in a series of decisions over the past thirty years that public school students should not be coerced—either by intentional institutional pressure or implied peer pressure—to join in group prayers.

That important precedent never has been intended as a slap against religion but as an acknowledgment of religion's central place in life. As Justice Kennedy wrote, "The First Amendment's religion clauses mean that religious beliefs and religious expression are too precious to be either proscribed or prescribed by the state."

Still, the justice is not so doctrinaire that he would advocate building an insurmountable wall between church and state. On the contrary, Justice Kennedy has been one court member who has suggested that public life could be enriched by acknowledging the country's religious tradition—as long as no one were coerced into participating.

Indeed, he took care to say that the rationale of this week's decision did not necessarily extend to church-state cases involving adults, who are less impressionable than young people. "A relentless . . . attempt to exclude religion from every aspect of public life could itself become inconsistent with the Constitution," he wrote.

Although the prayer case happened to reach the court first, it is just the tip of the iceberg. More than a half-dozen other cases, all raising church-state questions, also are pending before the justices. The Supreme Court will have ample opportunity next term to define further what is the appropriate role of religion in public life.

PART TWO

Reflections

1

Religion and the Court: A New Beginning?

Mary Ann Glendon

Mention the First Amendment to any lawyer, and the odds are excellent that he or she will assume you are talking about free speech. This habitual tendency to equate the First Amendment with speech goes beyond mere verbal shorthand. It is revealing of the pre-eminence that lawyers generally accord to speech on their "honor roll of superior rights." Constitutional-law professor Laurence Tribe, for example, reflects the view of many in the profession when he describes freedom of speech in his widely used text as "the Constitution's most majestic guarantee." As for the American public, opinion studies consistently show that they too value free speech highly. But most American men and women still place the freedom of speech exactly where the framers of the Bill of Rights put it—very close to, but just behind, the free exercise of religion.

What is more interesting than the bare findings of such surveys, however, is the way the latest one was reported by the press. One leading newspaper chose to focus on the information that a majority of Americans (consistent with long-standing constitutional tradition) do not regard the Constitution's speech guarantee as absolutely unlimited. This paper's five-column headline announced: "Study Finds Americans Willing to Curtail Some Free Speech." One might think that the fact that most Americans interpret the Bill of Rights somewhat differently from the litigation wing of the ACLU is about as newswor-

MARY ANN GLENDON is a professor of law at Harvard University and the author of *Rights Talk: The Impoverishment of Political Discourse* (The Free Press). This essay is reprinted by permission of the Institute on Religion and Public Life from the March 1992 issue of *First Things*.

thy as a report that the Pope has been seen at Mass. Yet the national press cannot quite get over it. Perhaps someday they will try a new angle on this old story. What, for example, would be the results of a poll among university professors, journalists, professionals of various sorts, entertainers, and other members of the knowledge class inquiring into how they rank constitutional values?

My guess is that the results of such a poll would closely resemble the hierarchy long implicit in the Supreme Court's decisions, and explicit in works by prominent constitutional-law specialists. That is, we would probably find many who would agree with Professor Tribe, as well as many others who would prefer Justice Louis Brandeis's famous dictum that "the right most cherished by civilized man [is] the right to be let alone," otherwise known as the right to privacy. One can only surmise where the freedom of religion would rank on such a list. Would it be treated as of only marginal significance, as Professor Douglas Laycock found it was by the authors of all the leading constitutional-law case books used in American law schools? Would it make the list at all? If not, could we expect to see excited headlines proclaiming, "New Study Finds Elites Willing to Dispense With Freedom of Religion"? Or, "Bill of Rights Would Not Be Ratified Today by Academics"?

To avoid any misunderstandings, let me make plain that I do not raise the question of a possible discrepancy between elite and popular belief systems in order to suggest that legal elites are to be faulted when they fail to conform to majoritarian sentiment. They perform indispensable services for our society by doing precisely that. Nor do I wish to dwell on the extent to which many intellectuals seem to be lapsing from the independent-mindedness on which they pride themselves into a rather uncritical conformity to the dogmas of knowledge-class culture. The relevance of knowledge-class attitudes to my subject is simply that awareness of some of these attitudes helps one to understand how and why the Supreme Court's religion-clause case law has now reached the state where it is described on all sides, and even by the justices themselves, as hopelessly confused, inconsistent, and incoherent.

As an aside, however, I would enter a note of skepticism concerning whether that body of law is really so incomprehensible as it is usually said to be. Admittedly, if what one is looking for is a reasoned elaboration of principles grounded in constitutional text or tradition, or if one expects to see a sustained collegial effort to discern the underlying purposes of the religion provisions and to interpret them in such a way as to promote those values, it is incoherent. Nevertheless, one can comprehend a good deal about court decisions by examining what judges do as well as what they say, and by comparing patterns of fact and outcomes in a line of related cases.

What I wish to suggest here is that one can also learn something about the underlying assumptions of the judges from their silences— what they treat as unimportant or what they choose not to mention at all. Viewed in this way, the Supreme Court's church-state jurisprudence is a museum of examples of a cognitive problem that is pervasive in our legal system. The problem is that, although we have a highly developed linguistic and conceptual apparatus for thinking about and dealing with individuals, market actors, and the state, we lack adequate concepts to enable us to take into consideration the social dimensions of human personhood, and the social environments that individual men, women, and children require in order to flourish.

S ociologists often use the somewhat cumbersome expression "mediating structures" to refer to what I prefer to call communities, i.e., families, neighborhoods, religious groups, and other groups of memory and mutual aid. Psychologists like Urie Bronfenbrenner who are more inclined to emphasize the role of these primary groups in fostering human development and socialization speak of "human ecology." Political theorists, for their part, sometimes use the metaphor "seedbeds of virtue" to underscore the dependency of our design for government on the nurture and education of its citizens and leaders, and hence on the vitality of the sorts of institutions where character is formed and competence acquired.

It is curious that the field of modern American law has rushed headlong into interdisciplinary relationships with economics, but has been slow to avail itself of the resources and insights of the other bodies of social thought I have just mentioned. Legal academics seem to have a preference for what they call the "hard" social sciences, by which they mean forms of inquiry that assume away most of the irrational, messy, and unpredictable aspects of human behavior that are the subjects of examination by the so-called soft social sciences. Chaos science, perhaps, will change all this in a generation or two, but at the present time, American courts and legal commentators have difficulty in taking a holistic or ecological view of the relationship between legal and social phenomena.

The individual-state-market framework, combined with the relentless present-mindedness that pervades our culture generally, makes it hard for legally trained individuals to take adequate account of any but the immediate implications of much of what they say and do. It is almost as though they had decided to set aside two troublesome elements that threaten to gum up our efforts to devise sensible rules, standards, principles, and policies for a complex, heterogeneous, modern state—the elements, namely, of "society" and "time."

Ironically, however, the peculiar excellence of the Anglo-American common-law tradition over centuries, that which distinguished it from continental "legal science," was its rejection of simplifying abstractions, its close attention to facts and patterns of facts, and its insistence that in deciding particular cases judges not only must strive to do justice between the parties before them, but must do so with a view toward maintaining principled continuity with the past, and providing guidance for parties similarly situated in the future. It was this unique combination of common sense and modest (as distinguished from "grand") theory that enabled England and the United States to develop and maintain a legal order possessing the toughness to weather political and social upheavals, yet the flexibility to adapt constructively and contribute to social change. When legal scholars distance themselves from those ways of thinking, they repudiate much of what is best in their professional tradition. They begin to resemble Thomas Reed Powell's famous caricature of the legal mind as "a mind that can think of something that is inextricably connected to something else without thinking of what it's connected to."

There is no great mystery about how American lawyers acquired the mental habits that prevent them from focusing on the social environments where the practices that sustain the democratic experiment are generated, shaped, and transmitted. For most of our history, there simply was no particular reason for statesmen and scholars to pay special attention to families, neighborhoods, religious groups, and other associations, or to the connections among them. These social networks were just there—in abundance, seemingly natural, like gravity, on whose continued existence we rely to keep us grounded, steady, and attached to our surroundings.

Certainly no one can blame the Founders for the fact that they took for granted the dense texture of eighteenth-century American society, with its family farms and businesses, its tight-knit communities, and its churches firmly woven into the social fabric. Nor would it be fair to say that the Founders underestimated the importance of the institutions whose durability they assumed. On the contrary, there is much evidence that they counted on families, custom, religion, and convention to help preserve and promote the habits and practices they believed to be required for the success of their experiment in ordered liberty. But it seems not to have occurred to our early leaders that there might come a time when the society's ability to produce virtuous citizens and statesmen would falter.

Things were quite different on the other side of the Atlantic, where the French revolutionaries had deliberately set out to try to eliminate every intermediate body standing between citizen and state. In this bicentennial of their founding period, when we are all trying to think of nice things to say about the French Revolution, it is appropriate to note that a happy by-product of all that revolutionary fury directed against the family, the guilds, the Church, and the commune system of local government was to bring into being a great school of social and political thought whose leading figures were concerned with what might happen when and if society actually did lose its intermediate structures. Burke, Tocqueville, and later Durkheim understood that this could not happen overnight (as the revolutionaries had hoped), but that it could be the long-term consequence of several fateful choices that in themselves seemed benign. What would the world be like, they asked, if nothing stood between the free, self-determining individual and the mighty, sovereign state?

The body of social theory these thinkers produced affords a useful perspective from which to consider the United States Supreme Court's religion decisions. For with hindsight we can see that in the 1940s, when the Court decided to make the religion language of the First Amendment binding (via the Fourteenth Amendment) on the states, industrialization, urbanization, and our special American history of geographic mobility had already begun to take a certain toll on families and other social structures. Our social capital, so to speak, was diminishing a bit. But we had plenty of it, and anyway, not everyone feels strongly about preserving capital.

We should not fault Supreme Court justices of the 1940s for failing to consider that this country might have been consuming its social capital somewhat faster than it was being replenished. After all, the Court began to apply the religion language to the states just at a time when the World War II effort had given the country an extraordinary sense of national unity. The members of the Court had every reason to embark on the incorporation project with a sense of complacency about the crisscrossing networks of associations and relationships that constitute the warp and woof of a civil society.

When several of those justices went on to become pioneers in the judicial-rights revolution that began in the 1950s, they continued to be somewhat cavalier about cultural foundations. In their zeal to protect certain preferred individual liberties, they seem in retrospect (like the French revolutionaries) to have given little thought to the structures that ultimately sustain a regime of rights. Where, one wonders, did they expect Americans to acquire that genuine respect for the dignity and worth of others that we now demand from our citizens to a higher degree than ever before? How were citizens of our increasingly diverse country supposed to internalize a sense of concern for fellow human beings in need that would be strong enough to support the expanded welfare activities of government? To pin so many of their hopes in this regard on the public schools, as some of the judges seem to have done, was seriously to underestimate the extent to which the public schools themselves depended, and still depend, on the support of, and interaction with, families and their surrounding communities.

What started out as mere judicial inattention to the role of religious groups in the American social ecosystem seems over time to have passed into a more studied indifference. Purely as a matter of judicial craftsmanship, it is striking in retrospect to observe how little intellectual curiosity was shown by most members of the Court in the challenge presented by the fact that the religion language of the First Amendment was made binding against the states at just the time when state and federal relations were undergoing momentous changes and the federal government was rapidly expanding its reach into towns and cities and local school districts. Transposing to this new context language that had been meant to apply only to the federal government posed an intriguing set of legal-political questions—real brain-teasers that should have called forth every ounce of energy, wit, technical skill, and imagination available to the Court. Yet in reading the decisions it is hard to escape the impression that—regardless of outcomes—serious issues were overlooked, important claims and arguments were rather lightly dismissed, and practical implications were regularly ignored.

The Court skipped right over formidable interpretive problems that required the kind of attention to language, history, and purposes that its members had lavished on many other parts of the Constitution: Are the establishment and free-exercise provisions two separate "clauses," each with its own set of values, and somewhat in tension with each other? Or is there, as the historical record suggests, a single religion clause whose establishment and free-exercise provisions serve one central value—the freedom of religion? Is free exercise an individual right, or does it also have associational and institutional aspects? Instead of grappling with these and other vitally important questions, Court majorities were content for a considerable period of time, in establishment cases, to use the metaphor of the "wall of separation" as a substitute for reasoned analysis. As for free exercise, it seems to have been left on the sidelines of the rights revolution. Indeed, free exercise in the broad sense took something of a battering in this period from Court majorities who gave a very expansive interpretation to the notion of "establishment" without pausing to consider the costs they might be inflicting on the associational aspects of free exercise.

From time to time, various justices have given us glimpses of the beliefs and assumptions about religion that undergirded their inclination to construe the establishment language in the First Amendment broadly: beliefs that religion is "inviolably private"; that it is an "individual experience"; and that a religion "worthy of the name" is the product of "choice." What is troubling about such presuppositions is that they leave out of consideration the free-exercise interests of members of religions to which the idea of a worshipping community is central. In addition, as Michael Sandel has pointed out, they fail "to respect persons [who consider themselves] bound by duties they have not chosen," the men and women who experience religious commitment more as a kind of "yoke" or "encumbrance" than as the product of a shopping expedition in the marketplace of ideas.

In the 1970s, Court majorities eventually shifted away from trying to maintain a "high and impregnable wall of separation" in establishment cases. Nevertheless, the Court's generally expansive understanding of what it means to establish religion continued to hinder legislative and local experiments with creative use of mediating structures to deliver social services. Nowhere have the deleterious effects of an excessively narrow view of free exercise and an inflated concept of establishment been more apparent than in the cases involving schools. In a judicial pincer movement, one line of decisions requires the public schools to be rigorously secular, while another has struck down most forms of public assistance to parents who desire to protect their children from an educational system that is often actively promoting values that are profoundly at odds with the family's religious convictions. The net result has been that a crucial aspect of religious freedom can be exercised only by families wealthy enough to afford private education after paying taxes to support public schools. Nor is private education an entirely safe harbor from intrusive and homogenizing governmental regulation.

All these trends culminated in, and were symbolized by, *Aguilar* v. *Felton*, the 1985 case in which the Court struck down a Great Society program designed to provide federal aid to educationally deprived children from low-income families. Under the specific program involved in *Aguilar*, public school teachers in New York City furnished remedial services and instruction to poor children with special needs in the city's private schools as well as to public school students. Of the private school children who were helped by this program, 84 per cent were in Catholic schools, and 8 per cent were in Hebrew day schools. After nineteen years of successful operation, this program was attacked by six taxpayers as a violation of the establishment provision, and was struck down by a 5–4 majority of the Supreme Court on the grounds that it impermissibly entangled church and state. The fatal entanglement arose from a judge-made "Catch 22": The program had to be monitored by the school district in order to assure that the public school teachers did not become involved in advancing religion, but the process of monitoring was itself an impermissible form of state involvement with religion.

Justice Sandra Day O'Connor's dissent in *Aguilar* could serve as a general indictment of the approach to establishment issues that had prevailed on the Court since the 1940s. She chided Justice William Brennan for his utter lack of interest in the facts of the case, for the abstract and perfunctory character of his analysis, for his failure to inquire into the practical operation of the program he struck down, and for his unconcern with the effects of the Court's decision on the lives and prospects of 20,000 poor special-needs children in New York City—not to mention children in similar programs in other parts of the country. She pointed out that the record showed not a single incident of religious "inculcation" by the public school teachers during the nineteen years that this large-scale program had been in operation. She noted, too, that this unblemished history was hardly surprising in view of another undisputed fact: three-quarters of the teachers in the program did not even have the same religious affiliation as the schools in which they taught. Nevertheless, as often in the past, a majority on the Court in *Aguilar* condemned a benign, carefully worked out legislative settlement by mechanically applying an abstract "test."

I t seems fair to observe that until the composition of the Court began to change in the mid-1980s, the decisions interpreting the religion language of the First Amendment showed few signs of giving the difficult issues in the area the care and concentrated attention that they needed and deserved. Then, with the departure of Justice Lewis Powell from the Court, and his replacement by Justice Anthony Kennedy, a period of change seemed to be opening. But the Court soon veered alarmingly in the direction of yet another simplistic approach—this time reflexive deference to the elected branches of government.

The most serious problem with the deferential approach to the legislature and executive now emergent is that, if applied with the same rigidity as was the old strict separationism, it is highly threatening to free-exercise concerns, especially where members of small, unpopular, or unconventional religions are involved. The Court's decisions in the Air Force yarmulke case [*Goldman* v. *Weinberger*, 475 U.S. 503 (1986)], the prison worship case [*O'Lone* v. *Estate of Shabazz*, 482 U.S. 342 (1987)], and most recently the peyote discharge case [*Employment Division* v. *Smith* (1990)] are troubling in this respect. The problem is not so much the bare results in those cases—reasonable people differ over whether some or all of them are justified by strong governmental interests. It is, rather, the majority's reasoning (or, more precisely, its lack of reasoning) in its inclination mechanically to subordinate free exercise to reasons of state without examining the governmental interest asserted and without reckoning the burden to free exercise.

One might imagine that a flexible and principled, as opposed to a rigid and mechanical, deference to the elected branches would have certain advantages over its predecessors, at least in the establishment cases. Unlike rigorous separationism, it would not carry overtones of those attitudes Justice Arthur Goldberg once described as "a brooding and pervasive devotion to the secular and a passive, or even active, hostility to religion." Such an approach would be more sensitive to the significant regional variations that exist in this country, and more respectful of local democratic decision-making. It would be apt to facilitate utilization of mediating structures which, as Peter Berger and Richard John Neuhaus have argued, can often deliver social services more efficiently, more economically, and more humanely than the state. And it would be likely to promote an important form of free exercise if it were to facilitate support of parental choice in education. It is unfortunate, I believe, that so much attention and energy have been expended for and against prayer in public schools, when the real issue is the current state of the public schools themselves, and the growing sense of many parents that they are losing the struggle for the hearts and minds of their children.

The peyote case, *Employment Division* v. *Smith*, however, looks very much like a decisive step by a Court majority toward an excessively rigid posture of deference in free-exercise cases. There, Justice Antonin Scalia, upholding the denial of unemployment benefits to Native Americans dismissed from their jobs for religiously inspired peyote use, wrote that "generally applicable religion-neutral laws that have the effect of burdening a particular religious practice need not be justified by a compelling governmental interest." Nevertheless, there is some basis for believing that *Smith* does not represent the Court's definitive adoption of a new approach. In the first place, Justice Scalia's opinion in *Smith* does not unambiguously purport to represent a comprehensive reordering of a body of law that took over forty years to become confused and unworkable. Furthermore, if one takes into consideration the views on religious freedom that have been expressed on various occasions by most of the individual justices who joined in the result in *Smith*, it is hard to believe that this one case represents their last word on a subject to which they have devoted so much thought in dissents and separate concurrences over the years. Keeping in mind that it took decades for the law in this area to achieve its present tangled state, it seems reasonable to expect a few fits and even false starts as the Court strives to work out a better way of dealing with the sensitive and important issues involved in these cases.

Prominent among the elements that one might expect to play a role in the process of developing a more principled and workable approach is Chief Justice William Rehnquist's judicial statesmanship, his demonstrated interest in religion-clause history, his often-expressed solicitude for the role of religion as a mediating structure, and his view of federalism. Another is Justice Byron White's longstanding call for a thorough reconsideration of the case law in this area—a process that has not yet taken place. Another is Justice Scalia's fidelity to constitutional text, a text that is no more neutral on the value of religion than it is on the value of free speech. Yet another factor is Justice Kennedy's constant alertness to the way in which purported "neutrality" can mask "hostility" to religion, a concern that in many cases cannot be alleviated without some scrutiny of the purpose and effects of laws that appear neutral on their face. A key role will undoubtedly be played by Justice O'Connor. Her willingness to listen, her careful attention to all points of view, her inclination to proceed cautiously case by case, her persistence in demanding justification, her attention to facts and practical consequences, all combine to bring the rich resources of the common-law tradition to bear on problems to which the Court in the past has given short shrift. Justice David Souter, for his part, shows every sign of being a judge in the common-law mode exemplified by Justice O'Connor.

It is possible, some would say probable, that a Court majority will once again—without much deliberation—brush the religion clause aside while it pursues an unrelated constitutional agenda. *Smith* may, as many fear, be the decisive step toward a reflexive majoritarianism as simplistic in its way as was the old separationist anti-majoritarianism. But on the other hand it may be that in time *Smith* will come to be seen as explicable mainly in relation to a strong national policy for dealing with a severe social problem. That is, just as *Bob Jones University* v. *United States* [461 U.S. 574 (1983)] (where a university's religiously based ban on interracial dating cost it its tax exemption) is more of an anti-discrimination case than a religion-clause case, so *Smith* may turn out to be primarily a drug case—a detour, rather than a landmark, in First Amendment case law. No doubt it is just in such "hard" cases where the Supreme Court ought to stand tall for religious liberty. Unfortunately, it is just in such cases that the Supreme Court, being human, is apt to falter. But not every judicial slip must initiate a cycle of decline.

My reading of the post-1987 religion cases is that they show a closely divided Court earnestly beginning to struggle with the formidable interpretive difficulties of the Constitution's religion language. The path they are taking may be erratic, but this group of justices is, at least, taking the religion clause seriously. Whether they will unite in a workable approach for a pluralistic society, and whether they will restore religion to its rightful place as the first among freedoms, remains to be seen.

2

Freedom of Conscience or Freedom of Choice?

Michael J. Sandel

One of the prevailing hypotheses of the contemporary public debate is that the reigning public philosophy is inadequate or impoverished in ways that a larger public role for religion might help to cure. In order to assess this claim, it may be helpful to examine the political theory of contemporary liberalism and to describe its stance toward religious practice and belief. In one respect, the liberal tradition seeks to secure for religion the most favorable conditions; given its emphasis on toleration and respect for conscience, liberal political theory promises the fullest religious liberty for each consistent with a similar liberty for all. In another respect, however, liberalism limits the reach of religion; its insistence that government be neutral among competing moral and theological visions, that political authority be justified without reference to religious sanction, would seem to confine religion to private life and to resist a public role.

The question whether government can be neutral among competing moral and religious conceptions is the subject of much debate within recent political philosophy. The goal here is threefold: first, to summarize this debate, and to argue, briefly, that government cannot be neutral in this sense; second, to show that, notwithstanding its inadequacy as theory, this version of liberalism is the one that has come

MICHAEL J. SANDEL is a professor of government at Harvard University. He is the author of *Liberalism and the Limits of Justice* and the editor of *Liberalism and Its Critics*. This essay is excerpted by permission from *Articles of Faith, Articles of Peace: The Religious Liberty Clauses and the American Public Philosophy*, edited by James Davison Hunter and Os Guinness (Washington, D.C.: The Brookings Institution, 1990). Notes have been omitted; some case names and authors' names given in notes have been inserted, within brackets, in the text.

to inform the constitutional law of religious liberty; and finally, to show how problems in the theory find expression in the law.

LIBERALISM AND THE UNENCUMBERED SELF

The version of liberalism with which I am concerned is prominent in contemporary moral, legal, and political philosophy. Its central idea is that government should be neutral on the question of the good life. Since people disagree on the best way to live, public policy should be, as Ronald Dworkin puts it, "independent of any particular conception of the good life, or of what gives value to life."

This version of liberalism is defined by the claim that the right is prior to the good, and in two senses: first, individual rights cannot be sacrificed for the sake of the general good; and second, the principles of justice that specify these rights cannot be premised on any particular vision of the good life. What justifies the rights is not that they maximize the general welfare or otherwise promote the good, but rather that they constitute a fair framework within which individuals can choose their own values and ends, consistent with a similar liberty for others.

The claim for the priority of the right over the good derives much of its moral force from a certain conception of the person. Unlike utilitarianism, which assumes a self simply defined as the sum of its desires, the liberal ethic affirms the notion of a choosing self, independent of the desires and ends it may have at any moment. Thus Kant appealed to the idea of a moral subject given prior to experience, capable of an autonomous will. And contemporary liberals rely on the similar idea of a self given prior to its purposes and ends.

For purposes of politics and law, this conception of the person seems compelling for at least two reasons. First, the image of the self as free and independent, unencumbered by aims and attachments it does not choose for itself, offers a powerful liberating vision. Freed from the sanctions of custom and tradition and inherited status, unbound by moral ties antecedent to choice, the liberal self is installed as sovereign, cast as the author of the only obligations that constrain. More than the simple sum of circumstance, we become capable of the dignity that consists in being persons of, in George Kateb's words, our "own creating, making, choosing." We are agents and not just instruments of the purposes we pursue. We are, according to John Rawls, "self-originating sources of valid claims."

A second appeal of the liberal self-image lies in the case it implies for equal respect. The idea that there is more to a person than the roles he plays or the customs she keeps or the faith he affirms suggests a basis for respect independent of life's contingencies. Liberal justice is blind to such differences between persons as race, religion, ethnicity, and gender, for in the liberal self-image, these features do not really define the identity in the first place. They are not constituents but merely attributes of the self, the sorts of things the state should look beyond. These considerations help clarify the connection between the aspiration to neutrality and the unencumbered self. If we conceive ourselves as free and independent selves, unclaimed by moral ties antecedent to choice, we must be governed by a neutral framework, a framework of rights that refuses to choose among competing purposes and ends. If the self is prior to its ends, the right must be prior to the good.

But how plausible is this self-conception? Can it make sense of our moral life, at least in those aspects relevant to politics and law? I shall first suggest some general reasons for thinking that it cannot, then turn to the specific case of religion.

One general difficulty with the liberal self-image is that it limits in advance the kind of community of which we are capable, and implausibly restricts the scope of moral and political obligation. Understood as unencumbered selves, we are free to join in voluntary association with others, whether to advance our private ends, or to enjoy the communal sentiments that such associations often inspire. We might call this community in the cooperative sense.

What is denied to the unencumbered self is the possibility of membership in any community bound by moral ties antecedent to choice; he cannot belong to any community where the self itself could be at stake. Such a community would engage the identity as well as the interests of the participants, and so implicate its members in a citizenship more thoroughgoing than the unencumbered self can know. More than a cooperative arrangement, community in this second, stronger sense describes a mode of self-understanding, a shared way of life that partly defines the identity of the participants. We might call it community in the constitutive sense.

One way of distinguishing communities in the constitutive sense from those that are merely cooperative is by reference to the moral and political obligations the participants acknowledge. On the liberal view, obligations can arise only in one of two ways: as "natural duties" we owe to human beings as such, or as voluntary obligations we incur by consent. The natural duties are the duties we owe persons *qua* persons—to do justice, to avoid cruelty, and so on. All other obligations, the ones we owe to particular others, are founded in consent, and can arise only by virtue of agreements we make, be they tacit or explicit.

Conceived as unencumbered selves, we must respect the dignity of all persons; but beyond this, we owe only what we agree to owe. Liberal justice requires that we respect people's rights (as defined by the neutral framework), not that we advance their good. Whether we must concern ourselves with other people's good depends on whether, and with whom, and on what terms, we have agreed to do so.

The liberal attempt to construe all obligation in terms of duties universally owed or obligations voluntarily incurred makes it difficult to account for a wide range of moral and political ties that we commonly recognize. It fails to capture those loyalties and responsibilities whose moral force consists partly in the fact that living by them is inseparable from understanding ourselves as the particular persons we are—as members of this family or city or nation or people, as bearers of that history, as citizens of this republic. Loyalties such as these can be more than values I happen to have, and to hold, at a certain distance. The moral responsibilities they entail may go beyond the obligations I voluntarily incur and the "natural duties" I owe to human beings as such. Those who share a common life informed by moral ties such as these may be said to comprise a community in the constitutive sense. The meaning of their membership cannot be redescribed in wholly voluntarist or contractarian terms without loss.

In the sections to follow, I explore this general objection to contemporary liberalism by considering the case of religion. I shall try to show that the version of liberalism I have summarized informs the current understanding of religious liberty in American constitutional law, and that difficulties in the theory show up in the practice. I shall try also to show that the reigning interpretation of religious liberty is not characteristic of the American constitutional tradition as such, but a recent development that departs from earlier understandings.

RELIGION AND THE CONSTITUTION: THE SEARCH FOR NEUTRALITY

After World War II, the U.S. Supreme Court assumed as its primary role the protection of individual rights against government infringement. Increasingly, it defined these rights according to the requirement that government be neutral on the question of the good life, and defended neutrality as essential to respecting persons as free and independent selves, unencumbered by moral ties antecedent to choice.

The principle of government neutrality found its first sustained application in cases involving religion. Time and again the Supreme Court has held that "in the relationship between man and religion, the State is firmly committed to a position of neutrality" [*Abington* v. *Schempp* (1963)]. "Government in our democracy, state and nation, must be neutral in matters of religious theory, doctrine, and practice. . . . The First Amendment mandates governmental neutrality between religion and religion, and between religion and nonreligion" [*Epperson* v. *Arkansas*, 393 U.S. 97 (1968)]. Whether described as "a strict and lofty neutrality" [*Everson* v. *Board of Education* (1947), J. Jackson dissenting], a "wholesome neutrality" [*Abington*], or a "benevolent neutrality" [*Waltz* v. *Tax Commission* (1970)], the principle "that the Government must pursue a course of complete neutrality toward religion" [*Wallace* v. *Jaffree* (1985)] is well established in American constitutional law.

In liberal political thought, religion offers the paradigmatic case for bracketing controversial conceptions of the good. The Supreme Court has conveyed its insistence on bracketing religion by invoking Jefferson's metaphor of a "wall of separation between church and state" [*Everson*]. While some complained that "a rule of law should not be drawn from a figure of speech" [*McCollum* v. *Board of Education* (1948), J. Reed dissenting], most see the wall as a symbol of resolve to keep religion from bursting the constitutional brackets that contain it. Since "the breach of neutrality that is today a trickling stream may all too soon become a raging torrent" [*Abington*], the "wall between Church and State . . . must be kept high and impregnable" [*Everson*].

It is striking to recall that, for all its familiarity, the requirement that government be neutral on matters of religion is not a longstanding principle of constitutional law, but a recent arrival, a development of the last forty years. Not until 1947 did the Supreme Court hold that government must be neutral toward religion [*Everson* v. *Board of Education*]. The American tradition of religious liberty goes back further, of course. [In a section that is omitted here the author traces the development of the principles of religious liberty and, later, government neutrality toward religion.]

RELIGION AND THE CONSTITUTION: JUSTIFYING NEUTRALITY

To assess the Court's conflicting applications of neutrality, it is necessary to consider the reasons for neutrality. What counts as neutrality partly depends on what justifies neutrality, and the Court has offered two different sorts of justification for insisting that government be neutral toward religion.

The first has to do with protecting the interests of religion on the one hand, and of the state on the other. "The First Amendment rests on the premise that both religion and government can best work to achieve their lofty aims if each is left free from the other within its respective sphere" [*McCollum*]. "We have staked the very existence of our country on the fact that complete separation between the state and religion is best for the state and best for religion" [*Everson*, J. Rutledge dissenting]. "In the long view the independence of both church and state in their respective spheres will be better served by close adherence to the neutrality principle" [*Abington*, J. Brennan concurring].

The religious interest served by separation lies in avoiding the corruption that comes with dependence on civil authority. A century and a half before Jefferson stated the secular case for a "wall of separation" between church and state, Roger Williams gave the metaphor a theological meaning. "When they have opened a gap in the hedge or wall of separation between the garden of the church and the wilderness of the world," he wrote, "God hath ever broke down the wall itself, removed the candlestick, and made His garden a wilderness, as at this day."

The Court has invoked the theological argument for separation only occasionally, and usually in combination with other arguments. In striking down school prayer [*Engel* v. *Vitale* (1962)], for example, Justice Hugo Black argued that the establishment clause "rested on the belief that a union of government and religion tends to destroy government and to degrade religion." The history of established religion "showed that many people lost their respect for any religion that had relied upon the support of government to spread its faith." The founders sought by the establishment clause to avoid the "unhallowed perversion" of religion by a civil magistrate. And Justice William Brennan [concurring in *Abington*] emphasized that separation is not only for the sake of the nonbeliever but also for "the devout believer who fears the secularization of a creed which becomes too deeply involved with and dependent upon the government."

The political interest served by separation is in avoiding the civil strife that has historically attended church-state entanglements. Providing public funds for religion brings "the struggle of sect against sect. . . . It is only by observing the prohibition rigidly that the state can maintain its neutrality and avoid partisanship in the dissensions inevitable when sect opposes sect over demands for public moneys" [*Everson*, J. Rutledge dissenting]. Opposing public school involvement in a "released time" program for religious instruction [*McCollum*], Justice Felix Frankfurter wrote that "the public school must be kept scrupulously free from entanglement in the strife of sects." [Dissenting] in a similar case, Justice Black vividly recalled the danger of sectarian strife that separation was meant to prevent. "Colonial history had already shown that, here as elsewhere zealous sectarians entrusted with governmental power to further their causes would sometimes torture, maim and kill those they branded heretics, atheists or agnostics" [*Zorach* v. *Clauson* (1952)].

Alongside the argument that neutrality is best for religion and best for the state is a different sort of argument, an argument in the name of individual freedom. On this justification, the state must be neutral not only to avoid compromising religion and provoking sectarian strife, but also to avoid the danger of coercion. This argument goes back to the eighteenth-century concern for freedom of conscience, and in its modern form emphasizes respect for persons' freedom to choose their religious convictions for themselves. It thus connects the case for neutrality with the liberal conception of the person.

In its modern, or voluntarist version, this argument for religious liberty first appears in *Cantwell* v. *Connecticut* (1940), the case that announced the incorporation of the religious-liberty clauses. "Freedom of conscience and freedom to adhere to such religious organization or form of worship *as the individual may choose* cannot be restricted by law" (emphasis added). The First Amendment "safeguards the free exercise of the chosen form of religion."

In banning Bible reading in the public schools [*Abington*], the Court found justification for neutrality in "the right of every person to freely choose his own course" with reference to religion, "free of any compulsion from the state." Justice Potter Stewart dissented from the result, but endorsed the view that neutrality is required for the sake of respect for individual choice, "a refusal on the part of the state to weight the scales of private choice."

Contemporary commentators have identified the voluntarist argument for neutrality as the primary justification for the separation of church and state. "The fundamental principle underlying both religion clauses is the protection of individual choice in matters of religion—whether pro or con" [Gail Merel]. "Since freedom of religious choice, not neutrality per se, is the fundamental establishment value, the neutrality tool is useful only insofar as it promotes that choice"

[Alan Schwarz]. "The moral basis of the antiestablishment clause is . . . equal respect," not for religious beliefs themselves but "for the processes of forming and changing such conceptions" [David A. J. Richards]. In short, the religious-liberty clauses secure "the core ideal of religious autonomy" [Laurence Tribe].

Perhaps the clearest statement of the voluntarist conception of religious liberty is the one that appears in Justice John Paul Stevens's opinion for the Court in a 1985 case [*Wallace* v. *Jaffree*] striking down Alabama's moment of silence for voluntary prayer in public schools. "The individual's freedom to choose his own creed is the counterpart of his right to refrain from accepting the creed established by the majority," Stevens wrote. "The Court has unambiguously concluded that the individual freedom of conscience protected by the First Amendment embraces the right to select any religious faith or none at all. This conclusion derives support not only from the interest in respecting the individual's freedom of conscience, but also from the conviction that *religious beliefs worthy of respect are the product of free and voluntary choice* by the faithful" (emphasis added).

As Stevens's opinion illustrates, the voluntarist justification of neutrality presupposes the liberal conception of the person. It holds that government should be neutral toward religion in order to respect persons as free and independent selves, capable of choosing their religious convictions for themselves. The respect this neutrality commands is not, strictly speaking, respect for religion, but respect for the self whose religion it is, or respect for the dignity that consists in the capacity to choose one's religion freely. Religious beliefs are "worthy of respect," not by virtue of what they are beliefs in, but rather by virtue of being "the product of free and voluntary choice," by virtue of being beliefs of a self unencumbered by convictions antecedent to choice.

By invoking the voluntarist conception of neutrality, the Court gives constitutional expression to the version of liberalism that conceives the right as prior to the good and the self as prior to its ends, at least where religion is concerned. We are now in a position to see how the promise of the theory, and also its problems, make themselves felt in the practice the theory informs. We turn first to the promise.

The voluntarist case for neutrality, insisting as it does on respect for persons, seems to secure for religious liberty a firm foundation. Unlike the theological case for separation of church and state, it does not depend on any particular religious doctrine. And unlike the political case for separation, it does not leave religious liberty hostage to uncertain calculations about how best to avoid civil strife. Under present conditions, such calculations may or may not support the separation of church and state. As Justice Lewis Powell has observed [*Wolman* v. *Walter*, 433 U.S. 229 (1977)], the risk "of deep political division along religious lines" is by now "remote." We do not live on the brink of the wars of religion that gave toleration its first occasion.

Even granting the importance of avoiding sectarian strife, a strict separation of church and state may at times provoke more strife than it prevents. The school-prayer decisions of the early sixties, for example, set off a storm of political controversy that twenty-five years have not stilled. A court concerned above all to avoid social discord might reasonably have decided those cases the other way.

The voluntarist case for neutrality, by contrast, does not tie religious liberty to such contingencies. In affirming a notion of respect for persons, it recalls the ideal of freedom of conscience. By emphasizing the individual's right to choose his beliefs, it points beyond religion to, as Tribe has said, "the broader perspective" of autonomy rights in general, including "the rights of privacy and personhood." It thus casts religious liberty as a particular case of the liberal claim for the priority of the right over the good and the self-image that attends it. Respecting persons as selves defined prior to the religious convictions they affirm becomes a particular case of the general principle of respect for selves defined prior to their aims and attachments.

But as we have seen, the image of the unencumbered self, despite its appeal, is inadequate to the liberty it promises. In the case of religion, the liberal conception of the person ill equips the Court to secure religious liberty for those who regard themselves as claimed by religious commitments they have not chosen. Not all religious beliefs can be redescribed without loss as, in Justice Stevens's words, "the product of free and voluntary choice by the faithful."

FREEDOM OF CONSCIENCE VERSUS FREEDOM OF CHOICE

The difference between the voluntarist account of religious liberty and freedom of conscience as traditionally conceived is revealing. For Madison and Jefferson, freedom of conscience meant the freedom to exercise religious liberty—to worship or not, to support a church or not, to profess belief or disbelief—without suffering civil penalties or incapacities. It had nothing to do with a right to choose one's beliefs. Madison's "Memorial and Remonstrance" consists of fifteen arguments for the separation of church and state, and not one makes any mention of "autonomy" or "choice." The only choice referred to in Jefferson's Bill for Establishing Religious Freedom "is predicated of God, not man."

Madison and Jefferson understood religious liberty as the right to exercise religious duties according to the dictates of conscience, not the right to choose religious beliefs. In fact, their argument for religious liberty relies heavily on the assumption that beliefs are not a matter of choice. The first sentence of Jefferson's bill states this assumption clearly: "The opinions and beliefs of men depend not on their own will, but follow involuntarily the evidence proposed to their own minds." Since I can only believe what I am persuaded is true, belief is not the sort of thing that coercion can compel. Coercion can produce hypocrisy but not conviction. In this assumption Jefferson echoed the view of John Locke, who wrote in *A Letter Concerning Toleration* (1685), "It is absurd that things should be enjoined by laws which are not in men's power to perform. And to believe this or that to be true, does not depend upon our will."

It is precisely because belief is not governed by the will that freedom of conscience is unalienable. Even if he would, a person could not give it up. This was Madison's argument in "Memorial and Remonstrance." "The Religion then of every man must be left to the conviction and conscience of every man; and it is the right of every man to exercise it as these may dictate. This right is in its nature an unalienable right. It is unalienable, because the opinions of men, depending only on the evidence contemplated by their own minds cannot follow the dictates of other men: it is unalienable also, because what is here a right towards men, is a duty towards the Creator."

Oddly enough, Justice Stevens cites this passage from Madison in support of the voluntarist view. But freedom of conscience and freedom of choice are not the same; where conscience dictates, choice decides. Where freedom of conscience is at stake, the relevant right is to exercise a duty, not make a choice. This was the issue for Madison and Jefferson. Religious liberty addressed the problem of encumbered selves, claimed by duties they cannot renounce, even in the face of civil obligations that may conflict.

In contemporary liberalism, by contrast, religious liberty serves the broader mission of protecting individual autonomy. On this view, government should be neutral toward religion for the same reason it should be neutral toward competing conceptions of the good life generally—to respect people's capacity to choose their own values and ends. But despite its liberating promise, or perhaps because of it, this broader mission depreciates the claims of those for whom religion is not an expression of autonomy but a matter of conviction unrelated to a choice. Protecting religion as a "life-style," as one among the values that an independent self may have, may miss the role that religion plays in the lives of those for whom the observance of religious duties is a constitutive end, essential to their good and indispensable to their identity. Treating persons as "self-originating sources of valid claims" may thus fail to respect persons bound by duties derived from sources other than themselves.

The case of *Thornton* v. *Caldor* [105 S.Ct. 2914 (1985)] shows how voluntarist assumptions can crowd out religious liberty for encumbered selves. By an 8–1 decision, the Supreme Court struck down a Connecticut statute guaranteeing Sabbath observers a right not to work on their Sabbath. Although the law gave all workers the right to one day off each week, it gave the Sabbath observers alone the right to designate their day. In this lack of neutrality the Court found constitutional infirmity.

Chief Justice Warren Burger, writing for the Court, noted that Sabbath observers would typically take a weekend day, "widely prized as a day off." But "other employees who have strong and legitimate, but non-religious reasons for wanting a weekend day off have no rights under the statute." They "must take a back seat to the Sabbath observers." Justice Sandra Day O'Connor echoed this worry in a concurring opinion: "All employees, regardless of their religious orientation, would value the benefit which the statute bestows on Sabbath observers—the right to select the day of the week in which to refrain from labor."

But this objection confuses the right to exercise a duty with the right to make a choice. Sabbath observers, by definition, do not select the day of the week they rest; they rest on the day their religion requires. The benefit the statute confers is not the right to choose a day of rest, but the right to exercise the duty of Sabbath observance on the only day it can be exercised.

Considered together with earlier decisions upholding Sunday closing laws, *Thornton* v. *Caldor* yields a curious constitutional conclusion: a state may require everyone to rest on Sunday, the day of the Christian Sabbath, so long as the aim is not to accommodate the observance of the Sabbath. But it may not give Sabbath observers the right to rest on the day of the week their religion requires. Perverse though this result may seem from the standpoint of promoting religious pluralism, it aptly reflects the constitutional consequences of seeing ourselves as unencumbered selves.

The Court has on occasion accorded greater respect to the claims of encumbered selves. When a Seventh-day Adventist was fired from her job for refusing to work on Saturday, her Sabbath, she was denied unemployment compensation under a rule requiring applicants to accept available work. The Supreme Court [in *Sherbert* v. *Verner* (1963)] decided in her favor, holding that the state could not force a worker to choose between her religious convictions and means of support. According to the Court, requiring the state to take account of Sabbath observance in the administration of its unemployment program did not prefer religion in violation of neutrality. Rather, it enforced "the governmental obligation of neutrality in the face of religious differences." In this case at least, the Constitution was not blind to religion but alive to its imperatives.

In cases involving conscientious objection to military service, the Court has interpreted federal law broadly and refused to restrict exemptions to those with theistic beliefs alone. The relevant test is "whether a given belief that is sincere and meaningful occupies a place in the life of its possessor parallel to that filled by the orthodox belief in God" [*United States* v. *Seeger*, 380 U.S. 163 (1965)]. What matters is not "conventional piety" [*Gillette* v. *United States*, 401 U.S. 437 (1971)] but an imperative of conscience rising above the level of a policy preference. The point of the exemption, according to the Court, is to prevent persons bound by moral duties they cannot renounce from having either to violate those duties or violate the law. This aim is consistent with Madison and Jefferson's concern for the predicament of persons claimed by dictates of conscience they are not at liberty to choose. As the Court wrote [in *Gillette*], "the painful dilemma of the sincere conscientious objector arises precisely because he feels himself bound in conscience not to compromise his beliefs or affiliations."

In *Wisconsin* v. *Yoder* (1972), the Court upheld the right of the Old Order Amish not to send their children to school beyond the eighth grade, despite a state law requiring school attendance until age sixteen. Higher education would expose Amish children to worldly and competitive values contrary to the insular, agrarian way of life that sustains Amish community and religious practice. The Court emphasized that the Amish claim was "not merely a matter of personal preference, but one of deep religious conviction" that pervades their way of life. Though "neutral on its face," Wisconsin's school attendance law unduly burdened the free exercise of religion, and so offended "the constitutional requirement for governmental neutrality."

Writing in dissent, Justice William Douglas asserted the voluntarist vision, arguing that the Amish children should be free to choose for themselves whether to continue in school or adopt the ways of their parents. "If a parent keeps his child out of school beyond the grade school, then the child will be forever barred from entry into the new and amazing world of diversity that we have today. The child may decide that that is the preferred course, or he may rebel." It is the child, not the parents, who should be heard if the Court is to respect "the right of the students to be masters of their own destiny."

The Court's occasional hospitality to the claims of encumbered selves did not extend to Captain Simcha Goldman, an Orthodox Jew whom the Air Force prohibited from wearing a yarmulke while on duty in the health clinic where he served. Justice William Rehnquist, writing for the Court [*Goldman* v. *Weinberger*, 475 U.S. 503 (1986)], held for the Air Force on grounds of judicial deference to the "professional judgment of military authorities" on the importance of uniform dress. Of the precedents he cited in support of deference to the military, all involved interests other than religious duties or conscientious imperatives. "The essence of military service 'is the subordination of the desires and interests of the individual to the needs of the service.'" Standardized uniforms encourage "the subordination of personal preferences and identities in favor of the overall mission." Having compared the wearing of a yarmulke to "desires," "interests," and "personal preferences" unrelated to religion, Rehnquist did not require the Air Force to show that an exception for yarmulkes would impair its disciplinary objectives. Nor did he even acknowledge that a religious duty was at stake, allowing only that, given the dress code, "military life may be more objectionable for petitioner."

The Court's tendency to assimilate religious liberty to liberty in general reflects the aspiration to neutrality; people should be free to pursue their own interests and ends, whatever they are, consistent with a similar liberty for others. But this generalizing tendency does not always serve religious liberty well. It confuses the pursuit of preferences with the exercise of duties and so forgets the special concern of religious liberty with the claims of conscientiously encumbered selves.

This confusion has led the Court to restrict religious practices it should permit, such as yarmulkes in the military, and also to permit practices it should probably restrict, such as Nativity scenes in the public square. In different ways, both decisions fail to take religion seriously. Permitting Pawtucket's crèche might seem to be a ruling sympathetic to religion [*Lynch* v. *Donnelly*, 465 U.S. 668 (1984)]. But as Justice Harry Blackmun rightly protested, the Court's permission came at the price of denying the sacred meaning of the symbol it protected.

What has preceded is an attempt to show how the version of liberalism implicit in contemporary constitutional law depreciates the claims of religion and fails to respect persons bound by duties they have not chosen. To this extent, this version of liberalism fails to secure the toleration it promises. But beyond the issue of toleration is the further question whether the liberal self-image is adequate to the demands of self-government. Is the unencumbered self too thin to sustain the obligations of citizenship? If so, is religion among the forms of identity likely to generate a fuller citizenship and a more vital public life? Or does it depend on the religion: might some religious convictions erode rather than enhance the civic virtues required of citizens in a pluralistic society? These are questions this essay can only suggest. Perhaps an attempt to address them would itself enrich the discourse of American public life.

3

Taking Religious Freedom Seriously

Michael W. McConnell

P assage of the religion clauses of the First Amendment ("Congress shall make no law respecting an establishment of religion or prohibiting the free expression thereof . . .") was one of the first effective exertions of political muscle by minority groups in the United States. James Madison, usually credited with their authorship, initially found the idea of a Bill of Rights "highly objectionable." During the early months of 1788, he tried to persuade his fellow Virginians that inclusion of a Bill of Rights in the new Constitution would be unnecessary, maybe even dangerous.

Madison began to reconsider, however, when he found himself under attack for this position among his constituents. Baptists, previously his enthusiastic supporters, were opposing the Constitution and threatening to support his opponent, James Monroe, in the congressional elections of that fall. Madison prudently changed his mind, and wrote to Baptist minister George Eve that he would now support "specific provisions made on the subject of the Rights of Conscience." In return, the Baptists held an election rally at their church at which Pastor Eve took "a very spirited and decided part" for Madison and reminded the crowd of his "many important services to the Baptists." (Those who think that church involvement in electoral politics began with Jesse Jackson and Pat Robertson do not know their American history.) Madison was duly elected to Congress, and he did not forget his pledge. He became the draftsman and floor leader for what would later be called the First Amendment.

MICHAEL W. MCCONNELL is William B. Graham Professor of Law at the University of Chicago. He has argued before the Supreme Court in cases involving the free exercise of religion. This essay is reprinted by permission of the Institute on Religion and Public Life from the May 1990 issue of *First Things*.

The Baptists had good reason to be concerned about religious freedom. As late as the 1760s, Baptists in Virginia were attacked, horsewhipped, fined, and jailed for preaching their faith. But they were not the only religious minority that felt threatened by the absence of a guarantee of religious freedom in the new Constitution. Some Quakers in Pennsylvania opposed the Constitution for fear that the new national government would not respect their conviction against military service. Representative Daniel Carroll of Maryland, one of only three Roman Catholics in the First Congress, spoke up for the proposed religion amendment, stating that "many sects have concurred in [the] opinion that they are not well secured under the present Constitution." It is symptomatic of the unusual religious circumstances of America that a Roman Catholic should become the spokesman for the diversity of religious sects.

Certain groups that one might assume would have been deeply involved in the passage of the religion clauses, such as the Jewish community, in fact were not. Jews have in recent times become perhaps the quintessential constituents of the religion clauses; but at the time the Constitution was written and ratified, there were fewer than 2,000 of them in America, and they played little role in the struggle for the First Amendment, either as victims of religious persecution or as advocates of religious freedom. It is true that Jews were excluded from public office in most states (Virginia and New York being the only exceptions as of passage of the First Amendment) and even from citizenship in otherwise pluralistic Rhode Island. But for the most part, Jews were tolerated and sometimes even welcomed. The Fundamental Constitutions of Carolina, issued in 1669, opened the colony to persons of "different opinions concerning matters of religion," specifically mentioning "Jews, heathens, and other dissenters from the purity of the Christian religion." Historians record that the small Jewish community in Puritan Connecticut received a respectful reception, even though the laws of the Empire mandated their exclusion. A Virginia newspaper in the early nineteenth century editorialized:

> Whether we view the Jews historically or religiously—as one of the earliest nations of the earth, still existing in observation of their ancient usages—or as the chosen people of God, selected in the first instance to receive the dispensations of his will, and after, to sustain for ages, his wrath and displeasure—the view is calculated to fill us with sentiments of awe, admiration, sympathy, and reverence.

How widespread such sentiments were we do not know; we do know that anti-Semitism grew with the waves of Jewish immigration later in the century.

In any event, the struggle for addition of protections for religious freedom in the Constitution was led by evangelical Protestants. Once proposed by the First Congress, the First Amendment met with easy and widespread approval, not because the majority believed in religious freedom as a matter of principle—most did not—but because the sheer number of religious denominations made each feel vulnerable to the combined efforts of the others. Anglicans were dominant in the South but a beleaguered minority in New England. Presbyterians were the most numerous denomination in New Jersey but experienced protracted difficulties with the authorities in Virginia, who deemed them fanatical and objected to their practice of itinerant preaching. Quakers had strength in numbers in the middle colonies but nowhere else. The First Amendment was a product of minority religions, but every religion was a minority religion in America.

That ought to tell us something about the purpose and original meaning of the religion clauses. They were not intended as an instrument of secularization, or as a weapon that the non-religious or antireligious could use to suppress the effusions of the religious. The Religion Clauses were intended to guarantee the rights of those whose religious practices seemed to the majority a little odd. "Enthusiastic" was the word often used to describe the Baptists of that day, with much the same meaning as our opprobrious term "fanatical" today. Nonbelievers were protected from majoritarian religion, too, but we must not think that was the exclusive, or even the primary, focus of the religious-freedom advocates of the founding period.

D espite the origins of the religion clauses, the Supreme Court has not tended to interpret them in light of the concerns and fears of minority religions. In the first religion-clause case decided on its merits, the Court in 1879 upheld conviction of a Mormon leader for carrying out his religious duty of polygamy. In the next case, a dozen years later, the Court upheld denial of the vote to anyone who supported polygamy, and that same year the justices sustained an Act of Congress abolishing the Mormon Church and expropriating its property. In the course of countenancing this, the most brutal act of official religious suppression in this country since adoption of the Bill of Rights, the Court added insult to injury by questioning whether any belief so bizarre as the Mormons' advocacy of polygamy could even be given the title of "religious" and thus claim the protections of the First Amendment. Only when the leaders of the church received a revelation repudiating the practice of polygamy, thus conforming to the usual family structure of the United States, were the Mormons allowed to practice what was left of their religion in peace.

Over the course of time the Supreme Court became more sensitive to those who do not share the majority's religious outlook. It for example gave extensive protection to the often annoying practices of the Jehovah's Witnesses, guaranteed access to unemployment compensation to those who celebrate the Sabbath on Saturday, allowed the Old Order Amish to remain separate from the secularizing influences of the upper grades of high school, and put an end to organized "nondenominational" prayer and Bible reading in the public schools. But the Court's record remained mixed. It has turned a blind eye to the claims of Orthodox Jews in two cases involving them as well as to plausible claims by Muslims, fundamentalists, Scientologists, practitioners of Native American religions, and others outside the religious mainstream.

On the establishment-clause front, the Court also entered decisions that run counter to the interest of religious minorities in maintaining a separate identity. One of the major subjects of the Court's attention has been the issue of aid to religious schools. Private religious-school systems were formed by minority religious groups precisely to avoid assimilation into the majority religious culture, originally Protestant, now largely secular. These schools are a principal means for preserving corporate religious identity. The decisions of many states to extend to students attending these schools some fraction of the support they would receive if they went to public schools have, however, repeatedly been struck down by the Supreme Court under the establishment clause. The effect of these decisions has been to force children of lower- and middle-income families into the melting pot of public education.

The Supreme Court evinces little recognition of the central place of religious pluralism, hence minority religions, under the First Amendment. As a matter of formal legal doctrine, the Court's interpretation of the free-exercise clause may seem to indicate the contrary. According to the Court, the free-exercise clause prohibits the government from enforcing laws and policies that burden the practice of religion unless they are the least restrictive means of achieving a compelling government purpose. While the clause applies equally to members of all faiths, it is particularly important to members of small, unknown, or unpopular religions, since more numerous and influential religions are better able to protect themselves in the political sphere. But while the free-exercise doctrine sounds protective—the language is as strong as that used to bar overt racial classification—the application falls considerably short of the words. Since 1972, the Court has rejected all claims for free-exercise exemptions, other than those involving unemployment compensation, which are governed by clear precedent going back to 1963. Far from requiring a compelling justification and a search for less restrictive alternatives, the Court appears to accept virtually any government reason for imposing a burden on religious practice.

The establishment-clause doctrine of the Court does not even give verbal support to religious pluralism. Under the so-called *Lemon* test (*Lemon* v. *Kurtzman*, 1971), government actions are condemned if they lack a secular purpose, if they "advance" religion, or if they threaten to "entangle" government with religion. It may well be that it is *Lemon* that is most responsible for the anemic enforcement of the Court's free-exercise doctrine, since a vigorous defense of the free exercise of religion is non-secular, advances religion, and often embroils government in issues of religion. To the degree we are serious about the *Lemon* test, we correspondingly downplay or ignore the free-exercise doctrine.

A recent case involving a Native American religion illustrates the point. In *Lyng* v. *Northwest Indian Cemeteries Protective Association* (485 U.S. 439 [1988]), members of the Yurok, Karok, and Tolowa Indian tribes of northern California challenged the decision of the U.S. Forest Service to build a logging road through an area called the "High Country," in which the Indians practice their spiritual devotions. On the basis of a study commissioned by the Forest Service and the evidence presented in court, the lower courts concluded—and the Supreme Court accepted—that construction of the road would "virtually destroy the Indians' ability to practice their religion." Moreover, it was essentially conceded that the government's interest in building the road was less than compelling; to many, the road looked like an utter boondoggle. It should have been an open-and-shut case for the free-exercise clause.

Instead a majority of the Court rejected the Indians' claim on the theory that the government can do whatever it wants with "its land." How the government's exercise of its property powers under Article IV, Section 3, Clause 2 somehow attained exemption from the Bill of Rights remains unexplained, but that was the Court's decision.

The significant point about the Indians' argument in *Ling* is that they were asking the government to violate all three of the prongs of the *Lemon* test. The secular considerations favored building the logging road; the Indians asked that non-secular reasons be considered as well. That violates *Lemon*. To preserve the sacred area in its pristine form would surely advance the Indians' religion. That violates *Lemon*. And to ask the government to regulate its land use in accordance with the religious significance some place on particular areas is to ask the government to be deeply entangled in religious affairs and to make delicate religious judgments. That violates *Lemon* too. The government evidently was faced with a choice between violating *Lemon* and saving the Indians' religion, or saving their religion and violating *Lemon*.

This dilemma is the predictable result of a legal formula that does not distinguish between advancing *religion* and advancing *religious freedom*. The *Lemon* test prohibits the government from "advancing" religion. But it *necessarily* advances religion to accommodate the secular dictates of public policy to the spiritual needs and concerns of religious minorities. The *Lemon* test is therefore a serious impediment to a policy of religious pluralism.

This is not to say that everything the Court has done under *Lemon* is wrong. There are, indeed, practices that advance a particular view of religion (usually, if not always, a generic Protestantism), and these *should* be invalidated. Spoken school prayers are the most notorious example; others include anti-solicitation statutes that target new religions, and statutes requiring the teaching of creationism. But the problem is that *Lemon* does not provide a means to distinguish between the good and the bad. By forbidding all government action that has the effect of "advancing religion" — even by preserving its free exercise — the *Lemon* test fosters secularism, not religious pluralism.

One justice, Sandra Day O'Connor, has called for abandoning the *Lemon* test and has proposed a new formulation expressly oriented to the needs of religious minorities. Her approach warrants quotation at length:

> The Establishment Clause prohibits government from making adherence to a religion relevant in any way to a person's standing in the political community. Government can run afoul of that prohibition in two principal ways. One is excessive entanglement with religious institutions, which may interfere with the independence of the institution, give the institution access to government or governmental powers not fully shared by nonadherents of the religion, and foster the creation of political constituencies defined along religious lines. The second and more direct infringement is government en-

dorsement or disapproval of religion. Endorsement sends a message to nonadherents that they are outsiders, not full members of the political community, and an accompanying message to adherents that they are insiders, favored members of the political community. Disapproval sends the opposite message.

While I do not think Justice O'Connor's proposed "endorsement" test will work as a practical test for deciding cases, it is significant, and hopeful, that she has addressed her attention to the religious "outsider," for whose protection the religion clauses were adopted. Perhaps this will mark a turning point for the Court as a whole.

Unfortunately, Justice O'Connor has gotten the matter only half right. She is correct that an important element of religious freedom is that those who maintain beliefs at variance with the mainstream should not be made to feel like "outsiders, not full members of the political community." But that is not all there is to religious freedom. It is equally important that those who maintain beliefs at variance with the mainstream should be permitted to *act* like outsiders, and to keep their distance from the mainstream. Assimilation and secularization are threats to religious pluralism equally as serious as intolerance and ostracism.

And this is where the Supreme Court is most prone to be insensitive. Overt official acts of intolerance are, thankfully, rare in this society, and would, I am confident, be squelched by the courts if they occurred. But America's secularized Protestant culture presses about us from all sides with subtle nudges to conform. It invites us, it tempts us, to become full insiders even when we are not.

A few examples may help. Captain Simcha Goldman was an Air Force officer and an Orthodox rabbi (*Goldman* v. *Weinberger*, 475 U.S. 503 [1986]). In keeping with his faith, he insisted on wearing a head covering at all times, including occasions when military uniform regulations forbade the wearing of headgear. Captain Goldman was not especially concerned that he would be made to feel like an outsider in this respect. In fact, one of the purposes behind the religious tradition of the skullcap, or yarmulke, is that it is an outward sign of obedience to God that sets Jews apart from others. At a profound spiritual level, Captain Goldman was an outsider to this community, and he wanted to act like one. His desire came into conflict with the military's rules, for the very purpose of those rules was to "encourage [!] the subordination of personal preferences and identities in favor of the overall group mission," and to "eliminate outward individual distinctions except for those of rank." Captain Goldman's ability to maintain his visible identity as a Jew—as an outsider—was at odds with military uniformity. He refused to doff his yarmulke, and was expelled from the Air Force as a result. And although seven of the nine justices concluded that the effect on military morale from allowing an exception would be minimal, the majority nonetheless upheld the Air Force's rules and decision.

More encouraging is the story of *Wisconsin* v. *Yoder* (1972), in which families belonging to the Old Order Amish community protested the requirement that their sons and daughters be forced to attend school beyond the eighth grade. As in the *Goldman* case, their principal concern was not that they would be made to feel like outsiders. Even more acutely than Captain Goldman, they *wanted* to be outsiders; their entire religious way of life is built around separation from what they view as a sinful world. They dress differently, abjure television and radio, drive buggies instead of automobiles, live in isolated rural communities, refrain from voting, decline Social Security and welfare benefits in favor of taking care of their own, and generally refuse to participate in the culture of the outside world. That is why they objected to high school. By the end of the eighth grade, their children had learned all they needed for life in the Amish community, and additional schooling would amount to enforced indoctrination into a world of which they heartily disapproved. To the credit of the Supreme Court, the justices understood the families' position and respected their right to remain as outsiders.

Less fortunate were the trustees of Georgetown University in Washington, D.C. Their standing as "outsiders" was considerably more attenuated than that of the Amish, for they wished to participate actively in the intellectual and cultural life of the capital by operating a first-class university. Their problem was that they wanted to do so in accordance with the moral precepts of the Roman Catholic Church, which recognizes Georgetown as one of only two pontifical universities in the United States. It might be said that the trustees wanted to be in the world but not of it.

One of their moral precepts is that homosexual practices are sinful. This belief is at odds with the law of the District of Columbia, which forbids discrimination on the basis of sexual preference. A group of Georgetown students formed a gay-rights group and approached the university with a request for recognition as an official student group, along with access to meeting rooms, offices, clerical help, and a subsidy. Georgetown refused. Its religiously grounded moral convictions did not permit the university to maintain a position of support for, or even neutrality toward, the advocacy of homosexuality as a legitimate sexual alternative. This refusal ran afoul of the District's law, and the District's law was held to override the university's right to enforce Catholic morality within a Catholic school.

My point is not that the gay students of Georgetown should be made to feel like outsiders, any more than the officials of the university should. For purposes of this discussion, let us assume that the District's position is correct and enlightened and that Georgetown is morally wrong. But the danger of suppressing the conscientious practice of a religious minority is greater than the advantage to be gained by allowing the majority's moral precepts to be enforced universally, without exception. In the wider society of the District of Columbia, homosexuals do not depend for their survival on extracting the support and subsidy of a private religious organization. They have the support and protection of the law, as well as the culture and the market. But Georgetown's ability to maintain its position, at variance with the mainstream, was on the line. Unlike the gay students, who could meet to their hearts' content in the wider community, Georgetown was faced with only two choices: compromise its religious faith or get out of town.

It behooves us to recognize that protecting religious minorities will sometimes mean protecting and perpetuating practices we deem morally repugnant. Religion is not necessarily inoffensive. But if we are committed to the proposition that the claims of God are not subject to the authority of civil government but commended to the consciences of believers, then we will be forced to tolerate some claims that seem to us very wrong. Only if we have very powerful reasons—a compelling justification—independent of any purpose of enforcing moral and religious homogeneity for its own sake can the government intervene.

It may not be inappropriate here to quote from Gamaliel, the revered first-century rabbi, writing at a time when the Jewish authorities were considering how to respond to a new and unsettling religious minority. "Men of Israel," he said,

> take care what you do with these men. For before these days Theudas arose, giving himself out to be somebody, and a number of men, about four hundred, joined him; but he was slain and all who followed him were dispersed and came to nothing. After him Judas the Galilean arose in the days of the census and drew away some of the people after him; he also perished, and all who followed him were scattered. So in the present case I tell you, keep away from these men and let them alone; for if this plan or this undertaking is of

men, it will fail; but if it is of God, you will not be able to overthrow them. You might even be found opposing God!

And the Book of Acts records that the Sanhedrin followed Gamaliel's advice and released the Christians from imprisonment. We need more of the spirit of Gamaliel in our constitutional law.

O ne place to begin is with the formal doctrine of the Supreme Court. The first step is to develop an interpretation of the two religion clauses that makes the free-exercise clause and the establishment clause consistent and complementary rather than antagonistic toward each other. This requires a return to the original purpose for prescribing constitutional protections for religious freedom: the protection of differences of opinion in matters of religion. The evil is not religion, but enforced religious uniformity.

A modified test might look like this: (1) A law or policy is unconstitutional if its purpose or likely effect is to increase religious uniformity either by inhibiting the religious practice of the person or group challenging the law (free-exercise clause) or by forcing or inducing a contrary religious practice (establishment clause); (2) a law or policy is unconstitutional if its enforcement interferes with the independence of a religious body in matters of religious significance to that body; (3) violation of either of these principles will be permitted only if it is the least restrictive means for (a) protecting the private rights of others, or (b) ensuring that the benefits and burdens of public life are equitably shared.

I believe that this would return to the original conception of religious freedom in the United States—not a freedom of submergence and invisibility, but a freedom of open, boisterous expression and celebration. Those who led the drive for religious freedom in America had a horror of religious authoritarianism, and their solution—possible only in a nation as diverse as this—was to allow each religious group "to flourish in accordance with the zeal of its adherents and the appeal of its dogma," to use Justice William O. Douglas's turn of phrase.

Those who have led the fight to preserve religious freedom in the succeeding years have never lost that horror of religious authoritarianism. But some of them have favored a different alternative—the alternative of a public, and often even a private, secularism. Some members of minority religions have taken this position, and it is easy to understand why: if religion is the point of division between themselves and the mainstream, then it is best to make religion as irrelevant as possible, so that the differences will become irrelevant. Some members of the Protestant majority have taken this position as well, perhaps because of an embarrassment at any public witness of the faith they prefer to keep private. And of course some of those who have no faith at all (if secularism is not a faith) have taken this position also, for it removes a source of competition for secular ideologies that they hope to see guide the culture.

Many who have taken this position, of whatever religious conviction, are sincere and even courageous opponents of religious authoritarianism. But their position, when taken to its extreme, is a demand for freedom *from* religion, not freedom *of* religion. And the society they would create is one not of religious diversity but of a dull and conformist secularism. It approaches what Justice Arthur Goldberg described as a "brooding and pervasive devotion to the secular and a passive, or even active, hostility to the religious."

Notwithstanding occasional excesses of the religious right, the greatest force for religious uniformity in the United States today is this devotion to the secular. It does not usually come in the form of a militant atheism, openly denying the possibility of a sovereign God. Most often it comes in the form of mores, sometimes reinforced by law, that make it uncomfortable or costly to put one's religious principles into practice in public. And for those who think their faith should control their life and action, the intolerance can be degrading, and all the worse because it will often be the outsider whom the culture labels "intolerant" and "closed-minded."

There is not much that the law can do about this form of intolerance. But at the very least, the law can serve as a reminder that our Constitution envisions a different course. As the equal-protection clause has contributed to an ethic of racial nondiscrimination and good will, so the religion clauses could contribute to an ethic of religious diversity, pluralism, and freedom. I believe it is increasingly true that the more committed believers of various religious faiths feel a sympathy and a solidarity with their counterparts in other religions far exceeding their sympathy with the secularized mainstream, and that they can, and will, make common cause in the fight against enforced secularization.

Perhaps there is nothing new in this. Colonel John Trumbull, the noted portrait painter, described in his *Autobiography* a remarkable dinner party at the home of Thomas Jefferson in 1793. Despite Jefferson's authorship of Virginia's Bill for Establishing Religious Freedom, he was anything but tolerant in matters of religion. Later in life, after his retirement from politics loosened his tongue, Jefferson referred to Athanasius and Calvin as "impious dogmatics," and their religion (that is, Catholicism and Reformed Protestantism) as a "counter-religion made up of the *deliria* of crazed imaginations." The theology of Judaism he called "degrading and injurious," and Jewish ethics he called "repulsive." His own particular view of national religious perfection would be for all to become Unitarians.

At the dinner party, Trumbull was "scarcely seated" when another guest began to berate him for his religion, which was Congregational. Though considering himself "in no degree qualified to manage a religious discussion," Trumbull made an attempt to defend his faith as best he could. The guest "proceeded so far at last, as to ridicule the character, conduct, and doctrines of the divine founder of our religion." Trumbull reports that Jefferson smiled and nodded approbation on his aggressive guest, while Trumbull himself became more and more annoyed and uncomfortable. Others at the party gave Trumbull no support, until David Franks took up the argument on Trumbull's side. Trumbull then remarked to his host:

Sir, this is a strange situation in which I find myself; in a country professing Christianity, and at a table with Christians, as I supposed, I find my religion and myself attacked with severe and almost irresistible wit and raillery, and not a person to aid me in my defense, but my friend Mr. Franks, who is himself a Jew.

We would do well to note the example and do likewise.

Bibliography

Amar, Akhil. "The Bill of Rights as a Constitution." *The Yale Law Journal* 100 (1991): 1131–1210.

Baker, John S., Jr. "The Establishment Clause as Intended: No Preference among Sects and Pluralism in a Large Commercial Republic." In *The Bill of Rights: Original Meaning and Current Understanding*, edited by Eugene W. Hickock, Jr. Charlottesville: University Press of Virginia, 1991.

Berns, Walter. *The First Amendment and the Future of American Democracy*. New York: Basic Books, 1976.

Bradley, Gerard V. "Beguiled: Free Exercise and the Siren Song of Liberalism." *Hofstra Law Review* 20 (1991): 245–319.

Cord, Robert L. *The Separation of Church and State: Historical Fact and Current Fiction*. Grand Rapids: Baker Book House, 1988.

Currie, David P. *The Constitution in the Supreme Court: The Second Century, 1888–1986*. Chicago: University of Chicago Press, 1990.

Curry, Thomas. *The First Freedoms: Church and State in America to the Passage of the First Amendment*. New York: Oxford University Press, 1986.

Dreisbach, Daniel L. *Real Threat and Mere Shadow: Religious Liberty and the First Amendment*. Westchester, Ill.: Crossway Books, 1987.

Freund, Paul. "Public Aid to Parochial Schools." *Harvard Law Review* 1680 (1969): 1680–1692.

Gaffney, Edward, Douglas Laycock, and Michael W. McConnell. "An Open Letter to the Religious Community." *First Things,* March 1991, 44–46.

Hall, Kermit, ed. *The Oxford Companion to the Supreme Court of the United States*. New York: Oxford University Press, 1992.

Howe, Mark DeWolfe. *The Garden and the Wilderness: Religion and Government in American Constitutional History*. Chicago: University of Chicago Press, 1965.

Hunter, James Davison. *Culture Wars: The Struggle to Define America*. New York: Basic Books, 1991.

———, and Os Guinness, eds. *Articles of Faith, Articles of Peace: The Religious Liberty Clauses and the American Public Philosophy*. Washington, D.C.: The Brookings Institution, 1990.

Kurland, Philip B., ed. *Church and State: The Supreme Court and the First Amendment*. Chicago: University of Chicago Press, 1975.

Laycock, Douglas. " 'Nonpreferential' Aid to Religion: A False Claim About Original Intent." *William & Mary Law Review* 27 (1986): 875–923.

509

Levy, Leonard. *The Establishment Clause: Religion and the First Amendment*. New York: Macmillan, 1986.

Malbin, Michael. *Religion and Politics: The Intentions of the Authors of the First Amendment*. Washington, D.C.: American Enterprise Institute for Public Policy Research, 1978.

McConnell, Michael W. "The Origins and Historical Understandings of Free Exercise of Religion." *Harvard Law Review* 103 (1990): 1410–1512.

―――. "Free Exercise as the Framers Understood It." In *The Bill of Rights: Original Meaning and Current Understanding*, edited by Eugene W. Hickock, Jr. Charlottesville: University Press of Virginia, 1991.

Miller, William L. *The First Liberty: Religion and the American Republic*. New York: Alfred A. Knopf, 1986.

Morgan, Richard E. *The Supreme Court and Religion*. New York: The Free Press, 1972.

Murray, John Courtney. "Law or Prepossessions?" *Law and Contemporary Problems* 14 (1949): 23–43.

Noonan, John T., Jr. *The Believer and the Powers That Are: Cases, History, and Other Data Bearing on the Relation of Religion and Government*. New York: Macmillan, 1987.

Pfeffer, Leo. *Church, State, and Freedom*. Rev. ed. Boston: Beacon Press, 1967.

Reichley, A. James. *Religion in American Public Life*. Washington, D.C.: The Brookings Institution, 1985.

Stokes, Anson Phelps. *Church and State in the United States*. 3 vols. New York: Harper & Bros., 1950.

Index of Cases

References may be in either the text or the footnotes on a page. Cases in bold type are among the twenty-five included in this book.

511

Index of Justices

References may be in either the text or the footnotes on a page.

515